AP EUROPEAN HISTORY

10th Edition

TestWare® Edition

Jere Link, Ph.D.
AP European History Instructor
The Westminster Schools
Atlanta, Georgia

Miles W. Campbell, Ph.D.
Professor and Chair
Department of History
New Mexico State University
Las Cruces, New Mexico

Niles R. Holt, Ph.D.
Professor of History
Illinois State University
Normal, Illinois

William T. Walker, Ph.D.
Associate Professor and Chair
Department of Humanities
University of the Sciences in Philadelphia
Philadelphia, Pennsylvania

Research & Education Association
Visit our website at: www.rea.com

Research & Education Association
61 Ethel Road West
Piscataway, New Jersey 08854
E-mail: info@rea.com

AP EUROPEAN HISTORY
with TestWare®

Published 2011

Copyright © 2009 by Research & Education Association, Inc.
Prior editions copyright © 2007, 2003, 2001, 1999, 1998, 1997, 1995, 1993, 1990 by Research & Education Association, Inc.
All rights reserved. No part of this book may be reproduced in any form without permission of the publisher.

Printed in the United States of America

Library of Congress Control Number 2008942822

ISBN-13: 978-0-7386-0626-2
ISBN-10: 0-7386-0626-X

Windows® is a registered trademark of Microsoft Corporation.

REA® and TestWare® are registered trademarks of
Research & Education Association, Inc.

CONTENTS

About Our Editor v
About Research & Education Association.. v
Acknowledgments... v
Study Schedule vi
Installing REA's TEST*ware*®...viii

Chapter 1
Excelling on the AP European History Exam... 1

AP EUROPEAN HISTORY COURSE REVIEW

Chapter 2
New Monarchies, the Renaissance, and the
Age of Exploration 11

Chapter 3
Reform, Counter-Reform, and the New Sciences... 37

Chapter 4
Overview of European Powers 65

Chapter 5
Absolutism, Constitutionalism, and Enlightenment... 105

Chapter 6
Revolution and the New European Order... 137

Chapter 7
The Heyday of Liberalism and Nationalism... 187

Chapter 8
The "Second Thirty Years' War": World Wars I and II.......................................227

Chapter 9
Postwar Europe: Cold War, Reconstruction, Decolonization and
Unification Efforts 317

Selected Readings 369

PRACTICE EXAMS

Practice Exam 1 373
Answer Key 405
Detailed Explanations of Answers 406

Practice Exam 2 429
Answer Key 454
Detailed Explanations of Answers 455

Practice Exam 3 479
Answer Key 509
Detailed Explanations of Answers 510

Practice Exam 4 537
Answer Key 566
Detailed Explanations of Answers 567

ANSWER SHEETS 593

INDEX 607

ABOUT OUR EDITOR

Dr. Jere Link teaches Advanced Placement European History at the college-preparatory Westminster Schools in Atlanta, Ga., where he is assistant coach for the Academic Quiz Team as well as the debate team, for which he coaches Lincoln-Douglas and extemporaneous speaking. Dr. Link attended the University of Texas at Austin, majoring in German. While attending the University of North Carolina in Chapel Hill, where he studied Comparative Literature and History, Dr. Link worked as a research lab assistant in biochemistry and edited and proofread medical and scientific journals. Following his winning a Fulbright Fellowship for study in Germany, Dr. Link completed his doctorate in 1988 and taught at Agnes Scott College and Virginia Polytechnic and State University before moving to the Westminster Schools in 1992. He received the Alumni Award for Teaching Excellence, the Merrill Family Award for Teaching, was named STAR teacher of Georgia in 1997 and earned runner-up STAR honors in 2004. He has published articles in Germany on literary politics and charities, and worked for the Southern Center for International Studies in Atlanta to produce a new text on modern Europe. His interests include classical music, good literature, theater, cooking, and his dog and cat.

ABOUT RESEARCH & EDUCATION ASSOCIATION

Founded in 1959, Research & Education Association (REA) is dedicated to publishing the finest and most effective educational materials—including software, study guides, and test preps—for students in elementary school, middle school, high school, college, graduate school, and beyond.

Today REA's wide-ranging catalog is a leading resource for teachers, students, and professionals.

We invite you to visit us at *www.rea.com* to find out how "REA is making the world smarter."

STAFF ACKNOWLEDGMENTS

In addition to our authors, we would like to thank Larry B. Kling, Vice President, Editorial, for supervising development; Pam Weston, Publisher, for production integrity and managing the publication to completion; John Cording, Vice President, Technology, for coordinating the design and development of REA's TestWare®; Diane Goldschmidt, Senior Editor, for coordinating revisions and pre-publication quality assurance; Anne Winthrop Esposito and Tamar Friedman, Senior Editors, and Molly Solanki, Associate Editor, for editorial contributions; Heena Patel and Michelle Boykins, Technology Project Managers, for their design contributions and software testing efforts; and Christine Saul, Senior Graphic Artist, for designing our cover.

We also extend our thanks to Caroline Duffy and Patricia Daly for copyediting the manuscript, and Aquent Publishing Services for typesetting this edition.

STUDY SCHEDULE
AP European History

Here is REA's suggested six-week study schedule to guide your prep for the AP European History Exam. Depending on how soon you will be sitting for the exam, you can expand or condense this timetable. If time is especially short, commit to covering the full historical review in one week instead of two, but we strongly recommend the two-week period. The key to gaining a firm command of the subject matter and thus the test itself is to set aside time each day for study. Once you commit to an activity, stick with it to the end. This will help ensure that you cover everything you need to be completely in control of the material—and the exam—come test day.

Week	Activity
1	Acquaint yourself with the AP European History Exam by reading Chapter 1. If you have a computer with an internet connection, check the College Board website (*http://apcentral.collegeboard.com*) to be sure you're completely in tune with all the procedural details. This way, you can walk into the test center with a clear mind and be able to focus exclusively on the task at hand.
	Take AP European History Practice Exam 1 on CD-ROM as a diagnostic to gauge your strengths and weaknesses. Carefully read through all of the detailed explanations (not just those questions that you answered incorrectly). Make a note of any sections that are difficult for you, or any questions that are still unclear after reading the explanations. Review the specific field of difficulty in the AP European History course review included with this book, or by using appropriate textbooks and notes.
2 **and** **3**	Now it's time to dive into our targeted course review. You'll need to cover an average of one chapter every two days for the next two weeks. Study the review material included in this book in Chapters 2 through 9. Do not study too much at any one time and don't let yourself fall behind. Pace yourself, so that you can better comprehend what you are reading. Remember that cramming is not an effective means of study.

Before you embark on Practice Exams 2, 3 and 4 in the remaining three weeks, be sure to block out a portion of the day that will be devoted strictly to this exercise. It's critical that you make each practice session as realistic as possible, which means that you should sit and take the test without interruption or distraction.

Measure your progress from exam to exam. Take note of where your performance improves, remains static, or falls off. Allow extra time to address the latter two categories.

4	Take AP European History Practice Exam 2 on CD-ROM. Read through all of the detailed explanations. Make a note of anything that you find difficult or unclear after reading the explanations. Use your AP European History course review and your textbooks, notes, or course materials to review those areas that need clarification.
5	Take AP European History Practice Exam 3 on CD-ROM. Read through all of the detailed explanations. Make a note of anything that you find difficult or unclear after reading the explanations. Use your AP European Review course review and your textbooks, notes, or course materials to review those areas that need clarification.
6	Take AP European History Practice Exam 4 in this book. Read through all of the detailed explanations. Continue reviewing any material that you are finding difficult. Compare your progress between each of the practice exams. Note any sections where you were able to improve your score, and sections where your score remained the same or declined. Use any remaining time to enhance your feel for the rhythm and flow of the exam by taking the printed version of practice exams 1, 2, and 3 in this book.

INSTALLING REA's TEST*ware*®

SYSTEM REQUIREMENTS

Pentium 75 MHz (300 MHz recommended) or a higher or compatible processor; Microsoft Windows 98 or later; 64 MB available RAM; Internet Explorer 5.5 or higher

INSTALLATION

1. Insert the AP European History TEST*ware*® CD-ROM into the CD-ROM drive.
2. If the installation doesn't begin automatically, from the Start Menu choose the RUN command. When the RUN dialog box appears, type *d:*setup (where *d* is the letter of your CD-ROM drive) at the prompt and click OK.
3. The installation process will begin. A dialog box proposing the directory "Program Files\REA\APEuroHistory" will appear. If the name and location are suitable, click OK. If you wish to specify a different name or location, type it in and click OK.
4. Start the AP European History TEST*ware*® application by double-clicking on the icon.

REA's AP European History TEST*ware*® is **EASY** to **LEARN AND USE**. To achieve maximum benefits, we recommend that you take a few minutes to go through the on-screen tutorial on your computer. The "screen buttons" are also explained there to familiarize you with the program.

SSD ACCOMMODATIONS FOR STUDENTS WITH DISABILITIES

Many students qualify for extra time to take the AP exams, and our TEST*ware*® can be adapted to accommodate your time extension. This allows you to practice under the same extended-time accommodations that you will receive on the actual test day. To customize your TEST*ware*® to suit the most common extensions, visit our website at *www.rea.com/ssd*.

TECHNICAL SUPPORT

REA's TEST*ware*® is backed by customer and technical support. For questions about **installation or operation of your software**, contact us at:

> **Research & Education Association**
> **Phone: (732) 819-8880 (9 a.m. to 5 p.m. ET, Monday–Friday)**
> **Fax: (732) 819-8808**
> **Website: http://www.rea.com**
> **E-mail: info@rea.com**

Note to Windows XP Users: In order for the TEST*ware*® to function properly, please install and run the application under the same computer administrator-level user account. Installing the TEST*ware*® as one user and running it as another could cause file-access path conflicts.

Chapter 1

Excelling on the AP European History Exam

Prepare with Confidence

If you're looking for a true edge on Test Day...

And if you're not willing to settle for second best...

...then this new edition of REA's AP European History test prep is for you.

REA gives you all the tools you'll need to master the Advanced Placement Examination in European History:

- Summary appraisals of the cultural, diplomatic, economic, political, and social strands that form the basis of the AP course and the exam.

- Unrivaled relevant, detailed, and properly apportioned, review of European history in a context that (a) accords with known exam coverage, (b) will serve to sharpen your classroom discussion and (c) will keep you from having to continually check your textbook for citations as you study.

- Handy timelines that not only summarize each period's key events but also explain their significance.

- Carefully chosen artwork that pictorially presents the progression of events, ideas and trends associated with a given period.

- Bibliography of additional study resources.

- Comprehensive index that speeds specific referencing.

- Practice exams 1, 2, & 3 provided on REA's exclusive TEST*ware*® CD, affording you the benefits of instantaneous, accurate scoring and enforced time conditions.

- Complete array of sample essay questions and answers.

Importantly, this book embraces the same principles of organization and coverage as those adopted by the AP Program's European History Development Committee, which is to say that REA, too, recognizes that early twenty-first century teaching on college and university campuses reflects a broad perspective in terms of the sweep of intellectual and cultural history; political and diplomatic history, and social and economic history.

In choosing REA, you're putting yourself in the company of tens of thousands of AP students who have benefited from our total preparation package year after year. Moreover, teachers across America and beyond find that this book offers a clear-eyed, no-nonsense narrative of the history of Europe. In fact, many AP instructors use it to supplement their classroom text and lectures precisely because it so comprehensively supports specific curriculum objectives for the AP course and exam.

About REA's TEST*ware*®

Practice exams 1 through 3 of this book are included in two formats: in printed format in this book, and in TEST*ware*® format on the enclosed CD. We strongly recommend that you begin your preparation with the TEST*ware*® practice exams. The software provides the added benefits of automatic, accurate scoring and enforced time conditions. The content and format of the actual European History exam are faithfully mirrored. See below for a detailed description of the format and content of the AP European History Exam.

About the Exam

The Advanced Placement European History examination is offered each May at participating schools and multi-school centers in the United States and more than 30 other countries.

The Advanced Placement Program is designed to allow high school students to pursue college-level studies while attending high school. Participating colleges and universities, in turn, grant credit and/or advanced placement to students who do well on the examinations.

Format of the AP European History Exam

The AP European History exam is approximately three hours and five minutes long. The exam is divided into two sections. Each section of the exam is timed and completed separately, and each counts for half of the student's score. None of the exam items focuses on the pre–1450 or the post–2001 period.

1. Multiple choice. This section consists of 80 multiple-choice questions to be answered in 55 minutes. The questions are designed to measure the student's ability to understand and analyze European History from the High Renaissance to the recent past. This section tests factual knowledge, scope of preparation, and knowledge-based analytical skills.

2. Free response. This section is composed of three essay questions designed to measure the student's ability to write coherent, intelligent, and well-organized essays on historical topics. The essays require the student to demonstrate mastery of historical interpretation and the ability to express views and knowledge in writing. The student may be required to relate documents to different areas, analyze common themes of different time periods, or compare individual and group experiences that reflect socio-economic, racial, gender, and ethnic differences.

Part A consists of a mandatory 15-minute reading period, followed by 45 minutes in which the student must answer a document-based essay question (DBQ).

In Parts B and C, the student is asked to answer two thematic questions in 70 minutes. Students choose one essay from the three essays in Part B and one essay from the three essays in Part C.

In determining the score for the free-response section, the DBQ is weighted 45 percent while the two thematic essays are weighted 55 percent. The entire free-response section counts for one-half of the final grade.

Content of the Exam

In general, the AP European History exam covers the following topics:

Political and Diplomatic History	30–40%
Social and Economic History	30–40%
Intellectual and Cultural History	20–30%

The exam encompasses the High Renaissance to the present. The time periods are covered as follows: 50% from 1450 to 1789, 50% from 1789 to present. Major late medieval events bearing upon post-1450 events may also be included. The number of questions covering the nineteenth and twentieth centuries is divided about evenly, which is approximately 25% of the total number of questions for each century.

In addition to studying the review presented in this book, test-takers should acquaint themselves with current issues affecting European society, thereby gaining the necessary perspective on modern European events.

You may find the AP European History exam considerably more difficult than many classroom exams. In order to measure the full range of your ability, the AP exams are designed to produce average scores of approximately 50 percent of the maximum possible score for the multiple-choice and essay sections. Therefore, you should not expect to attain a perfect or even near-perfect score.

For more in-depth information regarding the AP European History exam, please visit the College Board website at *www.collegeboard.com.*

How To Use This Book and TEST*ware*®
What do I study first?

To begin your studies, read over the introduction and the suggestions for test taking. Take Practice Exam 1 on CD-ROM to determine your strengths and weaknesses, and then study the course review material, focusing on your specific problem areas. The course review includes the information you need to know when taking the exam. Make sure to follow up your diagnostic work by taking the remaining practice exams on CD-ROM to become familiar with the format and feel of the AP European History Exam.

To best utilize your study time, follow our Study Schedule, which you will find in the front of this book. The schedule is based on a six-week program, but if necessary can be condensed to three weeks by collapsing each two-week interval into one week.

When should I start studying?

It is never too early to start studying for the AP European History examination. The earlier you begin, the more time you will have to sharpen your skills. Do not procrastinate! Cramming is *not* an effective way to study, because it does not allow you the time needed to learn the test material. The sooner you learn the format of the exam, the more time you will have to familiarize yourself with it.

SSD Accommodations for Students with Disabilities

Many students qualify for extra time to take the AP exams, and our TEST*ware*® can be adapted to accommodate your time extension. This allows you to practice under the same extended-time accommodations that you will receive on the actual test day. To customize your TEST*ware*® to suit the most common extensions, visit our website at *www.rea.com/ssd*.

Scoring REA's Practice Exams
Scoring the Multiple-Choice Section

For the multiple-choice section, use this formula to calculate your raw score:

_____ − _____ = _____

number right   number wrong*   raw score

*Do not include unanswered questions.

4

Scoring the Free-Response Section

For the free-response section, use this formula to calculate your raw score:

_____ + _____ + _____ = _____ (round to the nearest whole number)
DBQ   essay   essay
essay   #1   #2

Each essay question is given a score of 0–9 points. It might be helpful to have a teacher or another impartial person knowledgeable in European history decide how points should be awarded. A tough, objective appraisal is your best insurance against test-day surprises. Follow *all* AP requirements to properly calibrate your score.

Figuring Your Composite Score

To obtain your composite score, use the following method:

1.13 × _____ = _____ (weighted multiple-choice score—do not round)

2.73 × _____ = _____ (weighted free-response score—do not round)

Now, add the two weighted sections together and round to the nearest whole number. The result is your total composite score. Compare your score with this table to approximate your grade:

AP Grade	Composite Score Range
5	114–180
4	91–113
3	74–90
2	49–73
1	0–48

The overall scores are interpreted as follows:

AP Grade	Interpretation
5	Extremely well qualified
4	Well qualified
3	Qualified
2	Possibly qualified
1	No recommendations

Scoring the Official Exams

The College Board creates a formula (which changes slightly every year) to convert raw scores into composite scores grouped into broad AP grade categories. The weights for the multiple-choice sections are determined by the chief reader, who uses a process called *equating*. This process compares the current year's exam performance on selected multiple-choice questions to that of a previous year, establishing a level of achievement for the current year's group and a degree of difficulty for the current exam. This data is combined with historical trends and the reader's professional evaluation to determine the weights and tables.

The AP free-response problems are graded by teacher volunteers grouped at scoring tables and led by a chief faculty consultant. The consultant sets the grading scale that translates the raw score into the composite score. Past grading illustrations are available to teachers from the College Board and may be ordered using the contact information given in this book. These actual examples of student responses and a grade analysis can be of great assistance to both the student and the teacher as a learning or review tool.

When will I know my score?

In July, a grade report will be sent to you, your high school, and the college you chose to notify. The report will include scores for all the AP exams you have taken up to that point.

Your grade will be used by your college of choice to determine placement in its European History program. This grade will vary in significance from college to college, and is used with other academic information to determine placement. Normally, colleges participating in the Advanced Placement Program will recognize grades of 3 or higher. Contact your college admissions office for more information regarding its use of AP grades.

Studying for Your Exam

It is very important for you to choose the time and place for studying that works best for you. Some students may set aside a certain number of hours every morning, while others may study at night before going to sleep. Other students may study during the day, while waiting in line, or even while eating lunch. Only you can determine when and where your study time will be most effective. But be consistent, and use your time wisely. Work out a study routine and stick to it.

When you take the practice tests, create an environment as much like the actual testing environment as possible. Turn off your television and radio, and sit down at a quiet table free from distraction. Make sure to time yourself, breaking the test down by section.

As you complete each practice test, score your test and thoroughly review the explanations to the questions you answered incorrectly; however, do not review too much at one time. Concentrate on one problem area at a time by reviewing the question and explanation and by studying our review until you are confident that you completely understand the material.

Keep track of your scores. By doing so, you will be able to gauge your progress and discover general weaknesses in particular sections. You should carefully study the reviews that cover areas with which you have difficulty, as this will build your skills in those areas.

Test-Taking Tips

If you are not familiar with standardized tests such as the AP European History exam, there are many ways to acquaint yourself with this type of examination and help alleviate any test-taking anxieties. Listed below are ways to help you become accustomed to the AP exams, some of which may be applied to other standardized tests as well.

Become comfortable with the format of the exam. Stay calm and pace yourself. After simulating the test a couple of times, you will boost your chances of doing well, and you will be able to sit down for the actual exam with more confidence.

Read all of the possible answers. Just because you think you have found the correct response, do not automatically assume that it is the best answer. Read through each choice to be sure that you are not making a mistake by jumping to conclusions.

Use the process of elimination. Go through each answer to a question and eliminate as many of the answer choices as possible. By eliminating just two answer choices, you give yourself a better chance of getting the item correct, because there will be only three choices left from which to make your guess.

Work quickly and steadily. Work quickly and steadily and avoid focusing on any one question too long. Taking the practice tests in this book will help you learn to budget your time.

Beware of test vocabulary. Words such as *always, every, none, only*, and *never* indicate there should be no exceptions to the answer you choose. Words like *generally, usually, sometimes, seldom, rarely,* and *often* indicate there may be exceptions to your answer. When analyzing and writing your essay answer, be aware of words such as *analyze, assess, evaluate, compare, contrast, describe, discuss, explain,* and *identify.*

Learn the directions and format for each section of the test. Familiarizing yourself with the directions and format of the exam will save you valuable time on the day of the actual test.

Answer every question. There is no penalty for guessing, so answer every question before you run out of time, even if you are not sure of the answer.

The Day of the Exam

Before the Exam

On the day of the test, you should wake up early (preferably after a good night's rest) and have a good breakfast. Make sure to dress comfortably so that you are not distracted by being too hot or too cold while taking the test. Also, plan to arrive at the test center early. This will allow you to collect your thoughts and relax before the test and will spare you the anxiety that comes with being late.

Before you leave for the test center, make sure you have your admission form, social security number, and another form of identification, which must contain a recent photograph, your name, and signature (i.e., driver's license, student identification card, or current alien registration card). You will not be allowed to take the test if you do not have proper identification. Also make sure to bring your school code, as well as several sharpened No. 2 pencils with erasers for the multiple-choice questions and black or blue pens for the free-response questions.

You may wear a watch, but only one without a beeper or an alarm. No dictionaries, textbooks, notebooks, compasses, correction fluid, highlighters, rulers, computers, cell phones, beepers, PDAs, scratch paper, listening and recording devices, briefcases, or packages will be permitted, and drinking, smoking, and eating are prohibited while taking the test.

During the Exam

Once you enter the test center, follow all of the rules and instructions given by the test supervisor. If you do not, you risk being dismissed from the test and having your scores canceled.

After the Exam

When taking the exam, you may immediately register to have your score sent to the college of your choice, or you may wait and later request to have your AP score reported to the college of your choice.

Contacting the AP Program

For registration bulletins or more information about the AP European History Exam, contact:

AP Services
Educational Testing Service
P.O. Box 6671
Princeton, NJ 08541-6671
Phone: (609) 771-7300 or (888) 225-5427
E-mail: apexams@ets.org
Website: *www.collegeboard.com*

COURSE REVIEW

AP European History

Chapter 2

New Monarchies, the Renaissance, and the Age of Exploration

Background

Europe as an Idea and a Geographical Reality

Europe: From an Asian to a Roman Matter

Not yet united, though more unified today than ever before, Europe is technically a subcontinent of Asia. According to Greek mythology, the god Zeus abducted an Asian princess, Europa, to the island of Crete. This makes both him and Crete *European* before the fact. Other islands are also considered part of Europe: Sicily, Malta, the Balearics, Ireland, England, even Iceland. Europe and Asia were linked by the Silk Road, the Judeo-Christian tradition, Persian Zoroastrianism, the myth of Troy, and more. But Europe strove to distance itself from its Asian "mother" and African "sisters." Itself both an idea and an ideal, Europe under the Romans was subdivided into smaller units that prefigured later nations: Italia, Hispania, Germania, Gallia (which became Francia), Anglia, and so on. Two legacies of Rome helped keep the idea of an integral Europe alive, even in the fragmented feudal era: the ideal of a Roman empire, and the unity of Christendom, shaken from 1054 on, but able to unite nations intermittently against foreign threats, such as the Arabs, Vikings, Magyars, Mongols, Turks, and the ex-colonial reflux that has challenged Europe since 1945. So Europe's cultural and geopolitical significance elevated it from a lowly subcontinent to a major continent in its own right. Greek ideals of beauty, laws, science, and democracy have also shaped modern Europe, whose significance in world history owes something as well to its physical geography.

Physical Geography of Europe

The arbitrariness of the borders within Europe is explained by the spread of Christianity—and its losses. Whereas North Africa and the Near East once belonged to Roman Europe, their loss to Islam bracketed them out of European history in the seventh century. By 1400, the last pagans in Europe had been converted, but Christians had split into two factions: Orthodox or Greek in the East, and Latin or Roman Christians in the West. Since it was a Byzantine emperor who codified Roman law, we see the legacies of ancient Rome at work in defining all of Europe: through the sway of Roman law (and its roads), and in the building of bastions of Christianity, whether Roman or Greek, against threatening outsiders. Europe begins in the east with the Ural Mountains in Russia and ends in the west, just as arbitrarily, with an outpost of Viking wanderlust—Iceland. The islands of the Mediterranean Sea, Rome's *mare nostrum* ("our lake"), belong to Europe, as do the Black, Caspian, Baltic, Irish, and North seas; the English Channel; the Turkish, Scandinavian, and Gibraltar straits; and stretches of the Atlantic Ocean. The northern verge of Europe is the Arctic Circle beyond the Scandinavian archipelago.

Physical aspects of Europe give clues to its rise to worldwide preeminence in the nineteenth century. Though parts of northern Russia and Scandinavia are icebound for much of the year, much of Europe has navigable oceans, seas, inlets, bays, and rivers, so European history was largely written by its navies, which for five centuries explored, conquered, or traded with every other part of the globe. The coasts and waterways also brought seafood to tables—vital for Catholic and Orthodox Europe during fasts and on Fridays. Beyond the coasts, Europe had plentiful forests for exploitation, but where forests were absent or depleted, locals managed with other fuels, such as peat, and from the sixteenth century on, coal. It is no coincidence that trade, agriculture, and industry developed and thrived in areas blessed with coal and iron seams; such was the case in Silesia, Saxony, the Ruhr and Saar in Germany, north Italy, Lorraine in France, and the Midlands in England, as well as Sweden and the Urals, which had iron though not coal. Europeans mined silver, tin, mercury, salts, and other subterranean riches. Most of Europe lies in a temperate climate zone with adequate rain, so a variety of crops thrived: olives and citrus in the south; grapevines further north; hardy vegetables, hops, winter wheat, barley, millet, and rye everywhere; rice and cotton in some areas; sugar beets near coasts; and sugar cane on Spanish islands. In addition, apple, plum, cherry, pear, and other fruit trees grew in many areas. Pasturing of goats, sheep, cattle, water buffaloes, and other animals meant a steady supply of dairy products and, at slaughtering time, meat for the lucky. For hydration, with water supplies often tainted, Europeans had beer, wine, mead, fortified wines (port, Madeira), liqueurs, champagne, and distilled liquors (brandy, whiskey, vodka, and so forth) before the advent of tea, coffee, and chocolate in the seventeenth century.

We can infer much about a continent from knowledge of its physical properties. But it was Europe's culture that helped it to overtake the superior cultures of India and China in the early eighteenth century and become *the* world power of the nineteenth century. Long before that, however, Europe had to overcome the backwardness and isolation left by the so-called Dark or early Middle Ages (circa 476–1000), marred by noble feuds and foreign invaders.

The High and Late Middle Ages

The Middle Ages fell chronologically between the classical world of Greece and Rome and the early modern world. The High Middle Ages (circa 1000–1350) saw the revival of long-distance trade, the creation of a politico-military feudalism and agricultural manorialism, the construction of castles and cathedrals, the advancement of learning, and the initiation of the crusades. This age was cut short by the catastrophe of the Black Death, which, according to the theories of some historians, may not have resulted from the plague alone, but also from other diseases. European life was, by the contemporary standards of China, India, Japan, and much of the Islamic world, sordid and filthy: sewage flowed in the streets, homes were ill-lit and unheated under thatched roofs, and animals slept indoors in the winter. No wonder the plague was able to take hold so quickly and do so much damage. With the loss of 40 percent of its population, Europe entered a period labeled by Johan Huizinga the *Waning of the Middle Ages*. This survey of European history begins with the Late Middle Ages (1350–1450) and Early Modern Europe (circa 1450–1650).[1] The dominant power in Europe, until the late sixteenth century, was the Roman Catholic Church, so its structure needs to be sketched in first; later, we look at the other major social force in Europe: the power and wealth of the hierarchical nobility.

The Church and Corruption

The Roman Catholic Church was a pyramidal hierarchy with believers at the base. The faithful were ministered to by priests, who in turn were supervised by bishops under the rule of the pope, the "bishop of Rome." Monks, nuns, and friars played auxiliary roles and were also governed by a bishop. Despite church lore that Saint Peter was the first pope, the papacy did not possess much power or a viable structure until the seventh century. Over four centuries, the church developed the West's first bureaucracy (Curia, *Rota Romana*, and the College of Cardinals) to amass influence and power in a fragmented age; sent papal delegates (*nuncios*) to distant lands to collect dues owed to Rome and to discipline kings and bishops; and gladly let the pious deed it their land and wealth, with hints that such legacies might just insure the salvation of the generous. So the church grew powerful and wealthy. In 1200, Pope Innocent III was probably the most powerful ruler in Europe. But with power and wealth came temptation.

Corruption was widespread; many decisions within the church bureaucracy were influenced by money, friendship, or politics. Simony—the purchase of church offices irrespective of merit—was common. Pluralism allowed a man to hold several offices, even though he could not perform all their tasks; he might hire an assistant to do a job, or leave it undone. Not being ubiquitous, he could be charged with absenteeism. Those who hogged lucrative *benefices* were targets of church reformers and critics mindful of the vow of poverty. Critics noted how the clergy indulged in extravagant display, secular politics, and sexual improprieties, a trend that led to anticlericalism—hostility toward priests as men and ministers. With the church—despite its precarious situation—acting as a force for law, order, and the true faith throughout a divided Europe, critics seemed like criminals or heretics to most Christians.

---

[1] American students must be mindful of the fact that European universities start their "modern" era in 1477, whereas to Americans modernity does not begin until after our Civil War, that is, 1866 or 1867.

Conciliar Movement and Reformers

Reformers initiated efforts to have the church ruled, not by the pope, but by clergy as well as laymen. Marsiglio of Padua (1270–1342) argued in his book *Defender of the Peace* that the church was subordinate to the state and should be governed by a general council. Efforts after 1409 by councils at Pisa (1409) and Constance (1414–1418) united the church under one pope but failed to effect reform of abuses, as all such efforts ended in struggles between the pope and councils over power in the church. Pope Martin V and his successors rejected the conciliar movement and proceeded, through centralized papal power, to restore and beautify Rome as capital of Christendom.

John Wycliffe (1320–1384), an English friar, criticized the vices of the clergy, taxes collected by the pope, the doctrine of transubstantiation, and the authority of the pope. As he believed the church should follow only the Scriptures, he began translating the Bible from Latin into English. Wycliffe's ideas were used by peasants in the revolt of 1381, and his followers, Lollards, survived into the fifteenth century and may have still had adherents in England when Henry VIII split from the Romish church in the 1530s.

John Huss (1369–1415), a Czech priest with criticisms similar to Wycliffe's, produced a national following in Bohemia that rejected the authority of the pope. Huss was burned at the stake at the Council of Constance. However, owing to the fierce Hussite Wars, Bohemia gained unique concessions from the papacy in the early fifteenth century as to the taking of communion "under both forms" and the conduct of priests. Both Lollards and Hussites are considered, unhistorically, as "pre-Protestants," but to later Protestants, such as John Foxe, who cited them in his widely-read *Book of Martyrs* (1563), they served as heroes and handy precursors, justifying Protestant actions before the fact.

Lay Piety and Self-Reform

In the Rhine valley, the mystics Meister Eckhart (1260–1327) and Thomas à Kempis (1379–1471) sought direct knowledge of God through inner feelings, not church rituals. They fostered the regular meeting of lay people (all who were not clergy or under vows) in order to achieve a more heartfelt religion. Kempis's highly influential book, *The Imitation of Christ*, spread ideas of lay piety far and wide. Gerard Groote (1340–1384) fostered a communal life for laymen in the Low Countries. His Brethren of the Common Life ran schools and led lives guided by Christian principles of humility, tolerance, and love, all unconcerned with the institutional church. The church was not unaware of the need for reform, but the hard trials that the papacy suffered in its Babylonian Captivity at Avignon (1308–1377) and the Great Schism (1378–1415) had left it on the defensive, with little time or energy to devote to reforms, given the pressing need to reestablish the power of popes as princes of the Papal States and vicars of Christ on earth. Tragically, attempts to reform the church from within were blocked by other agendas: papal fear of councils, pushed by kings of France for selfish reasons; the need to finance wars against the heathen Turks; and successive invasions of Italy by foreign powers, from 1494 on.

A Tour of Europe in the Fifteenth Century

An educated person in the mid-fifteenth century might have bet that these rising nations would dominate Europe by 1800: the revived **papacy**; rich **Burgundy**; the largest "republic," **Poland-Lithuania**; the kingdom of **Aragon**, with its Mediterranean islands, Naples and Sicily; the city-states of **Venice**, **Florence**, **Genoa**, and **Milan**, if they united against Rome; and the kingdom of **France**, which had just won the Hundred Years' War (1337–1453). With the exception of France, the bettor would have lost the bets. Transported through time, our hypothetical gambler would have seen Prussia, Austria, "Muscovy" (Russia), and England as the great powers of 1800.

A map of 1460 looked like this:

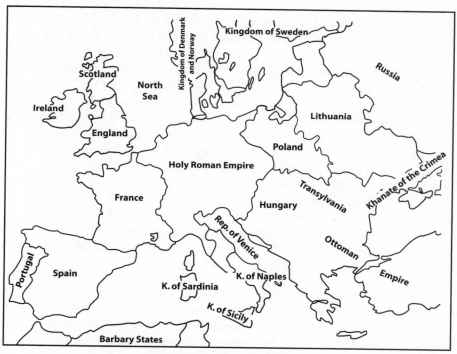

Map of Europe in the Fifteenth Century

This map does not include Muscovy (core of modern Russia), and few in the fifteenth century would have balked, since Russia seemed doomed to labor under the Tatar yoke, or Golden Horde. That Muscovy was Orthodox, and therefore part of Christendom, would not have impressed many as a reason to call Russia "European"—western ambassadors in the sixteenth and seventeenth centuries returned home with tales of a massive land sunk in barbarism, ice, and backwardness. The Renaissance, Reformation, Scientific Revolution, Baroque art and music—none of these penetrated Russia until the eighteenth century. Her neighbor to the west, Poland-Lithuania, was a more impressive power until the 1660s, when it lost the Ukraine to an expanding Russia. To the south, the kingdom of Hungary was still a force to reckon with, and the Ottoman Empire remained the greatest threat to European Christendom, especially after the fall of Constantinople (1453). In this era, the Dracul family, sometime rulers of Wallachia (now Romania), often had to change sides, sometimes allying with one liege, the king of Hungary, and at other times with their *other* liege lord, the Turkish sultan. Vlad III Dracula (son of the dragon) made his name for cruelty from 1456 to 1462. Legend says that he burned some enemies alive and impaled others. He blamed the ills of his land not on its three overlapping rulers, but on treacherous *boyars* (old nobles) who played politics so unscrupulously. To him, as to other princes of this era, uncertainty and the confusion of feudalism called for some blood-letting.

In the north, the kingdoms of Sweden, Norway, and Denmark went from uneasy personal union to open conflict with nearby dukes and that union of cities, the Hansa League, stretching from London to Novgorod in Russia.

Central Europe sported the crazy quilt of the Holy Roman Empire of the German Nation, whose 1356 constitution (the Golden Bull) made emperors elective—dependent on seven electors, the Diet in Regensburg, and many imperial knights and cities. Neither "holy, nor Roman, nor an empire" (a crack by the French writer and philosopher Voltaire in the eighteenth century), this loose federation of the Germanies was fragmented, too medieval for the emerging world of strong monarchies. Meanwhile, though the authorities of the Holy Roman Empire did not realize it, the elective nature of the papacy weakened the empire, as would prove true of the Polish monarchy in the eighteenth century. Signs of the instability attendant on elections were clear from papal history. In 1200, a pope gave orders to kings of Europe and served as a focal point for Christendom; in the 1300s, successive popes were held captive in Avignon, beholden to French kings. During the Great Schism (1378–1415), two or three popes vied for legitimacy, each backed by different European princes. The return of one pope to Rome in 1417, Martin V, marked a long struggle of this secular and spiritual prince to regain the power of the papacy, which centered at first on Italian interests, and then was restricted to the Catholic part of Europe in the Reformation.

Further west was the congeries of lands called "Burgundy," extending from Savoy in the south through Switzerland and eastern France to the Netherlands in the north. As in the rest of Europe, Burgundy subsumed relics of the feudal past: the free cities of Flanders, the separate cantons of Switzerland, and others. Though dukes of Burgundy pretended to rule this area, its lands owed allegiance to other princes, notably the kings of France, independent bishops, and the Holy Roman emperors. Conflicting, confusing claims of feudal lords to the same area characterized the medieval map, a fact that helped to cause the Hundred Years' War between France and England (discussed later in the chapter).

Owing to many factors, even chance, the four powers of the west—England, Spain, France, and (for a while) Portugal—unified first as near-modern centralized monarchies and dominated Europe from 1500 to 1800. A new concept was emerging, that of keeping contiguous lands together under one prince; it was a trend that bucked the pattern of the Middle Ages, when lords governed far-flung, noncontiguous tracts of land. In the sixteenth century, for example, the Orange-Nassau family owned estates in southern France, western Germany, and the Netherlands, this despite having to cross hostile lands to move from one estate to the other. England united first, under King Alfred, adding Wales after the twelfth century. Portugal won rounded borders in the wars of reconquest against Iberian Muslims. Then Spain secured the union of Castile and Aragon. And finally, the kings of France expanded and unified their domain through wise marriages (for example, to the heiress to Brittany), inheritance (Mary of Burgundy), wars, and diplomacy.

Activity:

Use the following outline map to identify key regions of Europe. Make notes on seas, capitals, and other important details, as you read. To test what you have read, find and label the following: Muscovy (Russia), Finland, Sweden, Norway, Denmark, the Baltic states, Poland, Hungary, Austria, the Black Sea, Germany, Italy, France, the Netherlands, Flanders/Belgium, Spain, Portugal, Switzerland, the Mediterranean, England, Scotland, Ireland, Iceland, and the North and Baltic seas.

The Social and Political Hierarchy of Early Modern Europe

The western church in the early modern era was a pyramid, with the pope at the top, then the cardinals in their college (and in the bureaucratic Curia), and then, in descending levels, the archbishops, bishops, abbots, and parish monsignors and priests. The church modeled its structure after the feudal pyramid that emerged following invasions from 840 to 955 by Vikings, Muslims, and Magyars.

Ideally, the feudal pyramid was surmounted by the Holy Roman Emperor, but as his power waned after the 1200s, Europe's rising leaders, the hereditary monarchs, took the top spot. These were noble families exalted by war or luck to be "first among equals"; other old noble families contended with them into the seventeenth century as "peers" of the realm.

In the Middle Ages, to be free was to be noble, and vice versa, but the vast majority were neither. Townsmen were subordinated usually to a lord, though they were free within town walls; all others were serfs (semifree) or slaves. A runaway serf could legally claim the "freedom of the city" if he managed to breathe city air for a year and a day, but the fact that roughly 95 percent of Europe's population lived in the countryside until 1800 indicates how difficult it was to gain (or buy) one's freedom from a lord. Nevertheless, early modern Europe saw the widespread endowment of many with "liberties": in western Europe, local lords freed peasants from bondage, though they were still liable for taxes, dues, and even forced labor. Starting in Flanders and Italy, townsmen could free themselves by buying their municipal liberties from an overlord, such as the Pope or Holy Roman Emperor, or a local potentate, such as an abbot or seigneur.

Peasants occupied the manorial base upon which feudalism rested—and on which it fed. In between that base and the pyramid above figured townsmen of indeterminate status. On the pyramid itself, which obscures the complex reality, nobles jockeyed for position. What was nobility? The Latin root, *nobilitas*, connotes a well-known family, one with a name, position, strength, and longevity, which required land sufficient for basic needs and luxuries, and thus the dependent manpower to work that land and provide servants. In the feudal order, a higher lord, the territorial prince, or the emperor had to recognize a family as noble. In the Middle Ages, this meant military service for generations; later a family could distinguish itself in other ways or even buy its patent of nobility.

Europe had many untitled nobles, but the following overview focuses on the titled nobility, who played more of a role in history. At the top, princes of the blood, nearest in consanguinity to the reigning royal family, could monopolize high posts in the army and diplomatic corps, or they could be idle parasites. Next were mediatized princes—once sovereign, but after a war or two, made dependent on another prince; this was common in the Russias and Germanies, and a factor in French politics until the eighteenth century. Next came dukes, earls, marquises, counts, and other titles, the bottom-most of which were barons, baronets, or knights. Roughly speaking, the higher the title, the more land the family owned, but this varied wildly. Except on the British isles, every child of a noble family inherited a title; only in Britain was primogeniture carried so far that only the eldest male got the title, so that his siblings, unless the girls married well, sank into the country gentry, an ill-defined, socially mobile factor in British society until the First World War. History is kinder to rising or ruthless families than to losers, so we must keep in mind that nobles were not necessarily rich; in fact, many poor nobles existed in Poland, Hungary, and lands with a high percentage of nobles. A family was derogated (deprived of its patent of nobility) for a misalliance (poor marriage), recourse to manual labor for sustenance, conviction of a felony, hopeless debt, or offense to a monarch. Princes Kropotkin and Bakunin, for example, were stripped of their nobility and imprisoned by Tsar Nicholas I for embracing anarchism and advocating rebellion in nineteenth-century Russia.

Having sketched in the hierarchy of the church and of noble-dominated society, we proceed to events providing the immediate background to the decade of the 1450s, with which the AP European History exam begins. The year 1453 marks a milestone on the timeline of European history, since, with one bit of license, we can locate three major events: the fall of Constantinople, the perfection of movable-type printing in Germany, and the end of the Hundred Years' War.

The Hundred Years' War

An important change in the waning of the Middle Ages was the slow move, in key areas, from the feudal order to the revolutionary notion of a centralized, dominant, hereditary monarchy. Instrumental in this evolution was the intermittent conflict between England and France known as the Hundred Years' War (1337–1453).

The English king was vassal of the French king for the duchy of Aquitaine, but the French king wanted control of that duchy; meanwhile, the English king, Edward III, had a claim to the French throne through his mother, a princess of France. Thus, each prince wanted to grab something belonging to the other.

In addition, French nobles sought opportunities to gain power at the expense of the French king. England exported its wool to Flanders, some of whose traditionally free cities were coming under control of the king of France. The rich woolen-producing cities of Bruges and Ghent sought to play off the friendlier English king against the French king; but Flemish nobles thought otherwise and looked to the French king for protection. Since kings and nobles shared the value of chivalry, which portrayed war as a glorious adventure, they could overlook economic interests underlying their political jockeying.

The war was fought in France, though the Scots (with French encouragement) invaded northern England. In a few major battles—Crecy (1346), Poitiers (1356), and Agincourt (1415)—English longbows triumphed over French crossbows, but otherwise fighting consisted of sieges and raids. The war became one of attrition: the French slowly wore down the English. Technological changes during the war included the use of the aforementioned English longbows and the increasingly expensive plate armor of knights.

Joan of Arc (1412–1431), a peasant girl who heard and saw Saints Michael, Margaret, and Catherine of Alexandria, rallied the French army to victory. Due to Joan's prowess, Charles VII was crowned king at Rheims, the traditional locale for this rite. Joan was captured by the Burgundians, allies of England, and sold to the English, who tried her for heresy (witchcraft). She was burned at the stake at Rouen. But the martial spirit with which she endowed French troops helped them to win the war.

Results of the Hundred Years' War

England lost all of its continental possessions, except Calais. Both England and France expended great sums of money; population, especially in France, declined. Both countries suffered internal disruption as soldiers plundered and local officials left to fight. The war disrupted trade everywhere, and England's wool trade to the Low Countries (modern-day Belgium and the Netherlands) slumped badly. To cover financial burdens, both countries raised taxes on the peasants.

In England, the need for money led kings to summon Parliament more often because the levying of taxes required parliamentary approval. These more frequent sessions, in turn, increased the power of the nobles, gentry, and merchants who made up the parliament. In addition, parliamentary procedures changed, giving nobles more control—specifically, the power of impeachment—over government. Representative government thus gained a tradition and foothold that enabled it to survive later challenges and crises.

Ongoing internal conflicts also affected England after the war. A series of factional struggles had led to the deposition of Richard II in 1399. After the war ended, the English nobility continued fighting in the War of the Roses (1450–1485), choosing sides as Lancastrians and Yorkists. Stark losses to old noble families on both sides later helped the Tudor dynasty to create a new nobility more beholden to them and less prone to feuding and plotting against the crown. The Tudors were related to both York and Lancaster, a reason that helped end this bloody civil war.

In France, noble factions contended for power with the king, who refused to deal with the new Estates-General (*Etats-généraux*).[2] By skillful maneuvers with their neighbors, kings of France won room for free play over and against their nobles; royal bankers such as Jacques Coeur were vital to the kings. In order to defeat the hated English, the French monarch wrested from nobles and clergy the right to levy direct taxes on salt (the *gabelle*) and on incomes (the *taille*) from which many nobles and clergy were exempt. With such concessions, the Estates-General gave away a power that the English parliament jealously guarded, namely the right to debate new taxes. The French king thus won control over a royal standing army so that reliance on his nobles became unnecessary.

In both countries, the war led to the growth of **nationalism**, a feeling of unity among the subjects of the king, who used propaganda to rally popular support. Hatred of the enemy united people, and military accomplishments fed national pride.

---

[2]The Estates-General were a national assembly representing the three estates—clergy, nobility, and commoners. They never attained the power of Parliament in England.

Literature also came to express nationalism, when written in the language of the people, instead of Latin. Geoffrey Chaucer (1340–1400) portrayed a wide spectrum of English life in the *Canterbury Tales*, while Francois Villon (1431–1463), in his poetry, emphasized the ordinary life of the French with humor and emotion.

The Rise of New Monarchies, the Renaissance, and the Age of Exploration

New Monarchs

After 1450, monarchs tried to strengthen their national power. The rulers of England, France, Spain, and Portugal were most successful, though the task was difficult. The economic stagnation of the late Middle Ages added to the rising costs of mercenary armies to force monarchs to seek new taxes, a matter traditionally requiring the consent of the nobles.

In addition, nobles, long the chief problem for kings, faced declining incomes and rising desires to control the government of their king. If not fighting external foes, they engaged in civil war at home with fellow nobles and the royal family. One of the consequences of the Black Death was a severe shortage of peasant labor and urban workers for more than thirty years, a fact that hurt the incomes of noble landlords and city employers alike. When princes and nobles sought to impose new taxes on peasants and new work conditions along with lower wages on urban workers, they faced massive peasant revolts (called *jacqueries* in France) and urban revolts of skilled laborers, especially in Flanders and north Italy (for example, the Ciompi revolt in Florence in 1378). In western Europe, nobles had to deal with free peasants, whom they sought to make bear the brunt of economic reversals through taxes and dues. In eastern Europe, the trend toward greater freedom reversed itself: in Brandenburg, Prussia, Poland, Austria, and especially Russia, serfdom was either reintroduced or drastically strengthened.

Opposition to Monarchical Power

Nobles claimed levels of independence under feudal traditions, which from Muscovy to Portugal allowed nobles to meet in a more or less representative forum in order to advise (and in some places, check) the prince. Furthermore, the core of royal armies consisted of nobles; only the appearance of mercenary armies of pikemen saved monarchs from total reliance on noble knights. Many of the higher clergy were noble born, and thus could be enlisted in conflicts with the prince. Facing opposition from the most powerful social groups, the upper clergy, and titled nobles, kings often sought alliances with the bourgeoisie of the towns to counteract the pretended powers of the noble assemblies—for example, the Cortes in Spanish lands, the Estates-General in France, Parliament in England, the Diet in the Holy Roman Empire, the Rijksdag in Sweden, the Sejm in Poland, and the *zemskii sobor* in Muscovy.

Help for France's Monarchy

The defeat of the English in the Hundred Years' War removed the external threat to France. Within France, Louis XI (1461–1483) dealt ruthlessly with nobles who opposed him, whether they acted individually or collectively in the Estates-General. He wanted to aggrandize his lands at the expense of his neighbors, so he could allow no noble dissent. The death of the Duke of Burgundy in 1477 removed the military power holding parts of eastern France, whose heiress, Mary of Burgundy, was unable to hold onto the duchy of Burgundy, Franche-Comté, or Artois, all of which fell to the French king. To the west, Louis maneuvered to force another heiress, Anne of Brittany, to marry him or his heir; after a decade of wrangling, deaths, and intrigues, Brittany fell to the greedy French crown. The kingdom of France, in two hundred years, had expanded to nearly its present size, thanks to successful wars and clever, ruthless kings.

Help for Spain's Monarchy

The marriage of Isabella of Castile (1474–1504) and Ferdinand of Aragon (1478–1516) created a nearly united Spain, whose boundaries were rounded out when Navarre was conquered in 1512, and the Muslims defeated at Granada in 1492. Lands absorbed retained many provincial rights under the new Spanish crown. To afford the luxury of a larger kingdom, Ferdinand and Isabella, even before the Age of Exploration (discussed later in the chapter), sought to enrich the country and pay for a larger army by encouraging local economic interests, such as sheep farming, which profited from a royally sponsored league, the *Mesta*. (Spanish merino wool became a prized commodity everywhere.) Cities and towns formed an alliance, the *Hermandad*, to oppose the old nobility. Finally, the church's authority within Spain and the queen's religious beliefs enabled the Inquisition (1479). Believing in *limpieza de sangre* (purity of blood), Isabella sought to root out all Jewish and Moorish influences from Spain, even among converts, whose sincerity she and the Grand Inquisitor doubted.

The strengthening of nearby Portugal's monarchy is discussed in "The Age of Exploration" section of this chapter.

The Renaissance

The Renaissance occurred mainly in Italy between 1300 and 1550. New learning and changes in styles of art were its two most pronounced characteristics. The Renaissance contrasts with the Middle Ages in that it was more secular. Also, the arts, literature, and scholarship emphasized the individual, not the group, and city-life, not the countryside, predominated. Italian city-states, such as Venice, Milan, Padua, Pisa, Rome, and especially Florence, were home to most Renaissance developments, which were limited to the elite of nobles, bankers, worldly upper clergy, and merchants.

Jacob Burckhardt's *The Civilization of the Renaissance in Italy* (1860) made this period popular, contrasting it starkly with the Middle Ages. Subsequent historians have found more continuity with medieval society and its traditions. Whether the term *renaissance* applies to a cultural event or merely a time period is still debated.

Definitions

Renaissance. French for "rebirth"; the word describes the reawakening or rebirth of interest in the heritage of the classical past.

Classical past. Greece and Rome in the years between 500 B.C.E. and 476 C.E. Humanist scholars were most interested in Rome from 200 B.C.E. to 180 C.E.

Humanism. The study of writings and ideals of the classical past. Rhetoric was the initial area of study, which soon widened to include poetry, history, politics, and philosophy. Civic humanism was the use of humanism in the political life of Italian city-states. Christian humanism focused on early Church writings instead of secular authors.

Individualism. Behavior or theory that emphasizes each person as contrasted with corporate or community behavior. Renaissance individualism sought great accomplishments and looked for heroes of history.

***Virtù*.** The essence of being a man by the display of courage and cleverness. One could display this ability in speech, art, politics, warfare, or elsewhere by seizing the opportunities available. For many, the pursuit of *virtù* was amoral.

Florentine or Platonic Academy. Located in a country villa, and supported by the Medici, the leading Florentine political family, this was a group of scholars who initially studied the works of Plato in Greek. The leading members were Marsilio Ficino (1433–1499) and Pico della Mirandola (1463–1494). They spread such Platonic concepts as the perfection of the circle (see chapter 3) and the plenitude of the universe.

Causes

Economics was the primary cause of the Renaissance. Northern Italy was very wealthy from serving as intermediary between the silk- and spice-producing East and the consuming West. Also, Italian merchants had built up great wealth in the cloth industry and had often turned to international banking. This wealth gave people leisure to pursue new ideas, and money to support the artists and scholars who produced the new works.

Political interaction also contributed to the sweeping changes. Struggles between the papacy, the Holy Roman Empire, and merchants during the Middle Ages had resulted in the independence of many small city-states in northern Italy. This fragmentation meant no single authority had the power to stop or redirect developments. The governments of the city-states, often in the hands of one man, competed by supporting artists and scholars. In many cities, governments became stronger and were dominated by despots (Milan had the Visconti and later the Sforza; Florence, the Medici) or oligarchies (Venice was ruled by the Council of Ten). Smaller city-states disappeared as continual wars led to larger territories dominated by one large city.

Historical influences played a vital role in encouraging the Renaissance as well. Italian cities were often built on ancient Roman ruins, and citizens knew of their heritage. During the many wars between Italian city-states, contestants sought justification for their actions even in classical history. In Florence, based on new readings of Roman authors, a civic republicanism took hold (circa 1380–1430) with the aim of restoring the Roman republic to its old glory, but in a new setting. The recourse to Roman law during disputes between popes and emperors led to study of other Roman writers. Finally, men fleeing the falling Byzantine Empire brought the study of Greek to Italy. The fusion of Greco-Roman cultures occurred at this time.

Renaissance Popes

After 1447, a series of popes supported the arts in Rome. Often criticized for their own lax adherence to the church's teachings on sexuality, these popes took more interest in political, military, and artistic activities than in church reform. Sixtus IV (1471–1484) started the painting of the Sistine Chapel, which his nephew, Julius II (1503–1513), whom Sixtus had promoted within the church, finished by employing Michelangelo to paint the ceiling. Julius successfully asserted his control over the Papal States in central Italy. These popes did not cause the Reformation, but they failed to do anything that might have averted it. One wonders, given divergent trends north of the Alps, what *could* have been done.

Literature, Arts, and Scholarship

Literature

Humanists, as orators and poets, were inspired by and imitated works of the classical past. Their literature was more secular and covered more subjects than that of the Middle Ages, though we must except Dante (1265–1321), whose great *Commedia* (1308–1321) defies cubby-holing. Dante Alighieri was a Florentine writer who spent much of his life in exile after being on the losing side in political struggles in Florence. His *Divine Comedy*, describing a journey through hell, purgatory, and heaven, shows that Reason can take people only so far, then God's grace and revelation take over. The culmination of the Middle Ages, Dante was *not* a Renaissance man, though Italians later claimed him as a precursor to their Renaissance.

Francesco Petrarch (1304–1374), who wrote in both Latin and Italian, encouraged the study of ancient Rome, collected and preserved the work of ancient writers, and produced much work in the classical literary style. He is best known for his sonnets, including many expressing his love for a married woman named Laura, and is considered the father of humanism.

Giovanni Boccaccio (1313–1375) wrote The Decameron, a collection of short stories in Italian, which were meant to amuse, not edify, the reader. The storytellers, having fled the plague in Florence, amuse each other with often bawdy tales written in the Tuscan dialect, which was becoming the basis of the modern Italian language.

Baldassare Castiglione (1478–1529) wrote *The Book of the Courtier*, which specified the qualities necessary for a gentleman who would need to lead an active, not contemplative, life, as in the Middle Ages. Abilities in conversation, sports, arms, dance, music, Latin, and Greek, he advised, should be combined with an agreeable personal demeanor. The notion that marks Castiglione's attitude to manners and life was *sprezzatura*—a lightness of touch, the ability to do something very well, with seeming ease, though much effort may have gone into the final product. This book, translated into many languages, greatly influenced Western ideas about correct behavior.

Art

Artists broke with the medieval past, in both technique and content. Medieval painting, which usually depicted religious topics and was used for religious purposes, was idealized. Its main purpose was to portray the essence or idea of the topic. Renaissance art still used religious topics but often dealt with secular themes and individuals. Oil paints, chiaroscuro, and linear perspectives all combined to achieve greater realism (for an example, see Figure 2-1).

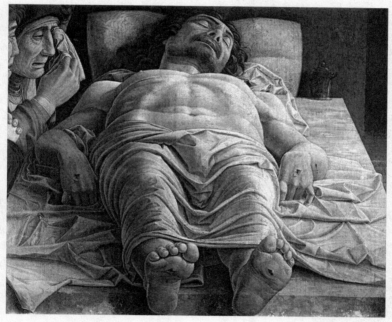

Galleria Brera, Milan, Italy

Figure 2-1. Andrea Mantegna's *Lamentation over the Dead Christ* (1490) shows, more than other works, how skillfully Italian Renaissance artists worked with the exciting ideas of perspective adumbrated earlier by Filippo Brunelleschi and Leon Battista Alberti. This down-the-body view still arrests and captivates us as realistic, just as it opens up a new emotional reaction.

Medieval sculpture was often affixed to churches and its figures designed to teach illiterate believers Bible and saints' stories. By copying classical models and using freestanding pieces, Renaissance sculptors produced works celebrating the individual and the "pagan" spirit of the day. Though some Renaissance statues were meant for exhibition in churches, many were not, making their way instead to private collections or, as with Benvenuto Cellini's *Perseus*, into public squares.

Medieval architecture included the use of pointed arches, flying buttresses, and fan vaulting to obtain great heights, while permitting light to flood the interior of the church or cathedral. The result gave a "feeling" for God rather than fostering an approach to him through Reason. Busy details filling every niche and the absence of symmetry also typify medieval work. Renaissance architects openly copied classical, especially Roman, forms, such as the rounded arch and squared angles.

Giotto (1266–1336) painted religious scenes using light and shadow, a technique called *chiaroscuro*, to create an illusion of depth and greater realism (see Figure 2-2). He is considered the father of Renaissance painting.

Capella degli Scrovengi, Padua, Italy

Figure 2-2. Giotto's *Flight into Egypt* (1303–1305) still shows signs of his late medieval culture—some stiffness, awkwardness in rendering facial emotions—yet his work broke new ground and he was recognized as a creative genius by no less than his contemporary, Dante.

Donatello (1386–1466), the father of Renaissance sculpture, produced the first statue cast in bronze since classical times. His *David* (1440) was also the first nude since antiquity (over a thousand years). No medieval statue dared to be so brazenly naked (see Figure 2-5).

Masaccio (1401–1428) emphasized naturalism in *Tribute Money* (see Figure 2-3) by showing realistic human figures in lifelike poses and by using perspective (the sense that objects that are farther away appear smaller).

Brancacci Chapel, Florence, Italy

Figure 2-3. Masaccio's *Tribute Money* (1428) shows a distinct advance over Giotto in the naturalness of poses and its delicate coloring.

Leonardo da Vinci (1452–1519) produced *The Last Supper* and *Mona Lisa*, as well as many mechanical designs, though few were constructed. (See Figure 2-4.)

Galleria degli Uffizi, Florence, Italy

Figure 2-4. Leonardo da Vinci's *The Annunciation* (1472) shows that three-dimensional composition for which Italian painters were renowned. His subject matter also reminds us that the Renaissance did not reject religion or religious subjects, nor did artists like da Vinci scorn rich Church patrons!

Raphael (1483–1520), a master of Renaissance grace and style, theory and technique, represented these skills in *The School of Athens*.

Michelangelo (1475–1564), a universal man, produced masterpieces in sculpture (*David*; see Figure 2-5) and painting (the Sistine Chapel ceiling). His work was a bridge to mannerism.

Galeria dell'Academia, Florence, Italy   *Victoria and Albert Museum, London, England*

Figure 2-5. Compare the different interpretations obvious in Donatello's *David* (1440) (right) and Michelangelo's *David* (1508) (left). Donatello depicts a graceful boy in a pose that his contemporaries did not find effeminate; whereas Michelangelo depicts a young man—concentrated in the moment perhaps before he joins the rock in one hand to the sling in the other.

Michelangelo and da Vinci, Alberti earlier and Cellini later, all exemplified the *uomo universale*—the ideal man who could do everything well, in all worthy fields. A few noble ladies had the resources and talents to be called Renaissance women: the writer Christine de Pizan, aristocratic patronesses of the arts and letters Isabella Gonzaga and Beatrice d'Este, the poet Vittoria Colonna, the painter Artemisia Gentilleschi, and others kept the Renaissance from being just an old-boys club.

Scholars

Scholars sought to know what is good and to practice it, as did those of the Middle Ages. However, Renaissance people sought more practical results and did not judge things solely by religious standards. Manuscript collections enabled scholars to study the primary sources and to reject all traditions that had been built up since classical times. Also, scholars participated in the lives of their cities as active politicians.

Leonardo Bruni (1370–1444), civic humanist, served as chancellor of Florence, where he used his rhetorical skills to rouse the citizens against external enemies. He also wrote a history of his city and was the first to use the term *humanism*.

Lorenzo Valla (1407–1457) authored *Elegances of the Latin Language*, the standard text in Latin philology, and also exposed as a forgery the *Donation of Constantine*, which had purported to give the papacy control of vast lands in Italy.

Machiavelli (1469–1527) wrote *The Prince*, which analyzed politics from the standpoint of reason, rather than faith or tradition. His work, amoral in tone, describes how a political leader can obtain and hold power by acting first in self-interest, but ultimately with the idea of the well-being of his land in mind. For one's country, one had to be strong at all costs; for both ends, one found *reasons of state* to do the necessary.

The Renaissance Outside Italy

Styles of the Italian Renaissance touched the rest of Europe in varying ways. In the Low Countries, artists such as Hieronymus Bosch (1450–1516) still produced works on religious themes, but the attention to detail in the paintings of Jan van Eyck (1385–1440) typifies the grafting of Renaissance ideas. The works of artist Pieter Brueghel the Elder (1525–1569) show an even stronger turn toward realism (see Figure 2-6), as do those of the Venetian school, with Giorgione and the mannerists active about the same time.

Gemaeldegalerie, Staatliche Museen zu Berlin, Berlin, Germany

Figure 2-6. Pieter Brueghel the Elder's *Netherlandish Proverbs* (1559) shows the homely, often humorous realism of many northern artists.

In Mainz, Germany, the invention of printing with movable type in the 1450s, attributed to Johann Gutenberg, facilitated the spread of new ideas throughout Europe, a breakthrough quickly exploited by such Renaissance printers as Aldus Manutius (1449–1515) of Venice. Albrecht Dürer (1471–1528) gave realism and individuality to the art of the woodcut, where he often combined words and images (see Figure 2-7).

Alte Pinakothek, Munich, Germany

Figure 2-7. Albrecht Dürer's *Four Holy Men* **(1526) shows his solid training as a wood engraver as well as the influence of his journeys in Italy. Dürer's subject, as with those of other northern artists, can be interpreted as a sign of the preponderance of Christian humanism north of the Alps; like Erasmus, Dürer remained Catholic. The four men are Saints John, Peter, Paul, and Mark, not the evangelists.**

Many Italian artists and scholars were hired in France. The Loire Valley chateaux of the sixteenth century and Francois Rabelais's (1494–1553) bawdy epic *Gargantua and Pantagruel* reflect Renaissance erudition and tastes.

The new interest in the past and new developments did not appear in England until the sixteenth century. Poetry and drama, culminating in the age of Shakespeare, is the most pronounced accomplishment of the Renaissance spirit in England.

In Spain, money from the Americas supported such building as the Escorial, the new royal palace, as well as El Greco (1541–1614), often considered a mannerist. His work is discussed in chapter 3.

Christian Humanism

The Renaissance outside Italy emphasized the study of the Bible and the church fathers more than secular authors of Rome and Greece.

Elements

Although they used the techniques of the Italian humanists in the analysis of ancient writings, language, and style, Christian humanists were more interested in providing guidance on personal behavior.

Work on Christian sources done between 1450 and 1530 emphasized education and the power of the human intellect to bring about institutional change and moral improvement. The many tracts and guides of Christian humanists were directed at reforming the church, but led many into criticisms of the church, which resulted in the Reformation. In addition, the discovery that traditional Christian texts had different versions proved unsettling to many believers.

Though many Christian humanists were not clergymen, most early reformers of the church during the Reformation had been trained as Christian humanists.

Christian humanism, with its emphasis on toleration and education, disappeared for a time owing to the increasing passion of the Reformation after 1530.

Leaders of Northern Humanism

Desiderius Erasmus (1466–1536), a Dutchman and the most notable figure of the Christian humanist movement, made new translations of the Greek and Latin versions of the New Testament in order to have "purer" editions. His *In Praise of Folly* satirizes the ambitions of the world, especially those of the clergy. A man known throughout intellectual circles of Europe, he emphasized the virtues of tolerance, restraint, and education at the time the church was fragmenting during the Reformation. Erasmus led a life of simple piety, practicing the Christian virtues, which led to complaints that he had no role for the institutional church. His criticisms of the church and clergy, though meant to lead to reforms, gave ammunition to those wishing to attack the church and, therefore, it is said, "Erasmus laid the egg that Luther hatched."

Thomas More (1478–1536), an English lawyer, politician, and humanist, wrote *Utopia* (a Greek word for "nowhere"). Mixing civic humanism with religious ideals, the book describes a perfect society, located on an imaginary island, in which war, poverty, religious intolerance, and other problems of the early sixteenth century do not exist. *Utopia* sought to show how people might live if they followed the social and political ideals of Christianity. Also, in a break with medieval thought, More portrayed government as very active in the economic life of the society, education, and public health. Though a critic of the church and clergy of his day, More was executed by Henry VIII, king of England, for refusing to countenance Henry's break with the pope in religious matters.

Jacques Lefevre d'Etaples (1455–1536), the leading French humanist, edited and published five versions of the Psalms, an edition that challenged the tradition of a single, authoritative Bible. Also, his work on St. Paul anticipated that of Martin Luther.

Francesco Ximenes de Cisneros (1436–1517), the Grand Inquisitor and thus the leader of the Spanish church, founded a university and produced the *Complutensian Polyglot Bible*, which had Hebrew, Greek, and Latin versions of the Bible in parallel columns. He also reformed the Spanish clergy and church so that most criticisms of the later reformers during the Reformation did not apply to Spain.

The Age of Exploration and Conquests

Motives

A number of factors combined to make the overwhelming risks of long-distance voyages in the Atlantic both more feasible and more desirable. Though we cannot discount the desire for adventure and glory, an idealist quest for new knowledge, or the Christian zeal behind converting nonbelievers, other factors most likely were preponderant:

1. Since the Middle Ages, the Mediterranean Sea had become a de facto Italian lake, with Venice, Genoa, Pisa, and other port cities monopolizing trade with North Africa and the Near East. The rest of Europe was well aware of the costs of these middlemen.

2. The incursions of the Turks, encroaching on the old Silk Road to China and India, then on the Black Sea, left in their wake higher tolls on goods shipped overland, so the discovery of free sea routes became desirable. Inventions and improvements in naval technology in the late Middle Ages also made such voyages more feasible: the compass, astrolabe, better charts, a pocket watch, and other devices helped.

3. The Renaissance revived Greek studies of the round earth and heavens, with good estimates now possible of the earth's real circumference and of actual distances.

4. Dynastic ties between Aragon and south Italy underlay the "conquest" of the papal throne by a Spanish noble family, the Borgias, so that the spirit and advances of Renaissance Italy easily voyaged to the Iberian peninsula.

Portugal

Prince Henry the Navigator (1394–1460) was inspired by both medieval and modern aims when he set up the first European school of navigation in his realm. The old *reconquista* and crusader spirit lived in him: he wished to conquer his neighbors and the North African Muslims, and also to retake the Holy Land (believing in legends of a lost Christian king, Prester John, in need of his chivalrous aid in Abyssinia). Also, Henry wanted to circumvent Genoese trade in west African gold and, if possible, make it to the east African gold and spice markets, thus eliminating all middlemen. In the 1440s, his captain, Joao Gonçalvez Zarco, made it around the Horn of Africa to Cape Verde and began the fateful practice of slave raids. Bartolomeu Dias rounded the southern tip of Africa in 1487, but left the more perilous voyage to India to his compatriot, Vasco da Gama, who reached India in 1498. The cargo from his first voyage may have netted investors an astonishing profit of about 600 percent. Soon, in addition to the African forts founded from the 1450s on, Portugal had footholds in Calicut and Goa, then in 1510 in the Spice Islands. Probably by accident, the explorer Cabral landed on Brazil in 1500. By this time, the Spanish pope, Alexander VI Borgia, had made a spectacular deal with Spain and Portugal in the Treaty of Tordesillas (1494): beyond a certain line (changed at least once), Spain would have legal claim to all "new" lands to the west, Portugal to the east of that line, which now included most of Brazil, all of Africa, the Indian Ocean, the Spice Islands, and so on.

Spain

Even more than the Portuguese, the Spanish came to be motivated by the desire to convert pagans and heathens, not to mention Muslims. But they were no less hungry for gold, silver, spices, and other highly profitable commodities. Once Portugal had secured an African route to the east, the Spanish resigned themselves to going west. Christopher Columbus (1446–1506), a Genoese sailor, brought to Spain a map by the Florentine Toscanelli suggesting a westerly route across the Atlantic to Japan, China, and India. Queen Isabella bankrolled his voyages, which took him to the West Indies, so named because Columbus mistakenly believed he had come upon islands off the coast of India. The discovery of naked Indians and placer gold excited the varied lusts of Spanish sailors and led to the next wave of voyages, including four more trips by Columbus, one making it to Panama.

Several other explorers sailed under the Spanish flag:

- The Italian Amerigo Vespucci made several voyages (1499–1502) exploring the soon-to-be-renamed American coast for Spain.

- Vasco Núñez de Balboa reached the Pacific Ocean in 1513.

- The Portuguese sailor Ferdinand Magellan sailed most of the way around the world for Spain (1519–1522) but met his death in the Philippines, leaving his captain, Juan Sebastian del Cano, to complete the voyage of circumnavigation.

- Hernan Cortes was able to conquer the Aztec empire in Mexico (1519–1521) with the aid of disaffected neighboring tribes.

- Francisco Pizarro conquered the Inca empire in Peru (1531–1534) with a cruel stratagem, and thus opened the path to the exploitation of the silver ore of Potosi. At about the same time, Spanish explorers discovered large silver deposits in Mexico, thus insuring a steady supply of wealth to the Spanish crown, which wisely took its fifth (*el quinto*).

Other Countries

Soon the English and French began their own fateful voyages; only a century later, the Dutch joined in the action. Two Portuguese brothers, John and Sebastian Cabot, hired themselves out to the English crown to explore North America in the 1490s, but English voyages of exploration to the Americas did not pick up again until the 1570s, under Queen Elizabeth; in the meanwhile, they had pioneered new routes to Russia via the White Sea. The French were represented in North America first by Jacques Carier in 1534, later by Samuel de Champlain and others.

Results of Voyages: Colombian Exchange

Obviously, Portugal and Spain brought back riches to the Old World: gold, silver, spices, silks, slaves, and more. Silver from the New World especially helped fuel the price revolution of the sixteenth century: Spanish prices doubled by 1560; by 1600 some prices had risen tenfold in Europe, which brought important changes to the social and economic fabric. The "rents" or income of landowners fell relative to commodity prices, so that nobles all over Europe scrambled for new sources of income, often at the expense of their peasants. In contrast, income for many city dwellers, especially merchants, rose appreciably, and with it, in many cases, their social or political clout, most often expressed by good marriages with "old money" or elevation into the nobility.

Europeans and New World "Indians" exchanged other things, including foods and diseases:

From the Americas to Europe: Corn, tomatoes, potatoes, turkeys, cashews, beans, chocolate, chili peppers, peanuts, pineapples, and, perhaps, syphilis (though some historians dispute this)

From Europe to the Americas: Wheat, cattle, horses, pigs, grapes, oranges, rice, chickens, geese, olives, bananas, sugar cane; and smallpox, measles, and other deadly diseases

Though syphilis took its deadly toll in Europe (the only "cure" being a dangerous use of mercury into the nineteenth century), the Americas clearly suffered most, with decimation of whole populations, some of which, in some places, were wiped out. Native Americans' lack of immunity to foreign diseases rewrote the history of the Americas, whereas Africans, long used to contact with Europeans, were, just as tragically, able to survive, thus becoming hardier candidates for enslavement.

← TIMELINE →

New Monarchies, Renaissance, and the Age of Exploration

Year(s)	Event	Significance
1308–1377	French kings keep several popes in the so-called Babylonian Captivity in Avignon.	The residence of several popes in Avignon undermines the authority of the papacy and helps national monarchs to grab more power over the church in their lands.
1340	Italy revives the honor of poet laureate.	Francesco Petrarch is crowned poet laureate in Rome, a symbolic milestone in Italian Renaissance as it marks the revival of an ancient Roman custom.
1347–1350	The Black Death decimates the population of Europe.	Europe loses roughly 40 percent of its population over three decades. Workers and peasants press for more freedom and higher wages, which leads to urban and rural riots (1378–1382) all over Europe.
1434	The Medici come to power in Florence.	Though Florence is a republic, the Medici family of bankers and wool merchants come to dominate politics in the fifteenth century. They are great art patrons.
1453	The sack of Constantinople occurs; the Hundred Years' War ends.	The loss of the capital of the Byzantine Empire makes the Turks the prime menace to Christian Europe. France's victory over England in the Hundred Years' War releases both countries to develop strong monarchies.
1450s	Johann Gutenberg and Johann Fust develop movable-type printing in Mainz, Germany (Holy Roman Empire).	The perfection of movable-type printing allows the printing and dissemination of cheaper books throughout Europe.
1454–1494	Milan and Venice sign Peace Treaty of Lodi; peace ends when French invade Italy in 1494.	The five powers of Italy enjoy forty years of peace, which according to some historians, makes the High Renaissance in the arts possible.
1480	Muscovy throws off the Tatar yoke.	Grand Duke of Muscovy stops paying tribute to the Mongol Tatars—a symbolic declaration of independence of the Russian states.
1494	Portugal and Spain sign the Treaty of Tordesillas.	Pope Alexander VI "divides the world" between Spain and Portugal with respect to further exploration (the line in the Atlantic is moved at one point to give Portugal Brazil).

(Continued)

1487/ 1499	Bartolomeu Dias reaches the Cape of Good Hope; Vasco da Gama comes back from India with precious cargo.	Dias, a Portuguese explorer, is first to reach, then round the Cape of Good Hope on the way to India. Da Gama's load of spices nets investors 600 percent profit, thus spurring on further voyages.
1519/ 1533	Hernan Cortes conquers the Aztec empire in Mexico; Francisco Pizarro conquers the Inca empire in and near Peru.	Spanish exploitation of New World silver and gold begins.
1527	The Sack of Rome occurs.	The imperial troops of Charles V sack Rome, marking the symbolic end to the artistic Renaissance—and of Italy's independence in European affairs.

Chapter 3

Reform, Counter-Reform, and the New Sciences

The Reformation

By generating new ideas about the relationships among God, individuals, and society, the Reformation destroyed western Europe's religious unity. Its course was greatly influenced by politics and led, in most areas, to the subjection of the church to local or national political rulers, because resentments, especially in Europe north of the Alps, often focused on the burden of a "foreign," international power, namely the papacy, dictating to distant peoples what to do, and how much money to send to Rome. It is no coincidence that the Protestant Reformation went hand in hand with both emergent nationalisms and the aggrandizement of local princes at the expense of the church, whose lands and wealth the princes gladly appropriated—in the name of Christ.

Earlier threats to the unity of the church had been made by John Wycliff and Jan Hus, and abuses of church practices and positions upset many people, including Christian humanists. Personal piety and mysticism, alternative approaches to Christianity that did not need the apparatus of the institutional church and the clergy had been attracting adherents since the late Middle Ages.

Martin Luther (1483–1546)

The Beginnings

Martin Luther was a miner's son from Saxony in central Germany. At the urging of his father, he studied for a career in law, but he underwent a religious experience while traveling that led him to become an Augustinian friar. Later, he became a professor at the fairly new University of Wittenberg in Saxony.

Religious Problems

Luther, to his chagrin, could not reconcile the idea of the sinful individual with the justice of God. How could a sinner attain the righteousness needed for salvation? In his reading of the Bible, especially Romans 1:17, Luther came to believe that personal efforts—good works and the sacraments—could not "earn" the sinner salvation; only through belief and faith could one obtain grace. *Justification by faith alone* was the road to salvation, Luther believed by 1515. God's grace was a free gift, not a reward.

Indulgences

Indulgences, started during the crusades, were practices or prayers given by the church to confessed sinners to help the sinners cancel their penalty in purgatory.[1] During the Avignon Captivity, popes unable to tap funds frozen in Italy resorted to charging money for some indulgences. This became an easy—and sordid—device to raise revenues long after the popes had returned to Rome. From 1508 on, popes sold indulgences to fund the new basilica of Saint Peter.

The practice of selling indulgences was not limited to the popes, however; clergy further down the church hierarchy took advantage of the practice as well. For example, in order to become archbishop of Mainz, a lucrative post, and one of the seven imperial electors, Albrecht of Brandenburg borrowed money from the Fuggers, a rich family of bankers, to bribe the cathedral chapter. In return, the Fuggers took as collateral part of Albrecht's yearly income and part of the sales of the indulgence known as "Peter's Pence." Albrecht licensed a Dominican friar named Tetzel to sell that indulgence in the lands of the new archbishop, some of which were near Wittenberg, with proceeds going to repay Albrecht's loan to the Fuggers. The popular belief was: "As soon as a coin in the coffer rings, the soul from purgatory springs," and Tetzel had many takers.

On October 31, 1517, Luther, believing that indulgences gave false hopes of salvation, nailed his Ninety-five Theses about indulgences to the door of the Wittenberg church for the sake of an academic debate. At this time, he was seeking to reform the church, not divide it.

Luther's Relations with the Pope and Governments

In 1519, Luther debated his criticisms of the church and was driven to say that only the Bible, not religious tradition or papal statements, determined correct religious practices and beliefs. In 1521, Pope Leo X excommunicated Luther for his beliefs.

In 1521, Luther appeared in the city of Worms before the Diet[2] of the Holy Roman Empire, including Emperor Charles V. He was again condemned. At the Diet of Worms, Luther made his famous statement about the basis for his writings: "Here I stand. I can do no other." After this, Luther could not go back; the break with the pope was permanent.

Frederick III of Saxony, where Luther resided, protected Luther in Wartburg Castle for a year. Frederick never accepted Luther's beliefs, but protected him because Luther was his subject. The weak political control of Emperor Charles V enabled Luther's success in avoiding the penalties of the pope and the emperor.

Luther's Writings

Thanks to the printing press, Luther was able to print his 95 theses in pamphlet form. More important were his three pamphlets of 1520 that outlined more than a program of reform: these could only lead to a break with the hierarchical Church. The

---

[1] Purgatory was a place, according to medieval Catholic doctrine, where souls with venial, or minor sins, could go to be purified, since Heaven was meant for souls pure of all sin.

[2] A diet, in European usage, was a representative assembly that met daily to discuss problems and advise princes.

angry pamphlet of 1524 against the Peasants' Revolt shows the earthy, often obscene side of Luther, but also an important point: that he intended no "Protestant Revolution," as did some of his followers.

- *Address to the Christian Nobility of the German Nation* (1520) argued that nobles, as well as clergy, were leaders of the church and should undertake to reform it.

- *Babylonian Captivity* (1520) attacked the traditional seven sacraments, replacing them with only two.

- *Freedom of the Christian Man* (1520) explained Luther's views on faith, good works, the nature of God, and the supremacy of political authority over believers.

- *Against the Murderous, Thieving Hordes of Peasants* (1524), responding to the peasants' revolt, said that political leaders, not the people, should control society.

By 1534, Luther had translated the Bible into German, making it accessible to many more people than was the Latin Bible and greatly influencing the development of the German language. His "A Mighty Fortress Is Our God" was the most popular hymn of the sixteenth century. The printing press enabled Luther's works to be distributed quickly throughout Germany, though he continued to publish in both Latin and German.

Subsequent Developments of Lutheranism

The increasing economic burdens placed on the peasants by their lords, combined with Luther's words that a Christian is subject to no one, allegedly led German peasants to revolt in 1524. The ensuing repression, supported by Luther, resulted in the deaths of 70,000–100,000 peasants and a central Lutheran tenet of obedience to princes.

At a meeting of the Holy Roman Empire's leaders in 1529, a group of rulers influenced by Luther's teachings "protested" the decision of the majority to force Protestants to give back Church property just stolen and to allow the Catholic Mass—hence the term "Protestant." *Protestant* eventually was applied to all Western Christians who did not maintain allegiance to the pope. After a failure of Protestants and Catholics to find a mutually acceptable statement of faith, the Augsburg Confession of 1530 came out as a summary of Lutheran beliefs. Led by Philip Melanchthon (1497–1560), "educator of Germany," Lutherans undertook educational reform, including establishing schools for girls.

The spread of Lutheranism brought new allies and wealth to local rulers. To protect themselves against the efforts of Emperor Charles V to reestablish Catholicism in Germany, Lutheran rulers formed a defensive alliance at Schmalkalden, the Schmalkaldic League, in 1531. In addition, wherever Lutheranism was adopted, the ruler seized church lands. This made a return to Catholicism difficult, since princes profiting thereby would never restore lands to the church willingly. (Denmark became Lutheran in 1523, Sweden in 1527.)

After the Schmalkaldic wars in the 1540s, which Charles V won but was unable to capitalize on because his treatment of defeated political rulers in Germany offended the nobility of the empire, the Peace of Augsburg (1555) established the permanent religious division of Germany into Lutheran and Catholic churches. The formula *cuius regio, eius religio* ("whose region, his religion") meant that the religion of any area would be that of the ruling political authority.

Other Reformers

Luther was not so much the father as the elder brother of the Reformation, because other reformers were speaking up by the early 1520s.

Ulrich Zwingli (1484–1531) introduced reform ideas in Zurich in Switzerland. He rejected clerical celibacy, veneration of saints, fasts, transubstantiation,[3] and purgatory. Scorning ritual and ceremony, Zwingli stripped churches of decorations, such as statues. In 1523, the governing council of the city accepted his beliefs. Zurich became a center for Protestantism and its spread throughout Switzerland. Zwingli, believing in the union of church and state, established in Zurich a system that required church attendance by all citizens and regulated many aspects of personal behavior—all enforced by courts and a group of informers. His model would greatly influence John Calvin in Geneva.

Efforts to reconcile the views of Zwingli and Luther, chiefly over the issue of the Eucharist, failed during a meeting in Marburg Castle in 1529.

Switzerland, divided into many cantons, also divided into Protestant and Catholic camps. A series of civil wars, during which Zwingli was captured and executed, led to a treaty in which each canton was permitted to determine its own religion.

Anabaptists

As the Bible became available to common folk in vernacular translations, many people adopted interpretations contrary to those of Luther, Zwingli, and the Catholics.

The Anabaptists were one such group. The Anabaptists rejected the validity of child baptism and believed that such children had to be rebaptized when they became adults (hence the name *Anabaptist*, which is derived from the Greek word for "baptize again"). For all others, they advocated adult baptism only. They also sought to return to the ideal of the early Christian church, which they felt was a voluntary association of believers with no connection to the state. Perhaps the first Anabaptists appeared in Zurich in 1525 under the leadership of Conrad Grebel (1498–1526), and were called Swiss Brethren.

In 1534, a group of Anabaptists led by Jan Matthys gained control of the city of Münster in Germany and forced other Protestants and Catholics to convert or leave. The Anabaptists, most of whom were workers and peasants who followed Old Testament customs, abolished private property and legalized polygamy. Combined armies of Protestants and Catholics recaptured the city and executed the leaders in 1535. Thereafter,

---

[3]This is the doctrine that the bread and wine are transformed by the priest, at the highpoint of the Mass, into the Body and Blood of Christ; but retain the appearances of bread and wine. The Lutheran idea of consubstantiation is more complex; the Zwinglians and Calvinists threw both out and decided that the Eucharist was only symbolic.

Anabaptism became a byword for other Christians of the danger of letting reform ideas influence workers and peasants. Subsequently, Anabaptists adopted pacifism and avoided involvement with the state whenever possible. Today, the Mennonites, founded by Menno Simons (1496–1561) and the Amish are the descendents of the Anabaptists.

John Calvin

John Calvin (1509–1564), a Frenchman, arrived in 1536 at Geneva, a Swiss city-state that had adopted an anti-Catholic position, but failed in his first efforts to further the reforms. Upon Calvin's return in 1540, however, Geneva became the center of the Reformation.

Calvin's *Institutes of the Christian Religion* (1536), a logical reworking of Christianity, had a universal more than a local or national appeal. Calvin differed from Luther in emphasizing predestination, namely, the doctrine that God ordained who would be saved before anyone was born. Like Zwingli, Calvin rejected most aspects of the medieval church's practices and sought a simple, unadorned church. He also believed that church and state should be united.

During his stay in Strasbourg, Calvin saw how the reformer Martin Bucer (1491–1551) had organized that city, and he followed Bucer's example when he returned to Geneva. As in Zurich, the church and city authorities in Geneva combined to enforce Christian behavior, such as prohibitions on gaming, immodest dress, and public baths as well as regular church attendance and "godly" conduct in all things. Calvinism came to stand for stern morality. Followers of Calvin became the most militant and uncompromising of all Protestants. Geneva became the home to Protestant exiles from England, Scotland, the Netherlands, and France, who later returned to their countries with Calvinist ideas.

Calvinism ultimately triumphed as the majority religion in Scotland, under the leadership of John Knox (1505–1572), and the United Provinces of the Netherlands. Puritans in England and New England also accepted Calvinism.

Reform in England

England underwent reforms in a pattern differing from the rest of Europe. Personal and political decisions by the rulers determined much of the course of the Reformation there.

The Break with the Pope

Henry VIII (1509–1547) married Katharine of Aragon, the widow of his older brother, but by 1526, he was certain that her inability to produce a son to inherit his throne was because he had violated God's commandments (Leviticus 18:16, 20:21) by marrying his brother's widow.

Soon, Henry fell in love with Anne Boleyn and decided to annul his marriage to Katharine in order to marry Anne. Pope Clement VII, whose pronouncement was needed for an annulment, was, after 1527, under the control of Charles V, Katharine's nephew. Efforts to secure the annulment, directed by Cardinal Thomas Wolsey (1474–1530), ended in failure and his disgrace. Thomas Cranmer (1489–1556), made archbishop in 1533, dissolved Henry's marriage, which permitted him to marry Anne in 1533.

Henry used Parliament to threaten the pope and eventually to legislate a break with Rome. The Act of Annates (1532) prevented payments of money to the pope. The Act of Restraint of Appeals (1533) forbade appeals to Rome, which stopped Katharine from appealing her divorce to the pope. The Act of Supremacy (1534) declared Henry, not the pope, as the head of the English church. Subsequent acts enabled Henry to dissolve the monasteries and seize their land, which represented perhaps 25 percent of the land of England.

In 1536, Thomas More, the English author and statesman, was executed for rejecting Henry's leadership of the English church; for this Thomas became a Catholic saint.

Protestant beliefs and practices made little headway during Henry's reign as he accepted transubstantiation, enforced celibacy among the clergy, and otherwise made the English church conform to most medieval practices.

Protestantism

Under Henry VIII's son, Edward VI (1547–1553), a child of ten at his accession, the English church adopted Calvinism. Clergy were allowed to marry, communion by the laity expanded, and images were removed from churches. Doctrine included justification by faith, the denial of transubstantiation, and only two sacraments.

English Catholicism

Under Mary (1553–1558), Henry's daughter and Edward's half-sister, Catholicism was restored and England reunited with the pope. More than 300 people were executed, including Archbishop Cranmer, for refusing to abandon their Protestant beliefs. Numerous Protestants fled to the Continent, where they learned about more advanced Protestant beliefs, including Calvinism at Geneva.

Anglicanism

Under Elizabeth I (1558–1603), Henry's daughter and Edward's and Mary's half-sister, the church in England adopted Protestant beliefs again. The Elizabethan Settlement required outward conformity to the official church but rarely inquired about inward beliefs. Some practices of the church, including ritual, resembled Catholic practices. Catholicism remained, especially among the gentry, but could not be practiced openly.

Some reformers wanted to purify (hence "Puritans") the church of its remaining Catholic aspects. The resulting church, Protestant in doctrine and practice but retaining most of the physical possessions, such as buildings, and many powers, such as church courts, of the medieval church, was called *Anglican*.

Reform Elsewhere in Europe

The Parliament in Ireland established a Protestant church much like the one in England. The landlords and people near Dublin were the only ones who followed their monarchs to Protestantism, as the mass of the Irish people were left untouched by the Reformation. Protestants in Ireland formed what is called the *Ascendancy*, an elite group that ruled the country for four centuries. Catholic stalwarts and priests became the religious, and eventually, the national, leaders of the rest of Irish people.

John Knox (1505–1572), upon his return from the Continent, led the Reformation in Scotland. The Scottish Parliament, dominated by nobles, established Protestantism in 1560. The resulting church was Calvinist in doctrine.

France, near Geneva and Germany, experienced efforts at establishing Protestantism, but the kings of France had control of the church there and gave no encouragement to reformers. Calvinists, known in France as Huguenots, were especially common among the nobility, and after 1562, a series of civil wars involving religious differences resulted.

The church in Spain, controlled by the monarchy, allowed no Protestantism to take root. Italian political authorities similarly rejected Protestantism.

The Counter-Reformation

The Catholic or Counter-Reformation brought changes to the portion of the Western church that retained its allegiance to the pope. Some historians see this as a reform of the Catholic Church, similar to what Protestants were doing, while others see it as a result of the criticisms of Protestants.

Efforts to reform the church were given new impetus by Luther's activities. These included new religious orders such as Capuchins (1528), Theatines (1534), and Ursulines (1535), as well as mystics such as Saint Teresa of Avila (1515–1582).

Saint Ignatius of Loyola (1491–1556), a former soldier, founded the Society of Jesus in 1540 to lead the attack on Protestantism. Called Jesuits, members of this society trained pursuant to ideas found in Ignatius's *Spiritual Exercises*, had dedication and determination, and became the leaders in the Counter-Reformation. In addition to serving in Europe, by the 1540s, Jesuits, including Saint Francis Xavier (1506–1552), traveled to Japan as missionaries. Jesuits viewed education as the principal weapon against Protestant heresy, and so their schools became some of the best in Europe and remained so for centuries.

Popes resisted reforming efforts because of fears as to what a council of church leaders might do to papal powers. The Sack of Rome in 1527, when soldiers of the Holy Roman Emperor captured and looted Rome, was seen by many as a judgment of God against the lives of Renaissance popes. In 1534, Paul III became pope and attacked abuses while reasserting papal leadership.

Convened by Paul III and firmly under papal control, the Council of Trent met in three sessions from 1545 to 1563. It settled many aspects of doctrine including transubstantiation, the seven sacraments, the efficacy of good works for salvation, and the role of saints and priests. It also approved the "Index of Forbidden Books," which was a list of books banned for general use, but accessible by scholars with special permission. Some books banned over the centuries were those of Montaigne, Galileo, and other intellectuals.

Other reforms came into effect. The sale of church offices was curtailed. New seminaries for more- and better-trained clergy were created. The revitalized Catholic Church, the papacy, and the Jesuits set out to reunite western Christianity and won back many lands in central Europe from the Protestants.

Part of the appeal of Counter-Reformation Catholicism was its emphasis on mysticism and saints' stories in theology, as well as its embrace of baroque styles in painting, music, and architecture. Whereas most Protestant sects shunned ornament and ostentation, Catholic reform used both, relying on the strategy that more believers are moved through the senses than through the bare Word of God. An example of the skillful blend of Church aims and baroque techniques is seen in the works of El Greco (see Figure 3-1).

Doctrines Compared

The Reformation induced many to rethink the beliefs of Christianity. Most of the major divisions of the Western church took differing positions on matters of doctrine. Some thinkers, such as Martin Bucer, the reformer in Strasbourg, believed many traditions, such as the ring in the marriage ceremony, were "things indifferent"—Christians could differ in their beliefs on such issues—but with the increasing rigidity of various churches, such views did not dominate.

Protestants and Catholics differed in their use of religious texts and their view of the clergy. Whereas Protestants emphasized the role of the Bible, Catholics included the traditions and saints' stories that evolved during the Middle Ages, as well as papal pronouncements. Catholics also retained the medieval view about the special nature and role of clergy, while Protestants emphasized the "priesthood of all believers," which meant that all individuals were equal before God. But only a few radical sects (for example, the Friends, or Quakers) rejected a clergy altogether; most Protestants wanted a preaching clergy that lived a more Christian life, which meant marriage for ministers.

Church governance varied widely. Catholics retained the medieval hierarchy of believers, priests, bishops, and pope. Anglicans rejected the authority of the pope and substituted the monarch as the supreme governor of the church. Lutherans rejected the authority of the pope but kept bishops, of whom the highest was the local prince. Most Calvinist churches were governed by ministers and a group of elders, a system called Presbyterianism. Anabaptists rejected most forms of church governance in favor of congregational democracy.

Santo Church of Tomé, Toledo, Spain

Figure 3-1. Domenikos Theotokopoulos, more commonly know as El Greco, is classed as a mannerist for his elongated figures and passionate colors. He is also an early baroque master. The *Burial of Count Orgaz* (1586), his masterpiece, shows the fervid piety of the Counter-Reformation and of loyal Spain; the profusion of saints and angels marks this apart from any contemporary painting by a Protestant.

Most Protestants denied the efficacy of most sacraments of the medieval church. However, the various churches were very divided over the Christian ritual of blessing and distributing bread and wine. Known by several different names—the Eucharist, the Mass, the Lord's supper, the communion, among others—the ritual was founded in the actions of Christ at the Last Supper. According to the doctrine of transubstantiation, the bread and wine retain their outward appearances but the substances are transformed into the body and blood of Christ; this was the Catholic doctrine. According to the doctrine of consubstantiation, nothing of the bread and wine is changed, but the believer realizes the presence of Christ in the bread and wine ("a piece of iron thrust into the fire does not change its composition but still has a differing quality"); this was a Lutheran doctrine. Others viewed the blessing and receiving of the bread and wine as symbolic, energizing the community of believers. Still others believed it served as a memorial to the actions of Christ, or was a thanksgiving for God's grant of salvation.

Teachings regarding the means of obtaining salvation also differed among the churches. Catholics believed in living life according to Christian beliefs and participating in the practices of the church—good works. Because Christ had been celibate, it seemed proper for Catholics that priests, nuns, and brothers should imitate his life in that fashion. Protestants chose to concentrate on the Pauline text (1 Corinthians 7: 8-9) about marrying rather than burning, so they emphasized the married life. Lutherans accepted the notion of justification by faith: salvation cannot be earned and a good life is the fruit of faith. Calvinists believed in predestination: salvation is known only to God but a good life can be some proof of predestined salvation.

The churches also held disparate views regarding relations of church to state. Catholics and Calvinists believed the church should control and absorb the state; a government in which God is seen as ruling the society is called a theocracy. Lutherans and Anglicans believed the state should control the church. Anabaptists considered the state a necessary evil that the church should ignore.

Because of the multiplication of warring Protestant sects and the defensive stance of Catholics, many ideas sprang up that grated against the orthodoxies of both Protestants and Catholics. Caspar Schwenckfeld (died 1561) taught a sacramental Lutheranism that made the miracle of the Eucharist central, an idea Luther rejected. Michael Servetus (died 1553) embraced Unitarianism, denying the Trinity, which incited Calvin to have him burned at the stake. And Lelio Sozzini (died 1562), moving from a Catholic position, rejected the Trinity as unscriptural. Anti-Trinitarianism continued to roil the waters for centuries.

Results

By 1560, attitudes were hardening, and political rulers understood the benefits and disadvantages of religion, be it Catholic or Protestant, as a political force. The map of Europe and its religions did not change much after 1560, by which time Catholic forces had retaken as much as two-fifths of the area "lost" earlier to Protestantism. Political rulers, be they monarchs or city councils, gained power at the expense of the church. The state thereafter could operate as an autonomous unit.

The Reformation and Counter-Reformation rekindled religious enthusiasm among the general population. While political and religious leaders of society instigated most of the reforms, regular citizens eventually accepted the changes with enthusiasm—an enthusiasm lacking in religious belief since far back into the Middle Ages.

All aspects of Western Christianity undertook to remedy the abuses that had contributed to the Reformation. The practices of simony and pluralism, as well as the ordination of immoral or badly educated clergy, were denounced and, by the seventeenth century, considerably remedied.

Protestantism, by emphasizing the individual believer's direct contact with God, rather than through the intermediary of the church, contributed to the growth of individualism, especially the idea of the inviolability of each person's conscience.

Thinkers have attempted to connect religious change with the rise of capitalism. Karl Marx, the nineteenth-century social theorist, believed that capitalism, which emphasized hard work, thrift, and the use of reason rather than tradition, led to the development of Protestantism, a type of Christianity especially attractive to the middle class, who were also capitalists. Max Weber, a later nineteenth-century sociologist, reversed the argument and believed that Protestantism, especially Calvinism, with its emphasis on predestination, led to great attention being paid to the successes and failures of this world as possible signs of future salvation. Such attention, and the attendant hard work, furthered the capitalist spirit.

Most writers today accept neither view but do believe that Protestantism and capitalism are related; however, too many other factors are involved to make the connection clear or easy. The number of successful Catholic and Jewish capitalists in the early modern age renders all such hypotheses facile.

The Wars of Religion

The period from 1560 to 1648 witnessed continuing warfare between Protestants and Catholics. Though religion was not the only reason for the wars—occasionally Catholics and Protestants were allies against other Catholics or Protestants—religion was the dominant cause of the bloodshed. In the latter half of the sixteenth century, fighting took place along the Atlantic seaboard between Calvinists and Catholics; after 1600, the warfare spread to Germany where Calvinists, Lutherans, and Catholics fought.

Warfare and the Effects of Gunpowder

The continual fighting among warring factions led to many changes in warfare. Technological advancements and the introduction of gunpowder made cannons more effective, so cities required elaborate and expensive fortifications for protection. As a result of the better fortifications, long sieges became necessary to capture a city. The infantry, organized in squares of three thousand men and armed with pikes and muskets, made the cavalry charge obsolete. Military leaders had to instill greater discipline in and command greater control of their armies in order to train the infantry or sustain a siege. An army once trained would not be disbanded owing to the expense of retraining. Thus, the order of command and modern ranks appeared, as did uniforms. Better discipline among the troops permitted commanders to attempt more actions on the battlefield, so more soldiers were necessary. Armies grew from the 40,000 of the Spanish army of 1600, to 400,000 in the French army at the end of the seventeenth century.

War and Destruction

Devastation of the enemy's lands became the rule. Armies, composed mostly of mercenaries, lived by pillage when not paid, and their ruler-employer often could not control them. Peasants, after such devastation, and after torture to reveal their valuables, often left farming and turned to banditry.

The Catholic Crusade

Charles I/V, before his death, was able to split his territories between his brother and his son. As King Charles I of Spain, he bequeathed to his son, Philip (1556–1598), the vast empire of Spain, Milan, Naples, the Netherlands, and the New World. As Emperor Charles V, he left to his brother, Ferdinand, the territories of Austria, Hungary, Bohemia, and the best claim to be elected Holy Roman Emperor. Both branches of the Habsburg family,[4] henceforward, cooperated in international matters.

Philip was a deeply religious, hard-working man of severe personal habits. Solemn (it is said he only laughed once in his life, at the report of the St. Bartholomew's Day massacre) and reclusive (he built the Escorial outside Madrid as a palace, monastery, and eventual tomb), he devoted his life and the wealth of Spain to making Europe once again Catholic. It was Philip, not the pope, who led the Catholic attack on Protestants. The pope and the Jesuits, however, did participate in Philip's efforts.

Sources of the Power of Philip II

Philip derived his power from several sources:

- The gold and silver of the New World flowed into Spain, especially following the opening of the silver mines at Potosí in Peru.

- Spain dominated the Mediterranean through a series of wars led by Philip's half-brother, Don John, against Muslim, largely Turkish, forces. Don John secured the Mediterranean for Christian merchants with a naval victory over the Turks at Lepanto off the coast of Greece in 1571.

- Spain annexed Portugal in 1580 following the death of the Portuguese king, who had no clear successor. This gave Philip the only other large navy of the day as well as Portuguese territories around the globe. This windfall proved to be a mixed blessing, however. The combined territories of Spain and Portugal upset the balance of power in Europe, thus making France and England, especially, bitter foes of Spanish pretensions; also, Spanish kings, until the throne of Portugal reverted to an acceptable family, were fully unable to police and exploit the overextended territory they had inherited, thus paving the way for the predations and seizures by English and Dutch privateers and pirates.

---

[4]The Habsburgs were the royal family from the crownlands of Austria whose eldest male was usually elected Holy Roman Emperor. Under Charles I, they ruled a fair part of Europe.

Nature of the Struggle

Calvinism was spreading in England, France, the Netherlands, and Germany. Calvinists supported each other, often disregarding their countries' borders.

England was ruled by two queens: Mary (1553–1558), who married Philip II, and then Elizabeth (1558–1603), while three successive kings of France from 1559 to 1589 were influenced by their mother, Catherine de' Medici. Queens as rulers in their own right had existed in the Middle Ages (Isabella of Castile being one of the last), but in the early modern age, except in England and Russia, they became increasingly rare, given the sway of the Salic Law—a law barring women from inheriting land—on the Continent.

Monarchs attempted to strengthen their control and the unity of their countries, a process that nobles often resisted.

Civil War in France

Francis I (1515–1547) obtained control of the French Church when he signed the Concordat of Bologna with the pope (1516), and therefore had no incentive to encourage Protestantism.

With the signing of the Treaty of Cateau-Cambrésis in 1559, the struggles of the Habsburgs and Valois[5] ended, leaving the French with no fear of outside invasion for a while, except that of ideas. John Calvin was a Frenchman and Geneva was near France, so Calvinist ideas spread in France, especially among the nobility. Three noble families—Bourbon, Chatillon, and Guise—sought more power and attempted to dominate the monarchs after 1559. Partly due to politics, the Bourbons and the Montmorency-Chatillons became Calvinist.

When Henry II (1547–1559) died as a result of injuries sustained in a tournament, he was succeeded, in succession, by his three sons (Francis II 1559–1560, Charles IX 1560–1574, and Henry III 1571–1589), each influenced by their mother, Catherine de' Medici (1519–1589), and often controlled by one of the noble families. Though the monarch was always Catholic until 1589, each king was willing to work with Calvinists (Huguenots) or Catholics if it would give him more power and independence.

The Wars

Nine civil wars occurred in France from 1562 to 1589. The wars became more brutal as killing of civilians supplanted military action.

The St. Bartholomew's Day Massacre on August 24, 1572, was authorized by Catherine de' Medici and her weak-willed son, King Charles IX, allegedly to preempt a planned attack by Protestants who were in Paris for a royal wedding. Their leader, Admiral Gaspard de Coligny, was severely wounded in an assassination attempt during the wedding festivities. Given the royal go-ahead, Catholics massacred nearly 20,000 Huguenots across France. The pope had a medal struck commemorating the

---

[5] The Valois' were the royal family of France. Feeling encircled by Habsburgs in Spain and the Germanies, they fought them for nearly a century.

event and ordered the ringing of happy church bells in Catholic lands. As a result of St. Bartholomew's Day and other killings, Protestants throughout Europe feared for their future.

Several important figures were assassinated by their religious opponents, including Kings Henry III and Henry IV. The two leading members of the Guise family were killed at the instigation of Henry III in 1588. Spain intervened with troops to support the Catholics, led by the Guise family, in 1590.

Henry of Navarre (1589–1610)

A Calvinist and Bourbon, Henry of Navarre became king in 1589 when Henry III was assassinated. A popular leader, Henry began to unite France but was unable to conquer or control Paris, center of Catholic strength. In 1593, he converted to Catholicism saying, "Paris is worth a mass." In this respect, he was a *politique*, a leader more interested in political unity than religious uniformity.

In 1598, Henry issued the Edict of Nantes, which permitted Huguenots to worship publicly, to have access to the universities and to public office, and to maintain fortified towns in France to protect themselves. The edict did not so much represent the triumph of religious tolerance as it did a truce in the religious wars.

The Revolt of the Netherlands

The Netherlands was a group of seventeen provinces clustered around the mouth of the Rhine and Scheldt rivers, and they were ruled by the king of Spain, as part of his Burgundian inheritance. Each province had a tradition of liberties, and each elected a stadtholder, a man who provided military leadership when necessary. The stadtholder often was an important noble and became the most important politician in the province.

Since the Middle Ages, the Netherlands had included many cities dominated by wealthy merchants. By 1560 the cities housed many Calvinists, including some who had fled France.

Philip II of Spain sought to impose on the Netherlands a more centralized government, as well as a stronger Catholic Church, following the decrees of the Council of Trent. His efforts provoked resistance by some nobles, led by William of Orange (1533–1584), who was called "the Silent" because he discussed his political plans with very few people. An agreement and pledge to resist, called the Compromise of 1564 and signed by people throughout the provinces, led to rebellion. The regent, Margaret of Parma, once hissed that the rebels were mere beggars; they took that insult and made it their nickname.

Philip sent the Duke of Alva (1508–1583) with 20,000 soldiers to suppress the rebellion. Alva established the "Council of Blood," which executed several thousand Calvinists as heretics. He also imposed new taxes, including a sales tax of 10 percent. Most significantly, the harsh Spanish Inquisition supplanted the milder Dutch/Flemish variety.

"Sea Beggars" resisted Alva along the coast, raiding ports, and landlubbers opened the dykes to frustrate the marches of the Spanish armies. In 1576, the unpaid Spanish sacked Antwerp, an event called the Spanish Fury, which destroyed Antwerp's commercial supremacy in the Netherlands.

The Calvinist northern provinces and the Catholic southern provinces united in 1576 in the Pacification of Ghent, but were unable to cooperate. They broke into two groups: the Calvinist Union of Utrecht (approximately modern-day Netherlands) and the Catholic Union of Arras (approximately modern Belgium). The division attracted international attention: a son of Catherine de' Medici attempted to become the leader of the revolt and the English sent troops and money to support the rebels after 1585.

The Spanish were driven out of the northern provinces in the 1590s, and the war ended in 1609, though Spain did not officially recognize the north's independence until 1648. The independent northern provinces, dominated by Holland, were called the United Provinces, and the southern provinces, ruled by the king of Spain, the Spanish Netherlands.

England and Spain

Mary (1553–1558)

The daughter of Henry VIII and Katharine of Aragon, Mary sought to make England Catholic. She executed many Protestants, earning her the name "Bloody Mary" from opponents. (In contrast, Elizabeth, who followed Mary to the throne, did not kill Protestants and was called "Good Queen Bess.") To escape persecution, many Englishmen went into exile on the Continent where, settling in Frankfurt, Geneva, and elsewhere, they learned more radical Protestant ideas.

Cardinal Reginald Pole (1500–1558) was one of Mary's advisers and symbolized the subordination of England to the pope. Mary married Philip II, king of Spain, and organized her foreign policy around Spanish interests. They had no children, and he did not take over personal control of England, a possibility the English people had greatly feared.

Elizabeth (1558–1603)

A Protestant of unclear beliefs, Elizabeth forged a religious compromise between 1559 and 1563 that left England with a church governed by bishops and practicing quasi-Catholic rituals, but maintaining a Calvinist doctrine. Supporters saw the compromise as a middle way between extremes, while opponents viewed it as an impossible melding of Protestantism and Catholicism.

Puritans who sought to purify the English church of the remnants of its medieval heritage were suppressed by Elizabeth's government, but not condemned to death. Catholics, who sought to return the English church to an allegiance to the pope, participated in several rebellions and plots, one of which was an attempt to establish Mary, Queen of Scots, on the English throne.

Mary, Queen of Scots, had fled to England from Scotland in 1568, after alienating nobles there. To Catholics, she was the legitimate queen of England.[6] Catholic plotting to put Mary on the throne led to her execution in 1587.

Elizabeth was excommunicated by the pope in 1570. A *politique* interested in the advancing English nation, Elizabeth did not "make windows into men's souls."

In 1588, as part of his crusade and to stop England from supporting rebels in the Netherlands, Philip II sent the Armada, a fleet of over 125 ships, to convey troops from the Netherlands to England as part of a plan to make England Catholic. The Armada was defeated by a combination of superior English naval tactics and a "Protestant wind" that made it impossible for the Spanish to accomplish their goal.

Spain and England signed a peace accord in 1604. England remained Protestant and an opponent of Spain as long as Spain remained a world power.

The Thirty Years' War

Though Calvinism had spread through Germany, the Peace of Augsburg, which settled disputes between Lutherans and Catholics in 1555, had no provision for Calvinists. Lutherans gained more territories through conversions and often took control of previous church states—a violation of the Peace of Augsburg. In 1609, a Protestant alliance under the leadership of the Calvinist ruler of the Palatinate[7] opposed a Catholic league led by the ruler of Bavaria. To appease his Calvinist nobles in Bohemia, the Habsburg emperor, Matthias, issued a Letter of Majesty in 1609 allowing them freedom of worship. But his family opposed his tolerant policies, and soon after electing the intransigent Ferdinand king of Bohemia in 1617, the Calvinist nobles of Bohemia realized they had made a big mistake.

The Bohemian Period (1618–1625)

When Ferdinand rescinded the Letter of Majesty in 1618, Bohemian nobles rose in revolt and declared him deposed, electing in his stead the Calvinist Frederick V of the Palatinate as their new king. Whether this was legal is disputed. When Ferdinand sent two representatives to Prague to protest his deposition, irate nobles threw them out of a high window of the Hradschin palace-fortress—the "defenestration of Prague."

Frederick's army was defeated by Ferdinand's at White Mountain in 1620; Bohemia was made Catholic, and the Spanish occupied the Palatinate. Had Frederick been allowed, as elector, to represent both the Palatinate and Bohemia, a four-to-three Protestant majority of votes might have yielded the unthinkable—a Protestant emperor!

The Danish Period (1625–1629)

The army of Ferdinand, who was now emperor, invaded northern Germany, raising fear among Protestants for their religion and local rulers for their political rights.

---

[6] The bastardy that tainted Elizabeth's ancestry, cancelled by an act of Parliament, was not forgotten by purists. Mary of Scotland was related without any taint to the Tudor house, so she seemed to have the better claim to the throne.

[7] The Palatinate was an area in southwest Germany governed by a branch of the Bavarian Wittelsbachs, a ducal house. Its position was strategic, a gateway between France, Switzerland, and the Holy Roman Empire.

Christian IV (1588–1648), king of Denmark, led an army into Germany in defense of Protestants but was defeated. Afterward, the emperor sought to recover all church lands secularized since 1552 and establish a strong Habsburg presence in northern Germany.

Not all issues pitted Protestants against Catholics. The Lutheran ruler of Saxony joined Catholics in the attack on Frederick at White Mountain, and the leading general for the Emperor Ferdinand was Albrecht of Wallenstein, a Protestant.

The Swedish Period (1629–1635)

Gustavus Adolfus (1611–1632), king of Sweden, monetarily supported by France and the United Provinces, hoping for a defeat of the Habsburgs, invaded Germany in defense of Protestantism. Sweden stopped the Habsburg cause at the battle of Breitenfeld in 1630, but Gustavus Adolfus was killed at the battle of Lützen in 1632.

The Swedish-French Period (1635–1648)

Catholic France, guided by Cardinal Richelieu (1585–1642), supplied money to Protestant princes and troops to Germany, as the war became part of a bigger war between France and Spain. Thus, a religious phase (1618–1635) was followed by the political phase (1635–1648) of the war in which balance-of-power considerations outweighed religious niceties.

Treaty of Westphalia (1648)

During the treaty talks, the presence of ambassadors from all of the belligerents, as well as many other countries, made settlement of nearly all disputes possible. Only the French-Spanish war continued, ending in 1659. It is significant that the papal ambassador was totally ignored in the negotiations: international politics had finally become secularized.

The Treaty of Westphalia reasserted the principles of the Peace of Augsburg, but with Calvinists included. The independence of the United Provinces from the king of Spain, and that of the Swiss Confederacy from the Holy Roman Empire were recognized. Most German states, numbering over three hundred, obtained virtual independence from the empire, though free cities and imperial knights had to maneuver between bigger states for position.

Germany suffered great destruction during the war, leading to a decline in population of perhaps one-third, more in some areas. Germany remained divided and without a strong government until the nineteenth century.

Results

The European wars that raged from 1560 to 1648 had political and religious consequences throughout the Continent:

- After 1648, religious goals were no longer the primary reason for which to go to war.

- The Catholic crusade to reunite Europe failed, largely owing to the efforts of the Calvinists. The religious distribution of Europe has not changed significantly since 1648.

- Nobles, resisting the increasing power of the state, usually dominated the struggle between themselves and their monarchs.

- France, then Germany, fell apart owing to the wars. France was reunited in the seventeenth century; Germany was not.

- In most political entities, *politiques*, such as Elizabeth I of England and Henry IV of France, who sought more to keep the state united than to ensure that a single religion dominated, came to control politics.

- The two branches of the Habsburg family—the Austrian and the Spanish—continued to cooperate in international affairs. Spain, though a formidable military power until 1648, began a decline thereafter, which ended its role as a great power of Europe.

Literature and the Arts

Literature

Cervantes (1547–1616), a Spaniard, was a former soldier concerned with the problems of religious idealism. His adventures in the wars of Spain, including enslavement in Muslim North Africa, contributed mightily to the subject and style of his great masterpiece, *Don Quixote* (1605), which satirized chivalric romances through the eyes of a worldly wise, skeptical peasant, Sancho Panza, and a wonderfully human, but perhaps mentally unstable, "knight errant" and religious idealist, Don Quixote.

William Shakespeare (1564–1616) is, like Cervantes, considered the finest writer in his literary tradition. He mixed country, court, and Renaissance ideas of the English in the late 1500s and early 1600s to produce tragedies, comedies, histories, and sonnets. In addition to the timelessness of his themes, Shakespeare had a gift for skillfully portraying the psychological aspects of his characters. The unique manner in which he utilized the English language permanently altered its future use.

Influenced by the Renaissance while traveling in Italy, Englishman John Milton (1608–1674) developed strong Puritan religious beliefs. His verse epic *Paradise Lost* (1667) studied the motives of those who reject God. Milton took an active part in the troubles in England from 1640 to 1660, as secretary to a committee of Parliament.

Michel de Montaigne (1533–1592), a Frenchman, became obsessed with death and the problems it raised. The inventor of the essay form, he adopted skepticism, embracing the doubt that true knowledge can be obtained, before turning to a belief in the value of individual self-study.

The Arts

Rejecting the balance and calm of Renaissance arts, mannerists, who dominated painting and sculpture in the latter part of the sixteenth century, emphasized dramatic and emotional qualities. A leading mannerist was Caravaggio (1571–1610), whose dissolute and violent life evidently fed the often shocking subject matter and bold treatments in his paintings (see Figure 3-2).

Galleria degli Uffizi, Florence, Italy

Figure 3-2. Michelangelo de Merisi, known as Caravaggio (1571–1610), led a short, action-packed life; his devotion to pleasure, including same-sex love, is portrayed in his sensual *Bacchus* **(1596).**

Seventeenth-century artists attempted to involve the viewer by emphasizing passion and mystery, as well as drama. Baroque, which emphasized grandeur and bold colors, was connected with the Counter-Reformation and monarchies, and was found primarily in Catholic countries. The works of Gianlorenzo Bernini (1598–1680), such as his columns in Saint Peter's Basilica in Rome, capture the appeal to emotion, the tension in the object, and the subjects' human energy. His sculpture *Ecstasy of Saint Teresa* is often depicted in textbooks as the quintessential example of Catholic Baroque fervor. In the Spanish Netherlands, Peter Paul Rubens (1577–1640) used religious and secular themes to convey strength and majesty.

In music, Claudio Monteverdi (1567–1643) moved from the dominance of medieval polyphony, which culminated in the masses of Italian composer Giovanni Palestrina, to help create the modern style of melody and counterpoint, prefigured in Renaissance madrigals. He is deemed the father of opera, owing to his *Orfeo* (1607) and even more to his masterpiece, *The Coronation of Poppaea* (1642). The Baroque style in music spread to France in the keyboard works of François Couperin and Jean-Baptiste Lully, to Spain in the harpsichord pieces of Domenico Scarlatti, and to Germany in the organ works and choral cantatas of Dietrich Buxtehude, Johann Pachelbel, and, best of all, Johann Sebastian Bach (1685–1750).

Science, Learning, and Society

Scientific *Revolution* or *Evolution*?

Astronomy, and to a lesser degree, physics, first produced the new ways of thought called *the scientific revolution* of the sixteenth and seventeenth centuries. Though its impact changed the world, this process was really a slow and steady "evolution" of scientific method and theories rather than a sudden or violent "revolution."

The "new science" called into question—and ultimately replaced—the ideas of the Greek natural philosopher Aristotle (384 B.C.E.–322 B.C.E.). Aristotle believed that the motionless earth occupied the center of the universe, and that the sun, planets, and stars revolved around it in circular orbits determined by crystalline spheres. Aristotle's system was further refined by Ptolemy, a second-century astronomer, to make it correspond to the observed movements of the stars and planets.

Accepting both the Platonic idea that the circle is a perfect figure and, also, the Renaissance belief in simple explanations, Nicolas Copernicus (1473–1543) suggested that the sun was at the center of the universe and that the earth and planets revolved around it in circular orbits. His *On the Revolutions of the Heavenly Spheres* was published in 1543, the year of his death. Copernicus's ideas that the universe was immense removed people from occupying the center of the universe, to inhabiting a small planet in a vast system. It also eliminated distinctions between the earth and the heavens.

Copernicus's views were not immediately accepted because they contradicted the words of the Bible. Although he posited circular orbits for the planets, his predictions of their locations were not accurate.

A Danish nobleman, Tycho Brahe (1546–1601), built the best observatory of his time, for which he collected extensive data on the location of the stars and planets. Brahe did not totally accept Copernicus's views, as he believed that the earth still occupied the center of the universe and that the other planets revolved around the sun, which, in turn, revolved around the earth. Brahe's discovery of a new star in 1572, and the appearance of a comet in 1577, shattered beliefs in an unchanging sky and crystalline spheres.

Johannes Kepler's (1571–1630) reworking of Copernicus's theory and Brahe's observations produced the idea that the planets move around the sun in elliptical, not circular, orbits. The three new laws of Kepler accurately predicted the movements of the planets and were based on mathematical relationships.

Astronomer and physicist Galileo (1564–1642) discovered four moons of Jupiter using a new invention of the time, the telescope. He also conducted other experiments in physics that related to the relationship of movement of objects and the mathematics necessary to describe the movement, such as that of the pendulum. A propagandist for science, Galileo defended his discoveries and mocked his opponents. The Catholic Church in Italy, where Galileo lived and worked, forced him to recant his views, which demonstrated the conflict of the older religious views and the new scientific approach.

Scientific Methodologies

The author of *Advancement of Learning* (1605) and an advocate of experimental approaches to knowledge, Francis Bacon (1561–1626) formalized empiricism, an approach to science that used inductive reasoning. Induction is the process whereby someone scrutinizes a set of facts and "induces" an hypothesis or theory that makes them cohere. An Englishman, Bacon himself did few experiments but believed empiricism would produce useful, rather than purely theoretical, knowledge.

Beginning from basic principles, René Descartes (1596–1650) believed that scientific laws could be found through deductive reasoning. Deduction is the logical process whereby a thinker moves from a theory given by reason alone to facts that will support (or deny) that theory. Formulating analytic geometry, Descartes knew that geometry and algebra were related and that equations could describe figures. Later developments merged inductive experimentalism with deductive mathematical rationalism to produce today's epistemology method, used to obtain and verify knowledge.

Connections with the Rest of Society

During the Renaissance, many universities instituted the study of mathematics and physics. Most of the great scientists involved in the changes in astronomy studied at universities, though in general the universities adhered to a medieval curriculum. The founding of scientific academies proved more conducive to original scientific research and thought. Probably the first academy devoted to the new science was the *Accademia dei Lincei*, founded in Rome in 1603.

Concerns outside the institutions of higher learning provided direction for scientific research. For example, the demands of explorers, especially those at sea, for more accurate measurements of the stars increased attention on the details of the heavenly movements. In addition, advances in warfare, particularly the development and use of artillery, required and permitted explanations involving precise measurements.

Initially, Protestant areas were more hostile than Catholic ones to the new learning. After Galileo, however, Catholic authorities led in trying to suppress new ideas.

Consequences

The new approaches of the scientific method spread to inquiries far beyond astronomy and physics. Many sought new explanations as well as order and uniformity in all aspects of the physical world and society. For example, William Gilbert (1544–1603), physician to Queen Elizabeth, showed the effects of magnetism and theorized on it as a force with special properties in 1600. William Harvey (1578–1657) demonstrated the circulation of blood and the role of the human heart.

Blaise Pascal (1623–1662), a French mathematician, developed new ideas, including the basis for calculus. He worried, however, about the increasing reliance on science, which he believed could not explain the truly important things in life, that is, those which can be perceived only by faith. Human beings, who had been at the center of the universe and the central link in the Great Chain of Being, became merely creatures in an unintelligibly vast universe.

Scientists slowly replaced the clergy as the people able to explain the happenings of the physical world. However, few of the discoveries and resulting inventions—except for the aids to explorers—had any consequences on the lives of Europeans.

Scientific Societies

Scientific societies were organized in many European countries in the seventeenth century. Italy began the first scientific societies in Rome, Naples, and Florence. English established the Royal Observatory at Greenwich in 1675 and the Royal Society in 1662; private donations and entrance fees from members financed the society. The French *Académie des Sciences* was founded in 1666. King Frederick I of Brandenburg-Prussia chartered the Berlin Academy of Sciences in 1700. Finally, Peter the Great of Russia founded the St. Petersburg Academy of Sciences in 1725. A key feature of the new academies was their willingness to share knowledge; central corresponding secretaries such as Marin Mersenne and Henry Oldenburg formed the nexus of international science via formal letters, and journals cropped up to publicize new findings.

Sir Isaac Newton (1642–1747) taught mathematics at Cambridge, was master of the Royal Mint in London, and for twenty-five years was the president of the Royal Society. Most of his work focused on astronomy, the dominant science of the seventeenth century. He worked with magnification, prisms, and refraction. He used lenses with different curvature and different kinds of glass. Newton's greatest contribution, however, was in formulating his principle of universal gravitation, which he explained in his *Principia Mathematica*, published in 1687. He claimed to have "subject[ed] the phenomena of nature to the laws of mathematics" and seen order and design throughout the entire cosmos.

Science and religion were not in conflict in the seventeenth and eighteenth centuries. Scientists universally believed they were studying and analyzing God's creation, not an autonomous phenomena known as "Nature." There was no attempt, as in the nineteenth and twentieth centuries, to secularize science. "Natural law," they believed, was created by God for man's use. A tension between the natural and the supernatural simply did not exist in their world view. The question of the extent of the Creator's involvement directly or indirectly in his creation was an issue of the eighteenth century, but there was universal agreement among scientists and philosophers as to the supernatural origin of the universe.

The scientific revolution of the sixteenth and seventeenth centuries tended to replace religion as the explanation of the educated for occurrences in the physical world. In contrast to religious articles of faith, the approach of science relied on experiment and mathematics. Learning, including the arts, moved away from Renaissance models to emphasize the emotions and individual variations.

Society (1650 to *ca.* 1789)

Demography

Exact figures for the population of Europe during the fifteenth and sixteenth centuries are not known, as complete censuses did not then exist. Following the Black Death and its endemic outbreaks in the fourteenth century, population remained stagnant until the sixteenth century, when, *ca.* 1550, it again reached preplague levels. Between 1550 and 1650, the population of Europe nearly doubled, and was checked only by widespread warfare. After 1650, growth leveled off for a century.

The following are population estimates for the year 1650:

England: 5.5 million

France: 18.0 million

Holy Roman Empire: 11.0 million

Italian peninsula: 12.0 million

Spain: 5.2 million

Sweden: 1.5 million

United Provinces: 1.5 million

Population in the cities grew much faster than did the population as a whole, as people migrated from the countryside. London grew from 50,000 in 1500 to 200,000 in 1650. Cities contained perhaps 10–20 percent of the total population of Europe.

The Family

The majority of households consisted of the nuclear family in the West, with more extended families in the East. A baby had a 25 percent chance of surviving to the age of one, a 50 percent chance of surviving to the age of twenty, and a 10 percent chance of reaching sixty. The average marriage age was twenty-seven for men and twenty-five for women, though nobles married younger. Few people married early enough or lived long enough to see their grandchildren.

The theory of family relationships, as expressed in sermons and writings, was one of patriarchy, with the father and husband responsible for, and in command of, the rest of the family. The reality of family relationships was more complex.

Romantic love did exist, but historians disagree as to its role in marriages. Women in urban areas shared in the work of their artisan and merchant husbands, but rarely operated a business on their own after the Middle Ages. The family was stable; divorce was very rare. Children were treated as sinful creatures, then as "little adults."

Witchcraft

Witch hunting, though found in the late Middle Ages, occurred primarily in the sixteenth and seventeenth centuries. All parts of society—the educated, the religious, and the poor—believed in witches.

Historians and anthropologists have theorized as to why people believed in witches, and why witch hunting occurred when and where it did. One theory is that people needed to have someone or something to blame when things went badly. Another explanation is that the increased concern with religion resulting from the Reformation and Counter-Reformation focused more attention on the role of the devil in life. Some studies have suggested witchcraft was more of a concern in areas that switched religions often.

A charge of witchcraft singled out the aberrant or nonconformists. Repression of sexuality may have led men to project fears and hopes onto women, who then had to be punished when things went awry. Though it is impossible to ascertain exact numbers, we do know that thousands of the so-called witches were executed, with numbers varying from place to place.

Food and Diet

Bread was the staff of life—the chief item in the diet of the laboring classes. The only vegetables were peas and beans, until vegetables from the Americas found their way to poorer tables after 1650. Meat and eggs were saved for special occasions, except among the rich. Beverages included beer and wine, as milk was considered unhealthy except for babies; water not only tasted awful but also tended to kill those who drank it.

Nobles and the bourgeois ate rich meats, fish, cheeses, and sweets, but consumed few vegetables or fruit. The English and later Dutch ate better than the rest of Europe, with the peoples of the Mediterranean the worst-off. Local famines were still common, as governments lacked the ability to move food from areas of surplus to those of dearth.

The Economy

Inflation, referred to as "the price revolution," began around 1500 and continued until the 1640s. The price of foodstuffs rose tenfold. The rise in population was the primary cause of the inflation, as there were more mouths to feed than food available. Another possible cause was the flow of silver from the Americas, which increased the amount of available spending money, thus encouraging merchants to raise prices.

Farmers sought to increase output as the price of food rose. In some places, farmers began cultivating land that had been idle since the Black Death of 1348. In England, enclosures produced larger, more efficient farms but resulted in fewer people living on the land. In Eastern Europe, landlords turned their lands into large wheat-exporting operations and began the process of converting peasants and laborers back into serfs.

Trade and industry grew everywhere. Certain areas began to specialize: for example, the lands south and east of the Baltic produced wheat for northwestern Europe, and the Dutch fleet dominated European trade.

Textiles, Europe's chief industry since the Middle Ages, underwent change. Regional specialization occurred on a larger scale. The putting-out system appeared, whereby the industry moved out of the cities into the countryside, and the process of production was divided into steps, with different workers doing each step. In this period, woolens and linens predominated, with most cottons imported from India or Egypt.

Mercantilism

The conscious pursuit by governments of policies designed to increase national wealth, reckoned in gold and silver, became common in the seventeenth century. The chief aim was to obtain a favorable balance of international payments. Governments sought to create industries in order to avoid importing items.

Mercantilism encompassed several basic assumptions:

1. Wealth is measured in terms of commodities, especially gold and silver, rather than in terms of productivity and income-producing investments.

2. Economic activities should increase the power of the national government in the direction of state controls.

3. Since a favorable balance of trade is important, a nation should purchase as little as possible from nations regarded as enemies. (The concept of the mutual advantage of trade was not widely accepted.)

4. Colonies exist for the benefit of the mother country, not for any mutual benefit that would be gained by economic development.

The philosophy of mercantilism had mixed results for the economy of Europe. On the one hand, the state encouraged economic growth and expansion. On the other, it tended to stifle entrepreneurship, competition, and innovation through monopolies, trade restrictions, and state regulation of commerce.

Since governments expected little from domestic society, taxes were, generally speaking, low enough not to discourage economic expansion. In addition, governments needed relatively few administrative officials in a day when communication and transportation was slow. Compare France, one of the most bureaucratic states of Europe in the eighteenth century, with France in the twentieth century: then, 12,000 civil servants meant one bureaucrat for every 1,250 people; today, it is one for every 70 people.

TIMELINE

Reform, Counter-Reform, and the New Sciences

Year(s)	Event	Significance
1380–1415	John Wycliffe and Jan Hus call for church reforms.	From England to Bohemia, ideas take root about the form of the Eucharist, morals of the clergy, and so forth. Wycliffe's followers go underground as Lollards in England; Hus is burnt at the stake for heresy, but his followers, Hussites, wage war and win concessions from the papacy.
1517	Martin Luther, a Catholic monk, posts his Ninety-five Theses on the door of the Wittenberg church.	Luther's Theses, in which he protests the sale of indulgences, puts him at odds with the politics of the Catholic Church and leads him to further acts of rebellion, which then spark the Protestant Reformation.
1520–1521	Luther publishes four pamphlets and is excommunicated by the pope.	Luther defines his doctrines of faith, grace, and scriptures alone; at the Diet of Worms, he refuses to recant his beliefs; the Pope excommunicates him, and the emperor puts him under imperial ban. As an outlaw to the Church and the Emperor, Luther had to seek refuge with the Elector of Saxony, and this saved him to publish a German Bible and to become the leader of the Reformation.
1527–1534	In his quest for a male heir, Henry VIII of England divorces the Holy Roman Emperor's aunt, Katharine, and marries Anne Boleyn.	Henry's divorce lead to the Act of Supremacy (1534) in which Parliament declares him "supreme bishop" of England, thus freeing him from the authority of the Pope.
1541	John Calvin publishes his *Institutes of the Christian Religion* in its French edition.	A trained lawyer, Calvin sees God as a stern judge who has predestined the elect as well as the damned from all time; Calvin directs his followers, called Calvinists, to work hard and live godly lives on earth, to found the New Jerusalem, the "City of God on earth." Calvin offers the prospect of salvation to merchants and workers who felt that the Catholic Church preferred poverty and idle lives to their work.
1543	Nicolas Copernicus publishes his heliocentric theory.	Copernicus's theory challenges the long-held belief in the Ptolemaic geocentric universe; however, his writing is not much read for sixty years.

1545–1563	The Council of Trent meets three times to settle issues of Catholic doctrine.	This church council, under papal rule, reaffirms most doctrines, ends the sale of indulgences, establishes new rules on the residency of bishops, and creates many new seminaries for better priest training.
1555	Holy Roman Emperor Charles V establishes the Peace of Augsburg.	Distracted by wars against the Turks and the French, Charles V is unable to crush German Protestants, so he grants the Peace of Augsburg, which enshrines the rule *cuius regio, eius religio* (he who rules the land decides its religion). He then abdicates in disgust.
1562–1598	Wars of religion in France begin following the end of the long Habsburg-Valois conflict.	The French royal family, often allied to the ultra-Catholic Guises, fights Huguenot families until Bourbon Huguenot Henri IV becomes king and converts to Catholicism to save France (see: *politiques*). His Edict of Nantes (1598) grants Huguenots some religious and political freedoms.
1566–1581	Calvinists in the Spanish Netherlands revolt against strictness of Philip II, leading to the Dutch wars of independence.	The Spanish are eventually driven out of the Calvinist northern provinces in the 1590s, and the warring ends in 1609, though Spain does not officially recognize the north's independence until 1648.
1587–1588	Mary, Queen of Scots, is executed by Elizabeth I of England; the English navy destroys the Spanish Armada.	Elizabeth I, to make England safe from papal plots and foreigners, executes Mary, Queen of Scots. Philip II launches Armada, but it fails. Elizabethan error marks a golden age for arts and power. The events further establish Elizabeth as a powerful ruler to be feared. Her reign marks a golden age in arts and literature.
1609	In his Letter of Majesty, Matthias, the Holy Roman Emperor, grants religious freedom to Bohemian Calvinist nobles.	The emperor's Letter of Majesty addresses a shortfall of the Peace of Augsburg, which had no provisions for Calvinists. Both a Catholic and a Protestant league form.
1609	The scientific revolution begins.	Johannes Kepler publishes three laws of planetary orbits. Galileo turns his new telescope to the heavens and publishes his findings of new celestial objects and "imperfect" matter. His ideas upset the church.

(Continued)

1618–1648	Thirty Years' War begins.	The Letter of Majesty is rescinded, which leads to the defenestration of deputies of the Holy Roman Empire in Prague. Leagues war over religion, then over the balance of power: Spanish and Austrian Habsburgs versus French and Protestant princes.
1648	Treaty of Westphalia is signed.	The anti-Habsburg side wins. The treaty grants religious rights to Calvinists, and recognizes as sovereign the Netherlands and Switzerland as well as more than three hundred states in the Holy Roman Empire. France becomes a new superpower.
1662–1725	Royal academies of science form throughout Europe.	Starting with the Royal Society in England, monarchs see advantages in supporting the new scientific spirit apparent in methods of Francis Bacon, René Descartes and, above all, Isaac Newton.
1667	John Milton publishes *Paradise Lost*.	In this great biblical epic, Milton tries to "justify the ways of God to man" and also to reconcile his Puritan past and Calvinist theology with the restored Anglican monarchy of Charles II. Satan is the hero.
1687	Newton publishes *Principia Mathematica*.	Newton's synthesis of new astronomy adds the all-important universal law of gravitation to the theories and observations of Copernicus, Brahe, Kepler, Galileo, and others.

Chapter 4

Overview of European Powers

Domestic Matters

France (*ca.* 1640–1789)

Louis XIV (reigned 1643–1715)

Louis XIV was vain, arrogant, and charming to the aristocratic ladies of his court. He was five feet five inches tall and wore shoes with high heels, but "for some reason" he looks taller, larger, and more masculine in his official portraits.

The king had great physical endurance in long hours of council meetings and endless ceremonies. He seemed indifferent to heat and cold and survived a lifetime of abnormal eating. Such a man was well suited to aspire to be an absolute prince.

The most significant challenge to royal absolutism in France in the seventeenth century was a series of three revolts (called *frondes,* meaning "a child's slingshot") by some of the nobility and judges of the *Parlement* (High Court) of Paris. Competition among the nobility, however, enabled the government to put down the revolts. All three occurred when Louis XIV was very young and left a lasting impression on him; he was determined that no revolt would arise during his reign, nor any minister dominate him.

The king believed in unquestioned authority. Louis deliberately chose ministers from among the middle classes in order to keep the aristocracy out of government. Only one member of the high aristocracy was ever admitted to the daily council at Versailles, where the king presided personally over deliberations of his ministers.

Council orders were transmitted to the provinces by *intendants,* who supervised all phases of local administration (especially courts, police, and the collection of taxes). In addition, Louis XIV nullified the power of some French institutions that might challenge his centralized bureaucracy.

Louis XIV never called the Estates-General, a national representative assembly like England's Parliament, but deprived of its function as tax consultant in 1439, when the Estates voted to give the king permanent direct taxes. His *intendants* arrested members of three provincial estates who criticized royal policy; the members of the *parlements* were too intimidated by the failure of the *frondes* to offer further resistance.

The king used numerous means to control the peasants, who accounted for 95 percent of the French population. Some peasants kept as little as 20 percent of their cash crops after paying the landlord, the government, and the church. Peasants also were subject to the *corvée,* a month's forced labor on the roads. Those not working the farms were conscripted into the French army or put into workhouses. Rebels were hanged or forced to work as galley slaves.

Jean-Baptiste Colbert, finance minister from 1661 to 1683, improved the economy and the condition of the royal treasury. He reduced the number of tax collectors, reduced local tolls in order to encourage domestic trade, improved France's transportation system with canals and a growing merchant marine, organized a group of French trading companies (an East India Company, a West India Company, the Levant Company, and the Company of the North), and paid bounties to shipbuilders to strengthen trade.

Palace of Versailles

Louis XIV moved his royal court from the Louvre in Paris to Versailles, twelve miles outside of Paris. The facade of his palace was a third of a mile long with vast gardens adorned with classical statuary; 1,400 fountains; and 1,200 orange trees.

In Paris, the court included six hundred people. At Versailles, it grew to ten thousand noblemen, officials, and attendants. Sixty percent of tax revenues were spent on Versailles and the upkeep of the court of Louis XIV. (This was reduced to 5 percent under Louis XVI, but popular prejudice enshrined the old percentage—enter the Revolution!)

The splendor of the court was in the beautiful gardens and baroque architecture of the palace, in the luxurious furnishings of the apartments, and in the magnificent dress of men and women who went there. Nobles and their ladies often spent half of their income on clothing, furniture, and servants.

Extravagant amusements occupied the time of the aristocratic court: tournaments, hunts, tennis, billiards, boating parties, dinners, dances, ballets, operas, concerts, and theater. To celebrate the birth of his son in 1662, the king arranged a ball at the *Place du Carrousel* that was attended by fifteen thousand people who danced under a thousand lights before massive mirrors.

Not all was fun and games at Versailles: the king intended to keep a tight rein on the old nobles of his realm through the charms and commands of Versailles. The old nobility, *noblesse d'épee* ("sword nobles") had, after all, long revolted against French kings, especially in the traumatic *frondes*. Thus, Louis did well to impoverish and emasculate them, afterward tying these old nobles to him by throwing positions in the army or diplomatic corps to their sons or ensuring good marriages for their daughters. He preferred the new nobility that he fostered, the *noblesse de robe* ("robe nobles"), because they were recruited from the grateful and hard-working middle classes—and they worked for their pay, often as magistrates and lawyers, hence the "robes." By pitting the old nobles against the new nobles, Louis proved himself to be a consummate tactician in domestic disputes.

Louis XIV's Policies Toward Christianity

The king considered himself the head of the French Church and claimed that the pope had no temporal authority over *his* Catholics. Louis sided with the Jesuits against the Jansenists—Catholics like mathematician Blaise Pascal who reaffirmed Saint Augustine's doctrine of inherent depravity, that is, that man is born a sinner and salvation is only for the elect of God.

About a million French citizens were Protestant. Louis attempted to eradicate Protestantism from France by demolishing Huguenot churches and schools, paying cash to Protestants to convert to Catholicism, and billeting soldiers in homes of those who refused to convert. In 1685, the king revoked the Edict of Nantes, which had given many religious freedoms to Protestants at the time of Henry IV. The revocation took away civil rights from Protestants. Their children were required by law to be raised as Catholics. Protestant clergymen were exiled or sent to the galleys. As many as 200,000 Huguenots fled from France—to England, Holland, Brandenburg (now in east Germany), and English colonies in America. Protestantism did survive in France, but it was greatly weakened.

Louis XV (reigned 1715–1774)

The reign of Louis XV saw a growing discontent among French citizens. Frenchmen of all classes desired more say in government and rejected royal absolutism. Many resented the special privileges of the aristocracy. All nobles and clergy were exempt from certain taxes. Many were subsidized with regular pensions from the government. The highest offices of government were reserved for aristocrats. Promotions were based on political connections rather than merit. Life at Versailles was wasteful, extravagant, and frivolous.

France had no uniform code of laws, and a lack of justice in the French judicial system rankled. The king had arbitrary powers to imprison. Royal bureaucrats were often petty tyrants, many serving their own interests. The bureaucracy of new nobles, under Louis XV, had become virtually a closed class within itself. One of his few stabs at reform was to abolish the insurrectionary *parlements* (twelve or thirteen in all) in 1770, after they rose en masse against him and royal authority. Some *philosophes (popularizers of the latest in science and philosophy)* applauded the insurrectionists and advocated a thorough overhaul of the judicial system.

Vestiges of the feudal and manorial systems continued to upset peasants, since they were taxed excessively in comparison to other segments of society. The *philosophes* gave expression to these grievances, and discontent grew.

Louis XV died, leaving many of the problems he had inherited. Corruption and inequity in government were even more pronounced. Ominously, crowds lined the road to Saint Denis, the burial place of kings, and cursed Louis's casket as they had his forebears'.

Louis XVI (reigned 1774–1792)

Louis XVI, the grandson of Louis XV, married Marie Antoinette (1770), daughter of the Austrian Empress Maria Theresa. He was honest, conscientious, and desirous of reform, but also indecisive and weak willed. He antagonized the old nobility when he sought fiscal reforms. As if to counteract their idleness and uppity behavior, in 1787 he granted toleration and civil rights to hard-working, docile Huguenots.

One of his first acts as king was to restore to the French *parlements* their judicial powers. This was a huge blunder. When he sought to impose new taxes on the under-taxed aristocracy, the *parlements* refused to register royal decrees.

So in 1787, the king summoned the Assembly of the Notables, a group of 144 representatives of the nobility and higher clergy. At Versailles, Louis XVI asked them to tax all lands, without regard to privilege of family; to establish provincial assemblies; to allow free trade in grain; and to abolish forced labor on the roads. The Notables refused to accept these reforms and demanded the replacement of certain of the king's ministers.

The climax of the crisis came in 1788 when the king was no longer able to get fiscal reform or new loans. He could not even pay the salaries of government officials. By this time, half of government revenues went to pay interest on the national debt (at 8 percent). Wars with England (see Chapter 5) had bankrupted France.

In 1789, for the first time in 175 years, the king called for a meeting of the Estates-General. When the Estates regrouped as the new National Assembly, the French Revolution was underway. Later, in the radical phase of the Revolution, the National Convention voted 366 to 361 to execute the king; Louis XVI went to the guillotine January 21, 1793.

Spain: Habsburg and Bourbon

Spain in the Seventeenth Century

The Treaty of Westphalia (1648; see Chapter 3) did not end the war between Spain and France. In the Treaty of the Pyrenees (1659), Spain ceded to France Artois in the Spanish Netherlands and territory in northern Spain. Marriage was arranged between Louis XIV, Bourbon king of France, and Maria Theresa, Habsburg daughter of Philip IV, king of Spain. (Louis XIV's mother was the daughter of Philip III of Spain.)

The population of Spain in the seventeenth century declined as Spain continued expelling Moors, especially from Aragon and Valencia. In 1550, Spain had a population of 7.5 million; by 1660 it was about 5.5 million.

Formerly food-producing lands were deserted. In Castile, sheep raising took the place of food production. Food was imported from elsewhere in Europe, and as domestic production declined, inflation increased. Historians have ascribed high taxes on peasants to wealthier Spaniards, who considered work a necessary evil to be avoided when possible. The upper classes preferred a life of cultured ease to one spent developing and caring for their estates. They purchased from the Crown patents of nobility, which carried with them tax exemptions.

Capitalism was almost nonexistent in Spain, as the nobility considered savings and investment beneath their dignity. What industry there was in Spain—silk, woolens, and leatherwork—was declining instead of growing.

Catholic orthodoxy and aristocratic exclusiveness were high values in Spanish society. In 1660, the clergy numbered two hundred thousand, an average of one for every thirty people.

The Spanish navy had all but ceased to exist by 1700, at which point it had only eight ships left plus a few borrowed from the Genoese. Most soldiers in the Spanish army were foreign.

Charles II (reigned 1665–1700)

Charles II, the last of the Spanish Habsburg kings, was only four when his father, Philip IV, died. His mother, Marie Anne of Austria, controlled the throne as head of the Council of Regency. Afflicted with many diseases and a weak constitution, the king was expected to die long before he did.

He intensely disliked the responsibilities of his office, and his timidity and lack of willpower made him one of the worst rulers in Spanish history.

In 1680, he married Marie Louise of France, and on her death he married Marie Anne of Bavaria. Since he had no child, Charles II's death in 1700 led to the War of the Spanish Succession.

Philip V (reigned 1700–1746)

The grandson of Louis XIV, Philip V was only seventeen when he became the first Bourbon king of Spain. The first dozen years of his reign were occupied with the War of the Spanish Succession, which ended successfully for him. He modernized the Spanish army and brought it to a strength of forty thousand men.

Philip V centralized Spanish government with the French *intendant* system, wherein his provincial governors were closely supervised by his royal government. He abolished many pensions and government subsidies and restored fiscal health to the Spanish government. His government encouraged industry, agriculture, and shipbuilding. He revived the Spanish Navy, and the fleet was substantial by the end of his reign.

Philip V married Marie Louise of Savoy, and when she died in 1714, he married Elizabeth Farnese of Parma. Philip V died during the War of the Austrian Succession and was succeeded by Ferdinand VI, who ruled an uneventful thirteen years (1746–1759).

Charles III (reigned 1759–1788)

By the time he ascended the Spanish throne, Charles III had already had political experience as the Duke of Parma and as king of the two Sicilies. He was an able ruler and enacted many reforms during his long reign. Moral, pious, and hard-working, Charles was one of the most popular of the Spanish kings.

He helped to stimulate the economy by eliminating laws that restricted internal trade and by reducing tariffs. He encouraged new agricultural settlements and helped establish banks for farmers. He helped to create factories and gave them monopolies: woolens, tapestries, glass, silks, and porcelain. He helped to establish schools to teach trades.

Spain was a strongly Catholic country and its intellectuals were not interested in the doctrines of the Enlightenment, repulsed by the irreligion of *philosophes*. An ambassador wrote in 1789 that in Spain "one finds religion, love for the king, devotion to the law, moderation in the administration, scrupulous respect for the privileges of each province and the individual."

Austrian Habsburgs and Central Europe

History of the Habsburgs

In 1273, Rudolph of Habsburg was elected Holy Roman Emperor, and Habsburgs ever after were nearly always elected emperor (Bavaria and Lorraine interrupted the winning streak). The empire was still intact in the eighteenth century, consisting of more than three hundred states, fifty-one free towns, and fifteen hundred free knights, each ruling a tiny state with about three hundred subjects and an annual income of $500. The largest states of the empire were the Austrian crown lands, with a population of 10 million inside the empire and 12 million outside; Prussia, with 5.5 million; Bavaria and Saxony, with 2 million each; and Hanover, with 900,000.

The custom was to select the ruler of Austria as the emperor because he alone had sufficient power to enforce imperial decisions. After the War of the Spanish Succession (1701–1713) and the Treaty of Utrecht (1713), the Spanish throne was occupied by a Bourbon, so Habsburg power was concentrated in Austria. The Habsburgs ruled the empire; Naples, Sardinia, and Milan in Italy; the Austrian Netherlands (now Belgium); Hungary; and Transylvania. Austria was not a national state; its lands included Germans, Hungarians, Czechs, Croats, Italians, Serbs, Rumanians, and others.

Government of Austria's Informal Empire

Since each part of the empire might have a different legal relationship to the emperor, there was no single constitutional system or administration for all parts of the realm. The emperor was Duke of Austria, Margrave of Styria, Duke of Carinthia, Lord of Swabia, Count of Tyrol, king of Bohemia, and king of Hungary, Transylvania, Croatia, Slavonia, and Dalmatia, in addition to his titles in Italy and the Austrian Netherlands. It is thus not surprising that government was divided to reflect national differences: separate chanceries for Austria (with two chancellors), Bohemia, Hungary, and Transylvania. There were also departments responsible for the affairs of Italy and the Austrian Netherlands.

In addition, the central government under the emperor consisted of the Privy Council that discussed high policy; the *Hofkammer*, which made decisions regarding finance and trade; the War Council; the Imperial Chancellery, which dealt with matters of empire; and the Court Chancellery, which dealt with domestic matters.

Feudalism in the Habsburg Lands

Lords of the manor had judicial and economic control over peasants. Peasants could not marry without the lord's consent; their children could not work or serve an apprenticeship outside the estate. Peasants could not contract a loan or sell anything without the lord's consent. They were obligated to the *corvée*, or compulsory labor, for as many as one hundred days a year. Peasants were obliged to buy products supplied by the lord at prices he set. They were obligated to pay tolls, customs duties, duties on transactions, quit-rents, and other taxes.

Music and Vienna

The most famous and popular of arts in the Habsburg Empire, especially Vienna, was music. Leopold I, a composer himself, was particularly significant as a patron of music. Royal concerts, ballets, and operas were part of the life of Vienna. Italians came to Austria, Bohemia, and Hungary to direct or improve their musical productions. The Slavs, Bohemians, and Magyars excelled in singing and playing of instruments. Adam Michna z Otradovic (1600–1676) composed hymns based on Czech poetry and the famous Saint Wenceslas Mass, honoring the Czech national hero.

Leopold I (reigned 1658–1705)

Emperor Leopold I was first cousin to Louis XIV of France and Charles II of Spain. He loved poetry and music, and was a patron of the arts. A devout Catholic, Leopold followed the advice of the Jesuits and sought to restrict severely his Protestant subjects. He employed German and Italian artists to build and decorate baroque churches and palaces.

One of Leopold's most severe tests was the Turkish invasion of Austria and siege of Vienna in 1683. However, with the help of the Poles under King Jan Sobieski, as well as the Germans, Austrians, and Hungarians, Leopold's forces drove back the Turks.

Emperor Leopold I was a key figure in the War of the Spanish Succession in three respects. His efforts against France helped to turn the tide of war and ensure that the same prince would not sit on both the thrones of France and Spain; he helped to elevate Brandenburg to the status of a major power by allowing its elector to add the title "king in Prussia" to his other titles, in reward for sending troops to the war; and Leopold, in using the services of one of the time's best generals, Prince Eugene of Savoy, helped Austria to expand southeast at the expense of the Turks, with whom Austria also was fighting.

Charles VI (reigned 1711–1740)

Following the reign of his brother, Joseph I (reigned 1705–1711), Charles VI, son of Leopold I, ascended the throne. Charles had a keen sense of duty and lived a moral life. He was meticulous, personally involved in the details of governing. One "detail" was the Pragmatic Sanction that he hawked around Europe to be signed by all princes in acknowledgment of his daughter's right to inherit the Habsburg crown lands. Most signed; one later reneged on his promise, calling it "a piece of paper."

Owing to a revolt by Hungarian nobles, he signed the Treaty of Szatmar with the Hungarians, recognizing their particular liberties and returning the Crown of Saint Stephen to Hungary. The Hungarian Chancellery thus became autonomous within the complicated Habsburg administration.

Maria Theresa (reigned 1740–1780)

Maria Theresa was not really "empress," although she was often referred to as such. First her husband, then her son was Holy Roman Emperor. Technically she was "Queen of Bohemia and Hungary, Archduchess of Austria, …" and so on.

Maria Theresa was a beautiful, courageous, high-minded, pious, and capable ruler. Her first reform was to increase the Austrian standing army from 30,000 to 108,000 by persuading the local estates to accept tax reforms. She gradually centralized the empire and increased the power of the Austrian government.

Maria Theresa was a conservative Catholic and considered the church and nobles to be the foundation of her state. She was concerned, however, with the freedom and well-being of her subjects, and political realism was the hallmark of her reign. The two most important international events of her forty-year reign were the War of the Austrian Succession (1740–1748) and the Seven Years' War (1756–1763).

Joseph II (reigned 1765–1790)

Joseph II was co-regent with his mother during the last fifteen years of her reign. He sought to be an "enlightened despot." He wanted to govern decisively and force-fully, but rationally, with the interests of his subjects in mind—at least as he envisioned them. He sought a full treasury, economy in government, and a strong military. One of his aims was to emulate the style and successes of Frederick II of Prussia. His mother's adviser, Prince von Kaunitz, provided a check on Joseph's ambitions. Kaunitz wrote to the emperor: "Despotic governments concern themselves with intimidation and punish-ment. But in monarchies [we must not forget] how much it is a joy worthy of a noble mind to govern free and thinking beings than to rule vile slaves."

Although the emperor was a devout Catholic, he expanded the state schools of Austria and granted religious toleration to both Protestants and Jews. Joseph II died at the age of forty-nine, having suffered military defeats from the Turks and fearing both the growing power of Russia and revolts in the Austrian Netherlands.

Prussia and the Hohenzollerns

Brandenburg-Prussia in 1648

The Thirty Years' War had devastated Germany. Brandenburg lost half its population through death, disease, and emigration.

Brandenburg was established in 950 AD, and its ruler was made an elector of the Holy Roman Empire in 1417. By the Thirty Years' War, despite its central location, Brandenburg was still insignificant. By marriage, the house of Hohenzollern had won widely separate parts of the empire. In the West, Hohenzollerns gained the duchy of Cleves and counties of Mark and Ravensberg, and in the East, the duchy of East Prussia.

The Treaty of Westphalia (1648) granted the elector eastern Pomerania, three tiny bishoprics and the archbishopric of Magdeburg. Nothing in its disparate territories foretold that Prussia would be a great power in Europe. Each province had its estates, representing towns and nobility. They had no common administration or culture. The sandy terrain had no natural frontiers for defense and was not economically productive. Its population was sparse, its soil poor. It was cut off from the sea and not on any existing trade route. Brandenburg was lampooned as the "sandbox of Europe."

Frederick William (reigned 1640–1688)

During his reign, Frederick William, the "Great Elector," established Prussia as a great power and laid the foundation for the unification of Germany in the nineteenth century. The nephew of Gustavus Adolfus of Sweden, and husband of the granddaughter of William the Silent, hero of Dutch independence (see Chapter 3), Frederick William sought to emulate the government organization of the Swedes and the economic policies of the Dutch.

Frederick had been well-educated. He was a strict Calvinist who settled twenty thousand Huguenot refugees on his estates. He granted toleration, moreover, to Catholics and Jews. He encouraged industry and trade and brought in foreign craftsmen and Dutch farmers. In each province, he established a local government, headed by a governor and chancellor, but with control from the central government in Berlin.

His most significant innovation was the building of a strong standing army. He was able to do this only through heavy taxes, the rate for which was twice that of the French during the height of Louis XIV's power. But the Prussian nobility were *not* exempt from those heavy taxes, as were the French aristocracy.

Frederick sought to encourage industry and trade, but was in danger of taxing them out of existence for his military. New industries were started to spread the tax burden: woolens, cottons, linen, velvet, lace, silk, soap, paper, and iron products. One of his achievements was the Frederick William Canal through Berlin, which linked the Elbe and Oder rivers and enabled canal traffic from Breslau and Hamburg to Berlin. He was the only Hohenzollern to be interested in overseas trade before Kaiser William II. But without ports and naval experience, the effort collapsed.

The central dynamic of Frederick William's life was his Calvinism through which he became convinced of direct protection and guidance from God in all he did. He highly valued learning and founded the Berlin Library. He was greatly alarmed at the threat to Protestantism implied in Louis XIV's revocation of the Edict of Nantes in 1685 and joined the League of Augsburg in 1686.

Frederick I (reigned 1688–1713)

The Great Elector's son (that is, Elector Frederick III and King Frederick I) was a weak, deformed man who won the affection of his people as did no other Hohenzollern. He loved the splendor of monarchy and an elaborate ceremony, with beautiful palaces and ornately dressed guards, who wore uniforms of white satin edged with gold lace. In his reign, the dye "Prussian blue" was invented and soon exploited in textile manufacture.

The city of Potsdam had been built by the Great Elector. Frederick I built new palaces in Berlin and Charlottenburg for his queen, Sophie Charlotte, who joined her husband in the many philosophical and religious discussions common in the palace.

Frederick I founded the University of Halle in 1692, a center for two of the great concepts of the time, Pietism and Natural Law.[1] The king welcomed as immigrants not only craftsmen, but also scholars such as Jacob Lenfant, historian of the Council of Trent, and Philip Speyer, a leading Pietist of his day. The Enlightenment philosopher Gottfried Wilhelm Leibniz persuaded Frederick to found an academy of science.

Much of Frederick I's reign was spent at war. Prussia participated in the War of the League of Augsburg (1688–1697) and the War of the Spanish Succession (1701–1713). For his services in the latter, the grateful emperor, Leopold, allowed him to take the title of king in Prussia, since East Prussia lay outside the boundaries of the empire and thus was not in the jurisdiction of the Austrian Habsburgs. He did not gain territory, but perpetuated the military tradition of his land. Costs of war were a heavy burden to the small state.

Frederick William I (reigned 1713–1740)

This king was quite different from his father. He cut the number of court officials drastically, not only for economy, but because he was impatient with ceremony. He believed Prussia needed a strong standing army and a plentiful treasury and proceeded to acquire both. Prussia's army grew from forty-five thousand to eighty thousand men during his reign, despite a population of only 2.5 million. Military expenditures consumed 80 percent of state revenues, compared with 60 percent in France and 50 percent in Austria. On the other hand, he spent only 2 percent of tax revenues to maintain his court, compared with 6 percent in Austria under Maria Theresa. Frederick built the fourth largest army in Europe, repaid all state debts, and left his successor a surplus of ten million thaler.

---

[1] Pietism was a movement within Lutheranism designed to overcome arid rituals by a return to a more ardent faith. Natural Law, already a concept in the Middle Ages, was now promoted as a viable alternative to Divine Law, which many felt restricted their inquiries.

Prussia maintained a large standing army in order to avoid war, if possible, and Frederick William I maintained this policy. The only time he went to war was when Charles XII of Sweden occupied Stalsund. Prussia immediately attacked and forced Sweden out. In 1720, Sweden agreed to the Prussian annexation of the port of Stettin and Pomeranian territory west of the River Oder.

Frederick William I continued Prussia's close relations with Holland and England. King George I of England was Frederick William's uncle and father-in-law. His mother was George I's sister and his wife was George's daughter.

Prussia developed the most efficient and incorruptible bureaucracy in Europe. In 1723, the king established a General Directory of four departments, each responsible for certain provinces. Taxes were high, but income from the royal estates (about one-third of the kingdom) largely paid for the army. The king made policy decisions and left it to the bureaucracy to work out the details.

Subordinate to the General Directory were seventeen provincial chambers. Merit promotions rewarded efficiency and diligence. The civil bureaucracy, like the military, was founded on the principle of absolute obedience and discipline. For oversight, every provincial chamber had a special royal agent, or Fiscal, to keep close watch on how well the king's orders were carried out. The Prussian bureaucracy employed only fourteen thousand poorly paid civil servants (about one-tenth of the proportion found in twentieth-century European nations). The king also required secret reports annually on all bureaucrats; hence, there was little or no bureaucratic corruption.

The king was a ceaseless worker and expected the same from those around him, including his son, the future Frederick the Great. The king entrusted his son's early education to his old governess, a Huguenot refugee who taught Frederick to speak French better than German. The king regimented his son's education from 6 A.M. to 10:30 P.M., and the young boy learned all the fifty-four movements of the Prussian drill before he was five years old. The value that Frederick William placed on education is also demonstrated by the fact that he established a thousand schools for peasant children.

Frederick the Great (Frederick II) (reigned 1740–1786)

Frederick the Great's father left him a prosperous economy, a full treasury, an income of seven million thaler, and an army of eighty thousand men. Unlike his father, Frederick loved French literature, poetry, and music. He played the flute and wrote poetry.

Frederick's philosophy of government soon became apparent. He wrote in 1740: "Machiavelli maintains that, in this wicked and degenerate world, it is certain ruin to be strictly honest. For my part, I affirm that, in order to be safe, it is necessary to be virtuous. Men are commonly neither wholly good nor wholly bad, but both good and bad." The king did not believe the state existed for the gratification of the ruler, but the ruler for the state: he must regard himself as "the first servant of the state." All his life, Frederick continued to ponder questions of religion, morality, and power. French literature dominated his reading.

In October 1740, Emperor Charles VI died; in December, Frederick ordered a sudden attack on Silesia, tearing up that "scrap of paper" guaranteeing Maria Theresa's throne. Thus began twenty-three years of warfare when the great powers of France, Austria, and Russia were aligned against Prussia. Their combined population was fifteen times Frederick's, yet Prussia emerged with enlarged territories of rich land and nearly twice its former population. But not without cost: Prussia alone saw 180,000 killed, and society was seriously disrupted. For a time, Frederick thought he would not survive "the ruin of the Fatherland." Instead, Prussia emerged as one of the great powers of Europe.

The king spent the remaining years of his life rebuilding and reforming what he had nearly destroyed. Frugality, discipline, and hard work, despite high taxation, were the values stressed throughout society. The king provided funds to rebuild towns and villages, used reserve grain for seed planting, and requisitioned horses for farming. He suspended taxes in some areas for six months as an economic stimulant. He started many industries. By 1773, 264 new factories were built, including sugar refineries, leather works, porcelain manufacturing plants, tobacco works, and so forth. The government drained marshes and settled hundreds of families to colonize former wastelands. He oversaw the reform of the judicial system in an attempt to produce a more equitable nation governed by law. His system was one of "constitutional absolutism" or enlightened despotism. In 1772, in the First Partition of Poland, Prussia acquired west Prussia, thus linking most of its territories.

The Dutch Republic

Historical Background

The Netherlands (now Holland and Belgium) were governed by the Spanish Habsburgs, but each of the seventeen provinces had its own special privileges and limited autonomy within the Spanish Empire.

During the Reformation, large numbers of Dutch converted to Calvinism ("Reformed" churches), especially in the North. Catholicism remained stronger in the South (now Belgium).

When Philip II, king of Spain, began demonstrating his determination to use the Spanish Inquisition to enforce laws against "heresy," the Netherlands began a revolt against Spain that continued intermittently for eighty years (1568–1648).

In 1578, the Duke of Parma restored many privileges of self-government to the ten southern provinces and large numbers of Calvinists moved north. In 1581, the seven northern Dutch provinces, under the leadership of William the Silent, declared themselves independent of Spain. In 1588, the great Spanish Armada sent to attack both the English and the Dutch was partially destroyed by a storm and then defeated by the English seadogs. This signal defeat emboldened England to seek more overseas trade.

Though James I established the first East Indies Company in 1600, with a seed capital of £20,000, the Dutch Estates-General showed their greater wealth from shipping in the founding of the Dutch East Indies Company in 1602 with ten times the capital, about £200,000. It was the first multinational corporation in the world and the first company to issue stocks.

In 1648, the Treaty of Westphalia recognized the independence of the Republic of the United Provinces. This had already been conceded by Spain in the Treaty of Munster, January 20, 1648.

Government of the Netherlands

The Dutch republic consisted of the seven northern provinces of which Holland was the wealthiest and most powerful. Each province and city was autonomous. National problems were governed by the States-General, which consisted of delegates from the provinces who could act only on the instructions of the provincial assemblies. Each province had a stadtholder, or governor, who was under the authority and instructions of the assembly. In times of crisis, the provinces would choose the same stadtholder, and he thereby became the national leader.

Dutch Economy

The seventeenth century was the golden age of the Dutch. Not only was it the Age of Rembrandt and other great painters, but the Netherlands was also the most prosperous part of Europe and the freest. The Dutch did not have government controls and monopolies to impede their freedom of enterprise. As a result, they became by far the greatest mercantile nation in Europe with the largest merchant marine in the world.

Medium-sized cities and ports such as Leyden, Haarlem, Gouda, Delft, and Utrecht (with populations from twenty thousand to forty thousand) were common in the Netherlands. Amsterdam was the richest city in Europe with a population of one hundred thousand. The quays and wharves of these Dutch cities were stocked with Baltic grain, English woolens, Indian silks and spices, Caribbean sugar, salted herring, and coal.

The Dutch had almost no natural resources, building their economy instead on the carrying on of trade, mercantile businesses, and other services. They were skilled in finishing raw materials. Coarse linens from Germany, for example, were bleached and finished into fine textiles. Other crafts at which the Dutch excelled included furniture and paper making, sugar refining, tobacco cutting, brewing, printing, and shipbuilding, as well as the manufacturing of fine woolens, pottery, glass, and armaments.

The Dutch taught accounting methods, provided banks, and instituted rational legal methods for settling disputes. Their low interest rate was a key to economic growth: 3 percent, half of the normal rate in England. The Dutch were discussed and written about all over Europe as champions of free enterprise and individual rights—in contrast to state absolutism, economic nationalism, mercantilism, and protective tariffs.

The Dutch East India and West India Companies were organized as cooperative ventures of private enterprise and the state. The provinces contributed part of the capital for these ventures, and the companies were subject to the authority of the States-General.

Dutch Wars and Foreign Policy

The Peace of Westphalia (1648) ended eighty years of war between Spain and the Netherlands and resulted in independence for the Dutch Republic and continued Habsburg rule of the Spanish Netherlands. After being freed from Spanish domination, the Dutch faced a series of wars against England over trading rights and colonial competition. Then, Louis XIV's efforts to move into the Low Countries brought the Dutch into a drawn-out war with France.

The accession of William and Mary to the throne of England in 1688 brought an end to the warfare between the Dutch and English. In the War of the Spanish Succession (1701–1713), England and Holland fought against France and Spain.

England, Scotland, and Ireland

Events Leading to the English Civil War

One of the underlying issues of the English Civil War (1642–1649) was the constitutional issue of the relation between king and Parliament: Could the king govern without the consent of Parliament or go against the wishes of Parliament? In short, the question was whether England was to have a limited, constitutional monarchy or the absolutism of France.

At issue theologically was the form of church government England was to have—whether it would follow the established Church of England's hierarchical, episcopal form of church government, or acquire a presbyterian form. The episcopal form meant that the king, the Archbishop of Canterbury, and the bishops of the church would determine policy, theology, and the form of worship and service. The presbyterian form of polity allowed for more freedom of conscience and dissent among church members. Each congregation would have a voice in the life of the church and a regional group of ministers, or presbytery, would attempt to ensure doctrinal purity.

The political implications for representative democracy were present in both issues. That is why most Presbyterians, Puritans, and Congregationalists sided with Parliament, and most Anglicans and Catholics sided with the king.

Charles I (reigned 1625–1649)

Charles I inherited both the English and Scottish thrones upon the death of his father, James I. He claimed a divine-right theory of absolute authority for himself as king and sought to rule without Parliament. In asserting that God alone made kings, and to Him alone kings are answerable, he also claimed absolute control over the Church of England.

The king demanded more money from Parliament, which refused and began impeachment proceedings against the king's chief minister, the Duke of Buckingham, later assassinated in 1628. Charles then levied a forced "loan" on many of the wealthier citizens of England and imprisoned seventy-six English gentlemen who refused to contribute. Sir Randolph Crew, chief justice of the King's Bench, was dismissed from office for refusing to declare those "loans" legal. Five of the imprisoned men applied for writs of habeas corpus (the right to be brought before a court or judge), asking whether the refusal to lend money to the king was a legal cause for imprisonment. The court returned them to jail without comment.

By 1628, both houses of Parliament—the House of Lords and the House of Commons—had united in opposition to the king.

The Petition of Right (1628)

Parliament in effect bribed the king by granting him a tax grant in exchange for his agreement to the Petition of Right. The petition stipulated that no one should pay any tax, gift, loan, or contribution except as provided by an act of Parliament; no one should be imprisoned or detained without due process of law; all were to have the right to the writ of habeas corpus; there should be no forced billeting of soldiers in the homes of private citizens; and martial law was not to be declared in England.

The Parliament of 1629

In the midst of a stormy debate over theology, taxes, and civil liberties, the king sought to force the adjournment of Parliament. But when he sent a message to the Speaker ordering him to adjourn, some of the more athletic members held the Speaker in his chair while the door of the House of Commons was locked to prevent the entry of other messengers from the king. The House then passed a number of resolutions: innovations toward Catholicism or Arminianism were to be regarded as treason; whoever advised any collection of taxes without consent of Parliament would be guilty of treason; and whoever should pay a tax levied without the consent of Parliament would be considered a betrayer of liberty and guilty of treason.

A royal messenger was allowed to enter the Commons and declared the Commons adjourned; a week later Charles I dissolved Parliament—for eleven years (1629–1640). Puritan leaders and leaders of the opposition in the House of Commons were imprisoned by the king, some for several years.

Religious Persecution

The established Church of England was the only legal church under Charles I, an Anglican with covert sympathies for Catholics. Within the Church of England (that is, the Anglican Church), specific ministers might be more Catholic, Arminian Protestant, or Puritan (with both Calvinist and Lutheran emphases).

William Laud, Archbishop of Canterbury, sought to enforce the king's policies vigorously. Arminian clergymen were to be tolerated, but Puritan clergymen silenced. Conventicles—secret meetings for worship in which the authorized Prayer Book was not used, only the Bible and the Psalter—were harshly suppressed, as was criticism of the king's religious policies. No book or pamphlet could legally be printed or sold without a license. Puritans who wrote secret pamphlets were punished harshly: in 1630, Alexander Leighton was whipped, pilloried, and mutilated for printing *An Appeal to Parliament* in which he challenged episcopacy. Three others had their ears cut off; one was branded on the cheek with the letters *SL* (Seditious Libeler). Several were executed.

National Covenant of Scotland (1638)

Dissatisfaction with royal absolutism reached a crisis in Scotland when representatives of the Scottish people met at Greyfriars Kirk in Edinburgh in 1638 to sign a national protest against the policies of Charles, who was also king of Scotland. Nobles and barons met and signed the National Covenant on one day, burgesses and ministers the next. The covenant affirmed the loyalty of the people to the Crown but declared that the king could not reestablish the authority of the episcopate over the church. (The Church of Scotland had had a presbyterian form of church government since the Reformation of the sixteenth century under John Knox; see Chapter 3.)

King Charles foolishly declared everyone who signed the National Covenant a rebel and prepared to move an army into Scotland.

War in Scotland

King Charles called out the militia of the northern counties of England and ordered the English nobility to serve as officers at their own expense. A troop of the king's horses entered Scotland only to find their way blocked by a large Scots army. They returned south of the border without fighting.

Charles signed the Pacification of Berwick with the Scots in June 1639, by which each side would disband its forces and a new General Assembly of the Church of Scotland and Scottish parliament would determine the constitution of the government. The Church General Assembly confirmed the actions of its predecessor; the Scottish parliament repealed laws in favor of episcopacy and increased its own powers; and the Scottish army remained in existence.

The Short Parliament

For the first time in eleven years, the king convened Parliament to vote on new taxes for the war with Scotland. Instead, the House of Commons presented to the king a long list of grievances, dating from 1629. These included violations of the rights of Parliament, violations of civil and property rights, and changes in church order and government. In anger, the king again dissolved Parliament, which had met only from April 13 to May 5, 1640.

The Scots Invade

The Scots immediately invaded the two northern counties of Northumberland and Durham unopposed. Charles called a Great Council of Lords, which had not met for over two hundred years. The council arranged a treaty with the Scots to leave things as they were.

The Long Parliament

The king was cornered: he had no money, no army, and no popular support. He summoned Parliament to meet in November 1640. The House of Commons immediately moved to impeach one of the king's ministers, Thomas Wentworth, Earl of Strafford.

Strafford's trial began in March 1641; after three weeks, there was still no verdict. He was accused of treason for subverting the fundamental laws of the realm with an arbitrary and tyrannical government. Treason was traditionally defined as an offense against the king, so the indictment read instead that he was guilty of "treason against the nation."

With mobs in the street and rumors of an army en route to London to dissolve Parliament, a bare majority of an underattended House of Lords passed a bill of attainder to execute the earl. Distraught, but fearing mob violence as well as Parliament itself, the king signed the bill and Strafford was executed. Archbishop William Laud was also arrested, and eventually tried and executed in 1645.

The House of Commons passed a series of laws to strengthen its position and to better protect civil and religious rights. The Grand Remonstrance listed 204 clauses of grievances against the king and demanded that all officers and ministers of the state be approved by Parliament. The Triennial Act provided that no more than three years should pass between parliaments. Another act provided that the current parliament should not be dissolved without its own consent. Various hated laws, taxes, and institutions were abolished, including the Star Chamber, the High Commission,[2] and the power of the Privy Council to deal with property rights. Ship money, a form of tax, was abolished, and tonnage duties were permitted only for a short time. The courts of common law were to remain supreme over the king's courts.

The Commons was ready to revoke the king's power over the Church of England, but members disagreed over what form the state church would take: episcopal, presbyterian, or congregational. Puritans were in the majority, but unable to make their views prevail. This deadlock was one of the reasons for divided allegiances of members of Parliament in the Civil War; some going for the king, some for the Puritan cause, and others in more radical directions.

Rebellion in Ireland and the Grand Remonstrance

It was at this juncture, with England on the brink of civil war, that Irish Catholics, oppressed by a Protestant minority, took the opportunity to murder thousands of their Protestant neighbors. The Commons immediately voted funds for a large army, but questions remained whether it was to be a parliamentary army or a royal army under the control of the king. This issue was eventually resolved by the Militia Ordinance of March 1642, which authorized Parliament to call up militias (heretofore the king's prerogative alone) and form them into a parliamentary army.

---

[2] The Star Chamber, created under Henry VII, was intended to provide more impartial justice and bring into line his 'overmighty subjects,' the old nobility. The High Commission was a more recent creation designed to enforce royal views on religion. In both cases, by the reign of Charles I, the people felt that these institutions were being used tyrannically to crush legitimate opposition.

The English Civil War (1642–1649)

With mobs in the streets and gentlemen carrying swords to protect themselves, men began identifying themselves as Cavaliers, in favor of the king, or Roundheads, if they supported Parliament.

In one of his most foolish actions as king, Charles then ordered his attorney general to prepare impeachment proceedings against five of the leading Puritans in the House of Commons. When the House refused to surrender their members to the custody of the king, Charles went in person to Parliament with four hundred soldiers to arrest the five members. While the five slipped away from Westminster to London, mobs turned out into the streets, including four thousand from Buckinghamshire who sought to defend one of the five, their hero, Sir John Hotham.

The king withdrew to Hampton Court and sent the queen to France for safety. In March 1642, Charles II went to York and the English Civil War began.

The Division of the Country

To some extent, every locality was divided between supporters of the king and supporters of Parliament. Geographically, the north and west of England sided with the king, and the south and east with Parliament. The Midlands were mixed in allegiance: eighty great nobles sided with the king, thirty against him. The majority of the gentry supported the king, but a large minority were for Parliament. Yeomen farmers tended to side with the higher-class landowning gentry of their areas; the peasants wanted to avoid fighting. In London, a few merchants were Royalist, but most businessmen sided with Parliament, and the city, strongly Presbyterian, supplied Parliament with men and money.

Parliament had two great advantages. First, the navy and merchant marine supported Parliament. They brought in munitions and revenue from customs as foreign trade continued. They hindered the coastal towns behind the king's lines. Second, Parliament had control of the wealthier and more strategic areas, including London, and was able to secure the three principal arsenals: London, Hull, and Portsmouth.

The King Attacks London

Charles put together a sizable force in August of 1642 and moved from Nottingham toward London, winning several skirmishes. He entered Oxford but was beaten back from London. Oxford then became his headquarters for the rest of the war.

Oliver Cromwell

Oliver Cromwell, a gentleman farmer from Huntingdon, led parliamentary troops to victory, first with his cavalry, which eventually numbered eleven hundred men, and then as lieutenant general in command of the well-disciplined and well-trained New Model Army.

Early Stages of the War

The early part of the war went in favor of the king. Lincolnshire, Cornwall, and Devon were occupied by two of the king's armies in 1643. The queen returned from

France with reinforcements and supplies. The king planned a three-pronged assault on London but was beaten back by the Earl of Essex. Charles sought allies among Irish Catholics, and Parliament sought aid from Presbyterian Scotland.

In January 1644, a well-equipped Scottish army of twenty-one thousand crossed into England, greatly upsetting the military balance. The Duke of Newcastle, the king's general, was forced into York and there besieged. Prince Rupert, nephew of the king and Count Palatine in Germany, came to his rescue from the West, but this action precipitated the battle of Marston Moor in July 1644. There, Cromwell decisively defeated the king's cavalry in a Royalist disaster. The North was now in parliamentary hands.

The king was not beaten yet, however. James Graham, Marquis of Montrose, raised troops for the king in the Scottish Highlands, much to the consternation of Lowlands Scots.

Parliament reconstructed and improved its army, giving Oliver Cromwell the top command. In June 1645, Charles marched into enemy territory and was crushed by Cromwell's troops, dubbed the "Ironsides," at Naseby. The king was then a fugitive and surrendered himself to the Scots in May 1646.

Controversy Between Parliament and the Army

The majority of Parliament was Presbyterian and wanted to extend the Scottish National Covenant to England. Many soldiers, however, were Independents who believed in democracy in politics and congregational control of the church.

During the Civil War, under the authority of Parliament, the Westminster Assembly convened to write a statement of faith for the Church of England that was Reformed or Presbyterian in content. Ministers and laymen from both England and Scotland participated for six years and wrote the *Westminster Confession of Faith*, still a vital part of Presbyterian theology.

When the war ended, Parliament ordered the army to disband without receiving the pay due to them. The army refused to disband, and in 1647 Parliament sought to disperse them by force. The plan was to bring the Scottish army into England and use it against the men who had won the war.

The army refused to obey and arrested the king when he was brought across the border. In August, the army occupied London, and some of their leaders wrote an "Agreement of the People" presented to the House of Commons. It called for a democratic republic with a written constitution and elections every two years, equal electoral districts and universal manhood suffrage, freedom of conscience, freedom from naval impressment, equality before the law, and no office of king nor House of Lords.

The Death of the King

On the night of November 11, 1647, the king escaped from Hampton Court and went to the Isle of Wight. He had made a secret agreement with the Scots that he would establish Presbyterianism throughout England and Scotland if they would restore him to his throne.

The Second Civil War followed in 1648, but it consisted only of scattered local uprisings and the desertion of part of the English fleet. The Scots invaded England, but were defeated by Cromwell at Preston, Wigan, and Warrington.

After these victories, the English army took control, again occupying London. The army arrested forty-five Presbyterian members of Parliament, excluded the rest, and admitted only about sixty Independents, who acted as the "Rump Parliament."

The army then tried Charles Stuart, formerly king, and sentenced him to death for treason. They charged him with illegal deaths and with governing in a tyrannical way instead of by the constitutional system of limited power that he had inherited. The execution of the king particularly shocked the Scots, because the English had specifically promised not to take the king's life when the Scots delivered him into English hands.

The Commonwealth (1649–1653)

After the execution of the king, Parliament abolished the office of king and the House of Lords. The new form of government was to be a commonwealth, or free state, governed by representatives of the people in Parliament. The entirety of the people, however, was not represented in Parliament. Large areas of the country had no representatives. The ninety Independents who controlled Parliament did not want elections. The Commonwealth was in effect a continuation of the Long Parliament under a different name. Parliament was more powerful than ever because there was neither king nor House of Lords to act as a check.

The Commons appointed a council of state and entrusted it with administrative power. Thirty-one of its forty-one members were also members of Parliament.

Opposition to the Commonwealth

Royalists and Presbyterians both opposed Parliament for its lack of broad representation and for regicide. The army was greatly dissatisfied that elections were not held, as one of the promises of the Civil War was popular representation.

The death of the king also provoked a violent reaction abroad. In Russia, the czar imprisoned English merchants. In Holland, Royalist privateers were allowed to refit. An English ambassador at The Hague and another in Madrid were murdered by royalists. France was openly hostile.

Surrounded by enemies, the Commonwealth became a military state with a standing army of forty-four thousand troops. The army, with career soldiers, was probably the best in Europe, and the most well paid. Forty warships were built in three years. The North American and West Indian colonies were forced to accept the government of the Commonwealth.

Ireland

In the summer of 1649, Cromwell landed in Dublin with an army of twelve thousand men. Despite a coalition of Protestant royalists and Irish Catholics, the Irish did not put together an army to oppose him. Instead, they relied on fortresses for safety. Drogheda was the scene of a gruesome massacre when Cromwell ordered the slaughter of the entire garrison of twenty-eight hundred. Another massacre took place at Wexford. This campaign of terror induced many towns to surrender; by the end of 1649, the southern and eastern coasts were in English hands. In 1650, Cromwell captured Kilkenny and left the rest of the conquest to others.

The lands of Roman Catholics who had taken part in the war were confiscated and given in payment to Protestant soldiers and others. Two-thirds of the land in Ireland changed hands, controlled mostly by Protestant landlords (the Ascendancy).

Scotland

Scottish Presbyterians, offended by the Independents' control of the English parliament and the execution of the king, proclaimed Charles II as their king. Charles accepted the National Covenant and agreed to govern a Presbyterian realm.

On September 3, 1650, Cromwell defeated the Scots at Dunbar, near Edinburgh, killing three thousand and taking ten thousand prisoner. The next year, King Charles II led a Scots army into England, but his forces were annihilated almost to the last man at Worcester. Charles was a fugitive for six weeks before escaping to France.

The Protectorate (1653–1659)

When it became clear that Parliament intended to stay in office permanently, without new elections, Cromwell took troops there and forced all members to leave, thus dissolving Parliament. Cromwell had no desire to rule either as king or military dictator. He called for new elections, but not under the old system; most officeholders in the new system were chosen by Independent or Puritan churches.

Cromwell then agreed to serve as lord protector with a council of state and a parliament. The new government permitted religious liberty, except for Catholics and Anglicans. Ironically, Cromwell invited Jews back to England in 1656 (they had been exiled in 1290). Part of his reasoning was pragmatic: he wanted a strong link to Dutch trade, and Amsterdam's Jews were only too eager to help out with this concession.

England was not strongly opposed to military rule, particularly after Cromwell divided the country into twelve districts with a major general in charge of each.

Oliver Cromwell died on September 3, 1658. After Cromwell's death, a new parliament was elected under the old historic franchise.

The Restoration (1660–1688)

The new parliament restored the monarchy, but the Puritan interregnum clearly showed that the English constitutional system required a limited monarchy, with the king as chief executive—but not as absolute ruler. Parliament in 1660 was in a far stronger position in its relationship to the king than it ever had been before.

Charles II (reigned 1660–1685)

The new king was dissolute, lazy, affable, and intelligent, as well as a cunning deceiver. He loved the sea and the navy and was interested in science and trade. Because he had so little interest in religion, he was willing to be tolerant.

While still on the Continent, Charles II issued the Declaration of Breda in which he agreed to abide by Parliament's decisions on the postwar settlement.

The Convention Parliament (1660)

Parliament pardoned all who had fought in the Civil War except for fifty people listed by name. Of these, twelve were executed for regicide.

Royalists whose lands had been confiscated by the Puritans were allowed to recover their lands through the courts, but those who had sold them could receive no compensation. That meant that both Roundheads and Cavaliers would be the landowners of England.

To raise money for the government, Parliament granted the king income from customs duties and an excise on beer, ale, tea, and coffee. Feudalism was abolished.

The Clarendon Code

Of England's nine thousand parish churches, two thousand were pastored by Presbyterian ministers, four hundred by Independents, and the rest by Anglicans. The Cavalier Parliament, elected early in 1661, sought to drive out all Puritans and exclude them from public life. They set to work passing a series of acts—collectively called the Clarendon Code—to do just that:

Corporation Act (1661). Excluded from local government anyone who refused to swear to the unlawfulness of resistance to the king or who did not receive communion according to the pattern of the Church of England.

Act of Uniformity (1662). Issued a new prayer book and ordered ministers either to accept it or resign their positions and livelihood. Twelve hundred pastors refused and vacated their churches.

Conventicle Act (1664 and 1670). Imposed harsh penalties on those who attended religious services that did not follow the forms of the Anglican Church.

Five-Mile Act (1665). Prohibited ministers from coming within five miles of a parish from which they had been removed as pastor.

In addition, Parliament passed a licensing act permitting the Archbishop of Canterbury and the bishop of London to control the press and the publishing of books.

The result of these acts of Parliament was an England divided into two groups: the Anglican Church and nonconformists. The church was purged of Puritans and regained its property. It levied tithes and controlled education at all levels. Nonconformists were excluded from the universities, from government, from many professions, and from membership in the House of Commons. Some, of course, became Anglicans outwardly but did not believe what they professed. Nonconformists became shopkeepers, artisans, small farmers, merchants, bankers, and manufacturers. Their diligence, thrift, and self-discipline brought prosperity. They were strengthened by the rise of Methodism in the eighteenth century.

Disasters for England

During the Restoration, England suffered a number of disasters. Wars with the Dutch cost the country enormously in ships and money. The bubonic plague hit London in 1665, killing sixty-eight thousand people. The Great Fire of London in 1666 destroyed thirteen thousand homes, eighty-four churches, and many public buildings, none of which were covered by insurance.

Scotland's Independence?

Scotland regained her independence at the restoration of Charles II in 1660. The Earl of Middleton was made the king's commissioner in the Scottish parliament and commander of the army in Scotland. Some Presbyterian ministers reminded the king of the National Covenant of 1638 and of his covenant-oath in 1651, pledging that Scotland be governed according to Presbyterian polity and principles. The king arrested the Marquis of Argyle, Presbyterian leader of the Covenanters, charged him with treason for "compliance with Cromwell's government," and had him executed.

Charles II declared himself head of the Church of Scotland and decreed that the episcopal form of hierarchical church government would be used in Scotland. In 1661, the Scottish parliament declared that the National Covenant was no longer binding and prohibited any renewal of a covenant or oath without royal permission.

A dictatorship was established in Scotland to enforce episcopacy and rule by approved bishops. The government demanded absolute obedience and used illegal detention to enforce it. Drastic fines were levied on hundreds of people suspected of sympathies to the Covenanters. Presbyterianism was outlawed and hundreds of ministers lost their positions. Perhaps as many as eighteen thousand ordinary people died for the cause of religious liberty in the persecution that followed. Dragoons were sent to prevent people from meeting in the fields and in "unlicensed" homes for the purpose of worshipping God and studying the Bible. Others were fined for not attending the parish church.

The last two years of Charles II's reign in Scotland were known as "the Killing Times" because of the wholesale slaughter of hundreds who were shot down without trial if they refused to take the oath of the Covenant.

Whigs and Tories

In Charles's reign, two factions of the ruling classes emerged that would reflect English political positions for centuries. The Whigs tended to support great aristocratic families and non-Anglican dissenters, such as Presbyterians, while the Tories supported the Anglican Church and the gentry of the countryside. Later, Whigs drew support from emerging industrial business interests, wealthy merchants, and other proponents of reform, while the Tories drew support from the landed interests and the Crown. Because Tories believed so strongly in the legitimacy of bloodlines, they were prepared to permit the royal house to be infiltrated by Catholics, as long as they were not too public about it. Charles II obliged, when he died in 1685, by receiving Roman Catholic absolution in relative privacy, on his deathbed.

James II (reigned 1685–1688)

The new king was the brother of Charles II. He had served as lord admiral and commanded an English fleet against the Dutch.

James II began his reign in a strong position. Parliament immediately voted the king an income from customs for life. But James, a staunch Roman Catholic, wanted to return England to "the faith." He appointed Catholics to high positions in his government. In 1685, he created the Court of Ecclesiastical Commission with power over the clergy and suspended the bishop of London from office. Three colleges at the University of Oxford were put under Catholic rule. (Oxford was an Anglican stronghold, so the king was undermining his support.)

In April 1687, James issued a *Declaration of Indulgence* that declared Catholics and nonconformists free to worship in public and to hold office. This was bold, but nonconformists knew that the king's intent was to enable Catholics to infiltrate government. Instead of supporting the king, the nonconformists secured a promise from the Anglicans that they would eventually be given toleration.

The Glorious Revolution of 1688

The leaders of Parliament were not at all willing to sacrifice the constitutional gains of the English Civil War and return to an absolute monarchy. Two events in 1688 goaded them to action.

In May, James reissued the Declaration of Indulgence with the command that it be read on two successive Sundays in every parish church. Seven bishops printed and distributed a petition to the king requesting that he withdraw his command. This was a technical violation of the law and the king ordered them to be prosecuted for publishing a seditious libel against his government. When a London jury reached a verdict of "not guilty," it was clear that the king did not have popular support.

On June 10, 1688, James's queen, Mary of Modena, gave birth to a son. The king and queen had been married for fifteen years and their other children had died. As long as James was childless by his second wife, the throne would go to one of his Protestant daughters, Mary or Anne. But the birth of a son, who would be raised Roman Catholic, changed the picture completely.

A group of Whig and Tory leaders, speaking for both houses of Parliament, invited William and Mary to assume the throne of England. William III was Stadtholder of Holland and son of a daughter of Charles I. Mary II was the daughter of James II by his first wife, Anne Hyde. They were both in the Stuart dynasty.

William was willing to assume the throne only if he had popular support and could retain his Dutch troops, despite the irritation their presence would cause in England.

The Dutch feared that Louis XIV of France would attack Holland while their army was in England, but the French attacked the Palatinate instead and eliminated that fear. Louis XIV offered to James II the French fleet, but James declined what would have been very little help. Louis thought that William's invasion would result in a civil war that would neutralize both England and Holland, but he was mistaken. On November 5, 1688, William and his army, aided by a "Protestant wind," landed at Torbay in Devon. James offered many concessions, but it was too late. He advanced with his army to Salisbury, then returned to London, and finally fled to France.

William assumed control of the government and summoned a free parliament, which met in February 1689. Whigs and Tories met in a conciliatory spirit, though party differences soon became evident. The Whigs wanted a declaration that the throne was vacant in order to break the royal succession and give the king a parliamentary title. The Tories declared that the king had abdicated so as to avoid admitting that they had deposed him. William and Mary were declared joint sovereigns, with administration given to him. The sovereignty of William and Mary, however, depended on their contract with Parliament, the justly celebrated Bill of Rights.

In 1689, Parliament established the **Bill of Rights**, which declared the following:

1. The king could not be Roman Catholic.

2. A standing army in time of peace was illegal without parliamentary approval.

3. Taxation was illegal without parliamentary consent.

4. Excessive bail and cruel and unusual punishments were prohibited.

5. The right to trial by jury was guaranteed

6. Free elections to Parliament would be held.

Parliament also passed other laws that affirmed or established basic freedoms or rights. The Toleration Act (1689) granted the right of public worship to Protestant non-conformists, though it did not permit them to hold office. The act did not extend liberty to Catholics or Unitarians, but normally they were left alone. The Trials for Treason Act (1696) stated that a person accused of treason had to be shown the accusations against him and had the right to the advice of counsel. The accused also could not be convicted except upon the testimony of two independent witnesses. In 1694, an act of Parliament established freedom of the press, but with strict libel laws.

Control of finances was in the hands of the House of Commons, which stopped uncontrolled grants to the king. The founding of the Bank of England in 1694 showed the influence of Dutch models. The bank worked closely with London merchants and the Commons.

The Act of Settlement in 1701 provided that should William or Anne—the other of James II's Protestant daughters—die without children (Queen Mary had died in 1694), the throne would descend, not to the exiled Stuarts, but to Sophia, Electress Dowager of Hanover, a granddaughter of King James I, or to her Protestant heirs.

Parliament also established that judges were independent of the Crown. Thus, England declared itself a limited monarchy and a Protestant nation.

Queen Anne (reigned 1702–1714)

William died childless in 1702, embroiled in the War of the Spanish Succession against his old enemy, Louis XIV. His successor, Queen Anne, was a devout Anglican, a semi-invalid who ate too much and who was too slow-witted to be an effective ruler. She had sixteen children, none of whom survived her. Her reign was occupied with the War of the Spanish Succession (1702–1713), and it ushered in the Augustan Age in arts and letters, also called the Silver Age (with the era of Shakespeare and contemporaries as the Golden). The Augustan Age was characterized by an elegant prose style, gentleman-writers, and the relentless march of heroic couplets in poetry and on the stage. The high style of the court and aristocracy was cultivated by all, including the elite made newly rich by trade and such adventurers as Daniel Defoe, whose "Robinson Crusoe" shows the enterprising spirit of the age.

The most important achievement of Queen Anne's reign was the Act of Union (1707), which united Scotland and England into one kingdom. The Scots gave up their parliament and sent forty-five members to the English House of Commons and sixteen to the House of Lords. However, they retained Presbyterianism as their national church.

Eighteenth-Century England

Following the Act of Settlement in 1701 and Queen Anne's death in 1714, the House of Hanover inherited the English throne in order to ensure that a Protestant would rule the realm. The Hanover dynasty produced George I (1714–1727); George II (1727–1760); George III (1760–1820); George IV (1820–1830); William IV (1830–1837); and Queen Victoria (1837–1901).

Because of the English Civil War, Commonwealth, and the Glorious Revolution, the Hanoverians were willing to rule as Kings-in-Parliament, which meant that to rule England, the king and his ministers had to have the support of a majority in Parliament. Robert Walpole, who served forty-two years in the English government, created the office of prime minister, a vital link between king and Parliament. Other famous eighteenth-century prime ministers were the Thomas Pelham-Holles, Duke of Newcastle; George Grenville; William Pitt the Elder, Earl of Chatham; Lord Frederick North; and William Pitt the Younger.

During the late eighteenth century, the British Empire suffered a major blow when it lost the North American colonies in the American War for Independence (1775–1783). The American victory sparked renewed hopes for autonomy or independence among another group long under British rule: the Irish.

The Irish had in the past attempted independence. In March 1689, James II arrived in Dublin with seven thousand French troops and was joined by Irish Catholics seeking freedom from England. Protestants fled to Londonderry, which withstood a siege of 105 days. In June 1690, William landed in Ireland with an army of thirty-six thousand troops and at the battle of Boyne completely defeated James, who fled to France.

Repercussions in Ireland were harsh: no Catholics could hold office, sit in the Irish parliament, or vote for its members. They could enter no learned profession except medicine, could not purchase land or hold long leases, and were subject to discriminatory taxation.

Not quite one hundred years later, as British troops were withdrawn from Ireland to be sent to America, an Irish militia formed, again with thoughts of independence. Ultimately, the British did grant concessions to the Irish between 1778 and 1783. Roman Catholics could inherit property and hold long-term leases. The Irish parliament was given its independence, but Protestants maintained control and the English Crown continued to appoint executive officials.

In 1800, the Irish parliament voted itself out of existence in exchange for one hundred seats in the British House of Commons and thirty-two places in the House of Lords. That year an Act of Union joined Ireland to Britain as the United Kingdom.

Eighteenth-century Scotland was the scene of Jacobite efforts to restore the Stuarts to the throne—but the efforts had their roots in the late seventeenth century. In 1688, the Scots declared that James had "forfeited" the Scottish throne, which they then offered to William and Mary with the understanding that Scotland would be Presbyterian. Some Highland clans, however, turned out in defense of James. They were defeated at the battle of Killiecrankie in July 1689. James's family (the Latin for James is Jacobus) gave rise to the doomed, romantic cause of the Jacobites.

The settlement with William and Mary was marred by the brutal Glencoe Massacre of 1692, in which the Campbell clan, aligning itself with William, slaughtered a large group of Macdonalds, who were more closely identified with the Jacobites. In 1715, James II's son raised an army of ten thousand Highlanders in revolt. James Francis Edward Stuart, the "Old Pretender," was soundly defeated and fled to France. In 1745, Stuart's son, Charles Edward, the "Young Pretender," obtained two ships from the French and sought to incite an uprising in Scotland, winning lasting fame as "Bonnie Prince Charlie."

Charles's spirit and ambition earned him the backing of several Highland chiefs. A natural leader, he won the respect of his men for enduring the hardships of the common soldier. Charles was able to capture the city of Edinburgh, but not the fortified castle. Soon he was forced to retreat north to Inverness. At Culloden, in April 1746, he was routed. Following the rebellion, the English carried out harsh reprisals, including many executions, and left parts of the Highlands devastated. They disarmed the Highlanders and even outlawed the wearing of the Highland kilt and tartan.

Scandinavia

Sweden in the Thirty Years' War

In 1630, King Gustavus Adolfus of Sweden drove the forces of the Holy Roman Empire from Pomerania, then part of eastern Germany. Swedish troops occupied all of Bohemia, organized a new Protestant Union, and invaded Bavaria. The king's success did not last long, however. Gustavus Adolfus was killed in 1632 in the battle of Lützen. And in the fall of 1634, imperial forces decisively defeated the Swedish army at Nordlingen. The Treaty of Prague (1635) restored Catholic and Protestant lands to their status as of 1627.

Catholic France allied with Protestant Sweden against the Habsburg Empire during the last phase of the Thirty Years' War (1635–1648). Sweden acquired western Pomerania as part of the Peace of Westphalia (1648), ending the Thirty Years' War.

Swedish Empire

Swedish power in the Baltic reached its zenith in the 1650s. The population of the Swedish Empire, including the German provinces, was only three million, half of whom were Swedish.

Sweden was not a large or productive country. Maintaining a strong standing army proved to be too much of a strain on the economy. Sweden sought to control the trade of the Baltic Sea with its important naval stores, but even at the height of Swedish power only 10 percent of the ships in the Baltic trade were Swedish; 65 percent were Dutch.

Swedish provinces in the Baltic and in Germany were impossible to defend against strong continental powers such as Russia, Prussia, and Austria.

Political Situation

After the death of Gustavus Adolfus in 1632, the government was effectively controlled by an oligarchy of the nobility ruling in the name of the Vasa dynasty. Christina, daughter of Gustavus Adolfus, became queen at age six and ruled from 1632 to 1654. At age twenty-eight, she abdicated the throne to her cousin and devoted the rest of her life to the Catholic faith and to arts.

Charles X Gustavus reigned from 1654 to 1660 during the First Northern War against Poland, Russia, and Denmark. Poland ceded Livonia to Sweden by the Treaty of Olivia (1660). Denmark surrendered to Sweden the southern part of the Scandinavian peninsula by the Treaty of Copenhagen (1660).

Charles XI (reigned 1660–1697) became king at age eleven. After he came of age, he spent the rest of his life attempting to regain powers lost to the Royal Council. For this, he secured the aid of the Lower Estates of the Rijksdag, which in 1693 declared that Charles XI was "absolute sovereign King, responsible to no one on earth, but with power and might as his command to rule and govern the realm as a Christian monarch." This was in dramatic contrast to the long struggles in Holland and England to constitutionally limit their kings.

Charles XII (reigned 1697–1718) came to the throne at age fifteen and reigned for twenty-one years. He spent most of his life at war, and in the Great Northern War (1700–1721), proved himself an outstanding military leader.

The Great Northern War pitted Charles XII against Denmark, Saxony, Poland, and Russia, which had formed an alliance to destroy the Swedish Empire. In February 1700,

Poland attacked Swedish Livonia, and Denmark invaded Holstein. The Swedish navy defeated the Danes and attacked Copenhagen, forcing Denmark to make peace.

Charles then shifted his attention to Estonia and routed a Russian invasion in the first battle of Narva, inflicting heavy losses. He spent the next several years fighting in Poland, defeating both the Poles and the Russians. But in 1709, the Russians, outnumbering Swedish forces two to one, defeated them. Tsar Peter the Great then took the Baltic provinces of Livonia and Estonia from Sweden.

Years of warfare, poor government, and high taxes finally led to Charles XII's alienation from his people. In 1718, he was killed by a stray bullet.

Eighteenth-Century Sweden

The loss of the empire meant a move to a more limited monarchy, and the new freedom led to a sharp increase in peasant enterprises and independence. The Swedish economy prospered. By 1756, the Rijksdag (Swedish parliament) considered itself the sovereign Estates of the realm and thus made the principal decisions of government, including establishing many civil liberties. The government returned temporarily to royal absolutism under Gustavus III, but he was assassinated in 1792.

Scandinavian Rotations

Finland was part of the Swedish Empire in the seventeenth century, and Norway was part of Denmark. In the early nineteenth century, Sweden gave up Finland but acquired Norway from Denmark as an autonomous part of a union of the two nations.

Russia

Ivan III (reigned 1442–1505)

Ivan III, or "Ivan the Great," put an end in 1480 to Mongol domination over Russia. He married Sophie Paleologue (1472), the niece of the last emperor of Constantinople. (The Byzantine Empire had been absorbed by the Ottoman Turks in 1453.) Ivan took the title of Caesar (that is, tsar) as heir of the Eastern Roman Empire. He encouraged the Eastern Orthodox Church and called Moscow the "Third Rome"; many Greek scholars, craftsmen, architects, and artists were brought to Russia.

Ivan IV (reigned 1533–1584)

Ivan IV, or "Ivan the Terrible," grandson of Ivan III, began westernizing Russia. A contemporary of Queen Elizabeth, he welcomed the English and the Dutch and opened new trade routes to Moscow and the Caspian Sea. English merchant adventurers opened Archangel on the White Sea and provided a link with the outer world free from Polish domination.

Ivan was a man of contradictions. It was he who made the old state councils (Duma and Sobor) more democratic, as a new *zemskii sobor* (1550), with representatives of the people. Yet Ivan seethed with paranoia, using a brutal, black-robed state police (the dread *oprichniki*) to terrorize the boyars, or powerful old nobles, and others into obedience and to take their property. It was under Ivan IV that Russia continued its expansion into contiguous territory and created an empire stretching into Siberia, toward the Pacific.

The death of Ivan IV in 1584 marked the end of the ruling Muscovite family and soon thereafter began the "Time of Troubles," a period of turmoil, famine, power struggles, and invasions from Poland. This era is epitomized in the story of Tsar Boris Godunov, immortalized in the drama by Alexander Pushkin (1825) and the opera by Modest Mussorgsky (1869).

The Romanov Dynasty

The Romanov dynasty ruled Russia from 1613 to 1917. Stability returned to Russia in 1613 when the *Zemskii Sobor* (estates-general representing the Russian Orthodox Church, landed gentry, townspeople, and a few peasants) elected Michael Romanov as tsar from 1613 to 1645.

Russia, with a standing army of seventy thousand troops, was involved in a series of unsuccessful wars with Poland, Sweden, and Turkey. In 1654, Russia annexed the Ukraine with its rich farmlands. The Ukrainians were supposed to be granted autonomy, but were not.

Under the Romanovs, Russia began a period of westernization. The Russian army was trained by westerners, mostly Scotsmen. Weapons were purchased from Sweden and Holland. Four Lutheran and Reformed churches and a German school were established in Moscow. Western skills, technology, clothes, and customs became accepted in Russia. By the end of the seventeenth century, twenty thousand Europeans lived in Russia, developing trade and manufacturing, practicing medicine, and smoking tobacco, while Russian boyars, forced by Peter the Great, began trimming their beards and wearing Western clothing.

Western books were translated into Russian. The Bible had long existed in Old Church Slavonic, but in 1649 monks were appointed by Tsar Alexis to translate it into Russian, a task not completed until the 1750s. The *raskolniki* ("old believers") refused to accept Western innovations or liturgy in the Orthodox Church and were severely persecuted: in twenty years, twenty thousand were burned to death. The hero of Fyodor Dostoevsky's *Crime and Punishment* is named Raskolnikov. Millions still called themselves "old believers" as late as 1917.

Peter the Great (reigned 1682–1725)

Peter was one of the most extraordinary people in Russian history. He was nearly seven feet tall with physical strength so great that he could bend a horse shoe with his bare hands. His restless energy kept him active, doing things incessantly, perpetually at work building boats, extracting teeth, dissecting corpses, shoemaking, cooking, etching, and writing dispatches and instructions, sometimes for fourteen hours a day. He did not understand moderation and could be cruel and vicious. He often whipped his servants, killed people who angered him, and even tortured his son to death. When he received good news, he would sometimes dance around and sing at the top of his voice.

Peter was born in 1672, the son of Tsar Alexis's second wife, Natalia. When Peter was four, his father died and the oldest son Theodore ruled until 1682, when he also died without heir. For seven years, Peter and his older half-brother ruled with the older half-sister Sophia as regent. Discovering a plot by Sophia to kill him, Peter, in 1689, banished her to a monastery and began ruling in his own right with his mother Natalia as regent. When she died in 1694, Peter took over the administration of the government.

The driving ambition of Peter the Great's life was to modernize Russia and he needed the West to accomplish that. At the same time he wanted to compete with the great powers of Europe on equal terms.

Peter visited western Europe in disguise in order to study the techniques and culture of the West. He worked as a carpenter in shipyards, attended gunnery school, and visited hospitals and factories. He sent back to Russia large numbers of European technicians and craftsmen to train Russians and to build factories, some of which were larger than any in the West. By the end of Peter's reign, Russia produced more iron than England (though not more than Sweden or Germany).

Wars of Peter the Great

Peter built up the army through conscription and a twenty-five-year term of enlistment. He gave flintlocks and bayonets to his troops instead of the old muskets and pikes. Artillery was improved, and discipline enforced. By the end of Peter's reign, Russia had a standing army of 210,000 men, despite a population of only thirteen million. Peter also developed the Russian navy.

In 1696, Peter sailed his fleet of boats down the Don River and took Azov on the Black Sea from the Turks.

The Great Northern War (1700–1721)

In 1699, Peter allied with Poland and Denmark against Sweden. At the first battle of Narva (1700), Sweden's Charles XII defeated the Russian army of thirty-five thousand, capturing its artillery and most of its senior officers. Peter learned his lesson and prepared for a rematch by melting down church bells for cannon. He won the second battle of Narva in 1704.

The main Swedish effort, though, was against Poland; war lasted for twenty years. In 1706, Sweden again defeated Russia at Grodno, but in 1709 Peter won at Poltava.

The Treaty of Nystad (1721) ended the war. Russia returned Finland to Sweden, but Livonia (Latvia) and Estonia became part of the Russian Empire. Russia now had possessions on the Baltic Sea and a "window on the West."

Saint Petersburg

Carving the great city of Saint Petersburg out of wilderness and making it one of the two capitals of Russia was one of Peter's crowning achievements. Construction began in 1703, using conscripted labor, and supervised by the tsar himself, who was bent on creating the "Venice of the North"—or at least a Russian Amsterdam. It became a cosmopolitan, lively city with French theater and Italian opera. Peter's palace copied Versailles's terraces, fountains, art gallery, and park. Saint Petersburg was built mostly of stone and brick, rather than wood.

The tsar ordered a number of noble families to move to Saint Petersburg and build their houses according to Peter's plans. At Peter's death in 1725, Saint Petersburg had a population of seventy-five thousand people, the largest city in northern Europe.

Reforms Under Peter the Great

In organizing the central government, Peter followed the Swedish model: Russia was divided into twelve provinces with a governor in charge of each. This decentralized many functions previously performed by the national government. Nevertheless, the tsar ruled by decree (*ukase*). Government officials and nobles acted under government authority, but Russia had no representative body. The Russian secret police ferreted out opposition and punished it as subversion.

Russia had a conditional land tenure system with the tsar as the theoretical owner of all land in a Russian-style feudal system where both nobility and serfs served the state. All landowners owed service for life to the state, either in the army, the civil service, or at court. In return for government service, they received land and serfs to work their fields.

Peter established and maintained a formidable military, which, by the end of his reign, accounted for 75 percent of the Russian government's budget. Conscription, which required each village to send recruits, guaranteed a steady supply of troops for the Russian army. By 1709, Russia manufactured most of its own weapons and had an effective artillery. The Russian navy, mostly on the Baltic, grew to a fleet of 850 ships, though it declined sharply after Peter's death. Peter further fortified his forces by establishing naval, military, and artillery academies.

The budget of the Russian government at the end of Peter's reign was three times its size at the beginning. Heavy taxes, on trade, sales, and rent provided much of the needed funds. The government also levied a head tax on every male. State-regulated monopolies brought income to the government as well, but stultified trade and economic growth and were counter-productive economically. Half of the two hundred enterprises begun during Peter's reign were state-owned; the rest were heavily taxed. (In addition to the heavy tax burden, Russian enterprise suffered from its reliance on industrial serfdom: the workers, who were bought and sold among factories, tended to create inferior products.)

Among Peter's other pursuits, he sought unsuccessfully to link Russia's main rivers by canals. Thousands died in the effort, but only one of his six great canals was completed: Saint Petersburg was linked to the Volga by canal in 1732.

Russian religion, of course, was not left untouched by Peter the Great. When the patriarch of the Russian Orthodox Church died in 1700, Peter abolished his authority and began treating the church as a government department. He eventually gave governing authority to a secular procurator and Holy Synod.

Main Eighteenth-Century Russian Tsars after Peter the Great

The following are the most notable of Peter the Great's eighteenth-century successors:

Anna (reigned 1730–1740). Dominated by German advisers, Anna was a wartime tsarina. Under her rule, the War of the Polish Succession (1733–1735) gave Russia firmer control over Polish affairs. War against the Turks (1736–1739) gave Azov to Russia once again. Russia agreed not to build a fleet on the Black Sea.

Elizabeth (reigned 1741–1762). The youngest daughter of Peter the Great, Elizabeth reigned during the golden age of the aristocracy as they freed themselves from some obligations imposed on them by earlier tsars. Russia entered the Seven Years' War (1756–1763) during Elizabeth's reign. Her death in 1762 allowed a pro-Prussian German prince to take over.

Peter III (reigned 1762). Peter's reign ended soon after it began when he was killed in a military revolt condoned by his German wife, who succeeded him to the throne.

Catherine II (reigned 1762–1796). Born Sophia Augusta Fredericka of Anhalt-Zerbst, and rechristened when she married Peter and turned Orthodox, Catherine II (Catherine the Great) continued the westernizing process begun by Peter the Great. The partitions of Poland (1772, 1793, and 1795) occurred under her rule, as did Russia's annexation of the Crimea from Turkey. Like Joseph II of Austria and Frederick II of Prussia, Catherine II was considered an enlightened despot, but in fact she only flirted with enlightened ideas, *philosophies*, and legal reform. After the terrible Pugachëv Revolt of 1773–1775, in which thousands of Cossacks and peasants ransacked southeastern Russia, Catherine's sham-enlightenment stopped. Her love affairs did not.

Italy and the Papacy

The Papacy

For the first time in its long history, the papacy became a negligible power in the seventeenth century. Several factors contributed to its decline:

1. The Protestant Reformation of the sixteenth century and the emergence of many Protestant principalities throughout Europe diluted the pope's sphere of influence.

2. The emphasis on limited constitutional government—adopted in the Protestant Reformation and accepted by many non-Protestants as well—made rulers and their people less willing to submit to the pope's authority.

3. The relatively few sanctions available to the pope in an international atmosphere of realpolitik (realistic politics) gave him little leverage over those he would choose to influence.

4. The spread of the Enlightenment sparked the beginnings of secularization in Europe.

5. The anticlericalism associated with the Enlightenment spread a desire to reduce the power and economic holdings of the church in traditionally Catholic countries. Anticlericalism reached a climax in the French Revolution.

6. The papacy lacked the leadership needed to counter the above. Most seventeenth- and eighteenth-century popes were more concerned about administering their own territories than with the wider political milieu.

The following are the most notable of the seventeenth- and eighteenth-century popes:

Pope Innocent X (1644–1655). He protested against the Peace of Westphalia (1648) because it acknowledged the rights of Lutherans and Calvinists in Germany, but diplomats at Westphalia paid him little attention.

Quiet obscurity characterized the next three popes, though they did clash with King Louis XIV over the prerogatives of the church versus the prerogatives of the Crown, particularly in the appointment of bishops.

Innocent XI (1676–1689). He was scrupulous in financial matters and worked actively against the Turkish invasion of Europe. He subsidized Poland's relief of Vienna in the great campaign against the Turks in 1683.

Clement XI (1700–1721). He sided with France in the War of the Spanish Succession and, in the course of the war, the papal states were invaded by Austria. Clement renewed the condemnation of Jansenism, which had made extraordinary progress in France. (Jansenism was an Augustinian Catholic reform movement akin to Protestant Calvinism in its theology.)

Clement XIV (1769–1774). He ordered the Jesuit Society dissolved (July 21, 1773), acquiescing in the program of enlightened despots and ministers, such as the instigator, the Marquis de Pombal of Portugal, to rid their realms of any power bases that might become dangerous states-within-the-state. The Jesuits were considered as such.

Pius VI (1775–1799). He felt the full force of French radical anticlericalism, which finally led to the French invasion of the papal states in 1796.

Seventeenth- and Eighteenth-Century Italy

Italy in the seventeenth and eighteenth centuries remained a geographic expression. Divided into small lands, Italy was under foreign influence. In the seventeenth century,

Spain controlled Lombardy in the North and Naples, Sicily, and Sardinia in the South. Lombardy was the most valuable to Spain because of its strategic importance, linking Spain with Austria and Flanders (through Franche-Comté). It served as a barrier to French invasion of Italy. Naples and Sicily were not scenes of foreign invasion as was the north of Italy.

Independent Italian States

By the eighteenth century, many of the independent Italian states were no longer of international importance. The Duchy of Tuscany had lost its earlier eminence in art and literature. The once-prosperous Republic of Genoa did not influence European affairs. The Republic of Venetia no longer challenged Turkey in the eastern Mediterranean. Savoy, however, began to play a large role in Italian and even European affairs that could not have been foreseen from the major players in the Italian Renaissance.

Savoy

Savoy was the only state with a native Italian dynasty. In the early sixteenth century, it was a battleground between the French and the Spanish, a prize sought by both.

Emmanuel Philibert, Duke of Savoy (reigned 1553–1580), was rewarded by the Holy Roman Emperor with the restoration of the independence of Savoy, which he made a modern state. Charles Emmanuel I (reigned 1580–1630) maintained this independence by playing off France diplomatically against Spain and *vice versa*. Neither country could permit the other to gain a foothold in strategic Savoy, so Savoy remained independent.

Victor Amadeus (reigned 1630–1637) married Marie Christine, the sister of Louis XIII of France, thus increasing French influence in Savoy. Victor Amadeus II (reigned 1675–1731) championed the Protestant Vaudois against Louis XIV. He joined William of Orange and the League of Augsburg against France. France defeated Savoy and forced it to change sides. But the Peace of Ryswick of 1697 confirmed Savoy's independence and left it the leading Italian state and an important entity in the balance of power. One of the greatest generals of the age was Prince Eugene of Savoy, who fought for the Habsburgs in brilliant campaigns that consolidated Austrian power in Hungary, Transylvania, and Croatia.

In 1713, Victor Amadeus was awarded Sicily and in 1720 exchanged Sicily with Austria for the island of Sardinia. Henceforth, he was known as the king of Sardinia.

Charles Emmanuel III (reigned 1731–1773) joined in the War of the Polish Succession in an unsuccessful attempt to drive Austria out of Italy; then Savoy sided with Austria in the War of the Austrian Succession and received part of Lombardy as a reward.

The French Revolution and Napoleon Bonaparte's invasion of Austrian territories in North Italy completely changed the situation for Italy, and in the nineteenth-century, Italian unification was achieved under a Sardinian king, Victor Emmanuel II.

The Ottoman Turkish Empire's Power in Europe

Christian Europe Versus Islamic Mediterranean

During the Middle Ages, the Islamic Empire included Spain, North Africa, and the Middle East. Expansion of Islam into Europe was blocked by France in the West (after 1492, by Spain) and by the Byzantine Empire in the East. When Constantinople fell to the Ottoman Turks in 1453, eastern Europe was prey to Islamic expansion.

Hungary and the Habsburg Empire became the defenders of Europe. Under Suleiman the Magnificent (died 1566), the Turks captured Belgrade and took over nearly half of eastern Europe. Ottoman power extended from the Euphrates River to the Danube. However, various problems combined to usher in a long decline, among which were overextension of the military, court intrigues, the resort to the brutal janissary system of forced impressment of kidnapped Christian boys into the army, and more.

Turkish Decline in the Seventeenth and Eighteenth Centuries

The Turkish sultan headed an autocratic and absolutist political system, often controlled by intrigue, murder, and arbitrary capital punishment. Most sultans were more concerned with their harem than with affairs of state.

Government finance was based more on spoils of war, tribute, and sale of offices than on a sound economy. The Turkish military and bureaucracy were dependent on the training and loyalty of Christian slaves, the famous janissaries (and elite corps of Turkish troops), and officials of the sultan's household.

Muhammad IV (reigned 1648–1687)

The reign of Muhammad IV was characterized by bloodshed. He and his grand vizier (a religious and political adviser) executed thirty thousand people in an attempt to purge all opposition to their will.

In 1683, the Turks, with a force of two hundred thousand men, besieged Vienna for six weeks, intending to take Vienna as they had Constantinople two centuries earlier. John Sobieski, king of Poland, with fifty thousand Polish troops, went to the relief of the city and the Habsburg Empire. The Turks massacred thirty thousand Christian prisoners and were then defeated in a terrible slaughter. Though the siege was horrible in its toll on lives, we may now in retrospect see why the Viennese were ironically thankful, since the Turks left coffee beans in their wake.

Mustapha II (reigned 1695–1703) and Ahmed III (reigned 1703–1730)

After prolonged and successful military operations, the Austrian troops, led ably by Prince Eugene of Savoy, succeeded in pushing the Turks out of much of the Balkans. The Treaty of Karlowitz (1699) recognized Austrian conquests of Hungary and Transylvania. The Ottoman Empire never recovered its former power.

In 1711, the Turks under the leadership of Ahmed III attacked the Russians and forced Peter the Great to surrender and restore the Black Sea part of Azov. But in 1716, Austria destroyed twenty thousand Turks while forcing them away from Belgrade, and overran Serbia. In the Treaty of Passarowitz (1718), the Turks ceded the rest of Hungary and the great fortress of Belgrade to Austria. The sultan Ahmed abdicated later, in 1730, in the face of a rebellion of the janissaries.

Ottoman Decline (1730–1789)

Starting in the 1730s, the Ottoman Empire entered its final decline. Austria and Russia coalesced to dismember the empire; Russia was successful, regaining Azov in 1737, but Austria was defeated and gave up Belgrade in 1739.

Domestic disputes compounded the Turkish troubles. The janissaries disintegrated as an effective military force when the sultan began selling the rank of janissary to anyone willing to pay for it. Because the national government was suffering such internal turmoil, provincial governors became more independent.

In the Treaty of Kuchuk-Kainardji (1774), Catherine the Great of Russia forced the Turks to surrender the Crimea and to recognize Russia's right to protect Orthodox Christians in the Balkans. Russia and Austria declared war on Turkey in 1788 and Austria recaptured Belgrade in 1789.

By the end of the eighteenth century, the Ottoman Empire was no longer an important power in Europe. However, competition to take over parts of eastern Europe, especially the Balkans, continued. Referred to as the "Eastern Question" in European history, those long-simmering territorial disputes played a causal factor in starting World War I.

◄─────────────── **TIMELINE** ───────────────►

Overview of European Powers

Year(s)	Event	Significance
1581–1583	Ivan IV begins successful conquest of Siberia.	Ivan the Terrible sends out mercenary forces to begin conquest of Siberia and its Muslim and pagan tribes, little knowing the mineral wealth that huge region would bring to Russia.
1609	The United Provinces establish the Bank of Amsterdam.	The United Provinces charter one of the first modern national banks: rather than small account holders, big savers and investors use it. State control helps regularize commercial transactions and monitor the currency.
1611	King James Bible is published.	One of the few good things produced by a committee, the King James Bible illustrates the glory of the English language, and helps anchor Protestant rites and tenets in England.
1642–1649	Civil war racks England, Scotland, and Ireland.	Charles I unwisely tries to force Anglican rites and Book of Common Prayer on Scottish Presbyterians and English Puritans. Civil war throughout the isles ultimately leads to Charles's execution when the parliamentary army wins.
1648–1653	Revolts (frondes) by old nobles and the Parlement of Paris rock France.	Louis XIV, still only a child, is traumatized by the frondes; the experience shapes his conviction as king not to be dominated by any minister and not to allow any room for revolt.
1640–1688	The Great Elector, Frederick William, rules Brandenburg.	The Great Elector rebuilds Brandenburg after the disasters of the Thirty Years' War by adopting the practices of absolutism: centralized government over the old provincial estate. He also builds an army that "wags the state."
1649–1660	Interregnum in England: Cromwell and his army rule the country. (Jews are allowed back in England, 1655.)	The victory of Parliament over Charles I ushers in a republic, but the overweening influence of the army and Cromwell makes this form of government unwelcome. Charles the II is restored to throne in 1660.

1652–1774	Dutch eminence in trading and trans-shipping annoys England into three wars.	England reacts to Dutch shipping success with the Navigation Acts of 1652 and 1660, which outlaw the use of Dutch ships from English ports (mercantilism at work).
1661	Louis XIV declares his resolve for personal rule.	Mindful of "undue" influence of two cardinals (Richelieu and Mazarin) on past kings, Louis decides to rule without a first minister: his declaration of absolutism is buttressed by the divine-right theories of Jean Bodin and Jacque-Bénigne Bossuet.
1683	Turks stage siege of Vienna.	The loss of Vienna would have meant a deadly blow to Habsburg power and a major psychological defeat for European Christians. But the Turkish siege was lifted by arrival of Polish king, Jan Sobieski, with troops. A major Austrian push until 1717 nets Habsburgs territory in Hungary and Transylvania; Turkish threat ends.
1685	Louis XIV revokes the Edict of Nantes.	Louis believes in one king, one law, one faith, so he revokes the old edict, causing many Huguenots to flee to England, Brandenburg, and the Netherlands. Consequently, an alliance forms against him.
1688–1689	King James II threatens to return England to the papist fold, leading to the Glorious Revolution.	James's threat leads Parliament to seat William of Orange and his Stuart wife, Mary, on the English throne. Parliament institutes the Bill of Rights and passes the Toleration Act.
1696	Peter the Great becomes sole ruler of the Russias (and reigns until 1725).	Peter ousts a sister and brother, and kills some of his bodyguard (streltsi) to become sole tsar. Disgusted by Russian backwardness, Peter spends his reign in Westernizing Russia.
1701	The English parliament passes the Act of Settlement.	Fearing Stuart pretenders (Jacobite rebellions 1715, 1745), Parliament passes the act to secure throne for Protestants. Thus, when Queen Anne dies, succession passes to the Hanover dynasty.
1701–1713	France and Spain wage the War of the Spanish Succession against much of the rest of Europe.	The Holy Roman Empire, England, and the Dutch join the fight against France and Spain to establish a better balance of power in Europe. The war results in great harm to France, and even greater harm to Spain.

(Continued)

1707	The Act of Union unites England and Scotland into one Britain.	The thrones of Scotland and England unite to avoid Jacobite pretensions, to strengthen their land holdings, and to bolster their economy.
1713–1714	The Treaties of Utrecht and Rastatt end the War of Spanish Succession.	War ends with major gains and victory for Britain and Austria. Britain gets Gibraltar and asiento, the right to ship slaves to the New World; Austria gains the Spanish Netherlands and lands in Italy.
1700–1721	Great Northern War pits Sweden against an alliance of Denmark, Saxony, Poland, and Russia.	Charles XII of Sweden, interested in gains in Poland and Prussia as well, beats Russians in first battle of Narva, but his defeat at Poltava (1709) means victory for Russia's Peter the Great, who thus secures the site of Saint Petersburg (1703 on) from the Swedes.
1713–1740	Foreign princes agree to Holy Roman Emperor Charles VI's Pragmatic Sanction.	The Pragmatic Sanction stipulates the right of Charles VI's his daughter Maria Teresa to inherit the Habsburg crown lands.
1740–1748	Frederick II of Prussia invades the Austrian province of Silesia, leading to the War of the Austrian Succession.	Frederick's disregard of the Pragmatic Sanction showed a new Machiavellian spirit in big-power politics: might justifies crimes. His seizure of Silesia led to much bloodshed, also to a Diplomatic Revolution in which France and Austria, old enemies, became friends in 1756.

Chapter 5

Absolutism, Constitutionalism, and Enlightenment

State Power, Wars, and Diplomacy

The Growth of the State

In the seventeenth century, the political systems of Europe began dividing into two types: absolutist and constitutional. While no country typified either type and all countries had parts of both, we may safely sort countries into camps. England, the United Provinces, and Sweden moved toward constitutionalism, while France adopted absolutist ideas.

Overseas exploration, begun in the fifteenth century, expanded in the sixteenth and seventeenth centuries. Governments supported such activity in order to gain wealth and to preempt other countries. The state, then as now, was often the greatest source of capital and the best guarantor of one's funds, so investing in state bonds began in earnest with the formulation of national banks: the Bank of Amsterdam in 1609 and the Bank of England in 1694.

Definitions

Constitutionalism meant rules, often unwritten, defining and limiting government. Constitutionalism, later becoming liberalism, sought to enhance the rights of the individual as a person and a citizen (not just a subject of the prince). Constitutional regimes usually had some means of group decision-making, such as a parliament, but a constitutional government need not be a democracy and usually was not. Consent of the governed—acceptance by citizens—provided the basis for the legitimacy of the regime.

Absolutism emphasized the role of the state and its fulfillment of a specific purpose, such as religion, or the glory of the monarch. The usual form of government of an absolutist regime was, in the seventeenth century, kingship, which gained its legitimacy from the notion of divine right—which held that the monarch was ordained by God and therefore answerable only to God—but its actuality from the obedience of subjects.

Nobles and bourgeois, depending on the country, provided the chief opposition to the increasing power of the state. In constitutionalist states, they often obtained control of the state, while in absolutist states they became servants of the state.

Political Thought

The collapse of governments during the wars of religion, and the subjection of one religious group to another, stimulated thought about the nature of politics and political allegiances. The increasing power of the monarchs raised questions about the nature and extent of that power.

Both Protestants and Catholics hatched theories of resistance to bad rulers. Martin Luther and John Calvin (see Chapter 3) had disapproved of such revolts, but John Knox's *Blast of the Trumpet against the Terrible Regiment of Women* (1558) approved rebellion against a heretical ruler. His text was directed against Mary, Queen of Scots, as a woman and a papist.

In France, Huguenot writers, stimulated by the Saint Bartholomew Day's Massacre (see Chapter 3), applied the concept of a *covenant* (contract) to the relationship between people and God and between subjects and monarch. If the monarch ceased to observe the covenant, the purpose of which was to honor God, the representatives of the people (usually the nobles or others in an assembly) could resist the monarch.

Catholic writers, such as Robert Cardinal Bellarmine, saw the monarch as the anointed given political and religious authority by God. The pope being God's vicar on earth, he could dispose of a monarch who put people's souls in jeopardy with heretical beliefs.

Jean Bodin (1530–1596), in response to the chaos of France during the civil wars, developed the theory of sovereignty. He believed that in each country one power or institution must be strong enough to make everyone obey; otherwise chaos results from the conflicts of institutions or groups of equal power. Bodin provided the theoretical basis for absolutist states.

Those who resisted the power of monarchs argued for the need to protect local customs, "traditional liberties," and "the ancient constitution." Nobles and towns appealed to the medieval past, when sovereignty had been shared by kings, nobles, and other institutions.

Struggles in the seventeenth century produced varying results. At the extremes, an absolutist country was ruled by a monarch from whom all power flowed, while a constitutional country could limit royal or executive power and determine the will of the people, or at least some of them, through a representative assembly. The absolutist French king, for example, tried to circumvent representative institutions, dominated the nobility, and ruled directly. The more constitutionally minded nobles and gentry of England controlled their government through the representative institution of Parliament. In Germany, various components of the Holy Roman Empire defeated the emperor and governed themselves independently.

England

Problems Facing English Monarchs

Religion

The English church was a compromise of Catholic practices and Protestant beliefs and was criticized by both groups. The monarchs, after 1620, gave leadership of the church to men with Arminian beliefs. Jacobus Arminius (1560–1609), a Dutch theologian, downplayed the Calvinist emphasis on predestination, along with its sternness. English Arminians also sought to emphasize the role of ritual in church services and to enjoy the "beauty of holiness," which their opponents took to be too Catholic. William Laud (1573–1645), Archbishop of Canterbury, accelerated the growth of Arminianism.

Opponents to this shift in belief were called Puritans, a term that covered a wide range of beliefs and people. To escape the church in England, Puritans began moving to the New World, especially Massachusetts. Both James I and Charles I made decisions that, to Puritans, favored Catholics too much.

Finances

In financial matters, inflation and Queen Elizabeth's wars had left the government short of money. Contemporaries blamed the shortage on the extravagant courts of James I and Charles I. James I sold titles of nobility, especially the new baronetcy, in an effort to raise money, but this annoyed nobles with older titles and debased the familial, blood-based ideal underlying nobility.

Monarchs lacked any substantial source of income and had to obtain the consent of Parliament to levy a tax, a process fraught with problems. First, Parliament only met when the monarch summoned it. Though the English Parliament had existed since the Middle Ages, long periods elapsed between meetings. Second, the men in Parliament—most of whom were nobles and gentry, with a few merchants and lawyers—usually wanted the government to remedy grievances in exchange for a new tax. In 1621, for the first time since the Middle Ages, Parliament used its power to impeach governmental servants to eliminate men who had offended its members. Third, the traditions of local independence among the forty English counties or shires stymied the king's taxation efforts. The landowners—nobles and gentry—controlled the counties and resented royal interference.

James I (reigned 1603–1625)

James I ended a short war with Spain and avoided other entanglements, despite the fact that his son-in-law, Frederick V of the Palatinate, was embroiled in the Thirty Years' War and had made his wife, James's daughter—the "Winter Queen"—a fugitive when he was forced to give up his flimsy claims to the throne of Bohemia. The Earl of Somerset and Duke of Buckingham served as favorites of the king, doing much of the work of government and dealing with suitors for royal actions. James is most remembered for his firm treatment of Puritans, who dared to tell him they wanted no bishops in the church.

He let them know his contrary logic: "No bishop, no king!" He was also known for his oversight of a commission to revise earlier biblical translations and create the master-piece with his name, the King James Bible (1611).

Charles I (reigned 1625–1649)

Though Henrietta Maria, a sister of the king of France and a Catholic, became his queen, Charles stumbled into wars with both Spain and France during the late 1620s. To raise money for those wars, he collected a "forced ban" from taxpayers with the promise that it would be repaid when a tax was voted by Parliament; he also billeted soldiers in subjects' houses. Those who resisted the king's directives were imprisoned.

However, Charles's actions led to confrontations with his opponents in Parlia-ment. In 1626, Parliament nearly impeached the Duke of Buckingham because of his monopoly of royal offices and his exclusion of others from power. In 1628, Parliament passed the Petition of Right, which declared illegal the royal actions in connection with the loans and billeting. Charles signed, but then prorogued Parliament in order to go back on his word.

During the 1630s, the king ruled without calling a parliament, and instituted a policy of "thorough anti-Puritanism"—strict efficiency and much central government activity. He raised money using old forms of taxation. For example, citing a medieval law that required all landowners with a certain amount of wealth to become knights, Charles fined those who had not been knighted. In addition, he forced all counties to pay money to outfit ships—"ship money"—previously an obligation only of coastal counties.

Breakdown

Charles, with the help of the William Laud, Archbishop of Canterbury, attempted to impose English ritual and the English prayer book on the Scottish church (1637). The Scots revolted and invaded northern England with an army in 1640. To pay for his army against the Scots, Charles called the Short Parliament, but was not willing to remedy any grievances or to change his policies. In response, Parliament did not vote for new taxes.

Charles then called another parliament, the Long Parliament, which attacked his ministers, challenged his religious policies, and refused to trust him with money. Arch-bishop Laud and the Earl of Strafford, the two architects of "thorough anti-Puritanism," were driven from power. The courts of Star Chamber and High Commission, which had been used to prosecute Charles's opponents, were abolished. When the Irish revolted, Parliament would not let Charles raise an army to suppress them, as it was feared he would use the army against his English opponents. John Pym (1584–1643) emerged as a leader of the king's opponents in Parliament, helping in 1641 to push through the Grand Remonstrance, a list of 150 grievances against Charles, and a path-breaking Militia Bill, giving Parliament control over the army in order to squelch the Irish rebel-lion. Charles ignored both.

Civil War

In August 1642, Charles abandoned all hope of negotiating with his opponents and, instead, declared war against them. His supporters were called royalists or Cavaliers; his opponents, parliamentarians or Roundheads, owing to the London apprentices among them who wore their hair cut short. Both sides produced great poetry.

Historians differ on whether to call this struggle the Puritan Revolution, the English Civil War, or the Great Rebellion. The war was precipitated by religious differences and the question of the extent of royal authority in government.

Charles's opponents allied with the Scots, who still had an army in England. Also, the parliamentarian New Model Army, with its general Oliver Cromwell (1599–1658), was superior to Charles's army. With the collapse of government, new religious and political groups, such as Levelers, Quakers, and Ranters, appeared. Charles tried to outmaneuver Parliament by switching sides to the Scots, but to no avail: by 1646 he had lost the war.

Following his defeat, Charles's opponents attempted to negotiate a settlement but, that failing, he was executed on January 30, 1649, and England became a republic for the next eleven years. The mounting tyranny of the Cromwell government and the army induced the people to recall Charles II from exile. He and his brother, James II, were unable or unwilling to solve pressing constitutional and religious issues in their lands, so when James sired a Catholic heir, Parliament called William III of the Netherlands and Mary II Stuart (James's estranged daughter) to be their new constitutional monarchs.

The search for a settlement thus ended in 1689, when the nobles, gentry, and merchants, acting through Parliament, assumed control over government and the monarch.

France

Problems Facing French Monarchs

Regions of France long had a measure of independence, and local *parlements* (more law courts than assemblies) could refuse to enforce royal laws. Centralization of government began when Louis XIII and Louis XIV replaced local authorities with *intendants*, civil servants who reported to the king and were beholden to him alone for pay and favors.

Huguenots, thanks to the Edict of Nantes, had unique rights, making them, in effect, a state within the state. Efforts to unify France under one faith (Catholic) faced internal resistance from Huguenots and threats from Protestant powers abroad.

By 1650, France had been ruled by only one competent adult monarch since 1559. The mothers of Louis XIII and Louis XIV, Maria de' Medici and Anne of Austria, respectively, governed as regents until the boys came of age. Both queens relied on chief ministers to help govern France: Cardinal Armand Jean de Richelieu (1585–1642) and Cardinal Jules Mazarin (1602–1661).

Henry IV (reigned 1589–1610)

Henry relied on the Duke of Sully (1560–1641), the first of a series of strong ministers in the seventeenth century. Sully and Henry increased the involvement of the state in the economy, acting on the theory of mercantilism (see Chapter 3). The government created monopolies for the production of gunpowder and salt, and only the government could operate mines. A canal was begun to connect the Mediterranean Sea to the Atlantic Ocean.

Louis XIII (reigned 1610–1643)

Owing to the weakness of France after the wars of religion, Maria de' Medici concluded a treaty with Spain in 1611. Cardinal Richelieu, upon whom she relied, then became the real power in France over Louis XIII. In order to keep the Habsburgs from gaining ascendancy in Germany, Richelieu supplied troops and money to Gustavus Adolfus, a Lutheran, after 1631. Richelieu is a prime example of a minister acting on the Machiavellian principles of "reasons of state" (that the state's needs override even moral commands) and the need for a "balance of power" among the major European powers.

The unique status of the Huguenots was reduced through warfare and the Peace of Alais (1629), when their separate armed cities, such as La Rochelle, were eliminated.

The nobility was reduced in power through the increasing use of *intendants*, constant attention to the law, and swift justice of Richelieu, who executed the Duke de Montmorency and the Marquis de Cinq-Mars for conspiring against him.

Louis XIV (reigned 1643–1715)

Breakdown

Cardinal Mazarin governed when Louis XIV was a minor. During the *frondes*, from 1649 to 1652, the nobility controlled Paris, drove Louis XIV and Mazarin from the city, and attempted to run the government. Noble ineffectiveness, the memories of the chaos of the wars of religion, and the overall anarchy convinced most people that a strong king was preferable to a warring nobility. The movement's lack of impact was symbolized by the name *fronde*, the term for a slingshot used by children to shoot rocks at carriages, but which caused no real damage.

Absolutism

By 1652, the French monarchy had developed the tools to implement a strong, centralized government. Louis XIV personally saw the need to increase royal power and his own glory, and dedicated his life to these goals. He steadily pursued a policy of "one king, one law, one faith." Through most of his reign, the populace accepted this policy.

Other Constitutional States

United Provinces

The seven provinces sent representatives to an estates-general dominated by the richest, Holland and Zeeland, but the body had few powers. Each province elected a stadtholder and a military leader. Usually, for the latter position, all of the provinces elected the same man: the head of the royal house of Orange-Nassau.

Some followers of Calvinism broke from that strict faith when Arminius proposed a theology that downplayed predestination. Though the stricter Calvinism prevailed, Arminians had full political and economic rights after 1632, and Catholics and Jews were also tolerated, though with fewer rights. In all of Europe, only the United Provinces and Poland-Lithuania allowed Jews civil rights.

The merchants dominating the Estates-General supported the lax Arminianism and wanted peace, while the house of Orange adopted strict Calvinism and sought a more aggressive foreign policy. In 1619, Jan van Oldenbarneveldt (1547–1619), representing the merchants, lost a struggle over the issue of renewing war with Spain to Maurice of Nassau, the head of the house of Orange. Until 1650, the house of Orange—first under Maurice, and then William II—dominated, and the Dutch supported anti-Habsburg forces in the Thirty Years' War. Then the merchants regained power, and in 1653 Jan de Witt (1625–1672) set about returning power to the provinces, which instituted the short-lived Dutch Republic.

The seventeenth century witnessed tremendous growth in the wealth and economic power of the Dutch. Formerly, the bourse (exchange) at Antwerp, established in 1531, had dominated trade in the North, but the sack of Antwerp and occupation of the southern Netherlands by Spanish troops hindered the industry of the South and helped to pass the torch to the northern provinces. The Bank of Amsterdam, founded in 1609, provided safe and stable control of money, which encouraged investments in many kinds of activities. Amsterdam became the financial center of Europe. The Dutch also developed the largest fleet in Europe devoted to trade more than war, and became the dominant trading country.

Sweden

Gustavus Adolfus (reigned 1611–1632) reorganized the government, giving nobles a dominant role in both the army and the bureaucracy. The central government was divided into five departments or "colleges," each with a noble at its head. The very capable Axel Oxenstierna (1583–1654) dominated this government.

The Rijksdag, an assembly of nobles, clergy, townsmen, and peasants, nominally had the highest legislative authority. The real power, however, lay with the nobles and the monarch. From 1611 to 1650, noble power and wealth greatly increased. In 1650, Queen Christina, who wanted to abdicate and become a Catholic (which eventually she did in 1654), used the power of the Rijksdag to coerce the nobles into accepting her designated successor.

As a result of Gustavus Adolfus's military actions, the Baltic Sea became "a Swedish lake," and Sweden became a world power. Swedish economic power resulted from exploitation of its copper mines, the best in Europe, and its iron seams.

In both the United Provinces and Sweden, the government was dominated by rich and powerful groups who used representative institutions to limit the power of the state and produce nonabsolutist regimes.

Age of Absolutism, West and East (1648–1789)

After 1648, the Bourbon dynasty emerged stronger than the Habsburgs, who had through their Spanish and Austrian branches dominated Europe for a century and a half. Though the Netherlands still prospered, England grew in power and wealth, and the eastern monarchies of Russia, Austria, and Prussia were on the rise. It is no exaggeration to label the century and a half from 1648 to 1789 as the French or Bourbon century.

Treaty of the Pyrenees (1659)

The war between France and Spain continued for eleven more years after the Thirty Years' War until, in the Treaty of the Pyrenees, Spain finally ceded to France part of the Spanish Netherlands and territory in northern Spain. A marriage was arranged between Louis XIV, Bourbon king of France, and Maria Theresa, daughter of the Habsburg king of Spain, Philip IV.

War of Devolution (First Dutch War, 1667–1668)

After the death of his father-in-law, Philip IV, Louis XIV claimed the Spanish Netherlands (Belgium) in the name of his wife. Louis used the Law of Devolution—a property rights law that granted inheritance to the heirs of a first marriage precedent to those of a second marriage—to support his claim of political sovereignty. Fifty thousand French troops invaded the Spanish Netherlands in 1667 without a declaration of war. As a defensive measure, England, Holland, and Sweden formed the Triple Alliance.

Treaty of Aix-la-Chapelle (1668)

The war ceased with the Treat of Aix-la-Chapelle, in which France received twelve fortified towns on the border of the Spanish Netherlands, but gave up Franche-Comté (Burgundy). Furthermore, the question of sovereignty over the Spanish Netherlands was deferred.

Second Dutch War (1672–1678)

Louis XIV sought revenge for Dutch opposition to French annexation of the Spanish Netherlands. As a Catholic king, he opposed Dutch Calvinism and republicanism.

France disputed the Triple Alliance by signing separate treaties with England (Charles II: Treaty of Dover, 1670) and with Sweden (1672).

In 1672, France invaded southern Holland with one hundred thousand troops. William III of Orange became head of state for Holland. The Dutch opened the dikes to flood the land, saving Holland and the city of Amsterdam from the French. At the war's end, the Peace of Nijmegen (1678–1679) granted Holland all of its lost territory, while Spain and France exchanged more than a dozen territories.

Invasion of the Spanish Netherlands (1683)

Looking east, Louis XIV saw traditionally French territories, such as Alsace and Lorraine, in the hands of the hated Habsburgs; also, operating on a dubious historical theory based on Charlemagne's empire, he viewed the Rhine River as the "natural frontier" of France—a policy to beset French politics for centuries. To wrest towns, including Strasbourg, from the Holy Roman Emperor, Louis prosecuted lawsuits, known as the "reunions," to gain those territories. When these failed, he started another war. France occupied Luxemburg and Trier and seized Lorraine while signing a twenty-year truce with the empire.

The League of Augsburg was formed in 1686 to counteract the French and restore the balance of power. Members included the empire, Holland, Spain, Sweden, the Palatinate, Saxony, Bavaria, and Savoy.

War of the League of Augsburg (1688–1697)

The War of the League of Augsburg renewed an old Anglo-French rivalry that continued until the defeat of Napoleon Bonaparte in 1815. France fought the two leading naval powers, Holland and England, in three theaters of war—the Rhineland, the Low Countries, and Italy. Louis's wanton destruction of large swaths of the Rhineland, including Heidelberg, left Germans with a lasting legacy of bitterness against the French that would tragically play itself out in the Franco-Prussian War (1870–1871), World War I (1914–1918), and World War II (1940).

The Anglo-French conflict played out in the New World as well. Known in North America as King William's War (1689–1697), English and French colonials clashed along the New York and New England frontiers.

Treaty of Ryswick (1697)

The War of the League of Augsburg ended with the Treaty of Ryswick, in which France, England, and Holland agreed to restore captured territories. Fortresses in the Spanish Netherlands were to be garrisoned with Dutch troops as a buffer zone between France and Holland. In addition, the treaty acknowledged as permanent French sovereignty over Alsace and Strasbourg.

War of the Spanish Succession (1701–1713)

Charles II, the last of the Habsburg kings of Spain, died childless on November 1, 1700. The Austrian Habsburg candidate expected reversion of the throne to his side of the family, but the king's will named Philip of Anjou, the grandson of France's Louis XIV and Maria Theresa, to be king of Spain. (In 1698, Charles had named Holy Roman Emperor

Leopold's grandson, the seven-year-old Electoral Prince Joseph Ferdinand of Bavaria, as his sole heir. The boy died a few months later. In October 1700, Charles signed the new will in favor of Philip.)

The Second Partition Treaty, signed by England, Holland, and France in May 1700, agreed that the son (later, Emperor Charles VI) of the Austrian Habsburg emperor, Leopold I, would become king of Spain and Philip of Anjou would be compensated with Italian territories. (The mother and first wife of Leopold were daughters of Spanish kings.)

Issues involved in the War of the Spanish Succession concerned the future of the Spanish Empire and slave trade. Other causes were the possible separation of Austrian Habsburg lands from Spain as well as the question of French/Bourbon strength in Spain.

In a sense, Charles II made war almost inevitable. Louis XIV had to fight for his grandson's claims against those of his enemy and Leopold had to do the same.

The Grand Alliance

William III, king of England and stadtholder of Holland, did not want to see the Spanish Netherlands fall into French hands. Since 1648, England had ensured that the mouth of the Scheldt River near Antwerp, the best natural harbor in all Europe, would be silted up to bolster English trade by ruining that of the Spanish Netherlands; William, speaking for Dutch and English interests, was just as interested in keeping the Scheldt closed to rival shipping. This issue underpinned English interest in Belgian neutrality.

England also faced Spanish and French competition in the New World. A merger of the Spanish and French thrones would result in a coalition of Spain and France against England and Holland in the Americas. In response, England, Holland, the Empire, and Prussia formed the Grand Alliance in September 1701.

War

France and Spain were stronger on land; England and Holland controlled the sea. But the battle of Blenheim, August 13, 1704, was a brilliant victory for England and the Duke of Marlborough, and one of the key battles of the war. It began a series of military reverses that prevented French domination of Europe.

At the great battle of Ramillies, May 23, 1706, Marlborough shattered the French army in four hours and held on to the Netherlands. In September 1709, in the bloody battle of Malplaquet, the Allies lost twenty-four thousand men and the French lost twelve thousand. This was the bloodiest European battle before those at Austerlitz (1805) and Solferino (1859).

The Allies invaded Spain and replaced Philip with Charles. The French and Spanish, however, rallied and drove the Allies from both countries, restoring the Spanish throne to the Bourbons.

The war was known as Queen Anne's War (1702–1713) in North America. There, England was faced for the first time with an alliance of its two great rival empires, Spain and France. Though the results in North America were inconclusive, English colonials were more reliable in fighting than were the Spanish and French colonists.

Treaty of Utrecht (1713)

The Treaty of Utrecht was the most important European treaty since the Peace of Westphalia in 1648. The Spanish Empire was partitioned and a Bourbon remained on the throne of Spain. Philip V (Philip of Anjou) retained Spain and the Spanish Empire in America. He explicitly renounced his claims to the French throne. The Habsburg Empire in Central Europe acquired the Spanish Netherlands (Austrian Netherlands thereafter) and territories in Italy. England took Gibraltar, Minorca, Newfoundland, Hudson's Bay, and Nova Scotia. France retained Alsace and the city of Strasbourg.

As a result of the treaty, the Habsburgs became a counterbalance to French power in western Europe, but no longer occupied the Spanish throne.

War of the Austrian Succession (1740–1748)

Charles VI died in 1740 and his daughter, twenty-three-year-old Maria Theresa (reigned 1740–1780) inherited the Austrian Habsburg Empire. Frederick the Great (reigned 1740–1786), had, at age twenty-eight, just inherited the Prussian throne from his father, Frederick William I. In 1740, Frederick suddenly invaded the Habsburg territory of Silesia, and England joined Austria against Prussia, Bavaria, France, and Spain. The War of Austrian Succession had begun.

Frederick's brilliant military tactics won many victories. His long night marches, sudden flank attacks, and surprise actions contrasted with the usual siege warfare.

The war was known in North America as King George's War (1744–1748). Colonial militia from Massachusetts captured Louisburg, the fortified French naval base on Cape Breton Island commanding the entrance to the Saint Lawrence River and Valley. Louisburg was returned to France after the war in exchange for Madras in India, which the French had captured.

The Treaty of Aix-la-Chapelle (1748) ended the war, and Prussia emerged as one of the great powers. By retaining Silesia, Prussia doubled its population.

The Seven Years' War (1756–1763)

Britain and France renewed hostilities as the French and Indian War (1754–1763) began at the entrance to the Ohio Valley. To leaders in those countries, the European war must have seemed a continuation of their colonial hostilities. At stake was control of the North American continent.

In Europe, Austria sought to regain Silesia with its important textile industry and rich deposits of coal and iron. The empire's Maria Theresa persuaded France's Louis XV to overlook their traditional Habsburg-Bourbon enmity and aid Austria in a war with Prussia. The French-Austrian alliance is known as the "Diplomatic Revolution."

Russia, under Tsarina Elizabeth (reigned 1741–1762), joined the alliance. She disliked Frederick the Great intensely and feared Prussian competition over Poland.

Great Britain provided Prussia with funds but few troops. Prussia was then faced with fighting almost alone against three major powers of Europe: Austria, France, and Russia. Their combined population was fifteen times that of Prussia.

The Seven Years' War was the hardest fought war in the eighteenth century. In six years, Prussia won eight brilliant victories and lost eight. Berlin was twice captured and partially burned by Russian troops. Still Prussia prevailed. In the process, Prussia emerged as one of the great powers of Europe and established the reputation of having the best soldiers on the Continent.

William Pitt the Elder led the British to victory. The Royal Navy defeated both the French Atlantic and Mediterranean squadrons in 1759. Britain's trade prospered, while French overseas trade dropped to one-sixth its prewar level. The British captured French posts near Calcutta and Madras in India, and defeated the French in Quebec and Montreal.

In 1762, Elizabeth of Russia died; her successor, Tsar Peter III, was a great admirer of Frederick the Great. Though he occupied the Russian throne only from January to July, he took Russia out of the war at a historically decisive moment.

In the Treaty of Hubertusburg (1763), Austria recognized Prussian claims to Silesia.

Treaty of Paris (1763)

In *this* Treaty of Paris, France lost all possessions in North America to Britain. (In 1762, France had ceded to Spain all French claims west of the Mississippi River and New Orleans.) France retained fishing rights off the coast of Newfoundland, Martinique, and Guadeloupe, and the sugar islands in the West Indies. Spain ceded the Floridas to Britain in exchange for the return of Cuba.

The American War for Independence as a European War (1775–1783)

Some European nations viewed the American War for Independence as an opportunity to further their own interests. France entered the French-American Alliance of 1778 in an effort to regain lost prestige in Europe and to weaken her British adversary. In 1779, Spain joined France in the war, hoping to recover Gibraltar and the Floridas.

Whatever were their motives, the Europeans contributed mightily to the American cause. French troops strengthened the forces of George Washington's Continental Army. The leadership of French field officers such as the Marquis de Lafayette aided in strategic planning. Admiral de Grasse's French fleet prevented the evacuation of Lord Cornwallis from Yorktown in the final decisive battle of the war in 1781. General-Count de Rochambeau's and Lafayette's French troops aided Washington at Yorktown.

Treaty of Paris (1783)

In *this* Treaty of Paris, Britain recognized the independence of the United States of America, and retroceded the Floridas to Spain. Britain left France no territorial gains by signing a separate and territorially generous treaty with the United States.

Summary of French Foreign Policy

France was the dominant European power from 1660 to 1713. Louis XIV, however, was unable to extend French boundaries to the Rhine River—one of his chief objectives.

From 1713 to 1789, no single European power dominated international politics; instead, the concept of balance of power prevailed. A readjustment of power was necessary in central and eastern Europe as a result of the decline of Sweden, Poland, and the Ottoman Empire. This period was characterized by a power struggle between France and England for colonial supremacy in India and in America.

Economic Developments

Traditional Economic Conditions

Poverty was the norm during the Middle Ages. Infant mortality rate was 50 percent and sometimes half the surviving children died before reaching adulthood. As late as 1700, the overall life expectancy was thirty years of age.

Subsistence farming was the dominant occupation historically, and famine was a regular part of life. One-third of Finland, for example, died in the famine of 1696–1697. France, one of the richest agricultural lands, experienced eleven general famines in the seventeenth century and sixteen general famines in the eighteenth century.

Contagious diseases such as smallpox, measles, diphtheria, typhoid, scarlet fever, bubonic plague, and typhus decimated towns and villages.

Political and economic freedoms associated with the Protestant Reformation and biblical work ethic gradually began to change the economy of Europe as innovation, hard work, frugality, and entrepreneurship became the norm.

Social Institutions Necessary for Commerce and a Prosperous Economy

A prosperous economy needs a moral system as a base for reliance on expectations and contracts. This was found both in traditional Catholic morality and in the Protestant Reformation. A modern economy could not function without confidence in people living up to their agreements with a sense of individual responsibility toward the following:

1. Credit

2. Representations as to quality

3. Promises to deliver products or to buy them when produced

4. Agreements to share profits

5. Honoring a bank check or bill of exchange

6. Obligations of contracts, whether written or oral

The legal system in society reinforced individual morality by legally enforcing contracts, including bills of exchange and bank checks, as well as insurance and payment of claims; by recognizing property claims and rights; and by barring confiscatory taxation.

Innovations in business arrangements abounded. Joint stock companies enabled enterprises to accumulate capital from many investors. Double-entry bookkeeping provided a check on clerks, enabling managers to detect errors. Bank notes were used as a medium of exchange. A divided Europe enabled merchants and businessmen to compete as they sought to locate themselves in places with a favorable business climate.

From Mercantilism to Laissez-Faire Capitalism

The wars of the seventeenth and eighteenth centuries involved dynastic disputes, balance-of-power struggles, and mercantilist competition for trade, raw materials, and colonies. Though economics was involved, it was not as important a factor as the more traditional power politics of international competition. It would have been less of a factor without some of the philosophical assumptions of mercantilism.

In the nineteenth century, economists and the governments that listened to them directed more thought toward encouraging economic initiative by average citizens to benefit themselves and, by extension, the entire country. Adam Smith's *The Wealth of Nations* (1776) had led the way to a more laissez-faire approach. Smith wrote at the beginning of the American War for Independence:

> To prohibit a great people … from making all that they can of every part of their own produce, or from employing their stock and industry in the way that they judge most advantageous to themselves, is a manifest violation of the most sacred rights of mankind.

The Dutch and the English were the first to view the concept of productivity as a measure of national wealth. Holland became one of the most productive countries in the seventeenth century, England in the eighteenth and nineteenth centuries. There was always a certain ambivalence, however, in the English attitude. The Navigation Acts (1651, 1660) reflected a restrictive, mercantilist, and nationalist attitude toward international trade.

In France, Jean Baptiste Colbert (1619–1683), economic adviser to Louis XIV, used the government to encourage economic productivity and foster the prosperity of France. But his dictatorial regulations were also counterproductive. For example, he forbade the emigration of skilled French workers and specified, in detail, methods of production. He also believed that foreign trade was a fixed quantity rather than one that grew with demand and lower prices. France, as most states, had high protective tariffs.

The lowering of interest rates also stimulated investment and productivity. Here England led the way: 1600, 10 percent; 1625, 8 percent; 1651, 6 percent; 1715, 5 percent; 1757, 3 percent.

Growth of Trade

The first Age of Exploration (1415–1600) had been driven by mercantilist and religious impulses: soldiers, merchants, and priests came not to colonize so much as to exploit native labor and wealth in the New World. In India and other settled areas, they sought footholds in port cities from which to trade as equals with local potentates. When the locals resisted, Europeans found their shipboard cannon a persuasive means to force potentates to come to terms and let them in on the action.

The second wave of exploration (1600–1800) was characterized by more great-power rivalry, as between France and England in India, and England and Holland for Portuguese concessions. It also brought the first great migration of Europeans to colonies in North and South America, as well as Australia, South Africa, and other "less-populated" places. This second wave cannot be understood without reference to trends in the home countries:

Population. The growth in population expanded domestic markets far in excess of overseas trade. European population at the beginning of the seventeenth century was 70 million; by the end of the eighteenth century, it had doubled. Productivity and economic growth increased at an even faster rate.

Innovation. Innovative scientific discoveries, such as the nature of oxygen, and technological inventions such as the spinning jenny and cotton gin stimulated trade. Likewise, three-masted trading vessels lowered the costs of transportation and made possible trading over greater distances. Canal and road building also stimulated trade and productivity.

Capitalism. Capitalist systems of banking, insurance, and investment made possible the accumulation of capital essential for discovery and economic growth.

Urbanization. Urbanization was both cause and effect in economic growth, since it required a network of market relationships. Towns with prosperous trade increased in population, while towns without trade quickly stagnated. In addition, urbanization provided the opportunity and market for commercial services such as banking, insurance, warehousing, and commodity trading, as well as medicine, law, government, and churches.

Agricultural Changes

Feudal and manorial patterns began, especially in England and the Netherlands, to be replaced by absentee landlords and commercial farms. Urbanization, increased population, and improvements in trade stimulated the demand for agricultural products.

The design of farm implements improved. All-metal plows came into use in England as did horse-drawn cultivators. Drainage and reclamation of swamp land was expanded, owing in large part to Dutch innovations in hydraulics engineering; indeed, so good were the Dutch at draining land (and mines) that they traveled throughout Europe hiring out their services, from the malarial swamps of Italy to the marshes of Russia.

The English systematically attempted experiments with crops, seeds, machines, breeds of animals, and fertilizers. Crop rotation, especially inasmuch as it included nitrogen-fixating crops, revolutionized European farming over two centuries. Instead of plowing odd strips of land and letting half of it lie fallow to be replenished, farmers consolidated strip land into large fields (enclosure movement) and reduced or eliminated unproductive fallow lands by rotating crops that leached the soil (for example, wheat, cotton, tobacco, and so on) with crops that fed the soil (turnips, clover, and such). If humans could not eat the latter, animals could, thus increasing dramatically their longevity, production of milk and meat, and that helpful byproduct, manure.

Improvements in Transportation

The construction of canals and roads was of fundamental importance to the expanding European economy. Though railroads were not developed until the 1830s, the canal lock was invented in Italy in the seventeenth century, and soon after Holland began building canals. Major rivers of France were linked by canals during the seventeenth century. In England, coastal shipping made canals less pressing, and so it was not until the eighteenth century that canals were built there.

All-weather roads were constructed after the mid-eighteenth century, when John Macadam (1756–1836) discovered that a graveled and raised roadbed could carry vehicles year round.

Industrial Technology

Technological advances enabled the development of European industry, and key among these inventions was the steam engine. Thomas Newcomen in 1706 invented an inefficient steam engine as a pump. James Watt, between 1765 and 1769, improved the design so that the expansive power of hot steam could drive a piston. Later, Watt translated the motion of the piston into rotary motion. The Newcomen-Watt steam engine might have waited ages for development, however, had it not been for the steady investment and cheery entrepreneurial vision of Watt's wealthy friend, Matthew Boulton.

The steam engine became one of the most significant inventions in history. No longer was it necessary to locate factories on mountain streams where water wheels were used to supply power. The steam engine's portability meant that both steamboats and railroad engines could be built to transport goods across continents. Ocean-going vessels were no longer dependent on winds to power them.

At the same time, mechanization of cotton manufactures revolutionized the textile industry. John Kay introduced the flying shuttle in 1733. Richard Arkwright perfected the spinning frame in 1769. James Hargreaves invented the spinning jenny in 1770. Samuel Crompton introduced the spinning mule in 1779. Edward Cartwright invented the power loom in 1785. Add Eli Whitney's cotton gin of 1793, and you have a cotton industry—with slave labor supplying the raw material—that would upset and undermine the superior cottons of India, where Britain fiercely sought preeminence by destroying Indian looms and engaging in other chicanery. Names of Indian towns still survive in certain cotton fabrics and prints: Madras, calico (from Calicut), bombazine, and so on.

Factors in Sustained Economic Growth

Several factors coalesced to foster sustained economic growth in the eighteenth-century Europe:

Innovation. As mentioned previously, innovation was a key element. It led to the extension of trade and discovery of new resources; reductions in the costs of production; introduction of new products and new ways of doing things; and the organization of production and marketing methods. By producing success, innovation itself overcame its own greatest obstacle: resistance to innovation.

Free enterprise. The development of free enterprise stimulated new ideas. This was easiest in countries where the state was not overly involved in the economy. In England, the Puritan Revolution of the 1640s challenged the royal right to grant monopolies and trade privileges. English common law afterward adopted the principle of free enterprise. With free enterprise came the responsibility of risk-taking with the possibilities of losses as well as profits.

Freedom of movement. The free movement of populations provided necessary labor resources. People "voted with their feet" and found their way to new jobs. The population of England in 1700 was about 5.5 million and only 6 million by 1750. Economic growth from 1750 to 1800 increased the population to 9 million—50 percent growth in a half century. Because of the Industrial Revolution of the nineteenth century, this figure doubled yet again to 18 million by 1850.

The Enlightenment (*ca.* 1700–1800)

The scientific revolution gravely undermined the foundation on which the traditional social order rested by producing a revolution in the world of ideas that radically challenged the status quo. The Enlightenment was a response to economic and political changes at work in European society.

The eighteenth century marked the first time a secular world view emerged among many intellectuals. In the past, some kind of a religious perspective had always ruled cultures east and west. This was true of the ancient Egyptians, Hebrews, Persians, Greeks, and Romans, as well as medieval Christendom and the Protestant Reformation. By contrast, the eighteenth century philosophers, who declared themselves "enlightened," thought that "light" came from man's ability to reason. They rejected the idea that light must come from God, either through the church (the Catholic position) or the Scriptures (the Protestant position). The Enlightenment opened the door to a secularized, anthropocentric universe instead of the traditional theocentric view.

The philosophical starting point for the Enlightenment was the belief in the autonomy of man's intellect apart from God, and concomitantly, that original sin was an irrelevant notion, so that one could dare to think of humans born as innocent and full of the potentiality to be reasonable. The most basic assumption was faith in reason rather than a conviction of sinfulness and a blind faith in revelation. The "enlightened" claimed, however, a rationality they were sometimes unwilling to concede to their opponents.

The Enlightenment believed in the existence of God as a rational explanation of the universe and its form, but that God was a deist Creator who created the universe and its laws, then was no longer involved in its mechanistic operation. The mechanistic operation was governed by "natural law." Enlightenment philosophers are sometimes characterized as being either basically rationalists or basically empiricists.

Rationalists

Rationalists stressed deductive reasoning or mathematical logic as the basis for their epistemology (source of knowledge). They started with "self-evident truths" or postulates, from which they constructed a coherent and logical system of thought:

René Descartes (1596–1650). Sought a basis for logic and thought he found it in man's ability to think: "I think; therefore, I am." This statement cannot be denied without thinking; therefore, it must be an absolute truth that man can think. Proof depends upon logic alone.

Baruch Spinoza (1632–1677). Developed a rational pantheism in which he equated God and nature. He denied free will and ended up with an impersonal, mechanical universe—a universe with no personal God or Heaven there for guidance or comfort.

Gottfried Wilhelm Leibniz (1646–1716). Worked on symbolic logic and calculus, and invented a calculating machine. He, too, had a mechanistic world-and-life view and thought of God as a hypothetical abstraction rather than a person.

Empiricists

Empiricists stressed inductive observation as the basis for their epistemology, in short, the scientific method. Their emphasis was on sensory experience. Two note empiricists were John Locke and David Hume:

John Locke (1632–1704). Pioneered in the empiricist approach to knowledge and stressed the importance of environment in development. He classified knowledge as (1) according to reason, (2) contrary to reason, and (3) above reason. Locke believed in some sort of God, but he rejected the Calvinist notion of sinful babies, asserting that babies were born with a *tabula rasa* (clean slate) of a mind with untapped potentials, until experience and reflection "wrote" on that mind.

David Hume (1711–1776). A Scottish historian and philosopher who began by emphasizing the limitations of human reasoning. He later became a dogmatic skeptic.

Thinkers of the Enlightenment believed in absolutes; they were not relativists. They believed in absolute truth, absolute ethics, and absolute natural law. And they believed optimistically that these absolutes were discoverable by man's rationality. It wasn't long, of course, before one rationalist's "absolutes" clashed with another's.

The Enlightenment believed in a closed system of the universe in which the supernatural was not involved in human life. This was in sharp contrast to the traditional view of an open system in which God, angels, and devils were very much a part of life.

Philosophes: Agents of Change

The new learning was promoted by a relatively small number of thinkers called *philosophes*—not philosophers in a traditional sense, but rather, social activists for whom knowledge was something to be converted into reform. They were not always original thinkers, but rather popularizers of leading reformist thought. The *philosophes* believed their task was to do for human society what the scientists had done for the physical universe: apply reason to society for the purpose of human improvement, and in the process, discover the natural laws governing God, humans, and society.

They were men and women of letters, such as journalists and teachers who frequented the salons, cafes, and discussion groups in France. They were cultured, refined, genteel intellectuals who had unbounded confidence in man's ability to improve society through sophistication and rational thought. They had a habit of criticizing everything in their path—including rationalism:

Francois-Marie Arouet (1694–1778). Known as Voltaire, was one of the most famous *philosophes*. He attended an elite Jesuit school and became well-known for his unusual wit and irreverence. His sharp tongue and "subversive" poetry led to an eleven-month imprisonment in the Bastille, the infamous French prison. Voltaire lived in England for several years and greatly admired the freedom in the relatively open English society. He accepted deism and believed in a finite, limited God whom he thought of as Watchmaker of the universe. Characteristically, Voltaire relied on ridicule rather than reason to present his case. Considered the most brilliant and influential *philosophe*, he argued for tolerance, reason, limited government, and free speech.

Denis Diderot (1713–1784). Served as editor of the *Encyclopedia,* the bible of the Enlightenment period. This twenty-eight volume work was a compendium of all new learning; no self-respecting reformer would be found without a set.

Baron de Montesquieu (1689–1756). Authored *The Spirit of the Laws* (1748), in which he articulated the separation-of-powers theory. Montesquieu believed such a separation would keep any individual (including the king) or group (including the nobles) from gaining total control of the government.

Jean-Jacques Rousseau (1712–1778). Lived in Geneva but spent time on the road, including four years in English exile, because of what the government considered radical ideas. Rousseau thought of man in a simpler state of nature as "the noble savage" and sought to throw off the restraints of civilization. He saw autonomous freedom as the ultimate good. Later in life he decided that if a person did not want Rousseau's utopian ideas, he should be "forced to be free," an obvious contradiction in terms. Rousseau has been influential in Western civilization for over two hundred years with his emphasis on a "general will" governing the social contract and freedom as a Bohemian ideal. His book on education, *Emile* (1762), is still popular, though he left five illegitimate children in an orphanage instead of putting his educational theories to work with his own children. His *Social Contract* (1762) was an attempt to discover the origin of society and to propose that the composition of the ideal society was based on a new kind of social contract, one where the "general will" (a vague concept) governed all.

The dissemination of Enlightenment thought was largely accomplished through *philosophes* touring Europe or writing and printing books and essays, the publication of the *Encyclopedia* (1751), and the discussions in the salons of the upper classes. The salons became the social setting for the exchange of ideas, and were usually presided over by prominent women, such as Madame Geoffrin and Julie de l'Espinasse.

Major Assumptions of the Enlightenment

Enlightenment thinkers accepted these basic principles:

- Human progress was possible through change of one's environment, that is, better people, better societies, better standard of living.

- Humans were free to use reason to reform the evils of society.

- Material improvement would lead to moral improvement.

- Natural science and human reason would discover the meaning of life.

- Laws governing human society would be discovered through application of the scientific method of inquiry.

- Inhuman practices and institutions would be removed from society in a spirit of humanitarianism.

- Human liberty would ensue as individuals became free to choose what reason dictated, or required, as good.

Chronology

The Enlightenment varied from country to country; the French Enlightenment was not the same as the English or German Enlightenment. Distinctions can also be made chronologically in the development of Enlightenment thought. The end of the seventeenth and first half of the eighteenth century saw a reaction against "enthusiasm," or emotionalism, and sought moderation and balance in a context of ordered freedom. From the mid-eighteenth century, the Enlightenment moved into a skeptical, almost iconoclastic phase where it was fashionable to deride and tear down. The last three decades of the eighteenth century were revolutionary, radical, and aggressively dogmatic in defense of various abstractions demanding a revolutionary commitment. "Love of mankind" made it one's duty to crush those who disagreed and thus impeded "progress." In short, the Enlightenment entered a utopian phase that became disastrous as it foreshadowed the French Revolution.

The "Counter-Enlightenment"

The "Counter-Enlightenment" is a comprehensive term of diverse, even disparate groups who disagreed with the fundamental assumptions of the Enlightenment and pointed out its weaknesses. This was not a "movement," merely a convenient category.

Theistic Opposition

German pietism, especially as advocated by Count von Zinzendorf (1700–1760), leader of the Moravian Brethren, taught the need for spiritual conversion and a religious experience. Methodism of the eighteenth century similarly taught the need for regeneration and a moral life that would demonstrate the reality of conversion. Methodism was led by an Anglican minister, John Wesley (1703–1791). The Great Awakening in the English colonies in America in the 1730s and 1740s, led by Jonathan Edwards, had a similar result.

Roman Catholic Jansenism in France argued against the idea of an uninvolved or impersonal God. Hasidism in eastern European Jewish communities, especially in the 1730s, stressed a joyous religious fervor in direct communion with God. Both of these were in sharp contrast to deism, which was at the same time gaining adherents in England.

Philosophic Reaction

Some philosophers questioned fundamental assumptions of rationalist philosophy. David Hume (1711–1776) struck at faith in natural law as well as faith in miracles. He insisted that "man can accept as true only those things for which he has the evidence of factual observation." Since *philosophes* lacked indisputable evidence for their belief in the existence of natural law, Hume believed in living with a "total suspension of judgment." This dogmatic skepticism soon troubled the German philosopher Kant, who set about to challenge and supplant Hume.

Immanuel Kant (1724–1794) separated science and morality into separate branches of knowledge. He said that science could describe the natural phenomena of the material world but could not provide a guide for morality. Kant's "categorical imperative" was an intuitive instinct, implanted by God in conscience. Both the ethical sense and aesthetic appreciation in human beings are beyond the knowledge of science. Reason is a function of the mind and has no content in and of itself.

Enlightenment Effect on Society

The Enlightenment fostered the idea that changes or reform must be instituted when institutions cannot demonstrate a rational base of operation. It thus challenged society in many areas of thought:

Religion. Deism or "natural religion" was inaugurated, which rejected traditional Christianity by promoting an impersonal God who did not interfere in the daily lives of the people. The continued discussion of the role of God led to a general skepticism associated with Pierre Bayle (1647–1706), a type of religious skepticism pronounced by David Hume, and a theory of atheism or materialism advocated by Baron d'Holbach (1723–1789).

Political theory. John Locke and Jean-Jacques Rousseau believed that people were capable of governing themselves, either through a political (Locke) or social (Rousseau) contract forming the basis of society. However, most philosophies opposed democracy, preferring a limited monarchy that shared power with the nobility.

Economic theory. The assault on mercantilist economic theory was begun by the physiocrats in France, who proposed a laissez-faire (nongovernmental interference) attitude toward land usage, which culminated in the theory of economic capitalism associated with Adam Smith and his slogans of free trade, free enterprise, and the law of supply and demand.

Education. Attempting to break from the strict control of education by the church and state, Rousseau advanced the idea of progressive education, where children learn by doing and where self-expression is encouraged. This idea was carried forward by Johann Pestalozzi, Johann Basedow, and Friedrich Frobel, and influenced a new view of childhood.

Psychological theory. In the *Essay Concerning Human Understanding* (1690), Locke offered the theory that all human knowledge was the result of sensory experience, without any preconceived notions. He believed that the mind at birth was a blank slate (*tabula rasa*) that registered the experience of the senses passively. According to Locke, since education was critical in determining human development, human progress was in the hands of society.

Gender theory. The assertion of feminist rights evolved through the emergence of determined women who had been denied access to formal education, yet used their position in society to advance the cause of female emancipation. The Enlightenment salons of Madame de Geoffrin and Louise de Warens are an example of self-educated women taking their place alongside their male counterparts. One woman fortunate enough to receive education in science was Emilie du Chatelet, an aristocrat trained as a mathematician and physicist. Her scholarship resulted in the translation of Isaac Newton's work from Latin into French. The writing of Lady Mary Montagu and Mary Wollstonecraft promoted equal political and educational rights for women. Madame Marie Roland was a heroic figure throughout the early but critical periods of the French Revolution, as she attacked the evils of the ancient regime.

Era of "Enlightened Despotism"

Most *philosophes* believed that human progress and liberty would ensue as absolute rulers became "enlightened." The rulers would still be absolute, but use their power benevolently, as reason dictated. However, the reforms of the rulers were usually directed at increasing their power rather than the welfare of their subjects. Their creed was "Everything for the people, nothing by the people."

Most *philosophes* opposed democracy. According to Voltaire, the best form of government was a monarchy in which the rulers shared the ideas of the *philosophes* and respected people's rights. Such an enlightened monarch would rule justly and introduce reforms. Voltaire's influence, as well as that of other *philosophes*, on Europe's monarchs produced "enlightened despots" who nonetheless failed to bring about lasting political change. The most important were Frederick II, or Frederick the Great, of

Prussia (1740–1786), Catherine II, or the Great, of Russia (1762–1796), and Joseph II of Austria (1765–1790).

Influence of the American Revolution

The American Revolution acted as a "shining beacon" to Europeans anxious for change, and helped prove that people could govern themselves without the help of monarchs and privileged classes.

France, center of Enlightenment thought, was particularly vulnerable. Eighteenth-century ideas of the "rights of man" and "consent of the governed" were discussed widely in salons, as well as in the rest of Europe. French reformers believed that their nation was a perfect example of everything wrong with society. *Philosophes* and their admirers were galvanized into action.

Finally, the concept of revolution was validated as a legitimate means to procure social and political change, when it could not be affected through existing avenues. The American Revolution, however, was not radical, but a conservative movement that kept the existing social order and property rights, and led to a constitutional system built on stability and continuity.

Culture of the Baroque and Rococo

Age of the Baroque (1600–1750)

The baroque style emphasized grandeur, spaciousness, unity, and emotions in a work of art. The splendor of Versailles typifies baroque architecture: gigantic frescoes unified around the emotions in a single theme. The glory and stark passions of Johann Sebastian Bach's *Saint Matthew's Passion* are the crown of baroque music. Art reflects a *weltanschauung*—way of looking at the world dominant in a given age. To grasp the seventeenth and eighteenth centuries, you need to see how values, philosophy, and attitudes of the age are reflected in baroque art, architecture, and music. Although the baroque began in Catholic Reformation countries as a way for the arts to use emotions and the senses to bring the faithful closer to God, it soon spread to Protestant nations. Some of the great baroque artists and composers were Protestant (for example, Bach and George Frederic Händel).

Baroque Architecture

Michelangelo's work provided the initial inspiration for baroque architecture. A dynamic, unified treatment of the elements of architecture combined in the baroque. Oval or elliptical plans were often used in baroque church design. Giovanni Bernini (1598–1650) was perhaps the leading early baroque sculptor, architect, and painter. Bernini's most famous architectural achievement was the colonnade for the piazza in front of Saint Peter's in Rome. Louis XIV brought Bernini to Paris to plan a design for the completion of the palace of the Louvre, but the final design selected was that of Claude Perrault (1613–1688).

Louis XIV's magnificent palace at Versailles was particularly the work of Louis LeVau (1612–1670) and Jules Mansart. The geometric design of the palace included the gardens, which excel in symmetry and balance, and many fountains.

Baroque Art

Baroque art concentrated on broad, bold areas of light and shadow rather than on linear arrangements as in the High Renaissance. Color was an important element because it appealed to the senses and was more true to nature. The baroque was not as concerned with clarity of detail as with the overall dynamic effect. It was designed to give a spontaneous personal experience.

Masters of baroque painting were Michelangelo Merisi, known as Caravaggio, (1573–1610) from near Milan, and Diego Velazquez (1599–1660) from Seville. They are known for the concrete realism of their subjects. Their work is forceful and dramatic with sharp contrasts of light and darkness (*chiaroscuro*). In addition to Caravaggio's *Bacchus* (see Chapter 3), consider Velazquez's famous *Las Meninas* (1656), showing the royal family in an eccentric way not atypical of baroque artists out for effect (see Figure 5-1).

Museo del Prado, Madrid, Spain

Figure 5-1. Diego Velazquez's *Las Meninas* (1656) shows how elaborate fashion, the use of perspective to indicate distance and secrecy, and the deceptive quality of mirrors combine to make a great baroque painting.

Dutch Art

The seventeenth century was the most significant in history for Dutch painting. Most of the Dutch painters came from the province of Holland. Rembrandt van Rijn and Jan Steen came from Leyden; Cuyp from Dordrecht; Van Goyen from The Hague; and Jan Vermeer from Delft.

The artistic center of the Netherlands was Amsterdam, where the Dutch school of painters was noted for landscape and portrait painting, and especially for "genre painting" in which scenes of everyday life predominate. The Calvinist influence in Holland is reflected in their celebration, but not idealization, of God's Creation. The realistic portrait paintings show mankind as great and noble, but also flawed, or, as the Reformed churches put it, "fallen creatures in a fallen world." Nevertheless, the flawed creation was still to be enjoyed and the Dutch artists' pictures of Dutch life in the seventeenth century show it to be intensely joyful and satisfying in human relationships.

The Dutch painters were masters of light and shadow as were the later French impressionists. They captured the subtlety and realism of an ordinary scene under the vast expanse of the sky, a storm at sea, or a rain shower "drifting across a distant landscape pursued by sunshine." It is interesting to contrast the work of the Dutch painters with that of artists from the equally great Flemish contemporary school in the Spanish Netherlands, which was strongly influenced by the Counter-Reformation baroque. Peter Paul Rubens from Antwerp is a good example.

The unique style of Rembrandt Van Rijn (1606–1669), the great Dutch painter, could not be considered typically baroque. Consider the two paintings in Figure 5-2: one shows the impact of the new science and medicine on realistic artists, the other the enduring power of Bible stories to shape the imaginations of Europeans.

Mauritshuis, The Hague, The Netherlands   *The Hermitage, St. Petersburg, Russia*

Figure 5-2. In his *Anatomy Lesson of Dr. Tulp* (1632) (left), Rembrandt makes the sight of a corpse being dissected acceptable as an aesthetic subject by the calm, dignified poses of the living and the dead; in his emotionally powerful *Return of the Prodigal Son* (right), Rembrandt taps in to the biblical literacy of his Protestant audience to make both moral and all-too-human points about this story and its characters.

Another exemplar of the Dutch baroque, which tended to be less dramatic and more mundane in subjects than French, Italian, or Spanish variants, was Jan Vermeer (1632–1675) of Delft in Holland. His very personal works let us into the world of professional painters and their models, as in his *Girl with the Pearl Earring* (1665; see Figure 5-3).

Mauritshuis, The Hague, The Netherlands

Figure 5-3. Vermeer may have made use of a strange invention, the camera obscura, a box with a lens for casting "purified" images on a black background. The eerie quality of the light in such masterpieces as the *Girl with the Pearl Earring* (1665) suggests this possibility.

Baroque Music

A major assumption underlying baroque music was that the text should guide the music rather than let music dominate the text, as was done formerly. The idea that music can depict a situation and express the emotion and drama involved was a major innovation. Instead of writing lyrics appropriate to a musical composition, the lyrics or libretto came first, determining the texture and structure of the composition. Dissonance was used freely to make the music conform to the emotion in the text. Special devices of melody, rhythm, harmony, and texture all contributed to the emotional effects.

The baroque was a conscious effort to express a wide range of ideas and feelings vividly in music. These were intensified by sharp contrasts in the music and a variety of moods experienced: anger, excitement, exaltation, grandeur, heroism, wonder, a contemplative mood, mystic exaltation, and so on.

Bach's *Saint Matthew Passion* illustrates this with a frenzied effect of cruelty and chaos obtained by a double chorus of four voices singing, "Crucify him! Crucify Him!" The jubilant "Easter Oratorio" reflects the triumph of the Resurrection. Violins and violas maintain a steady progression of pizzicato chords to depict the gentle knocking of Christ in the cantata, "Behold I stand at the door and knock."

The splendor and grandeur of baroque art and architecture could be captured in baroque music. Giovanni Gabrieli (1554–1612) pioneered the shift from Renaissance to baroque when he placed four groups of instruments and choirs, each complete in itself, in the galleries and balconies of Saint Mark's Cathedral in Venice. The baroque followed his lead and Gabrieli laid the foundation for the modern orchestra.

The concerto, involving interaction between a solo instrument and a full orchestra, was also an innovation of the baroque. Antonio Vivaldi (1678–1741) pioneered the concerto and standardized a cycle of three movements. The major-minor key system of tonality was also developed during the baroque period.

The baroque developed a new counterpoint different from that of the Renaissance. There was still a blending of different melodic lines, but those melodies were subordinate to the harmonic scheme. Bach was supremely successful in balancing harmony, counterpoint, and melody with polyphony. Georg Friedrich Händel (1685–1759) was a master of baroque grandeur, especially in dramatic oratorios. He brought to life in his music a poetic depth, and his use of the chorus profoundly affected his mostly English audiences. (His name is often anglicized.) Händel was like a painter who was at his best with gigantic frescoes that involved his audience in the whole uplifting experience.

Rococo

The term "rococo" comes from a French word meaning "shell" or "decorative scroll." It describes a tendency toward elegance, pleasantness, and even frivolity. It is in contrast to the serious grandeur of the baroque. It has more decorative than grand or sublime elements; simpler, but not plain. The effect is more sentimental than emotional.

The center of the rococo movement was France, and Antoine Watteau (1684–1721) was one of the most famous rococo painters. His works are elegant, delicate, innocent, and sensual at the same time, as his soul-stirring portrait of Gilles the clown shows (see Figure 5-4).

Figure 5-4. *Gilles* **(1717 or 1718) shows a melancholy, moonstruck Pierrot, a stock figure in the hugely popular dramatic form of** *commedia dell'arte*, **an Italian export to all points from Russia to England, still alive in the twentieth century with Punch and Judy puppets (England) and allusions in Russian poets Aleksandr Blok and Anna Akhmatova. Viewers can interpret Gilles's haunting look as a sign of Watteau's encroaching death, but it is likelier that Watteau is paying homage to the "genius" of his patron, an actor and inn owner who had been a successful Pierrot on stage. Other** *commedia* **figures can be seen in the background, and since** *commedia* **mixed slapstick comedy with melodrama, no simple interpretation will do.**

Characteristics of the rococo can be found in the compositions of both Franz Josef Haydn (1732–1809) and young Wolfgang Amadeus Mozart (1759–1791), whose masterworks, beginning about age fourteen, shade more into the classical age.

TIMELINE

Absolutism, Constitutionalism, and Enlightenment

Year(s)	Event	Significance
1576	Jean Bodin publishes *Six Books of the Commonwealth*.	In wake of Saint Bartholomew's Day Massacre (1572), Bodin tries to show that division of powers results in anarchy, thus stability and order require indivisible sovereignty in one power, for example, a monarch. Later, absolutists Thomas Hobbes and Jacques-Bénigne Bossuet take up this strong argument.
1610–1643	Cardinal Richelieu (following the lead of the Duke of Sully) institutes the *intendant* system.	The *intendants*, who are paid by the king to collect taxes, enforce laws, and recruit for the army, foster absolutism by ridding the monarch of rival power bases, in this case provincial governors and estates-general.
1620	Francis Bacon publishes his *New Organon*.	Bacon outlines his method of (a) clearing away idols of the mind that inhibit free thought and observation and (b) induction from the facts to theory.
1637	René Descartes publishes *Discourse on Method*.	Descartes outlines his method of deduction from first principles, with his dictum triumphant: "I think; therefore, I am."
1659	France and Spain sign the Treaty of Pyrenees.	The treaty ends war between France and Spain (*cf.* Cateau-Cambrésis, 1559) and gives Louis claims to Spanish lands as part of his wife's dowry. The War of Devolution follows (1666) as does the War of the Spanish Succession (1701).
1690	John Locke publishes treatises on government and on *tabula rasa*.	Locke advocates a limited monarchy and the rights to life, liberty, and property. His *Essay on Human Understanding* argues the *tabula rasa*, that infant brains are slates to be written on by experience and by reflection.
1727	Johann Sebastian Bach composes the *Saint Matthew Passion*.	One of the crowning achievements of the baroque, Bach's Passion combines the perfection of the contrapuntal art with lovely, naive musical effects to show different feelings and events.
1733	Voltaire publishes *Letters on the English*.	Voltaire begins a life of arguing against arbitrary power and obscurantist religion; exiled for insulting a noble, he lavishes praise on England's freedoms—as he sees them.

(Continued)

1748	Baron de Montesquieu publishes *The Spirit of the Laws*.	Montesquieu, a member of the Bordeaux *parlement*, saw these law courts as valuable intermediary powers between the king and his people; this was *his* idea of separation of powers: checks and balances.
1751–1762	Denis Diderot and collaborators publish the massive *Encyclopedia*.	*Encyclopedia* offers a compendium of new learning and useful sciences. Diderot is threatened by the Catholic Church, but protected by the king's mistress, Madame de Pompadour.
1754–1763	England and France fight the Seven Years' (or French and Indian) War.	England and France fight in the colonies: India, North America, and Caribbean sugar islands. France is routed, losing Canada and India to Britain.
1756	France and Austria ally with one another, forming the Diplomatic Revolution.	Reversing 250 years of enmity, France and Austria ally against Prussia and England to right the balance of power. Prussia launches a preemptive strike against Austrian ally, Saxony.
1761	Rousseau's two major publications	Rousseau's *Social Contract* argues that the "general will" knows best what is good for the people (not a majority vote); his *Emile* shows that boys, at least, are best educated when left free to run and play.
1763	Warring nations sign the Treaties of Hubertusburg and Paris.	Treaty of Hubertusburg ends the Seven Years' War, granting Silesia (formerly of Austria) to Prussia. The Treaty of Paris ends the French and Indian War, allowing Britain to keep most of its wartime gains, but giving back to France some of the Caribbean sugar islands for the sake of balance of power.
1776	Adam Smith publishes the *Wealth of Nations*. The American colonies rebel.	Smith's treatise (capitalist bible) argues that wealth is more than gold and silver, that comes from land; while frowning on state interference in the market, he knows that merchants collude to fix prices and all else, so he is no doctrinaire free-trader! England loses its colonies.
1769–1778	Newcomen-Watt steam engine is invented, improved upon, and financed for markets.	Newcomen's steam engines were being used instead of animals in the 1710s to pump water more efficiently from mines, but Watt's separate condenser of 1769 made a great stride forward; and Matthew Boulton's investments made the steam engine an affordable and much more efficient source of power than animals or humans.

1769–1793	Richard Arkwright's spinning frame, James Hargreaves's spinning jenny, Edward Cartwright's power loom, and Eli Whitney's cotton gin mechanize the production of cotton threads and fabrics.	These technological advances help establish England as an economic powerhouse.
1781	Joseph II issues the Edict of Toleration in Habsburg crown lands.	Joseph II, one of several coeval "enlightened despots," alienates the church, nobles, and even peasants by a radical program that includes toleration of Protestants and Jews, as well as the confiscation of idle church lands in favor of hard-working priests and nuns who teach, tend hospitals, and so on.

Chapter 6

Revolution and the New European Order (1789–1848)

The French Revolution I (1789–1799)

The shape of the modern world first became visible during ten years of upheaval in France, between 1789 and 1799. Radical ideas about society and government had emerged earlier in response to the success of new scientific methods and new ideas. Armed with scientific knowledge of the physical universe, as well as a new view of the human capacity to detect Truth, social critics assailed the existing modes of thought governing political, social, religious, and economic life.

The modern world that came of age was characterized by rapid, revolutionary change that paved the way for economic modernization and political centralization throughout Europe. Ideas and institutions created by revolutionaries would be codified and extended by Napoleon Bonaparte, who conquered and almost converted parts of European society to his revolutionary, but not to his nationalist, agenda.

Causes of the French Revolution

Cumulative Discontent with the Ancient Regime

Changing expectations of "enlightened" society were manifested in the rise in criticism of government inefficiency, corruption, and privilege. The old model of social strata failed to correspond to the realities of wealth and ability in French society. The clergy (First Estate) and nobility (Second Estate) represented only two percent of the population of twenty-four million; but privileges made them essentially tax exempt. The rest of the population (Third Estate) consisted of the bourgeois, urban workers, and the mass of peasants, who all bore the burden of taxation and feudal obligations. As economic conditions worsened in the eighteenth century, the French state became poorer, overdependent on the poorest and most depressed sections of the economy for support, at the very time that this tax base had become saturated.

The mode of absolute government practiced by the Bourbon dynasty was wed to the "divine right of kings" (see Chapter 5). This in turn produced a government that was irresponsible and inefficient, with a tax system that was unjust and inequitable, without any means of redress because of the absence of any meaningful representative assembly. The legal system was confusing and frustratingly slow, with no uniform or codified laws.

The economic environment of the eighteenth century produced a major challenge to the state-controlled French economy (mercantilism), as businessmen and bankers assailed the restrictive features of this economic philosophy. With the growth of new industrial centers and the development of modern capitalist thought, the middle classes began to assert themselves, demanding that their economic power be made commensurate with political and social power—both of which were denied to them. Within France, the estates allowed the few to monopolize economic benefits, while the many were ignored. Thus, an inequitable and inefficient tax system hit those least able to pay, and the mass of peasants had additional burdens—performing feudal services for the privileged classes and paying outdated feudal taxes and fees.

Intellectual currents of the eighteenth century were responsible for creating a climate of opposition based on the political theories of John Locke, Jean-Jacques Rousseau, Baron de Montesquieu (see Chapter 5) and other *philosophes*; the economic ideas of the French physiocrats and Adam Smith (today considered the father of modern capitalism); and the general reform-minded direction of the century.

Immediate Cause: Financial Mismanagement

The coming of revolution seemed a paradox in one of the largest and richest nations in Europe, with a population of about twenty-four million and a capital, Paris, considered the center of all culture and civilization. Dissatisfaction with how France was administered reached a crisis during the reign of Louis XVI (reigned 1774–1792).

The deepening public debt was of grave concern. It stemmed from (1) colonial wars with England (1754–1763 and 1778–1783), (2) French participation in the American War of Independence, (3) maintenance of large military and naval establishments, and (4) the gross inefficiencies of tax farming in a country where the richest were exempt from their fair tax burden. Unable to secure loans from leading banking houses in Europe (owing to a poor credit rating), France edged closer to bankruptcy.

Between 1730 and the 1780s, an inflationary spiral raised prices dramatically, as wages failed to adjust accordingly. Government expenses continued to outstrip tax revenues. The government's "solution" to the debt problem was to increase the rates of taxation or decree new taxes. The French tax system could not produce the amount of taxes needed to save the government from bankruptcy because of the corruption and inefficiency of the system. The legal system of parlements (courts), controlled now by robe and sword nobles alike (see Chapter 4), blocked tax increases as well as new taxes in order to force the king to share power with the Second Estate.

As France slid into bankruptcy, Louis XVI summoned an Assembly of Notables (1787) in the mistaken hope they would either approve the king's new tax program or consent to the removal of their exemption from the payment of taxes. They refused to agree to either proposal.

Estates-General Summoned

Designed to represent the three estates of France, this ancient feudal body, created in 1302, virtually gave away any claim to power when in 1439 it gave the king, still fighting the Hundred Years' War, a direct royal tax, the *taille*, thus obviating one of the principal reasons for the estates to meet and vitiating its main hold over the monarchy. The estates were moot after 1614. When the parlements insisted that new taxes must be approved by this body, Louis XVI reluctantly ordered it to assemble at Versailles by May 1789. Each estate was expected to elect its own representatives. As a gesture to the size of the Third Estate, the king doubled the number of its representatives. However, the Parlement of Paris decreed that voting in the Estates-General would follow "custom and tradition," that is, by estate unit voting. Therefore, the First and Second estates, with similar interests to protect, would control the historic meeting despite the increased size of the Third Estate.

Election fever hit France for the first time. The 1788–1789 election campaign is often considered the precursor of modern politics. Each estate was expected to compile a list of suggestions and complaints called *cahiers* and present them to the king. These lists of grievances emphasized the need for reform of government and civil equality. Campaigning proceeded through debate and pamphlets. The most influential writer was the Abbé Sieyès and his pamphlet *What is the Third Estate?* The answer: everything.

The election campaign took place amidst the worst subsistence crisis since the 1709 frost: widespread grain shortages, two poor harvests, inflated bread prices, and wild rumors of hoarding by the hated tax farmers (private agents licensed by the government to collect taxes for the treasury).

On May 5, 1789, the Estates-General met and were outraged by the voting method, that is, by unit and not per capita. Each estate was ordered by the king and the Parlement of Paris to meet and vote separately. The Third refused and insisted on the entire assembly remaining together.

Phases of Revolution

The National Assembly (1789–1791)

After a deadlock over voting methods, the Third Estate declared itself the true National Assembly of France (June 17). They were immediately locked out of their meeting place by order of Louis XVI. Instead, they assembled in an indoor tennis court, where they swore an oath never to disband until they had given France a constitution (*Tennis Court Oath*). The Third Estate had assumed sovereign power on behalf of the nation. Defections from the First and Second estates then caused the king to recognize the National Assembly (June 27), after dissolving the Estates-General. At the same time, Louis XVI ordered troops to surround Versailles.

The Paris revolution began. Angry because of food shortages, unemployment, high prices, and the fear of military repression, workers and tradesmen began to arm themselves. On July 14, they stormed the ancient fortress of the Bastille in search of weapons. The fall of this hated symbol of royal power gave the Revolution its baptism of blood. The king recalled his troops from Versailles. The spirit of rebellion spread to the French countryside, triggered by rumors and hysteria. A feeling of fear and desperation called "The Great Fear" took hold in the country. Peasants attacked manor houses, symbols of noble power, in an effort to destroy legal records of their feudal obligations. The middle classes responded to this "rabble" violence by forming the National Guard, a militia to protect property rights. Hoping to put an end to further violence, the National Assembly voted to abolish feudalism in France and declare the equality of all (August 4). A virtual social revolution had taken place peacefully. The assembly then issued a constitutional blueprint, the Declaration of the Rights of Man and the Citizen (August 26), a guarantee of due process of law and the sovereignty of the people. The National Assembly now proceeded to its twin functions of governing France on a day-to-day basis and writing a constitution.

Among the achievements of the National Assembly were the following:

1. Secularization of religion. Church property was confiscated to pay off the national debt. The Civil Constitution of the Clergy (1790) created a national church with eighty-three new bishoprics. All clergy were to be democratically elected by the people and have their salaries paid by the state. The practical result was to polarize the nation over religion.

2. Governmental reform. To make the country easier to administer, the assembly divided the country into eighty-three departments (replacing the old provincial boundary lines) governed by elected officials. With a new system of law courts, France now had a uniform administrative structure: eighty-three dioceses, departments, and judicial districts.

3. Constitutional changes. On June 20, 1791, Louis XVI fled from Paris with his wife, Marie Antoinette, and their children. Fearing the new Constitution of 1791, he wanted help from Marie Antoinette's brother with troops across the border in the Austrian Netherlands. They were caught short of their goal at Varennes and taken back as prisoners to Paris. The National Assembly now had an excuse to transform France into a constitutional monarchy with a unicameral legislature. Middle-class control of the government was assured through indirect voting and property qualifications. The king had ruined all chances for the return to an absolute monarchy through his bumbling and his openly traitorous actions.

The Legislative Assembly (1791–1792)

While the National Assembly had been homogeneous in composition, the new government began to reflect the emergence of political factions competing for power. The most important political clubs were republican: the Jacobins (radical urban) and Girondins (moderate provincial). The sansculottes (working-class extreme radical) were a separate faction with a very radical economic agenda.

The focus of political activity during the life of the new Legislative Assembly was the question of war. Influenced by nobles who had fled France beginning in 1789 (the *émigrés*), the two largest continental powers, Prussia and Austria, issued the

Declaration of Pillnitz (August 1791), declaring the restoration of French monarchy as their goal. Meanwhile, the sharply polarized atmosphere, mounting political and economic chaos, and unpopular monarch fueled republican sentiment within France, as war against all monarchs was promoted to solve domestic problems. Ideological fervor and anti-Austrian sentiment drove the Legislative Assembly to declare war on Austria (April 1792). Unprepared, French revolutionary forces proved no match for the Austrian military. The Jacobins blamed their defeat on Louis XVI, believing him to be part of a conspiracy with Prussia and Austria. Mobs reacted to the threat, made by invading armies, to destroy Paris (Brunswick Manifesto) if any harm came to the royal family, by seizing power in Paris and imprisoning the king. The Legislative Assembly came under attack and obliged the radicals by suspending the 1791 Constitution, ordering new elections based on universal male suffrage, for the purpose of summoning a national convention to give France a republican form of government.

The National Convention (1792–1795)

Meeting in September 1792, the National Convention abolished the monarchy and installed a republic. On the day of the convention's first session, a mixed army of old-guard officers and untried recruits managed to beat German and Austrian forces at the great battle of Valmy. The poet Goethe, in the Duke of Brunswick's camp, proclaimed that, from that day forward, they were witnessing a new age in history. Louis XVI was charged with treason, found guilty, and executed on January 21, 1793; later that year, Queen Marie Antoinette met the same fate.

By the spring of 1793, the new republic was in a crisis. England and Spain had joined Austria and Prussia in opposing the Revolution. Food shortages and counter-revolution in western France threatened the radicals' grip. A power struggle ensued between Girondins and Jacobins, until the Jacobins ousted their political enemy and installed an emergency government to deal with external and internal challenges to the Revolution. The Committee of Public Safety, directed by Maximilien Robespierre, responded to food shortages and related economic problems by decreeing a planned economy (Law of the Maximum), which would enable France to urge total war against its external enemies. Lazare Carnot, known as "the Organizer of Victory," was placed in charge of reorganizing the army. The entire nation was conscripted into service (*levée en masse*), since war was now defined as a national mission.

The most notorious event of the French Revolution was the Reign of Terror (1793–1794), the government campaign against internal enemies and counter-revolutionaries. Revolutionary tribunals were created to hear the cases of the accused brought to "justice" under the new Law of Suspects. Approximately twenty-five thousand people in France lost their lives. Execution by guillotine became a spectator sport. A new political culture began to emerge, called the Republic of Virtue. This was Robespierre's grand scheme to de-Christianize France and inculcate revolutionary virtue. The Terror spiraled out of control, consuming Jacobin leaders Georges Danton, Camille Desmoulins, and Jacques Hébert, until no one could feel secure under Robespierre's dictatorship. On July 27, 1794, Robespierre was denounced in the convention, arrested, and executed the next day, along with his close associate, Louis-Antoine Saint-Just.

The fall of Robespierre was followed by a dramatic swing to the right called the Thermidorian Reaction (1794). Tired of terror and virtue alike, moderate bourgeois politicians regained control of the convention and readmitted the Girondins. A retreat from the excesses of revolution began. A new constitution was written in 1795, which set up a republican form of government. A new Legislative Assembly would choose a five-member executive, the Directory, from which the new regime was to take its name. Before its rule came to an end, the convention removed economic controls, which dealt a death blow to the sansculottes. Finally, the convention decreed that, at least for the first two years of operation, the new government reserve two-thirds of the seats in the Legislative Assembly for themselves.

The Directory (1795–1799)

The Constitution of 1795 set the tone and style of government in France: voting and holding office were reserved to property owners. The middle class was in control. They wanted peace in order to secure wealth and establish a society in which money and property would become the only requirements for prestige and power. These goals confronted opposition from the aristocracy, which in October 1795, attempted a royalist uprising. It might have succeeded were it not for the young Napoleon Bonaparte, who happened to be in Paris and loyally helped the government put down the rebellion. The sansculottes also attacked the government and its economic philosophy, but, leaderless and powerless, they were doomed to failure. Despite growing inflation and public discontent, the Directory ignored a growing shift in public opinion. When elections in 1797 produced a triumph for the royalist right, the Directory annulled the results and thus shed its last pretense of legitimacy.

Military success overshadowed the weak, corrupt Directory. French armies annexed the Austrian Netherlands, the left bank of the Rhine, Nice, and Savoy. The Dutch republic was made a satellite of France. The greatest military victories were won by Napoleon Bonaparte, who drove the Austrians out of northern Italy and forced them to sign the Treaty of Campo Formio (October 1797) in return for which the Directory agreed to Napoleon's scheme to conquer Egypt and threaten English interests in the East.

The Directory hung on for two more years, thanks to military successes. But a steady loss of support resulted from a government that was bankrupt, rife with corruption, and unwilling to halt an inflationary spiral that was aggravating the impoverished masses of French peasants. The Directory was crushing the spirit of revolution, and the resultant fear gave rise to a conspiracy to save the Revolution and forestall a royalist return to power. Led by the famous revolutionary the Abbé Sieyès, the conspirators invited Napoleon to join their movement, which he did upon returning from Egypt. On 18 *Brumaire* (the second month of the revolutionary calendar) 1799, they ousted the Directory. The conspirators quickly promulgated a new constitution, which established the Consulate Era.

European Reaction to the Events of 1789–1799

Throughout Europe, liberals and radicals hailed the birth of liberty and freedom in France. Among those who defended the French Revolution were the German philosophers

Immanuel Kant and Johann Gottlieb Fichte and the English scientist Joseph Priestly. The romantic poet William Wordsworth captured the sense of liberation and hope inspired by the French Revolution:

> Bliss it was in that dawn to be alive But to be young was very heaven.

Not all reactions were favorable, however. Conservatives predicted that social anarchy would ensue if French revolutionaries succeeded. Edmund Burke's 1790 *Reflections on the Revolution in France* remains to this day the classic statement of the conservative view of change.

Results

The first ten years of revolution in France destroyed the old social system; replaced it with a new one based on equality, ability, and the law; guaranteed the triumph of capitalist society; gave birth to the notion of secular democracy; laid the foundations for the establishment of the modern nation-state; and gave the human race what it had never had before, except from religion: hope of a better life.

The French Revolution II: The Era of Napoleon (1799–1815)

The shift to a new group in power did not prepare anyone in France for the most dramatic changes that would distinguish this era from the changes of the past ten years. France was about to be mastered by a legend, and Europe overrun by a mythical titan.

Background of Napoleon's Life

Napoleone Buonaparte was born on Corsica, August 15, 1769, to a prominent Italian family a year after France annexed the island. He pursued a military career while advocating Corsican independence. He associated with Jacobins and advanced rapidly in the army when vacancies resulted from the emigration of aristocratic officers. His first marriage was to Josephine de Beauharnais, whom he divorced after a childless marriage. In 1810, Napoleon arranged a marriage of state with Marie Louise, daughter of the Austrian emperor. Their son was known as Napoleon II, "King of Rome."

Napoleon was a military genius whose specialty was artillery. He was also a charismatic leader with the nationalist's clarity of vision and the romantic's urge for action. Napoleon galvanized a dispirited, divided country into a unified and purposeful nation at the price of individual liberty.

Role in Directory Government (1795–1799)

In 1793, Napoleon was instrumental in breaking the British siege of Toulon. Because of his loyalty to the Revolution, he was made commander of the Army of the Interior, after saving the new Directory from being overthrown by a Parisian mob in 1795. He led an army to Italy in the Campaign of 1796 against the First Coalition

(1792–1797), where he defeated the Austrians and Sardinians, imposing the Treaty of Campo Formio (1797) on Austria, effectively ending the First Coalition. England was thereby isolated.

The election results of 1797 forced the Directory to abandon the wishes of the country and establish a dictatorship of those favorable to the Revolution. After defending the government, Napoleon launched his invasion of Egypt (1798), only to have his navy destroyed by England's Lord Nelson at the battle of the Nile. Napoleon and the French army were isolated in North Africa. He abandoned his troops in Palestine when he heard that he might be charged with malfeasance by elements of the government at home.

Popular indignation against the Directory, along with financial disorder and military losses, produced a crisis atmosphere. Fearing a return to monarchy, a cabal headed by the Abbé Sieyès decided to save the Revolution by overthrowing the Directory. Napoleon was invited to furnish the armed power, and his name, to the takeover (Coup d'État of 18 *Brumaire*, November 9, 1799).

Consulate (1799–1804): Napoleon, an Enlightened Despot?

The new government was installed on December 25, 1799, with a constitution that concentrated supreme power in the hands of Napoleon.

Executive power was vested in three consuls, but the First Consul (Napoleon) behaved more as an enlightened despot than revolutionary statesman. His aim was to govern France by demanding obedience, rewarding ability, and organizing everything in orderly hierarchical fashion.

Napoleon's domestic reforms and policies affected every aspect of society and had an enduring impact on French history. Among the features were the following:

1. Strong central government and administrative unity, based on a meritocracy

2. Religious unity (Concordat of 1801 with the Roman Catholic Church)

3. Financial unity (Bank of France), emphasizing balanced budget and rigid economy in government

4. Economic reform to stimulate the economy, provide food at low prices, increase employment, and allow peasants to keep the land they had secured during the revolution

5. Educational reforms based on a system of public education under state control (new polytechnic schools, a University of France)

Napoleon's efforts toward legal unity provided the first clear, complete codification of French law (Code Napoleon), which made permanent many achievements of the French Revolution. It stipulated equality before the law, freedom of conscience, property rights, abolition of serfdom, and the secular character of the state. Its major regressive provisions denied women equal status with men, and denied true political liberty.

Thus, in the tradition of enlightened despotism, Napoleon repressed liberty, subverted republicanism, and restored absolutism to France, while, however, making parts of government and society more efficient and productive.

Empire (1804–1814): Enlightenment Abandoned for Wars and Conquest

After being made Consul for Life (1801), Napoleon decided that only an empire could secure France its position relative to other European states. On December 2, 1804, with the pope present as a virtual prisoner, Napoleon crowned himself emperor in Notre Dame Cathedral, an event famously recorded in the painting by Jacques-Louis David (see Figure 6-1).

Musée du Louvre, Paris, France

Figure 6-1. *Consecration of the Emperor Napoleon I and Coronation of the Empress Josephine in the Cathedral of Notre-Dame de Paris on 2 December 1804.*

Militarism and Empire Building

Beginning in 1805, Napoleon engaged in constant warfare that put his troops in enemy capitals from Lisbon and Madrid to Berlin and Moscow, temporarily giving him the largest empire since Roman times. Napoleon's Grand Empire consisted of an enlarged France and satellite kingdoms, as well as coerced allies. At times only England fought him; at times Austria as well fought him. Then Sopain (1808) and Russia (1812) joined the Allied Powers against Napoleon. By 1814, most powers were against Napoleon, with the notable exceptions of Denmark and Saxony.

The military campaigns of the Napoleonic Years included the War of the Second Coalition (1798–1801), the War of the Third Coalition (1805–1807), the Peninsular War

(1808–1814), the War of Liberation (1809), the Russian Campaign (1812), the War of the Fourth Coalition (1813–1814), and the Hundred Days (March 20–June 22, 1815).

French-ruled subject peoples viewed Napoleon as a tyrant who repressed and exploited them for France's glory and advantage. Enlightened reformers believed Napoleon had betrayed the ideals of the Revolution.

The downfall of Napoleon resulted from his inability to conquer England; economic distress caused by the Continental System (a boycott of British goods); the Peninsular War with Spain; the German War of Liberation; and the invasion of Russia. The actual defeat of Napoleon was the result of the Fourth Coalition and the battle of Leipzig ("Battle of Nations") in 1813. Napoleon was exiled to the island of Elba as a sovereign prince with an income from France.

After learning of Allied disharmony at the Vienna peace talks, Napoleon escaped from Elba and launched his "Hundred Days" by seizing power from the restored French king, Louis XVIII.

Napoleon's gamble ended at Waterloo in June 1815. He was then exiled as a prisoner of war to the South Atlantic island of Saint Helena, where he died in 1821.

Evaluation

The significance of the Napoleonic era lies in its mix of revolutionary and imperial ideas. Although Napoleon ruled France for only fifteen years, his impact had lasting consequences on French and world history. He consolidated revolutionary institutions. He thoroughly centralized the French government. He made a lasting settlement with the church. He also spread the positive achievements of the French Revolution to the rest of the world.

Napoleon also repressed liberty, subverted republicanism, oppressed conquered peoples, and caused terrible suffering.

The Napoleonic legend, based on his memoirs, suggests an attempt by Napoleon to rewrite history by interpreting past events in a positive light.

← ── TIMELINE ── →
Revolution and the New European Order (1789–1815)

Year(s)	Event	Significance
1770–1774	Louis XV suspends refractory parlements and initiates judicial reform.	When the provincial parlements gang up with the chief Parlement of Paris to protest the king's use of a royal corvée and defend their narrow privileges, Louis XV dissolves the parlements—an act some interpret as royal despotism, others as a much-needed reform; Louis XVI reverses this decision and reinstates the retrograde parlements.
1781	Jacques Necker issues his *Comte Rendu* for the king—in 100,000 copies.	To woo the support of the king and parlements for fiscal reform, Necker doctors the books to show a surplus of ten million *livres* in the hope of concealing an actual deficit of forty-six million. This backfires, he is dismissed, and the subject of reform becomes taboo.
1787–1788	The king calls an Assembly of Notables to advise on the financial crisis.	Aware that the king wants to tax the nobles and clergy, the Assembly refuses to act, and demands the recall of the Estates-General (first meeting since 1614).
1789	The Estates-General meets but is hamstrung by voting procedures.	After an electoral campaign in which dossiers of grievances are amassed, the Estates-General meets, but the decision of one-vote-per-Estate angers the Third Estate, which vastly outnumbers the other two, but will now be outvoted.
June 1789	National Assembly is formed and recognized by king.	With the Tennis Court Oath, the Third Estate vows to form an assembly; defections from the First and Second cause the king to give in.
July 14, 1789	French workers and tradesmen storm the Bastille.	Louis XVI, afraid of the new Assembly and Paris workers, orders troops to surround both Versailles and Paris. This leads to the storming of Bastille! The fall of this hated symbol of royal power gives the Revolution its baptism of blood.
Summer 1789	"The Great Fear" sweeps the countryside, leading to the Night of Renunciation (August 4); the National Assembly issues the Declaration of Rights of Man and the Citizen.	Rumors of royal troops being sent to kill peasants cause peasants to storm chateaux and burn feudal documents. In response, nobles arise in the assembly on August 4 to renounce forever their feudal privileges, thus ending feudal order in France. On August 26, Declaration of Rights of Man and the Citizen makes France a constitutional monarchy.

(Continued)

1789–1790	The National Assembly confiscates church lands and issues the Civil Constitution of the Clergy.	To pay off the old war debt, the assembly orders the confiscation of church lands (cf.: Reformation) and issues *assignats* (bonds) using them as collateral. The Civil Constitution of the Clergy (1790) ties church to the state with wages and appointments; half the French clergy refuses to swear required oath and become "outlaws" (big mistake by Revolution).
1791	The royal family flees; German princes issue the Declaration of Pillnitz.	The royal family's attempts to reach the Austrian Netherlands and secure troops from Marie Antoinette's brother are thwarted when they are captured at Varennes, returned to Paris, and placed under house arrest. The German princes' declaration threatening invasion and sack of Paris if the royal family is hurt radicalizes the Revolution.
September 1792	The National Convention makes France a republic. French forces defeat German and Austrian troops at the battle of Valmy.	The National Convention, elected through universal male suffrage, votes death to the monarchy; on the same day, a French army with many raw recruits beats the professional forces of German princes, signaling a victory for the concept of a citizen-army.
1792–1793	Revolution at war! France declares war on Austria and invades the Austrian Netherlands and Rhineland.	The Revolution is now bent on exporting its ideals via the sword and cannon; also, September massacres in Paris illustrate the growing fear of spies and *aristos*.
1793–1794	France is seized by the Reign of Terror!	Maximilien Robespierre, as head of the Committee of Public Safety, and his associate Saint-Just inaugurate the Terror to root out spies and counter-revolutionaries. Tens of thousands, most of whom are innocent of the charges against them, are guillotined.
1795–1799	The five-man Directory becomes the executive office of the government, after the fall of Robespierre.	The Directory permits the White Terror against revolutionaries. Corruption and excess characterize the Directory's rule.
1796–1799	Revolutionary armies invade Italy, Holland, Egypt.	Often under general Napoleon Bonaparte, armies take the Revolution to Holland, Switzerland, north Italy, and even to Egypt, where the British navy routs the French. Napoleon leaves troops to certain death in Egypt and Palestine to return to Paris to foil a coup.

1798	William Wordsworth and Samuel Taylor Coleridge publish *Lyrical Ballads*.	Wordsworth and Coleridge, in a famous preface, announce the agenda and ideals of English romantics: natural language, clearly expressed feelings, and so on.
November 9, 1799	Napoleon joins other conspirators and stages the coup of 18 *Brumaire*.	After the overthrow of the Directory, Napoleon becomes the First (and only) Consul ruling France.
1801	Napoleon and the church come to terms in the Concordat.	Rome recognizes France and renounces claims demanding the return of church lands; Napoleon grants to the church the supervision of French schools.
1804	Napoleon institutes reforms.	Code Napoleon revises laws and regularizes them; careers are now open to merit rather than birth; and a secular school system is founded, with new attention to math and sciences (polytechnics).
1805–1807	France wages the Napoleonic Wars.	After making himself emperor, Napoleon renews wars with Europe. Though defeated at Trafalgar, he scores victories at Austerlitz, Jena, and Friedland. The Treaty of Tilsit nearly destroys Prussia, and neutralizes Russia.
1806–1811	Napoleon imposes the Continental Blockade on all his conquests and satellite states.	Napoleon sets up the blockade to punish England, but England merely switches trade to the Americas. Napoleon's actions alienate German princes and Russia.
1808/1812	Napoleon commits his greatest military blunders.	The invasion of Spain in 1808 and of Russia in 1812 overstretch France's resources and lead to Napoleon's defeat at the battle of Leipzig, October 1813.
1814–1815	Congress of Vienna meets.	England, Austria, Russia, and Prussia meet to decide Napoleon's fate. His Hundred Days intervene, ended by Waterloo. Then France, represented by Charles-Maurice de Talleyrand-Périgord, joins the other countries to redraw the map of Europe based on balance of power, legitimacy, and a conservative acceptance of Napoleon's changes.

The Postwar Settlement: The Congress of Vienna (1814–1815)

The Congress of Vienna met in 1814 and 1815 to redraw the map of Europe after Napoleon, and provide some way of preserving the peace. While Europe was spared a general war through the remainder of the nineteenth century, the failure of the statesmen who shaped its future in 1815 to recognize the forces unleashed by the French Revolution, such as nationalism and liberalism, only postponed the ultimate confrontation between two views of the world: change and accommodation versus maintaining the status quo.

The "Big Four" Meet the Wily Fifth

The Vienna settlement was the work of representatives of the four nations that had done the most to defeat Napoleon: Austria, England, Prussia, and Russia:

Klemens, Prince Metternich. Representing Austria, Metternich epitomized conservative views. He resisted change and was generally unfavorable to ideas of liberals and reformers because of the impact such forces would have on the multinational Habsburg Empire; but he was willing to recognize unavoidable changes from the previous years.

Robert Stewart, Lord Castlereagh. As England's representative, Stewart saw his principal objective as achieving a balance of power on the Continent by surrounding France with larger and stronger states.

Karl von Hardenberg. As chancellor of Prussia, Hardenberg sought to recover Prussian territory lost to Napoleon in 1807 and gain additional territory in northern Germany (all of the rebel kingdom of Saxony).

Tsar Alexander I. Representing Russia, Alexander was a mercurial figure who vacillated between liberal and reactionary views. The one specific "nonnegotiable" goal he advanced was a "free" and "independent" Poland, with himself as its king.

Joining the Big Four was Charles-Maurice de Talleyrand-Périgord, who represented disgraced France, his fat king, and the sweet life before 1789. With a club foot, like that of the poet Lord Byron, he managed with great charm to betray every master from Louis XVI to Napoleon for gain and power. Napoleon once called him "a sack of crap in a silk stocking." But he was as good a diplomat as Metternich. Though Talleyrand, as foreign minister, was left out of early deliberations, he became a mediator when interests of Prussia and Russia clashed with those of England and Austria. He thereby brought France into the deliberating elite.

The "Dancing Congress"

This gathering of Europe's princes and princelings was held amid much pageantry. Parties, balls, and extramarital dalliances were intended to generate favorable opinion and occupy the lesser delegates, since they had little of note to do.

Principles of Settlement

Legitimacy

"Legitimacy" meant returning to power most of the ruling families deposed by more than two decades of revolutionary warfare. The Bourbons were restored in France, Spain, and Naples; old dynasties to Holland, Sardinia, Tuscany, and Modena; and the pope to his states. But Metternich allowed the 1803 reorganization of the now-defunct Holy Roman Empire to stand, even though his family was one of the many that thereby lost power and lands. He also recognized the new king of Sweden, a French general named Bernadotte.

Compensation

"Compensation" meant territorial rewards to states that had made sacrifices to defeat Napoleon. England received far-flung naval bases (Malta, Ceylon, and Cape of Good Hope). Austria recovered the Italian province of Lombardy and was awarded adjacent Venetia as well as Galicia (from Poland), and the Illyrian Provinces along the Adriatic. Russia was given most of Poland, with the tsar as king, as well as Finland and Bessarabia. Prussia was awarded the Rhineland, three-fifths of Saxony and part of Poland. Sweden was given Norway. Talleyrand brokered the important Poland-Saxon trade-off.

Balance of Power

"Balance of power" meant arranging the map of Europe so that never again could one state, such as France, upset the international order and cause a general war.

Delegates achieved the encirclement of France through several measures:

- A new kingdom of Holland was created uniting Belgium (Austrian Netherlands) to the old United Provinces, now a much larger state north of France.

- Prussia received Rhenish lands bordering the eastern French frontier.

- Switzerland received a guarantee of perpetual neutrality.

- Austria received control over the Germanies through the new German Confederation (the Bund) of thirty-nine states, with Austria always president of the Diet of the Confederation

- Piedmont-Sardinia had its former territory restored, with the addition of Genoa.

Enforcement Provisions (Concert of Europe)

Arrangements to guarantee the enforcement of the status quo as defined by the Vienna settlement now included two provisions. The "Holy Alliance" of Czar Alexander of Russia, an idealistic and unpractical plan, existed only on paper; no one except Alexander took it seriously. The "Quadruple Alliance" of Austria, England, Prussia, and Russia provided for concerted action to stop any threat to the peace or balance of power.

England defined concerted action as the "Great Powers" meeting in "congress" to solve each problem as it arose, so that no state would act unilaterally and independently of the other great powers. France was always believed to be the possible "repeat offender" and next violator of the Vienna settlement.

Austria believed concerted action meant the great powers defending the status quo as established at Vienna against any change or threat to the system. Thus, liberal or nationalist agitation was unhealthy for the body politic.

Congress System

From 1815 to 1822, European international relations were controlled by meetings held by the great powers to defend the status quo: the Congresses of Aix-la-Chapelle (1818), Troppau (1820), Laibach (1821), and Verona (1822).

The principle of collective security required unanimity among members of the Quadruple Alliance. The history of the Congress System points to the ultimate failure of this key provision in light of the serious challenges to the status quo after 1815.

Evaluation

The Congress of Vienna has been criticized for ignoring the liberal and nationalist aspirations of many peoples. Hindsight suggests that statesmen at Vienna may have been more successful in stabilizing the international system than those charged with the same task in the twentieth century. Not until the unification of Germany (1870–1871) was the balance of power upset; not until World War I in 1914 did Europe have another general war. But hindsight also instructs us that the statesmen at Vienna underestimated the new nationalism generated by the French Revolution and did not understand the change that citizen armies and national wars had affected among people concerning political problems. In addition, the men at Vienna in 1815 underestimated the growing liberalism of the age and failed to see that an industrial revolution was beginning to create a new alignment of social classes, with new needs and issues.

The Industrial Revolution

In the late nineteenth century, the English historian Arnold Toynbee began to refer to the period since 1754 as "the Industrial Revolution." The term was intended to describe a time of transition when machines began to significantly displace human and animal power in methods of producing and distributing goods.

These changes began slowly, almost imperceptibly, gaining momentum with each decade, so that by the midpoint of the nineteenth century, industrialism had swept across Europe west to east, from England to eastern Europe. Few countries avoided industrialization, because of its promise of material improvement and national wealth.

The economic changes that constitute the Industrial Revolution have done more than any other movement in Western civilization to revolutionize life, by imparting to the world's cultures a uniqueness never before, or perhaps since, matched or duplicated.

England Begins the Revolution in Energy and Industry

Essentially, the Industrial Revolution describes a process of economic change from an agricultural and commercial society into a modern industrial society. This was a gradual process, where economic, social, and political changes nonetheless produced a veritable revolution, which Arnold Toynbee was the first to identify. He placed the origins of this remarkable transition in England.

Roots of the Industrial Revolution could be found in (1) the Commercial Revolution (1500–1700) that spurred the great economic growth of Europe brought about by the Age of Exploration, which in turn helped to solidify the economic doctrines of mercantilism; (2) the effect of the Scientific Revolution, which produced the first wave of mechanical inventions and technological advances; (3) the increase in population in Europe from 140 million people in 1750 to 266 million people by the mid-nineteenth century (more producers, more consumers); and (4) the political and social revolutions of the nineteenth century, which began the rise to power of the middle classes, and provided leadership for the economic revolution.

England began this economic transformation by employing her unique assets:

1. A supply of cheap labor, the result of the enclosure movement that robbed yeomen farmers of land, so that some agricultural laborers were now available for hire in the new industrial towns, though many remained in the countryside as dependent laborers

2. A good supply of coal and iron, indispensable for the growth of industry and energy

3. The availability of large supplies of capital from profitable commercial activity in the preceding centuries, ready to be invested in new enterprises

4. A class of inventive people who possessed technological skill, and whose independence and nonconformity allowed them to take risks

5. Ready access—thanks to its position as a colonial and maritime power—to the raw materials needed for the development of many industries

6. A government whose Whig party was especially sympathetic to industrial development, with established financial institutions ready to make loans available

7. A wartime record of success that left England unharmed and free to develop new industries, which even prospered from economic dislocations caused by the Napoleonic Wars

Early Progress

The revolution, if it may be so called, fed on scarcities, bottleneck frustrations in manufacturing processes, problems in transportation, and other examples that Necessity is indeed the mother of Invention. One early improvement may suffice: Abraham Darby needed to transport coal to his iron mine nine miles away; coal, turned into coke, was the new means to smelt iron. Carts dragged over roads were slow and laborious. He came up with the brilliant idea of laying tracks for the cart's wheels to glide along. This was 1709. Note that the need to replace wood as an energy source led to the use of coal, and its byproduct, coke, which increased coal mining and resulted in the invention of the steam engine and the locomotive as inventions that sought to solve practical problems.

Other innovations occurred in the cotton and metallurgical industries, because those industries lent themselves most easily to mechanization. Mechanical inventions beginning in 1733, lasting until 1793, enabled the cotton industry to mass-produce quality goods.

The development of steam power allowed the cotton industry to expand and transformed the iron industry. The factory system, created in response to new energy sources and machinery, was perfected to increase the amount of manufactured goods.

A transportation revolution ensued in order to distribute productive machinery as well as deliver raw materials to the eager factories. This led to the growth of canals, the construction of hard-surfaced "macadam" roads, the commercial use of the steamboat demonstrated by Robert Fulton, and the railway locomotive made commercially successful by George Stephenson.

Subsequent revolution in agriculture made it possible for fewer people to feed all, thus freeing people to work in factories or in the many new fields of communications, distribution of goods, or services like teaching, medicine, and entertainment.

Spread of Industrialization to Europe and the World

During the first fifty years of the nineteenth century, industrialization swept across Europe west to east, from England to eastern Europe. In its wake, all modes of life would be challenged and transformed.

Challenges to the Spread of Industrialism

Continental economic growth had been retarded by the Napoleonic Wars.

Because England was so technically advanced, European countries found it difficult to compete. However, catching up to England was made easy by avoiding the costly mistakes of early British experiments and by using the power of strong central governments and national banks to promote native industry. But on the Continent there was no large labor supply in cities; iron and coal deposits were not as concentrated as in England, except in a few places (Ruhr, Saar, Silesia, Lorraine, and so on).

Route of Industrialization

England was the undisputed economic and industrial leader until the mid-nineteenth century. The industrialization of the Continent occurred mostly in the latter half of the nineteenth century, and, in the southern and eastern regions, in the twentieth century.

By 1830, industrialism had begun to spread from England to Belgium, France, and other areas. These successful industrial operations were due to the exportation from

England of machines, management, and capital. Germany was slower in following English methods until a tariff policy was established in 1834 (the *Zollverein*), which induced capital investment by and in German manufacturers.

Growth of Industrial Society

The undermining of Western society's traditional social structure (that is, clergy, nobility, and commoners) was the result of the Industrial Revolution.

The Bourgeoisie: The New Plutocracy

The middle class was the major contributor as well as principal beneficiary of early industrialism. Those of the middle class measured success in monetary terms and tended to be indifferent to the human suffering of the new wage-earning class. The industrial bourgeoisie had two levels: (1) upper bourgeoisie, that is, great bankers, merchants, and industrialists who demanded free enterprise and tariffs; and (2) lower bourgeoisie, that is, small industrialists, merchants, and professional men who demanded stability and security from government.

To the chagrin of traditionalists, increasing numbers of the old aristocracy of birth intermarried with wealthy bourgeois, thus forming the nucleus of a new plutocracy. The new upper class, long a fact in British society, began to infiltrate, and later rule, society in France, north Italy, Belgium, the Germanies, Austria—in other words, areas where industry was making strides and society was already in ferment.

The Factory Worker: The New Wage-Earning Class

The Industrial Revolution created a unique category of people dependent on their job alone for income, a job from which they might be dismissed without cause. The factory worker had no land, no home, and no source of income but his job. During the first century of the Industrial Revolution, the factory worker was completely at the mercy of the law of supply and demand for labor.

Working in the factory meant more self-discipline and less personal freedom for workers. The system tended to depersonalize society and reduced workers to an impersonal status. The statistics with regard to wages, diet, and clothing suggest overall improvement for the workers, with some qualifications, since some industries were notoriously guilty of social injustices. Contemporary social critics complained that industrialism brought misery to the workers, while others claimed life was improving. Until 1850, workers as a whole did not share in the wealth produced by the Industrial Revolution. Matters improved as the century advanced, as union action combined with general prosperity and a developing social conscience to improve working conditions, wages, and hours first of skilled labor, and later of unskilled labor.

Social Effects of Industrialization

The most important social result of industrialism was increased urbanization. New factories acted as a magnet, pulling people away from rural roots to achieve the most massive population transfer in history; thus were born the factory towns and cities that grew into large industrial centers.

The role of the city changed in the nineteenth century from manageable governmental and market centers to large industrial centers with all the problems of urbanization.

Workers in cities became aware of their numbers and common problems, so cities made the working class a powerful force by raising their consciousness and enabling them to unite for political action, often to remedy their economic dissatisfaction. It is in this urban setting that the century's great social and political dilemmas were framed: working class injustices, gender exploitation, and standard-of-living issues.

Family structure and gender roles in the family were altered by industrialism. Families as an economic unit were no longer tied to both production and consumption, but to consumption alone. New wage economy meant that families were less closely bound together than in the past; the economic link was broken. Productive work was taken out of the home and sent elsewhere. As factory wages for skilled adult males rose, women and children were separated from the old workplaces. A new pattern of family life emerged. Until mid-century, women and children continued to work, but not always where men worked.

Gender-determined roles in the home and domestic life emerged slowly. Married women came to be associated with domestic duties, while men tended to be the sole wage earner in the middle classes. Single women and widows had much work available, but that work commanded low wages and low skills and provided no protection from exploitation.

Marriage as an institution economy began to change. Women were now expected to create a nurturing environment to which family members returned after work. Married women worked outside the home when family needs, illness, or death of a spouse required. The leading mode of employment for working women in the nineteenth century was in domestic service; work on farms probably came second; third, work in factories and workhouses.

Evaluation

The Industrial Revolution harnessed water power, coal, oil, and electricity, all of which now replaced more and more human work. The amount of wealth available for consumption increased. Vast amounts of food, clothing, and energy were produced and distributed to workers of the world. Luxuries were made accessible, life expectancy increased, and leisure time became more enjoyable.

But workers would not begin to share in this dramatic increase in the standard of living until the second half of the nineteenth century, when evils associated with the factory system (low wages, poor working conditions, and so forth) were addressed. In the first century of industrialism, the wealth created went almost exclusively to entrepreneurs and the owners of capital—the upper and middle classes.

Impact of Ideologies or "Isms" on Europe

The mindset of Western civilization was challenged in the first half of the nineteenth century by the appearance of new thought systems. Moving beyond the Enlightenment, men sought to catalog, classify, and categorize their thoughts and beliefs. Several systems of thought acted as agents of change in the nineteenth century, some continuing into the twentieth century to change and redefine the modern world.

Romanticism

Romanticism was a reaction to rigid classicism, rationalism, and deism. Strongest between 1800 and 1850, the Romantic movement differed from country to country, and from individual to individual. Because it emphasized change, it was considered revolutionary. It was an atmosphere in which events came to affect not only the way humans thought and expressed themselves, but also the way they lived socially and politically.

Characteristics

Romanticism appealed to emotion more than to reason (that is, truth and virtue can be found as much by the heart as the head). It rejected classical emphasis on order and the observance of rules (that is, let the imagination create new forms and techniques).

It also rejected the Enlightenment view of nature as a precise harmonious whole (that is, nature is alive, vital, changing, filled with the divine spirit), as well as the cold, impersonal ideas of deism (that is, it viewed God as inspiring nobility of soul and deplored the decline of Christianity).

Romanticism rejected the enlightened view of the past, which ran afoul of real human history (that is, it viewed the world as an organism that was growing and changing with each nation's history unique); it expressed optimism about life and the future.

Romantics enriched European cultural life by encouraging personal freedom and flexibility. By emphasizing feeling, they enabled humanitarian movements to form and fight slavery, poverty, and industrial evils.

Romantic Literature, Art, Music, and Philosophy

The English Romantics William Wordsworth and Samuel Taylor Coleridge epitomized the movement, along with Robert Burns; George Gordon, Lord Byron; John Keats; Percy Bysshe Shelley; Alfred, Lord Tennyson; and Sir Walter Scott. The greatest German figures were Johann Wolfgang von Goethe, Heinrich Heine, Johann Gottfried von Herder, and Friedrich von Schiller. French romantics were Honoré de Balzac, Alexandre Dumas, Victor Hugo, and Stendhal (aka Henri Beyle). The outstanding Russian exponents were Aleksandr Pushkin and Nikolay Gogol.

The leading romantic painters in popular taste were the Frenchman Jacques-Louis David, the Englishmen Turner and John C. Constable, and the Spaniard Francisco G. Goya. Examples of their work shown in Figure 6-2 show how romanticism can never be conceived as a monolithic movement.

One side of romantic art, then, preferred the dreamy, religious, nature-worshipping self; the other found fodder in violence, death, disaster, and patriotic remembrance, as can be seen in the paintings of Goya, Gericault, Turner, and Delacroix (see Figure 6-3).

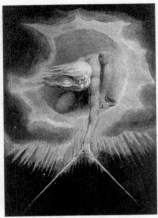

Musée du Louvre, Paris, France

British Museum, London, England

Nationalgalerie, Berlin, Germany

Musée du Louvre, Paris, France

Figure 6-2. David's *Oath of the Horatii* (1784) (top, left) may be neoclassical, but here we also see how the recently revived melodrama adds emotionalism to a classical subject from Livy. William Blake's *Ancient of Days* (1794) (top, right) shows a religious fervor in the movement, as Caspar David Friedrich in his *Two Men Looking at the Moon* (1819) (bottom, left) typifies the romantic obsession with sublime landscapes and lone reveries. Madame Vigée LeBrun, the first modern woman to practice painting as a profession, shows the romantic exaltation of a work by another woman, Madame de Stael's *Corinne* (1807), as seen through her eyes in her painting of 1808 (bottom, right).

Music did not change as dramatically as did literature. Composers still observed the classical forms, but began incorporating new ideas and innovations. Ludwig van Beethoven was a transitional figure for pure romantics, such as Hector Berlioz, Fryderyk Chopin, Franz Schubert, Robert Schumann, and Karl Maria von Weber.

Romantic philosophy stimulated an interest in idealism, the belief that reality consists of ideas, as opposed to materialism. This school of thought (philosophical idealism), founded by Plato, was developed through the writings of:

1. Immanuel Kant, whose work *Critique of Pure Reason* advanced the theory that reality was twofold—physical and spiritual. Reason can discover what is true in the physical, but not in the spiritual, world.

Prado Museum, Madrid, Spain

Musée du Louvre, Paris, France

The National Gallery, London, England

Musée du Louvre, Paris, France

Figure 6-3. Goya's *The Third of May* (1808) (top, left) shows the inhumanity of the Napoleonic war-machine as it mowed down Spanish insurgents. Theodore Gericault's famous *Raft of the Medusa* (1818) (top, right) shows both the despair and the desperate hopes attendant upon a shipwreck. J.M.W. Turner's wistful *Fighting Temeraire* (1839) (bottom, left) shows the passing of a great ship from the Napoleonic Wars, destined for dry dock amid the new squalor of industry. Eugene Delacroix's sumptuous *Death of Sardanapalus* (1827) (bottom, right) depicts not only the horror of a massacre, but also the Byronic disdain and boredom of the sated monarch.

2. Johann Gottlieb Fichte, a disciple of Kant, and Friedrich Schelling, collaborator of Fichte. Fichte is considered a great egotist among the Idealists (the "I" is all), whereas Schelling was the great religious mystic, one sought out by the future King Max of Bavaria for inspiration.

3. Georg Wilhelm Hegel, its greatest exponent. Hegel believed that an impersonal God rules the universe and guides humans along a progressive evolutionary course by means of dialectic, a process by which one thing is constantly reacting with its opposite (the thesis and antithesis), producing a result (synthesis), that automatically meets another opposite and continues the series of reactions. Hegel's philosophy exerted a great influence on Karl Marx, who turned the Hegelian dialectic upside down to demonstrate that the ultimate meaning of reality was a material end, not a higher or spiritual end, as Hegel suggested.

Impact

Romanticism challenged the clear simplicity and unity of thought that had characterized the eighteenth century. A single philosophy no longer expressed all the aims and ideals of Western civilization. Romanticism provided a more complex, perhaps truer, view of the real world, but it in turn would be challenged for its excesses in the subsequent realist and impressionist movements.

Conservatism

Conservatism arose in reaction to the violence, terror, and disorder unleashed by the French Revolution. Early conservatism was allied to the restored monarchical governments of Austria, France, and Russia. Support for conservatism came from the traditional ruling classes. Intellectual ammunition came from the pens of the Englishman Edmund Burke, the Frenchmen Joseph de Maistre and Louis de Bonald, the Austrian Friedrich von Gentz, and several early romantics. In essence, conservatives believed in order, society and the state, faith, and tradition.

Characteristics

Conservatives saw history as a continuum that no one generation could break. They believed society was organic, not contractual. Society was not a machine with replaceable parts. Stability and longevity, not progress and change, marked a good society. The only legitimate sources of political authority were God and history. Conservatives rejected social-contract theory (see Chapter 5) because contracts did not make authority legitimate.

Concentrating on individuals ignored social ties and undermined the concept of community, which was essential to life. Conservatives said self-interest lead to social conflict, not social harmony. They preferred *noblesse oblige*: help from on high.

Conservatives argued that measuring happiness and progress in material terms ignored the spiritual side of humans. Charity, mixed with moral injunctions, not revolution, was helpful.

Conservatives rejected the philosophy of natural rights and believed that rights did not pertain universally, but were determined and allocated by each state.

Conservatives denounced the *philosophes* and reformers for ignoring emotional realities and for underestimating the complexity of human nature. To conservatives, society was hierarchical, that is, some humans were better able to rule and lead than those who were denied intelligence, education, wealth, and birth. The motto of conservatives before the 1860s was "Throne and Altar."

Impact

Conservatism was basically "anti-" in its propositions. It never had a feasible program of its own. The object of their hatred was a liberal society, which they claimed was antisocial and morally degrading. While their criticisms contained much justification, conservatives ignored the positive features of liberal society. Conservative criticism did poke holes in liberal ideology, and pointed toward a new social tyranny, the aggressive and heartlessly selfish middle classes.

Liberalism

The theory of liberalism was the first in the history of Western thought to teach that the individual is a self-sufficient being, whose freedom and well-being are the sole reasons for the existence of society. Liberalism was more closely connected to the spirit and outlook of the Enlightenment than to other "isms" of the early nineteenth century. While the general principles and attitudes associated with liberalism varied considerably from country to country, liberals tended to come from the middle classes or bourgeoisie, and favored increased liberty for their class and, indirectly, for the masses of people, as long as the latter did not in turn ask for so much freedom that they endangered the security of the middle class. Liberalism was reformist and political rather than revolutionary.

Characteristics

Liberals held that individuals were entitled to seek their freedom in the face of arbitrary or tyrannical restrictions imposed upon them. Humans had certain natural rights, and governments should protect them. These rights included the right to own property, freedom of speech, freedom from excessive punishment, freedom of worship, and freedom of assembly.

Liberals further argued that these rights were best guaranteed by a written constitution, with careful definition of the limits to which governmental actions could go. Examples include the American Declaration of Independence (1776) and the French Declaration of Rights of Man (1789).

Another view of liberalism was presented by individuals who came to be known as the Utilitarians. Their founder, Jeremy Bentham, held the pleasure-pain principle as the key idea—that humans were ordained to avoid pain and to seek pleasure. He equated pleasure with good, pain with evil. The good or bad of any act, individual, or group, was found by balancing the pleasure against pain it caused. Thus, one came to test the utility of any proposed law or institution, that is, "the greatest happiness of the greatest number."

Liberals advocated economic individualism (that is, laissez-faire capitalism), heralded by Adam Smith in his 1776 masterpiece, *Wealth of Nations*. They regarded free enterprise as the most productive economy, and the one that allowed for the greatest measure of individual choice.

Economic inequality will exist and is acceptable, liberals held, because it does not detract from the individual's moral dignity, nor does it conflict with equality of opportunity and equality before the law.

Economic liberalism claimed to be based on the realities of a new industrial era. The "classical economists" (Thomas Malthus and David Ricardo) taught that there were inescapable forces at work—competition, the pressure of population growth, the iron law of wages, and the law of supply and demand—in accordance with which economic life must function. It was the duty of government to remove any obstacle to the smooth operation of these natural forces.

On the international level, liberals supported the balance-of-power system and free trade, because each track allowed individual nations the opportunity to determine its own course of action.

Liberals believed in the pluralistic society, as long as it did not block progress. War and revolutionary change, they argued, disrupted progress and enlarged the power of government.

Education was an indispensable prerequisite to individual responsibility and self-government. Until later in the century, most liberals felt that the vote and other civic rights depended on one's stake in society and one's abilities to understand public affairs, which boiled down to the need to own property (especially land) and to be educated.

Early Nineteenth Century Advocates of Liberalism

In England, liberals included political economists, Utilitarians, and individuals like Thomas Babington Macaulay and John Stuart Mill; in France, Benjamin Constant, Victor Cousin, Jean Baptiste Say, and Alexis de Tocqueville; in Germany, Wilhelm von Humboldt, Friedrich List, Karl von Rotteck, and Karl Theodor Welcker.

Impact

Liberalism contributed to the various revolutionary movements of the early nineteenth century. It found concrete expression in over ten constitutions secured between 1815 and 1848 in states of the German Confederation. Its power was demonstrated in the reform measures that successive British governments adopted during these same decades. It affected German student organizations and permeated Prussian public life.

Alexis de Toqueville spoke for many liberals when he warned against the masses' passion for equality, and their willingness to sacrifice political liberty in order to improve their material well-being. These fears were not without foundation. In the twentieth and twenty-first centuries, the masses have often shown themselves willing to trade freedom for authority, order, economic security, and national power. For instance, laws passed in the United States since the 9/11 terrorism attacks reflect the willingness of citizens to sacrifice liberty for security.

Nationalism

The regenerative force of liberal thought in early nineteenth century Europe was revealed in the explosive force of nationalism. Nationalism raised the level of consciousness of people having a common language, common soil, common traditions, a common history, a common culture, and a shared human experience, to seek political unity around an identity of what or who constitutes the nation. The French revolutionary era roused and made militant often dormant nationalist germs not only in conquering France, but also in conquered or threatened Spain, Austria, Germany, Poland, and Russia.

Characteristics

Early nationalist sentiment was romantic, exuberant, and cosmopolitan, as opposed to the more intense, hate-filled nationalism of the latter half of the nineteenth century.

The breakdown of society's traditional loyalties to church, dynasties, and region began during the eighteenth century. Impelled by revolutionary dogma, nationalists advocated new loyalties—that people possessed the supreme power (sovereignty) of the nation and were, therefore, the true nation united by common language, culture, history, and so on. Only then would people develop the sense of pride, tradition, and common purpose that would come to characterize modern nationalism.

Nationalism, conceived as loyalty to one's nation, did not originate in the early nineteenth century. People had been fighting for, and living and dying for, their countries for ages (and still are today). It wasn't until the early nineteenth century that this feeling evolved into something more intense and more demanding than it had been. The focus of the loyalty changed from dynastic self-interest to individual self-interest as part of a greater collective consciousness.

Impact

Nationalist writers examined the language, literature, and folkways of their people, thereby stimulating nationalist feelings. Emphasizing the history and culture of all European peoples tended to reinforce and glorify national sentiment.

Most early nineteenth-century nationalist leaders adopted the ideas of the German philosopher-historian, Johann Gottfried Herder (1744–1803), who is regarded as the father of modern nationalism.

Herder taught that every person is unique and possesses a distinct national character, or *Volksgeist*, which evolved over many centuries; no one culture or person is superior to any other; and all national groups are parts of that greater whole, humanity.

Herder's doctrine of the indestructible *Volksgeist* led to a belief that every nation had the right to become a sovereign state encompassing all members of the same nationality. Since most western states contained people of many different nationalities, and few states contained all the members of any one nationality, nationalism came to imply, for radicals, the overthrow of almost every existing government.

Evaluation

Because of its inherently revolutionary tenets, nationalism was suppressed by the established authorities. Yet it flourished in Germany, where conservative and reactionary nationalists competed with a more liberal nationalism associated with intellectuals like Johann Gottlieb Fichte, Georg Wilhelm Hegel, Wilhelm von Humboldt, and Leopold von Ranke. In eastern Europe, conservative nationalists stressed the value of their unique customs and folkways, while western nationalists demanded liberal political reforms. The influence of the Italian nationalist Giuseppe Mazzini and the

French nationalist Jules Michelet in stimulating nationalist feeling in the West was a key ingredient.

It should be noted that there was always a fundamental conflict between liberalism and nationalism. Liberals were rationalists who demanded objectivity in studying society and history, while nationalists relied on emotion and would do anything to exalt the nation, even subvert individual rights. By the late nineteenth century, nationalism was promoting competition and warfare between peoples and threatening to douse liberal ideas of reason and freedom.

Socialism

With the chief beneficiary of industrialism being the new middle class, the increasing misery of the working classes disturbed the conscience of concerned liberal thinkers (Bentham and Mill), who proposed a modification of the concept of laissez-faire economics. Other socially aware thinkers, observing the injustice and inefficiencies of capitalistic society, began to define the social question in terms of equality and the means to be followed in order to secure this goal. As cures for the social evils of industrialism were laid out in detail, the emerging dogma came to be called socialism.

Characteristics

Since biblical times, men have worried about social justice, but it was not until the nineteenth century that it possessed a broader intellectual base and a greater popular support than it had enjoyed in the past. The difficulty with the existing system, according to social critics, was that it permitted wealth to be concentrated in the hands of small elite of persons and deprived workers of a just share in what was rightfully theirs. A social mechanism had to be developed so that a just distribution of society's wealth could be attained. The result was a variety of approaches.

The Utopian Socialists (from *Utopia,* Thomas More's ideal of society; see Chapter 2) were the earliest to propose an equitable solution to improve the distribution of society's wealth. While they endorsed the productive capacity of industrialism, they denounced its mismanagement. Society was to be organized as a community rather than a clash of competing, selfish individuals. All the goods a person needed could be produced in one community.

Generally, Utopians advocated some kind of harmonious society, some form of model community, social workshops, or the like, where the ruthless qualities of an individualistic capitalism would disappear.

Utopian ideas were generally regarded as idealistic and visionary, with no practical application. With little popular support from the political establishment or the working classes, the movement failed to produce any substantial solution to the social question. Leading Utopians were Henri de Saint-Simon (1760–1825), Charles Fourier (1772–1837), Robert Owen (1771–1858), and Louis Blanc (1811–1882).

Anarchists rejected industrialism and the dominance of government. Auguste Blanqui (1805–1881) advocated terrorism as a means to end capitalism and the state.

Pierre Joseph Proudhon (1809–1865) attacked the principle of private property because it denied justice to the common people.

Christian Socialism began in England circa 1848. Believing that the evils of industrialism would be ended by following Christian principles, the advocates of this doctrine tried to bridge the gap between the antireligious drift of socialism and the need for Christian social justice for workers. The best-known Christian Socialist was the novelist Charles Kingsley (1814–1875), whose writings exposed the social evils of industrialism. Later, in Austria, Christian Socialism took a sinister, racist turn.

"Scientific" Socialism, or Marxism, was the creation of Karl Marx (1818–1883), a German scholar who, with the help of Friedrich Engels (1820–1895), intended to replace utopian hopes and dreams with a brutal, militant blueprint for socialist working-class success. The principal works of this revolutionary school of socialism were *The Communist Manifesto* and *Das Kapital* (*Capital*).

The theory of dialectical materialism enabled Marx to explain history. By borrowing Hegel's dialectic (discussed earlier), substituting materialism and realism in place of Hegel's idealism, and inverting the methodological process, Marx was able to justify his theoretical conclusions.

Marxism formulated key propositions:

1. The economic interpretation of history, that is, all history has been determined by economic factors (mainly who controls the means of production and distribution).

2. The class struggle, that is, throughout history, there has been a struggle between rich and poor, or exploiters and the exploited.

3. The theory of surplus value, that is, the true value of a product is labor and, since the worker receives a small portion of his just labor price, the difference is surplus value, "stolen" from him by the capitalist.

4. Socialism is inevitable, that is, capitalism contains the seeds of its own demise (overproduction, unemployment, and so on); the rich grow richer, the poor poorer, until the gap between classes (proletariat and bourgeoisie) is so great that workers will rise up in revolt and overthrow the bourgeoisie to install a "dictatorship of the proletariat." As modern capitalism is dismantled, the creation of a classless society guided by the principle "From each according to his abilities, to each according to his needs" will take place.

Evaluation

Ideologies (isms) are interpretations of the world from a particular viewpoint. They are, or imply, programs of action, and thrive where belief in general standards and norms has broken down. The proliferation of thought systems, and movements based on them, after 1815 suggests that the basic division of society at that time was between those who accepted the implications of the intellectual, economic, and political revolutions of the eighteenth and early nineteenth centuries, and those who did not. Polarization in ideology was the result.

Europe in Crisis (1815–1833): Repression, Reform, and Revolution

The peace settlement crafted by the Congress of Vienna signaled the triumph of the conservative order, socially and politically. Dangerous ideas (liberalism and nationalism) associated with the French Revolution and Napoleonic period had been "contained" by the territorial provisions of the 1815 agreement. The status quo had been once again defined. Order and stability were to be expected from the European state system.

Underestimating the power of ideas, conservative leaders after 1815 faced a dramatic confrontation between those sponsoring the "new" ideas (which required political change) and those of the traditional ruling classes, reluctant to make any accommodation with the believers in "new" ideas. The result in most states was government-sponsored repression followed by revolution. Few states chose to answer the call for liberal reform. Only nationalist impulses in Greece and Belgium were successful, for reasons that hardly comforted liberals. The intellectual climate of romanticism provided a volatile atmosphere in which these events unfolded, because this artistic and historical movement strangely accommodated warring political ideologies, from liberal to reactionary.

Postwar Repression (1815–1820)

Initially, the great powers followed the lead of the Austrian statesman Prince Metternich (1773–1859) in suppressing any expression of liberal faith. Most leaders attempted to reinstitute conservative means of governmental control, in order to prevent reforms that would further increase people's participation in government. The literate middle class, supported by urban workers, demanded reform, and at least the latter group was willing to use violence to obtain it.

England

The Tory (conservative) government that defeated Napoleon was in control of England. Facing serious economic problems that had produced large numbers of industrial unemployed, the conservatives tried to follow a reactionary policy.

The Corn Law of 1815 effectively halted the importation of cheaper foreign grains, aiding the Tory landholding aristocracy, but increasing the cost of bread, and driving the poor and unemployed to protest and demand parliamentary reform.

The Coercion Acts of 1817 suspended habeas corpus for the first time in English history, provided for arbitrary arrest and punishment, and drastically curtailed freedom of the press and public mass meetings.

The Peterloo Massacre of 1819 occurred when members of a large crowd, who were listening to reformers demand repeal of the Corn Laws and other changes, were killed, with hundreds of others injured when police authorities broke up the meeting.

The Six Acts of Parliament in 1819, in response to Peterloo, were a series of repressive measures that attempted to remove the instruments of agitation from the hands of radical leaders and to provide the authorities with new powers.

The Cato Street Conspiracy of 1820 took place when a group of extreme radicals plotted to blow up the entire British cabinet. (This has been a recurring threat in English politics, from the Gunpowder Plot of 1605 to attempts on the life of Margaret Thatcher in the 1980s.) It provided new support for repression by the Tories, as well as discrediting the movement for parliamentary reform.

By 1820, England was on the road to becoming a reactionary, authoritarian state, when protests among younger Tories argued that such repressive legislation was not in the English tradition, and that the party itself might need to change its direction.

France

France emerged from the chaos of the revolutionary period (1789–1815) as the most liberal power on the Continent. The period from 1815 to 1830 is referred to as the Restoration, signifying the return of the legitimate royal dynasty of France—the Bourbons, who reputedly never learned and never forgot anything.

Louis XVIII (reigned 1814–1824) governed France as a constitutional monarch by agreeing to observe the "Charter" or constitution of the Restoration period. This moderate document managed to limit royal power, grant legislative powers, protect civil rights, and uphold the Code Napoleon and other pre-Restoration reforms.

Louis XVIII wished to unify the French, who were divided into those accepting the Revolution and those who did not. The leader of the refuseniks was the Count of Artois (1757–1836), brother of the king and leader of the ultra-royalists. The 1815 White Terror saw royalist mobs murder thousands of former revolutionaries.

New elections in 1816 for the Chamber of Deputies resulted in the ultra-royalists being rejected, in favor of a moderate royalist majority dependent on middle-class support. The war indemnity was paid off, France was admitted to the Quadruple Alliance (1818), and liberal sentiment began to grow.

In February 1820, the Duke of Berri, son of Artois and in line for the throne, was murdered. Royalists charged that liberals were responsible and that the king's policy of moderation had encouraged all of those on the left.

Louis XVIII began to move the government more to the right, as changes in the electoral laws restricted the franchise to the most wealthy, and censorship was imposed. Liberals were driven out of legal political life and into near-illegal activity. The triumph of Reaction came in 1823, when French troops were authorized by the Concert of Europe to crush the Spanish Revolution and restore another Bourbon ruler, Ferdinand VII.

Austria and the Germanies

Until his ouster in 1848, Prince Metternich ruled Austria and the German Confederation. He epitomized conservative ideology. To no other country or empire were the programs of liberalism and nationalism potentially more dangerous. Given the multiethnic composition of the Habsburg Empire, any recognition of the rights and aspirations of any national group would probably usher in the dissolution of the empire.

It was Napoleon who reduced more than three hundred German states to thirty-nine, and the Congress of Vienna that preserved this arrangement under Austrian domination. The purpose of the German Confederation (the Bund) was to guarantee the independence of member states and, by joint action, preserve German states from domestic disorder or revolution. A diet (an assembly) at Frankfurt acted as a diplomatic center presided over by Austria, as president.

The two largest states in the confederation were Austria and Prussia. Austria, through Metternich's antiliberal and nationalist pathology, held the line against any change in the status quo. Prussia followed suit in most matters, with the single exception being its leadership of the Customs Union (organized 1818–1834), in which Austria was not welcome. The century-old rivalry between Austria and Prussia bubbled underground.

Prussia was ruled by the Hohenzollerns, an aggressive royal family when it came to expanding the borders of this northern German state, sometimes at the expense of other German rulers. For a short time after 1815, liberals looked to Prussia as a leader of German liberalism because of reforms in government enacted after a humiliating defeat at the hands of Napoleon. However, these reforms were intended to improve the efficiency of government and were not the portent of a general trend. The Prussian government and its traditional ruling classes (*Junkers*) decided to follow the lead of Metternich in repressing liberal-nationalist agitation, despite the king's promise of a constitution in 1815.

Liberal-nationalist agitation was very vocal and visible in German universities in the first half of the nineteenth century. Student organizations, such as the *Burschenschaften*, openly promoted political arrangements that seemed radical-revolutionary. At the Wartburg Festival (1817), students burned symbols of authority. Such agitation continued until 1819, when a theology student, Karl Sand, a *Burschenschafiler*, stabbed to death Germany's most popular playwright, August von Kotzebue, because he was considered a bad moral influence on youth and was suspected of being a Russian agent (he did send long reports to the tsar, but this was hardly treason).

The Carlsbad Decrees (1819) were pushed through by Metternich to end seditious activity by German liberals and nationalists. The supplementary Vienna Act of 1820 even provided that any prince offended by opinions or actions in another principality could use the machinery of the Confederation to prosecute the offending prince.

Russia

From 1801 to 1825, Tsar Alexander I governed in traditional authoritarian style. A man of many moods, this Russian emperor thought he was called upon to lead Europe into a new age of benevolence and good will. After the Congress of Vienna, he became increasingly reactionary, mystically Christian, and subservient to Metternich.

Alexander was torn between an attraction to the ideas of the Enlightenment and reform, and a very pragmatic adherence to traditional Russian autocracy (absolutism).

With the help of a liberal adviser, Mihkail Speransky, the tsar made plans to liberalize Russian government, owing to the tsar's admiration for Napoleon's administrative genius. But such liberal policies alienated the nobility, so Speransky was dismissed in 1812.

Alexander came to regard the Enlightenment, the French Revolution, and Napoleon in biblical terms, seeing all as anti-Christian. Turning to a reactionary adviser, General Arakcheev, he let loose the dogs of repression. His regime would tolerate no opposition or criticism. The early years of possible liberal reform had given way to conservative repression.

Revolutions I (1820–1829)

Nationalism, liberalism, and socialism were all factors in the outbreak of revolution in the first half of the nineteenth century. All three isms were opposed by conservative groups (royalists, clergy, landed aristocracy) rooted in the way of life before the Revolution. Promoting forces of change was a younger generation, the heirs of the Enlightenment who believed in progress.

The International System: The Concert of Europe

At the 1815 Congress of Vienna, enforcement provisions of the settlement were designed to guarantee stability and peace in the international arena. The Quadruple Alliance (Austria, England, Prussia, and Russia) that had defeated Napoleon was to continue through a new spirit of cooperation and consultation that would be referred to as the "Concert of Europe." At the suggestion of Lord Castlereagh, Britain's foreign minister, foreign policy issues affecting the international order would be worked out in meetings or congresses so that no one nation could act without the consent of the others. But under the leadership of Metternich, the congress system became a means to preserve the political status quo of autocracy in Europe against all ideas. The congress system was short-lived because continental powers could not always agree on cooperative action, and the English refused to support interference in the domestic affairs of nation-states. In the end, each nation became guided by its own best interests.

The Congress System of Conferences

The Congress of Aix-la-Chapelle (1818) arranged for the withdrawal of the allied army of occupation from France, and the admission of France into the Concert of Europe (resulting in the Quintuple Alliance). The Jewish Rothschild brothers had their first international success at this conference, being the go-betweens for French indemnity payments to the Allies—for a low handling fee and interest. The Rothschilds had started as Hessian moneylenders, but then the founding five brothers branched out from Frankfurt in Germany to Paris, London, Naples, and Vienna to set up branches. Working in secret and at great peril, they helped the anti-Napoleonic coalition to overthrow the tyrant. All were made barons by Francis I, first Austrian emperor, in 1816. With close ties to Metternich and many princes, the Rothschilds prospered mightily in the nineteenth century.

The Congress of Troppau (1820) was summoned by Metternich because of the outbreak of revolution in Spain. A policy statement (Protocol of Troppau), which would authorize armed intervention into any state that underwent revolutionary change, was opposed by England.

The Congress of Laibach (1821) authorized Austrian troops to crush revolution in the kingdom of the Two Sicilies, where revolutions had spread from Spain. No decision was made concerning Spain.

The Congress of Verona (1822) was called because of continuing unrest in Spain and the outbreak (1821) of revolution in Greece. When Russia, Prussia, and Austria agreed to support French intervention in Spain, the new English foreign minister, George Canning (1770–1827)—a replacement for Castlereagh, who had committed suicide—withdrew England from the Concert of Europe. Verona marked the effective end of the congress system.

The Monroe Doctrine and the Concert of Europe

British fears that Metternich would attempt the restoration of Spain's colonies, then revolting in Latin America, prompted Canning to suggest, then support, the foreign policy of the United States of America known as the Monroe Doctrine (1823), which prohibited further colonization and intervention by Europe in the Western Hemisphere.

England hoped to replace Spain in establishing her own trading monopoly with these former Spanish colonies. Throughout the nineteenth century, British commercial interests dominated Latin America, in spite of the Monroe Doctrine.

Latin America in Revolution

Inspired by the French Revolution and Napoleon, Latin American nationalism between 1804 and 1824 witnessed the end of three centuries of Spanish colonial rule and the emergence of new heroes such as Toussaint L'Ouverture, José San Martin, Bernardo O'Higgins, Simon Bolivar, and Miguel Hidalgo in Haiti, Argentina, Chile, and Mexico, respectively.

The Revolutions of the 1820s

Spain (1820–1823). In January 1820, a mutiny of army troops arose in opposition to the persecution of liberals by the restored monarch, King Ferdinand VII. The Congress of Verona (1822) authorized a French army to invade Spain and crush the revolutionaries, who wanted to revive the liberal constitution of 1812.

Italy (1820–1821). Incited to revolution by the activities of secret liberal-nationalist organizations (*carbonari*), liberals revolted in Naples in 1820, protesting the absolute rule of Ferdinand I of the kingdom of the Two Sicilies. The Congress of Laibach (1821) authorized Austria to invade and suppress the rebels. An attempted uprising (1821) in Piedmont was crushed by Austrian forces.

The Greek Revolt (1821–1830). The revolution that broke out in Greece in 1821, while primarily a nationalist uprising rather than a liberal revolution, was part of an issue known as "The Eastern Question." Greece was part of the Ottoman Empire, whose vast territories were receding in the early nineteenth century. The weakness of the Ottoman Empire, and the political and economic ramifications of this instability for the balance of power in Europe, kept the major powers in a nervous state of tension.

Because of conflicting interests, the great powers were unable to respond in a pragmatic way for years. The revolt dominated European organs of opinion throughout the 1820s. It immediately set afire the sensitivities of romantics in the West. A Greek appeal to Christian Europe did not move Prussia or Austria, but did fuse England, France, and Russia into a united force that defeated a combined Turkish-Egyptian naval force at Navarino Bay (1827). Greek independence was recognized through the Treaty of Adrianople (1829). In the process, the poet George Gordon, Lord Byron (1788–1824), died in Greece fighting for independence—and unsuccessfully fighting a fever.

Russian intervention on the side of Greek revolutionaries was based on Russian national interest (that is, any diminution of Ottoman power increased Russian chances of further expansion into the Turkish Empire).

Greek nationalism triumphed over the conservative Vienna settlement, and three of the five great powers had aided a movement that violated their agreement of 1815. The self-interests of the great powers demonstrated the growing power of nationalism in the international system.

The Decembrist Uprising in Russia (1825). The sudden death of Tsar Alexander on December 1, 1825, resulted in a crisis over the succession to the throne and produced the first significant uprising in Russian history. The expected succession of Constantine, older brother of Alexander I, believed to be more liberal than the late tsar, did not occur. Instead, the younger brother Nicholas, the antithesis of all things liberal, prepared to assume the throne that Constantine had secretly renounced.

Hoping to block Nicholas's succession, a group of moderately liberal junior military officers staged a demonstration in late December 1825, in Saint Petersburg, only to see it quickly dissipated by artillery attacks ordered by Tsar Nicholas I.

The Decembrists were the first noble opponents of the autocratic Russian system who called attention to popular grievances in Russian society. The insurrection hatched in Nicholas I a pathological dislike for liberal reformers.

Nicholas promulgated a program called *Official Nationality*, with the slogan "Autocracy, Orthodoxy, and National Unity," to lead Russia back to its historic roots. Through it, Nicholas I became Europe's most reactionary monarch.

On the domestic front, Russia became a police state with censorship and state terrorism. The government allowed no representation, no comment on public affairs, and no education that was not strictly prescribed and carefully monitored. A profound alienation of Russian intellectual life ensued that gave birth to that special Russian class, the intelligentsia.

In foreign affairs, the Russian regime demonstrated the same extreme conservatism. It crushed the Polish Revolution of 1830–1831, and Russian troops played a key role in stamping out Hungarian nationalism in the Habsburg Empire, during the revolutionary uprisings of 1848–1849. Russia's traditional desire for expansion at the expense of the Ottoman Empire produced a confrontation between France and Russia over who was entitled to protect Christians and the holy places in the Near East. When the sultan of Turkey awarded France the honor, Nicholas I was prepared to go to war against Turkey to uphold Russia's right to speak for Slavic Christians. The result was the Crimean War (1854–1856), which Russia lost. Nicholas died (1855) during this war.

England Chooses Reform over Revolution

The climax of repression in England was the passing of the Six Acts (1819). Yet even as Parliament enacted those laws, young conservatives were questioning the wisdom of their party elders (the Duke of Wellington, Lord Castlereagh) and calling for moderation. During the 1820s, a group of younger Tories would moderate their party's unbending conservatism.

George Canning and Robert Peel promoted reform, in opposition to the reactionary policies of earlier Tory leaders. With the help of liberal Whig politicians, the younger Tories found enough votes to put England on the road to liberal reform.

Canning inaugurated a liberal policy in foreign affairs, including abandonment of the congress system. Peel reformed prisons and the outdated criminal code, as well as established an efficient metropolitan police force (thus, police officers came to be called "bobbies," nicknamed after Peel).

Parliament acted as well. It liberalized mercantile and navigation acts, enabling British colonies to trade with nations other than England. It repealed the 1673 Test Act, a religious test that barred non-Anglicans from participation in government. (It was defiance of the Test Act that led to the election of Irish leader Daniel O'Connell, a Catholic, to the British parliament.) The Catholic Emancipation Act (1829) granted full civil rights to Roman Catholics.

The momentum for liberal reform continued into the 1830s, as Britain realized that accommodation with the new merchant and financial classes was in the spirit of English history. The acid test of liberal reform, however, would come to focus on the willingness of Parliament to repeal the Corn Laws and reform itself.

Revolutions II (1830–1833)

The conservative grip on Europe following the turbulent 1820s was loosened when revolution broke out in France in 1830. By then, forces of liberalism and nationalism had become so strong that they constituted threats to the security of many governments. In eastern Europe, nationalism was the greater danger, while in the West the demands of middle-class liberals for political reforms grew louder.

France: The July Revolution

The death of Louis XVIII in 1824 brought his brother, head of the ultra-royalists, to the throne as Charles X, and set up France for a new Old Regime—or else revolution.

Attempting to roll back revolutionary gains, Charles X alienated moderate forces on the right as well as the left. Continued violations of the Charter enabled French voters to register their displeasure in the elections of 1827 by giving the liberals a substantial gain in the Chamber of Deputies.

In 1829, when Charles X appointed a ministry led by the Prince de Polignac, the personification of Reaction in France, liberals considered this a dire insult. Elections in 1830 produced a stunning victory for them. Charles responded by issuing the Four Ordinances, which would have amounted to a royal coup d'état had the radicals of Paris, mostly workers and students raising barricades in the narrow streets, not revolted with the intention of establishing a republic. Charles abdicated and fled France.

The liberals in the Chamber of Deputies, under the leadership of Adolphe Thiers, preferred a constitutional cocktail—without Bourbon. With the leadership of Talleyrand and the Marquis de Lafayette, hero of the American revolution, they agreed on Louis-Philippe, head of the Orleans family and royal cousin to Charles X. Once again, Talleyrand had successfully betrayed a master.

Bourgeois (upper-middle-class) bankers and businessmen now controlled France. Louis-Philippe was "the bourgeois king" who would tilt government toward these interests. While the July monarchy of Louis Philippe was politically more liberal than the Restoration government, socially it proved to be quite conservative.

The news of the successful July Revolution in France served as a spark ("When France sneezes, the rest of Europe catches cold") igniting revolution throughout Europe.

Belgian Independence (1830–1831)

Since its merger with Holland in 1815, Belgium had never reconciled itself to rule by a country with a different language, religion, and economic life. Inspired by the news of the July Revolution in France, and an opera about a revolt in 1647 Naples, revolt against Dutch rule broke out in Brussels, led by students and workers. The Dutch army was defeated and forced to withdraw from Belgium by the threat of a Franco-British fleet. A national congress wrote a liberal constitution. In 1831, Leopold of Saxe-Coburg (reigned 1831–1865) became king of the Belgians. In 1839, the great powers declared the neutrality of Belgium, including the Scheldt River.

Poland (1830–1831)

The new tsar, Nicholas I (reigned 1825–1855), had a good opportunity to demonstrate his extreme conservatism in foreign policy when an insurrection broke out in

1830 in Warsaw. This nationalist uprising challenged the historic Russian domination of Poland. The Poles drove out the Russian garrison, and a revolutionary government deposed the tsar as king and proclaimed the independence of Poland.

Nicholas ordered the Russian army to invade; it ruthlessly crushed the nationalist rebellion. Poland became "a land of graves and crosses."[1] The Organic Statute of 1832 made Poland an integral part of the Russian Empire. The great composer Fryderyk Chopin (1810–1849) happened to be out of the country when the revolt occurred. When it was crushed in 1831, he was in Stuttgart, Germany, and there he composed his great *Revolutionary Etude* to a homeland he would never see again.

Italy (1831–1832)

Outbreaks of discontent occurred in northern Italy, centering on Modena, Parma, and the Papal States. The inspiration for Italian nationalists to dream of unification came from (1) Giuseppe Mazzini and his secret revolutionary society called *Young Italy*; and (2) the *Carbonari*, the secret societies that advocated the use of force to achieve national unification. Too disorganized, Italian revolutionaries were easily crushed by Austrian troops acting on Metternich's principle of international intervention. Still, the Italian *risorgimento* (resurgence of the Italian spirit) was well under way.

Germany (1830–1833)

The Carlsbad Decrees of 1819 effectively restricted freedom in the Germanies. Hearing of France's July Revolution, German students and professors led demonstrations that forced temporary grants of constitutions in several states. These expressions of liberal sentiment and nationalist desires for German unification were easily crushed by the German Confederation, as steered by Metternich with his influence over Prussia.

Great Britain: Reform Continues

The death of George IV and accession of William IV in 1830 resulted in a general parliamentary election in which the opposition political party, the Whigs, scored major gains with their platform calling for parliamentary reform. With the Tory party divided, the king asked the leader of the Whigs, Earl Grey (1764–1845), to form a government.

Immediately, the Whigs introduced a major reform bill designed to increase the number of voters by 50 percent and to eliminate underpopulated electoral districts ("rotten boroughs") and replace them with representatives for previously unrepresented manufacturing districts and cities, especially in the industrial Midlands.

After a national debate, new elections, and a threat from William IV to alter the composition of the House of Lords, Parliament enacted the Great Reform Bill of 1832. While the Reform Bill did not resolve all political inequities in British political life, it marked a beginning. Subsequent reforms would redraw the landscape of British society.

---

[1] From the play "Iridion" (1835) by Zygmunt Krasinski.

Evaluation

Neither the forces of revolution nor those of Reaction were able to maintain the upper hand between 1789 and 1848. Liberalism and nationalism, socialism and democracy, were on the march, but the forces of conservatism and reaction were still strong enough to contain them. The polarization of Europe was becoming clear: the liberal middle-class West, which advocated constitutionalism and industrial progress; and the authoritarian East, committed to preserving the status quo. The confrontation would continue until one or the other side would win out decisively.

The Revolutions of 1848

The year 1848 is considered the watershed of the nineteenth century. The revolutionary disturbances of the first half of the century reached a climax in a new wave of revolutions that extended from Scandinavia to southern Italy, from France to central Europe. Only England and Russia avoided violent upheaval.

The issues were substantially the same as in 1789. What was new in 1848 was that these demands were far more widespread and irrepressible than before. Whole classes and nations demanded to be fully included in society. The French Revolution of 1789 came at the end of a period ("ancien régime"), while the revolutions of 1848 signaled the beginning of a new age. Being aggravated by a rapid growth in population and the social disruption of industrialism and urbanization, a massive tide of discontent swept across the western world.

The 1848 upheavals shared the strong influences of romanticism, nationalism, and liberalism, as well as a new factor of economic dislocation and instability throughout most of Europe. Some authorities believe that it was the absence of liberty that was most responsible for the uprisings.

Several similar conditions existed in several countries:

1. Severe food shortages caused by poor harvests of grain and potatoes (for example, the Irish Potato Famine)

2. Financial crises caused by a downturn in commerce and industry

3. Business failures

4. Widespread unemployment

5. A sense of frustration and discontent among urban artisan and working classes as wages diminished

6. A system of poor relief that was overburdened

7. Living conditions that deteriorated in cities

8. The power of nationalism in the Germanies and Italies, as well as eastern Europe, to inspire the overthrow of existing governments

Middle-class predominance in the unregulated economy continued to drive liberals to push for more reform of government and for civil liberty. They pursued this by enlisting the help of the working classes in putting more pressure on the government to change. The marriage of liberals and workers would be short-lived.

Republicanism: Victory in France and Defeat in Italy

In France, working-class discontent and liberals' unhappiness with the corrupt regime of Louis Philippe—especially his minister François Guizot—erupted in street riots in Paris on February 22 and 23, 1848. With workers in control of Paris, Louis Philippe abdicated on February 24, and a provisional government proclaimed the Second French Republic.

Heading the provisional government was the liberal Alphonse Lamartine (1790–1869), a poet who favored a moderate republic and political democracy. Lamartine's bourgeois allies had little sympathy for the working poor and did not intend to pursue a social revolution.

Working-class groups were united by their leader Louis Blanc (1811–1882), a socialist who expected the provisional government to deal with the unemployed and anticipated the power of the state to improve life and the conditions of labor. Pressed by the demands of Blanc and his followers, the provisional government established national workshops (*ateliers*) to provide work and relief for thousands of unemployed workers.

An election in April resulted in a National Assembly dominated by moderate republicans and conservatives under Lamartine, who regarded socialist ideas as threats to private property. When Lamartine's government closed the national workshops, Parisian workers, feeling that their revolution had been nullified, took to the streets again.

Later called the "June Days," this new revolution (June 23–26, 1848) was unlike previous uprisings in France. It marked the inauguration of genuine class warfare; it was a revolt against poverty and a cry for the redistribution of property. It foreshadowed the great social revolutions of the twentieth century. The revolt was extinguished after General Cavaignac was given dictatorial powers by the government. The June Days confirmed the political predominance of conservative property holders, including well-off peasants, in French life.

The Constitution of the Second Republic provided for a unicameral legislature (manned by the current members of the National Assembly) and executive power vested in a popularly elected president. When the election returns were counted, the candidate of the government, General Cavaignac, was soundly defeated by a "dark horse," Prince Louis Napoleon Bonaparte (1808–1873), a nephew of the great emperor. On December 20, 1848, Louis Napoleon was installed as president of the Republic.

It was clear that voters turned to the name Bonaparte for stability and greatness. They expected him to prevent further working-class disorders. However, the election of Louis Napoleon doomed the Second Republic. He was a Bonaparte, dedicated to his own fame and vanity—not republican institutions. On December 2, 1851, Louis

Napoleon staged a bloody coup d'état to kill the republic; a year later, in 1852, he became Emperor Napoleon III. France once again had, like a courtesan, flirted with republicanism only to drop it for a stronger, better-paying leader.

Italian nationalists and liberals wanted to end Austrian, Bourbon (Naples and Sicily), and papal domination, to unite these disparate areas in a unified liberal nation. A revolt by liberals in Sicily in January 1848 was followed by the granting of liberal constitutions in Naples, Tuscany, Piedmont, and the Papal States. Milan and Venice expelled their Austrian rulers. In March 1848, following the news of the revolution in Vienna, a fresh outburst of revolution against Austria occurred in Lombardy and Venetia, with Sardinia-Piedmont declaring war on Austria. Simultaneously, Italian patriots attacked the Papal States, forcing Pope Pius IX to flee to Naples for refuge.

The temporary nature of these successes was illustrated by the speed with which conservative forces regained control. In the North, Austrian Field Marshal Joseph von Radetzky swept aside opposition, regaining Lombardy and Venetia and crushing Sardinia-Piedmont. In the Papal States, the establishment of the Roman Republic (February 1849) under the leadership of Giuseppe Mazzini and the protection of Giuseppe Garibaldi failed when French troops took Rome in July 1849, after a heroic defense by Garibaldi. Pope Pius IX returned to Rome cured of his liberal leanings. In the South and in Sicily, the revolts were suppressed by the former rulers.

Within eighteen months, the revolutions of 1848 had failed throughout Italy. Among explanations for these failures were the failure of conservative, rural people to support the revolution; the divisions in aim and technique among the revolutionaries; the fear the radicals aroused among moderate groups of Italians, who would be needed to guarantee the success of any revolution; and the general lack of experience and administrative ability on the part of the revolutionists.

Nationalism Resisted in the Austrian Empire

The Austrian Empire was vulnerable to revolutionary challenge. Declared in 1804, as the Holy Roman Empire was dying (death: 1806), the new Austrian Empire was a collection of subject nationalities (more non-Germans than Germans) stirred by acute nationalism, its government was reactionary (liberal institutions were nonexistent), and its reliance on serfdom doomed the mass of people to misery. As soon as news of the February Days in France reached the borders of the empire, rebellions began. The long-suppressed opponents of the government believed the time had come to introduce liberal institutions into the empire.

Vienna

In March 1848, Hungarian criticism of Habsburg rule was initiated by the Magyar nationalist Louis Kossuth (1802–1894), who demanded Hungarian independence. Students and workers in Vienna rushed to the streets to demonstrate on behalf of a more liberal government. The army failed to restore order, and Prince Metternich, symbol of reaction, resigned and fled the country. Emperor Ferdinand I (reigned 1835–1848) granted a moderately liberal constitution, but its shortcomings dissatisfied more radical elements, and continual disorder prompted the emperor to flee from Vienna to Innsbruck, where he relied on his army to restore order in the empire. Austrian imperial troops remained loyal to the Habsburgs. Prince Felix von Schwarzenberg, Chancellor of Austria, was put in charge of restoring control.

A people's committee ruled Vienna, where a liberal assembly gathered to write a constitution. In Hungary and Bohemia, revolutionary outbreaks were successful.

The inability of the revolutionary groups in Vienna to govern effectively made it easier for the Habsburgs to lay siege to Vienna in October 1848. The rebels surrendered, and Emperor Ferdinand abdicated in favor of his young nephew, Francis Joseph (reigned 1848–1916), who promptly restored royal absolutism.

The imperial government had been saved at Vienna through the loyalty of the army and the lack of ruling capacity on the part of the revolutionaries. The only thing the revolutionaries could agree on was their hatred of the Habsburg dynasty.

Bohemia

Nationalist feeling among Bohemians (Czechs) had been smoldering since the Hussite Wars. They demanded a constitution and autonomy within the Habsburg Empire.

A Pan-Slav Congress meeting in June 1848 attempted to unite all Slavic peoples, but accomplished little, because divisions were more decisive among them than was unified opposition to Habsburg control. During the congress's doomed but symbolically important tenure, Austrian military leader General-prince Alfred von Windischgrätz bombed Prague into submission, accidentally killing his own wife in her palace. Prague submitted to military occupation, followed by a military dictatorship in July, after all revolutionary groups were crushed.

Hungary

The kingdom of Hungary was a state of about twelve million under Habsburg authority. Magyars or Hungarians, who represented about five million subjects of the emperor, enjoyed a privileged position in the empire. The remaining seven million Slavic, Jewish, Polish, Romanian, and other natives were powerless.

In March 1848, Louis Kossuth took over direction of the movement and tamed a more radical rebellion. The nationalists declared autonomy in April, but failed to win popular support for the revolution, because of tyrannical treatment of Slavic minorities. Since the government in Vienna was distracted by revolutions everywhere in the empire in the summer and fall of 1848, Kossuth had time to organize an army to fight for Hungarian independence.

Austria declared war on Hungary on October 3, 1848, and Hungarian armies drove to within sight of Vienna. But desperate resistance from Slavic minorities forced the Hungarians to withdraw. Hungary was invaded by an Austrian army from the West, in June 1849, and a Russian army (Nicholas offered assistance to new emperor Francis Joseph) from the North. Along with Serbian resistance in the South and Romanian resistance in the East, the opposition proved too much for Kossuth's Hungarian Republic (proclaimed in April 1849), which was defeated. Kossuth fled into exile, while thirteen of his guards were executed. Not until Austria was defeated by Prussia, in 1866, would Hungary be in a position again to demand equality with Austria.

Italy

Charles Albert, king of Sardinia, having granted his people a constitution, and hoping to add the Habsburgs's Italian holdings to his kingdom, declared war on Austria. Unfortunately, the Sardinian army was twice defeated in battle (at Custozza and Novara) by Austrian General Radetzky.

King Charles Albert abdicated in favor of his son, Victor Emmanuel, who was destined to complete the unification of Italy (1859–1870).

The revolutions of 1848 failed in Austria for several reasons. The subject nationalities sometimes hated each other more than they despised Austria. Habsburgs used the divisions between the ethnic groups as an effective weapon against each. The imperial army had remained loyal to its aristocratic commanders, who favored absolutism. There were too few industrial workers and an equally small middle class. Workers could not exert political power, and the middle class feared working-class radicalism and rallied to the government as defender of the status quo.

Liberalism Halted in the Germanies

The immediate effect of the 1848 revolution in France was a series of liberal and nationalistic demonstrations in the German states (March 1848), with rulers promising liberal concessions. The liberals' demand for constitutional government was coupled with another demand: a union or federation of the German states. While demonstrations by students, workers, and the middle class produced the promise of a liberal future, the permanent success or failure of these "promises" rested on Prussian reaction.

Prussia, the Frankfurt Parliament, and German Unification

Under Frederick William IV (reigned 1848–1861), Prussia moved from revolution to reaction. After agreeing to liberalize the Prussian government following street rioting in Berlin, the king rejected the constitution written by a special assembly. The liberal ministry resigned and was replaced by a conservative one. By fall, the king felt powerful enough to substitute his constitution, which guaranteed royal control of government, with a three-class system of indirect voting that excluded all but landlords and wealthy bourgeois from office. This system prevailed in Prussia until 1918. Finally, the government ministry was responsible to the king and the military services swore loyalty to the king alone.

Self-appointed liberal and nationalist leaders called for elections to a constituent assembly, from all states belonging to the Bund, for the purpose of unifying the German states. Meeting in May 1848, the Frankfurt parliament was dominated by intellectuals, professionals, lawyers, businessmen, and writers. After a year of deliberating the issues of (1) monarchy or republic, (2) federal union or centralized state, and (3) boundaries (that is, only German-populated or mixed nationalities), the assembly produced a constitution.

The principal problem facing the Frankfurt Assembly was to obtain Prussian support. The smaller German states generally favored the Frankfurt Constitution, as did liberals throughout the large- and middle-sized states. Austria made it clear that it was opposed to the work of the assembly and would remain in favor of the present system.

Assembly leaders made the decision to stake their demands for a united Germany on Frederick William IV of Prussia. They chose him as emperor in April 1849, only to have him reject the offer because he was a divine-right monarch, not subject to popularly elected assemblies. Without Prussia, the German states could not succeed, so the Frankfurt parliament dissolved without achieving much aside from the airing of liberal desires.

Frederick William IV had his own plans for uniting Germany. After refusing Frankfurt's offer, which he considered a "crown from the gutter," he offered his plan to German princes, wherein Prussia would play a prominent role, along with Austria. When Austria demanded allegiance to the Bund, the Prussian king realized pushing his plan would involve him in a war with Austria and her allies (including Russia). In November 1850, Prussia agreed to forego the idea of uniting the German states at a meeting with Austria later called the "Humiliation of Olmütz." Austria had confirmed its domination of the German Bund.

Great Britain and the Victorian Compromise

The Victorian Age (1837–1901) is named for the long reign of Queen Victoria, who succeeded her uncle, William IV, at age eighteen and married her cousin, Prince Albert of Saxe-Coburg und Gotha (the official name of the royal family until anti-German sentiment made them change it to Windsor in 1917). The early years of her reign coincided with continued liberal reform of the government accomplished through an arrangement known as the "Victorian Compromise." This was a political alliance of the middle class and aristocracy to exclude the working class from political power. The middle class gained control of the House of Commons, the aristocracy controlled the government, the House of Lords, the army, and the Church of England. The process of accommodation was working successfully.

Highlights of the Compromise Era

Parliamentary reforms continued after passage of the 1832 Reform Bill. Parliament enacted laws abolishing slavery throughout the empire (1833). The Factory Act (1831) forbade the employment of children under the age of nine. The New Poor Law (1834) required the needy who were able and unemployed to live in workhouses. The Municipal Reform Law (1835) gave control of the cities to the middle class. The last remnants of the mercantilist age fell with the repeal of the Corn Laws (1846) and repeal of the old Navigation Acts (1849).

Working-class protest arose in the wake of their belief that passage of the Great Reform Bill of 1832 would bring prosperity. When workers found themselves no better off, they turned to collective action. They linked the solution of their economic plight to a program of political reform known as "chartism," from the charter of six points that they petitioned Parliament to adopt: universal male suffrage, secret ballot, no property qualifications for members of Parliament, salaries for members of Parliament, annual elections for Parliament, and equal electoral districts.

During the age of Victorian Compromise, these ideas were considered dangerously radical. Both the middle class and aristocracy vigorously opposed the working class political agenda. Chartism as a national movement failed. Its ranks were split between those who favored violence and those who advocated peaceful tactics. The return of prosperity, with steady wages and lower food prices, robbed the movement of momentum. Yet the chartist movement came to constitute the first large-scale, working-class political movement that workers would eventually adopt if they were to improve their situation.

After 1846, the middle class dominated England; this was one of the factors that enabled England to escape the revolutions that shook Europe in 1848. The ability of the English to make meaningful industrial reforms gave the working class hope that its goals could be achieved without violent social upheaval.

Evaluation

The revolutions of 1848 began with much promise, but they all ended in defeat for a number of reasons. They were spontaneous movements that lost popular support as the people lost enthusiasm. Initial successes by the revolutionaries were due less to their strength than to the hesitancy of governments to use superior force. Once this hesitancy was overcome, the revolutions were smashed. They were essentially urban movements, so conservative landowners and peasants tended to nullify the spontaneous actions of the urban classes. The middle class, which led the revolutions, came to fear the radicalism of working-class allies. While in favor of political reform, the middle class drew the line at social engineering—to the dismay of the laboring poor. Divisions among national groups, and the willingness of one nationality to deny rights to others, helped destroy revolutionary movements across Europe. Because liberals and nationalists did *not* cooperate across borders, princes easily succeeded, since, thanks to Prince Metternich, they were more than willing to cooperate across borders to maintain their powers and control.

However, the results of the conflicts of 1848–1849 were not entirely negative. Universal male suffrage was introduced in France; serfdom remained abolished in Austria and German states; parliaments were established in Prussia and other German states, though dominated, to be sure, by princes and aristocrats; and Prussia and Sardinia-Piedmont emerged with new determination to succeed in their respective unification schemes.

The revolutions of 1848 to 1849 brought to a close the era of liberal revolutions that had begun in France in 1789. Reformers and reactionaries alike learned a lesson from the failures of 1848. They learned that planning and organization was necessary, that rational argument and revolution would not always assure success. With 1848, the Age of Revolution sputtered out. The Age of Romanticism was about to give way to an Age of Realism in which blood and iron would remake the world, not airy ideals.

Epilogue: The View from Mid-Nineteenth Century Europe

A new age was about to follow the revolutions of 1848–1849, as Otto von Bismarck, one of the dominant political figures of the nineteenth century, was quick to realize. If the mistake of these years was to believe that great decisions could be brought about by speeches and parliamentary majorities, the sequel would soon show that in an industrial era, new techniques involving ruthless force were all too readily available. The period of realpolitik—of realistic, iron-fisted politics and diplomacy—was about to happen.

By 1850, all humankind was positioned to become part of a single, worldwide, interacting whole. Given Europe's military technology and industrial productivity, no part of the world could prevent Europeans from imposing their will.

The half century after 1850 would witness the political consolidation and economic expansion that paved the way for the brief global domination of Europe. The conservative monarchies of Sardinia-Piedmont and Prussia united Italy and Germany by military force, and gave birth to new power relationships on the Continent. Externalizing their rivalries produced conflict overseas in a new age of imperialism, which saw Africa and Asia fall under the domination of the West.

Nationalism overtook liberalism as the dominant force in human affairs after 1850. Nationalists would be less romantic and more hardheaded. The good of the nation and not the individual became the new creed. The state would be deified.

After 1848–1849, the middle class ceased to be revolutionary. It became concerned with protecting its hard-earned political power and property rights against radical political and social movements. And the working classes also adopted new tactics and organizations. They turned to trade unions and political parties to achieve their political and social goals, or else to the violence, immediate and threatened, of anarchism and Marxist socialism.

A great era of human progress was about to begin—material, political, scientific, industrial, social, and cultural—shaping of the contours of the world.

TIMELINE

Reaction and More Revolutions (1815–1849)

Year(s)	Event	Significance
1815	The Congress of Vienna redraws Europe.	The Congress creates the new German Confederation of thirty-nine states, and the kingdoms of Holland, and of Sweden with Norway; and gives the Rhenish provinces to Prussia; the north Italian provinces to Austria; Bessarabia and most of Poland to Russia; and part of Saxony to Prussia.
1815–1822	The congress system, instituted at Vienna, controls international relations in Europe.	Prince Metternich enforces the congress system whereby major decisions are made in concert of the great powers. His principle of armed intervention works to suppress revolts in Spain and Italy, as well as liberal and nationalist dissent in the Germanies. However, Britain is hostile to his bullying and policies, so it drops out.
1818–1834	Prussia pioneers in formation of toll-free trade union.	Urged on by ministers with liberal and nationalist ideas, Prussia in a series of treaties lures many German states into a *zollverein* to get rid of internal trade barriers and help German goods compete against low-priced British imports.
1821–1827	The Greeks successfully wage wars of independence.	Greece revolts against Turkish rule. Russia, Britain, and France look on benignly; Prince Metternich is trumped for first time. The great powers recognize Greek independence—a cause of the liberals and romantics—in 1827.
1825	Decembrist Revolt in Russia fails.	Noble officers in Russia, imbued with liberal fever caught in revolutionary wars, scheme to create either a constitutional monarchy or a republic in Russia. The sudden death of Alexander I sparks an ill-planned revolt, easily crushed by Tsar Nicholas I. The revolt is deemed first revolution in Russian history and leads to Reaction.
1829	In England, George Stephenson inaugurates the world's first rail line.	The first rail line, with its steam-powered locomotive, ushers in a new age of transportation and communication.
1829	Parliament in England declares Catholic emancipation.	The Tory government, stealing a march on liberals (a trend in nineteenth-century British politics) grants political rights to Catholics, since dissenting Protestants had just won such rights. The action postpones revolution in Ireland.

(Continued)

1815–1846	Conservatives (Tories) in English parliament enact Corn Laws to protect grain prices and landowners.	The laws hurt urban workers. Calls for their repeal (successful in 1846) show the growing impact of liberalism in European politics.
1830	From Paris, revolution spreads to Belgium, Germanies, and Poland.	All the rebellions are crushed, except that in Belgium, which wins its independence, thanks to neutrality secured by Britain in 1839. The French revolution enthrones "bourgeois king," who favors upper bourgeoisie and some liberal principles.
1832	English parliament enacts the Great Reform Bill.	Liberals, allied to industrialists, demand and get reforms to the electoral map, parts of which have been unchanged since the Middle Ages. The reforms create new parliamentary seats in the industrial Midlands; eliminate old rotten and pocket boroughs; and increase the electorate by adding leaseholders (formerly, only landowners could vote).
1840s	The "Hungry Forties" give birth to new ideas on socialism.	Economic slump, financial crisis, and famine (in Ireland and east Germany), among other disastrous conditions, sow the seeds of discontent. Literature takes on a new realism in urban novels (Charles Dickens, Honoré de Balzac, Sue), and such tracts as Joseph Proudhon's *What is Property?* (Answer: Theft). Also, universities are overcrowded and young men cannot get work, thus creating revolutionary fodder.
1848	Revolution sweeps Europe—again!	A crackdown on liberal banquets sparks revolt in Paris, where workers ally themselves to bourgeois liberals. News spreads and revolts break out in Baden, Berlin, Vienna, Budapest, Italy, Saxony, and Prague, but *not* Russia or Britain.
1848	Congresses and parliaments crop up all over.	Germans convene parliament at Frankfurt to discuss new order; pan-Slavs met in Prague to discuss ways to unite all Slav peoples, but especially those oppressed by the Habsburgs. Everywhere, liberals write constitutions that princes sign—reluctantly.
1848	During the "June Days," workers in Paris revolt when government closes the *ateliers*.	The June Days mark the first break of urban workers with the liberals, an ominous sign. General Cavaignac crushes the revolt, but the liberals have lost face. In the elections that follow, voters choose Napoleon's nephew, indicating that peasants are still conservative.

Fall 1848	Reactionary forces regain power in key countries.	Armies in all lands (except Baden) remain loyal to side-lined princes. Seeing liberal weakness, princes start to regain power: the Roman Republic is attacked by pope with French troops; the Frankfurt parliament is attacked by a mob.
1848–1849	The new Austrian emperor sends troops to rewin Prague, north Italy, and other territories; French troops save the pope; Russian troops crush the Hungarian revolt; Prussian troops crush revolts in Saxony, Baden, and Hesse, among others.	Austria, France, Russia, and Prussia invoke Metternich's old principle of militarily defending the status quo.
1850	Reaction back! The era of realpolitik begins.	Princes return to thrones and reverse many liberal gains, but now see that they must compromise with the new wealth of liberal bourgeoisie: realist politics takes over.

Chapter 7

The Heyday of Liberalism and Nationalism (1850–1900)

The Failure of the Revolutions (1848–1849)

By the summer of 1848, the revolutionary effort had been spent and the earlier gains of the late winter and spring had been reversed or challenged in many countries. The June Days in France coincided with the dissolution of the Pan-Slavic Congress in Prague by Austria's General Alfred Windischgrätz. By October, Windischgrätz had suppressed the revolution in Vienna, and the armies of Austria's General Radetzky were moving successfully against the Italians. In the fall and winter (1848–1849), the revolutions were stifled in France, Prussia, Austria, Italy, and all other affected states.

Several factors contributed to the failure of the revolutions of 1848:

- On a military level, armed forces had remained loyal to the old leadership and demonstrated a willingness to assist in the suppression of revolution. (In one instance where troops had sworn an oath on the new constitution, the Grand Duchy of Baden imported Prussian troops, who did the dirty work of crushing the revolution there.)

- In western Europe, liberal political reforms appeased the revolutionaries. In most instances, the majority of citizens in the West indicated that they were opposed to radical economic and social change.

- In central Europe, revolutions that had been led by the middle class did not show much interest in radical solutions to social and economic problems. When workers and students demanded a full revolution, the middle class became alienated from the movement they had led; they desired change only through a constitutional process. This breach in the revolutionary camp was detected and exploited by the old regime.

- In eastern and southern Europe, nationalist revolutions lacked organization and, above all, the military capacity to resist the professional armies of the Austrian Empire and, ominously, the Russians as well, who were invited to crush the lingering revolution in Hungary while Austrian armies were tied down in several other theaters of war.

By 1849, the revolutions had been suppressed or redirected. Only in France with the Second French Republic (1848–1852) and in Prussia (the Constitution of 1850) did some of the earlier gains endure in obvious ways. But in other places, agendas of liberals and nationalists seethed and fermented in ways that demanded a sort of Hegelian compromise or synthesis. Though the 1850s were branded as reactionary, the seeds of change had germinated by the 1860s, in which, from Russia to Ireland, older regimes were forced to adopt some of the agenda points of liberals and nationalists.

Realpolitik and the Triumph of Nationalism

Cavour and the Unification of Italy

After the collapse of the revolution of 1848, the leadership of Italian nationalism passed to King Victor Emmanuel II of Piedmont-Sardinia; his prime minister, Count Camillo de Cavour; and the often-exiled *Carbonaro* soldier, Giuseppe Garibaldi, whose ties to Piedmont were erratic. They replaced Giuseppe Mazzini of the Young Italy society; the former Sardinian king, Charles Albert; the once liberal Pius IX; and the neo-Guelf movement, which had looked to the papacy to unify Italy. The new leaders did not entertain romantic illusions about the process of transforming Sardinia into an Italian kingdom; they were practitioners of the politics of realism, realpolitik.

Cavour (1810–1861) was a Sardinian who served as editor of *Il Risorgimento*, a newspaper that argued that Piedmont should organize the new Italy. Between 1852 and 1861, Cavour served as Victor Emmanuel II's prime minister. In that capacity, Cavour transformed Sardinian society through the implementation of a series of liberal reforms designed to modernize the Sardinian state and attract the support of liberal states such as Great Britain and France. Among Cavour's reforms were (1) the Law on Convents and the Siccardi Law, which were directed at curtailing the influence of the Roman Catholic Church; (2) reform of the judicial system; (3) the implementation of the *Statuto*, the Sardinian constitution modeled on the liberal French constitution of 1830; and (4) support for economic development projects, such as port, rail, and highway construction.

In 1855, under Cavour's direction, Sardinia joined Britain and France in the Crimean War against Russia. At the Paris Peace Conference (1856), Cavour addressed the delegates on the need to eliminate the foreign (Austrian) presence in the Italian peninsula and attracted the attention and sympathy of the French emperor, Napoleon III.

Cavour and Napoleon III met at Plombières (July 20, 1859). The Plombières Agreement stated that, in the event that Sardinia went to war with Austria—presumably after being attacked or provoked—France would provide military assistance, and with victory Sardinia would annex Lombardy, Venetia, Parma, Modena, and a part of the Papal States. In addition, the remainder of Italy would be organized into an Italian confederation under the direction of the pope, France would receive Nice and Savoy, and the alliance would be finalized by a marriage between the two royal families. The Plombières Agreement was designed to bring about a war with Austria and to assist Sardinia in developing an expanded northern Italian kingdom. The concept of an Italian confederation under the papacy was contributed by Napoleon III and demonstrates his lack of understanding of Italian political ambitions and values during this period.

After being provoked, the Austrians declared war on Sardinia in 1859. French forces intervened and the Austrians were defeated in the battles of Magenta (June 4) and Solferino (June 24), one of the bloodiest battles of European history to that point. Napoleon III's support wavered for four reasons: (1) Prussia's mobilization and its expressed sympathy for Austria; (2) the outbreak of uncontrolled revolts in some north Italian states; (3) the forcefulness of the new Austrian military efforts; and (4) the lack of public support in France for his involvement, with mounting criticism from the French Catholic Church, which opposed the war against Catholic Austria.

Napoleon III, without consulting Cavour, signed a secret peace with the Austrian emperor Franz Josef (the Truce of Villafranca) on July 11, 1859. Sardinia received Lombardy but not Venetia; other terms indicated that Sardinian influence would be restricted and Austria would remain a power in Italian politics. The terms of Villafranca were clarified and finalized with the Treaty of Zürich (1859).

In 1860, after popular referenda in Parma, Modena, Romagna, and Tuscany in favor of Piedmont-Sardinia, Cavour arranged their annexation. The actions of these duchies were recognized by the Treaty of Turin between Napoleon III and Victor Emmanuel II; Nice and Savoy were transferred to France. With these acquisitions, Cavour anticipated the need for a period of tranquility to incorporate these territories into Piedmont-Sardinia.

Giuseppe Garibaldi and his followers, the Red Shirts, landed in Sicily (May 1860) and extended the nationalist activity to the south. Within three months, they had taken Sicily, and by September 7, Garibaldi was in Naples, and the kingdom of the Two Sicilies had fallen under Sardinian influence. Cavour distrusted Garibaldi, but Victor Emmanuel II encouraged him. Garibaldi favored a republican form of government for Italy, but he was persuaded that only the king of Piedmont-Sardinia could unify the peninsula, so he greeted Victor Emmanuel as king at a famous meeting, then retired to the island of Caprera, refusing all attempts of the new Italy to honor him.

In February 1861, in Turin, Victor Emmanuel was declared king of Italy and presided over an Italian parliament that represented the entire Italian peninsula with the exception of Venetia and the Patrimony of Saint Peter (Rome). Cavour died in June 1861.

Venetia was incorporated into the Italian kingdom in 1866 as a result of an alliance between Otto von Bismarck's Prussia and the kingdom of Italy that preceded the German Civil War between Austria and Prussia. In return for opening a southern front against Austria, Prussia, upon its victory, arranged for Venetia to be transferred to Italy.

Bismarck was indirectly helpful in the acquisition of Rome by Italy in 1870, when the Franco-Prussian War broke out and the French garrison, which had been in Rome providing protection for the pope, was withdrawn to serve on the front against Prussia. Italian troops seized Rome, and in 1871, as a result of a plebiscite, Rome became the capital of the kingdom of Italy, and the pope made himself "prisoner of the Vatican."

Bismarck and the Unification of Germany

After 1815, Prussia emerged as an alternative to a Habsburg-based Germany. Germany was politically decentralized into thirty-eight to thirty-nine independent states. This situation had been sanctioned by the Peace of Westphalia in 1648.

Prussia had absorbed some smaller states during the eighteenth and early nineteenth centuries, and controlled indirectly such enclaves as the Anhalt duchies, surrounded by Prussian territory.

Otto von Bismarck (1815–1898) entered the diplomatic service of William I as the revolutions of 1848 were being suppressed. In 1862, Bismarck emerged as principal adviser and minister to the king, who sought to form a Prussian-based (Hohenzollern) Germany. In the 1860s, Bismarck supported a series of military reforms to improve the Prussian army, but he was thwarted by liberals in the Prussian parliament. At one juncture, he announced, intending to humiliate them, that Germany would not be made great by speeches and such—the fault of (their) revolutions of 1848—but rather through "blood and iron" (meaning, wars and industry). When the parliament continued to refuse to grant him a new budget to modernize the army, he boldly defied them, ruling with the old budget through a "hole in the constitution."

In 1863, the Schleswig-Holstein crisis broke. Holstein was part of the German Confederation, but both provinces, occupied by Germans, were also under the personal rule of Christian IX of Denmark. The Danish government advanced a new constitution specifying that Schleswig and Holstein must be annexed by Denmark. German reaction was predictable, and Bismarck arranged for a joint Austro-Prussian military action. Denmark was defeated and agreed (Treaty of Vienna, 1864) to give up the provinces. Schleswig and Holstein were to be jointly administered by Austria and Prussia.

Questions of jurisdiction provided the rationale for estranged relations between Austria and Prussia. In 1865, the two reached a temporary settlement in the Gastein Convention, which stated that Prussia would administer Schleswig, and Austria manage Holstein. In 1865 to 1866, Bismarck made diplomatic preparations for the impending struggle with Austria. Italy, France, and Russia did not interfere, and Britain was not expected to involve itself in a central European war. Key states in the Confederation allied with Austria, fearing Prussian preponderance in any new Germany. These included the kingdoms of Saxony, Bavaria, Württemberg, and Hanover; the grand duchies of Baden and Darmstadt; the principality of Hesse-Kassel and Nassau; and the free city of Frankfurt. Only a few minor northern states joined with Prussia: the grand duchies of Oldenburg and Mecklenburg-Schwerin, and the duchies of Strelitz and Brunswick, among others. Anyone not looking too closely at military technicalities might have bet on the Austrian side, but the Prussian army, brilliantly reorganized and modernized by its chief of staff, Helmuth von Moltke, had the advantage in rail lines, the newest rifles, and more.

The German Civil War (also known as the Seven Weeks' War) was devastating to Austria and her allies. The humiliating defeat at Koniggratz (July 4, 1866) showed the ineptitude of Austrian forces when confronted by the Prussian army led by Moltke. Within two months, Austria had to agree to the peace terms, which were drawn up at Nikolsburg and finalized by the Peace of Prague (August 1866).

The peace treaty stipulated three major terms: Austria was excluded from all German affairs—the *kleindeutsch* plan had prevailed over the *grossdeutsch* plan (which would have included Austria); Venetia was ceded to Italy; and Austria had to pay an indemnity to Prussia. Some of Austria's allies suffered far more: Hanover, part of Darmstadt, Kassel, Nassau, and Frankfurt were simply annexed by the victors. Blind king George of Hanover had to stumble his way to exile in Austria, defiant to the end as Bismarck used his sequestered wealth for Prussian political purposes.

In the next year, 1867, the North German Confederation was established by Bismarck. It was designed to facilitate the movement toward a unified German state and included most German states, except for the south German powers, Baden, Württemberg, and Bavaria, which soon signed military alliances with Prussia, in anticipation of difficulties with France; the king of Prussia served as president of the Confederation.

In 1870, the deteriorating relations between France and Germany became critical over the Ems Dispatch. William I, while vacationing at Ems, was approached by the French diplomat Count Benedetti, who demanded a Prussian pledge not to interfere on the issue of the vacant Spanish throne. William I refused to give such a pledge and informed Bismarck of these developments through a telegram from Ems. Bismarck doctored this telegram and leaked it to the friendly press, which reacted as he had wished, with anti-French sentiment, since the telegram seemed to show that the French had insulted the king of Prussia. Bismarck also leaked proof that Benedetti had been part of a French plan to annex Belgium and Luxemburg (part of the latter had belonged to the German Confederation until an 1867 crisis).

Bismarck exploited the situation by initiating a propaganda campaign against the French. Subsequently, France declared war and the Franco-Prussian War (1870–1871) commenced. Prussian victories at Sedan and Metz proved decisive; Napoleon III and his leading general, Marshal MacMahon, were captured. Paris continued to resist, under the tragic and anarchist government of its Commune, but fell to the Prussians in January 1871. The Treaty of Frankfurt (May 1871) ended the war and resulted in France ceding Alsace-Lorraine to Germany and a German occupation until an indemnity was paid.

The German Empire was proclaimed on January 18, 1871, with William I elected as emperor of Germany by all the princes. Bismarck became imperial chancellor. Bavaria, Baden, and Württemberg were incorporated into the new Germany.

Inter-European Relations (1848–1878)

Since the Napoleonic era, the peace in Europe had been sustained by fears and memories of the devastation and disruption caused by the French Revolution and Napoleonic Wars. The primary structure that maintained the peace was the Concert of Europe, a rather loose and ill-defined understanding among the great powers that they would join to resolve problems that threatened the status quo; it was believed that the powers would undertake joint action to prohibit any drastic alteration in the European system or balance of power. The credibility of the Concert of Europe was undermined by the failure of the powers to take action against the revolutions of 1848 in time. Between 1848 and 1878, the peace among the European powers was interrupted by the Crimean War (1854–1856) and challenged by the crisis centered on the Russo-Turkish War of 1877–1878.

The Crimean War

The origins of the Crimean War involved a dispute between two groups of Christians (and their protectors) over privileges in the Holy Land. At this time, Palestine was part of the Ottoman Turkish Empire. In 1852, the Turks negotiated an agreement with the French to provide enclaves in the Holy Land to Roman Catholic religious orders; this arrangement appeared to jeopardize already existing agreements that provided access to Greek Orthodox religious orders. Tsar Nicholas, unaware of the impact of his action, ordered Russian troops to occupy the Danubian principalities; his strategy was to withdraw once the Turks agreed to clarify and guarantee the rights of the Greek Orthodox orders. The role of Britain in this developing crisis was critical; Nicholas mistakenly assumed that the prime minister, Lord Aberdeen, would be sympathetic to the Russian policy. Aberdeen, heading a coalition cabinet, sought to use the Concert of Europe to settle the question. However, Lord Palmerston, home secretary, supported the Turks; he was suspicious of Russian intervention in the region. Consequently, misunderstandings about Britain's policy developed. In October 1853, the Turks demanded that Russia withdraw from the occupied principalities; the Russians failed to respond, so the Turks declared war. In February 1854, Nicholas advanced a draft for a settlement of the conflict; the Turks rejected it, and Great Britain and France joined the Ottoman Turks and declared war on Russia.

With the exception of naval encounters in the Gulf of Finland, this war was conducted on the Crimean peninsula in the Black Sea. In September 1854, more than fifty thousand British and French troops landed in the Crimea, determined to take the Russian port city of Sebastopol. While this war has been remembered for the work of Florence Nightingale and the "Charge of the Light Brigade," it was a conflict in which there were more casualties from disease and weather than from combat. In December 1854, Austria, with great reluctance, became a cosignatory of the Four Points of Vienna, a statement of British and French war aims. The Four Points specified that (1) Russia should renounce any claims to the occupied principalities, (2) the 1841 Straits Convention, which had declared that no warships were to be allowed in the Straits, would be revised, (3) navigation in the mouth of the Danube River (on the Black Sea) should be internationalized, and (4) Russia should withdraw any claim to having a special protective role for Orthodox residents in the Ottoman Empire. In 1855, Piedmont joined Britain and France in the war. In March 1855, Nicholas I died and was succeeded by Alexander II, who was opposed to continuing the war. In December 1855, the Austrians, under excessive pressure from the British, French, and Piedmontese, sent an ultimatum to Russia in which they threatened to renounce their neutrality. In response, Alexander II indicated that he would accept the Four Points.

Representatives of the belligerents convened in Paris between February and April 1856. The resulting Peace of Paris had the following major provisions: Russia had to acknowledge international commissions that were to regulate maritime traffic on the Danube, recognize Turkish control of the mouth of the Danube, renounce all claims to the Danubian principalities of Moldavia and Wallachia (this later led to the establishment of Romania), agree not to fortify the Aaland Islands, renounce its position as protector of Orthodox residents of the Ottoman Empire, and return all occupied territories to the Turks. The Straits Convention of 1841 was revised through the neutralization of the Black Sea. The Declaration of Paris specified the rules that would regulate commerce during periods of war. Lastly, the signatories recognized and guaranteed the independence and integrity of the Ottoman Empire. Russia felt betrayed by Austria, a fact that would lead to the First World War, but Prussia under Bismarck wisely, but cruelly, affected a rapprochement with Russia by helping it to crush the Polish Rebellion of 1863. The special Russo-German friendship would fail only after the fall of Bismarck.

The Eastern Question to the Congress of Berlin

Another challenge to the Concert of Europe developed in the 1870s with a stream of Balkan crises. Once again, the conflict initially involved Russia and Ottoman Turks, but it quickly became a conflict with Britain and Russia serving as principal protagonists. British concerns over Russian ambitions in the Balkans reached a critical level in 1877 when Russia went to war with the Turks.

In 1876, Turkish forces under the leadership of Osman Pasha defeated the Serbian army. Serbia requested assistance from the great powers and, as a consequence of their political pressure, the Turks agreed to participate in a conference in Constantinople; the meeting resulted in a draft agreement between the Serbs and Turks. However, Britain quietly advised the sultan to scuttle the agreement, which he did. In June 1877, Russia dispatched forces across the Danube. During the next month, Osman Pasha took up a defensive position there. During the siege, sympathy in the West shifted toward the Turks, and Britain and Austria became alarmed over the extent of Russian influence in the region. In March 1878, the Russians and Turks signed the Peace of San Stefano, but implementation of its provisions would have resulted in Russian hegemony in the Balkans, dramatically altering the balance of power in the Mediterranean. Specifically, it provided for the establishment of a large Bulgarian state under Russian influence; the transfer of Dobrudja, Kars, and Batum to Russia; the expansion of Serbia and Montenegro; and the establishment of an autonomous Bosnia-Herzegovina under Russian control.

Britain, under the leadership of Prime Minister Benjamin Disraeli, denounced the San Stefano Accord, dispatched a naval squadron to Turkish waters, and demanded that San Stefano be scrapped. Otto von Bismarck, now chancellor of Germany, intervened and offered his services as mediator.

Delegates of the major powers convened in Berlin in the summer of 1878 to negotiate a settlement. Prior to the meeting, Disraeli had concluded a series of secret arrangements with Austria, Russia, and Turkey. The combined impact of these accommodations was to restrict Russian expansion, reaffirm the independence of Turkey, and maintain British control of the Mediterranean. The specific terms of the Treaty of Berlin resulted in the following: (1) recognition of Romania, Serbia, and Montenegro as independent states; (2) the establishment of the autonomous principality of Bulgaria; (3) Austrian acquisition of the right to occupy militarily Bosnia and Herzegovina; and (4) the transfer of Cyprus to Great Britain.

The Russians, who had won the war against Turkey and had imposed the harsh terms of the San Stefano Treaty, found that they left the conference with very little (Kars, Batum, and Dobrudja) for their effort. Although Disraeli was the primary agent of this anti-Russian settlement, the Russians blamed Bismarck for the dismal results. Their hostility toward Germany led Bismarck (1879) to embark upon a new system of alliances that realigned European diplomacy and rendered any additional efforts of the Concert of Europe futile.

In his last hurrah, the Reinsurance Treaty of 1887, Bismarck tried to appease his old Russian allies with assurances that Germany would rally to Russia's side should Austria attack, but anti-Russian sentiment had invaded the highest circles in Berlin and Potsdam, including the heir to the throne, so when Wilhelm II became king of Prussia and German emperor, he took the first opportunity to sack the pro-Russian Bismarck (1890). The path was now clear for the other powers to alienate Germany and Austria, thus precipitating the First World War.

Capitalism and the Emergence of the New Left (1848–1914)

Economic Developments: The New Industrial Order

During the 1800s, Europe experienced the full impact of the Industrial Revolution. The new economic order not only altered the working lives of all Europeans, but also changed the very fiber of European culture. Shifts in demography were radical, the process of urbanization was irreversible, and the transformation of European values and living was dramatic. The Industrial Revolution improved aspects of the lives of a greater number of Europeans; at the same time, it led to a factory system with undesirable working and living conditions and abuses of child labor. While the advantages of industrialism were evident, the disadvantages were more subtle; the industrial working class was more vulnerable than peasants because of the fragile nature of the industrial economy. This new economy was based on a dependent system that involved (1) the availability of raw materials, (2) an adequate labor supply, and (3) a distribution system that successfully marketed the products; distribution was in itself dependent upon the ready availability of money throughout the economy. If any requirement was impeded or absent, the industrial workforce was confronted with unemployment and poverty. The industrial system was based on developing capitalism, which itself was grounded in an appreciation of material culture. The standard of living, neomercantilist attitude toward national power, and accumulation of wealth were manifestations of this new materialism.

As the century progressed, the inequities of the system became increasingly evident. Trade unionism and socialist political parties emerged that attempted to address these problems and improve the lives of the working class. In most of these expressions of discontent, the influences of Utopian Socialism or Marxism were evident and can be detected readily. Socialism was steeped in economic materialism that had emerged in the eighteenth century and came to dominate the nineteenth and twentieth centuries. Economics was a component in the rise of scientism; by its very nature, it advanced the values of material culture.

Materialism and Realism (1850–1914)

Marx and Scientific Socialism

From 1815 to 1848, Utopian Socialists, such as Charles Fourier, Robert Owen, and Louis de Rouvroy Saint-Simon, advocated a political-economic system based on romantic concepts of the ideal society. The failure of the revolutions of 1848 discredited the Utopians, so the new "Scientific Socialism" advanced by Karl Marx (1818–1883) became the new ideology of protest and revolution. Marx, a German philosopher, developed a communist philosophy that ironically depended on the goodness of men; this Rousseau-influenced position argued that men were basically good but had been corrupted by artificial institutions (states, churches, and so on) from which they had evolved. Marx stated that the history of humanity was the history of class struggle, and that the process of the struggle (the dialectic) would continue until a classless society was realized; the Marxian dialectic was driven by the dynamics of materialism. Further, he contended that the age of bourgeois domination of the working classes was the most severe and oppressive phase of the struggle. The proletariat, or industrial working class, needed to be educated and led toward a violent revolution that would destroy the institutions that perpetuated the struggle and the suppression of the majority. After the revolution, the people would experience the dictatorship of the proletariat, during which the Communist Party would provide leadership. Marx advanced these ideas in *The Communist Manifesto* (1848), *Critique of Political Economy* (1859), and *Capital* (1863–1864). In most instances, his arguments were couched in scientific form; Marx accumulated extensive data and developed a persuasive rhetorical style. In the 1860s, Marxism was being accepted by many reformers. He lived most of his adult life in London exile, where he died in 1883.

The Anarchists

Anarchism emerged in the nineteenth century as a byproduct of the Industrial Revolution. Its early proponents, William Godwin (1756–1836) and Pierre-Joseph Proudhon (1809–1865), argued that anarchism, a system in which there would be no property or authority, would be attained through enlightened individualism. Proudhon, in *What is Property?* (1840), stated that anarchism would be achieved through education and without violence. After the revolutions of 1848 to 1849, Mikhail Bakunin, a Russian, stated that violent, terrorist actions were necessary to move people to revolt against their oppressors; anarchism has been associated with violence since Bakunin. A variation of anarchism, syndicalism, was developed by Georges Sorel in France. Syndicalism, sometimes referred to as anarcho-syndicalism, involved direct economic actions in order to control industries. The general strike and industrial sabotage were employed frequently by the syndicalists, whose influence was restricted to France, Spain, and Italy.

The Revisionist Movement

A reconsideration of Marxism commenced before Marx's death in 1883. That year a group of British leftists organized themselves as the Fabian Society and declared that, while they were sympathetic to Marxism—indeed, they considered themselves Marxists—they differed from the orthodox on two major points:

1. They did not accept the inevitability of revolution in order to bring about a socialist, that is, communist, society; democratic societies possessed the mechanisms that would lead to the gradual evolution of socialism.

2. They did not accept the Marxist interpretation of contemporary history; they contended the historical processes endured and were difficult to redirect and

reform, while Marxists tended to accept the notion that world revolution was imminent.

Sidney and Beatrice Webb, George Bernard Shaw, Keir Hardie were among those who formed the Fabian Society. Later it would split over the Boer War, but its members would serve in every Labour Party ministry.

In Germany, the Social Democratic Party (SDP) had been established by orthodox Marxists. In the 1890s, Edward Bernstein (1850–1932), influenced by the Fabians, redirected the efforts and platform of the SDP toward the revisionist position. Within a few years, the SDP extended its credibility and support to acquire a dominant position in the *Reichstag* (Germany's legislative assembly). In 1912, it became the largest party, which may have led German militarists in 1914 to consider continental war better than "turning red."

The French socialist Jean Jaurès (1859–1914) led his group to revisionism; their moderation led to an increase of seats in the Chamber of Deputies and their acceptance for criticisms and proposals during the tumultuous years of the Dreyfus Affair (discussed later in the chapter). He was murdered on the eve of the First World War, a symbolic defeat for the pacifism of most Social Democrats in Europe.

While orthodox Marxists (such as Lenin) denounced the revisionist movement, the majority of socialists in 1914 were revisionists who were willing to use the democratic process to bring about their goals. Unfortunately, a byproduct of their compromise position was a willingness to be seduced by nationalist propaganda and thus to support the First World War.

Britain and France

During the second half of the nineteenth century, Britain and France enjoyed economic prosperity, experienced periods of jingoistic nationalism, and were confronted with demands for an expanding democracy. Britain, under the leadership of Lord Palmerston, William Gladstone, and Benjamin Disraeli, represented a dichotomy of values and political agendas. On one hand, Britain led Europe into a new age of imperialism and almost unbridled capitalism; on the other, Gladstone and the Liberal Party advocated democratic reforms, an anti-imperialist stance, and a program to eliminate or restrict unacceptable working and social conditions. In France, the evolution of a more democratic order came into question with the collapse of the Second French Republic and the development of the Second Empire. However, in 1871, the Third Republic was established, and the French moved closer to realizing democracy.

The Age of Palmerston

From 1850 to 1865, Lord Palmerston dominated politics in Great Britain in a range of positions, including foreign secretary, home secretary, and prime minister. In foreign affairs, Palmerston was preoccupied with colonial problems such as the Sepoy Mutiny of 1857, troubles in China, and British interests in the American Civil War; he tended to express little interest in domestic affairs. This period witnessed the realignment of parties within British politics; the Tory Party was transformed into the Conservative Party under Disraeli, and the Whigs became the Liberal Party, with Gladstone serving as its leader. It should be noted that John Bright, a manufacturer, anti-Corn Law advocate, and leader of the Manchester School (the English school of industrial capitalism), contributed significantly to the development of the Liberal Party. These changes in party organization involved more than appellations. The new structure more clearly represented distinct ideological positions on many substantive issues. The new political structure was facilitated by Palmerston's (Whig) lack of interest in domestic issues and Lord Derby's (Tory) indifference to politics; he was preoccupied with his study of the classics and horse racing.

Until 1858, the British East India Company managed India for the government. During the 1850s, a new rifle, the Enfield, was introduced. The procedure for loading the Enfield required that cartridge covers be removed with the teeth prior to inserting them in the rifle. Rumors circulated that the covering was made from the fat of cows and swine; these rumors of taboo grease alarmed the Hindu and Muslim troops. Troops mutinied in Calcutta in 1857 and within months over a third of India was in the hands of rebels and Europeans were being killed. A British-led force of about three thousand troops under Sir Hugh Rose suppressed the mutiny, which lacked cohesion in its aims, organization, and leadership. By January 1858, Britain had reestablished its control of India; the East India Company was dissolved and replaced by the direct authority of the government.

During the 1850s and 1860s, Palmerston sought to clarify British commercial access to China. In 1858, with the support of French troops, the British army took forts on the Peiko River and, in 1860, captured Peking. As a result, China agreed to open Tientsin and other ports to the European powers.

The American Civil War (1861–1865) curtailed the supply of unprocessed cotton to British mills. This adversely affected the British economy, resulting in significant unemployment and factory closings. The American war also led to a discussion within Britain on fundamental issues of liberty, slavery, and democracy. A crisis between Britain and the United States developed over the Trent Affair (1861), during which a British ship was boarded by American sailors. In the end, the British government and people supported the Union cause because of ideological considerations; even those in the areas affected by the shortage of cotton supported the North.

Disraeli, Gladstone, and the Era of Democratic Reforms

After Palmerston's death in 1865, significant domestic developments occurred that expanded democracy in Great Britain. The leaders of this period were William Gladstone (1809–1898) and Benjamin Disraeli (1804–1881). Gladstone, initially a Conservative, emerged as a severe critic of the Corn Laws and, as budgetary expert, became chancellor of the exchequer under Palmerston. As leader of the Liberal Party (to 1895), Gladstone supported Irish Home Rule, fiscal responsibility, free trade, and the extension of democratic principles. He was opposed to imperialism, the involvement of Britain in European affairs, and the further centralization of the British government. Disraeli argued for an aggressive foreign policy, the expansion of the British Empire, and, after opposing democratic reforms, the extension of the franchise.

After defeating Gladstone's effort to extend the vote in 1866, Disraeli advanced the Reform Bill of 1867 as a clever move to "steal the thunder" of the Liberals, that is, beat them at their own game and win more votes for Conservatives. This bill, based on the Reform Bill of 1832, was enacted with two reforms:

1. There would be a redistribution (similar to reapportionment) of seats that would provide a more equitable representation in the House of Commons; the industrial cities and boroughs gained seats at the expense of some depopulated areas in the North and West.

2. The right to vote was extended to include all adult male citizens of the counties who paid twelve pounds or more rent annually or who earned five pounds or more annually as leaseholders.

The consequence of this act was that almost all men over twenty-one years of age who resided in urban centers were granted the right to vote. In 1868, the newly extended electorate provided the Liberals with a victory, and Gladstone commenced his first of four terms as prime minister. So Disraeli's gambit backfired—in the short run.

Gladstone's first ministry (1868–1874) was characterized by a wave of domestic legislation reflecting the movement toward democracy. Among the measures that were enacted were five acts:

1. The Ballot Act (1872) provided for the secret ballot; this act realized a major chartist demand of the 1830s (see chapter 6).

2. Civil Services Reform (1870) introduced the system of competitive examination for government positions.

3. The Education Act (1870) established a system of school districts throughout the country, and provided assistance in the organization of school boards, and for the establishment of schools in poverty stricken regions. Free elementary education in Britain would not be realized until 1891, however.

4. The Land Act (1870) was an attempt to resolve economic and social inequities in Ireland. However, it did not succeed in providing Irish tenants with reasonable safeguards against arbitrary eviction or the imposition of drastic increases in rent.

5. The University Act (1870) eliminated the use of religious tests that provided a quota of seats in universities for members of the Anglican Church.

Between 1874 and 1880, Disraeli served as prime minister, and while he was concerned with foreign issues, he did succeed in extending the new "Tory Democracy" to domestic issues. Tory Democracy represented Disraeli's views on how the Conservative Party would support necessary domestic action on behalf of the common good. It seems now an extension of the aristocratic sense of *noblesse oblige* ("nobility obliges its own to engage in charitable behavior") to the political arena.

In 1875, through Disraeli's support, the following measures were passed: (1) laws that lessened the regulation of trade unions; (2) the Food and Drug Act regulating the sale of these items; (3) the Public Health Act, which specified government require-ments and standards for sanitation; and (4) the Artisan's Dwelling Act, which provided subsidies for public housing. These measures represented a degree of government interference in the private sphere that Old Liberals found abhorrent; but eventually these Tory acts were proven to be wise, and this helped the Labour Party to rise at the expense of the hidebound Liberals.

While a few Conservatives, such as Lord Randolph Churchill, attempted to extend Tory Democracy and incorporate it permanently within the Conservative program, most of the Conservative Party abandoned this approach after Disraeli's death in 1881.

During his remaining ministries (1880–1885, 1886, and 1892–1895), Gladstone was preoccupied with Ireland. However, a further extension of the franchise occurred in 1884 with the passage of the Representation of the People Act granting the vote to adult males in the counties on the same basis as in the boroughs. In 1885, another redistribution of seats in the House of Commons was approved on the ratio of one seat for every fifty thousand citizens.

The Second French Republic and the Second Empire

Louis Napoleon became the president of the Second Republic in December 1848. It was evident that he was not committed to the republic; in May 1849, elections for the Legislative Assembly indicated that the people did not believe in the republic, either. In this election, conservatives and monarchists scored significant gains; republicans and radicals lost power in the assembly. During the three-year life of the Second Republic, Louis Napoleon demonstrated his skills as a gifted politician through the manipulation of the various factions in French politics. He employed a tactic introduced by his uncle, the plebiscite: a simple up-or-down vote on a question of vital interest to the people. Enemies of Napoleon referred to this procedure, fraught with manipulative tactics and propaganda, as Caesarism. His deployment of troops in Italy to rescue and restore Pope Pius IX was condemned by republicans but strongly supported by the monarchists and moderates. As a consequence of French military intervention, a French garrison under General Oudinot was stationed in Rome until the fall of 1870, when it was recalled dur-ing the Franco-Prussian War. Like Julius and Augustus Caesar before him, Napoleon III, as he was known, knew that the appearance of religious devotion could help rulers remain in power.

Napoleon initiated a policy that minimized the importance of the Legislative Assem-bly, capitalized on the developing Napoleonic legend, and courted the support of the army, the Catholic Church, and a range of conservative political groups. The Falloux Law returned control of education to the church. Further, Louis Napoleon was confronted with Article 45 of the constitution, which stipulated that the president was limited to one four-year term; he had no intention of relinquishing power. With the assistance of a core of dedicated supporters, Louis Napoleon arranged for a coup d'état on December 1 to 2, 1851. The Second Republic fell and was soon replaced by the Second Empire.

Napoleon drafted a new constitution, which resulted in a highly centralized government centered on himself. He was to have a ten-year term, and power to declare war, to lead the armed forces, to conduct foreign policy, and to initiate and pronounce all laws; the new Legislative Assembly would be under the control of the president. On December 2, 1852, he announced that he was Napoleon III, emperor of the French.

The domestic history of the Second Empire is divided into two periods: 1851 to 1860, during which Napoleon III's control was direct and authoritarian, and 1860 to 1870, the decade of the Liberal Empire, during which the regime was liberalized through a series of reforms. During the Second Empire, living conditions in France generally improved. The government instituted agreements and actions that stimulated the movement toward free trade (Cobden-Chevalier Treaty of 1860), improved the economy (through the Crédit Mobilier and Crédit Foncier, the one for bank notes, the other for mortgages), and conducted major public works programs in French cities with the assistance of such talented leaders as Baron Haussmann, the prefect of the Seine. Even though many artists and scholars (Gustave Flaubert, Victor Hugo, and Jules Michelet) were censored and, on occasion, prosecuted for their work, the artistic and scholarly achievements of the Second Empire were impressive. While Flaubert and Charles-Pierre Baudelaire, and in music, Jacques Offenbach, were most productive during these decades, younger artists, such as Paul Cézanne, Edouard Manet, and Pierre-August Renoir began their careers and were influenced by the culture of the Second Empire. The progressive liberalization of the government during the 1860s resulted in extending the powers of the Legislative Assembly, restricting church control over secondary education, and permitting the development of trade unions. In large part, this liberalization was designed to divert criticism from Napoleon III's unsuccessful foreign policy. French involvement in Algeria, the Crimean War, the process of Italian unification, the establishment of colonial presences in Senegal, Somaliland, and Indo-China (Laos, Cambodia, and Viet Nam), and the ill-fated Mexican adventure (the short-lived rule of Maximilian, Archduke of Austria), resulted in increased criticism of Napoleon III and his authority. Scandals involving the Crédit Mobilier, for instance, exposed the thorough corruption of Napoleon's favored elites.

The Second Empire collapsed after the capture of Napoleon III during the Franco-Prussian War (1870–1871). After a regrettable Parisian experience with a communist type of government, the Third French Republic was established; it would survive until 1940.

Imperial Russia

The autocracy of Nicholas I's regime was not threatened by the revolutions of 1848. The European revolutionary experience of 1848 to 1849 reinforced the conservative ideology at the heart of the Romanov regime. In 1848 and 1849, Russian troops suppressed disorganized Polish attempts to reassert their nation's power and culture; in 1849, Russian troops brutally suppressed stragglers of the Hungarian revolution.

Russian involvement in the Crimean War met with defeat. France, Britain, and Piedmont emerged as victors; Russian ambitions in the eastern Mediterranean had been thwarted by a coalition of western European states. In 1855, Nicholas I died and was succeeded by Alexander II (reigned 1855–1881), who feared the forces of change and introduced reforms in order to remain in power.

Fearing the transformation of Russian society from below, Alexander II instituted a series of reforms that contributed to radical changes in the social contract in Russia. With the regime in disarray after defeat in the Crimean War, Alexander II, in March 1856, indicated that serfdom had to be eliminated. After years formulating the process for its elimination, Alexander II pronounced in 1861 that serfdom was abolished. Further, he issued the following reforms:

1. The serf (peasant) would no longer be dependent upon the lord.

2. All people were to have freedom of movement and be free to change their means of livelihood.

3. The serf could enter into contracts and own property.

A lingering problem with emancipation, not solved until 1905, was the requirement that freed serfs pay for their freeing in the so-called redemption payments. Theoretically set to end in 1910, these heinous charges had to be collected by the *mir* (commune); Alexander II should have foreseen the resentment and noncompliance that ensued.

In fact, the lives of most peasants were not radically affected by these reforms. Most lived in local communes that regulated the lives of members; thus, the needs of commune life undermined the reforms of Alexander II. Another significant development was the creation of the *zemstvos*, assemblies that administered localities; through the *zemstvos*, the rural nobility retained control. Nevertheless, the elective role of towns, nobles, and peasants in the *zemstvos*, however imperfectly realized, introduced notions of democracy to Russia; also, the power of local taxation enabled some *zemstvos* to provide social services for rural Russia for the first time in its history—fire brigades, repair of bridges and roads, and schools were some of the *zemstvo* reforms. Next, Alexander reformed the judiciary system. The new judiciary was to be based upon such enlightened notions as jury trial, the abolition of arbitrary judicial processes, and the equality of all before the law. In fact, the only substantive change was the improvement in the efficiency of the Russian judiciary; however, the reforms did lead to expectations that were later realized. Finally, Alexander reformed the army (1864–1874) in significant ways: the abolition of harsh corporal punishment (running the gauntlet) was one, the institution of army schools for illiterate peasant conscripts, another.

The reforms of Alexander II did not resolve the problems of Russia. During the 1860s and 1870s, criticism of the regime mounted. Moderates called for Russia to proceed along Western lines in a controlled manner to address political and economic problems; radicals argued that the overthrow of the system was the only solution to the problems confronting the Russian people. Quite naturally, Alexander II and other members of the elite maintained that Russia would solve its own problems within the existing structure and without external intervention. Economic problems that plagued

Russia were staggering. Under the three-field system, one-third of agricultural land was not being used; the population was increasing dramatically, but food protection was not keeping pace. Peasants were allowed to buy land and live outside of the communes; however, even with the establishment of the Peasant Land Bank (1883), most peasants were unable to take advantage of this opportunity to become property owners. During years of great hardship, the government did intervene with emergency measures that temporarily reduced, deferred, or suspended taxes and/or payments.

While agriculture appeared to have no direction, nor to have experienced much growth during this period, Russian industry, particularly in textiles and metallurgy, did develop. Between 1870 and 1900, as the result of French loans, Russia expanded its railroad network significantly. In large part, the expansion of Russian industry resulted from direct governmental intervention. In addition to constructing railroads, the government subsidized industrial development through a protective tariff and by awarding major contracts to emerging industries. From 1892 to 1903, Count Sergei Witte served as minister of finance. As a result of his efforts to stimulate the economy, Russian industry prospered during most of the 1890s. During this same period, the government consistently suppressed the development of organized labor. In 1899, a depression broke and the gains of the 1890s quickly were replaced by the increased unemployment and industrial shutdowns; the outbreak of the Russo-Japanese war in 1904 further aggravated this already very difficult situation.

The last years of the reign of Alexander II witnessed increased political opposition that was manifested in demands for reforms from an ever more hostile group of intellectuals, the emergence of a populist movement, and attempts to assassinate the tsar. Some demands for extending reforms came from within the government from such dedicated and talented ministers as D. A. Miliutin, a minister of war, who reorganized the Russian military system during the 1870s. However, reactionary ministers such as Count Dmitri Tolstoy, minister of education, did much to discredit progressive policies emanating from the regime; Tolstoy repudiated academic freedom and advanced an antiscience bias. As the regime matured, it placed greater importance on traditional values. This attitude fostered nihilism, a viewpoint that rejected romantic illusions of the past in favor of a rugged realism and that was being advanced by such writers as Ivan Turgenev in his *Fathers and Sons* (1862).

The notion of the inevitability and desirability of a social and economic revolution was promoted through the Russian populists. Originally, populists were interested in an agrarian utopian order in which the lives of peasants would be transformed into an idyllic state, but government persecution of the populists, who had no national base of support, resulted in the radicalization of the movement. In the late 1870s and early 1880s, leaders such as Andrei Zhelyabov and Sophie Perovskaya became obsessed with the need to assassinate Alexander II. In March 1881, they succeeded, killing Alexander in Saint Petersburg by bombing his carriage.

Alexander III (reigned 1881–1894) then became the tsar, advocating a national policy based on "Orthodoxy, Autocracy, and National Unity." Alexander III selected as his primary aides conservatives such as Count Dmitri Tolstoy, now minister of the

Interior, Count Delianov, minister of education, and Constantine Pobedonostsev, who headed the Russian Orthodox Church. Alexander III died in 1894, succeeded by the last of the Romanovs to hold power, Nicholas II (reigned 1894–1917). Nicholas II displayed a lack of intelligence, wit, and political acumen, and the absence of a firm will throughout his reign. Nicholas tended to be swayed by stronger personalities, such as his wife Alexandra's, and her favorite monk, Rasputin's. The crisis confronting imperial Russia required extraordinarily effective and cohesive leadership; with Nicholas II, the situation became more severe and, in the end, unacceptable.

The opposition to the tsarist government became more focused and threatening with the emergence of the Russian Social Democrats and the Social Revolutionaries; both were Marxist. Vladimir Ilyich Ulyanov, known as Lenin, led the Bolsheviks, a splinter group of the Social Democrats. Until the impact of the 1899 depression and the horrors associated with the Russo-Japanese War, groups advocating revolutions commanded little support. Even when the Revolution of 1905 occurred, Marxist groups did not enjoy political gains. By winter 1904 to 1905, however, the accumulated consequences of inept management of the economy and in the prosecution of the Russo-Japanese War reached a critical stage. A group under the leadership of the radical priest Gapon marched on the Winter Palace in Saint Petersburg (January 9, 1905) to submit a list of grievances to the tsar; troops fired on the demonstrators on this "Bloody Sunday." In response to the massacre, a general strike broke out, evidently called by unions and the germs of the first soviets; it was followed by peasant revolts through the spring. During these same months, Russian armed forces were defeated by the Japanese and a lack of confidence in the regime became widespread. In June 1905, naval personnel on the battleship *Potemkin* mutinied while the ship was in Odessa. With this startling development, Nicholas II's government lost its nerve. In October 1905, Nicholas issued the October Manifesto that called for the convocation of a duma, or assembly, which would serve as an advisory body to the tsar; extended civil liberties to include freedom of speech, assembly, and press; and announced that Nicholas II would reorganize his government.

The leading revolutionary forces differed in their responses. The monarchist constitutionalists, the Octobrists, indicated that they were satisfied with the arrangements; the more liberal Constitutional Democrats, also known as the Cadets, demanded a more liberal representative system. The Duma convened in 1906 and, from its outset to the outbreak of the First World War, was paralyzed by its own internal factionalism, which was exploited by the tsar's ministers. By 1907, Nicholas II's ministers had recovered real power. Russia experienced a general though fragile economic recovery that was evident by 1909 and lasted until the war.

The Habsburgs in Decline: Austria-Hungary

After the disruptions of the revolution of 1848 to 1849, the Austrian government had to address several major issues with which it was confronted: (1) whether a *kleindeutsch* or *grossdeutsch* Germany was best, (2) how to suppress the national aspirations of ethnic groups that resided in the Balkans, and (3) how to manage an empire that was not integrated because of historic tradition and cultural diversification.

During the 1850s, Habsburg leadership deferred any attempt to resolve problems, and in so doing, lost the initiative. To the north, Bismarck was developing the Prussian army in anticipation of a struggle with Austria over the future of Germany; in the Balkans, Hungarians and Czechs, while smarting from the setbacks of 1849, were agitating for national self-determination or, at the least, for a semiautonomous state. In 1863 to 1864, Austria became involved with Prussia in a war with Denmark. This war was a prelude for the German Civil War of 1866 between Austria and Prussia; Prussia prevailed. The impact of these developments on the Austrian government necessitated a reappraisal of its national policies. Without doubt the most significant development was the *Ausgleich*, or Compromise, which transformed Austria into the Austro-Hungarian Empire. The Hungarians would have their own assembly, cabinet, and administrative system, and would support and participate in the imperial army and imperial government. Not only did the *Ausgleich*, assimilate the Hungarians and nullify them as a primary opposition group, it also led to a more efficient government.

From 1867 to 1914, Austria-Hungary continued to experience difficulties with the subject nationalities and with adjusting to a new power structure in central Europe in which Austria-Hungary was secondary to Germany. At the same time, it enjoyed a cultural revival in which its scholars (Sigmund Freud and Heinrich Friedjung), painters (Gustav Klimt and Hans Makart), dramatists (Hugo von Hofmannsthal), composers (Johannes Brahms and Gustav Mahler), and writers (Rainer Maria Rilke, Adalbert Stifter, and Stefan Zweig) were renowned throughout the world.

Balkan States and Disintegration of the Ottoman Empire

During the period from 1848 to 1914, the influence of the Ottoman Empire eroded steadily due to its internal structure and system, the ineptitude of its leaders, the lack of cohesion within the empire, the development of nationalist ambitions among many ethnic groups in the region, and the expansionist policies of Austria-Hungary and Russia in the Balkans, and of Great Britain in the eastern Mediterranean.

By 1914, Romania, Serbia, Bulgaria, and Montenegro were established as sovereign states, Austria had annexed Bosnia and Herzegovina, Britain held Cyprus, and Russia had extended its influence over the new Bulgaria.

Origins and Motives of New Imperialism (1870–1914)

During the first seven decades of the nineteenth century, European powers did not pursue active imperial expansion. Internal European development preoccupied the powers, which viewed colonies as liabilities because of costs associated with their administration. However, this attitude to extra-European activity began to change in the 1870s and, within twenty years, most European states were conducting aggressive imperial policies. This sharp departure from previous policy resulted from economic, political, and cultural factors. By the 1870s, European industrial economies had grown to a level where they required external markets to distribute the products that could not be absorbed within their domestic economies. Further, excess capital was available, and foreign investment, while risky, appeared to offer the promise of high return. Finally, the need for additional sources of raw materials served as a rationale and stimulant for imperialism. In part, these economic considerations arose from the existing political forces of the era and, at the same time, motivated the contemporary political leadership to be sympathetic in their reappraisal of imperialism. Politicians were also influenced by the missionary societies that sought government protection, if not support, in extending Christianity through the world; British and French missionary societies were vehement in their antislavery position. Further, European statesmen, cognizant of a new distribution of power in Europe, were interested in asserting their national power overseas through the acquisition of strategic—and many not so strategic—colonies. Benjamin Disraeli and Lord Salisbury of England, Adolphe Thiers and Jules Ferry of France, and Bismarck of Germany were influenced by yet another factor: European cultural sentiments of the 1870s and 1880s. The writings of John Seeley, Pierre-Paul Leroy-Beaulieu, and others suggested that the future status of the powers was dependant on the extent and significance of imperial holdings; these thoughts were later amplified by the social and national Darwinists. Exploration and imperial policies were supported by the public throughout the era; national pride and economic opportunities were the factors upon which this popular support was based.

Unlike colonial policies of earlier centuries, the "New Imperialism" of the 1870s was comprehensive in scope and, as Disraeli argued in 1872, a call to "greatness" where a nation was to fulfill its destiny. From Disraeli to Rudyard Kipling to Lord Churchill, there were few leaders who would differ sharply from this view. On the Continent, the New Imperialism was opposed most vigorously by orthodox Marxists; even the revisionist groups such as the Social Democratic Party and, during the Boer War, the English Fabian Society, supported imperial policies.

The Scramble for Colonies

The focus of most European imperial activities in the late 1800s was Africa. Since the 1850s, Africa had commanded the attention of explorers such as Richard Burton, Carl Peters, David Livingston, and others who were interested in charting the unknown interior of the continent, and, in particular, in locating the headwaters of the Nile River. Initially, European interest in these activities was romantic; with John Hanning Speke's discovery of Lake Victoria (1858), Livingston's survey of the Zambezi, and Henry Morton Stanley's work on the Congo River, Europeans became enraptured with the greatness and novelty of Africa south of the Sahara.

While Disraeli was involved in the intrigue that would result in British acquisition of the Suez Canal (1875), Britain found itself becoming increasingly involved in establishing itself as an African power. During the 1870s and 1880s, Britain was involved in a Zulu war and announced the annexation of the Transvaal, which the Boers regained after their victory of Majuba Hill (1881) over the British. At about the same time, Belgium established its interest in the Congo; France, in addition to seizing Tunisia, extended its influence into French Equatorial Africa, which was the Ubangui River Basin; and Italy established colonies in East Africa that would later be extended. During the 1880s, Germany, feeling the need to keep up with the other great powers, acquired the African colonies of German East Africa, the Cameroons, Togoland, and German

South West Africa. All these imperial activities heightened tensions among European powers. Consequently, the Berlin Conference (1884–1885) was convened, resulting in an agreement that specified the following:

1. The Congo would be controlled by Belgium through an international association.

2. Colonial powers would allow others more access to the Niger and Congo rivers.

3. European powers could acquire African territory through by first occupying it and then notifying the other European states of their occupation and claim. This policy involved the new principle of interior control, whereby each power had to show that it did not control only the coast, but also had major interests—military, mercantile, or missionary—in the interior.

Between 1885 and 1914, the principal European states continued to enhance their positions in Africa. Without doubt, Britain was the most active and successful. From 1885 to 1890, Britain expanded its control over Nigeria, moved north from the Cape of Good Hope, and became further involved in East Africa. By this time, Salisbury was the leader of the Conservative Party and, in office, he fostered imperial expansion. Gladstone was still an anti-imperialist and leader of the Liberal Party; he found imperialist forces so formidable that he had to compromise his position on occasion when prime minister. During the 1880s, an Islamic revolution under the Mahdi, an Islamic warrior, developed in the Sudan. In 1884, Gladstone sent General Charles Gordon to evacuate Khartoum; Gordon and the city's defenders were slaughtered by the Mahdi's forces in January 1885. The British found themselves confronted with a continuing native insurrection in the Sudan that was not fully squelched until Lord of Khartoum Herbert Kitchener's victory at Omdurman in 1898. The French were also active during this period; they unified Senegal, the Ivory Coast, and Guinea into French West Africa and extended it to Timbuktu, and moved up the Ubangui toward Lake Chad. While the British had difficulties in the Sudan, the French had to suppress a native insurrection in Madagascar, which was prolonged to 1896.

British movement north of the Cape of Good Hope resulted in a different type of struggle—one that involved Europeans fighting one another rather than a native African force. The Boers from the United Provinces of the Northern Netherlands had settled in South Africa in the middle of the seventeenth century. With the discovery of gold (1882) in the Transvaal, many English Cape settlers moved into the region. The Boers, under the leadership of Paul Kruger, restricted the political and economic rights of British settlers and developed alternative railroads through Mozambique that would lessen the Boer dependency on the Cape colony. Relations between the British and Boers steadily deteriorated; in 1895, the Jameson Raid, an ill-conceived action not approved by Britain, failed to result in restoring the status of British citizens. The crisis mounted and, in 1899, the Boer War began; from 1899 to 1903, the British and Boers fought a war that was costly to both sides. Britain prevailed and, by 1909, the Transvaal, Orange Free State, Natal, and the Cape of Good Hope were united into the Union of South Africa.

Another area of increased imperialist activity was the Pacific, where the islands appealed to many nations. In 1890, the American naval captain Alfred Mahan published

The Influence of Sea Power Upon History, in which he argued that history demonstrated that those nations that controlled the seas prevailed. During the 1880s and 1990s, ships required coaling stations. While Britain, the Netherlands, and France demonstrated that they were interested in Pacific islands, the most active states in this region during the last twenty years of the nineteenth century were Germany and the United States. Britain's Pacific interests were motivated primarily in sustaining its control of Australia. The French were interested in Tahiti; after a dispute over the Samoan Islands, France, Germany, and the United States divided the islands among themselves. The United States acquired the Philippines in 1898; Germany gained part of New Guinea, and the Marshall, Caroline, and Mariana islands.

European powers were also interested in the Asian mainland. In 1900, the Boxer Rebellion erupted in Peking, a native reaction to Western influence in China. An international force was organized to lift the siege of the Western legations. Most powers agreed with the American Open Door Policy that recognized the independence and integrity of China and provided economic access for all powers. Rivalry over China (Manchuria) was a principal cause for the outbreak of the Russo-Japanese War in 1904.

The Age of Bismarck (1871–1890)

The Development of the German Empire

During the period from the establishment of the German Empire in January 1871 to his dismissal as chancellor of Germany in March 1890, Otto von Bismarck dominated European diplomacy and established an integrated political and economic structure for the new German state. Bismarck established a statist system reactionary in its political philosophy and based upon industrialism, militarism, and innovative social legislation. German adaptation during the *Gründerjahre* (founder-years of the new industrial order, 1870–1875) was staggering; remarkable increases in productivity and industrialization took place during the first twenty years of the German Empire's history.

Until 1866, the German Confederation consisted of thirty-odd sovereign states that tended to identify with regional rather than national concerns; to a large degree, this condition reflected the continuing impact of the Peace of Westphalia (1648). With the unification of Germany, a German state became reality, but the process of integration of regional economic, social, political, and cultural interests had not yet occurred. Bismarck, with the consent and approval of Wilhelm I, the German emperor, developed a constitution for the new nation that provided for the following:

1. The Emperor was the executor of state and, as such, established domestic and foreign policies; he was also the commander of the armed forces. The chancellor (similar to a prime minister) held office at the discretion of the emperor.

2. A bicameral legislature consisted of the *Reichstag*, a lower body that represented the nation (the *Volk*); and the *Bundesrat*, an upper body that represented all the states. During Bismarck's tenure, the *Bundesrat* identified with

reactionary positions and served to check any populism rising up from the *Reichstag*.

During the 1870s and 1880s, Bismarck's domestic policies aimed at the establishment of a united, strong German state capable of defending itself in a French war of revenge that would be designed to restore Alsace-Lorraine to France. The legislature enacted laws to regularize the monetary system, establish an imperial bank and strengthen existing banks, develop universal German civil and criminal codes, and require compulsory military service. All of these measures contributed to the integration of the German state.

The political system was multiparty. The most significant political parties of the era were (1) the Conservatives, who represented the *Junkers* (ruling class) of Prussia; (2) the Progressives, who unsuccessfully sought to extend democracy through sharp criticism of Bismarck's autocratic procedures; (3) the National Liberals, who represented the German middle class, identified with German nationalism, and provided support for Bismarck's policies; (4) the Center Party (also known as the Catholic Party), which approved Bismarck's policy of centralization and promoted the political concept of particularism, which advocated regional priorities; and (5) the Social Democrats (SDP), Marxists who advocated sweeping social legislation, the realization of genuine democracy, and the demilitarization of the government. Bismarck was unsuccessful in stopping the influence of the Center Party through his anti-Catholic *Kulturkampf*, his cultural war against Catholics led by him and waged by laws passed in the Prussian parliament; and he failed to thwart the growth of the Social Democrats, whom he outlawed from 1878 to 1890.

In order to develop public support for the government and minimize threats from the left, Bismarck instituted a protective tariff, which maintained domestic production, and many social and economic laws, which provided social security, regulated child labor, and improved working conditions for all Germans. In this, his policies resembled the Tory Democracy of Britain.

European Diplomacy

Bismarck's foreign policy centered on the principle of maintaining the diplomatic isolation of France. After a few years of recovery from defeat in the Franco-Prussian War, the French regained their confidence and publicly discussed the feasibility of a war of revenge to regain Alsace-Lorraine. In 1875, the War-In-Sight Crisis occurred between the French and Germans. While the countries avoided war, the crisis clearly indicated the delicate state of Franco-German relations. In the crisis stemming from the Russo-Turkish War (1877–1878), Bismarck tried to serve as "honest broker" at the Congress of Berlin. Russia did not succeed at the conference and incorrectly blamed Bismarck for its failure. Early the next year, a cholera epidemic affected Russian cattle herds and Germany placed an embargo on the importation of Russian beef. The Russians were outraged by this action and launched an anti-German propaganda campaign in their press. Bismarck, desiring to maintain the peace and a favorable diplomatic environment, concluded a secret defensive treaty with Austria-Hungary in 1879. The Dual Alliance was significant because it was the first "hard" diplomatic alliance of the era. A "hard" alliance involved the specific commitment of military support; traditional or "soft" alliances involved pledges of neutrality or to hold military conversations in the event of a war. The Dual Alliance, which had a five-year term and was renewable, directed that one signatory would assist the other in the event that one power was attacked by two or more states.

In 1881, a similar agreement, the Triple Alliance, was signed between Germany, Austria-Hungary, and Italy. In the 1880s, relations between Austria-Hungary and Russia deteriorated over Balkan issues. Bismarck, fearing a war, intervened and, by 1887, had negotiated the secret Reinsurance Treaty with Russia. This was a "hard" defensive alliance with a three-year renewable term. Since these were "defensive" arrangements, Bismarck was confident that, through German policy, the general European peace would be maintained, and through the sustained diplomatic isolation of France, the security of Germany ensured. Bismarck also acted to neutralize the role of Great Britain in European affairs through the implementation of a policy that, in most but not all instances, was supportive of British interests.

In 1888, the emperor, Kaiser Wilhelm I, died, but his successor, Frederick III, also died within a few months. Frederick's son, Wilhelm II (reigned 1888–1918), came to power and soon found himself in conflict with Bismarck. Wilhelm II was intent upon administering the government personally and viewed Bismarck as an archaic personality. Early in 1890, two issues developed that led to Bismarck's dismissal. First, Bismarck had evolved a scheme for a fabricated coup by the Social Democratic Party; his aim was to use this situation to create a national hysteria through which he could restrict the SPD through legal action. Second, Bismarck intended to renew the Reinsurance Treaty with Russia to maintain his policy of French diplomatic isolation. Wilhelm II opposed both plans; in March 1890, Bismarck, who had used the threat of resignation so skillfully in the past, suggested that he would resign if Wilhelm II did not approve his actions. The kaiser accepted his resignation; in fact, Bismarck was dismissed. Diplomatic developments after 1890 radically altered the balance of power in Europe. The position of chancellor of Germany was filled by four less-talented statesmen, including Count von Caprivi (1890–1894), Prince Hohenlohe (1894–1900), Prince Bernhard von Bülow (1900–1909), and Theobald Bethmann-Hollweg.

The Movement Toward Democracy in Western Europe (1870 to 1914)

Great Britain

Even after the reforms of 1867 and 1884, the movement toward more democracy in Great Britain continued unabated. Unlike other European nations where the focus on democracy was limited to gaining the vote, British reform efforts were more complex and sophisticated, involving social and economic reforms as well as further changes in the political process; reformers desired not only participation in the system but also representation. During the 1880s and 1890s, new groups emerged that wanted to extend the definition of democratic government to embrace new social and economic philosophies. From women's suffrage and the condemnation of imperialism to the redistribution of wealth and demise of nationalism, these groups represented a broad spectrum of radical and reformist ideologies. Among the most significant was the Fabian Society (1883), which advanced a revisionist Marxism and whose members included Sidney and Beatrice Webb, the Scottish politician Keir Hardie (who later led the Labor Party), George Bernard Shaw, H. G. Wells, and the young Ramsay MacDonald, who became the first Labour prime minister. The Fabians argued for evolutionary political transformation that would result in full political democracy and economic socialism. In 1884, the Social Democratic Federation was formed by H. M. Hyndman. In 1893, Keir Hardie established the Independent Labour Party that rapidly became a vocal third party in British politics. The Labour Party attracted trade unionists, socialists, and those who thought that the Conservative and Liberal parties had no genuine interest in the needs of the public.

During the early years of the twentieth century, both the Conservatives and the Liberals advanced more aggressive social and economic programs. The Conservatives, through the efforts of Arthur James Balfour, promoted the Education Act of 1902, which they argued would provide enhanced educational opportunities for the working class. In fact, this act was criticized roundly for not providing what it promised. In 1905, the Liberals under Henry Campbell-Bannerman came to power. Government ministries were staffed by such talented leaders as Herbert Asquith, Sir Edward Grey, David Lloyd George, and Winston Churchill.

The most significant political reform of this long-lived Liberal government was the Parliament Act of 1911, which eliminated the veto powers of the House of Lords and resulted in the House of Commons becoming the unquestioned center of national power. The catalyst for this "parliamentary revolution" was the Budget of 1909, which was two-pronged in providing for some social security laws (modeled more or less on Germany's example) and in funding a bigger, better navy (meant to cow the Germans into stopping their naval race). This was a clever budget, since it had one half to which Conservatives could not well object (the navy) and which the king supported. When the Lords threatened vetoes, the king pulled out his trump card: he would flood the Lords with newly created peers. The Lords grudgingly agreed to their own emasculation. All revenue bills approved by the House of Commons would automatically become law thirty days after being sent to the House of Lords. If the Lords voted favorably, the law would be enacted earlier. The Lords had lost their old veto power over revenue bills.

Nonrevenue bills opposed by the Lords would be enacted if passed by three consecutive sessions of Commons. It was not difficult to transform such measures into revenue bills. Finally, the life span of Parliament was reduced from seven to five years.

The British political climate during this period was volatile. Issues relating to trade unions, Ireland, and women's suffrage tended to factionalize politics. The Liberal Party, which was in power from 1905 to the early 1920s, came to be institutionalized and in the process came to be identified as "the government." To many, programs advanced by the Conservative and Labour parties provided the basis for debate and decision. The Liberal Party was withering because it lacked clarity of platform and encapsulated the unrealized domestic goals, the ambiguities of bureaucracy, and the horrors of war.

The most serious problem that Britain experienced from 1890 to 1914 was the "Irish Question." Gladstone, in his final ministry, argued unsuccessfully for Irish Home Rule. In Ireland, opposition to British rule and its abuse of power was evident through the program of the National Land League, established in 1879 by Michael Davitt. This organization stimulated and coordinated Irish opposition to British and Irish landlords. The efforts of the National Land League resulted in support for Irish Home Rule. During the 1880s, Charles Stewart Parnell led the Irish delegation to the House of Commons. Parnell, through the support of Gladstone, attained some gains for the Irish, such as the Land Reform Act and the Arrears Act. In 1890, Parnell became involved in a divorce case and the scandal ruined his career; he died the next year. In 1893, Gladstone devised the Irish Home Rule bill, which was passed by the Commons, but rejected by the Lords. The Irish situation became more complicated when Protestant counties of the North started to enjoy remarkable economic growth in the 1890s; they were adamant in their rejection of all measures of Irish Home Rule. In 1914, an Irish Home Rule Act was passed by both the Commons and the Lords, but the Protestants refused to accept it; implementation was deferred until after the First World War.

The Third French Republic

In the fall of 1870, Napoleon III's Second Empire collapsed when it was defeated by Prussian and allied German armies in the Franco-Prussian War. Napoleon III and his aides were captured; he abdicated and fled to England. Political moderates created the National Assembly (1871–1875) and recognized Adolphe Thiers as its chief executive. At the same time, a radical political entity, the Paris Commune (1870–1871), came into existence and exercised unusual power during the Prussian siege of Paris. After the siege and the peace agreement with Prussia, the Commune refused to recognize the authority of the National Assembly. Led by Marxists, anarchists, and republicans, the Paris Commune repudiated conservative and monarchist control of the National Assembly; from March to May 1871, the Commune fought a bloody struggle with troops of the National Assembly. Thousands died, and when Paris surrendered to Assembly troops, thousands more were executed—accepted estimates place the number of executions at twenty thousand during the first week after Paris fell on May 28, 1871. It was within this historic framework that France began a program of recovery that led to the formulation of the Third Republic in 1875. The National Assembly sought to (1) put the political house in order; (2) establish a new constitutional government; (3) pay off an indemnity imposed by the Treaty of Frankfurt (1871) and, in doing so, remove German troops from French territory; and (4) restore the honor and glory of France. For decades, however, pretenders to the throne from all three royal houses—Bourbon, Orleans, and Bonaparte—muddied the waters.

In 1875, the National Assembly adopted a constitution that provided for a republican government with a president (few powers), a Senate and a Chamber of Deputies, which was the center of political power. Politicians and factions who led France during the 1870s and 1880s had to address the dominant forces of French society and politics, such as the immense influence of the bourgeoisie (upper-middle class), intent upon establishing and sustaining a republic; the mounting hostility between the Catholic Church and government (anticlericalism was frequently manifested in the proceedings of the Chamber of Deputies); the unpredictability of multiparty politics; and, finally, the extreme nationalism that gripped France and resulted in continuing calls for a war of revenge against Germany in order to regain Alsace-Lorraine.

During the early years of the republic, Leon Gambetta (1838–1882) led the republicans. Beginning in the 1880s, a series of crises challenged the Third Republic and threatened its continuity. The Boulanger Crisis (1887–1889), the Panama Scandal (1894), and the Dreyfus Affair (1894–1906) were grave domestic problems; in all these developments, the challenge to republicanism came from the right. Support for republicanism in this time of troubles came primarily from (1) the able leadership of the government, and (2) the continuing commitment of the bourgeoisie to republicanism.

Since the founding of the Third Republic, monarchists and conservatives schemed to overthrow the regime; however, until the appointment of General Georges Boulanger (1837–1891) as minister of war in 1886, the antirepublican cause lacked a clear leader. Boulanger won over the army by improving the conditions of military life. His popularity was high in 1888, when supporters urged him to lead a coup; he delayed and by the spring of 1889, the republicans had mounted a case against Boulanger. He was directed to appear to respond to charges of conspiracy; Boulanger broke, fled to Belgium, and committed suicide in 1891.

The Boulanger Crisis resulted in renewed confidence in the republic, but what popular gains it made were unraveled in 1892 to 1894 with the Panama Scandal. The French had been involved with the engineering and the raising of capital for the Panama Canal since the 1870s; the heroic engineer of the Suez Canal (1859–1869), Ferdinand de Lesseps, was chosen to lead this enterprise. Early in the 1890s, promoters of the project resorted to the bribery of government officials and of members of the press who had access to information that indicated the work on the canal was not proceeding as had been announced. In 1892, the scandal broke and for months the public thought the entire government was corrupt. However, by 1893, elections to the Chamber of Deputies resulted in socialist gains. Monarchists did not attract much public support.

Without a doubt, the most serious threat to the republic came in the Dreyfus Affair. In 1894, Captain Alfred Dreyfus was assigned to the French General Staff of the Army. A scandal broke when it was revealed that classified information had been provided to German spies. Dreyfus, a Jew, was charged, tried, and convicted. Later, a small group of generals determined that the actual spy was Major Marie-Charles Esterhazy; however, he was acquitted in order to save the pride and reputation of the army. Monarchists used this incident to criticize republicanism; the republicans countered when the great naturalist, novelist, and journalist, Emile Zola, took up Dreyfus's cause and wrote an open letter in his newspaper entitled *J'accuse*, which condemned the General Staff's actions and pronounced Dreyfus innocent. Leftists supported the republic, and in 1906, the case was closed when Dreyfus was declared innocent and returned to the ranks. Rather than cause the collapse of the republic, the Dreyfus Affair demonstrated the intensity of anti-Semitism in French society, the level of corruption in the French army, and the willingness of the Catholic Church and monarchists to join a conspiracy against a scapegoat. The republicans launched an anticlerical campaign that culminated in the separation of church and state in the Combes Laws (1905).

From 1905 to 1914, the socialists under Jean Jaurès gained seats in the Chamber of Deputies. The Third Republic endured the crises that confronted it and, in 1914, enjoyed the support of the vast majority of French citizens.

Lesser States of Europe

During the decades prior to 1914, the Low Countries exhibited differing approaches to extending democracy. An appreciation of democracy was evident in Belgium under the leadership of Leopold I (reigned 1865–1909) and Albert I (reigned 1909–1934); during their reigns, the franchise was extended, social and economic reforms were introduced, and equity was used in reconciling the Flemish and French-speaking Belgians. To the north, the Netherlands was slow to adopt democracy. By 1896, only 14 percent of the Dutch had the vote and it would not be until 1917 that universal manhood suffrage would be enacted.

Denmark experienced a struggle between the old guard represented by Christian IX (reigned 1863–1906), who opposed parliamentary government, and the Social Democrats, who advocated democratic principles. The Danish Constitution of 1915 provided a basic democratic political system. Sweden, after a decade of debilitating debate, recognized the independence of Norway in 1905; Norway moved quickly toward democracy, granting women the vote in 1907, one of the first places in the world to do so. Sweden, under Gustavus V (reigned 1907–1950), inaugurated a fully democratic system in 1909.

In southern Europe, advocates of democracy did not meet with any substantive success prior to 1914. In Spain, Portugal, and Italy, the monarchist establishments were preoccupied with survival. Though they promulgated the occasional reform, the monarchs had no intention to move toward full democracy.

European Cultural Developments (1848–1914)

The great political and economic changes of this period were accompanied by cultural achievements that included the development of a literate citizenry and substantive innovations in science, literature, art, music, and other areas of intellectual activity. In large part, these developments occurred as a reaction against the mechanistic sterility of the scientism and positivism of the age; however, some achievements, such as

Charles Darwin's theories of evolution and natural selection, ironically extended the exaggerated claims of scientism. From Darwin, Richard Wagner, Friedrich Nietzsche, and Sigmund Freud to Claude Monet, Richard Strauss, Igor Stravinsky, Oscar Wilde, Thomas Mann, and James Joyce, intelligent Europeans of the era pursued differing, and at times opposing, approaches in their quest for truth. For much of the nineteenth century, after romanticism had exhausted its charms, artists sought to master reality by giving a ruthlessly truthful rendering of it, the so-called movement of realism in the arts and letters. Though realism's practitioners were self-consciously "bohemian" in their lifestyles, their efforts oddly paralleled the go-getting worldly realism of many staid liberals, especially the captains of industry and trade who triumphed after mid-century. Later, many philosophers became critical of liberal democracy, which they identified with mass culture and political ineptitude. Artists attempted to escape their plight through moving into symbolism with their pen or brush; there, they were free to express their fantasies of hope and despair.

Realism

Western art had had realistic tendencies since the Renaissance, and a number of writers in the seventeenth century, such as William Shakespeare, Miguel de Cervantes, J.J.C. von Grimmelshausen, and others, can lay claim to a considerable amount of realism in their works. But until the 1830s, idealizing tendencies in the arts and letters always prevailed and dominated the arbiters of taste and all the teaching academies. It is with the rise of the megalopolis (big city) that we begin to see a more programmatic realism develop, fed by two major innovations: photography and mass-circulation, often sensationalistic, journalism.

The modern techniques of photography were developed in France by Joseph-Nicéphore Niépce and Louis Daguerre in the 1820s and 1830s; the word "photography" was coined by the British astronomer Sir John Herschel in 1839, when the details of the photographic process were made known by Daguerre. The need for technical fine-tuning and fights over patents kept photography from becoming commercially viable, and popular, until the 1850s when the pioneer Nadar (pseudonym for Gaspard Tournachon) opened studios and inaugurated the rage for personal (and business) photos. In one respect, we may look at the realism of photography as a double-pronged challenge to the plastic arts: one either had to go away from realism into fantasy, or had to embrace its potential and perhaps go further than society photographers dared.

The other innovation spurring on realism in arts and letters was the development of the mass-circulation (later, illustrated) "penny press." Newspapers had been a fact of life in Europe since the early 1600s, but in all countries they were hampered by strict censorship, costs of paper, slow printing presses, and (often) a stamp tax. The mass-circulation press, already thriving in the new United States, was introduced into England and France in the 1830s, but in England most evaded the onerous stamp tax, and were thus both illegal and radical. With the end of the stamp tax in Britain in 1855, the era of the popular press took off. In the 1840s, the steam-powered rotary press was perfected; in the 1860s, illustrated newspapers became possible, thanks to advances in the daguerreotype, supplanted in the 1880s by Otto Mergenthaler's invention of the linotype.

Alongside these innovations there developed the mindset of the first realists in the aesthetic realm. As early as the 1830s, Charles Dickens in England and Honoré de Balzac in France were producing novels more realistic than the public was used to; in the 1840s, the author Eugene Sue (1804–1857) wed sensationalist realism to melodramatic excess in his bestsellers *Mysteries of Paris* and *The Wandering Jew* of the 1840s. In general, the early realism of even the masters Dickens and Balzac contains more sentimentality and melodramatic plotting than was used by the later naturalists, who affected to be cold, more scientific, bland.

Realism in the arts begins, more or less, with Gustave Courbet (1819–1877), whose *Burial at Ornans* (1850) shows a Catholic funeral in the countryside without extraneous emotion, artificial poses, or any of the other traits of academic painting of the time (see Figure 7-1). It can be profitably compared with the equally impressive *Burial of Count Orgaz* by El Greco, a masterpiece of the Spanish baroque.

Musée d'Orsay, Paris, France

Figure 7-1. Gustave Courbet's *Burial at Ornans* (1850) shows a real, somewhat mundane, Catholic funeral procession without a dramatic focus; the deceased is not even shown. The normalcy, even every-dayness, of the scene would have shocked contemporaries used to more drama, more moral uplift.

Other exemplars of the realist school in painting were Edouard Manet and Edgar Degas of France, and Ilya Repin of Russia. Manet shocked the art world with two realist masterpieces, one after the other: the *Luncheon on the Grass*, exhibited at the Salon des Refusés of 1863, and his saucy *Olympia* (see Figure 7-2), exhibited at the Salon of 1865. By the time that Degas painted his sad *Absinthe Drinker* (see Figure 7-3) of 1876, realism was no longer as shocking. In Russia, realism went hand in glove with an awakened nationalism, also the new populism that saw the future of Russia (for good or ill) in its majority of peasants. Repin's *Barge Haulers on the Volga* (1872) is justifiably famous as a subtle exposé of the inhuman working conditions prevalent even in postemancipation Russia (see Figure 7-4).

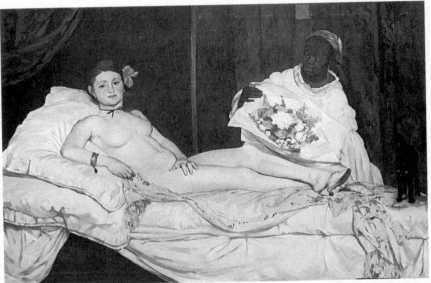

Musée d'Orsay, Paris, France

Figure 7-2. Edouard Manet's *Olympia* (1862) shows a nude more brazen than any in the Renaissance or rococo, since she presents to us an unabashed sensuality, even the businesslike, bemused smile of the courtesan; the necklace, shoes, black maid, and bird all bespeak a sordidness beyond the merely naughty.

Musée d'Orsay, Paris, France

Figure 7-3. Edgar Degas's *Absinthe Drinker* (1875-76) relies on the viewer's knowledge of the stupefying effects of absinthe, outlawed in the early twentieth century for causing insanity.

The Russian Museum, St. Petersburg, Russia

Figure 7-4. Ilya Repin's starkly lit, dramatically composed *Barge Haulers on the Volga* (1872–1873) was based on his travels around Russia looking for the real life of real people. That this self-indicting composition could be shown at all speaks well of the liberal interlude of Tsar Alexander II.

Darwin, Wagner, Freud, and the Emergence of a New Tradition

In 1859, Charles Darwin's (1807–1882) *The Origin of Species* was published; it provided scientific evidence for evolution, a theory bandied about for decades before. Darwin's contributions to the theory were based (1) on the data that he provided in its defense and (2) in the formulation of a well-structured explanation of the mechanism of natural selection (survival of the fittest). The reaction to *The Origin of Species* was diverse and tenacious; some discussants were concerned with the implication of the theory on religion, while others were interested in applying aspects of the theory to the understanding of contemporary social problems. Within the Darwinian camp, factions emerged that supported or rejected one or more components of the theory. Samuel Butler and George Bernard Shaw accepted evolution but rejected natural selection; Thomas Huxley was Darwin's most consistent and loyal supporter. Herbert Spencer (1820–1903) developed a Social Darwinism that enjoyed a widespread vogue in scholarly and popular circles. One obvious consequence of Darwin's theory was that it necessitated a reevaluation of ideas relating to man's place in the cosmos. The doctrine of creation was challenged and thus the authenticity of prevailing religion was endangered.

In classical music, the erratic Richard Wagner (1813–1883) was both a musical genius-innovator and a vulgar polemicist. Wagner developed an aestheticism with one fundamental element: it demanded absolute artistic integrity. He shifted styles several times during his career; his *Ring* cycle revived old German epics and advanced a national myth about the history of the German people. He is much criticized for his anti-Semitic attitude, but, a walking contradiction, he attracted ardent Jewish supporters.

Sigmund Freud (1856–1939) established a new approach to human behavior, psychoanalysis. He accepted the impressionist interpretation that reality is not material, but is based on moods, concepts, and feelings that shift. In Vienna, Freud developed his concepts that the unconscious was shaped during the formative years, that sexuality was a dominant life force, and that free will may not exist. Freud argued his theories in

Origins of Psychoanalysis and *Civilization and Its Discontents*. The scholarly establishment rejected his unorthodox views as threats to the rationalist tradition of the West.

In science, new developments challenged the certainty and security of the old models. Max Planck's *Quantum Physics*, Albert Einstein's *Theory of Relativity*, and the findings of Niels Bohr, Hendrik Lorentz, and Ernest Rutherford, all in physics, led to a new generation of scientists reexamining many assumptions of the past. Just as earth-shaking was the rediscovery in 1900 by three biologists studying heredity—Carl Correns, Hugo De Vries, and Ernst von Tschermak—of the 1866 paper of the monk Gregor Mendel. Mendel's findings on the transmission of various traits in sweet peas opened up the new discipline of genetics and provided invaluable support for Darwin's theories.

Impressionism and Symbolism: Forces of the New Art

The turbulence within European cultural life during the fifty years prior to the outbreak of the First World War can be seen most evidently in the new attitudes that emerged in art and literature. Not only did intellectuals find themselves looking for a new synthesis through which to offer new vision and hope, but they were also liberated from limitations imposed on their predecessors through new ideas on optics and physics. Developments in optics enabled artists to look at nature in different ways from those of photographic realism. Painters were now free to pursue the dictates of their imaginations. Impressionism developed in France during the 1870s; Claude Monet, Edouard Manet, Pierre-August Renoir, and others pioneered the new art. Impressionism soon gave way to post-impressionism and later expressionism. At the turn of the century, more radical artistic forms such as symbolism and cubism enjoyed notoriety, if not much acceptance.

Realism itself did not die out, of course; it only branched into new areas, as can be seen in Arnold Böcklin's evocative *Island of the Dead* (1880; see Figure 7-5) and Gustave Caillebotte's arresting *Man on Balcony, Boulevard Haussmann* (1880; see Figure 7-6).

Museum der Bildenden Kuenste, Leipzig, Germany

Figure 7-5. Arnold Böcklin (1827–1901) was a Swiss painter who spent most of his career in Germany. His *Island of the Dead (1880–1886)* is available in different versions at different museums. The composer Sergey Rachmaninov was inspired to write a tone-poem on seeing this evocative work.

Private Collection, Switzerland

Figure 7-6. Gustave Caillebotte (1848–1894) was a French impressionist much influenced by developments in photography. His *Man on Balcony, Boulevard Haussmann* (1880) is reminiscent of Caspar David Friedrich's from-the-rear portraits.

Impressionism was never a monolithic school or movement, as can be seen in different works by Monet (see Figure 7-7) and Georges Seurat (see Figure 7-8). Each was influenced by different revelations of modern optics, namely what passing impressions might be like to the eye, and how to represent color through dots that mirror the workings of the eye's rods and cones.

Musée Marmottan–Claude Monet, Paris, France

Figure 7-7. Claude Monet (1832–1883) tried to render the "impression" of the moment by painting quickly, on site. His masterful and very influential *Impression: Sunrise* (1873) rejects the filled-in realism that had dominated European art since the Italian Renaissance. What could be seen as gaps or unevenness actually merge to make vagueness artistically more truthful, impressionists thought.

The National Gallery, London, England

Figure 7-8. Georges Seurat (1859–1891) accomplished great things in his short life, mainly the completion of masterpieces that illustrate a different kind of impressionism, his pointillism. The *Sunday Afternoon on the Isle of Grande-Jatte* is best known, but his *Bathers at Asnières* (1884) is equally astute in forcing the eye to connect dots of color.

Literature was transformed through the writings of such innovators as Oscar Wilde (*The Picture of Dorian Gray*), Thomas Mann (*Death in Venice*), Marcel Proust (the first volume of his great series of novels, *In Search of Time Past*, 1913–1927), and the young James Joyce (*Portrait of the Artist as a Young Man*, and the collection of short stories, *Dubliners*). These writers were interested in themes that had great personal value and meaning. Whereas Joyce emerged as the most seminal stylist of the twentieth century, Proust, building on such astute psychological writers as Fyodor Dostoevsky, may well be the greatest writer of the century, period.

← TIMELINE →

Liberalism, Nationalism, and Imperialism (1850–1913)

Year(s)	Event	Significance
1851	Louis Napoleon stages a coup d'état on December 2, 1851.	Impatient with the machinery of the Second Republic, Louis Napoleon as its president overthrows its government to rule alone. He has the support of peasants in the 1848 election and subsequent plebiscites; he garners the support of the church in the Falloux Law of 1850. In 1852, he declares himself Emperor Napoleon III.
1851	Crystal Palace is built to house industrial exhibitions.	The Great Exhibition of 1851 lasts until 1936. The Crystal Palace becomes the symbol of progress through its exhibits of the latest in technology and industry. In this bizarre structure, Victorian ideals of hard work and thrift are symbolized.
1853–1856	Europe becomes embroiled in the Crimean War.	The Crimean War grows out of a dispute between Russia and France over holy places in Palestine and becomes a struggle over the "sick man of Europe," Turkey: its European possessions, the Straits of the Bosporus and Dardanelles, and more. Britain, France, and Piedmont ally to defeat Russia.
1858–1870	France and Piedmont plan Italian unification.	Impressed by Piedmontese in Crimean War, Napoleon III embraces Italian unification (to twit Austria). He meets Prime Minister Camillo de Cavour of Piedmont in 1858 and promises military support to Italy if Piedmont gives up Nice and Savoy. When war erupts between Italy and Austria in 1859, France sends in troops, Austria loses, and Piedmont gets Lombardy. Italy adds the northern duchies in 1860 to 1861; Venetia falls to Italy in 1866, and Rome in 1870.

(Continued)

1859	Charles Darwin publishes *The Origin of Species*, which delineates his well-founded theory of natural selection.	Charles Darwin's work adds substance to the old theory of evolution. It creates an uproar from conservative camps over degradation of religion and leads to the rise of Social Darwinism to explain poverty and degeneration of "races."
1860–1862	Legislation to upgrade the army fails in Prussia.	For three years, the liberal Prussian diet opposes the illiberal army-upgrade provisions requested by Regent (then King) Wilhelm. When Otto von Bismarck becomes prime minister in 1862, he evades parliament by using the old budget of 1858. This is the first instance of Bismarck's sly brilliance and underhandedness in dealing with domestic politics.
1861	Tsar Alexander II emancipates the Russian serfs.	Alexander II concludes that Russia lost the Crimean War because it is backward and consequently institutes major reforms, starting with the emancipation of the serfs. Redemption payments, however, sour this reform with the onus of having to pay off one's freedom for forty-nine years!
1866	The German Civil War erupts.	Austria and Prussia clash over Schleswig-Holstein. Austria and allies lose to Prussia and allies. The North German Confederation forms without Austria.
1867	A second Reform Bill extends suffrage in Britain; Germany and Austria extend suffrage as well.	The Tory government, stealing a march on Liberals, grants more votes to the middle classes; Bismarck grants universal male suffrage in the North German Confederation; Austria-Hungary gets a new, more liberal constitution with an effective voting system. This change made Austria for the first time a more liberal state, but also opened the floodgates to the resentments of the working classes.
1870–1871	Franco-Prussia War occurs.	Prussia leads all Germany in war against France in order to unify north and south. France loses war and Alsace-Lorraine; Germany is united on January 18, 1871, by vote of princes to create the German Empire.

1871	Paris Commune comes to power—briefly.	As France fights for its life from capitals in Bordeaux and Versailles, anarchists take over Paris and attempt to install a radical democracy. French chief executive Adolphe Thiers sends troops to crush the Commune, and executes about twenty thousand Communards. The legacy of this revolution was made a socialist myth by Karl Marx and Friedrich Engels.
1873–1896	Europe and United States suffer through worldwide economic depression.	The depression causes the collapse of Vienna Exchange and U.S. banks, creating a ripple effect; markets overheat in France and Germany after indemnity payments from the Franco-Prussian War. Industry and agriculture suffer, so most nations resort to protectionist tariffs. The depression marks the end of liberal economics as the dominant policy.
1877–1878	Russo-Turkish War leads to Congress of Berlin.	Russian victory over Turkey threatens the balance of power, which leads the Congress of Berlin to strip Russia of its gains. Thus, Serbia gains its independence, and Bosnia is awarded to Austria. Russia leaves angry. Bismarck forms the Dual Alliance with Austria.
1878–1890	Bismarck institutes antisocialist laws and social insurance legislation.	After anti-Catholic *Kulturkampf* backfires (1873–1879), Bismarck drops old allies, the National Liberals, to court Catholic Center Party (old enemy) with tariffs; he courts the Conservatives with the same, as well as with antisocialist laws. In the 1880s, he enacts radical social insurance laws—the first in the world—in an attempt to keep workers docile. Social insurance was successful, but Bismarck's attacks on the Socialists backfired—they won the largest bloc of seats in the elections of 1912.
1880s	Jules Ferry secularizes French education.	Ferry's laws privilege secular schools, thus removing the Catholic Church from its last official role in French government and from one of its chief roles in French society.

(Continued)

1881	Alexander II is assassinated by radical populists.	The assassination ends reforms in Russia and begins a period of anti-Semitic pogroms and bleak reaction.
1880s	European powers scramble for colonies in Africa!	After Congress of Berlin (1878) gives Britain Cyprus, and Tunisia to France, powers scramble to divvy up Africa. The Brits move into Egypt and Sudan, after taking control over Suez Canal from the French; Italy goes for Libya, Belgium for Congo, and so on. By 1914, only two lands are independent: Abyssinia and Liberia. The powers meet at the 1885 Berlin Conference to regulate further forays, mainly by Belgium, France, and Britain.
1894–1906	The Dreyfus Affair rocks France.	Reports of leaks of French army secrets to German embassy leads to the court martial of Captain Alfred Dreyfus, falsely accused of treason. Further leaks keep the case alive, as does Dreyfus's wife, who agitates in press. Zola takes up Dreyfus's cause in 1898. France is split between pro- and anti-Dreyfus factions. Only a new government is able to end the affair by acquitting Dreyfus in 1906. The affair leads to anti-church laws of 1905 and 1906, since the church sided with army and nobility in excoriating Dreyfus.
1896	Theodor Herzl publishes *Judenstaat*.	Herzl, an Austrian journalist, is disgusted by anti-Dreyfus demonstrations in Paris. His *Judenstaat* is a major Zionist document, advocating a Jewish state, since "Christian" states are hostile, even to assimilated Jews.
1898	Russian Social Democratic Party (RSPD) is formed.	The RSPD forms on strictly Marxist lines. Lenin forms the Bolsheviks in 1903 on a "majority" vote to outwit the Mensheviks (minority RSPD). Russian Social Democrats live in exile, plotting revolution.

1898–1904	Britain and France affect rapprochement in colonial affairs.	After a showdown in Sudan (1898), Britain and France resolve colonial disputes in Africa and elsewhere. Warmer relations ultimately lead to the 1904 Entente Cordiale, an informal alliance of the two great powers.
1900	Science marks major milestones!	Max Planck publishes his path-breaking paper in quantum physics five years before Einstein. Three biologists of heredity rediscover 1866 paper of Gregor Mendel, thus giving birth to the modern science of genetics.
1905	Russian Revolution occurs.	Disasters in Russo-Japanese War lead to a yearlong revolution against tsardom. Ultimately, Nicholas II is forced to concede a constitution (October Manifesto) and a representative assembly (Duma) to Russia.
1909	Budget of 1909 sparks parliamentary crisis.	Liberals raise so-called death taxes on the wealthy to pay for (a) a new navy, wanted by Tories, and (b) social insurance, a sop to the Labour Party. When the House of Lords threatens to veto the budget, the king counters with a threat to flood the Lords. The Lords acquiesce, and the House of Lords Act of 1911 ends peremptory veto of Lords over bills.
1911–1913	Literary advances explore social taboos.	Thomas Mann's *Death in Venice* (1911) broaches taboo of homosexuality, as does Marcel Proust's masterpiece, *In Search of Lost Time*, whose first volume, *Swann's Way*, appears in 1913.

Chapter 8

The "Second Thirty Years' War": World Wars I and II (1890–1945)

International Politics and the Coming of the War (1890–1914)

During the generation prior to the outbreak of the World War I in the summer of 1914, conflicts and strained relations among the great powers increased in frequency and intensity. There can be no question that the primary factors contributing to this crisis were the heightened nationalism and the mindless militarism of the period.

The Polarization of Europe

In 1890, Otto von Bismarck was dismissed as German chancellor by the immature, impetuous, and inexperienced Kaiser Wilhelm II. The particular issues that led to Bismarck's fall involved the renewal of the Reinsurance Treaty (1887) with Russia, and his scheme to undermine the Social Democratic Party (SPD) in German politics. Bismarck's dismissal called into question the continuing dominance of a German agenda over European affairs. The intricate alliance system that Bismarck had constructed was directed at maintaining the diplomatic isolation of France, but in lesser hands his old balance of power would shift radically to an imbalanced international scene.

Germany failed to renew the Reinsurance Treaty, so, consequently, Russia looked elsewhere to lessen its perceived isolation. In 1891, the French and Russians undertook secret negotiations, and by 1894, these deliberations resulted in the Dual Entente, a comprehensive military alliance. This agreement was sustained through 1917 and allowed France to pursue a more assertive foreign policy. From the Russian perspective, the agreement abated fears of isolation and of the development of an anti-Russian coalition. A few years after Bismarck's dismissal, the imperative of German foreign policy in the late nineteenth century—the diplomatic isolation of France—was no longer a reality.

In 1895, a new Conservative government came to power in Great Britain. Led by Lord Salisbury, who served as prime minister and foreign secretary, this government included a range of talented statesmen: Joseph Chamberlain, Lord Landsdowne, and the young Arthur James Balfour. The Salisbury government was interested in terminating the long-standing policy of "splendid isolation" that had prevailed as Britain's response to European alliances. Salisbury came to argue that new realities of world politics and economics deemed it advisable for Britain to ally itself with a major power. While coming under criticism for its role in the Boer War (1899–1902) in South Africa, the British government sought an Anglo-German alliance. Germany declined their advances because (1) the Germans were sympathetic to the Boers, (2) the Germans questioned the ability of the British army, (3) they believed that the British would never be able to reach an accommodation with the French or Russians, and (4) Wilhelm II was involved in a major naval building program, an effort that would be jeopardized if the Germans were allied to the world's greatest naval power, Britain.

Consequently, Britain pursued diplomatic opportunities that resulted in the Anglo-Japanese Alliance (1902), the Entente Cordiale or Anglo-French Entente (1904), and the Anglo-Russian Entente (1907).

The Anglo-Japanese Alliance of 1902 was an agreement between the two powers to adopt a position of benevolent neutrality in the event that the other member state was involved in war. This arrangement was sustained through World War I.

The Entente Cordiale (1904), also known as the Dual Entente, was a settlement of long-standing colonial disputes between Britain and France over African territories. The countries agreed that northeast Africa (Egypt and the Anglo-Egyptian Sudan) would be a British sphere of influence, and northwest Africa (Morocco), a French sphere. This was a colonial settlement, not a formal alliance; neither power pledged support in the event of war. However, the Entente Cordiale was of critical significance because it drew Britain into the French-oriented diplomatic camp.

While Anglo-French relations improved in 1904–1905, the historically tense Anglo-Russian relationship was aggravated by the Russo-Japanese War (1904–1905). The Dogger Bank Incident, in which Russian ships fired on and sunk British fishing boats in the North Sea, resulted in a crisis between the powers. Britain, which had adopted a sympathetic posture toward Japan responded by deploying the Home Fleet and curtailing activities of the Russian fleet. The crisis was resolved when Russia agreed to apologize for the incident and pay compensation. In 1905, a Liberal government came to power in Britain, and Russia was absorbed in its own revolution that liberalized, temporarily, the autocratic regime. Negotiations between these powers were facilitated by the French; in 1907, Britain and Russia reached a settlement, the Anglo-Russian Entente, on outstanding colonial disputes. They agreed on three points:

1. Persia would be divided into three zones: a northern sector under Russian influence, a southern sector under British control, and a central zone that could be mutually exploited for its now-valuable oil reserves.

2. Afghanistan was recognized as part of the British sphere of influence.

3. Tibet was recognized as part of China and free from foreign intervention.

By 1907, France, Britain, and Russia had formed a Triple Entente that effectively balanced the Triple Alliance of Germany, Austria-Hungary, and Italy. While Britain was not formally committed to an alliance system, Sir Edward Grey, British foreign minister from 1905, supported secret conversations between British and French military representatives. Thus, in terms of military power and economics, Germany became isolated by 1907.

The Rise of Militarism

After 1890, Europeans began to view the use of military power as not only feasible but also desirable to bring a resolution to the increasingly hostile political conditions in Europe. The apparent inability of diplomats to develop lasting settlements furthered this perception. The idea that a European war was inevitable became acceptable to many.

Within the structure of European states, militarists enjoyed increased credibility and support. The general staffs became preoccupied with planning for an anticipated struggle, and their plans affected national foreign policies. Germans, under the influence of General Count Alfred von Schlieffen, developed the Schlieffen Plan by 1905. It was predicated on the assumption that Germany would have to conduct a two-front war with France and Russia. It specified that France must be defeated quickly through the use of enveloping tactics that involved the use of German armies of about 1.5 million men. After victory in the West, Germany would then look to the East to defeat the Russians, who would be slower to mobilize. The French developed the infamous Plan XVII, approved by Marshall Joseph Joffre. They thought that a German attack would be concentrated in Alsace-Lorraine and that the French forces should be massed in that area; the élan of the French soldiery would result in a victory.

The Arms Race

This wave of nationalist militarism also manifested itself in a continuing arms race that threatened the balance of power, owing to revolutionary technological developments. Field weapons such as mortars and cannons were improved in range, accuracy, and firepower; the machine gun was perfected and produced in quantity. The new submarines and airplanes were recognized as having the capacity to improve strategy.

In naval weaponry, the rivalry between the British and Germans over capital ships not only exacerbated the deteriorating relationship between them, but also led to restrictions on the national domestic expenditures during peacetime in order to pay for the increasingly costly battleships and cruisers. In 1912, the British-sponsored Haldane Mission was sent to Berlin to negotiate an agreement; the Germans were suspicious and distrustful of the British and were not receptive to any proposal.

Imperialism as a Source of Conflict

During the late nineteenth century, the economically motivated "New Imperialism" further aggravated relations among the European powers. The struggle for an increased share in world markets, the need for raw materials, and the availability of capital for overseas investment sharpened the rivalry among European nations and, on several occasions, spawned crises. Crises over Fashoda in the Sudan (1898–1999), Morocco (1906 and 1911), and the Balkans (1908) demonstrated the impact of imperialism in heightening tensions among European states and in creating an environment in which conflict became more acceptable.

The Fashoda Crisis developed between France and Britain when the French, under the influence of Foreign Minister Theophile Delcassé, ordered Commandant Marchand and a small number of troops to march across Africa and establish a French "presence" near the headwaters of the Nile. Marchand arrived in Fashoda (now Kodok) in 1898; it was located on the White Nile, south of Khartoum in the Anglo-Egyptian Sudan. A British army under General Kitchener, having defeated a native rebel army in the battle of Omdurman, advanced to Khartoum, where he learned of the French force at Fashoda. Kitchener marched on Fashoda and a major crisis ensued. In the end, the French withdrew and recognized the position of the British in the Anglo-Egyptian Sudan; however, for months there was a serious threat of war over this issue.

The first Moroccan Crisis (1905–1906) developed when Wilhelm II traveled to Tangier (March 1905), where he made a speech in support of the independence of Morocco; this position was at odds with that agreed to by the British and the French in the Entente Cordiale, but initially the German position prevailed because of lack of organization in the Franco-Russian alliance. However, in 1906, at the Algeçiras Conference, the German effort was thwarted and the French secured their position in Morocco. Russia, Britain, and Italy supported the French on every important issue. German diplomatic isolation—save for the Austrians—became increasingly evident.

The Balkan Crisis of 1908 showed European imperialist rivalry at home. Since the Congress of Berlin in 1878, the Austro-Hungarian Empire had administered the Balkan territories of Bosnia and Herzegovina. Austrian influence in this area was opposed by Russia, which considered the region a natural area of Russian influence. Specifically, Russians hoped to capitalize on the collapse of the Ottoman Empire and gain access to the Mediterranean. In 1908, the decadent Ottoman Empire was suffering domestic discord that attracted the attention of both Austria and Russia. These powers agreed that Austria would annex Bosnia and Herzegovina, and that Russia would be granted access to the Turkish Straits and thus the Mediterranean. Great Britain intervened and demanded that there be no change in the status *quo vis-à-vis* the Straits. Russia backed down from a confrontation, but Austria proceeded to annex Bosnia-Herzegovina. The annexation was condemned by Pan-Slavists, who looked to Russia for assistance; a crisis developed, and it appeared that war between Austria and Russia was likely. However, the Russians disengaged from the crisis because of lack of preparedness for a major struggle and because of clear indications that Germany would support Austria. The Balkan Crisis was another example of European rivalries and the rapid recourse to saber-rattling on the part of great powers. Further, it demonstrated that the fundamental regional problem—the nationalism among the peoples of the Balkans—was not addressed.

After local disturbances, the Agadir Crisis (1911) broke when France announced that its troops would be sent to several Moroccan towns to restore order. Germany, fearing French annexation of all of Morocco responded by sending the Panther, a German ship, to Agadir. After exchanging threats for weeks, the French and Germans agreed to recognize Morocco as a French protectorate and to transfer two sections of the French Congo to Germany.

An Assassination, Then a War

During the late nineteenth and early twentieth centuries, the Ottoman Empire was in a state of collapse. At the same time, Austria and Russia were interested in extending their influence in the region. Further, nationalism among the ethnic groups in the Balkans was rapidly developing. In addition to the previously mentioned Balkan Crisis of 1908, the region was involved in the Italian-Turkish War (1911) and the Inter-Balkan Wars of 1912 and 1913.

On June 28, 1914, Archduke Franz Ferdinand, heir to the Austro-Hungarian throne, and his wife were assassinated while on a state visit to Sarajevo, the capital of Bosnia. Their assassin was a radical Serb, Gavrilo Princip, who opposed Franz Ferdinand's plan to integrate the Slavs more fully into the government. The assassination triggered a crisis between Austria-Hungary and Serbia that would ignite a series of events that in just two months would envelop Europe in war.

The Culture of Illiberalism

Between 1848 and 1914, Europeans underwent revolutionary changes in their culture. These alterations were based on a new sense of reality, and values in which materialism and the notion of human progress were manifested in the pragmatism of the era. Nationalism, science and technology, and the rapid expansion of the population were primary factors that contributed to these changes and to the expansion of European culture throughout the world. The growth in the European standard of living was uneven. Western Europe developed most comprehensively, central Europe—especially German urban centers—witnessed remarkable growth during the last decades of the period; but southern and eastern Europe lagged behind and, by 1914, the standard of living had not much improved from the previous century.

Reaction to these and other changes varied, ranging from the new politics of Marxism, anarchism, and trade unionism, all opposed to the adverse consequences of capitalism and industrialism, to the emergence of impressionism, expressionism, and symbolism in reaction to the perceived intellectual sterility of mechanistic positivism. Nineteenth-century Europe, which was identified with hope, progress, and rationality, gave way to the uncertainty, violence, and irrationality of the twentieth century. These varied movements are often lumped together under the rubric of illiberalism—not just a rejection of liberal values, but also of the liberals' lifestyles, seen stereotypically as staid, obese, moralistic, and bourgeois. Because of the rise of mass politics, some of this illiberalism was manifested in racist, anti-Semitic, and misogynist political movements as well as hyperprotectionist economic policies. But in the arts and letters, many of the avant-garde rejected these illiberal tendencies, which fit all too snugly with the agendas of the ruling elites and militarists. That they also rejected the certainties and smugness of liberal politics makes it difficult to cubbyhole turn-of-the-century arts and letters neatly.

The art of the young, in self-conscious revolt against "the fathers," may be divided into a few key movements: expressionism, symbolism, and naturalism. Whereas the old liberal order had demanded the suppression, even repression, of emotions, the expressionists or post-impressionists reveled in dramatic emotions. Some examples may be seen in the works of Vincent van Gogh (1853–1890) of the Netherlands, Paul Gauguin (1848–1903) of France, and Edvard Munch (1863–1944) of Norway (see Figures 8-1–8-3).

Kröller-Mueller Müseum, Otterlo

Figure 8-1. Vincent van Gogh's famous *Café Terrasse at Night* (1888) shows how his command of brushstrokes and vibrant colors helps to transmit stronger emotions than the old Academic art could usually muster.

Albright-Knox Art Gallery, Buffalo, NY

Figure 8-2. Paul Gauguin's interest in the supposedly unrepressed South Sea cultures is often foregrounded in discussions of his lush, uninhibited works, but his startling *Yellow Christ* (1889) takes the viewer into taboo areas of religious and perhaps irreligious emotion.

© 2007 The Munch Museum/The Munch-Ellingsen Group/Artists Rights Society (ARS), NY

Figure 8-3. Edvard Munch seemed to view the staid, often stifling society of Norway as a covered pot about to boil over in violence and frenzied emotion, as can be seen in his famous *The Scream*; even in his more complex *The Dance of Life* (1899–1900), the feeling of bottled-up emotions may be detected.

The turn of the century also produced art and architecture of a dreamier nature, the art-for-art's-sake often labeled aestheticism or symbolism. A specific branch of this aestheticism was the movement known variously as art nouveau and *Jugendstil*. A great exemplar of this tendency was Gustav Klimt (1862–1918) of Austria (see Figure 8-4).

Historisches Museum der Stadt Wien, Vienna, Austria

Figure 8-4. Gustav Klimt's take on *Jugendstil* often shows the dreamworld of the very rich in Vienna, as in his portrait of *Emilie Flöge* (1902); in other works, he indulges in a frank and lusty eroticism.

In the world of letters, a gamut of styles, not reconcilable to a single program, produced symbolist works that were resolutely antirealist, even escapist, as well as the hyperrealism grit of naturalism. Oscar Wilde, the scandalous aesthete, wrote charming fairy tales for children, but also the erotic and violent drama *Salomé* (1894). Maurice Maeterlinck (1862–1949) was perhaps the most influential symbolist playwright of the generation, with his dreamy *Pelléas et Mélisande* (1892), turned into an opera by Claude Debussy, and the children's classic, *Bluebird* (1909). The acknowledged master of naturalism was the novelist Emile Zola (1840–1902), whose shocking *The Dram-Shop* (1877), *Nana* (1880), and *Germinal* (1885) try to offer up an un-retouched "slice of life" showing, respectively, the worlds of alcoholism, prostitution, and mining.

Both styles were able to stir up the public, or at least the avant-garde, to react emotionally to the stifling conventions of bourgeois and petty-bourgeois life as well as the looming threats posed by illiberal mass politics and shrill militarism. The year 1913, for instance, saw four major events that in hindsight may be seen to herald the end of the old order, for good or ill. Marcel Proust (1871–1922) published the first volume of his magnum opus, *In Search of Lost Time*; titled *Swann's Way*, the volume presents a panorama of French life, from the provinces to Paris, from the heights of the often decadent aristocracy to the middling levels of the often hypocritical bourgeoisie. Though many passages suggest that Proust looks back nostalgically, many others are quite mordant and sarcastic. In Germany, in 1913, an old play, Georg Büchner's *Woyzeck* (1837), was revived on many stages to great effect; its grim portrayal of the shabby, tragic lives of the lower classes, ending in violent acts, showed the continuing relevance of naturalism. Finally, the premiere of Igor Stravinsky's (1882–1971) ballet *The Rite of Spring* in Paris in 1913 caused a scandal with its irregular rhythms, percussive emotions, and bizarre choreography based on Russian puppets. The portrayal of a barbaric tribe engaged in human sacrifice now looks like an accurate description of much of the ensuing world war.

The fourth cultural milestone of 1913 took place in the United States but reflected the preponderance of European standards then in the art world. The fabled Armory Art Show in New York City showcased, alongside American painters, the latest (or so they thought) in European art, including Paul Cézanne, Claude Monet, and Georges Seurat; the modern was now all the rage. But that show could not hold all the latest art of Marcel Duchamp (1887–1968), Henri Matisse (1869–1954), Wassily Kandinsky (1866–1944), Ernst Kokoschka (1886–1980), or Pablo Picasso (1881–1973). Though their styles show a remarkable range in modernism, these artists can be said to represent cubism, expressionism, and fauvism (see Figures 8-5–8-7).

Figure 8-5. Pablo Picasso's iconographic *Les Demoiselles d'Avignon* (1906–1907) shows the influence of African tribal masks and trick photography in his evolution of cubism.

Philadelphia Museum of Art, Philadelphia, PA

Figure 8-6. Marcel Duchamp's path-breaking *Nude Descending a Staircase* defined the special nature of cubism as a way to see the world through geometrical reductions.

Tretyakov Gallery, Moscow, Russia

Figure 8-7. The Russian émigré Wassily Kandinsky learned much in Germany from pioneer expressionists such as Klee, but his *Composition VII* (1913) seems closer to cubism.

World War I and Europe in Crisis (1914–1935)

The Origins of World War I

In August 1914, most of the world's major powers became engaged in a conflict that most people welcomed romantically and believed would last only a few months. Instead, a war of global dimensions evolved that saw the clash of outdated military values with modern technological warfare. A war that most welcomed and that no one seemed to be able to win lasted over four years and resulted in twelve million deaths.

The origins of World War I can be traced to numerous root causes as far back as the creation of Germany in 1871. This new German state destroyed Europe's traditional balance of power and forced its diplomatic and military planners back to their drawing boards to rethink collective strategies to maintain a military and diplomatic balance. From 1871 to 1914, a number of developments took place that heightened tensions between the major powers.

Balance of Power and Europe's Alliance System

One of the major themes of nineteenth-century European diplomacy was an effort by the major powers to organize their international relationships in such a way as to keep any single or collective group of nations from gaining a dominant diplomatic or military advantage on the Continent. From 1871 to 1890, this balance was maintained through the network of alliances created by German chancellor Otto von Bismarck; it centered on his *Dreikaiserbund* (League of the Three Emperors), which isolated France, and the Dual (Germany, Austria) and Triple (Germany, Austria, Italy) alliances. Bismarck's fall in 1890 resulted in new policies that saw Germany move closer to Austria, while England and France (Entente Cordiale, 1904), and later Russia (Triple Entente, 1907), drew closer.

Arms Buildup and Imperialism

Germany's defeat of France in the Franco-Prussian War (1870–1871), coupled with Kaiser Wilhelm II's decision in 1890 to build up a navy comparable to that of Great Britain, created an arms race that overheated Europe. Add European efforts to carve out colonial empires in Africa and Asia—plus a new nationalism and the growing romanticization of war—and the unstable international environment after 1890 becomes easier to understand.

Immediate Cause of World War I

The Balkan Crisis

The Balkans (*balkan* is Turkish for "mountain"), a region that today embraces the former Yugoslavia, Albania, Greece, Bulgaria, and Romania, was notably unstable. Part of the rapidly decaying Turkish Empire, it saw two forces at work: ethnic nationalism of a number of small groups who lived there and intense rivalry between Austria-Hungary and Russia over spheres of influence. Friction between Austria and Serbia increased after Austria annexed Bosnia-Herzegovina in 1908. In 1912, with Russia's blessing, the Balkan League (Serbia, Montenegro, Greece, and Bulgaria) went to war with Turkey. Serbia, which sought a port on the Adriatic Sea, was rebuffed when Austria-Hungary and Italy backed the creation of an independent Albania. Russia, meanwhile, grew increasingly protective of its southern Slavic cousins, supporting Serbia's and Montenegro's claims to Albanian lands. Just weeks after the outbreak of World War I, the new Albanian state collapsed.

The Outbreak of World War I

Assassination and Reprisals

On June 28, 1914, the Archduke Franz Ferdinand (1863–1914), heir to the Austrian throne, was assassinated by Gavrilo Princip, a young Serbian nationalist. Princip was working for the Serbian Army Intelligence in Sarajevo, then the capital of Bosnia and ominously close to the Serbian border. Austria's rulers felt the murder provided them with an opportunity to move against Serbia and end anti-Austrian unrest in the Balkans. Austria consulted with the German government on July 6 and received a "blank check" to take whatever steps were necessary to punish Serbia, which stood accused of harboring radical anti-Austrian groups like the "Black Hand." On July 23, 1914, the Austrian government presented Serbia with a ten-point ultimatum that required Serbia to suppress and punish all forms of anti-Austrian sentiment there. On

July 25, 1914, three hours after mobilizing its army, Serbia accepted most of Austria's terms; it asked only that Austria's demand to participate in Serbian judicial proceedings against anti-Austrian agitators—a demand that Serbia described as unprecedented in relations between sovereign states—be adjudicated by the International Tribunal at The Hague.

The Conflict Expands

Austria immediately broke off official relations with Serbia and mobilized its army. Meanwhile, between July 18 and 24, Russia let the Austrians and Germans know that it intended to back Serbia. France, Russia's ally, voiced support of Russia's moves. Last-ditch attempts by Britain and Germany to mediate the dispute and avoid a European war failed. On July 28, 1914, Austria went to war against Serbia, and began to bombard Belgrade the following day. At the same time, Russia gradually prepared for war against Austria and Germany, deciding on full mobilization on July 30. This meant that Russia would amass troops not only on the Austrian border but also on the German—though they were not yet enemies.

Germany and the Schlieffen Plan

German military strategy, based on the plan of the chief of the General Staff, Count Alfred von Schlieffen, viewed Russian mobilization as an act of war. The Schlieffen Plan was based on a two-front war with Russia and France predicated on a swift, decisive blow against France, while maintaining a defensive position against slowly mobilizing Russia, which would be dealt with after France. Attacking France required the Germans to march through neutral Belgium, which would later bring England into the war as a protector of Belgian neutrality.

War Begins

Germany demanded that Russia demobilize in twelve hours and appealed to its ambassador in Berlin. Russia's offer to negotiate the matter was rejected, and Germany declared war on Russia on August 1, 1914. Germany asked France its intentions and Paris replied that it would respond according to its own interests. On August 3, Germany declared war on France. Berlin asked Belgium for permission to send its troops through Belgian territory to attack France, which Belgium refused. On August 4, England, which agreed in 1839 to protect Belgian neutrality, declared war on Germany; Belgium followed suit. Between 1914 and 1915, the alliance of the Central powers (Germany, Austria-Hungary, Bulgaria, and Turkey) faced the Allied powers of England, France, Russia, Japan, and in 1917, the United States. A number of smaller countries were also part of the Allied coalition.

The War in 1914

The Western Front

After entering Belgium, the Germans attacked France on five fronts in an effort to encircle Paris rapidly. France was defeated in the battle of the Frontier (August 14–24) in Lorraine, the Ardennes, and the Charleroi-Mons area. However, the unexpected Russian attack in East Prussia and Galicia from August 17 to 20 forced Germany to transfer important forces eastward to halt the Russian drive.

To halt a further German advance, the French army, aided by Belgian and English forces, counterattacked. In the battle of the Marne (September 5–9), they stopped the German drive and forced a retreat. Mutual outflanking maneuvers by France and Germany created a battlefront that would determine the demarcation of the western front for the next four years. It ran, in uneven fashion, from the North Sea to Belgium and from northern France to Switzerland.

The Eastern Front

Russian forces under Rennenkampf and Samsonov, generals who disliked each other and refused to cooperate properly, invaded east Prussia and Galicia in mid-August. With only nine of eighty-seven divisions in the East, the German defense faltered. Generals Paul von Hindenburg and Erich Ludendorff, aided by two corps from the western front, were sent on August 23 to revive the Eighth Army in east Prussia.

In the battles of Tannenberg (August 25–31) and Masurian Lakes (September 6–15), the Russian Second Army, under Samsonov, met the German Eighth Army. Suffering from poor communications and Rennenkampf's refusal to send the First Army to aid him, Samsonov surrendered with ninety thousand troops and committed suicide. Moving northward, the German Eighth Army now confronted Rennenkampf's First Army. After an unsuccessful encounter with the Germans, Rennenkampf rapidly retreated, suffering significant losses.

Russia's Southwest Army, under the command of Nikolai Ivanov, enjoyed some successes against Austro-Hungarian forces in Galicia and southern Poland throughout August. By the end of 1914, it was poised to strike deeper into the area.

The Germans retreated after their assault against Warsaw in late September. Hindenburg's attack on Lodz ten days after he was appointed commander in chief of the eastern front (November 1) was a more successful venture; by the end of 1914 this important textile center was in German hands.

The War in 1915

The Western Front

With Germany concentrating on the East, France and England launched a series of small attacks through the year that resulted in few gains and heavy casualties. Wooed by both sides, Italy joined the Allies and declared war on the Central powers on May 23 after signing the secret Treaty of London (April 26). This treaty gave Italy Austrian provinces in the North and some Turkish territory. Italian attacks against Austria in the Isonzo area toward Trieste were unsuccessful because of difficult terrain, and failed to lessen pressure on the Russians in the East.

The Eastern Front

On January 23, 1915, Austro-German forces began a coordinated offensive in east Prussia and in the Carpathians. The two-pronged German assault in the North was stopped on February 27, while Austrian efforts to relieve their besieged defensive network at Przemysl failed when it fell into Russian hands. In early March, Russian forces under Ivanov drove deeper into the Carpathians with inadequate material support.

German forces, strengthened by troops from the western front under General Field Marshall August von Mackensen, began a move on May 2 to strike at the heart of the Russian front. They used the greatest artillery concentration of the war as part of their strategy. In June, Mackensen shifted his assault toward Lublin and Brest-Litovsk, while the German Twelfth, Tenth, and Niemen armies moved toward Kovno in the Baltic. By August 1915, much of Russian Poland was in German hands.

In an effort to provide direct access to the Turks defending Gallipoli, Germany and Austria invaded Serbia in the fall, aided by their new ally, Bulgaria. On October 7, the defeated Serbian army retreated to Corfu. Belated Allied efforts to ship troops from Gallipoli to help Bulgaria failed.

Command Changes

Allied frustration resulted in the appointment of Marshal Joseph Joffre as French commander in chief, and Field Marshal Douglas Haig as British commander in December 1915.

The Eastern Mediterranean

Turkey entered the war on the Central power side on October 28, 1914, which prevented the shipment of Anglo-French aid to Russians through the Turkish Straits.

The western stalemate caused Allied strategists to look to the eastern Mediterranean to break the military deadlock. Winston Churchill, Britain's first lord of the Admiralty, devised a plan to seize the Straits of the Dardanelles to open lines to Russia, take Constantinople, and isolate Turkey. These unsuccessful efforts to take the "soft underbelly of Turkey" occurred between February 19 and March 18, 1915.

On April 25, Allied forces invaded Gallipoli Peninsula in a different attempt to capture the Straits. Turkish troops offered strong resistance and forced the Allies (after suffering 252,000 casualties) to begin a three-week evacuation that began on December 20, 1915.

The Middle East (1914–1916)

In an effort to protect its petroleum interests in the Persian Gulf, an Anglo-Indian force took Basra in southern Iraq in November 1915. The following year, British forces moved north and took Al Kut (Kut al Irnara) from Turkey on September 28. To counter failures on the western front, British forces tried to take Baghdad but were stopped by the Turks at Ctesiphon. Turkish forces besieged Al Kut on December 8 and captured it in April 1916. Two-thirds of the ten thousand captured British prisoners of war (POWs) died of Turkish mistreatment.

The War in 1916

The Western Front

In order to break the stalemate on the western front and drain French forces in the effort, the Germans decided to attack the French fortress town of Verdun.

The battle for Verdun lasted from February 21 to December 18, 1916. From February until June, German forces, aided by closely coordinated heavy artillery barrages, assaulted the forts around Verdun. The Germans suffered 281,000 casualties while the French, under Marshal Henri Petain, lost 315,000 successfully defending their position.

To take pressure off the French, an Anglo-French force mounted three attacks on the Germans to the left of Verdun in July, September, and November. After the battle of the Somme (July 1–November 18), German pressure decreased, but at great loss. Anglo-French casualties totaled 600,000.

The Eastern Front

Initially, the Allies had hoped for a general coordinated attack on all fronts against the Central powers. Now efforts centered on relieving pressure at Verdun and on the Italians at Trentino.

Orchestrated by Russian General Aleksei Brusilov, the Brusilov Offensive (June 4–September 20) envisioned a series of unexpected attacks along a lengthy front to confuse the enemy. By late August, he had advanced into Galicia and the Carpathians. The number of enemy troops dead, wounded, or captured totaled 1.5 million. Russian losses numbered 500,000.

Romania entered the war on the Allied side as a result of Russian successes and the secret Treaty of Bucharest (August 17). This treaty specified that Romania would get Transylvania, Bukovina, the Banat, and part of the Hungarian Plain if the Allies won. The Romanian thrust into Transylvania was pushed back, and on December 6, a German-Bulgarian army occupied Bucharest as well as the bulk of Romania.

Central Powers Propose Peace Talks

The death of Austrian Emperor Franz Josef on November 21 prompted his heir, Charles I, to discuss the prospect of peace terms with his allies. On December 12, the four Central powers, strengthened by the fall of Bucharest, offered four separate peace proposals based on their recent military achievements. The Allies rejected them on December 30 out of a belief that they were insincere.

War on the High Seas (1914–1916)

Britain's naval strategy in the first year of the war was to disrupt German shipping worldwide with the aid of the French and Japanese. Germany sought ways to defend itself and weaken Allied naval strength. By the end of 1914, Allied fleets had gained control of the high seas, which caused Germany to lose control of its colonial empire.

Germany's failure in 1914 to weaken British naval strength prompted German naval leaders to begin to use the submarine (U-boat) as an offensive weapon to weaken the British. On February 4, Germany announced a war zone around the British Isles, and advised neutral powers to sail there at their own risk. On May 7, 1915, a German submarine sank a British passenger vessel, the *Lusitania*, because it was secretly carrying arms. There were 1,202 casualties, including 139 Americans.

The United States protested the sinking as a violation of the Declaration of London (1909), which laid out rules of actions and rights for neutrals and belligerents in war. After four months of negotiations, Germany agreed not to sink any passenger vessels without warning, and to help all passengers and crew to lifeboats. Germany shifted its U-boat activity to the Mediterranean.

The main naval battle of World War I was the battle of Jutland/Skagerrak (May–June 1916). This confrontation pitted twenty-eight British dreadnoughts and nine cruisers against sixteen German dreadnoughts and five cruisers. In the end, the battle was a draw, with England losing fourteen ships and Germany eleven. It forced the German High Sea Fleet not to venture out of port for the rest of the war. Instead, German naval command concentrated on use of the U-boat.

New Military Technology

Germany, Russia, and Great Britain all had submarines, though the Germans used their U-boats most effectively. Designed principally for coastal protection, they increasingly used them to reduce British naval superiority through tactical and psychological means.

By the spring of 1915, British war planners finally awoke to the fact that the machine gun had become the mistress of defensive trench warfare. In a search for a weapon to counter trench defenses, the British developed tanks as an armored "land ship," and first used them on September 15, 1916, in the battle of the Somme. Their value was not immediately realized because there were too few of them to be effective, and interest in them waned. Renewed interest came in 1917.

Airplanes were initially used for observation purposes in the early months of the war. As their numbers grew, mid-air struggles using pistols and rifles took place, until the Germans devised a synchronized propeller and machine gun on its Fokker aircraft in May 1915. The Allies responded with similar equipment and new squadron tactics during the early days of the Verdun campaign in February 1916 and briefly gained control of the skies. They also began to use their aircraft for bombing raids against zeppelin bases in Germany. Air supremacy shifted to the Germans in 1917.

During the first year of the war, the Germans began to use zeppelin airships to bomb civilian targets in England. Though their significance was neutralized with the development of the explosive shell in 1916, zeppelins played an important role as a psychological weapon in the first two years of the war.

In the constant search for methods to counter trench warfare, the Germans and the Allied forces experimented with various forms of internationally outlawed gas. On October 27, 1914, the Germans tried a nose-and-eye irritant gas at Neuve-Chappelle, and by the spring of 1915 had developed an asphyxiating lachrymatory chlorine gas that they used at the battle of Ypres. The British countered with similar chemicals at the battles of Champagne and Loos that fall. Military strategists initially had little faith in gas since its use depended heavily on wind conditions, which could change the direction of the gas at any moment. However, as they desperately struggled to find ways to break the deadlock on the western front, they devised tactics and protection methods that enabled them to integrate the use of gas into their strategy.

The Russian Revolutions of 1917

Two events that would have a dramatic impact on the war and the world were the February and October Revolutions in 1917. The former toppled the Romanov dynasty and spawned that country's brief flirtation with democracy under the temporary Provisional Government. It collapsed later that year as a result of the October Revolution, which brought Lenin (born Vladimir Ilyich Ulyanov) and his Bolshevik faction to power.

Plagued for centuries by a backward autocracy and a rural serf economy, Russia seemed on the verge of dramatic change after Tsar Alexander II (reigned 1855–1881) freed the serfs in 1861. Emancipation, however, coupled with other important government and social reforms, created chaos nationwide and helped stimulate a new class of violent revolutionaries bent on destroying the tsarist system. Terrorists murdered Alexander II, which prompted the country's last two rulers, Alexander III (reigned 1881–1894) and Nicholas II (reigned 1894–1917) to turn the clock backward politically.

The Russo-Japanese War and the 1905 Revolution

In February 1904, war broke out between Russia and Japan over spheres of influence in Korea and Manchuria. Russia's inability to support its military forces in Asia, coupled with growing battlefield losses, prompted a nationwide revolution after police fired on peaceful demonstrators in January 1905. A groundswell of strikes and demonstrations swept the country and neutralized the government, on the verge of collapse. Nicholas II survived because he agreed in his October Manifesto to create a constitution, share power with a legislature (the Duma), and grant civil rights. This decree defused the crisis and enabled the government to rebuild its political base.

Era of Reaction and Reforms (1906–1912)

Once the tsar reduced the threat to his throne, he issued the Fundamental Laws (May 6, 1906), which severely limited the power of the Duma. Regardless, over the next eleven years, four increasingly conservative dumas met and started a tradition of constitutional government for the country. This, with the emergence of workers' and soldiers' soviets (councils), and political parties (Cadets, Octobrists; see Chapter 7), created an atmosphere of change for Russia. To counter this mood, the tsar appointed Pyotr Stolypin as prime minister (1906–1911) to initiate reforms for the peasants and develop a private agricultural system throughout the country. These efforts, and an industrial boom, influenced Russia's economic potential for the better.

Rasputin and Upheaval (1912–1914)

The death of Stolypin in 1911, coupled with a governmental system incapable of dealing with new labor unrest associated with industrial development, brought to the fore a semiliterate holy man, Grigorii Rasputin. He seemed to possess powers to save the tsar's hemophiliac son, Alexei, and obtained tremendous influence over the royal family.

Russia at War: The Home Front (1914–1917)

Russia's entrance into World War I was met with broad public acceptance and support. Serious problems, however, plagued the government, the military, and the economy that threatened to undermine a military effort that most expected would win the war in a matter of months.

The Military. The draft increased Russia's armed forces from 1,350,000 to 6,500,000 during the war, though the government was only able to equip fully a small percentage of these troops. In addition, the country's military leaders differed whether to concentrate forces on the Austrians or Germans. While in the field, commanders were handicapped by inadequate communication and maps. As a result, German drives in the spring and summer of 1915 saw Russian spirit collapse as defensive efforts proved ineffective. However, by the end of that year, High Command personnel changes, aided by new industrial output, enabled the Russians briefly to turn the tide of battle.

The Civilian Economy. At first, Russian agricultural production proved adequate for the war's needs, but in time, with growing labor shortages, production of foodstuffs fell by one-third. The military received about one-half of their grain requests because of the collapse of the transport system. Regardless, by 1917, the country still had enough food for its military and civilian population. Skilled labor shortages, the loss of Poland, and inadequate planning kept industry from producing the material necessary to supply the military. Consequently, despite a trade surplus in 1914, Russia encumbered a trade deficit of 2.5 billion rubles by 1917 from its Allies. This, added to prewar debts, incurred mainly to the French, would sour postwar relations, when the new Bolshevik regime refused to honor "tsarist" debts.

Government and Bureaucracy. As problems mounted, the tsar responded by assuming direct command of his army at the front in September 1915, leaving government in the hands of his wife and Rasputin. Those in government who were critical of the tsar's policies were dismissed, so the country lost effective leaders. The Duma, forced to assume more leadership responsibilities, formed the Progressive Bloc, a coalition mainly of Cadets and Octobrists, in an effort to try to force the tsar to appoint more competent officials. The tsar's refusal to accept this group's proposals led to increasing criticism of his policies. In November 1916, distant relatives of the tsar and a Duma member secretly murdered Rasputin.

The February Revolution

The February Revolution, so named because the Russian calendar at the time was thirteen days behind that of the West, was a spontaneous series of events that forced the collapse of the Romanov dynasty.

Riots and Strikes. Growing discontent with the government's missteps in the war led to more unrest in the country. Roughly 1,140 riots swept Russia in January and

February, prompting officials to send extra troops into Petrograd (old Petersburg) to protect the royal family. Particularly troublesome were food riots. Military and police units ordered to move against the mobs either remained at their posts or joined them out of sympathy.

The Duma. Though ordered by the tsar not to meet until April, Duma leaders began to demand dramatic solutions to the country's problems. Its president, M. V. Rodzianko, was in constant consultation with the tsar about the crisis. On March 12, he informed Nicholas II that civil war had broken out and that he needed to create a new cabinet responsible to the legislature. Though dissolved on March 11, the Duma met in special session on March 13 and created a Provisional Committee of Elders to deal with the unrest. After two days of discussions, the committee decided that the tsar must give up his throne, and on March 15, 1917, Rodzianko and A. I. Guchkov, leader of the Octobrist Party, convinced the tsar to abdicate. He agreed and turned the throne over to his brother, Grand Duke Michael, who gave it up the following day.

The Provisional Government in Russia (March–November, 1917)

From March through November 1917, a temporary Provisional Government ruled Russia. It tried to move the country toward democracy and keep Russia in the war as a loyal western ally, a fateful, even fatal, move, given antiwar sentiment.

Leadership

Heading the new government were Prince George Lvov, a Cadet and *zemstvo* leader, as prime minister; Paul Miliukov, head of the Cadets, as foreign minister; A. I. Guchkov, an Octobrist, as minister of war; and Alexander Kerensky, conservative Socialist Revolutionary and a leader in the Petrograd Soviet, as minister of justice.

Problems

The Provisional Government contained many of the elite who had little contact or sympathy with the problems or concerns of workers or peasants. Its leaders, particularly Miliukov, felt the government had to remain a loyal ally and stay in the war to maintain international credibility. Despite pressure to redistribute land, Lvov's government felt that it did not have the authority to deal with that issue. Instead, the problem was left to a constituent assembly to convene within a year. The Provisional Government did, however, implement some far-reaching reforms, including full political and religious freedom, election of local officials, an eight-hour working day, and legal improvements.

The Petrograd Soviet

On the eve of Nicholas II's abdication, a shadow government, the Petrograd Soviet, was formed among the capital's workers, and took control of city administration. Briefly, it shared the Tauride Palace with the Provisional Government.

Creation. On March 13, delegates were elected to a soviet of worker's deputies, renamed the Soviet of Workers and Soldiers Deputies. It was made up of thirteen hundred representatives, and grew to three thousand the following week with the addition of military delegates. Because of its size, the Petrograd Soviet created an executive committee, headed by N.S. Chkeidze, a Menshevik,[1] to make its most important decisions.

Policies. In response to an unsuccessful request to the Provisional Government to absolve soldiers from potentially treasonous actions during the March Revolution, the Petrograd Soviet issued Order No. I (March 14) that granted them amnesty and stated that officers were to be elected by their units. It later issued Order No. II for units throughout the country. These decrees, hesitatingly approved later by the Provisional Government, caused a significant collapse of discipline in the armed forces.

Lenin Returns to Russia

Lenin (1870–1924) became involved in revolutionary activity after the execution of his brother for an assassination plot against Alexander III. A fervent Marxist, he split with the Menshevik wing of the Russian Social Democratic Party and formed his Bolshevik (majority) faction in 1903. Lenin felt the party should be led by a committed elite. He spent much of the period between 1905 and 1917 in exile, and was surprised by the February Revolution. However, with the aid of the Germans, he and some followers were placed in a sealed train and transported from Switzerland via Stockholm to Russia.

The April Theses. On April 16, Lenin arrived at Petrograd's Finland Station and went into hiding. The next day he proposed his April Theses to Bolshevik leaders, who rejected them. Lenin felt that the Bolsheviks should oppose the Provisional Government and support the theme "All Power to the Soviets." The soviets, he concluded, should control government as the war became a revolution against capitalism, with all soldiers on both sides joining the struggle. In addition, he wanted the country's land, factories, and banks to be nationalized, and the Bolshevik Party should begin to call itself the Communist Party.

The First Coalition

Paul Miliukov's decision on May 1 to assure the Allies that his country would not sign a separate agreement with Germany but continue to fight until a "decisive victory" was won, incited demonstrations that forced his resignation and the Lvov government to disavow his note. The Petrograd Soviet now permitted members to join a new provisional government, known as the First Coalition and formed under Prince Lvov; it included nine nonsocialists and six socialist representatives. Some of its prominent members were Alexander Kerensky, now minister of war and the navy; Victor Chernov, a Socialist Revolutionary, now minister of agriculture; M. I. Tereshchenko, previously finance minister, now foreign minister; and H. Tsereteli, the Menshevik leader and head of the Petrograd Soviet, as minister of posts and telegraph. In many instances, the coalition's new socialist members felt more loyal to the Petrograd Soviet than to the government itself.

---

[1] The Mensheviks were the so-called minority wing of the Russian Social Democrats, a label given to them by the Bolsheviks (majority wing) based on votes at the 1903 convention. Trotsky was once their leader.

July Crises

Because of Allied pressure, the Provisional Government decided to mount an offensive on the eastern front to counter French military failures and mutinies on the western front.

The July Offensive. Kerensky (the minister of war), determined to revive the Russian army, toured the front to rally forces and created special "shock" battalions to lead them into battle. On July 1, Russian forces attacked the Austrians in the Lvov area of Galicia and scored some successes, though within twelve days the Russian advance was halted, and a week later, Austro-German troops began to push the Russians back. Their retreat turned into a panic and desertions became rampant. The Provisional Government restored the death penalty on July 25 to stop this rupture in discipline, though it did little to stop the army's collapse.

The Second Coalition

In the midst of the July Offensive, the First Coalition collapsed. On July 16, four Cadet members resigned because of the coalition's decision to grant the Ukraine quasi-federal status, while later Prince Lvov stepped down as prime minister over the land question and efforts to strengthen Soviet influence in the cabinet. Kerensky became Prime Minister, and on August 22 he announced that elections for the Constituent Assembly would be on November 25, and that it would open on December 11.

The July Days. Prompted by the failure of the July offensive and resignation of Kadet ministers from the cabinet, military units and workers mounted a spontaneous protest against the Provisional Government on July 16. After hesitating, the Bolsheviks agreed to lead the demonstrations, which saw more than five hundred thousand people march on the Tauride Palace, demanding that the Petrograd Soviet seize power. Soviet leaders refused, and on July 18 troops loyal to the Provisional Government put the demonstrations down. Afterward, the government claimed that Bolshevik leaders were German agents and tried to arrest them. Many top Bolsheviks went underground or fled abroad.

The Kornilov Affair. In an effort to rebuild support for his government, Kerensky decided to call a meeting of delegates representing numerous organizations from throughout the country in late August. The rifts that developed there led to the Kornilov crisis several weeks later.

The Moscow State Conference, convened on August 26, attracted two thousand delegates representing the Duma, military, the soviets, professions, and other groups. The Bolsheviks opposed the meeting and responded with a general strike.

The conference accentuated the growing difference between Kerensky and the conservatives, who looked to the government's commander in chief, General Lavr Kornilov, as a leader. Kornilov represented those who decried the collapse of military discipline and left the Moscow Conference convinced that Kerensky did not have the ability to restore order and stability to the nation and the military.

Mutual suspicion between Kerensky and Kornilov, despite indirect, unofficial negotiations between the two, ended in Kornilov's dismissal. He responded by ordering his Cossack and "Savage" divisions to march to Petrograd to stop a Bolshevik coup. The Petrograd Soviet rallied to save the revolution and freed the Bolsheviks from prison to help with defense preparations. Kornilov's coup collapsed, and he surrendered on September 14. Kerensky now became supreme commander in chief.

The Third Coalition

Kerensky restructured his government as a temporary Directory of Five, and declared Russia a Republic. Thirteen days later, he convened twelve hundred representatives from the country to rebuild his power base. From it emerged the Third Coalition government on October 8 that consisted of Socialist Revolutionaries, Mensheviks, Kadets, and ministers without ties to any faction. The conference also decided to establish a Council of the Russian Republic or preparliament with 555 delegates that would open on October 20. Bolsheviks and other leftists opposed these efforts, which weakened Kerensky's efforts.

The Bolshevik October Revolution

The Kornilov Affair and Kerensky's failure to rebuild support for the Provisional Government convinced the two Bolshevik leaders, Lenin and Leon Trotsky that now was the time for them to attempt to seize power.

Lenin's Decision to Seize Power

After learning that the Second All-Russian Congress of Soviets of Workers and Soldiers Deputies would open on November 7, Lenin began to think of a simultaneous seizure of power, since he was convinced that while the Bolsheviks could dominate that Second Soviet Congress, they would not be able to do the same with the Constituent Assembly that was to open later. On October 23–24, he returned from Finland to meet with the party's Central Committee to plan the coup. Though he met with strong resistance, the committee agreed to create a political bureau (the Politburo) to oversee the revolution.

Trotsky and the Military Revolutionary Committee

Trotsky, head of the Petrograd Soviet and its Military Revolutionary Committee, convinced troops in Petrograd to support Bolshevik moves. While Trotsky gained control of important strategic points around the city, Kerensky, well-informed of Lenin's plans, finally decided on November 6 to move against the plotters.

The Coup of November 6–7

In response, Lenin and Trotsky ordered their supporters to seize the city's transportation and communication centers. The best girls' school in Russia, the Smolny Institute, was made headquarters for Lenin and Trotsky, while the Winter Palace was captured later that evening, along with most of Kerensky's government.

The Second Congress of Soviets

The Second Congress opened on November 7, with Lev Kamenev, member of Lenin's Politburo, as head. Over half the 650 delegates were Bolshevik supporters, and the newly selected 22-member Presidium had 14 Bolsheviks. Soon after the congress opened, many moderate socialists walked out in opposition to Lenin's coup, leaving Bolsheviks and the Left Socialist Revolutionaries in control of the gathering. Lenin now used the rump congress as the vehicle to announce his regime.

It was announced that the government's new cabinet, officially the Council of People's Commissars (*Sovnarkom*), responsible to a Central Executive Committee, would include Lenin as chairman or head of government, Trotsky as foreign commissar, and Josef Stalin as commissar of nationalities. The Central Executive Committee would be the government's temporary legislature. The congress also issued two decrees on peace and land: the first called for immediate peace without any consideration of indemnities or annexations, while the second adopted the Socialist Revolutionary land program that abolished private ownership of land and decreed that a peasant could only have as much land as he could farm. Village councils would oversee distribution.

The Constituent Assembly

The Constituent Assembly, promised by the Provisional Government as the land's first elected legislature, presented grave problems for Lenin, since the Bolsheviks could not win a majority of seats. Regardless, Lenin allowed elections to be held on November 25 with universal suffrage. Over forty-one million Russians voted. The Socialist Revolutionaries got 58 percent of the vote, the Bolsheviks got 25 percent, the Kadets and other parties got 17 percent. For the next seven weeks, the Bolsheviks did everything possible to discredit the election results. When the assembly convened on January 18, 1918, in the Tauride Palace, the building was surrounded by Red Guards and others. The assembly voted down Bolshevik proposals and elected Victor Chernov, a Socialist Revolutionary, as president. The Bolsheviks walked out. After it adopted laws on land and peace, and declared the country a democratic federal republic, the assembly adjourned until the next day. When the delegates later returned, they found the Tauride Palace ringed again by troops, who announced that the Constituent Assembly was dissolved.

World War I: The Final Phase (1917–1918)

In early 1917, the new French commander, General Nivelle, changed the earlier policy of attrition against the Germans and began to plan distracting Somme attacks with a major assault at Champagne. These plans caused friction with British field marshal Douglas Haig, who had a different strategy and resented serving under Nivelle.

The French Offensive

The Champagne offensive began near Reims on April 16. By May 9, it failed at the second battle of the Aisne, so mutinies broke out in the French army (May 3–20) that forced the replacement of Nivelle for Marshal Henri Petain, who restored order.

The British Offensive

To shore up the failing French battle effort, General Haig began a series of attacks in Flanders that resulted in the capture of Messines Ridge. Against French wishes, Haig began new, unsuccessful assaults (the third battle of Ypres, July 31–November 4) that were designed to capture the Flemish port cities of Ostend and Zeebrugge. These attempts ultimately failed. He did succeed in capturing the Passchendaele Ridge and seriously damaged the strength of the German Fourth Army, though his own troops suffered heavy loses.

The Italian Front and the Battle of Caporetto

In response to increased Italian attacks against Austro-Hungary in the Isonzo area in August and September 1917, the German High Command decided to strengthen Central power resistance with troops from the eastern front. Consequently, on October 24, a Central power campaign began at Caporetto, which resulted in an Italian retreat through November 12 and the capture of 250,000 Italians. The loss convinced the Allies to form a Supreme War Council at Versailles to enhance Allied cooperation.

The Tank Battle of Cambrai

From November 20 to December 3, the largest tank battle of the war took place at Cambrai involving four hundred British tanks. After breaking through the German Hindenburg line, a German counter offensive on November 30 pushed the British back.

The Middle and Near East (1917)

Mesopotamia. The British revived their Mesopotamian campaign in 1917 and retook Al Kut on February 23. They captured Baghdad on March 11.

British forces in Palestine unsuccessfully attacked Gaza on March 26–27, and reassaulted it with the same consequences on April 17–19. In the third offensive against Gaza from October 31 to November 7, Turkish forces retreated, which opened the way for a British attack on Jerusalem. While Colonel T. E. Lawrence worked to stir Arab passions against the Turks, General Sir Edmund Allenby took Jerusalem on December 9–11.

The United States Enters the War

American Neutrality. Woodrow Wilson, the U.S. president, issued a declaration of neutrality four days after war broke out in 1914, and offered to work to settle differences.

The United States and Freedom of the Seas. As the war expanded into the Atlantic, Allied efforts to stifle Central power trade and the German use of the submarine created problems for the United States. In October 1914, President Wilson asked both sides to abide by the Declaration of London (1909), which, as mentioned previously, laid out rules of actions and rights for neutrals and belligerents in war. Germany and its allies agreed to accept its terms because of their inferior naval strength, while the Allied powers refused.

Germany and Submarine Warfare. Throughout the latter part of 1915 and 1916, the United States was able to restrict most German submarine activity in the Atlantic because Berlin wanted to avoid any crisis that might bring America into the war. However, the failure of peace initiatives at the end of that year convinced German leaders, who felt their submarine fleet was now capable of a successful full blockade of England, to reinstitute unlimited submarine warfare in the Atlantic on January 31, 1917. Though they knew this policy would probably bring the United States into the war, they felt they could defeat Great Britain well before the United States could significantly alter its course.

The Zimmermann Telegram. On March 2, British intelligence published the Zimmermann Telegram, a note from the German foreign minister to his ambassador in Mexico that ordered him to seek an alliance with that country that would allow Mexico to seize the American Southwest if the United States entered the war. The message—revealed several days after Americans died on the *Lusitania* from a U-boat attack—along with the creation of a democratic government in Russia helped convince the president and American public opinion that it was now time to enter the war. The United States entered the war on April 6, 1917.

Russia Leaves the War

A cornerstone of Bolshevik propaganda throughout 1917 was a promise to end the war after they seized power. Once in control, Soviet authorities issued a decree that called for immediate peace "with no indemnities or annexations" at the Second Congress of Soviets on November 8, 1917.

The Armistice at Brest-Litovsk. As order collapsed along the eastern front, the Soviet government began to explore cease-fire talks with the Central powers. Trotsky, commissar of foreign affairs, offered negotiations to all sides, and signed an initial armistice as a prelude to peace discussions with Germany at Brest-Litovsk on December 5, 1917.

Trotsky and Initial Peace Negotiations with Germany. Trotsky, who replaced Adolf Joffe as principal delegate soon after talks began, felt he could utter a few revolutionary phrases and close up shop. He was shocked by German demands for Poland, Lithuania, and Kurland when negotiations opened on December 22, 1917. This prompted him to return to Moscow for consultations with the Bolshevik leadership.

Soviet Differences over Peace Terms. Three different perspectives emerged over the German peace terms among the Soviet leadership. One group, led by Nikolai Bukharin, wanted the conflict to continue as a revolutionary war designed to spread Bolshevism. Lenin, however, felt the country needed peace for his government to survive. Western revolution would take place later. Trotsky wanted a policy of no war and no peace.

At a Bolshevik meeting on January 21, 1918, the Soviet leadership barely selected Bukharin's proposal, while the Central Committee overrode this decision on January 24 in favor of Trotsky's proposal.

Negotiations Resume at Brest-Litovsk. Trotsky returned to the peace talks and tried to stall them with his "no war, no peace" theme. He left Brest-Litovsk on February 10, and eight days later, the Germans responded with broad attacks all across the eastern front that met with little opposition.

The Soviet Response and the Treaty of Brest-Litovsk. On the day the German offensive began, Lenin barely convinced party leaders to accept Germany's earlier offer. Berlin responded with harsher ones, which the Soviets grudgingly accepted, and were integrated into the Treaty of Brest-Litovsk of March 3, 1918. According to the treaty's terms, in return for peace, Soviet Russia lost its Baltic provinces, the Ukraine, Finland, Byelorussia, and part of Transcaucasia. The area lost totaled 1.3 million square miles and included 62 million people.

The Allied Breakthrough

By the end of 1917, the Allied war effort seemed in disarray. French and Italian governments had changed hands in an effort to revive war spirits, while an Anglo-French force arrived to stop the Central advance after Caporetto. To strengthen Allied resolve, the United States declared war on Austro-Hungary on December 6, 1917, while the Allies developed new mining policies to handicap German U-boat movements.

The American Presence: Naval and Economic Support

The United States, which originally hoped that it could simply supply the Allies with naval and economic support, made its naval presence known immediately and helped Great Britain mount an extremely effective blockade of Germany and, through a convoy system, strengthened the shipment of goods across the Atlantic.

Despite the difficulties of building a military from scratch, the United States was slowly able to transform its peacetime army of 219,665 men and officers into a force of 2 million. An initial token group, the American Expeditionary Force under General John J. Pershing arrived in France on June 25, 1917; by the end of April 1918, 300,000 Americans a month were being placed as complete divisions alongside British and French units.

The German Offensive of 1918

Emboldened by their victory over Russia, the German High Command decided to launch an all-out offensive against the Allies in France to win the war.

Strengthened by forces from the Russian front, Erich Ludendorff, the Germans' principal war planner, intended to drive his divisions, which outnumbered the Allies sixty-nine to thirty-three, between the British and the French and push the former to the English Channel.

Beginning on March 21, 1918, Ludendorff mounted four attacks on Allied forces in France: Somme, Lys, Aisne, and Champagne-Marne—lasting into July. The success of the assaults so concerned the Allies that they appointed French chief of staff Ferdinand Foch generalissimo of Allied Forces on April 14. In the third attack on Aisne, the Germans came within thirty-seven miles of Paris. However, the appearance of fresh, though untried American forces, combined with irreplaceable German manpower losses, began to turn the war against the Germans. Four days after the decisive German crossing of the Marne, Foch counterattacked and began to plan for an offensive against the Germans.

The Allied Offensive of 1918

Stirred by the successes on the Marne, the Allies began their offensive against the Germans at Amiens on August 8, 1918. Ludendorff, who called this Germany's "dark day," soon began to think of ways to end the fighting. By September 3, the Germans retreated to the Hindenburg line. On September 26, Foch began his final offensive and took the Hindenburg line the following day. Two days later, Ludendorff advised his government to seek a peace settlement. Over the next month, the French took Saint Quentin (October 1), while the British occupied Cambrai, Le Cateau, and Ostend. Other fronts also crumbled. On September 14, Allied forces attacked in the Salonika area of Macedonia and forced Bulgaria to sue for peace on September 29.

On September 19, Britain's General Allenby began an attack on Turkish forces at Megiddo in Palestine and quickly defeated them. In a rapid collapse of Turkish resistance, the British took Damascus, Aleppo, and finally forced Turkey from the war.

On October 24, the Italians began an assault against Austria-Hungary at Vitto Veneto and forced Vienna to sign armistice terms on November 3.

The Armistice with Germany

Several days after Ludendorff advised his government to seek peace, Prince Max of Baden assumed the German chancellorship. On October 4, he asked President Wilson for an armistice, based on the U.S. president's "Fourteen Points" of January 8, 1918. The Allies hesitatingly agreed to support the president's terms, with qualifications, which were given to the Germans on November 5. On November 11 at 11 A.M., the war ended on the western front.

Collapse of Monarchy and Creation of a German Republic

The dramatic collapse of German military fortunes seriously undercut the credibility of Wilhelm II and strengthened the country's politicians. Alarmed by the threat of revolution after the German naval rebellion at Kiel on October 28, politicians tried to get the kaiser to abdicate in hopes that this would enable Germany to get better terms from the Allies. The kaiser fled to army headquarters in Belgium, while on November 9 the chancellorship was transferred to Friedrich Ebert after his fellow socialist, Philipp Scheidemann, announced the creation of a republic on the same day.

The Paris Peace Conference of 1919–1920

To a great extent, the direction and thrust of discussions at the Paris Peace Conference were determined by the destructive nature of war and the responsibilities, ideals, and personalities of the principle architects of the settlements: President Woodrow Wilson of the United States, Prime Minister David Lloyd George of Great Britain, Prime Minister Georges Clemenceau of France, and Prime Minister Vittorio Orlando of Italy.

As politicians, they reflected the mood of victorious Europe's population, who wanted the principal Central powers, Germany and Austria-Hungary, punished severely for this inhuman calamity. Total losses are not accurately known, but the following estimates illustrate the staggering number of casualties:

Country	Dead	Wounded
Russia	1,700,000	7,450,000
France	1,363,000–1,500,000	4,660,800–4,797,800
British Empire	908,000–1,000,000	2,190,235–2,282,235
Italy	460,000–500,000	1,697,000–1,737,000
United States	100,000–116,708	87,292–104,000
Germany	1,774,000–2,000,000	5,142,588–5,368,558
Austria-Hungary	1,200,000–1,250,000	5,770,000–5,820,000

Woodrow Wilson and the Fourteen Points

Not handicapped by financial or territorial concerns, Wilson idealistically promoted his Fourteen Points—particularly the last, which envisioned a League of Nations—as the basis of the armistice and the peace settlement. Issued January 8, 1918, the points were

1. Open covenants of peace

2. Freedom of the seas

3. Removal of trade barriers

4. Arms reduction

5. Settlement of colonial claims

6. Evacuation of Russia

7. Restoration of Belgium

8. Return of Alsace-Lorraine to France

9. Adjustment of Italy's borders along ethnic lines

10. Autonomy for the peoples of Austria-Hungary

11. Evacuation and restoration of the Balkans

12. Autonomy for the non-Turkish parts of the Turkish Empire

13. Independent Poland with an outlet to the sea

14. A League of Nations

Secret Allied Agreements Concluded During World War I

Throughout the war, the Allied powers had concluded secret agreements designed to encourage countries to join their side or to compensate for war efforts. In March 1915, England and France had promised to Russia Constantinople, the Turkish Straits, and the bordering areas as long as they were openly accessible. In April of the following year, England and France had promised one another, respectively, spheres in Mesopotamia and Palestine, as well as Syria, Adana, Cilia, and southern Kurdistan. The Sykes-Picot Treaty in May 1916 better defined both countries' Arabian spheres, but the Balfour Declaration of 1917, promising Jews a national homeland in Palestine, seemed to contradict Sykes-Picot. Russia was to have rights in Armenia, portions of Kurdistan, and northeastern Anatolia. The Allies gave Italy and Romania significant territories to encourage them in their war effort in April 1915 and August 1916, while the English promised to support Japan's desire for Germany's Asian possessions. France and Russia agreed to promote one another's claims at a future peace conference.

Preliminary Discussions

The unexpected end of the war, combined with the growing threat of Communist revolution throughout Europe, created an unsettling atmosphere at the conference. After the Bolshevik victory in Russia, delegates from the United States, England, France, Italy, and later Japan hurriedly began informal peace discussions on January 12, 1919. This group was transformed into a Council of Ten, consisting of two representatives from each country. This body conducted most of the talks in Paris until March 24, 1919, when the "Big Four" of Wilson (United States), Clemenceau (France), Lloyd George (England), and Orlando (Italy) took over discussions. Initially, the Allied powers had hoped for a negotiated settlement with the defeated powers, which necessitated hard terms that would be negotiated down. However, delays caused by uncertainty at the beginning of the talks, Wilson's insistence that the League of Nations be included in the settlement, and fear of European-wide revolution resulted in a hastily prepared, dictated peace settlement.

France and the Rhineland Conflict. Once talks began among the Big Four, France insisted on the return of Alsace-Lorraine from Germany and the creation of an independent buffer state along the Rhine to protect it from Germany. The United States and Great Britain opposed these claims because they felt it could lead to future Franco-German friction. In return for an Allied guarantee of France's security against Germany, France got the Saar coal mines and the demilitarization of the Rhine, with portions occupied by the Allies for fifteen years.

German Disarmament. Lloyd George and Wilson saw German arms reduction as a prelude to a European-wide plan after the conference. They also opposed the draft, though agreed with the French about the need for a small German army.

Reparations. Each major power had different views on how much compensation Germany should pay for war indebtedness. At British insistence, civilian losses were added to the military ones. The "War Guilt" clause, Article 231, was included to justify heavy reparations, while determination of the amount was left to a reparations commission. Though Article 231 noted that Germany and her allies were all responsible for the war, Article 232 ominously restricted the payment of reparations to Germany alone, leaving the door wide open to resentments and frictions later.

The Treaty of Versailles

The Treaty of Versailles, which was only between Germany and the Allies, had fifteen sections and almost 450 articles. Any country that ratified it in turn accepted these terms as well as the League of Nations' Covenant in the first article. The treaty's fifteen sections were: (1) Covenant of the League of Nations, (2) Boundaries of Germany, (3) Other Territories of Germany, (4) Germany's Overseas Boundaries and Rights, (5) Germany's Military and Naval Restrictions, (6) Prisoners of War, (7) War Guilt, (8) Reparations, (9) Costs of the War, (10) Customs Agreement and Other Covenants, (11) Aerial Navigation, (12) Freedom of Movement on Europe's Waterways, (13) Labor Organizations, (14) Guarantees, and (15) Mandates for German Colonies and Other General Provisions.

Most Significant Clauses. The treaty's war-guilt statements were the justification for its harsh penalties. The former emperor, Wilhelm II, was accused of crimes against "international morality and the sanctity of treaties," while Germany took responsibility for itself and for its allies for all losses suffered by the Allied powers and their supporters as a result of German and Central power aggression.

Germany had to return Alsace and Lorraine to France and Eupen-Malmédy to Belgium. France got Germany's Saar coal mines as reparations, while the Saar Basin was to be occupied by the major powers for fifteen years, after which a plebiscite would decide its ultimate fate. Poland got a number of German provinces and Danzig, now a free city, as its outlet to the sea. Germany lost all colonies in Asia and Africa.

The German army was limited to one hundred thousand men and officers with twelve-year enlistments for the former, twenty-five for the latter. The General Staff was abolished. The navy lost its submarines and most offensive forces, and was limited to fifteen thousand men and officers with the same enlistment periods as the army. Aircraft and blimps were outlawed. A reparations commission was created to determine Germany's war debt to the Allies, which it figured in 1921 to be $31.4 billion, to be paid over an extended period of time. In the meantime, Germany was to begin immediate payments in goods and raw materials.

German Hesitance to Sign the Treaty. The Allies presented the treaty to the Germans on May 7, 1919, but Foreign Minister Count Brockdorff-Rantzau refused to sign it, precipitating a crisis on both sides. Germans stated that its terms were too much for the German people and that it violated the spirit of Wilson's Fourteen Points. After some minor changes were made, the Germans were told to sign the document or face an Allied advance into Germany. The treaty was signed on June 28, 1919, at Versailles.

Treaties with Germany's Allies

After the conclusion of the Treaty of Versailles, responsibility for concluding treaties with the other Central powers fell on the shoulders of the Council of Foreign Ministers and later, the Conference of Ambassadors.

The Treaty of St. Germain (September 10, 1919). The Allied treaty with Austria legitimized the breakup of the Austrian Empire in the latter days of the war and saw Austrian territory ceded to Italy and the new states of Czechoslovakia, Poland, and Yugoslavia. The agreement included military restrictions and debt payments.

Treaty of Neuilly (November 27, 1919). Bulgaria lost territory to Yugoslavia and Greece; the treaty also included clauses on military limitations and reparations.

Treaty of Trianon (June 4, 1920). The agreement with Hungary was delayed because of its Communist revolution in 1919 and Romania's brief occupation of Budapest. In the agreement, Hungary lost two-thirds of its prewar territory to Romania, Yugoslavia, and Czechoslovakia, and became an almost purely Magyar nation. Reparations and military reduction were also in the accord.

Treaty of Sevres (August 10, 1920). Turkey lost most of its non-Turkish territory, principally in the Middle and Near East, and saw the Straits and the surrounding area internationalized and demilitarized. The Turkish revolution of Mustafa Kemal Pasha ultimately saw its terms neutralized, and renegotiated, as the Treaty of Lausanne (July 24, 1923) with Turkey gaining territory in Anatolia, Smyrna, and Thrace.

Problems of Allied Unity: Japan, Italy, and the United States

During and after the meetings in Paris that resulted in the Treaty of Versailles, disputes arose among the Allies that caused friction among them later.

Japan. During the treaty talks, Japan asked for Germany's Shantung Province in China, its Pacific colonies, and a statement on racial equality in the League Covenant. Japan got what it essentially wanted on the first two requests, despite protests from China on Shantung. However, Japan's request for a racial-equality clause met strong opposition from the United States and some members of the British Commonwealth, who feared the impact of the statement on immigration. The proposal was denied, principally at the instigation of President Wilson.

Italy. Italians came to Paris expecting realization of the secret Treaty of London (1915), plus more. When Orlando proved stubborn on this matter, Wilson appealed directly to the Italians regarding the issue, which prompted the Italian delegation to leave the conference temporarily. Italy got the Tyrol, as well as Istria and some Adriatic islands in the Treaty of Rapallo (December 12, 1920). Dalmatia, however, went to Yugoslavia, while Fiume was seized by the Italian patriot/poet Gabriele D'Annunzio, on September 12, 1919. After a fourteen-month occupation, he departed, leaving its destiny to Italy and Yugoslavia. The Treaty of Rome (January 27, 1924) divided the city between the two, with Italy getting the lion's share of the area.

The United States. Although public and political sentiment was initially in favor of the treaty and its League, Wilson's failure to include Senate representatives in the negotiating, and fear of presidential usurpation of congressional war powers created suspicion between Republicans and the president. These suspicions, coupled with concern over the obligations of the United States in future European affairs (particularly those cited in Article X—which would, according to its opponents, give the United States no freedom of choice in deciding whether or not to intervene in world crises) prompted the Senate to reject it twice in 1919 and 1920, though by only seven votes on the latter occasion. The United States concluded a separate peace with Germany in 1921 and never joined the League, though it was active in some of its corollary organizations.

Political Developments in Postwar Europe (1918–1929)

England

The Economy (1918–1922). England had a set of problems unique to its status as a nation absolutely dependent on trade and commerce for its economic well-being.

With the war at an end, the coalition government of David Lloyd George held the first parliamentary elections since 1910. Known as the "Coupon" or "Khaki" elections, the question of victory, the nature of the settlement with Germany, and the prime minister himself were the election's burning issues. Before it took place, the Representation of the Peoples Act granted women over age thirty the right to vote. Lloyd George and his Conservative coalition won a landslide victory, winning 478 seats, while his opponents gained only 87.

Afterward, England enjoyed an economic boom fueled by government policies and economic production based on prewar conditions. Unfortunately, government retrenchment, blended with tax increases and overproduction, resulted in a severe recession by the end of 1921. It began in 1920 with almost seven hundred thousand unemployed by the end of that year and jumped to two million by the end of 1921. Until the Depression, unemployment averaged 12 percent annually. This resulted in the passage of the Unemployment Insurance Acts (1920, 1922) for workers, and the construction of two hundred thousand subsidized housing units.

During the Easter Rebellion of 1916, the extremist Sinn Fein faction gained prominence in Ireland. In 1918, three-quarters of its members elected to the British parliament declared Irish independence in Dublin. This prompted civil war between the Irish Republican Army and the Black-and-Tans, England's special occupation forces. The Lloyd George government responded with a Home-Rule division of Ireland with two legislatures, which only the northern six counties accepted. In October 1921, London created the Irish Free State, from which Ulster withdrew, as part of the new British Commonwealth.

Politics (1922–1924). The economic problems and the debate over Ireland caused Conservatives to withdraw from Lloyd George's coalition. Andrew Bonar-Law replaced him as head of a new Conservative government, though ill health forced him to resign in 1923, followed briefly by Stanley Baldwin. Continued unemployment and labor problems, coupled with a refusal to adopt more protectionist trade policies, resulted in a significant decline in support for Conservatives in the elections of November 1923.

Baldwin resigned, followed in office by Ramsey MacDonald, head of the Labour Party. His minority government lasted nine months, and fell principally because of his efforts to establish formal ties with Russia.

Stanley Baldwin (1924–1929). After MacDonald, Stanley Baldwin again became prime minister, this time with a solid electoral victory (411 seats) and strong Conservative backing. In 1925, the economic crisis abated somewhat, with an increase in prices and wages. However, the country's return to the gold standard, which made the pound worth too much, affected British trade. In May 1926, a general strike in support of miners who feared a dramatic drop in their already low wages swept the country. Baldwin refused to concede to the miners' demands, broke the strike, and in 1927 sponsored the Trade Unions Act, which outlawed such labor action. On the other hand, the government passed a number of pieces of social legislation that further allowed support for housing construction and expanded pensions through its Widows', Orphans', and Old Age Pensions Act (1925). It also passed new legislation in 1928 that gave women the same voting privileges as men. In foreign affairs, Baldwin cancelled the 1924 commercial agreement with the Soviet Union (formed in 1922; see discussion later in the chapter), and, as a result of Soviet espionage activities, broke formal ties with the Soviet Union in 1927.

France

The human toll of the war deeply affected France, exacerbating a slowdown in population growth that had begun in the nineteenth century. Robbed of its youth, the Third Republic reflected in its political life and foreign policy a country ruled by an aging leadership that sought comfort in its rich past.

The Bloc National (1919–1924). The election of November 1919 caused a momentary shift right with moderate conservatives winning almost two-thirds of the seats in the Chamber of Deputies. The new government, headed by Premier Alexandre Millerand, was a coalition known as the Bloc National. Aristide Briand replaced Millerand in January 1921 but was removed a year later because of lack of firmness on the German reparations question and was succeeded by Raymond Poincaré.

France had borrowed heavily during the war and spent great sums afterward to rebuild its devastated economy. Unfortunately, it relied on German reparations to fund many of these costs. Problems with these repayments created a financial crisis that saw French public debt increase, accompanied by a steady decline in the value of the franc.

Growing Franco-German differences over Germany's willingness to meet its debt payments created friction between both countries and toppled the government of Aristide Briand. In December 1922, Poincaré declared Germany in default on its reparations payments. In January, France and Belgium occupied the Ruhr, a valley in northwestern Germany, long an industrialized area based on its rich coal and iron deposits. Efforts to obtain payments in kind via Franco-Belgium operation of the Ruhr's mines and factories failed because of passive resistance by German workers in the area. The Ruhr's occupiers gained little more in payments than they had through normal means, and found the cost of occupation expensive. Consequently, the French government had to raise taxes 20 percent to cover the cost of the occupation.

The *Cartel des Gauches* (1924–1926). Poincaré's Ruhr occupation policy had divided voters, while tax increases helped defeat the Bloc National in the May 1924 elections, though it did gain 51 percent of the popular vote. A radical-socialist coalition, the *Cartel des Gauches*, had majority control of the Chamber of Deputies. It selected Edouard Herriot, a radical leader, as premier, while Millerand continued as president, and Aristide Briand as foreign minister. Millerand's interference in policy questions forced his removal on June 10, 1924, with his successor, Gaston Doumergue, serving as president until 1931.

France's economy was plagued by a declining franc and inflation. Herriot's efforts to raise direct taxes, force higher levies on the rich, and lower interest rates on government bonds met with radical opposition, which sought indirect tax increases and cuts in government expenditures. Herriot was removed from office on April 10, 1925, and replaced by mathematician Paul Painlevé, who served for eight months.

Briand, who dominated French foreign affairs until 1932, pursued a policy of reconciliation with Germany and better relations with Europe's other pariah, the Soviet Union. France granted diplomatic recognition to Soviet Russia in 1924, though relations quickly worsened because of the difficulty in getting the tsarist debt question resolved and the Soviets' use of their Paris embassy for espionage activities.

The *Union Nationale* (1926–1928). The most crucial domestic problem faced by the *Cartel des Gauches* was the declining franc, which by 1926 was worth only one-tenth of its prewar value. Its fall caused a political crisis so severe that the country had six cabinets over a nine-month period. Consequently, on July 15, 1926, Briand resigned his premiership, succeeded by Poincaré, who formed a *Union Nationale* Cabinet that had six former premiers in it. This coalition was backed by Radicals as well as Conservatives and centrists in the legislature. To resolve the franc problem, the Chamber granted Poincaré special authority. Over the next two years, he dramatically raised taxes and was able to get capital that had been taken out of the country reinvested in government bonds or other areas of the economy. By 1928, the franc had risen to 20 percent of its prewar value, and Poincaré was considered a financial miracle worker. Unfortunately, the political and psychological scars left by the crisis would haunt France for two more decades.

Weimar Germany (1918–1929)

The collapse of the German war effort in the second half of 1918 ultimately created a political crisis that forced the abdication of the kaiser and the creation of a republic on November 9. Since Berlin was seething with unrest, representatives met instead in provincial, culturally rich Weimar in Thuringia—hence the name.

Provisional Government. From the outset, the Provisional Government, formed of a coalition of Majority and Independent Socialists, was beset by divisions from within and threats of revolution throughout Germany. The first chancellor was Friedrich

Ebert, the Majority Socialist leader. On November 22, state leaders agreed to support a temporary government until elections could be held for a nationally elected legislature, which would draw up a constitution for the new republic.

Elections for the new National Constituent Assembly, which was to be based on proportional representation, gave no party a clear majority. A coalition of the Majority Socialists, the Catholic Center Party, and the German Democratic Party (DDP) dominated the new assembly. On February 11, 1919, the assembly met in historic Weimar and selected Friedrich Ebert president of Germany. Two days later, Phillip Scheidemann formed the first Weimar Cabinet and became its first chancellor.

On August 11, 1919, the assembly promulgated a new constitution, which provided for a bicameral legislature. The upper chamber, the Reichsrat, represented the Federal states, while the lower house, the Reichstag, with 647 delegates elected by universal suffrage, supplied the country's chancellor and cabinet. A president was to be elected separately for a seven-year term. As a result of Article 48 of the constitution, he could rule through emergency decree, though the Reichstag could take this authority from him.

Problems of the Weimar Republic (1919–1920). The new government faced serious domestic problems that severely undercut its authority. Forced acceptance of the hated *Friedensdiktat* ("the dictated peace") gravely compromised its prestige, while the unsuccessful, violent Communist Spartacist Rebellion (January 5–11, 1919) in Berlin created a climate of instability. This was followed three months later by the brief Communist takeover of Bavaria, and the rightist Kapp Putsch (March 13–17, 1920) in the capital the following year.

Territorial, manpower, and economic losses from the war, coupled with a $31.4 billion reparations debt, had a severe impact on the German economy and society, and handicapped the new government's efforts to establish a stable environment.

In an effort of good faith based on hopes of future reparation payment reductions, Germany borrowed heavily and made payments in kind to fulfill its early debt obligations. The result was a spiral of inflation, later promoted by the Weimar government to underline Allied insensitivity to Germany's plight that saw the devaluation of the mark from 8.4 marks to the dollar in 1919 to 7,000 marks to the dollar by December 1922. After the Allied Reparations Commission declared Germany in default on its debt, the French and the Belgians occupied the Ruhr on January 11, 1923.

Chancellor Wilhelm Cuno encouraged the Ruhr's Germans passively to resist the occupation, and printed worthless marks to pay laid-off workers, which dropped from 40,000 to the dollar in January 1923 to 4.2 trillion to the dollar eleven months later. The occupation ended on September 26 and helped prompt stronger Allied sympathy to Germany's payment difficulties, though the inflationary spiral had severe economic, social, and political consequences.

Weimar Politics (1919–1923). Germany's economic and social difficulties deeply affected its infant democracy. From February 1919 to August 1923, the country had six chancellors.

In the aftermath of the Kapp Putsch, conservative demands for new elections resulted in a June defeat for the ruling coalition that saw the Democrats (DDP) lose seats to the German National People's Party (DVP), headed by Gustav Stresemann, and the Majority Socialists lose seats to the more revolutionary Independent Socialists. Conservatives blamed the Weimar Coalition for the hated Versailles *Diktat* with its war guilt and reparations terms, while leftists felt the government had forgotten its social and revolutionary ideals.

Growing right-wing discontent with the government resulted in the assassination of the gifted head of the Catholic Center Party, Matthias Erzberger, on August 29, 1921, and the murder of Foreign Minister Walter Rathenau on June 24, 1922. These were two of the most serious of over 350 political murders in Germany in this period. An example of the radical-right politics in this period was a little-noticed new party in Munich, the National Socialist German Workers' Party, formed in 1920. Its early message was vaguely socialist and intensely nationalist, fueled by the postwar instability and desire for revenge against the Big Four, who had treated Germany—so the right-wing thought—shamefully. After an abortive putsch in Munich in November, 1923, the party's leader, Adolf Hitler, went to prison, not to make an impression on the nation until 1929.

The Policies of Gustav Stresemann. The dominant figure in German politics from 1923 to 1929 was Gustav Stresemann, founder and leader of the DVP. Though he served as chancellor from August 12 to November 23, 1923, his prominence derives from his role as foreign minister from November 1923 until his death on October 3, 1929. He received the Nobel Peace Prize for his diplomatic efforts in 1926.

As chancellor, Stresemann felt that the road to recovery and treaty revision lay in adherence to the Versailles settlement and positive relations with France and its allies. Consequently, on September 26, he ended passive resistance in the Ruhr and began to search for a solution to Germany's reparations payment problem with France. To restore faith in the currency, the government introduced a new one, the *rentenmark*, on November 20, 1923, that was equal to one billion old marks, and was backed by the mortgage value of Germany's farm and industrial land.

In an effort to come up with a more reasonable debt payment plan for Germany, the Western Allies developed the Dawes Plan that accepted the need for Germany to pay its war debts and blended England's desire for balance with France's needs for repayment assurances. According to its terms, Germany was to begin small payments of a quarter of a billion dollars annually for four years, to be increased if its economy improved. In return, the Allies agreed to help revitalize Germany's ailing economy with a $200 million American loan and withdrawal from the Ruhr.

The crowning achievement in Stresemann's efforts to restore Germany to normal status in the European community was the Locarno Pact, December 1, 1925.

Weimar Politics (1924–1928). Reichstag elections were held twice in 1924. The May 4 contest reflected a backlash against the country's economic woes and saw the Communists win 3.7 million votes and the dark-horse Nazis almost 2 million, at the expense of moderates. The December 7 elections were something of a vote on the Dawes Plan and economic revival, and saw the Nazis and the Communists lose almost a million votes apiece.

Following the death of President Ebert on February 28, 1925, two ballots were held for a new president, because no candidate won a majority on the first vote. On the second ballot on April 26, a coalition of conservative parties was able to get its candidate elected. War hero Paul von Hindenburg was narrowly elected against a centrist coalition and the Communists, who had a much smaller showing. Hindenburg, who some conservatives hoped would turn the clock back, vowed to uphold Weimar's constitution.

The elections of May 20, 1928, saw the Social Democrats get almost one-third of the popular vote, which, blended with other moderates, created a stable majority in the Reichstag, which chose Hermann Müller as chancellor. The Nazis, who held fourteen Reichstag seats at the end of 1924, lost one, while Communist strength increased.

Italy

Like other countries that had fought in the World War I, Italy had suffered greatly and gained little. Its economy, very weak even before the war broke out, relied heavily on small family agriculture, which contributed 40 percent of the country's gross national product (GNP) in 1920. Consequently, many of the social, political, and economic problems that plagued the country after the war could not be blamed solely on the conflict itself.

Italian Politics (1918–1919). Given growing discontent over the country's troubled economy, the Italian public looked to the parties that offered the most reasonable solutions. Strengthened by universal suffrage, and new proportional representation in Parliament, the Socialists doubled the number of seats to 156 in the Chamber of Deputies in the elections of November 16, 1919. The new Catholic People's Party gained 99 positions. The former had little faith in the current state and longed for its downfall, while the latter mixed conservative religious ideals with a desire for political moderation. Most important, no strong majority coalition emerged in this or the Parliament elected in May 1921 that was able to deal effectively with the country's numerous problems.

Government of Giovanni Giolitti (1920–1921). From June 9, 1920, until June 26, 1921, Italy's premier was Giovanni Giolitti, a prewar figure who had dominated Italian politics between 1901 and 1914. His tactics, to resolve Italy's international conflicts and stay aloof of its domestic conflicts, exacerbated the country's problems. Though a liberal, he was notorious for shady tactics and Machiavellian means. Socialists took advantage of his inaction and promoted strikes and other labor unrest in August and September 1920 that became violent and divided the country and the Socialist movement. Giolitti let the strikes run their course, and worked successfully to lower the government's deficit by 50 percent.

Benito Mussolini and Italian Fascism. Benito Mussolini, named by his Socialist blacksmith father after the Mexican revolutionary, Benito Juarez, was born in

1883. After a brief teaching stint, he went to Switzerland to avoid military service but returned and became active in Socialist politics. In 1912, he became editor of the party's newspaper, *Avanti*. After the outbreak of the world war, he broke with the party over involvement in the war and began to espouse nationalist ideas that became the nucleus of his fascist movement. He then opened his own newspaper, *Popolo d'Italia* ("The People of Italy") to voice his ideas. Mussolini was drafted into military service in 1915 and was badly wounded two years later. After recuperating, he returned to his newspaper, where he blended his feelings about socialism and nationalism with an instinct for violence.

Italy's postwar conflict with its allies at the Paris Peace Conference over fulfillment of the terms of the 1915 Treaty of London and the demand for Fiume played into Mussolini's hands. He supported the D'Annunzio coup (a failed attempt by a group of veterans to retake what they considered an Italian city) as a gambit toward power.

Capitalizing on the sympathy of unfulfilled war veterans, disaffected nationalists, and those fearful of communism, Mussolini formed the *Fasci di combattimento* ("Union of Combat") in Milan on March 23, 1919. Initially, this movement had few followers and did badly in the November 1919 elections. However, Socialist strikes and unrest enabled him to convince Italians that he alone could bring stability and prosperity to the country.

Fascism's greatest growth came during the Socialist unrest in 1920. Strengthened by large contributions from wealthy industrialists, Mussolini's black-suited *squadristi* attacked Socialists, Communists, and ultimately the government itself. His followers won thirty-five seats in the legislative elections in May 1921, which also toppled the Giolitti cabinet.

The center of fascist strength was in the streets of north Italy, which Mussolini's followers, through violence, came to control. He now transformed his movement into the Fascist Party, dropped his socialist views, and began to emphasize the predominance of Italian nationalism.

The resignation of the cabinet on February 9, 1922, underlined the government's inability to maintain stability. In the meantime, Fascists seized control of Bologna in May and Milan in August. In response, Socialist leaders called for a nationwide strike on August 1, 1922, which Fascist street violence stopped in twenty-four hours. On October 24, 1922, Mussolini told followers that if he was not given power, he would "march on Rome." Three days later, Fascists began to seize control of other cities, while twenty-six thousand began to move toward the capital. The government responded with a declaration of martial law, which the king, Victor Emmanuel III, refused to approve. On October 29, the king asked Mussolini to form a new government as premier of Italy.

Mussolini's Consolidation of Power. Using tactics similar to those of D'Annunzio to seize Fiume earlier, Mussolini built a government made up of a number of sympathetic parties, forming a coalition cabinet that included all major parties except the Communists and Socialists. After he assured the Chamber of Deputies that his government intended to respect personal liberties, but with "dignity and firmness," it approved his government in a 306 to 116 vote. Nine days later, the Chamber granted him quasi-dictatorial powers for a year.

To enhance his control of the government, one of Mussolini's assistants, Baron Giacomo Acerbo, successfully introduced a bill to the Chamber on July 21, 1923 (later approved by the Senate), stating that the party getting the largest number of votes in a national election with a minimum of 25 percent of the votes cast would control two-thirds of the seats in the Chamber. Mussolini also began to remove non-Fascists from his cabinet, the civil service, and other organs of government. The king kept his throne, though Mussolini now became head of state.

In violence-marred elections on April 6, 1924, the Fascists gained 60 percent of the popular vote and two-thirds of the Chamber's seats. In response to Fascist campaign tactics, Giacomo Matteotti, a Socialist Chamber member, attacked the Fascists for their misdeeds on May 30. Several days later, Fascist supporters kidnapped and murdered him, provoking his supporters, unwisely, to walk out of the Chamber in protest. Momentarily, Italy was stunned, and Mussolini was vulnerable. The opposition asked the king to dismiss Mussolini, but he refused.

Consolidation of the Dictatorship. On January 3, 1925, Mussolini accepted responsibility for events of the past year. He warned that he would quickly resolve the instability caused by his opponents. What followed was a new reign of terror that arrested opponents, closed newspapers, and eliminated basic civil liberties for Italians. On December 24, 1925, the legislature's powers were greatly limited, while Mussolini got more powers as the new head of state. Throughout 1926, Mussolini intensified his control over the country with legislation that outlawed strikes and created the syndicalist corporate system. A failed assassination attempt prompted the Law for the Defense of the State of November 25, 1926, that created a special court to deal with political crimes and introduced the death penalty for threats against the king, his family, or the head of state.

The Fascist Party. In December 1922, Mussolini created a Grand Council of Fascism, which in 1928 became the most important organ of government in Italy. The structure of the Fascist Party did not reach final form until November 12, 1932. It was defined as a "civil militia" with the *Duce* (Mussolini) as its head. The party's provincial secretaries, appointed by Mussolini, oversaw local party organizations, the *Fasci di Combattimento*. There were also separate Fascist youth organizations such as the *Piccole Italiane* (under age 12) and the *Giovane Italiane* (over age 12) for girls; and the *Balilla* (ages 8–14), the *Avanguardisti* (ages 14–18), and the *Giovani Fascisti* (ages 18–21) for boys. After 1927, only those who had been members of the *Balilla* and the *Avanguardisti* could be party members.

The Syndicalist-Corporate System. In an effort to institutionalize his theories about labor and management, Mussolini began to adopt some of the syndicalist theories of his followers. What emerged was a legal superstructure of labor-employer syndicates followed later by government-coordinated corporations to oversee the economy.

On April 3, 1926, the Rocco Labor Law created syndicates or organizations for all workers and employers in Italy. It also outlawed strikes and walkouts. Later altered, it created nine syndicate corporations: four for workers and four for employers in each of the major segments of the economy and a ninth for professionals and artists. This system was tinkered with until 1934, when a total of twenty-two such corporations were in place. The syndicalist system operated within a theoretical context, the ideal of *autarky*—self-sufficiency of the nation in economics, with the greatest reduction of dependence on trade.

Foreign Policy. Some have called the first decade of Mussolini's reign the "time of good behavior." This was more because of his deep involvement in domestic affairs than his creative desire for foreign stability. The nation's wish for postwar peace and stability led Mussolini to have Italy participate in all of the international developments in the 1920s aimed at securing normalcy in relations with its neighbors.

In the fall of 1923, Mussolini used the assassination of Italian officials, who were working to resolve a Greek-Albanian border dispute, as a pretext to seize the island of Corfu. Within a month, however, the British and the French convinced him to return the island for an indemnity. Only in the 1930s did Mussolini feel powerful enough to attempt greater things.

Soviet Russia

Soon after the Bolshevik seizure of power, opposition forces began to gather throughout Russia that sought to challenge Soviet authority or use the occasion to break up the Russian Empire. Partly to shore up his regime's fortunes, Lenin made the fateful move in 1919 of establishing the *Comintern* (the Third International Workingmen's Association). Its aim was to coordinate communist parties in the world, but its means included the rigorous exclusion of the then more powerful Social Democrats of the world.

Origins of the Russian Civil War (1918). After Brest-Litovsk, Lenin's government agreed to ship part of a group of Czech POWs through Vladivostok to the western front. On May 14, 1918, a brawl took place between these units and Hungarian POWs at Chelyabinsk in the Ural Mountains that led to a Czech rebellion against Soviet authorities and the seizure of the Urals area and eastern Siberia by late summer.

In the spring of 1918, Russia's old war allies had begun to land forces in Russia at major shipping points such as Murmansk, Archangel, and Vladivostok to protect supplies they had sent the Provisional Government. The Czech rebellion stirred the Allied leaders meeting at Paris to upgrade their efforts in Russia to aid the Czechs and other Communist opponents in a limited, and hopefully, noncombative manner. They began to land military contingents at the above ports, at Baku, and in Odessa to support a victor that would revive the eastern front and, to a lesser degree, counterbalance Lenin's threatening Communist movement.

Opposition to the Soviet takeover had begun immediately after Lenin's seizure of Petrograd. General M. V. Alexeev had formed a volunteer army, whose command was shared and later taken over by General Anton Denikin, who fled to the Don River basin area in early 1918. Another center of White resistance was created first by Socialist Revolutionaries at Omsk, followed later by a government there under Admiral Alexander Kolchak, who was backed by Czech forces and would declare himself supreme commander of White forces in the civil war. In time, most of the major White commanders would recognize Kolchak's authority. General Eugene Miller created a White opposition outpost at Archangel, and General Nicholas Yudenich another in Estonia.

To meet these threats, Lenin appointed Trotsky as commissar of war on March 13, 1918, with orders to build a Red Army. By the end of the year, using partial conscription, the new Soviet forces began to retake some areas captured by the Whites.

The Russian Civil War (1919–1920). The White forces, constantly weakened by lack of unified command and strategy, enjoyed their greatest successes in 1919, when Denikin, operating from the South, took Kharkov and later Odessa and Kiev. On the other hand, Yudenich was driven from Petrograd, while Denikin eventually lost Kharkov and Kiev. Kolchak had been defeated, and Omsk was taken by November.

By early 1920, White fortunes had begun to collapse. On January 4, Kolchak abdicated in favor of Denikin, and was turned over by his Czech protectors to the Soviets, who executed him on February 7. In the meantime, Denikin's capital, Rostov, was taken by the Red Army and his command was taken over later by General Peter Wrangel, whose forces were beaten that fall. Both armies were evacuated from the Crimea.

The Polish-Soviet War (1920). The new Polish state under Marshal Joszef Pilsudski sought to take advantage of the civil war in Russia to retake territory lost to Russia during the Polish partitions in the late eighteenth century. Polish forces invaded the Ukraine on April 25 and took Kiev two weeks later. A Soviet counteroffensive reached Warsaw by mid-August but was stopped by the Poles. Both sides concluded an armistice on October 12 and signed the Treaty of Riga on March 12, 1921, that placed Poland's border east of the Curzon Line—a new border proposed by British Foreign Secretary Lord Curzon but not considered seriously until Stalin took up the "Line" in 1942.

Domestic Policy and Upheaval (1918–1921). In order to provide more food to cities, the Soviet government implemented a "War Communism" program that centered on forced grain seizures and class war between kulaks (roughly defined middle-class peasants) and others. All major industry was nationalized. These policies triggered rebellions against the seizures, which, between 1918 and 1921, sharply decreased the amount of land under cultivation and the total grain produced.

The civil war and War Communism had brought economic disaster and social upheaval throughout the country. On March 1, 1921, as the Soviet leadership met to decide on policies to guide the country in peace, a naval rebellion broke out at the Kronstadt naval base. The Soviet leadership sent Trotsky to put down the rebellion, which he did brutally by March 18.

The New Economic Policy (1921–1927). The Kronstadt rebellion strengthened Lenin's resolve to initiate new policies approved at the Tenth Party Congress that would end grain seizures and stimulate agricultural production. Termed the New Economic

Policy (NEP), the government maintained control over the "commanding heights" of the economy (foreign trade, transportation, and heavy industry) while opening other sectors to limited capitalist development. It required the peasants to pay the government a fixed acreage tax and allowed them to sell the surplus for profit. Once the government had resolved the inconsistencies in agricultural and industrial output and pricing, the NEP began to yield near-1913 production levels. The country remained dominated by small farms and peasant communes. Industrial production also improved, though it was handicapped by outdated technology and equipment that hindered further output or expansion beyond 1913 levels.

The Death of Lenin and the Rise of Josef Stalin. Lenin, the founder of the Soviet State, suffered a serious stroke on May 26, 1922, and a second in December of that year. As he faced possible forced retirement or death, he composed a secret "testament" that surveyed the strengths and weaknesses of his possible successor, Stalin, who he feared would abuse power. Unfortunately, his third stroke prevented him from removing Stalin from his position as general secretary. Lenin died on January 21, 1924.

Josef Stalin (1879–1953) was born Josef Vissarionovich Dzugashvili in the Georgian village of Gori. He became involved in Russian Marxism as early as 1900; later he became Lenin's expert on minorities. Intimidated by the party's intellectuals, he took over some seemingly unimportant party organizations after the revolution and transformed them into important bases of power. Among them were Politburo (Political Bureau), which ran the country; the Orgburo (Organizational Bureau), which Stalin headed, and which appointed people to positions in groups that implemented Politburo decisions; the Commissariat of the Workers' and Peasants' Inspectorate, also under Stalin's control, which tried to eliminate party corruption; and the Secretariat, which worked with all party organs and set the Politburo's agenda. Stalin served as the party's general secretary after 1921.

Leon Trotsky. Born Lev Davidovich Bronstein, Trotsky (1879–1940) was a Jewish intellectual active in Menshevik revolutionary work, particularly in the 1905 Revolution. He joined Lenin's movement in 1917 and soon became his right-hand man. He was chairman of the Petrograd Soviet, headed the early Brest-Litovsk negotiating team, served as foreign commissar, and was father of the Red Army. A brilliant organizer and theorist, Trotsky was also brusque and, some felt, overbearing.

The Struggle for Power (1924–1925). The death of Lenin in 1924 intensified a struggle between Stalin and Trotsky and their respective supporters for control of the party. Initially, the struggle, which began in 1923, appeared to be between three men: Lev Kamenev, head of the Moscow Soviet; Zinoviev, party chief in Petrograd and head of the Comintern; and Trotsky. All three were Jewish, and though Stalin was a budding anti-Semite, the former two, allied with Stalin, presented a formidable opposition group to Trotsky.

The struggle centered on Trotsky's accusation that the trio was drifting away from Lenin's commitment to revolution by "bureaucratizing" the party. Trotsky believed in "permanent revolution," blending a commitment to world revolution and building socialism with the development of a heavy industrial base in Russia. Stalin responded with the concept of "Socialism in One Country," which committed the country to building up its socialist base, regardless of the status of world revolution.

In the fall of 1924, Trotsky attacked Zinoviev and Kamenev for the drift away from open discussion in the party and for not supporting Lenin's initial scheme to seize power in November 1917. As a result, Trotsky was removed as commissar of war on January 16, 1925, and two months later the party accepted "Socialism in One Country" as its official governing doctrine.

The Struggle for Power (1925–1927). Zinoviev and Kamenev, who agreed with the concept of permanent revolution, began to fear Stalin and soon found themselves allied against him and his rightist supporters, Nikolai Bukharin; Alexis Rykov, chairman of the Council of People's Commissars (the cabinet); and Mikhail Tomsky, head of the trade unions.

The XIV Party Congress rebuffed Kamenev and Zinoviev, and accepted Bukharin's economic policies. It demoted Kamenev to candidate status on the Politburo, while adding a number of Stalin's supporters to that body as well as the Central Committee. Afterward, Kamenev and Zinoviev joined Trotsky in his dispute with Stalin. As a result, Trotsky and Kamenev lost their seats on the Politburo, while Zinoviev was removed as head of the Comintern.

In early 1927, Trotsky and his followers accused Stalin and the Right of a "Thermidorian Reaction," Menshevism, and recent foreign policy failures in England and China. Trotsky and Zinoviev lost their positions on the Central Committee, which prompted them to participate in anti-rightist street demonstrations on November 7, 1927. Both were then thrown out of the party, followed by their supporters. Trotsky was forced into exile in Central Asia, while Zinoviev and Kamenev, humiliated and defeated, begged successfully to be allowed to return to the fold.

At the XV Party Congress, Stalin indicated that the party would begin gradually to collectivize the country's predominantly small-farm agricultural system. His shocked rightist allies, now outnumbered by Stalinists on the Politburo, sought an uncomfortable alliance with the defeated Left. Over the next two years, the major old rightist allies of Stalin, Bukharin, Rykov, and Tomsky lost their Politburo seats and other party positions, and ultimately, party membership. Brief exile followed in some cases.

Soviet Constitutional Development. Soviet Russia adopted two constitutions, one in 1918 and one in 1924. The first reflected the ideals of the state's founders and created the Russian Soviet Federative Socialist Republic (RSFSR) as the country's central administrative unit. An All-Russian Congress of Soviets was the government's legislative authority, while a Central Executive Committee (CEC), aided by a cabinet or Council of People's Commissars wielded executive power. The Communist Party was not mentioned in the 1918 or 1924 constitutions. The 1924 document was similar to the earlier one, but reflected changes brought about by the creation of the Union of Soviet Socialist Republics (U.S.S.R., or the Soviet Union) two years earlier. The CEC was divided into a Council of the Union and a Council of Nationalities, while a new Supreme Court and Procurator was added to the governmental structure. The new constitution also created a Supreme Court and a Procurator responsible to the CEC.

Foreign Policy (1918–1929). Soviet efforts after the October Revolution to openly foment revolution throughout Europe and Asia, its refusal to pay tsarist debts, and international outrage over the murder of the royal family in 1918 isolated the country. However, adoption of the NEP required more integration with the outside world to rebuild the broken economy.

Russia and Germany, Europe's post-World War I pariahs, drew closer out of necessity. By the early 1920s, Russia was receiving German technological help in weapons development while the Soviets helped train German pilots and others illegally. On April 16, 1922, Soviet Russia and Germany agreed to cancel their respective war debts and to establish formal diplomatic relations in the Treaty of Rapallo.

By 1921, the British concluded a trade accord with the Soviet government and in 1924 extended formal diplomatic recognition to the Soviet Union. Strong public reaction to this move, coupled with the publication of the "Zinoviev Letter" of unknown origin, helped topple the pro-Soviet MacDonald government, because the letter encouraged subversion of the British government. Great Britain formally severed relations in 1927 because of Communist support of a British coal mine strike, discovery of spies in a Soviet trade delegation, and Soviet claims that it hoped to use China as a means of hurting England.

The Soviets worked to consolidate their sphere of influence acquired earlier in Mongolia, and helped engineer the creation of an independent, though strongly pro-Soviet, People's Republic of Mongolia in 1924.

In China, in an effort to protect traditional Asian strategic interests and take advantage of the chaotic war-lord atmosphere in China, the Soviets helped found a Chinese Communist Party (CCP) in 1921. However, when it became apparent that Sun Yat-sen's revolutionary Kuomintang (KMT) was more mature than the infant CCP, the Soviets encouraged an alliance between its party and this movement. Sun's successor, Chiang Kai-shek, was deeply suspicious of the Communists and made their destruction part of his effort to militarily unite China.

Europe in Crisis: Depression and Dictatorship (1929–1935)

England

Ramsay MacDonald and the Depression (1929–1931)

In the required elections of May 30, 1929, Conservatives dropped to 260 seats, Labour rose to 287, and Liberals got 59. Ramsay MacDonald formed a minority Labour government that would last until 1931. The most serious problem facing the country was the Depression, which caused unemployment to reach 1.7 million by 1930 and more than 3 million, or 25 percent of the labor force, by 1932. To meet growing budget deficits caused by heavy subsidies to the unemployed, a special government commission recommended budget cuts and tax increases. Cabinet and labor union opposition helped reduce the total for the cuts (from 78 million pounds to 22 million pounds), but this could not help restore confidence in the government, which fell on August 24, 1931.

The "National Government" (1931–1935)

The following day, King George VI helped convince MacDonald to return to office as head of a National Coalition cabinet made up of four Conservatives, four Labourites, and two Liberals. The Labour Party refused to recognize the new government and ejected MacDonald and Viscount Philip Snowden from the party. MacDonald's coalition swept the November 1931 general elections winning 554 of 615 seats.

The British government abandoned the gold standard on September 21, 1931, and adopted a series of high tariffs on imports. Unemployment peaked at three million in 1932 and dropped to two million two years later.

In 1931, the government implemented the Statute of Westminster, which created the British Commonwealth of Nations, and granted its members political equality and freedom to reject any act passed by Parliament that related to a dominion state.

MacDonald resigned his position in 1935 because of ill health and was succeeded by Stanley Baldwin, whose conservative coalition won 428 seats in November.

France

The Government of André Tardieu (1929–1932)

On July 27, 1929, Raymond Poincaré resigned as premier because of ill health. Over the next three years, the dominant figure in French politics was André Tardieu, who headed or played a role in moderate cabinets.

Tardieu tried to initiate political changes along American or British lines to create a stable two-party system that would help France deal with the world economic crisis. He convinced the Laval government and the Chamber of Deputies to accept electing its members by a plurality vote, though the Senate rejected it. In 1930, the government passed France's most important social welfare legislation, the National Workingmen's Insurance Law. It provided various forms of financial aid for illness, retirement, and death.

The Depression did not hit France until late 1931, and it took the country four years to begin to recover from it. At first, the country seemed immune to the Depression, and the economy boomed. Its manufacturing indices reached a peak in 1929 but began gradually to slide through 1932. The economy recovered the following year and dropped again through 1935.

Return of the Cartel des Gauches (1932–1934)

The defeat of the moderates and the return of the leftists in the elections of May 1, 1932, reflected growing concern over the economy and failed efforts of the government to respond to the country's problems.

France remained plagued by differences over economic reform between Radicals and Socialists. The latter advocated nationalization of major factories, expanded social reforms, and public works programs for the unemployed, while the Radicals sought a reduction in government spending. This instability was also reflected in the fact that there were six cabinets between June 1932 and February 1934.

The government's inability to deal with the country's economic and political problems saw the emergence of a number of radical groups from across the political spectrum. Some of the more prominent were the fascist *Solidarité Française*, the *Cagoulards* (*Comité Secret d'Action Revolutionnaire*), the *Parti Populaire Française* (PPF), and the *Jeunesses Patriotes*. Not as radical, though still on the right were the *Croix de Feu* and the *Action Française*. At the other extreme was the French Communist Party.

The growing influence of these groups exploded on February 6, 1934, around a scandal involving a con man with government connections, Serge Stavisky. After his suicide on the eve of his arrest in December 1933, his reported involvement with high government officials stimulated a crescendo of criticism that culminated in riots between rightists and leftists that resulted in several dead and many injured. The demonstrations and riots, viewed by some as a rightist effort to seize power, brought about the collapse of the Edouard Daladier government. He was succeeded by former president Gaston Doumergue, who put together a coalition cabinet dominated by moderates as well as radicals and rightists. It contained six former premiers and Marshal Philippe Pétain of World War I fame.

Struggle for Stability (1934–1935)

The accession of Doumergue (who had been president from 1924 to 1931) with his "National Union" cabinet, stabilized the public crisis. The new premier (influenced by Tardieu) used radio to try to convince the public of the need to increase the power of the president, Albert Lebrun (1932–1940), and to enable the premier to dissolve the legislature. Discontent with Doumergue's tactics resulted in resignations from his cabinet and its fall in November 1934.

Between November 1934 and June 1935, France had two more governments. The situation stabilized somewhat with the selection of Pierre Laval as premier, who served from June 1935 through January 1936. Laval's controversial policies, strengthened by the ability to pass laws without legislative approval, were to deflate the economy, cut government expenditures, and remain on the gold standard. Laval's government fell in early 1936.

Germany

The Young Plan

One of the last accomplishments of Gustav Stresemann before his death in 1929 was the Young Plan, a new reparations proposal that required Germany to make yearly payments for fifty-nine years that varied from 1.6 billion to 2.4 billion Reichsmark. In return, the Allies removed foreign controls on Germany's economy and agreed to leave the Rhineland the following year. Efforts by conservative extremists to stop Reichstag adoption of the Young Plan failed miserably, while a national referendum on the reactionary bill suffered the same fate. It was in this contest that Adolf Hitler distinguished himself as a fine orator.

Germany and the Depression

The Depression had a dramatic effect on the German economy and politics. German exports, which had peaked at 13.5 billion marks in 1929, fell to 12 billion marks in 1930, and to 5.7 billion marks two years later. Imports suffered the same fate. The country's national income dropped 20 percent during this period, while unemployment rose from 1,320,000 in 1929 to 6 million by 1932. This meant that 43 percent of the German work force was without jobs (compared to 25 percent of the work force in the United States).

The Rise of Adolf Hitler and Nazism

The history of Nazism is deeply intertwined with that of its leader, Adolf Hitler.

Adolf Hitler was born on April 20, 1889, in the Austrian village of Braunau-am-Inn. A frustrated artist, he moved to Vienna where he unsuccessfully tried—twice—to become a student in the Academy of Fine Arts. He became an itinerant artist, living in hovels, until the advent of the world war, which he welcomed. He had moved to Munich and enlisted in the German army. His four years at the front were the most meaningful of his life up to that time, and he emerged a decorated corporal with a mission now to go into politics to restore his country's bruised honor.

In 1919, Hitler joined the German Workers Party (DAP), which he took over and renamed the National Socialist German Workers Party (NSDAP). In 1920, the party adopted a twenty-five-point program that included treaty revision, anti-Semitism, and economic and other social changes. They also created a defense cadre of the *Sturmabteilung* (SA), paramilitary "storm troopers," or "brown shirts," which was to help the party seize power. Some of the more significant early Nazi leaders were Ernst Röhm, who helped build up the SA; Dietrich Eckart, first head of the party paper, the *Völkischer Beobachter*; Alfred Rosenberg, who replaced Eckart as editor and became the party's chief ideologist; Hermann Göring, World War I flying ace who took over the SA in 1922; and Rudolf Hess, who became Hitler's secretary.

The Beer Hall Putsch (1923)

In the midst of the country's severe economic crisis in 1923, the party, which now had fifty-five thousand members, tried to seize power, first by a march on Berlin, and then, when this seemed impossible, on Munich's government center. The march was stopped by police, and Hitler and his supporters were arrested. Their trial, which Hitler used to voice Nazi ideals, gained him a national reputation—for a while. Though sentenced to five years imprisonment, he was released after eight months. While incarcerated, he dictated *Mein Kampf* to Rudolf Hess.

The Nazi Movement (1924–1929)

Hitler's failed coup and imprisonment convinced him to seek power through legitimate political channels, which would require transforming the Nazi Party. To do this, he reasserted singular control over the movement from 1924 to 1926. Party districts were set up throughout Germany, overseen by *gaulieter* (district heads) personally appointed by Hitler.

The party grew from 27,000 in 1925 to 108,000 in 1929. New leaders emerged at this time, including Joseph Goebbels, who became party chief in Berlin and later Hitler's propaganda chief, and Heinrich Himmler, who became head of Hitler's private body guard, the *Schutzstaffel* (SS), in 1929.

Weimar Politics (1930–1933)

Germany's economic woes and the government's seeming inability to deal with them underlined the weaknesses of the country's political system and provided the Nazis with new opportunities.

In March 17, 1930, the alliance of Social Democratic, DVP, and other parties collapsed over who should shoulder unemployment benefit costs. A new coalition, under Heinrich Brüning, tried to promote a policy of government economic retrenchment, and deflation, which the Reichstag rejected. Consequently, President Hindenburg invoked Article 48 of the constitution, which enabled him to order the implementation of Brüning's program. The Reichstag overrode the decree, which forced the government's fall and new elections.

Reichstag Elections of September 14, 1930

The September 14 elections surprised everyone. The Nazis saw their 1928 vote jump from 800,000 to 6.5 million (18.3 percent of the vote), which gave them 107 Reichstag seats, second only to the Social Democrats, who fell from 152 to 143 seats. Brüning, however, continued to serve as chancellor of a weak coalition with the support of Hindenburg and rule by presidential decree. His policies failed to resolve the country's growing economic dilemmas.

Presidential Elections of 1932

Hindenburg's presidential term expired in 1932, and he was convinced to run for reelection to stop Hitler from becoming president. In the first ballot of March 13, Hitler got only 30 percent of the vote (11.3 million) to Hindenburg's 49.45 percent (18.6 million). Since German law required the new president to have a majority of the votes, a runoff was held on April 10 between Hindenburg, Hitler, and the Communist candidate, Ernst Thälmann. Hindenburg received 19.3 million votes (53 percent), Hitler 13.4 million (37 percent), and Thälmann 2.2 million votes.

The Von Papen Chancellorship

On June 1, Chancellor Brüning was replaced by Franz von Papen, who formed a government from aristocratic conservatives and others that he and Hindenburg hoped would keep Hitler from power. He held new elections on July 31 that saw the Nazis win 230 Reichstag seats with 37 percent of the vote (13.7 million), and the Communists 89 seats. Offered the vice chancellorship and an opportunity to join a coalition government, Hitler refused. Papen, paralyzed politically, ruled by presidential decree and dissolved the Reichstag on September 12. In the elections of November 6, the Nazis got only 30 percent of the vote and 196 Reichstag seats, while the Communists made substantial gains (120 seats from 89). Papen resigned in favor of Kurt von Schleicher, one of the president's closest advisers, as the new chancellor.

Hitler Becomes Chancellor

Papen joined with Hitler to undermine Schleicher, and convinced Hindenburg to appoint Hitler as chancellor to head a new coalition cabinet with three seats for the Nazis.

Hitler dissolved the Reichstag and called for new elections on March 5. Using presidential decree powers, he initiated a violent anticommunist campaign that included the lifting of some press and civil freedoms. On February 27, the Reichstag burned, enabling Hitler to get Hindenburg to issue "Ordinances for the Protection of the German State and Nation" that removed all civil and press liberties as part of a "revolution" against communism. In the Reichstag elections of March 5, the Nazis got only 43.9 percent of the vote and 288 Reichstag seats but, through an alliance with the Nationalists, gained majority control of the legislature.

Hitler now intensified his campaign against his opponents, placing many of them in newly opened concentration camps. He convinced Hindenburg to issue the Enabling Act on March 21 that allowed his cabinet to pass laws and treaties without legislative backing for four years. The Reichstag gave Hitler its full legal approval two days later, since many felt it was the only way legally to maintain some influence over his government.

Once Hitler had full legislative power, he began a policy of *Gleichschaltung* (coordination) to bring all independent organizations and agencies throughout Germany under his control. He outlawed all political parties or forced them to dissolve, and on July 14, 1933, the Nazi Party became the only legal party in Germany. In addition, German state authority was reduced and placed under Nazi-appointed governors, while the party throughout Germany was divided into *Gaue* (districts) under a Nazi-selected *gauleiter*. In addition, non-Aryans and Nazi opponents were removed from the civil service, the court system, and higher education. Finally, the secret police or Gestapo (*Geheime Staatspolizei*) was created on April 24, 1933, under Göring to deal with opponents and operate concentration camps. The party had its own security branch, the *Sicherheitsdienst* (SD) under Reinhard Heydrich.

On May 2, 1933, the government declared strikes illegal, abolished labor unions, and later forced all workers to join the German Labor Front (DAF) under Robert Ley. In 1934, a special People's Court was created to handle cases of treason. *Gleichschaltung* was a success.

Hitler Consolidates Power

A growing conflict over the direction of the Nazi "revolution" and the power of the SA *vis-à-vis* the SS and the German army had been brewing since Hitler took power. Ernst Röhm, head of the SA, wanted his forces to become the nucleus of a new German army headed by himself, while the military, Hitler, and the SS sought ways to contain his growing arrogance and independence. The solution was the violent Röhm purge on the night of June 30, 1934 ("The Night of Long Knives"), coordinated by the Gestapo and the SS, that resulted in the arrest and murder of Röhm plus eighty-four SA leaders, as well as scores of other opponents that Hitler decided to eliminate under the cloud of his purge.

The final barrier to Hitler's full consolidation of power in Germany was overcome with the death of Hindenburg on August 2, 1934. Hitler now combined the offices of president and chancellor, and required all civil servants and workers to take a personal oath to him as the "Führer of the German Reich and people."

Religion and Anti-Semitism

A state Protestant church of "German Christians" under a bishop of the Reich, Ludwig Müller, was created in 1934. An underground opposition "Confessing Church" formed as well, under the leadership of Martin Niemöller, but its members suffered severe persecution. On July 8, 1933, the government signed a concordat with the Vatican that promised to allow traditional Catholic rights to continue in Germany. But the Nazis severely restricted Catholic religious practice, which created growing friction with the Vatican.

From the inception of the Nazi state in 1933, anti-Semitism was a constant theme and practice in all *Gleichschaltung* and nazification efforts. Intimidation and harassment of Jews was coupled with rigid enforcement of civil service regulations that forbade employment of non-Aryans. This first wave of anti-Semitic activity culminated with the passage of the Nuremberg Laws of September 15, 1935, that deprived Jews of German citizenship and outlawed sexual or marital relations between Jews and other Germans, thus effectively isolating them from the mainstream of German society.

International Affairs

Hitler's international policies were closely linked to his rebuilding efforts to give him a strong economic and military base for an active, aggressive, independent foreign policy. On October 14, 1933, Hitler had his delegates walk out of the Disarmament Conference[1] because he felt the Allied powers had reneged on an earlier promise to grant Germany arms equality. The Reich simultaneously quit the League of Nations. On January 26, 1934, Germany signed a nonaggression pact with Poland, which ended Germany's traditional anti-Polish foreign policy and broke France's encirclement of Germany via the Little Entente.[2] This was followed by the Saarland's vote in a plebiscite

---

[1] From 1932 to 1937, League of Nations members, the United States and the Soviet Union met to discuss ways to disarm, but this ended in deadlock because of the remilitarization of Nazi Germany.

[2] In 1920–1921 France made agreements with Romania, Czechoslovakia, and Yugoslavia to encircle Germany diplomatically and try to guarantee that Germany would never again launch an attack on France. Poland later adhered informally to this loose union, so German diplomacy was motivated in part by the desire to outflank France.

to return to Germany. The culmination of Hitler's foreign policy moves, though, came with his March 15, 1935, announcement that Germany would no longer be bound by the military restrictions of the Treaty of Versailles, that it had already created an air force (Luftwaffe), and that the Reich would institute a draft to create an army of five hundred thousand men. Allied opposition to this move was compromised by England's decision to conclude a naval pact with Hitler on June 18, 1935, that restricted German naval tonnage (excluding submarines) to 35 percent of that for England.

Italy

Fascist Economic Reforms

Increased economic well-being and growth were the promised results of Mussolini's restructuring of the economic system, while the general goals of the regime were to increase production through more efficient methods and land reclamation, with less dependency upon outside resources.

Efforts to increase the land under cultivation through reclamation projects were handicapped by Mussolini's emphasis on model propaganda projects, though the government had reclaimed 12 million acres by 1938. In fact, the small farmer suffered under these policies, because of Mussolini's quiet support of the larger landowner. In 1930, for example, 87.3 percent of the population controlled 13.2 percent of the land. The large farm owners, who made up only 0.5 percent of the population, controlled 41.9 percent of the land, while the mid-level farmer, who made up 12.2 percent of the population, controlled 44.9 percent of the countryside. Regardless, grain products did increase from 4,479 metric tons in 1924 to 8,184 metric tons in 1938, which enabled the government to cut grain imports by 75 percent. On the other hand, land needed to produce other agricultural products was used to increase wheat and grain output.

To aid firms affected by the Depression, the government created the *Instituto per la ricostruzione industriale* (IRI), which helped most big companies while smaller unsuccessful ones failed. The result was that the vast majority of Italy's major industry came under government oversight. Italian production figures were unimpressive during this period, with increases for industrial production rising between 1928 and 1935. Steel output dropped, while pig-iron, oil products, and electrical output enjoyed moderate increases in the 1930s.

Overall, Mussolini's economic programs raised the country's national income 15 percent from 1925 to 1935, with only a 10 percent per capita increase during this period. The value of exports dropped from 44,370,000 lira in 1925 to 21,750,000 lira in 1938 because of the decision in 1927 to peg the lira to an artificially high exchange rate.

Church and State

Until Mussolini's accession to power, the pope had considered himself a prisoner in the Vatican. In 1926, Mussolini's government began talks to resolve this issue, which resulted in the Lateran Accords of February 11, 1929. Italy recognized the Vatican as an independent state, with the pope as its head, while the papacy recognized Italian independence. Catholicism was made the official state religion of Italy, and religious teaching was required in all secondary schools. Church marriages were now fully legal, while the state could veto papal appointments of bishops. The clergy would declare loyalty to the Italian state; in addition, the government agreed to pay the church a financial settlement of 1.75 billion lira for the seizure of church territory 1860–1870.

A conflict soon broke out over youth education, and in May 1931 Mussolini dissolved the Catholic Action's youth groups. The pope responded with an encyclical, *Non abbiamo bisogno*, which defended these groups and criticized the Fascist deification of the state. Mussolini agreed later that year to allow Catholic Action to resume limited youth work.

Foreign Policy

The appointment of Hitler as chancellor of Germany in early 1933 provided Mussolini with his most important thrust of diplomatic action since he came to power, while it underlined the currency of fascism as a ruling ideology and strengthened his claim to revision of the 1919 Paris Peace Conference accords.

Since the late 1920s, Mussolini began to support German claims for revision of the Treaty of Versailles to strengthen ties with that country and to counterbalance France, a nation he strongly disliked. These goals were current in his Four Power Pact proposal of March 1933 that envisioned a concert of powers—England, France, Italy, and Germany—with arms parity for the Reich. French opposition to arms equality and treaty revision, plus concerns that the new consortium would replace the League of Nations, resulted in an extremely weakened agreement signed in June, but which only Italy and Germany ultimately accepted.

In an effort to counter the significance of France's Little Entente with Czechoslovakia, Yugoslavia, and Romania, Mussolini concluded the Rome Protocols with Austria and Hungary on March 17, 1934, which created a protective bond of friendship between the three countries.

The first test of the new alliance between Italy and Austria came in July 1934, when German-directed Nazis tried to seize control of the Austrian government. Mussolini, opposed to German annexation of Austria, mobilized Italian forces along the northern Renner Pass as a warning to Hitler. The coup collapsed from lack of direct German aid.

In response to Hitler's announcement of German rearmament in violation of the Treaty of Versailles on March 16, 1935, France, England, and Italy met at Stresa in northern Italy on April 11–14 and concluded agreements that pledged joint military collaboration if Germany moved against Austria or along the Rhine. The three states criticized Germany's recent decision to remilitarize and appealed to the Council of the League of Nations on the matter.

Ethiopia (Abyssinia) had become an area of strong Italian interest in the 1880s. Italy had slowly brought the country's coastal region under its control until its shameful defeat at Ethiopian hands at Adowa in 1896. In 1906, the international community had recognized the autonomy of Ethiopia, which, in 1923, joined the League of Nations. Mussolini, driven by a strong desire to avenge the humiliation at Adowa and to create an empire to thwart domestic concerns over the country's economic problems, now searched for the proper moment to seize the country. Acquisition of Ethiopia would enable him to join Italy's two colonies of Eritrea and Somalia, which could become a new area of Italian colonization.

Mussolini, who had been preparing for war with Ethiopia since 1932, established a military base in Ethiopian territory. Beginning in December 1934, minor conflicts took place between the two countries, which gave Mussolini an excuse to plan for the full takeover of the country in the near future.

Mussolini refused to accept arbitration over Ethiopia and used Europe's growing concern over Hitler's moves there to cover his own secret designs in Ethiopia. On October 2, 1935, Italy invaded Ethiopia, while the League of Nations, which had received four appeals from Ethiopia since January about Italian territorial transgressions, finally voted to adopt economic sanctions against Mussolini. Unfortunately, the League failed to stop shipments of oil to Italy and continued to allow it to use the Suez Canal. On May 9, 1936, Italy formally annexed the country and joined it to Somalia and Eritrea, which now became known as Italian East Africa.

Soviet Russia

The period from 1929 to 1935 was a time of tremendous upheaval for the Soviet Union as Stalin tried to initiate major programs of collectivization of agriculture and massive industrial development.

Collectivization of Soviet Agriculture

At the end of 1927, Stalin, concerned over problems of grain supply, ordered the gradual consolidation of the country's twenty-five million small farms, on which 80 percent of the population lived, into state-run collective farms. The goals of his First Five-Year Plan (1928–1932) were to raise agricultural output by 150 percent over five years and to transform 20 percent of the country's private farms into collectives.

In an effort to link agricultural efficiency with heavy industrial development, Stalin decided by the end of 1929 to rapidly collectivize the country's entire agriculture system. Because of earlier resistance from peasants between 1927 and 1929, Stalin ordered war against the kulaks (middle-class peasants). Some sources claim that as many as five million kulaks were internally deported during this period.

These events, combined with forced grain seizures, triggered massive, bloody resistance in the countryside. Though half of the nation's peasants were forced onto collectives during this period, they destroyed a great deal of Russia's livestock in the process. In the spring of 1930, Stalin called a momentary halt to the process, which prompted many peasants to leave the state farms.

Over the next seven years, the entire Soviet system was collectivized, and all peasants forced onto state farms. The two major types of farms were the *sovkhoz*, where peasants were paid for their labor, and the *kovkhoz*, or collective farm, where the peasants gave the government a percentage of their crops and kept the surplus. The three types of *kovkhozs* were the *artel*, the most common, where the peasant had a small garden plot; the *toz*, where he owned his tools and animals; and the *commune*, where the state owned everything. One of the most important components of the collective and the state farm system was the Machine Tractor Station (MTS), which controlled the tractors and farm equipment for various government-run farms.

Direct and indirect deaths from Stalin's collectivization efforts totaled 14.5 million. Grain production levels did not reach 1928 levels until 1935. The efforts did, however, break the back of rural peasant independence and created a totalitarian network of control throughout the countryside. They also undercut Stalin's own base of support within the party.

Industrialization

Stalin, concerned that Russia would fall irreparably behind the West industrially, hoped to achieve industrial parity with the West in a decade. At this time, Russia was barely on par with Italy in pig-iron and steel production. To stimulate workers, labor unions lost their autonomy, and workers, including impressed peasants, were forced to work at locations and under conditions determined by the state. A special "Turnover" tax was placed on all goods throughout the country to help pay for industrialization.

The industrialization goals of the First Five-Year Plan, supported hopefully by a flourishing agricultural system, were to increase total industrial production by 236 percent, heavy industry by 330 percent, coal by 200 percent, electrical output by 400 percent, and pig-iron production by 300 percent. Workers were to increase their efforts over 100 percent. Efficiency was also a hallmark of this program, and production costs were to drop by over a third, and prices by a quarter.

In most instances, the plan's unrealistic goals were not met. Still, steel production doubled, though it fell short of the plan's goals, as did oil and hard-coal output. Total industrial production, however, did barely surpass the plan's expectations.

The Second Five-Year Plan (1933–1937) was adopted by the XVII Party Congress in early 1934. Its economic and production targets were less severe than the first plan, and thus more was achieved. The model for workers was Alexei Stakhanov, a coal miner who met 1,400 percent of his quota in the fall of 1935. A Stakhanovite movement arose to stimulate workers to greater efforts. By the end of the second plan, Soviet Russia had emerged as a leading world industrial power, though at great cost. It gave up quality for quantity and created tremendous social and economic discord that affected the Soviet Union until its demise. The tactics used by Stalin to institute his economic reforms formed the nucleus of his totalitarian system, while reaction to them within the party led to the Great Purges.

Party Politics and the Origin of the Purges

The upheaval caused by forced collectivization, blended with the remnants of the rightist conflict with Stalin, prompted the Soviet leader to initiate one of the country's periodic purges of the party. Approved by the top leadership, suspected opponents were driven from party ranks, while Zinoviev and Kamenev were briefly exiled to Siberia. Continued uncertainty over the best policies to follow after the initiation of the Second Five-Year Plan ended with the murder at the end of 1934 of Sergei Kirov, Stalin's supposed heir and Leningrad party chief. Though the reasons for Kirov's murder are unclear, his more liberal tendencies, plus his growing popularity, made him a threat to the Soviet leader. In the spring of 1935, the recently renamed and organized secret police, the NKVD (Russian for People's Commissariat for Internal Affairs), oversaw the beginnings of a new, violent purge that eradicated 70 percent of the 1934 Central Committee, and a large percentage of the upper military ranks. Stalin sent between eight million and nine million to camps and prisons, and caused untold deaths before the purges ended in 1938.

Foreign Policy (1929–1935)

During the period from 1929 to 1933, the Soviet Union retreated inward as it funneled the bulk of its energies into domestic economic growth. Nevertheless, Stalin remained sensitive to growing aggression and ideological threats abroad such as the Japanese invasion of Manchuria in 1931 and Hitler's appointment as chancellor. As a result, Russia left its cocoon in 1934, joined the League of Nations, and became an advocate of "collective security," while the Comintern adopted Popular Front tactics, allying with other parties against fascism, to strengthen the Soviet Union's international posture. At the diplomatic level, in addition to League membership, the Soviet Union completed a military pact with France.

International Developments (1918–1935)

The League of Nations

Efforts to create a body to arbitrate international conflicts gained ground in 1899 when the First Hague Conference created a Permanent Court of International Justice to handle such matters. At a similar meeting in 1907, delegates expressed concern over Europe's growing arms race, though no country was willing to give the Permanent Court adequate authority to serve as a legitimate arbitrator. Leon Bourgeois, a French statesman, however, pushed for a strong international peacekeeping body, but no major efforts toward this goal were initiated until 1915, when organizations supporting a League of Nations arose in the United States and Britain. Support for such a body grew as the war lengthened, and creation of such an organization became the cornerstone of President Woodrow Wilson's postwar policy, enunciated in his "Fourteen Points" speech before Congress on January 8, 1918. His last point called for an international chamber of states to guarantee national autonomy and independence. At the Paris Peace Conference, the major Allied leaders created a Commission for the League to draft its constitution, while the Covenant of the League was placed in the Treaty of Versailles.

The Preamble of the League's Covenant. This statement defined the League's purposes: to work for international friendship, peace, and security. To attain this, its members agreed to avoid war, maintain peaceful relations with other countries, and honor international law and accords.

The Organization of the League of Nations. Headquartered in Geneva, the League came into existence after the Allies passed a resolution announcing their intentions on January 25, 1919, and the signed the Treaty of Versailles on June 28, 1919.

The twenty-six-article Covenant determined terms of membership and withdrawal (two-thirds vote to join and two years notice to resign) and means to amend the Covenant (unanimous vote of the League's council with majority approval from its assembly).

The League's council originally consisted of five permanent members: France, Italy, England, Japan, and the United States, though the U.S. seat was left vacant because the U.S. Senate refused to ratify the Treaty of Versailles. Germany filled the vacancy in 1926. The council also had four one-year rotating seats (increased to six seats in 1922, and to nine seats in 1926). The council, with each member having one vote, could discuss any matter that threatened international stability, and could recommend action to member states. It also had the right, according to Article 8 of the League Covenant, to seek ways to reduce arms strength, while Articles 10 through 17 gave it the authority to search for means to stop war. It could recommend through a unanimous vote ways to stop aggression, and could suggest economic sanctions and other tactics to enforce its decisions, though its military ability to enforce its decisions was vague. It met four times a year from 1923 to 1929, and then three times annually thereafter.

The League's legislative body had similar debating and discussion authority, though it had no legislative powers. It initially had forty-three members, which rose to forty-nine by the mid-1930s, though six others, including Germany, Italy, and Japan, withdrew their membership during the same period. The Soviet Union, which joined in 1934, was expelled six years later.

The League's judicial responsibilities were handled by the World Court, which was located at The Hague in The Netherlands. Created in 1921 and opened the following year, it would consider and advise on any case from any nation or the League, acting as an arbiter to prevent international conflict. The court's decisions were not binding: it relied on voluntary submission to its decisions. It initially had eleven judges (later fifteen) selected for five-year terms by the League.

The day-to-day affairs of the League were administered by the general secretary and his bureaucracy, the Secretariat, which was composed of an international collection of League civil servants.

Lesser known functions of the League dealt with the efforts of its International Labor Organization (ILO), which tried to find ways to reduce labor-management and class tensions, and the Mandates Commission, which oversaw territories taken from the Central powers and were administered—as a prelude to independence—under mandate from League members. In addition, the League tried to provide medical, economic, and social welfare aid to depressed parts of the world.

The Washington Conference (1921–1922)

The first postwar effort to deal with problems of disarmament was the Washington Conference (November 1921–February 1922). Its participants, which included the major powers in Europe and Asia plus the meeting's sponsor, the United States, discussed a number of problems that resulted in several separate agreements.

The Washington Naval Treaty (Five-Power Treaty). England, France, Italy, Japan, and the United States agreed to halt battleship construction for ten years, while limiting or reducing capital shipping levels to 525,000 tons for the United States and England, 315,000 tons for Japan, and 175,000 tons for Italy and France.

England, France, Japan, and the United States agreed not to seek further Pacific expansion or increased naval strength there and to respect the Pacific holdings of the other signatory powers.

The Nine-Power Treaty. To grant China some sense of autonomy not offered at the Paris Peace Conference, China, Belgium, England, France, Italy, Japan (after Japan's agreement to return Kiachow to China), the Netherlands, Portugal, and the United States signed an agreement guaranteeing China's independence and territorial autonomy.

The Locarno Pact (1925)

After the failure of the European powers to create some type of international system to prevent aggression, the powers undertook regional efforts, prompted by Germany's visionary foreign minister, Gustav Stresemann. In early 1925, Stresemann approached England and France about an accord whereby Germany would accept its western borders in return for early Allied withdrawal from the demilitarized Rhine area. Stresemann also wanted League membership for his country. While England responded with guarded regional interest, France hesitated. Six months after consultation with its eastern allies, Paris countered with a proposal that would include similar provisions for Germany's eastern borders, secured by a mutual assistance pact between, France, Great Britain, and Italy. These countries, along with Belgium, Czechoslovakia, and Poland, met for two months in Locarno, Switzerland, and concluded a number of separate agreements.

Treaty of Mutual Guarantees (Rhineland Pact). Signed on October 16, 1925, by Belgium, England, France, Germany, and Italy, the treaty guaranteed Germany's western boundaries and accepted the Versailles settlement's demilitarized zones. Italy and Great Britain agreed militarily to defend these lines if flagrantly violated.

Arbitration Settlements. In the same spirit, Germany signed arbitration dispute accords with Czechoslovakia, Belgium, France, and Poland; these accords mirrored the Geneva Protocol and required acceptance of League-determined settlements.

Eastern Accords. Since Germany would not finalize its eastern border, France separately signed guarantees with Poland and Czechoslovakia to defend their frontiers.

Germany Joins the League. The Locarno Pact went into force when Germany joined the League on September 10, 1926, acquiring, after some dispute, the United

States' permanent seat on the Council. France and Belgium began to withdraw from the Rhineland, though they left a token force there until 1930.

The Pact of Paris (Kellogg-Briand Pact)

The Locarno Pact heralded a new period in European relations known as the "Era of Locarno" that marked the end of postwar conflict and the beginning of a more normal period of diplomatic friendship and cooperation. It reached its peak, idealistically, with the Franco-American effort in 1928 to seek an international statement to outlaw war. The seed for this new proposal arose on the eve of the tenth anniversary of the American entrance into the world war, and centered on interest in a mutual statement outlawing war as a theme in national policy. In December 1927, Frank Kellogg, the U.S. secretary of state, proposed that this policy be offered to all nations in the form of a treaty. On August 27, 1928, fifteen countries, including the United States, France, Germany, Italy, and Japan, signed this accord with some minor limitations, which renounced war as a means of solving differences and as a tool of national policy. Within five years, fifty other countries signed the agreement. Unfortunately, without something more than idealism to back it up, the Kellogg-Briand Pact had little practical meaning.

The Waning Search for Disarmament

The Depression did not diminish the desire for disarmament. In fact, it added a new series of problems and concerns that made the search for a lasting resolution on disarmament more difficult, and with growing threats of aggression in Asia and Europe, these efforts were destroyed.

London Naval Disarmament Treaty. In March 1930, Great Britain and the United States sought to expand the naval limitation terms of the Five-Power Treaty of 1922. France and Italy could not agree on terms, while England, the United States, and Japan accepted mild reductions in cruiser and destroyer strength.

World Disarmament Conference. The starting point for implementation of the 1924 Geneva Protocol was a disarmament conference, which, though envisioned for 1925, did not convene until February 5, 1932. At this conference, attended by the Soviet Union and the United States, initial discussions centered on a French proposal for a protective monitoring system and required arbitration before considering disarmament. On the other hand, the United States asked for a one-third reduction of current treaty shipping strength. Germany countered with demands for arms parity before disarmament. Though these demands were a front for more complex issues, the Germans left the conference when rebuffed in September 1932, only to be lured back later by a statement from five of the powers that agreed, in spirit, to Germany's demand. Hitler's accession to power on January 30, 1933, halted any further consideration of this point, which prompted Germany's withdrawal from the conference and the League. This, and France's continued insistence on predisarmament security guarantees, neutralized conference efforts, and it closed in failure in June 1934.

League and Allied Response to Aggression

By 1931, international attention increasingly turned to growing acts or threats of aggression in Europe and Asia, and transformed Europe from a world that hoped for eternal peace to a continent searching desperately for ways to contain growing aggression.

The League's Lytton Report and Manchuria. On September 19, 1931, the Japanese Kwantung Army, acting independently of the government in Tokyo, began the conquest of Manchuria after fabricating an incident at Mukden to justify their actions. Ultimately, they created a puppet state, Manchukuo, under the last Chinese emperor, Henry Pu Yi. China's League protest resulted in the creation of an investigatory commission under the Earl of Lytton that criticized Japan's actions and recommended a negotiated settlement that would have allowed Japan to retain most of its conquest. Japan responded by resigning from the League in 1933.

The Stresa Front. Hitler's announcement on March 15, 1935, of Germany's decisions to rearm and to introduce conscription in violation of the Treaty of Versailles prompted the leaders of England, France, and Italy to meet in Stresa, Italy (April 11–14) to discuss a response. They condemned Germany's actions, underlined their commitment to the Locarno Pact, and reaffirmed the support they collectively gave for Austria's independence in early 1934. Prompted by these actions, the League Council also rebuked Germany and created an investigatory committee to search for economic means to punish the Reich. Britain's decision, however, to protect separately its naval strength *vis-à-vis* a German buildup in the Anglo-German Naval Treaty of June 18, 1935, effectively compromised the significance of the Stresa Front.

Italy and Ethiopia. By the end of 1934, Italy had begun to create a number of incidents in Ethiopia as a prelude to complete absorption of that country. The emperor of Ethiopia, Haile Sellasie, appealed to the League on the matter in January 1935. Anglo-Franco efforts to mediate the crisis failed, while Ethiopia continued to look to the League to contain Italian aggression. Mussolini was convinced that he could act with impunity when he realized that the League was reluctant to do more than make verbal objections to the Italian actions. Consequently, on October 3, 1935, Italy invaded Ethiopia, which prompted the League to declare the former country the aggressor. Ineffective economic sanctions followed on October 19. Independent Anglo-French efforts to halt separately Italian aggression by granting Mussolini most of Ethiopia (with economic predominance) failed in December because of a strong public outcry over the terms. Italy completed its conquest in early May 1936, annexing Ethiopia on May 9.

World War II, the Cold War, and a New World Order (1935–1945)

Authoritarian and Totalitarian States

The Soviet Union and Stalin

The 1936 Soviet Constitution recognized the success of socialism. It gave the people civil rights, such as freedom of speech, customary in democracies. In addition, it guaranteed a right to work, rest, leisure, and economic security. In fact, these rights were largely ignored by Stalin's government, or they existed only within the limits set by the ruling Communist Party of which Stalin was general secretary.

Stalin's absolute dictatorship and inability to tolerate any opposition or dissent was revealed to the world by the Great Purge Trials (1936–1938). In 1936, sixteen old Bolsheviks—including Gregory Zinoviev (first head of the Communist International) and Lev Kamenev—were placed on trial, publicly confessed to charges of plotting with foreign powers, and were executed. In 1937, Marshal Michael Tukhachevski and a group of the highest-ranking generals were accused of plotting with the Germans and Japanese, and executed after a secret court-martial. Other purges and trials followed, including the 1938 trial of Nicolai Bukharin, Alexei Rykov, and other prominent Bolsheviks charged with Trotskyite plots and wanting to restore capitalism.

These events tended to discredit Russia as a reliable factor in international affairs. By the late 1930s, the Soviet Union presented two images to the world: one a totalitarian regime of absolute dictatorship and repression exemplified by the Great Purges and the other of undeniable economic progress during a period of world depression. Industrial production increased an average of 14 percent per annum in the 1930s, and Russia went from fifteenth to third in production of electricity. The Bolshevik model was, however, one of progress imposed from above at great cost to those below. This fact helps explain the reluctance of British and French leaders throughout the 1930s to rely on the Soviet Union when they had to deal with acts of aggression by Hitler and Mussolini.

Events in Nazi Germany

The Nazi Third Reich was a brutal dictatorship enabled by Hitler's appointment as chancellor in 1933. By 1936, Hitler had destroyed the government of the Weimar Republic, suppressed all political parties except the Nazi Party, and consolidated Germany under his control as führer (leader). The party established mass organizations such as the Nazi Labor Front and the Hitler Youth. The Nazis also instituted propaganda campaigns and a regime of terror against political opponents and Jews (who were made scapegoats for Germany's problems). Germany had become a police state by 1936. In 1938, the Nazis used the assassination of a German diplomat by a Jewish youth as the excuse for extensive pogroms. During the night of November 9–10, soon called *Reichskristallnacht* ("Night of Broken Glass"), gangs of Nazi hoodlums murdered scores of Jews and damaged or destroyed much Jewish property. Persecution of the Jews escalated, culminating in the horrors of war-time concentration camps and the mass murder of millions.

Hitler achieved final control over the armed forces and the foreign office in 1937–1938. He moved against Blomberg, the minister of war, and Fritsch, the commander in chief of the army, taking advantage of scandals in which they were involved (in the case of Fritsch, the accusations were false). Hitler made himself minister of war and established the High Command of the Armed Forces under his personal representative, General Keitel. At the same time, Joachim von Ribbentrop was made minister of foreign affairs, giving the Nazis complete control over the German Foreign Office. Like most dictators, Hitler preferred yes-men to competent colleagues and subordinates.

The Nazi regime enjoyed success in part, at least, because it was able to reduce unemployment from 6 million in 1932 to 164,000 by 1938 through the so-called four-year plans aimed at rearming Germany and making its economy self-sufficient and free of dependence on any foreign power (see: *autarky* as a concept for Fascist Italy). The improving economic condition of many, together with Hitler's successes in foreign affairs, gave him a substantial hold over the German people.

By the beginning of World War II, Germany had been transformed into a disciplined war machine with all dissent stifled, and most of its citizens ready to follow the führer wherever he might lead.

Fascist Italy: The Corporate State

The pattern of Mussolini's dictatorship, followed to a degree by Hitler, was that of the "corporate state." Political parties and electoral districts were abolished. Workers and employers alike were organized into corporations according to the nature of their business. The corporations and the government (with the balance heavily favoring the employers and the government) generally determined wages, hours, conditions of work, prices, and industrial polices. The structure was completed in 1938 with the abolition of the Chamber of Deputies in the parliament and its replacement by a Chamber of Fasces and Corporations representing the Fascist Party and the corporations.

Fascism provided excitement and superficial grandeur but no solution to Italy's economic problems. Italian labor was kept under strict control. No strikes were allowed, and by 1939 real wages were below those of 1922. Emphasis on foreign adventures and propaganda concerning a new Roman Empire were used to maintain a regime of force and brutality. By way of contrast, Mussolini's state was more authoritarian (emphasis on public control), Hitler's more totalitarian (control over public and private sectors).

Other Authoritarian Regimes

The democratic hopes of those who established independent states in eastern and central Europe following World War I remained unfulfilled in the 1930s. Authoritarian monarchies—military regimes or governments on the fascist model—were established everywhere: Poland by 1939 was under a military regime established by General Joszef Pilsudski, Hungary under Admiral Horthy, and Greece by General Metaxas. Bulgaria, Romania, and Yugoslavia were ruled by authoritarian monarchies. In Spain, General Francisco Franco established a fascist dictatorship after the Spanish Civil War (1936–1939). In Austria, the clerical-fascist regime of Kurt von Schuschnigg ruled until the *Anschluss* (annexation by Germany) in 1938, and in Portugal, Antonio Salazar ruled as dictator.

Democracies

Great Britain

The national coalition government under Ramsey MacDonald governed from October 1931 to June 1935, when Stanley Baldwin formed a Conservative cabinet. Baldwin was succeeded by Neville Chamberlain (1937–1940), whose government used a policy of appeasement to deal with the problem of German and Italian aggression.

France: The Popular Front

In France, a coalition of Radical Socialists, Socialists, and Communists campaigned in 1936 on a pledge to save the country from fascism and solve problems of the Depression by instituting economic reforms. The Popular Front government, under Socialist Leon Blum, lasted just over a year. Much reform legislation was enacted, including a forty-hour work week, vacations with pay, collective bargaining, compulsory arbitration of labor disputes, support for agricultural prices, reorganization of the Bank of France, and nationalization of armaments and aircraft industries. Blum was attacked by conservatives and fascists as a radical and a Jew ("Better Hitler than Leon Blum"). The Popular Front government was defeated by the Senate, which refused to vote the government emergency financial powers. Edouard Daladier then formed a conservative government, which began to devote its attention to foreign affairs, collaborating with Britain's Chamberlain in the appeasement policy. Democracy was preserved from the fascist attacks of the early 1930s, but the Popular Front was not as successful in making permanent changes as might have been hoped, and it was a demoralized and dispirited France that had to meet the German attack on Poland in 1939.

Other Democratic States

Czechoslovakia was the one state of eastern Europe that maintained a democratic, parliamentary regime. It came under heavy attack from Nazi Germany following the annexation of Austria and was ultimately deserted by its allies, France and Britain, whose leaders forced Czech compliance with the terms of the Munich Agreement of 1938 (see later discussion). Switzerland maintained a precarious neutrality throughout the 1930s and World War II with the help of the League of Nations, which freed Switzerland of any obligation to support even sanctions against an aggressor. The Netherlands tried in World War I and after to maintain both a democratic republic and international neutrality, but internal weakness in the 1930s rendered its attempts to remain sovereign futile. Sweden also maintained its democratic existence by a firm policy of neutrality. Denmark and Norway were seized by the Germans early in 1940 and remained under German control during World War II. All of the Scandinavian countries were models of liberal democratic government.

Culture in the Late 1930: Engagement

In the twentieth century, feelings of fragmentation and uncertainty permeated European arts and letters. Some of this derived from Sigmund Freud, who maintained that most human behavior is irrational, and Albert Einstein, whose theories of relativity undermined long-held certainties of Newtonian physics. The Dutch historian Johan Huizinga noted in 1936: "Almost all things which once seemed sacred and immutable have now become unsettled. The sense of living in the midst of a violent crisis of civilization, threatening complete collapse, has spread far and wide" (Huizinga, *In the Shadow of Tomorrow,* 1936). Intellectuals came increasingly to see the world as an irrational place in which old values and truths had little relevance. Some became "engaged" in resistance to fascism and Nazism. Some like Arthur Koestler flirted with communism but broke with Stalin after the Great Purges. Koestler's *Darkness at Noon* (1941) is an attempt to understand the events surrounding those trials. German intellectuals such as Ernst Cassirer and Erich Fromm escaped Nazi Germany and worked in exile. Cassirer, in his *The Myth of the State* (1946), noted that the Nazis manufactured myths of race, leader, party, and so forth that disoriented reason and intellect. Fromm published *Escape from Freedom* in 1941, which maintained that modern man had escaped *to* freedom from the orderly, structured world of medieval society but was now trying to escape *from* this freedom and looking for security once again. The artist Pablo Picasso expressed his hatred of fascism by his painting of Guernica, a Spanish town subjected to aerial bombardment by the German air force as it intervened in the Spanish Civil War.

Existentialism is the philosophy that best exemplified European feelings in the era of the world wars and after. Three nineteenth-century figures influenced this movement: Fyodor Dostoyevsky, Soren Kierkegaard, and Friedrich Nietzsche. Martin Heidegger (though he rejected the term), Karl Jaspers, Jean-Paul Sartre, and Simone de Beauvoir are noted figures in twentieth-century existentialism, which sought to come to grip with life's central experiences and the trauma of war, death, and evil.

Figure 8-8. Giorgio de Chirico seems to do a riff on Italy's Roman past and Renaissance image in his *Disquieting Muses* (1916), which uncannily prefigures much of the grandiose nonsense of Mussolini's theatrics.

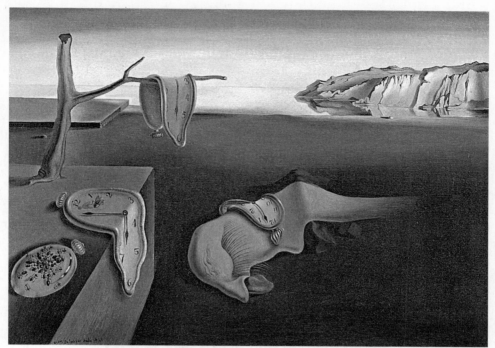

Figure 8-9. Salvador Dali shows landscapes of a dreamworld that more often borders the nightmare than the wish-fulfilling daydream, as in *Persistence of Memory* (1931).

Even before fascism took hold in much of Europe, artists recreated an atmosphere of malaise and unsettled values. During World War I, Giorgio de Chirico (1888–1978), a pioneer of surrealism, depicted the juxtaposition of the old classical world with new uncertainties in *The Disquieting Muses* (1916; see Figure 8-8). Surrealism borrowed much of its icons and images from the dreamworlds exposed by Freud, as is clear in Salvador Dali's (1904–1989) famous *Persistence of Memory* (1931; see Figure 8-9).

As Europe reeled from the effects of the World War I's carnage, it was Germans, ironically, who registered best the horrors of war and later fascism as bestiality, as is shown in the works of Ernst Ludwig Kirchner (1880–1938) and Georg Grosz (1893–1959; see Figure 8-10).

Another direction, which led to postmodernism, was taken by the Belgian René Magritte (1898–1967), whose cool modernism mixes a surrealist vision with a more distanced aesthetic (see Figure 8-11).

Figure 8-10. Georg Grosz, in his *Lovesick* (1916), anticipates his art of the 1920s, with its journalistic muckraking in images.

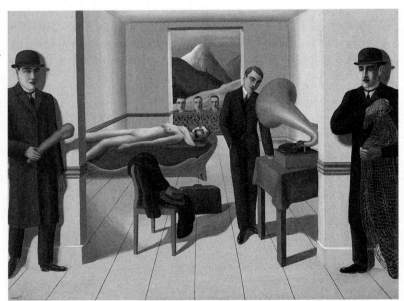

Figure 8-11. René Magritte's images suffered perhaps from their "posterization" in the 1960s, when every college room felt naked without a Magritte, but such a work as *The Menaced Assassin* (1927) calls to mind his arresting vision, eloquent without being preachy.

International Relations: The Road to War

Several factors need to be understood concerning the events leading to World War II.

First, more than one country was to blame: Germany, Italy, Japan, and the Soviet Union were not satisfied with the peace settlement of 1919, so they used force to achieve change, from the Japanese invasion of Manchuria in 1931 to the outbreak of war in 1939 over Poland. Hitler, bit by bit, dismantled the Treaty of Versailles in central and eastern Europe. Responsibility has also been placed to some degree on Britain and France and even the United States for following a policy of appeasement, which they had hoped would satisfy Hitler's demands. Nor may we underestimate the impact of the worldwide Depression, which destabilized even the most stable democracies and further brutalized the existing authoritarian and totalitarian regimes around the world.

Second, Britain and France as well as other democratic states were influenced in their policy by a profound pacifism based on their experience with the loss of life and devastation in World War I and by a dislike of the Stalinist regime in Russia.

Third, while the Soviet Union was a revisionist power, it was profoundly distrustful of Germany, Italy, and Japan. The threat to their interests led the Soviet leaders to pursue a policy of collective security through the League of Nations (which they joined in 1934). Only after evidence of Anglo-French weakness did Stalin in 1939 enter an agreement with Hitler. This event, like the Great Purges, only heightened suspicion of Soviet motives and was later to become the subject of debate and recrimination in the Cold War that followed World War II.

Finally, the policy of appeasement implemented by Britain's Neville Chamberlain was not based on any liking for Hitler, whom he considered "half-crazed," but on a genuine desire to remove causes of discontent inherent in the Versailles settlement and thus create conditions where peace could be maintained. His error lay in his belief that Hitler was open to reason, preferred peace to war, and would respect agreements.

The Course of Events

Using a Franco-Soviet agreement of 1935 as an excuse, Hitler, on March 7, 1936, repudiated the Locarno agreements and reoccupied the Rhineland (an area demilitarized by the Treaty of Versailles). Neither France (which possessed military superiority at the time) nor Britain was willing to oppose these moves.

The Spanish Civil War (1936–1939) is often seen as a "dress rehearsal" for World War II because of outside intervention. The government of the Spanish Republic (established in 1931) caused resentment among conservatives by its programs, including land reform and anticlerical legislation aimed at the Catholic Church. Labor discontent led to disturbances in industrial Barcelona and the surrounding province of Catalonia. Following an election victory by a popular front of republican and radical parties, rightwing generals in July began a military insurrection. Francisco Franco, stationed at the time in Spanish Morocco, emerged as the leader of this revolt, which became a devastating civil war lasting nearly three years.

The democracies, including the United States, followed a course of neutrality, refusing to aid the Spanish government or to become involved. Nazi Germany, Italy, and the Soviet Union did intervene despite nonintervention agreements negotiated by Britain and France. German air force units were sent to aid the fascist forces of Franco and participated in bombardments of Madrid, Barcelona, and Guernica (the latter incident being the inspiration for Picasso's famous painting, which became an anti-fascist symbol known far beyond the world of art). Italy sent troops, tanks, and other material. The Soviet Union sent advisers and recruited soldiers from among antifascists in the United States and other countries to fight in the international brigades with the republican forces. Spain became a battlefield for fascist and antifascist forces with Franco winning by 1939 in what was seen as a serious defeat for antifascist forces everywhere.

The Spanish Civil War was a factor in bringing together Mussolini and Hitler in a Rome-Berlin Axis. Already Germany and Japan had signed the Anti-Comintern Pact in 1936. Ostensibly directed against international communism, this was the basis for a diplomatic alliance between those countries, and Italy soon adhered to this agreement, becoming Germany's ally in World War II.

Italy, in addition to its involvement in Spain, in 1935 launched a war to conquer the African kingdom of Ethiopia (as discussed earlier in the chapter). The democracies chose not to intervene in this case, either, despite Emperor Haile Selassie's plea to the League of Nations. By 1936, the conquest was complete.

In 1937, there was Nazi-inspired agitation in the Baltic port of Danzig, a city basically German in population, but which had been made a free city under the terms of the Treaty of Versailles and was desired by Poland.

In 1938, Hitler renewed his campaign against Austria, which he had unsuccessfully tried to subvert in 1934. Some within the Austrian government pressured Austrian chancellor Kurt von Schussnigg to make concessions to Hitler, and when this did not work, German troops annexed Austria (the *Anschluss*). Again Britain and France took no effective action, and about six million Austrians were added to Germany—most so-called Aryans being quite willing.

Hitler turned next to Czechoslovakia. Three million people of German origin lived in the Sudetenland, a borderland between Germany and Czechoslovakia given to Czechoslovakia in order to provide it with a more defensible boundary. These ethnic Germans (and other minorities of Poles, Ruthenians, and Hungarians) agitated against the democratic government (the only one in eastern Europe in 1938) despite its enlightened minority policy. Hitler used the Sudeten Nazi Party to deliberately provoke a crisis by making demands for a degree of independence unacceptable to the Czech authorities. He then claimed to interfere as the protector of a persecuted minority. In May 1938, rumors of invasion led to warnings from Britain and France followed by assurances from Hitler. Nevertheless, in the fall the crisis came to a head with renewed demands from Hitler. Chamberlain twice flew to Germany in person to get German terms. The second time, Hitler's increased demands led to mobilization and other measures toward war. At the last minute, a four-power conference was held in Munich with Hitler, Mussolini, Chamberlain, and Daladier in attendance. At Munich, Hitler's terms were accepted. Neither Czechoslovakia nor the Soviet Union was in attendance. Britain and France, despite the French alliance with Czechoslovakia put pressure on the Czech government to force it to comply with German demands. Hitler signed a treaty agreeing to this settlement as the limit of his ambitions. At the same time, the Poles seized control of Teschen, and Hungary (with the support of Italy and Germany, and over the protests of the British and French) seized 7,500 square miles of Slovakia. By the concessions forced on her at Munich, Czechoslovakia lost the frontier defenses and was totally unprotected against any further German encroachments.

In March 1939, Hitler annexed most of the rump Czech state, while Hungary conquered Ruthenia. About the same time, Germany annexed Memel from Lithuania. In April, Mussolini, taking advantage of distractions created by Germany, landed an army in Albania and seized that Balkan state in a campaign lasting about one week.

Disillusioned by these continued aggressions, Britain and France made military preparations and gave guarantees to Poland, Romania, and Greece that they would come to the aid of the latter, if attacked. The two democracies also opened negotiations with the Soviet Union for an arrangement to obtain that country's aid against further German aggression. Hitler, with Poland next on his timetable, also began a cautious rapprochement with the Soviet Union. Probably Russian suspicion that the Western powers wanted the Soviet Union to bear the brunt of any German attack led Stalin to respond to Hitler's overtures. Negotiations that began quietly in the spring of 1939 continued with increasing urgency as summer approached and with it, the time of Hitler's planned attack on Poland. On August 23, 1939, the two countries stunned the world with the announcement of a Nazi-Soviet treaty of friendship. A secret protocol provided that in the event of a "territorial rearrangement" in eastern Europe the two powers would divide Poland. In addition, Russia would have the Baltic states (Latvia, Lithuania, and Estonia) and Bessarabia (lost to Romania in 1918) as part of her sphere. Stalin agreed to remain neutral in any German war with Britain or France.

World War II began with the German invasion of Poland on September 1, 1939, followed by British and French declarations of war against Germany on September 3.

World War II

The Polish Campaign and the "Phony War"

The German attack (known as *blitzkrieg* or "lightning war") overwhelmed the poorly equipped Polish army, which could not resist German tanks and airplanes. The outcome was clear after the first few days of fighting, and organized resistance ceased within a month.

In accordance with the secret provisions of the Nazi-Soviet Treaty of August 1939, Russia and Germany shared Polish spoils. On September 17, the Russian armies attacked the Poles from the east. They met the Germans two days later. Stalin's share of Poland extended approximately to the Curzon Line (a line proposed in 1919 by and named for British foreign minister Lord Curzon, but which was never implemented). Russia also made demands on Finland. Later, in June 1940, while Germany was attacking France, Stalin occupied the Baltic states of Latvia, Lithuania, and Estonia.

Nazi Germany formally annexed the port of Danzig, the Polish Corridor, and some territory along the western Polish border. Central Poland was turned into a German protectorate called the Government-General.

Following the successful completion of the Polish campaign, the war settled into a period of inaction on the part of both Germans and the British and French known as the "phony war" or *sitzkrieg*. The British and French prepared for a German attack on France and Belgium such as that at the beginning of World War I, but failed to take any offensive action. Germany extended some peace-feelers, but these met with no success. At sea, a campaign began between the British navy and German submarines, which began to prey on Allied shipping. The British were also concerned with finding a way to prevent vital Swedish iron ore from reaching Germany via a route that led over northern Norway and then continued by ship down the Norwegian coast to German Baltic ports. Any effective blockade would have involved violation of Norwegian territorial waters, however, and this the Chamberlain government was reluctant to do.

The "Winter War" between Russia and Finland

The only military action of any consequence during the winter of 1939–1940 resulted from Russian demands made on Finland, especially for territory adjacent to Leningrad (then only twenty miles from the border). Finnish refusal led to a Russian attack in November 1939. The Finns resisted with considerable vigor, receiving some supplies from Sweden, Britain, and France, but eventually by March had to give in to the superior Russian forces. Finland was forced to cede the Karelian Isthmus, Viipuri, and a naval base at Hangoe. Britain and France prepared forces to aid the Finns, but by the time they were ready to act the Finns had been defeated.

The German Attack on Denmark and Norway

The period of inactivity in the war in the West came suddenly to an end. On April 8, 1940, the British and French finally announced their intent to mine Norwegian coastal waters to blockade German ships transporting Swedish iron ore. On April 9, as the Norwegians were about to protest this action, the Germans struck, attacking Denmark and Norway simultaneously. Denmark was quickly occupied. In Norway, German forces landed by air at strategic points with the main forces coming by sea. The British and French responded by sending naval and military forces to Narvik and Trondheim in an effort to assist the Norwegians and to capture some bases before the Germans could overrun the entire country. They were too slow and showed little initiative, and within a few weeks they withdrew their forces, taking the Norwegian government with them into exile in London.

The Battle of France

On May 10, Germany launched its main offensive against France. First, it attacked Belgium and the Netherlands simultaneously. Just as the Germans anticipated, British and French forces advanced to aid the Belgians. At this point, the Germans departed from the World War I strategy by launching a surprise armored attack through Luxembourg and the Ardennes Forest (considered by the British and French to be impassable for tanks). As these forces moved toward the English Channel coast, they divided the Allied armies, leaving the Belgians, British Expeditionary Force, and some French forces virtually encircled. The Dutch could offer no real resistance and collapsed in four days after the bombing of Rotterdam—one of the first raids intended to terrorize civilians. Queen Wilhelmina and her government fled to London. The Belgians, who had made little effort to coordinate plans with the British and French, surrendered May 25, leaving the British and French in serious danger from the Germans who were advancing to the Channel coast; however, Hitler concentrated on occupying Paris. This provided just enough time for the British to effect an emergency evacuation of some 230,000 of their own men as well as about 120,000 French from the port of Dunkirk and the adjacent coast. This remarkable evacuation saved the lives of the soldiers, but all supplies and equipment were lost, including vehicles, tanks, and artillery—a very severe blow to the British Army.

Churchill Becomes British Prime Minister

Even before the offensive against France, on May 7–8 members of the House of Commons launched an attack on Prime Minister Chamberlain, prompted by the bungling of the Norwegian campaign, but extending to the conduct of the war to that point. Chamberlain, a man of peace who had never properly mobilized the British war effort or developed an effective plan of action, fell from power. A government was formed under Winston Churchill, whose warnings of the German danger and the need for British rearmament all during the 1930s made him Chamberlain's logical successor. The opposition Labour Party agreed to join in a coalition with Clement Attlee becoming deputy prime minister. Several other Laborites followed his lead by accepting cabinet posts. This gave Britain a government that would eventually lead the nation to final victory but which could do little in 1940 to prevent the defeat of France.

France Makes Peace

Paris fell to the Germans in mid-June. In this crisis, Paul Reynaud succeeded Eduard Daladier as premier, but he was unable to deal with the defeatism of some of his cabinet. On June 16, Reynaud resigned in favor of a government headed by aged Marshal Philippe Pétain, one of the heroes of World War I. The Pétain government quickly made peace with Hitler, who added to French humiliation by dictating the terms of the armistice to the French at Compiegne in the same railroad car used by Marshal Ferdinand Foch when he gave terms to the Germans at the end of World War I. The collapse of France in so short a time came as a tremendous shock to the British as well as to Americans. The French had built fortifications along their northern borders, the Maginot Line, but did not extend them fully along the Belgian border in order to spare Belgian pride and not insinuate that Belgium either posed a threat or could not defend itself. The failure was not due to treachery or cowardice, but to poor morale, a defensive "Maginot" mentality, and a failure by French leaders to think in modern terms or to understand as did the Germans the nature of modern mechanized warfare.

Mussolini chose the moment of French defeat to attack France, declaring war on both France and Britain on June 10. He gained little by this action, and Hitler largely ignored the Italian dictator in making peace with France.

Hitler's forces now occupied the northern part of France, including Paris. He allowed the French to keep their fleet and overseas territories, probably in the hope of making them reliable allies. Pétain and his chief minister Pierre Laval established their capital at Vichy and followed a policy of collaboration with their former enemies. A few Frenchmen, however, joined the Free French movement started in London by the then relatively unknown General Charles de Gaulle.

From the French Defeat to the Invasion of Russia

Germany's "New Order" in Europe. By mid-1940s, Germany, together with its Italian ally, dominated western and central Europe. Germany began with no plans for a long war, but continued resistance by the British made necessary the belated mobilization of all resources. Hitler saw that Germany had to exploit conquered lands, where collaborators were used to make puppet governments subservient. Some were called "Quislings," after the traitor Vidkun Quisling, who was made premier of Norway during the German occupation. Germany began the policy of forcibly transporting large numbers of conquered Europeans to work in German war industries. Jews were often forced to do slave labor for the war effort, but more and more were rounded up and sent to the new death camps to be slaughtered systematically as part of Hitler's "final solution" to the so-called Jewish problem. Some information about the extermination of Jews was leaked to the Allies as early as 1942, but governments either did not believe that such reports could be true or else kept the matter secret, so as not to undermine morale on the home fronts. The full horror of these atrocities was not revealed until Allied troops entered Germany in 1945.

The Battle of Britain. With the fall of France, Britain remained the only power of consequence at war with the Axis. Hitler began preparations for invading Britain (Operation "Sea Lion"). Air control over the English Channel was vital if an invasion force was to be transported safely to the English Coast. The German air force (Luftwaffe) under Herman Göring began its air offensive against the British in the summer of 1940. The British, however, had used the year between Munich and the outbreak of war to good advantage, increasing their production of aircraft to six hundred per month, almost equal to German production. The Spitfire and Hurricane fighters, the Royal Air Force's mainstay, were designed and produced later than similar German planes and proved superior. The British had developed radar in time to use it to give early warning of attacks. British intelligence was also effective in deciphering German military communications and in providing ways to interfere with the navigational devices used by their bombers. The Germans concentrated on British air defenses, then on ports and shipping, and finally in early September they began the attack on London. The Battle of Britain was eventually a defeat for the Germans, who were unable to gain superiority over the British, although they inflicted great damage on both British air defenses and major cities. Despite damage and loss of life, British morale remained high and war production continued. German losses determined that bombing alone could not defeat

Britain. Operation "Sea Lion" was postponed October 12 and never seriously taken up again, although the British did not know this and had to continue for some time to give priority to their coastal and air defenses.

Involvement of the United States. The Churchill government worked actively to gain help from the United States, and those efforts elicited a sympathetic response from President Franklin Roosevelt, although in his efforts to enact "measures short of war" to aid Britain, Roosevelt had to deal with strong isolationist sentiment in the United States exemplified by the America First movement, to whose tenets Wendell Willkie, his Republican opponent in the 1940 presidential election, adhered. In November 1939, Congress amended neutrality legislation in order to lift the ban on the sale of arms to belligerents. Late in 1940, when a crisis arose with respect to protection for British shipping, Roosevelt negotiated an agreement by which Congress was persuaded to transfer to the British fifty World War I destroyers in return for naval bases on British possessions in the Western Hemisphere. In 1941, when British assets in the United States had been depleted, the U.S. president and Congress enacted the Lend-Lease Program to provide resources for continued purchases of weapons and supplies by the British. Later the program was extended to supply Russia and other powers that became involved in the struggle against the Axis. The United States also introduced its first peacetime draft and began a tremendous program of military expansion. It obtained bases in Greenland and Iceland, and American warships began to convoy Allied shipping as far as Iceland. The United States was already waging an "undeclared war" against Germany months before the Pearl Harbor attack led to formal American involvement.

Germany Turns East. During the winter of 1940–1941, having given up Operation "Sea Lion," Hitler began to shift his forces to the East for an invasion of Russia (Operation "Barbarossa"). The Nazi-Soviet alliance of August 1939 was opportunistic, and German fears were aroused by Russia's annexation of the three Baltic states in June 1940, by the attack on Finland, and by Russian seizure of the province of Bessarabia from Romania. Russian expansion toward the Balkans dismayed the Germans, who hoped for more influence there. In addition, Hitler's ally Mussolini had, on October 28, 1940, begun an ill-advised invasion of Greece from bases in Albania that the Italians had seized earlier. Within a few weeks the Greeks, repulsed the Italians and drove them back into Albania.

The Balkan Campaign. These events prompted Hitler to make demands early in 1941 on Bulgaria, Hungary, and Rumania, which led these powers to become German allies accepting occupation by German forces. Yugoslavia resisted and the Germans attacked on April 6, occupying it despite considerable resistance. They then advanced to the aid of the Italians in Greece, which was quickly overrun despite aid from British forces in the Middle East. The Greek government took refuge on Crete some sixty miles off the coast, but that island was also captured from its British garrison. On May 20, German parachute troops and airborne forces established footholds at key points on the island. The defenders were unable to repel the Germans and at the end of May, and Crete was evacuated by the British, with the Greek government also going into exile in London.

Barbarossa: The Attack on Russia. The German invasion of Russia began June 22, 1941. The invasion force of three million included Finnish, Romanian, Hungarian, and Italian contingents and advanced on a broad front of about two thousand miles. In this first season of fighting, the Germans seized White Russia and most of the Ukraine, advancing to the Crimean Peninsula in the south. They surrounded the city of Leningrad (although they never managed to capture it). German units came within twenty-five miles of Moscow. Government offices were evacuated. In November, the enemy actually entered the suburbs, but then the long supply lines, early winter, and Russian resistance (strong despite heavy losses) brought the invasion to a halt. During the winter, a Russian counterattack pushed the Germans back from Moscow and saved the capital. Then on December 7, the United States was brought into the war by the surprise Japanese attack on the U.S. naval base at Pearl Harbor, and the entire balance of power in this conflict would ultimately change.

The Far Eastern Crisis

With severe economic problems stemming from the Depression, Japanese militarists gained more influence over the civilian government, which was unable to control its armed forces—especially the Kwantung army, which garrisoned the Japanese-controlled railroad lines in the Chinese province of Manchuria. Believing a policy of expansion onto the Asian mainland would help solve Japan's difficulties and bring ultimate prosperity, the officers of the Kwangtung army engineered an explosion on one of the railroad lines. On September 18, 1931, using this as an excuse, the Japanese occupied all of Manchuria. On July 7, 1937, a full-scale Sino-Japanese war began with a clash between Japanese and Chinese at the Marco Polo Bridge in Beijing. An indication of Japanese aims came on November 3, 1938, when Prince Konoye's government issued a statement on "A New Order in East Asia." This statement envisaged the integration of Japan, Manchuria (now the puppet state of Manchukuo), and China into one "Greater East Asia Co-Prosperity Sphere" under Japanese leadership. In July 1940, the Konoye government was re-formed with General Hideki Tojo (Japan's leader in World War I) as minister of war. Japan's policy of friendship with Nazi Germany and Fascist Italy was consolidated with the signing of a formal alliance in September 1940. The war in Europe gave Japan further opportunities for expansion: it obtained concessions from the Vichy government in French Indochina and established bases there.

All of these events led to worsening relations between Japan and the two states in a position to oppose her expansion—the Soviet Union and the United States. Despite border clashes with the Russians, Japan avoided any conflict with that state, and Stalin wanted no war with Japan after he became fully occupied with the German invasion. The United States viewed Japanese activities with increasing disfavor, especially the brutal war against China. In response to Japanese aggression, the U.S. government did not renew a trade treaty and embargoed exports of scrap metals, oil, and other materials necessary to the Japanese war effort. By 1941 the two countries were in a tense critical situation, and though the American government did not know the details at the time, in Japan decisions had already been made that would lead to the attack on U.S. naval forces that had been moved to Hawaii as a deterrent to further Japanese expansion. There has been much controversy surrounding the Japanese attack on the Pearl

Harbor naval base on December 7, 1941. Here it is sufficient to say that United States forces were caught off guard and suffered a disastrous defeat that fortunately was not as complete as the Japanese had planned. It did, however, put the United States on the defensive for a year. In a few weeks, Japanese forces were able to occupy strategic islands (for example, the Philippines and Dutch East Indies) as well as territory on the Asian mainland (Malaya, with the British naval base at Singapore, and all of Burma to the border of India).

The Japanese attack not only brought the United States into war in the Pacific but also resulted in German and Italian declarations of war on the United States. Henceforth, the United States would be a full-fledged participant in World War II.

The "Turning of the Tide"

The basic strategy for winning the war had evolved well before Pearl Harbor. Prewar American strategic planning provided for several possibilities, always keeping in mind the defense of the Western Hemisphere as the major goal. During 1940–1941, as it became more and more apparent that the United States would become involved as an ally first of Britain and then the Soviet Union, plans changed accordingly. A two-front war became increasingly likely, and U.S. strategists decided—with British concurrence—that priority should be given to the war in Europe (a "Germany first" policy), because the danger to both Britain and the Soviet Union seemed more immediate than the threat from Japan. As it turned out, the United States mobilized such great resources that it produced sufficient forces to go on the offensive in the Pacific at the same time as it was meeting the requirements of the European theater. Thus, the war against Japan ended only a few weeks after the German surrender.

American involvement in the war was ultimately decisive, for it meant that the greatest industrial power of that time was now arrayed against the Axis powers. The United States became, as President Roosevelt put it, "the arsenal of democracy." American aid was crucial to the immense effort of the Soviet Union. Despite almost unanimous expert opinion that the Russians would collapse under German attack, Roosevelt had his personal assistant Harry Hopkins visit Russia and assess the situation, and based on Hopkins's recommendations, he extended Lend-Lease aid to Russia. By 1943, supplies and equipment were reaching Russia in very considerable quantities via routes through the Persian Gulf and overland and also through the Russian Arctic port of Murmansk. The latter route was exceedingly dangerous because of the proximity of German forces based in Norway, and on one or two occasions, losses were so great that convoys had to be temporarily suspended until their defenses could be improved. Nevertheless, in this modern war where the supply and equipment of vast forces over great distances was a major factor, American industrial strength was decisive.

The Second German Offensive in Russia: Stalingrad

Despite losses that included their richest farm land, one-half of their industry, and millions of the population, the Russians not only stopped the Germans and their allies just short of Moscow, but in a winter offensive also drove the center German army group back some eighty miles from the capital. However, with Hitler in personal control,

German forces launched a second offensive in the summer of 1942. This attack concentrated on the southern part of the front, aiming at the Caucasus Mountains and vital oil fields around the Caspian Sea. At Stalingrad on the Volga River, the Russians halted the Germans. Weeks of bitter fighting ensued in the streets of the city itself. With the onset of winter, Hitler refused to allow the strategic retreat urged by his generals. As a result, Russian forces crossed the river north and south of the city and surrounded twenty-two German divisions. On January 31, 1943, following the failure of relief efforts, the German commander Friedrich Paulus surrendered the remnants of his army. From then on, the Russians were, with only few exceptions, always on the offensive.

The North African Campaigns

After entering the war in 1940, the Italians invaded British-held Egypt from Libya. In December 1940, the British general Wavell launched a surprise attack, driving back the Italian forces about five hundred miles and capturing 130,000 Italian troops. Then Hitler intervened, sending General Erwin Rommel with the *Afrika Korps* to reinforce the Italians. Rommel, exploiting the weakness of the British following the dispatch of forces to aid the Greeks, launched a counteroffensive that put his forces on the border of Egypt. Then Rommel in turn had to give up his reserves for the Russian campaign. He managed to recover from a second British attack, however, and by mid-1942 had driven to El Alamein, only seventy miles from Alexandria.

A change in the British high command now placed General Bernard Montgomery in immediate command of the British Eighth Army. After thorough preparations, Montgomery attacked at El Alamein, breaking Rommel's lines and starting a British advance that was not stopped until the armies reached the border of Tunisia.

Meanwhile, British and American leaders, realizing that the forces at their disposal in 1942 would not be sufficient to invade France and start the drive on Germany itself (which was their ultimate goal), decided that they could launch a second offensive in North Africa (Operation "Torch"), which would clear the enemy from the coast and make the Mediterranean once again safe for Allied shipping. To avoid fighting French forces that garrisoned landing areas at Casablanca, Oran, and Algiers, Allied command under the American general Dwight Eisenhower made an agreement with the French admiral Darlan. Darlan did, indeed, assist the Allies to a degree, but there was a public outcry in Britain and the United States at an alliance with a person who condoned fascism. Darlan was assassinated in December, leading to a struggle for leadership among the French in North Africa, de Gaulle's Free French, the French Resistance, and other factions. Roosevelt and Churchill publicly supported senior French officer General Henri Giraud, who had just escaped from imprisonment by the Germans, against the independent and imperious de Gaulle, who was especially disliked by Roosevelt and was not kept informed of the African operation or allowed to participate. De Gaulle proved his political as well as military talent by completely outmaneuvering Giraud, and within a year he was the undisputed leader of all the French elements.

French forces soon joined the war against the Axis. The Germans and Italians were a different matter. Hitler quickly sent German forces under General von Arnim to occupy Tunisia before the Anglo-American forces could get there from their landing points. It was only a matter of time before these forces, together with those commanded by Rommel, were forced into northern Tunisia and forced to surrender. American forces, unused to combat, suffered reverses at the battle of the Kasserine Pass but gained valuable experience. The final victory came in May 1943, about the same time as the Russian victory at Stalingrad.

Winning the Battle of the Atlantic

Another turning point came in the drawn-out battle against German submarines in the North Atlantic. Relatively safe shipping routes across the North Atlantic to Britain were essential to the survival of Britain and necessary if a force was to be assembled to invade France and strike at Germany proper. At times early in the war, the Germans sank ships at a higher rate than the two Allies could replace them, but gradually they began to develop effective countermeasures. New types of aircraft, small aircraft carriers, more numerous and better-equipped escort vessels, new radar and sonar (for underwater detection), efficient radio direction finding, decipherment of German signals, plus the building of more ships (including the mass-produced "Liberty Ship" freighter) turned the balance against the Germans despite their development of improved submarines. Again the tide of battle turned by early 1943 and the Atlantic became increasingly dangerous for German submarines.

A Turning Point

Success in these three campaigns—Stalingrad, North Africa, and the Battle of the Atlantic—gave new hope to the Allied cause and ensured that eventually victory would be won. Combined with the beginning of an offensive in late 1942 in the Solomon Islands against the Japanese, these events made 1943 the turning point of the war.

Allied Victory

At the Casablanca Conference in January 1943, Roosevelt and Churchill developed a detailed strategy for the further conduct of the war. The decision to clear the Mediterranean was confirmed, and Sicily was to be invaded to help achieve this purpose. This led almost inevitably to Italy. Historians differ as to the significance of these decisions. The Italian campaign did knock Italy out of the war and caused Hitler to send forces to Italy that might otherwise have opposed the 1944 landing in Normandy, and it did bring about the downfall of Mussolini and Italian surrender. It also ensured, by using up limited resources such as landing craft, that the Allies could not open a second front in France in 1943—a fact most unpalatable to Stalin, whose armies were fighting desperately against the bulk of the German army and air force. Also, drawing off of forces from Italy to ensure a successful landing in France made it extremely difficult to achieve decisive victory in Italy and meant a long drawn-out and costly campaign there against skillful and stubborn resistance by the Germans under Field Marshal Albert Kesselring. Allied forces did not capture Rome until June 4, 1944. With a new Italian government now supporting the Allied cause, resistance movements in Northern Italy became a major force in helping to liberate that area from the Germans.

The Second Front in Normandy. At Tehran in November 1943, a conference attended by all three Allied leaders (Stalin had previously declined to leave Russia), the decision reached by Roosevelt and Churchill six months earlier to invade France in May 1944 was communicated to the Russians. Stalin promised to open a simultaneous Russian offensive.

Despite the claims of General George Marshall and General Sir Alan Brooke (the American and British chiefs of staff, respectively), Roosevelt and Churchill decided on General Dwight Eisenhower, their North African commander, to be supreme commander of the coming invasion. Eisenhower arrived in London to establish Supreme Headquarters Allied Expeditionary Forces (SHAEF) and to weld together an international staff to command the invasion. He proved extremely adept at getting soldiers of several nations to work together harmoniously. Included in the invasion army were American, British, Canadian, Polish, and French contingents.

The Normandy invasion (Operation "Overlord") was the largest amphibious operation in history and was preceded by elaborate preparations and an enormous buildup of men and supplies. Plans included an air offensive with a force of ten thousand aircraft of all types, a large naval contingent and preinvasion naval bombardment of the very strong German defenses, a transport force of some four thousand ships, artificial harbors to receive supplies after the initial landings, and several divisions of airborne troops to be landed behind enemy coastal defenses the night preceding the sea-borne invasion. The landings took place beginning June 6, 1944. The first day, 130,000 men were successfully landed. Strong German resistance hemmed in Allied forces for about a month. Then the Allies, numbering about 1 million, managed a spectacular breakthrough. By the end of 1944, the Allies had seized all of France. A second invasion force landed on the Mediterranean coast in August, freed southern France, and linked up with Eisenhower's forces. By the end of 1944, Allied armies stood on the borders of Germany ready to invade from east and west.

The Eastern Front: Poland. Russian successes brought their forces to the border of Poland by July 1944. Russia had broken off relations with the Polish government in exile in London, however, after the Poles had voiced their suspicions that the Russians and not the Germans might have caused the mass executions of a large number of Polish officers in the Katyn Forest early in the war.

Stalin's armies crossed into Poland July 23, 1944, and three days later the Russian dictator officially recognized a group of Polish Communists (the so-called Lublin Committee) as the government of Poland. As Russian armies drew near the suburbs of Warsaw, the London Poles (who controlled a large, well-organized resistance movement in Warsaw and hoped to improve their position by a military effort) launched their underground army in an attack on the German garrison. Stalin's forces waited outside the city while the Germans brought in reinforcements and slowly wiped out the Polish underground army in several weeks of heavy street fighting. The offensive then resumed and the city was liberated by the Red Army, but the local influence of the London Poles was now nil. Needless to say, this incident aroused considerable suspicion concerning Stalin's motives and led both Churchill and Roosevelt to begin to think through the political implications of their alliance with Stalin.

Greece, Yugoslavia, and the Balkans. By late summer of 1944, the German position in the Balkans began to collapse. The Red Army crossed the border into Romania, leading King Michael II to seize the opportunity to take his country out of its alliance with Germany and to open the way to advancing Russians. German troops were forced to make a hasty retreat. At this point, Bulgaria changed sides. German forces in Greece, threatened with being cut off, withdrew in October and British forces moved in to take their place. The British hoped to bring about the return of the Greek government in exile from London.

From October 9 to 18, Winston Churchill visited Moscow to try to work out a political arrangement regarding the Balkans and Eastern Europe. (Roosevelt was busy with his campaign for election to a fourth term.) Dealing from a position of weakness, Churchill wrote out some figures on a sheet of paper: Russia to have the preponderance of influence in certain countries like Bulgaria and Romania, Britain to have major say in Greece, and a fifty-fifty division in Yugoslavia and Hungary. Stalin indicated agreement. The Americans refused to have anything to do with a spheres-of-influence arrangement.

In Greece, Stalin maintained a hands-off policy when the British used force to impose a settlement there. The Communist-led Greek resistance refused to agree to the return of the government in exile. Fighting between the factions broke out. In December, Churchill went to Athens to deal personally with the situation. British forces suppressed the Communist revolt and a regency was established under the archbishop of Athens to end the political dispute. The British task was simplified by the fact that Russia gave no support to the Greek Communists but treated Greece as a British sphere of influence.

The German Resistance and the 1944 Attempt to Assassinate Hitler. It was obvious before the Normandy invasion that Germany was losing the war. German officers and civilians had formed a resistance movement. As long as Hitler's policy was successful, it had little chance of overthrowing him. Four years of aerial bombardment, however, had reduced German cities to rubble by early 1944 and virtually destroyed the Luftwaffe. The Russians were on the offensive, and many German officials did not like to think, after what had happened in Russia, what the Russian armies might do if they reached German soil. Hitler was in direct control and disregarded professional advice that might have provided a better, less costly defense. Knowing the war was lost after the success of the Normandy invasion, the German Resistance plotted to assassinate Hitler. The leaders were retired General Ludwig Beck, Carl Goerdeler (former mayor of Leipzig), and Count Claus Schenck von Stauffenberg—a much-decorated young staff officer who undertook the dangerous task of planting the bomb in Hitler's headquarters on July 20, 1944. Hitler miraculously survived the explosion and launched a reign of terror in reprisal, with imprisonment, torture, and death for anyone even suspected of a connection with the plot. His survival ensured that the war would be fought out on German soil to the bitter end.

Final Questions of Strategy. In Eisenhower's headquarters, there was some dispute over the best way to invade Germany and end the war. Because of the rapid drive across France, supplies were insufficient for a broad advance into Germany. General Montgomery argued that his forces should be given priority and allowed to push ahead into the North German Plain as the quickest way to end the war. Eisenhower's decision to reject this and advance on a broad front took into account his fear that German forces might retreat into mountain areas in southern Germany and in these easily defensible positions, prolong the war.

Before the Allied could launch a final attack, however, the Germans launched an offensive of their own beginning December 16. Hitler gathered his last reserves and sent them to attack the Allies in the Ardennes Forest region with the goal of breaking through between the Allied forces and driving to the English Channel coast. The offensive became known as the Battle of the Bulge. Bad weather for days made impossible the effective use of Allied air power. Allied lines held, however, and by the end of the first week of January 1945, the German offensive had been broken. Whether the battle had any value is open to argument. In Yugoslavia, it certainly worked, and Tito (Communist resistance leader) emerged as head of government and managed to maintain a position of independence not achieved by any other East European country.

The End of the War in Europe

In early spring of 1945, the Allied armies crossed the Rhine. The Americans used a railway bridge at Remagen, which they captured just before the Germans had time to destroy it. As Americans, British, and other Allied forces advanced into Germany, the Russians attacked from the east. While Russian armies were slogging into Berlin, Hitler committed suicide in the ruins of the bunker where he had spent the last days of the war. Power was handed over to a government headed by Admiral Karl Doenitz. On May 7, General Alfred Jodl, acting for the German government, made the final unconditional surrender at General Eisenhower's headquarters near Reims.

The Yalta and Potsdam Conferences

The future treatment of Germany, and Europe generally, was determined by decisions of the "Big Three" (Churchill, Roosevelt, and Stalin) at wartime conferences. At Casablanca, Churchill and Roosevelt laid down a policy of unconditional surrender, to which Stalin acceded later. The Big Three then met at Teheran in November of 1943. Here the two Western allies told Stalin of the May 1944 date for the planned invasion of Normandy. In turn, Stalin confirmed a pledge made earlier that Russia would enter the war against Japan after the war with Germany was concluded. Political questions were barely touched upon. Poland and other topics were raised but not dealt with. Roosevelt reflected the views of his military leaders who were concerned with the quickest ending to the war. Hence he was willing to postpone political decisions on the Balkans and Eastern Europe and concentrate on a second front in France and the shortest road to Berlin. This was agreeable to Stalin, since any postponement would only better his position by allowing time for the Red Army to take control of the areas in question. Churchill seems to have had in mind political questions far more than his American colleague (hence his October 1944 visit to Moscow and spheres-of-influence agreement with Stalin referred to earlier in the chapter), but as American participation in the war grew, British influence declined, and he had to defer to the wishes of the Americans. It was not softness on communism, as charged by some critics of wartime diplomacy, but rather a desire for a quick military decision, that prompted Roosevelt to cooperate as he did with Stalin despite the fears of Churchill.

The Yalta Conference was the second attended by Churchill, Roosevelt, and Stalin. It lasted from the February 4 to 11, 1945. A plan to divide Germany into zones of occupation, which had been devised in 1943 by a committee under Deputy Prime Minister Clement Attlee, was accepted with the addition of a fourth zone taken from the British and American zones for the French to occupy. Berlin, which lay within the Russian zone, was divided into four zones of occupation also. Access to Berlin by the Western powers was not as clearly worked out as it should have been.

Such lack of precision was characteristic of other parts of the Yalta agreements as well, leading to future disputes and recriminations between the Western powers and the Russians. Stalin suggested a figure of $20 billion in reparations to be taken from German heavy industry and other assets, and Roosevelt and Churchill agreed this might be a goal but felt it might have to be modified later depending on conditions in Germany. A Declaration on Liberated Europe promised to assist liberated nations in solving problems through elections and by "democratic" means.

Regarding Poland, Churchill and Roosevelt had to allow Stalin to do what he pleased. An eastern frontier was established, corresponding roughly to the old Curzon Line drawn after World War I. Poland, in turn, was allowed to occupy territory in the West up to the line of the Oder and Neisse rivers. These boundaries were not, however, agreed upon as permanent boundaries but rather were left open to later negotiation, when a peace treaty could be made with Germany. In fact, they became permanent when relations between the wartime allies broke down and the Cold War began.

It was agreed that the nucleus of the postwar Polish government would be Stalin's Lublin Committee. The only concession was to add a number of "democratic leaders" (London Poles), but these, as it turned out, were powerless to affect the course of events and prevent an eventual total takeover of Polish government by the Communists.

In the Far East, in return for his agreement to enter the war against Japan after Germany's defeat, Stalin was promised the southern part of Sakhalin Island, the Kurile Islands, a lease on the naval base at Port Arthur, a preeminent position in control of the commercial port of Dairen, and the use of Manchurian railroads.

There has been much dispute over these concessions and whether they were really necessary. Looking back, it is easy to see that Japan was close to defeat with American and Allied forces near enough to commence a destructive aerial bombardment of Japanese cities and to blockade the main islands. At that time, however, considering how tenaciously the Japanese fought in the Pacific island campaigns, the Allies believed that the war might last a long time. An invasion of the main islands of Japan was planned by the American command with estimates of massive casualties. Any help from the Russians that might pin down numerous Japanese forces in Manchuria was deemed extremely desirable. No one could be sure of the secret atomic bomb—which, though nearing completion in American laboratories, had not yet been tested experimentally much less tried in actual combat.

The third summit meeting of the Big Three took place at Potsdam outside Berlin after the end of the European war but while the Pacific war was still going on. The conference began July 17, 1945, with Stalin, Churchill, and the new American President Harry Truman attending. (Roosevelt had died shortly after the conclusion of the Yalta meeting.) While the conference was in session, the results of the British general election became known: Churchill was defeated, his place taken by his wartime deputy prime minister, the Labour leader Clement Attlee. The meeting confirmed arrangements regarding Germany. A Potsdam Declaration, aimed at Japan, called for immediate Japanese surrender and hinted at the consequences that would ensue if that were not forthcoming. While at the conference, American leaders received news of the successful testing of the first atomic bomb in the New Mexico desert, but the Japanese were given no clear warning that such a destructive weapon might be used against them.

The Atomic Bomb and the Defeat of Japan

Development of an atomic bomb became a theoretical possibility following the first splitting of uranium atoms by Otto Strassmann and Fritz Hahn at the Kaiser Wilhelm Institute in Berlin just before the war (a woman physicist, Lise Meitner, was involved in the earlier thought and work behind this, but she had been forced out of Germany by Hitler's racist laws). The news spread quickly and both the British and Americans became concerned that the Germans might develop a weapon based on this principle, and therefore began an effort to build an atomic bomb first. In Britain, a research project known as Tube Alloys was begun, and valuable work had been done by the time the United States entered the war. At that point, the decision was made to concentrate the work in the United States with its vastly greater resources of power and industrial capacity. The Manhattan Engineering District under Major General Leslie Groves was established to manage the immense research, development, and production effort needed to develop an atomic weapon. By early 1945, it appeared that a weapon would soon be available for testing, and in July the successful test was completed.

President Truman established a committee of prominent scientists and leaders to determine how best to utilize the bomb. They advised the president that they could not devise any practical way of demonstrating the bomb. If it was to be used, it had to be dropped on Japan, and Truman then made the decision to do this. On August 6, 1945, the bomb was dropped by a single plane on Hiroshima and the city disappeared, with the instantaneous loss of seventy thousand lives. In time, many others died from radiation poisoning and other effects. Since Japan did not surrender, the United States dropped a second bomb on Nagasaki, obliterating that city. Even the most fanatical Japanese leaders saw what was happening and surrender then came quickly. The only departure from unconditional surrender was to allow the Japanese to retain their emperor (Hirohito), but only with the proviso that he would be subject in every respect to the orders of the occupation commander. The formal surrender took place September 2, 1945, in Tokyo Bay on the deck of the U.S. battleship *Missouri*, and the occupation of Japan began under the immediate control of the American commander General Douglas MacArthur.

TIMELINE

Two World Wars (1914–1945)

Year(s)	Event	Significance
1890	Kaiser Wilhelm II dismisses Otto von Bismarck as chancellor of Germany.	Insisting on a pro-Russian policy in the face of anti-Russian sentiment by the army and the new kaiser, Bismarck is sacked. In retirement, he is able to criticize the new policies of his successors in foreign policy. Ultimately, Bismarck's careful balance of power in Europe falls apart, making Germany feel encircled.
1894	France and Russia form an alliance.	Bismarck's "nightmare of coalitions" starts. Starved of German funds, Russia turns to France for investment capital, which leads to a diplomatic rapprochement. With enemies on two sides, German military leaders begin to plan for a two-front war; the Schlieffen Plan of 1905 evolves: attack France first, Russia second.
1904–1907	The Triple Entente emerges.	In 1904, Britain and France come to an agreement on all colonial issues, forming a near-alliance. In 1907, divvying up Persia into areas of influence, Britain and Russia likewise come to terms. Thus, the Triple Alliance (Austria, Germany, and Italy) is now faced with the more formidable Triple Entente (Britain, France, and Russia).
1908–1913	Young Turks revolt, Austria feuds with Russia, and the Balkan wars occur.	The revolution by "young Turks" leads to internal reforms, but more external weakness: Russia wanted the Straits, Austria the right to annex Bosnia-Herzegovina (Russia loses out). Wars in the Balkans underline Turkish feebleness and Austro-Russian hatreds.

(Continued)

1908–1913	Austria thwarts Serbia's land and sea claims.	Serbia is incensed by Austria's takeover of Bosnia-Herzegovina; it then struggles to get a seaport, but is further angered by Austria's move in 1913 to set up a new kingdom, Albania—thwarting Serbia once again. A secret society, the Black Hand, plots to get revenge on Austria.
June 28, 1914	Archduke Franz Ferdinand of Austria-Hungary is assassinated by a Serbian nationalist.	Following the assassination, Austria demands reprisals of Serbia, which rejects Austria's outrageous demands.
July–August 1914	Conflict between Austria and Serbia escalates into World War I.	Austria declares war on Serbia after getting "blank check" from Germany to do it thought necessary. Russians, upset over an attack on their ally, Serbia, mobilize on western front, which includes Germany. Germans declare war on Russia, and France steps in. When Germans violate Belgian neutrality, Britain enters the war, with ally, Japan.
1914–1916	War rages on the western and eastern fronts.	The western front soon settles into trench warfare, after the botched Schlieffen Plan fails to take Paris; larger swings occur on the eastern front with Russia, which by 1916 is seriously mismanaging its war effort.
1915–1917	Germans engage in submarine warfare; the United States enters the war.	The loss of American lives on the allegedly neutral liner the *Lusitania* (May 1915) causes Germany to back down, until the blockade forces them to declare unrestricted submarine warfare again (February 1917). The United States declares war a few months later.
1916	Combatants attempt to break stalemates on all fronts.	German fleet is bottled up by British blockade. Though their use of submarines helps, the battle of Jutland ends in a stalemate (1916). The fight for Verdun marks the bloodiest battle on the western front (1916). Allied attempts to force a Turkish front at Gallipoli fails utterly; and the Brusilov offensive in the East only buys more time for the tsar to show his gross incompetence.

March–November 1917	Revolutions take Russia out of war.	In March 1917, bread shortages, riots, and other strife lead the tsar to abdicate. The Provisional Government run by liberal Kadets and Socialist Revolutionaries keep Russia in the war despite huge problems in supplies and morale, In November 1917, Bolsheviks take over Saint Petersburg, then country with promises of "Land, Bread, Peace!"
March 1918	Russia and Germany agree to the Treaty of Brest-Litovsk.	To get out of "bourgeois" war, Russia's Bolshevik government is forced to accept German demands for huge swaths of land in western Russia—after the war.
November 11, 1918	Truce ends Word War I.	After last-ditch German offensives fail, and sailors mutiny, Germany agrees to end hostilities. The army screams foul since no foreign troops were on German soil. (Later, legends arose of "dagger-stab" in back by Social Democrats in government.)
1919–1923	Paris Peace Conference crafts the Treaty of Versailles.	The Big Four (Britain, France, Italy, and the United States) settle most questions and borders controversially. Treaty with Germany allegedly imposes a "harsh peace," with reparations, losses to navy and army, and the hated "War Guilt" clauses (Articles 231–232) that say Germany and its allies are guilty, but only Germany must pay reparations for decades.
1919–1920	Communist regimes arise in the West, but are short lived.	Communists riot in Berlin and take over governments in Bavaria, Hungary, and elsewhere. Though crushed, these revolts lead the Far Right to use Communist threat in propaganda of the 1920s and 1930s.
1920s	Democracies struggle in the West—and the East.	Britain and France face economic problems through the 1920s, with government instability; only one republic—Czechoslovakia—survives in the East, while the others become authoritarian.

(Continued)

1922	Fascists take over the Italian government.	In 1919, Italy is threatened by strikes and work stoppages by the new Communist Party and disgruntled veterans returning from war to broken promises. Industrialists and landowners hire thugs to restore order; among them are the *fasci di combattimento* of Mussolini. By 1922, Mussolini is ready to "march on Rome" to resolve deadlock in corrupt Italian politics. Made prime minister by the king, he jockeys to make his rule permanent thus killing parliamentary government in Italy.
1922–1925	German chancellor Gustav Stresemann implements new foreign policy.	Germany shocks Europe by making a deal with Soviet Russia involving exchanges of military technology and such (Treaty of Rapallo). In 1925, Germany agrees at Locarno to recognize its western borders, but not its eastern, thus opening the way to vengeful plans later.
1923	France occupies the Ruhr.	When Germany defaults on reparations, France invades the Ruhr and takes over industry to milk money from factories and mines. The German government responds by printing money to pay laid-off workers. By November, inflation has rendered the mark nearly worthless, and the savings of the middle classes are wiped out. The Dawes Plan by an American banker comes in to stabilize economy and mark.
1923–1924	Mussolini consolidates power over Italy.	Acerbo Law pushed through Italian parliament in 1923 guaranteeing power to any party getting 25 percent of vote. Fascists win the next election and extend Mussolini's powers. Chief opponents, the Socialists, are stunned when leader Giacomo Matteotti is murdered. Mussolini takes credit and proceeds to make Italian society and economy fascist.

November 9, 1923	Beer-Hall Putsch occurs.	A little-known far-right party, the National Socialists (Nazis), plots with wartime hero Erich Ludendorff to take over government in Bavaria from a Munich beer hall. The government is alerted to the plans, and the army crushes the coup in streets. The Nazi leader, Adolf Hitler, is arrested and charged with treason.
1925–1931	Britain reinstitutes the gold standard, but then abandons it again.	To improve its flagging economy, the British government goes back on the gold standard, which promptly makes British exports overvalued and harms the economy. This leads to the general strike of 1926. Finally, a new government abandons the standard in 1931.
1929	Mussolini and the pope agree to the Lateran Accords.	Though the church has opposed Mussolini and the Fascists, Mussolini strikes a deal with the pope: Vatican is made a separate state and given recompense for land seizures of 1860–1870, while the church has to acknowledge Fascist control over Italy.
1929–1932	World is rocked by the Great Depression.	New York stock market crash of 1929 ripples into Europe via reparations cycle with Britain, France, and Germany, all of whom experience a slowdown of trade. Starved of loans, German economy plummets; deprived of reparations, British and French stop repaying World War I loans from United States and buying U.S. goods.
1930–1933	The governments of Heinrich Brüning, Franz von Papen, and Kurt von Schleicher fail to revive economy or solve parliamentary deadlock between Far Left (Communists) and Far Right (Nazis).	This leads to Hitler being called to chancellorship January 30, 1933, in a desperation move to find a workable government.

(Continued)

1933–1934	Hitler sidelines domestic opposition.	Hitler uses Reichstag fire to outlaw Socialists and Communists; forces through the Enabling Act to make the Nazi Party supreme; starts a series of "solutions" to Jewish problem with boycott and April 7 law against Jews in the civil service; disbands trade unions; and forges the Concordat with Vatican to neutralize Catholic opposition (July 1933). His paramilitary army, the SA, grows too large and unruly, so Hitler purges its leaders (and many enemies) in late June 1934. The army capitulates to him as its führer.
1935–1938	Hitler neutralizes foreign opponents.	Hitler leaves League of Nations to re-arm (violating the Treaty of Versailles); invades demilitarized Rhine to reclaim it (1936); plans war in 1937; orchestrates both the annexation of Austria (1938) and Sudeten crisis that enables him to annex German parts of Czechoslovakia (Munich conference, 1938).
1935–1939	Hitler escalates war against German Jews.	Nuremberg Laws (1935) outlaw intermarriage; other laws push Jews out of professions and public places. On *Kristallnacht* (November 9–10, 1938), Hitler orders the SA and SS to destroy Jewish businesses and synagogues. Borders are closed to Jewish emigration; all Jews are forced to where yellow stars.
1935–1936	Mussolini attacks Ethiopia.	In revenge for humiliation of Adowa (1896), Mussolini launches war against Ethiopia; the League of Nations does little to sanction him or new oil imports. Italy formally annexes Ethiopia in May 1936.

1936–1939	Fascists take over Spain.	Alarmed by secularism of the Spanish Republic (1931–1939), General Francisco Franco and his army wage a civil war for three years, aided by from Fascist Italy and Germany. Western democracies offer no formal aid to Franco's opposition, and Franco wins what could be called the dress rehearsal for World War II. Nazis try out new bombers on Basque village of Guernica, leading to Pablo Picasso's painting (1937).
March 1939	Hitler takes the rump of the Czech state, Danzig, and the Polish Corridor.	In response to Hitler's actions, France and Britain start to prepare for war.
August–September 1939	Hitler prepares for war; World War II begins.	In August, Hitler and Stalin surprise the world by signing a nonaggression pact; this buys Stalin time after his rash purges of the Soviet army, but also helps him to grab his share of Poland later. On September 1, having secured his eastern flank, Hitler invades Poland with the *blitzkrieg*, and conquers the country in three to four weeks. France and Britain declare war.
1940	War resumes on northern and western fronts.	After a "phony war" of several months (*sitzkrieg*), Hitler resumes his conquests with invasions of Denmark, Norway, Benelux countries, and France. The Maginot Line does not protect France, which surrenders. Germany divides France into two zones: occupied and collaborationist (Vichy regime). Hitler begins the Battle of Britain with fearsome air raids.
1941	Germany antagonizes two new enemies.	After successes in Greece, Yugoslavia, and elsewhere, Hitler decides to invade Russia (Operation Barbarossa), June 1941; in December, the Japanese bombardment of U.S.-owned Pearl Harbor leads Hitler rashly to declare war on United States first.

(*Continued*)

1942–1945	Hitler implements his "Final Solution."	After mass shootings prove inefficient and negatively impact morale, Hitler and Himmler decide to build death camps in occupied Poland for mass murder of Jews, his maniacal wartime goal. About six million Jews are forced by train to these camps and gassed, then their bodies are cremated. Camps also detain and murder political dissidents, gypsies, homosexuals, and others.
Late 1942	Allies begin to turn back the fascist tide.	In summer of 1942, United States defeats the Japanese at the pivotal battle of Midway; November, Russians turn back German advances at Stalingrad, and British reverse German-Italian gains in North Africa with the second battle of El Alamein. Americans land in Morocco for an advance through Africa, then to Sicily and Italy.
1943	Wartime conferences commence.	At Casablanca then Tehran, the Allies meet to discuss how to end war and what to do with losers after. Decisions on the second front (France) anger Stalin. Allies decide to divide Germany into occupation zones; Russia is to enter the war in the Pacific three months after war against Hitler is won in the West.
1944	Britain and Soviet Union meet in the Moscow ministerial conference.	In the absence of the United States, Britain and the Soviet Union decide on spheres of influence in Balkans: some parts will be under the hegemony of the Soviet Union, others under Britain. This spheres policy results in a Cold War clash over Greece and Turkey in 1947.
1945	The Allies meet at Yalta and Potsdam.	At these final wartime conferences, the Allies discuss the fate of Poland, zones, reparations, and other controversial issues. War ends in the West on May 8; in the Pacific, after two atomic bombs on Japan, on August 15. By this time, the Cold War between the two great victors, the United States and the Soviet Union, has begun.

Chapter 9

Postwar Europe: Cold War, Reconstruction, Decolonization, and Unification Efforts (1945–2001)

Europe after World War II (1945–1953)

General Nature of the Peace Settlement

After the Second World War, the combatants did not craft a clear-cut peace settlement, as they had after the First World War with the Versailles and other treaties that made up the Paris Peace Settlement of 1919. What peace planning there was had been done at the major wartime conferences among leaders of Great Britain, the United States, and the Soviet Union (the Big Three). Then, in the years immediately following the German surrender, a series of de facto arrangements evolved, shaped by the occupation of Germany and the opening years of the so-called Cold War that followed the breakdown of the wartime alliance of Western powers (Britain, France, and the United States) with the Soviet Union.

The Atlantic Charter

Anglo-American ideas about the postwar world were expressed in the Atlantic Charter, a general statement of goals laid out by President Franklin Roosevelt and Prime Minister Winston Churchill at their meeting off the coast of Newfoundland in August 1941. The charter outlined the following postwar objectives: restoration of the sovereignty and self-government of nations conquered by Adolf Hitler's Germany, free access to world trade and resources, cooperation to improve living standards and economic security, and a peace that would ensure freedom from fear and want and stop the use of force and aggression as instruments of national policy.

Postwar Planning during World War II

At the Casablanca Conference (1943), the Allies announced the policy of requiring unconditional surrender by the Axis powers. This ensured that at the end of the war all responsibility for government of the defeated nations would fall on the victors, and they would have a free hand in rebuilding government in those countries. However, the Allies did not engage in any detailed planning before the time arrived to meet this responsibility. For the most part, they addressed the issue as needs arose.

At their meeting in Teheran (1943), the Big Three did discuss the occupation and demilitarization of Germany. They also laid the foundation for a postwar organization—the United Nations Organization—which, like the earlier League of Nations, was supposed to help regulate international relations and keep the peace and ensure friendly cooperation between the nations of the world.

One postwar plan for Germany was initially accepted by Roosevelt and Churchill in September 1944, then quietly discarded when its impracticality became apparent to all. This was the Morgenthau Plan, named after U.S. Secretary of the Treasury Henry Morgenthau. This harsh scheme would have largely destroyed Germany as an industrial power and returned it to an agricultural/pastoral economy. Both British and Americans quickly realized that Germany could not return to eighteenth-century, pre–Industrial Revolution conditions. They also realized that the resources of German heavy industry would be necessary to the recovery and vitality of the rest of Europe. This episode did point to the importance of a healthy German economy to Europe as a whole, and Allied recognition of this.

At the Yalta Conference early in 1945, the Big Three agreed on a number of matters, tentatively. The eastern boundary of Poland was set approximately at the old Curzon Line that had been proposed at the end of World War I to run roughly along ethnic lines separating Poles and Russians. Poland was to occupy formerly German territory in the West, including the old Polish Corridor, Danzig (Gdansk), and territory up to the Oder and Neisse rivers. Germany was to be disarmed and divided into four zones of occupation: Russian, British, and American, and a zone for France taken from what had originally been designated British and American territory. The principle of German reparations was established but no firm figure was set. Half of the reparations were to go to the Soviet Union.

At Yalta, the Big Three also reached agreement with regard to a government for Poland. The Communist Lublin Committee established by Stalin was to be the nucleus of a provisional government with the addition of representatives of other "democratic" elements (that is, the London Polish Government recognized by Britain and the United States). An oral agreement for the "earliest possible establishment through free elections of governments responsive to the will of the people" cost Stalin little: the other powers had no way to ensure the integrity of such elections if held. The Declaration on Liberated Europe, with its promise of rights of self-determination, provided a false sense of agreement.

The territorial arrangements with regard to Poland and the eastern boundary of Germany, agreed to provisionally at Yalta, were confirmed at Potsdam in July 1945 following the German surrender. Although the arrangements were to be provisional pending a formal peace treaty with Germany, they became permanent when the Allies could not reach agreement on a German treaty.

At Potsdam, the Big Three also agreed to sign peace treaties as soon as possible with former German allies. They established a Council of Foreign Ministers to draft the treaties. The council held several meetings in 1946 and 1947 and signed treaties with Bulgaria, Finland, Hungary, Italy, and Romania. These states paid reparations and agreed to some territorial readjustments as a price for peace. The council members could not reach agreement on Japan or Germany, however. In 1951, the Western powers led by the United States concluded a treaty with Japan without Russian participation. The latter made its own treaty in 1956. A final meeting of the Council of Foreign Ministers broke up in 1947 over Germany, and no peace treaty was ever signed with that country. One result of that meeting was the formal dissolution of the state of Prussia, now wiped off the map. The division of Germany for purposes of occupation and military government became permanent with the three western zones joining and eventually becoming the Federal Republic of Germany and the Russian zone becoming the German Democratic Republic.

Arrangements for the United Nations (UN) were confirmed at Yalta: the large powers would predominate in a Security Council where they would have permanent seats together with several other powers elected from time to time from among the other members of the UN. Any action by the Security Council would require the consent of all the permanent members (thus giving the large powers a veto). The General Assembly was to include all members.

Eastern Europe (1945–1953)

The Soviet Union

The ability of the Soviet Union to withstand the terrific pressure of the German invasion and to recover, drive back, and destroy the bulk of the German invaders indicated its great strength. Despite these victories, the Russian government faced tremendous problems. Much of European Russia had been devastated and about twenty-five million people made homeless. Recovery was achieved using the same drastic, dictatorial methods implemented by the Communists during the 1930s. Josef Stalin's dictatorship became more firmly entrenched than ever as it purged any potential opposition. In March 1946, the Supreme Soviet (Russian for "council") adopted a fourth five-year plan (see chapter 7 for previous plans) intended to increase industrial output to a level 50 percent higher than before the war. Toward that end, the government collected industrial equipment from areas occupied by the Red Army. In 1947, the state planning commission announced that while goals had not been met in 1946, the goal for 1947 had been surpassed: a bad harvest and food shortage in 1946 had been relieved by a good harvest in 1947, and in December 1947, the government announced the end of food rationing. At the same time, the government enacted a drastic currency devaluation that brought immediate hardship to many people but strengthened the Soviet economy in the long run. As a result of these and other forceful measures, the Soviet Union was able within a few years to make good most of the wartime damage and to surpass prewar levels of production. While this was being done at home, Stalin pursued an aggressive foreign policy and established a series of Soviet satellite states in Eastern Europe.

The Communization of Eastern Europe

The fate of Eastern Europe (including Bulgaria, Czechoslovakia, Hungary, Poland, Romania, and the Russian zone of Germany) from 1945 on was determined by the presence of Russian armies in that area. Stalin undoubtedly wanted a group of friendly nations on his western border from which invasion had come twice during his lifetime. The Russian Communists were also determined to support the advance of a Communist system similar to that developed in Russia into the countries of Eastern Europe. The presence of the Red Army allowed Russia to do this, just as the presence of American forces in Japan determined the postwar course of that nation.

Communization of Eastern Europe and the establishment of regimes in the satellite areas of the Soviet Union occurred in stages over a three-year period after the end of the war. Coalitions with other parties existed first, with the Communists forming a front with socialist and peasant parties. Initial measures were taken to punish those who, during the wartime occupation, had collaborated with the Nazis on measures such as land reform. Eventually all opposition parties were ousted and in each case the government became one totally dominated by the local Communist Party.

Poland: A Test Case. As agreed at Yalta, the Lublin Committee was expanded into a provisional government by the inclusion of Stanislas Mikolajczyk and other leaders from the London Polish government in exile. Communists occupied ministries controlling police, internal affairs, and the military, ensuring that power eventually remained in their control. The Polish Workers (Communist) Party knew it had very little backing among Polish people, who were strongly Catholic and anti-Russian, and they maintained tight control over them from the beginning. Elections agreed to at Yalta were finally held in 1947, but under conditions that made the victory of the Communists inevitable. This tragic period is beautifully re-created in Andrzej Wajda's great film *Ashes and Diamonds* (1958). Mikolajczyk, frustrated in his efforts to influence the government, resigned, went into opposition, and then finally fled the country later in 1947.

Hungary. Toward the end of the war, with German control weakened by defeats at the hands of the Russians, the Hungarian government changed hands and a new regime concluded an armistice on January 20, 1945. Hungary then changed sides and joined the Allies in the war against Germany. In November 1945, a general election gave victory to the anti-Communist Smallholders Party, whose leader, Zoltan Tildy, formed a coalition government. The government found itself in increasing economic difficulties, and by 1947 the Communists—with Soviet support—began a purge and takeover of the government. In February 1947, Bela Kovacs, secretary general of the Smallholders Party, was arrested and charged with plotting against the Soviet occupation forces. A general election held in August gave the Communists a majority. In January 1948, the Communists engineered a fusion of Communists and Social Democrats into a United Workers Party in which the Communists were dominant. Although the Smallholders Party still held some seats in the cabinet, effective power was in the hands of Deputy Premier Matyas Rakosi (Communist). A new constitution was promulgated August 7, 1949. The Communist regime was now firmly established and began a program of nationalization of industry followed by a five-year plan on the Russian model.

The refusal of the Roman Catholic Church in Hungary to make concessions to the government led to the arrest and trial of Josef Cardinal Mindszenty, who was sentenced in February 1949 to life imprisonment. Other bishops continued their opposition to the government for about two years before they finally took an oath of allegiance to the people's republic in July 1951.

Bulgaria. Postwar developments in Bulgaria were decisively influenced by the Red Army, which invaded the country in 1944. The Soviet-sponsored government established in September contained only a few Communists, but they occupied key positions of power. Bulgaria formally capitulated on October 28, 1944, and remained under occupation by the Red Army. An election held in November 1945 gave overwhelming support to a Communist-controlled coalition called the Fatherland Front. In 1946, the Communists made a sweeping purge of the government, executing or removing some fifteen hundred high-ranking officials of the Old Regime and many more lesser government officials. A referendum in September formally rejected any restoration of the monarchy, and later that same month Bulgaria was declared a people's republic.

With considerable government interference, a constituent assembly was elected with a Communist majority. Veteran Communist Georgi Dimitrov returned from Moscow to become premier in February 1947. In that year, a Bulgarian Peace Treaty was signed at Paris requiring Bulgaria to pay indemnities and limiting the size of its armed forces. During 1947, the government began a program of nationalization by taking over banks and industries. In December, Soviet forces ended their occupation, leaving behind a firmly entrenched Communist regime, which signed a treaty of friendship with the Soviet Union the following year.

Romania. During the war, Romania was governed by a pro-fascist regime that allied the country with the Axis. With Russian armies invading the country, King Michael dismissed the government and accepted armistice terms from the Allies. The Russians occupied the capital of Bucharest in August 1944. As in other areas of Eastern Europe, a coalition government was first formed with Communists participating along with other parties, but from the beginning the Communists held the real power. In November 1945, a general election took place preceded by a campaign of government violence against opposition parties. During 1947, the leaders of opposition parties such as the National Peasant Party were arrested and sentenced to prison for espionage and treason and their parties dissolved. At the end of the year, King Michael abdicated under Communist pressure. Following elections in 1948, a new constitution was adopted patterned after the Russian model. Relations with Western powers became virtually nil because of accusations of espionage made against Western diplomats. By the end of 1949, Romania had become completely Communist and a satellite of the Soviet Union.

East Germany. In the Russian zone in Eastern Germany, a Soviet satellite state was also established. During the Nazi period, a number of German Communists fled to Moscow. When the Red Army invaded Germany, these exiles returned under the leadership of Wilhelm Pieck and Otto Grotewohl. As relations broke down between the four occupying powers, the Soviet authorities gradually created a Communist state in their zone. Elections in May 1948 resulted in a constituent assembly with a two-thirds majority of Communists. By the end of the month, the assembly had approved a draft constitution. On October 7, 1948, a German Democratic Republic was established. Pieck became president and Grotewohl head of a predominantly Communist cabinet. The Soviet military regime was replaced by a Soviet Control Commission. In June 1950, an agreement with Poland granted formal recognition of the Oder-Neisse line as the boundary between the two states. Economic progress was unsatisfactory for most of the population, and on June 16 to 17, 1953, riots occurred in East Berlin that were crushed by Soviet forces using tanks. Soon after, the East German government announced a program of economic reform that eventually brought some improvement.

Special Cases. Czechoslovakia is an example of a country whose government tried to remain relatively free and democratic, while at the same time attempted to reach agreement with the Soviet Union that would provide the basis for peaceful coexistence with Russia after the war. The government in exile in London under President Eduard Benes maintained good relations with Moscow during the war. In April 1945, Benes appointed a national front government that was a genuine coalition of parties. The government moved to Prague on May 10, 1945. It carried out a sweeping purge of those who had collaborated with the Germans. In addition, on August 3 all those ethnic Germans living in the Sudetenland and elsewhere in the country were deprived of their citizenship and eventually expelled. The period from October 1945 to June 1946 was devoted to choosing a national assembly and establishing a permanent government. Elections held in May 1946 gave the Communists 114 of 300 assembly seats and the Communist Klement Gottwald formed a coalition cabinet. Benes was unanimously reelected president of the republic. On July 7, 1947, the Czech government decided to accept Marshall Plan aid and to participate in the carrying out of the plan. At this point, Soviet pressure caused the Czech government to break off this policy and withdraw.

The period of genuine coalition government lasted about three years in Czechoslovakia. But as elsewhere in Eastern Europe, the Communists seized total control of the government, eliminating other political elements. The Communist coup was carried out February 26, 1948. The Communist Party had prepared by infiltrating members into government services and trade unions. With Russian support, they then put pressure on President Benes to agree to a cabinet under Klement Gottwald, which would be primarily Communist. On March 10, a major obstacle to communization was removed when Foreign Minister Jan Masaryk (son of Thomas Masaryk, founder of the Czech Republic) was killed in a fall from his office window, which the authorities reported as suicide. A far-reaching purge in the next several months transformed a democratic Czechoslovakia into a "people's democracy" with a single party government. On May 9, a constituent assembly adopted a new constitution. National elections, in which only a single list of candidates (Communist) appeared on the ballot, confirmed the Communist victory. President Benes resigned June 7 because of ill health and died shortly after on September 3. On June 14, Gottwald became the new president and on January 1, 1949, a Soviet-style five-year plan of industrial development began with the aim of making the country independent of the West.

In June 1949, a campaign began against the Roman Catholic Church, which as elsewhere in Eastern Europe proved to be a source of opposition to the Communist program. The government formed its own Catholic Action Committee to take control of the local church from Archbishop Joseph Beran and the Catholic hierarchy. On October 14, the government assumed full control of all Catholic affairs. The Catholic clergy were required to swear a loyalty oath to the Communist state.

Czech politics followed a course of increasingly repressive measures paralleling that of Stalin during his last years in the Soviet Union. In 1950, a series of purges was carried out against enemies of the government, including some of its own members who were accused of anti-Soviet, pro-Western activities. Beginning in April, the Czech military was completely reorganized on Soviet lines. In March 1951, further purges were carried out to remove "Titoist" elements (a reference to the Yugoslav Communist leader Marshal Tito whose independent policy had earned him the enmity of Stalin). Reports of economic difficulties, including a severe shortage of coal and the failure of a program to collectivize farming, were made public by the government in 1952. Simultaneously, a mass treason trial opened in November. At the trial, Rudolph Slansky, former Czech Communist Party secretary general, pleaded guilty to treason, espionage, and sabotage.

In Yugoslavia, Marshal Tito and his Communist partisan movement emerged from the war in a strong position because of their effective campaign against the German occupation. Tito was able to establish a Communist government and, despite considerable pressure from Stalin, pursue a course independent of the Soviet Union unique among the countries of Eastern Europe.

Elections held November 11, 1945, gave victory to Tito's Communist-dominated National Front. A few days later, the Yugoslav monarchy was abolished and the country declared to be the Federal People's Republic of Yugoslavia. A new constitution was adopted January 31, 1946. The new regime was recognized by the Western powers despite its Communist nature and pro-Soviet inclination. Enemies of the new regime were dealt with severely. General Drazha Mihailovich, leader of an anti-Tito wartime resistance movement, was captured, tried, and executed July 17. Archbishop Stepinac, the Catholic leader of Croatia, was arrested on charges of collaborating with the Germans and sentenced to seventeen years imprisonment at hard labor.

In 1947, Yugoslavia appeared to follow the lead of the other East European states when it concluded treaties of friendship and alliance with a number of these states and became a founding member of the Communist Information Agency (Cominform)—an organization created to take the place of the old Communist International that had been abolished by Stalin in 1943 as a gesture of goodwill to his wartime allies. In April 1948, Tito announced the start of a five-year plan of development. Tito followed a policy independent of the wishes of Stalin, causing the Russian dictator to try to exert pressure on Yugoslavia and finally to recall Russian advisers and break off relations. On June 28, 1948, the Cominform formally expelled Yugoslavia.

Tito retained the support of his own party, however, when he denied Cominform charges against him at a congress of the Yugoslavian Communist Party and received a vote of confidence. The dispute continued in 1949 when the satellites of Eastern Europe broke off economic relations with Yugoslavia. In September, the Soviet Union denounced its Treaty of Friendship with Tito's regime. Tito's position was shown to be secure, however, when elections in March 1950 gave overwhelming victory to his People's Front candidates. Tito followed a policy of informal rapprochement with the West. He announced his opposition to Chinese intervention in the Korean War. He established diplomatic relations with Greece and withdrew support from the Communist guerrillas waging war against the government there. Tito also made overtures to Italy to repair relations with that country. In November 1951, Tito even went so far as to make an agreement with the United States for the latter to supply equipment, material, and services to the Yugoslavian army. In July 1952, the United States agreed to supply tanks, artillery, and jet aircraft to the Yugoslavs despite the fact that Tito—while retaining independence of Stalin—remained staunchly Communist.

Western Europe (1945–1953)

Italy

In Italy, following the end of hostilities with Germany, the leaders of the Resistance in the North ousted Premier Ivan Bonomi and placed one of their own leaders, Ferruccio Parri, in power. Parri was the leader of a faction—the Party of Action—that was socialist in its program. Although he was a man of great moral stature, he was a poor administrator and did not appeal to the public. He was left politically isolated when the Socialist leader Pietro Nenni made an alliance with the Communists. Meanwhile, more conservative forces had been gathering strength, and in November 1945, Parri was forced to resign.

The monarchy that had governed Italy since the time of unification in the mid-nineteenth century was discarded in favor of a republic. On May 9, 1946, King Victor Emmanuel III, compromised by his association with Mussolini's Fascist regime, resigned in favor of his son, who became King Umberto II. His reign was short-lived, for a referendum in June 1946 established a republic. In simultaneous elections for a constituent assembly, three parties predominated: the Social Democrats with 115 members, the Communists with 104, and the Christian Democrats with 207. Under the new regime, Enrico de Nicola formed a coalition government.

The Christian Democrats and their leader Alcide de Gasperi dominated Italian politics for the next several years. On February 10, 1947, a peace treaty was signed at Paris. Italy paid $350 million in reparations and suffered some minor losses of territory. Trieste, which was in dispute between Italy and Yugoslavia, became a free territory. Gasperi's government followed a policy of cooperation with the West and kept Italy non-Communist. In April 1948, in the first elections under the new constitution, the Christian Democrats won an absolute majority of seats in the Italian parliament. (Historians believe that the new U.S. spy agency, the Central Intelligence Agency (CIA), tampered with this election.) The issue of communism remained very much alive, and there was considerable Communist-inspired unrest, especially after an attempt was made on the life of the Communist leader Palmiro Togliatti. The Marshall Plan helped stabilize the situation in Italy. In 1948, Italy received $601 million in aid vital to the Italian economy. On April 4, 1949, Italy signed the North Atlantic Treaty and became a member of the North Atlantic Treaty Organization (NATO), firmly allied to the West. The Gasperi era came to an end in 1953. He won a narrow electoral victory as the head of a coalition in June and resigned July 28 after a vote of no confidence. He died a year later, August 19, 1954.

France

In the last two years of the war, France recovered sufficiently under the leadership of General Charles de Gaulle to begin playing a significant military and political role once again. In July 1944, the United States recognized de Gaulle's Committee of National Liberation as the de facto government of those areas liberated from the German occupation. As the war ended, this provisional government put through a purge of collaborators, including Marshal Pétain and Pierre Laval, who had headed the Vichy regime during the war.

In October 1945, elections for a constituent assembly showed the strength of left-wing forces: Communists, 152; Socialists, 151; and the Popular Republican Movement (MRP), 138. De Gaulle, after a period in which he tried to work with the more radical forces, resigned in January 1947 and went into retirement. In May 1946, a popular referendum rejected the proposed constitution. In June, a new assembly was elected, dominated by the MRP with the Communists second and the Socialists third. A revised constitution was adopted in October establishing a Fourth Republic, much like the Third, with a weak executive dominated by a strong legislature. This situation resulted in cabinet instability with a series of governments over the next several years. Communist agitation and obstructionism combined with economic difficulties created an increasingly wide split between Communist and non-Communist members of the cabinet that resulted in the exclusion of five Communist members in May 1947.

Meanwhile, de Gaulle had assumed control of a nationwide *Rassemblement du Peuple Français* (RPF) intended to unify non-Communist elements and reform the system of government. For a time, the RPF grew in strength at both the local and national level although de Gaulle himself remained out of office. Then, with the lessening of the Communist danger and improvements in the economy, moderates began to oppose what they perceived to be de Gaulle's authoritarian tendencies. By 1953 the RPF had faded from the scene, and de Gaulle returned to retirement.

Economically, France became a welfare state. De Gaulle, during his provisional government, inaugurated this welfare state to associate the working classes with a new spirit of national unity and to deprive the Communists of their propaganda advantage. During the year and a half following de Gaulle's retirement, the three parties (Socialist, Communist, and MRP) that dominated politics during that period agreed on a program building on reforms begun during the Popular Front of the 1930s. This program, which included nationalization of coal mines, banking, insurance, gas, and electricity as well as allowances for dependent children, was the beginning of a comprehensive system of social security legislation that eventually covered more than 50 percent of the French people.

These changes were accepted by all subsequent regimes as a fait accompli. Although excessively bureaucratic and regulatory, the welfare state did provide a cushion of security for the French population during the period of inflation and economic hardship in the immediate postwar years prior to the advent of the Marshall Plan.

The establishment of a national planning office under Jean Monnet was a significant achievement that provided the French government with a framework for guiding economic development—something both Italy and West Germany lacked. This was important in directing French resources effectively when production began to rise during the prosperous years of the 1950s.

In foreign affairs, France played a role in the occupation of Germany, but the Fourth Republic faced worse problems abroad when it attempted to assert its authority over Indochina and Algeria. The Indochina situation resulted in a long and costly war against nationalists and Communists under Ho Chi Minh. French involvement ended with the Geneva accords of 1954 and French withdrawal. The Algerian struggle reached a crisis in 1958 that resulted in the return to power of General de Gaulle and the creation of a new Fifth Republic.

Germany

In May 1945, when Germany surrendered unconditionally, the country lay in ruins and faced the Herculean task of recovering economically and politically from the tragic consequences of the Hitler era. About three-quarters of houses had been gutted by air raids, industry was in a shambles, and the country was divided into zones of occupation ruled by foreign military governors. Economic chaos was the rule, currency was virtually worthless, food was in short supply, and the black market flourished for those who could afford to buy in it. By the Potsdam agreements, Germany had lost about one-quarter of its prewar territory. In addition, some twelve million expelled people of German origin driven from their homes in countries like Poland and Czechoslovakia had to be fed, housed, and clothed along with the indigenous population.

Demilitarization, denazification, and democratization were the initial goals of the occupation forces. All four wartime allies agreed on the trial of leading Nazis for a variety of war crimes and "crimes against humanity." An international military tribunal was established at Nuremburg to try twenty-two major war criminals, and lesser courts tried many others. The four prosecuting powers gathered massive evidence of the crimes of the Hitler era from captured German archives, interviews, and other documents, and introduced it into evidence. Most of the defendants were executed, although a few like Rudolf Hess were given life imprisonment. At the time and later, commentators from east and west—journalists, legal scholars and others—raised questions about two main areas; the legality of these unprecedented proceedings, and the cogency of the charges against the Nazi regime. Some charges against the defendants, such as the waging of aggressive war and genocide, were new to jurisprudence. Some also questioned whether the trials were not simply "victors' justice." Also, one of the prosecuting powers was the Soviet Union, which many felt was guilty of some of the same crimes charged against the Nazi defendants.

The denazification program had mixed results. It started out as an effort to find everyone who had any connection to the Nazi Party. This included so many that the proceedings became bogged down. It became apparent after a time that not all could be investigated because of the sheer magnitude of the task. Some important Nazi officials were found and punished. Often it was easier to prosecute those less involved, and some important offenders escaped. There was quiet sabotage and a conspiracy of silence by a cynical population. Eventually wider amnesties were granted. The process never officially ended, but simply faded away, as former Nazis quietly took normal jobs and even major positions in the new Federal Republic.

The reestablishment of German government in the Western zones met with more success. As relations between the three Western powers and the Soviets gradually broke down in Germany, East and West became separate states. In the West, the British and American zones were fused into one in 1946, with the French zone joining in 1948. Political parties were gradually reestablished. First local government was once again run by Germans under close supervision, then gradually more independence was accorded to the Germans to govern themselves at the higher state level. Political parties were authorized by the end of 1945. In January 1946 elections for local offices in the American zone, the Christian Democrats were first and the Social Democrats second. Elections in the British and French zones brought the same results.

During 1947, the Council of Foreign Ministers met twice to work out a treaty for Germany. Both failed, and the occupying powers began to go their own way in their zones—the Russians to create a Communist satellite in East Germany and the British, Americans, and French to create a West German Federal Republic.

In February 1948, a bi-zonal charter granted further powers of government to the Germans in the American and British zones. During 1948, the Allied Control Council (comprised of the military commanders in the four zones) broke down. A major issue was the issuance of a new currency in the western zones, after which the old currency in the East dropped to nearly a fourth of its former value. The Russian delegate walked out of the council after charging that the three Western powers were undermining four-power cooperation. Later that year, the Russians and East Germans, in an effort to force the Western powers out of their zones in Berlin, began a blockade of the city, which was located within the Russian zone. The Allies used an airlift to supply the city, and eventually, after some months, the blockade was called off.

Meanwhile, reconstruction in western Germany proceeded. On June 1, 1948, the three Western powers and Belgium, the Netherlands, and Luxembourg reached and agreement calling for international control of the Ruhr industrial area, German representation in the European Recovery Program (Marshall Plan), and the drafting of a federal constitution for a western Germany.

In April 1949, the three Western powers agreed on an occupation statute for Western Germany that gave the Germans considerable autonomy at the national level while reserving wide powers of intervention to the occupying powers. In May, a parliamentary council representing the state governments adopted a basic law for a Federal Republic of Germany with its capital at Bonn. Elections in August gave the Christian Democrats a slight lead over the Social Democrats, and the next month Konrad Adenauer (a Christian Democrat) became chancellor of the new West German government. Theodor Heuss (a Free Democrat) was elected president. For the next fourteen years, Adenauer (who was seventy-three at the start) and the Christian Democrats remained in power.

West Germany regained complete independence and sovereignty within a short period of time. As a result of the Korean War (which started in 1950) and fear of Soviet aggression in Europe, the process moved rapidly. The Western powers felt that West German rearmament was necessary to the defense of western Europe. German leftists were upset, as can be seen at the end of Rainer Werner Fassbinder's film *The Marriage of Maria Braun* (1978). West Germany became firmly allied with the West and eventually with the military organization within NATO.

It should be noted that West German economic recovery had made it the strongest industrial power of western Europe. Wartime damage to German industry was less than appeared on the surface, and despite early taking of industrial assets as reparations, recovery was rapid once the Marshall Plan came into being. Even the expellees from the East were an asset as they provided extra labor—sometimes skilled. A program of industrial expansion with careful planning and investments, aided by the willingness of the population to accept relatively modest living standards and to work hard, paid dividends. There was little labor strife and for several years no need to provide for military expenditures. By 1950, industrial production surpassed prewar production. All of this made West Germany a great potential asset in the defense of western Europe. Germans refer to this era as the *Wirtschaftswunder*—economic miracle.

The possibility of West German rearmament aroused strong protests from the Soviet Union and opposition within West Germany itself from the Social Democrats. Nevertheless, in March 1954 President Heuss signed a constitutional amendment allowing German rearmament. By the end of the year, Germany and France had worked out their disagreements over the Saar, and France joined the other Western powers in agreeing to German membership in the Western alliance. On May 5, 1955, West Germany gained sovereign status and joined NATO four days later, and the division of Germany into two separate states was complete.

Great Britain

During the war, Great Britain mobilized its resources and more thoroughly and efficiently allocated manpower than the Germans. The whole population was affected. Rationing of food and other necessities created hardships that had been shared equally by rich and poor alike. There was little black market activity. During the war, the standard of living for the poor had actually risen. No reversal of this equality of sacrifice and opportunity was possible. Even before the war ended, the parties in power agreed to a program of restoring the balance of trade, directing investment of resources to ensure efficiency, and outlaying vast amounts of money for social services. As early as 1942, a report known for its author, Sir William Beveridge, proposed "full employment in a free society" and social security "from the cradle to the grave."

As the war ended in May 1945, elections were held that returned a Labour government under Clement Attlee in July. The new government enacted an extensive program increasing unemployment insurance and providing insurance for old age and various contingencies. It established a comprehensive medical and health service for the entire population, extended educational facilities, built new planned housing projects, and made efforts to rehabilitate depressed areas.

In addition, Labour nationalized the Bank of England, coal mines, transportation, iron and steel, and utilities (including electricity, gas, and communications). The Conservatives accepted much of this program but centered criticism on Labour's program of nationalizing the "commanding heights" of the economy—especially the iron and steel industry.

In order to complete this extensive series of reforms before its mandate expired in five years, Labour enacted a parliament bill that reduced the power of the House of Lords to delay legislation from three years to one year. Inheritance and income taxes were sharply increased to pay for the new measures.

Labour found its majority reduced to 7 from 148 in the 1950 elections. In view of the very slim margin of voting power, Labour passed no additional important reform legislation. Another election, in 1951, returned a Conservative majority to Parliament, and Winston Churchill became prime minister again. The new regime immediately reversed the nationalization of iron and steel. Other measures survived, however, especially the universal health care program, which proved to be one of the most popular parts of the Labour achievement. Thus, the activities of the Labour government firmly established the welfare state in Britain. In April 1955, Churchill resigned for reasons of age and health and turned over the prime minister's office to Anthony Eden.

The Marshall Plan

European recovery from the effects of the war was slow for the first two or three years after 1945. Economic difficulty made for weakness in the face of communism, which, with Russian support, had taken over in Eastern Europe and threatened to take over in western Europe as well if something was not done. In 1947, in a commencement address at Harvard University, George C. Marshall, the wartime army chief of staff who was now secretary of state under President Harry Truman, proposed an aid program for western European countries and others if they desired to join. It would revitalize the economies of the European nations and strengthen them to better resist communism. The European Recovery Program (Marshall Plan), which began the next year, showed substantial results in all the western European countries that took part. By 1950, France and Italy were well above their 1938 levels of production, although population increases of about 10 percent ate up some of the gains. In Britain, Marshall Plan aid was of considerable importance. The most remarkable gains, however, were in West Germany. By early 1949, less than a year after the currency reform in the western zones, West German production was about 85 percent of 1936 levels. The country soon experienced gains so great as to constitute what many called an "economic miracle." In western Europe during the first two years of the Marshall Plan, about $8 billion of American aid is estimated to have resulted in an overall expansion of some $30 billion annual output of goods and services.

The Movement toward West European Economic Unity

In May 1951, French Foreign Minister Robert Schuman came forward with the Schuman Plan for a European coal and steel community. This called for a pooling of resources in heavy industry and the elimination of tariffs throughout western Europe (including France, West Germany, Italy, Belgium, the Netherlands, and Luxembourg). By April 1951, the western European nations had signed a treaty incorporating the proposals of the Schuman Plan and creating the community from which other steps toward European unity grew (Common Market, General Agreement on Trade and Tariffs, and so on). The five-year period of implementation gave vested interests in each country time to adjust to new conditions.

The Cold War

The question of Poland initiated the breakdown of the wartime alliance between the United States and Britain on the one hand and the Soviet Union on the other even before the war ended. It became plain that Stalin intended to install the Communists of the Lublin Committee as a Polish government. Ultimately, all of Eastern Europe was made Communist within two or three years from the end of the war in 1945. With regard to postwar Germany, the Allies intended to institute common policies for the whole of the country and had no plan to divide it. However, seemingly irreconcilable differences between the Soviet Union and the Western democracies were present from the beginning of the occupation—differences going back to the revolution in Russia in 1917 that had embittered and complicated international relations through the 1920s and 1930s.

The Allied powers of World War II were an exception to the rule of hostility between capitalism and communism. The alliance, however, turned out to be one of expediency only. It therefore broke down when the common enemy was no longer a threat. More fundamental differences came to the fore again and made cooperation difficult if not impossible. In addition, given Stalin's fears and suspicious nature, it is little surprise that these conditions gave way to the Cold War, a period of occasional limited conflict and tension short of outright military conflict. Early in 1946, in a notable speech at Westminster College in Fulton, Missouri, Winston Churchill gave voice to the feelings of many when he announced that "from Stettin in the Baltic to Trieste in the Adriatic, an iron curtain has descended across the Continent."

Conflict in Germany

After German surrender, British and American armies withdrew from areas of Germany and Eastern Europe to within the zones of occupation agreed to in the spring of 1945. The Allies created the Allied Control Council (comprised of allied military governors) to establish common policies for Germany, but almost immediately there were difficulties with the Russians—a situation made no easier by the fact that there were additional differences between Britain, France, and the United States. In the eastern zone, the Russians made it plain they intended to communize the area in the same manner as in Eastern Europe. Early in 1946, they forced through a unification of the Social Democratic Party and the Communists in which the Socialists, although originally much stronger, lost any separate identity or ability to influence policy.

The Russians followed their own economic policy, too. Reparations were a cause of recrimination. At the wartime conferences, the Big Three had discussed but not formally agreed to charging Germany $20 billion in reparations, half of which would go to Russia. The Western powers had no intention, however, of allowing exports of supplies and equipment from their zones to proceed to a point where they would be forced to import goods just to keep their populations alive and at a minimal standard of living. Eventually the Americans and British halted any further deliveries from their zones to that of the Russians.

In their own zone, the Russians not only dismantled factories and shipped industrial equipment to the Soviet Union but also took reparations from current production, which was specifically forbidden in the Potsdam agreements. The Soviets operated their zone as a single economic entity, violating the agreement that Germany was to be treated as a single unit for purposes of trade. They failed to furnish information and statistical returns for their zone. The Western powers were moved to respond. In May 1946, General Lucius Clay, American military governor, suspended reparations deliveries to the Russian zone in retaliation for Russian intransigence on the control council. In December 1946, in a speech at Stuttgart, Secretary of State James Byrnes announced the fusion of the American and British zones into an entity called Bizonia, which the French later joined. The Western powers also raised the permitted level of German production and began to move from treating the Germans as conquered enemies to preparing them for a future role as allies of the West.

Breakdown of the Council of Foreign Ministers. Meanwhile, the Council of Foreign Ministers charged with drafting a peace treaty with Germany failed to reach agreement. The council's last meeting was held November 25 to December 15, 1947, after which it adjourned never to meet again. It had limited successes in arranging treaties with minor states but completely failed to reach any compromise that would unite Germany. Likewise, the Allied Control Council broke down. The last meeting was held in March 1948 when the Russian representative, Marshal Sokolovsky, walked out in protest over an Anglo-American invitation to the French to join their zone of Bizonia.

In the same year, Russia and its East German ally precipitated a great crisis in the form of a blockade of the western sectors of Berlin, which led to the Berlin airlift. Russian action was prompted by a currency reform in the western zones, but more broadly was aimed at forcing the Western powers to desist from their plan to establish a federal government that would eventually become independent.

The Containment Policy

There were other areas of Western-Soviet disagreement. Iran, which had been occupied during the war to provide a route for transport of Lend-Lease supplies to Russia, was to be evacuated after the end of hostilities. From 1945 until 1947, Russian forces remained in the northern part of the country and gave aid to a separatist movement seeking independence from the rest of Iran. Russia also put pressure on Turkey for control of the vital straits from the Black Sea to the Mediterranean—an area long contested by the great powers. In the Far East, the Soviets, although prevented by the American occupation from playing any important role in postwar Japan, did create a Communist regime in North Korea. They had occupied the northern part of the Korean peninsula in the days preceding the Japanese surrender, and they later resisted efforts by the UNO to reunite the area with South Korea. In addition, the activities of the Chinese Communists (behind which the United States tended to see the machinations of the Soviet Union) and the outbreak of civil war with the Nationalist government under Chiang Kai-shek, did nothing to improve relations.

By 1947, the American government adopted a policy of "containment" to deal with this problem of Soviet Communist expansion. The Truman administration was strongly influenced by the reports of diplomat George Kennan, whose position as counselor at the embassy in Moscow gave him a chance to express his opinion of Russian intentions and how to deal with them. Kennan also wrote in 1947, under the pseudonym of "X," a widely read article entitled "The Sources of Soviet Conduct," published in the influential journal *Foreign Affairs*, in which he suggested a patient but firm, long-term policy of resisting Soviet expansionism. When General George C. Marshall was made secretary of state by President Truman in 1947, he established a Policy-Planning Staff in the State Department and made Kennan the first head.

The Truman Doctrine and Aid to Greece. The Truman administration and its successors translated containment into a policy of military alliances, foreign aid, and American bases abroad to ring and contain the Soviet Union militarily, as well as a policy of resisting Communist-inspired wars of "liberation" in unstable areas of the world. The new policy was applied in Greece. In February 1947, the British government made known to Washington that it could no longer give aid to Turkey or to the royalist government installed in Greece by Britain in 1944 to 1945. The Greek government was experiencing attacks from Communist-led guerillas. On March 12, President Truman spoke to Congress. His message was a clear warning to the Soviet Union: the United States, he announced, "would support free peoples who are resisting subjugation by armed minorities or by outside pressure." The president asked for $400 million to aid Turkey and Greece. Congress complied, and the aid thus proved effective in Greece.

The Chinese Civil War and the Establishment of the People's Republic of China. During World War II, the United States followed a policy of trying to bring about cooperation in the war against the Japanese between the Nationalist Government of Chiang Kai-shek and the Communists under Mao Zedong. The war ended with the Nationalist government recognized as the legitimate government, but the Communists had a strong position in north China and a military force that had proved effective behind enemy lines and was therefore in a good position to compete with the government forces for control of former Japanese-occupied territory. With American help, the Nationalists succeeded in garrisoning the cities of Manchuria and other occupied areas, but the Communists controlled much of the surrounding territory. They were able to get additional weapons and supplies from the surrendering Japanese.

The uneasy truce that prevailed during the war almost immediately broke down. The Truman administration sent a diplomatic mission under Marshall to mediate the conflict. Marshall was able to arrange a temporary truce, but even his considerable skill as a mediator proved inadequate to keep the truce from breaking down again into full-scale civil war.

Aid to the Nationalists: The Wedemeyer Mission. Despite the shortcomings of Chiang Kai-shek's regime, and in the atmosphere of the Cold War, the United States believed that it had to aid the Nationalists to prevent a Communist takeover. A mission was sent under General Albert Wedemeyer, supplies and equipment were provided, and loans made to support the Chinese currency and alleviate inflation. All this was to no avail as the Communist forces defeated the Nationalist armies in a series of battles and eventually drove them from the mainland to the island of Taiwan (Formosa). In October 1949, even before the campaign was finally completed, the Communists established the Chinese People's Republic with the capital once again at Peking (Beijing). The Chinese Communist victory was seen at the time by the American government and by many others in the West as a disaster in the Cold War and a defeat for containment.

The Korean War

In 1945, the Soviet Union declared war on Japan after the dropping of the atomic bomb. During that brief period, Russian armies invaded Manchuria and occupied the northern part of Korea to approximately the thirty-eighth parallel (latitude 38° north). American forces occupied the southern part of Korea at the same time they occupied Japan itself. The Soviets and the Americans agreed to divide Korea for administrative purposes along the thirty-eighth parallel, and Korea was split into two states: a Communist People's Republic of Korea in the North and a UN-backed Republic of South Korea below the thirty-eighth parallel. Efforts to unify the country through elections failed. South Korea was allowed to have only a small army equipped with no heavy weapons because of fears that President Syngman Rhee might use such an army to attack the North in his own effort to unify the country. The North Koreans, however, did create an army, which was supplied with some heavy weapons, such as tanks, by the Russians. By early 1950, it appeared that the United States, which had withdrawn all its forces to Japan, would not defend South Korea, and the Russians encouraged the North Koreans to launch an invasion and make all Korea Communist.

NSC-68

In the United States, the Truman administration had been conducting a general review of the situation created by the Cold War in Europe and elsewhere. The conclusions reached were stated in a secret National Security Council study called *NSC-68*, which was completed in April 1950. The thesis was that the Soviet Union was an aggressor bent on overrunning Europe and Asia. To counter this, the United States should proceed to develop a thermonuclear (hydrogen) bomb. It should also obtain bases from which the bomb could be delivered against the Soviet Union. United States troops, the document said, should reinforce NATO. Despite obvious reluctance on the part of Europeans who had suffered from German depredations during the war, West Germany should be rearmed. The report further proposed a considerable buildup of American armed forces along with corresponding increases in the military budget. The sudden beginning of the Korean War in June 1950 only confirmed the need for a military program that otherwise might have been difficult to sell to Congress. The United States had already in 1947 created a separate air force and unified the three branches of the armed services under an overall Department of Defense. Congress also authorized the creation of the Central Intelligence Agency (CIA), which began to function in the Cold War as not only a collector of intelligence but also more and more as a clandestine arm of the government: carrying out secret, often illegal, operations abroad justified as being necessary to combat the clandestine operations of the Soviet Union and its satellites.

The North Korean Invasion

In June 1950, as the North Korean invasion of South Korea got underway, the United States decided on a policy of intervention. Taking advantage of a temporary absence of the Russian delegates, the United States was able to propose intervention and to get UN support. Before the war was over, seventeen Western or Western-oriented countries had sent contingents to Korea. South Korean and U.S. forces sent from Japan supplied most of the UN army. General Douglas MacArthur, commander of occupation forces in Japan, was made overall UN commander. After initial defeats and withdrawals, MacArthur carried out an amphibious landing at Inchon near the South Korean capital of Seoul. This force and the main Eighth Army driving north managed to surround and in a few weeks virtually destroy the invading army.

The Decision to Cross the Thirty-Eighth Parallel

By early fall of 1950, the UN forces were back to the thirty-eighth parallel and the question arose whether to stop there or continue north and reunify the whole of Korea. Despite warnings against this from the Chinese Communists sent through India, the leaders of the UN forces made the decision to continue north. Some forces had actually reached the Manchurian border when in November the Chinese Communists entered the battle, creating what MacArthur called a new war. Initially surprised by the Chinese attack, the UN forces were driven back below the thirty-eighth parallel again. The commander of the Eighth Army, General Walton Walker, was killed at this time, but under a new commander, General Matthew Ridgway, the army recovered, recaptured Seoul, and reached a line approximately at the thirty-eighth parallel once again.

During this period of Chinese intervention, the Truman administration had been increasingly in conflict with General MacArthur over what should be U.S. policy. Washington feared that widening the war to China proper might cause intervention by the Russians. In April 1951, after repeated warnings, President Truman relieved MacArthur of his command.

Instead of expanding the war, the two sides began long and difficult negotiations for an armistice. Eventually, in July 1953, North Korea signed an agreement with South Korea and her allies that still remains in force. No formal peace treaty was ever made, and the Korean War concluded with the situation essentially as it was before the North Korean invasion began. The Korean War prevented the United States from recognizing or establishing formal relations with the Chinese Communist regime (as Great Britain and other European nations had quickly done) until the time of the Nixon administration in the early 1970s.

Strengthening of NATO

One result of the Korean War was the strengthening of the NATO alliance begun in 1949. A mood approaching panic set in after the North Korean invasion began. The

United States expressed its fear that NATO would be too weak to resist a possible Russian attack that might come while American forces were engaged in the Far East. The United States insisted on a policy of rearming West Germany. Eventually, western European nations accepted West German rearmament but only after agreement to make German forces part of a European defense under NATO control. This policy of military buildup changed the emphasis of foreign aid under the Marshall Plan. In the first two years, the aid was primarily economic with few strings attached. Later, it became increasingly military aid.

Loss of European Overseas Empires

World War II created disruptions for the European powers that resulted in irresistible pressures for independence from their colonies overseas. Belgian, British, Dutch, French, and Portuguese empires in Asia and Africa virtually disappeared in the space of about fifteen years following the war. In some instances, withdrawal was accomplished by a relatively peaceful transfer of power (as with the final British withdrawal from India in 1947), but in other cases the colonial power resisted separation and long, bitter military conflicts resulted. In every case, independence created internal problems with which new governments had to struggle, often with violence ensuing and often with foreign intervention.

British Overseas Withdrawal

Palestine, Israel, and the Arab-Israeli Conflict

Britain received a mandate from the League of Nations following World War I to govern Palestine. Britain had earlier indicated in the Balfour Declaration of November 2, 1917, that it favored the creation of a Jewish "national home" in Palestine. The British position there was complicated by their involvement in the creation of Arab states such as Saudi Arabia and Transjordan, which were adamantly opposed to any Jewish state in Palestine. Violent clashes of Jews and Arabs occurred there between the world wars.

Creation of Israel. Following World War II, a considerable number of the Jews who had survived the Nazi Holocaust migrated to Palestine to join Jews who had settled there earlier. Conflicts broke out with the Arabs. British occupying forces tried to suppress the violence and to negotiate a settlement between the factions. In 1948, after negotiations failed to achieve agreement, the British, feeling they could no longer support the cost of occupation, announced their withdrawal. Zionist leaders then proclaimed the independent state of Israel and took up arms to fight the armies of Egypt, Syria, and other Arab states that had invaded the Jewish-held area. The new Israeli state quickly proved its technological and military superiority by defeating the invaders. Over five hundred thousand Arabs were displaced from their homes in establishing Israel. Efforts to permanently relocate them failed, and they became a factor in the continued violence in the Middle East.

The Jews of Israel created a parliamentary state on the European model with an economy and technology superior to that of their Arab neighbors. The new state was thought by many Arabs to be simply another manifestation of European imperialism made worse by religious antagonisms.

Other Arab-Israeli Wars. Several other Arab-Israeli wars have served to keep the Middle East in turmoil. In 1956, the Israelis chose the opportunity created by the ill-fated Anglo-French attempt to retake the Suez Canal (discussed later in the chapter) to launch their own attack on Egypt. Public opinion eventually forced the withdrawal of the British and French, and although the Israelis had achieved military successes, they found themselves barred from use of the canal by Egypt, which was now in control.

The Palestine Liberation Organization. Although defeated in the Six-Day War of 1967, the Arabs refused to sign any treaty or to come to terms with Israel. Palestinian refugees living in camps in states bordering Israel created grave problems. The Palestine Liberation Organization (PLO) formed to fight for the establishment of an Arab Palestinian state on territory taken from Israel on the west bank of the Jordan River. The PLO resorted to terrorist tactics both against Israel and other states in support of their cause.

The Egyptian Revolution. The British exercised control over Egypt from the end of the nineteenth century and declared it a British protectorate in December 1914. In 1922, Egypt became nominally independent, and in 1936 an Anglo-Egyptian treaty provided for British forces to withdraw to the Suez Canal zone, where they might keep ten thousand troops. Britain could expand the force in time of war. During World War II, the presence of British forces in Egypt, which was the British headquarters in the Middle East, resulted in fighting on Egyptian territory despite efforts by Egypt to remain neutral.

The government under King Farouk did little to alleviate the overriding problem of poverty after the war. In 1952, a group of army officers, including Gamal Abdel Nasser and Anwar Sadat, plotted against the government, and on July 23, overthrew the king. For a short time, the plotters ruled through a figurehead—General Muhammad Naguib; the Revolutionary Command Council held the real power. Colonel Nasser, the outstanding figure of the group, replaced Naguib as premier in April 1954. A treaty with Britain later that year resulted in the withdrawal of all British troops from the canal zone.

The Suez Canal Crisis. Nasser made several agreements in 1955 and 1956 with Communist-bloc nations, establishing trade relations and obtaining weapons. The United States and Britain then withdrew offers of aid in building the Aswan Dam on the Nile River. Nasser in turn nationalized the Suez Canal shortly after the British garrison there had been withdrawn. A crisis ensued when Israeli forces suddenly invaded Egypt. Britain and France, ignoring UN attempts to mediate, gave an ultimatum to Israel and Egypt to cease fighting and withdraw from the canal zone. When this failed, the two powers began a bombardment and invaded the area. Pressure from both the United States and the Soviet Union caused Britain, and then France and Israel to cease fire. A UN force was then formed to police the canal zone and the ceasefire. Eventually, foreign forces withdrew from Egypt, except that the Israelis remained in possession of the Gaza Strip.

India and Pakistan

British rule in India, the largest and most populous of the colonial areas ruled by Europeans, came to an end in 1947 with a transfer of power. Pressure for self-government had grown in the 1930s, and the British had granted a constitution, a legislature, trained an Indian civil service, and made other concessions to Indian nationalism. During World

War II, Britain promised dominion status to India after the war. This did not satisfy the Indian Congress Party, whose leaders wanted full and immediate independence. Complications ensued when Muslim leaders, representing some one hundred million Muslims, did not want to live in a state dominated by Hindus and the Congress Party and insisted on a state of their own.

Partition. The British decided to partition the subcontinent into two separate dominions, which quickly became independent republics: India, predominantly Hindu with a population of 350 million; and Pakistan, predominantly Muslim with a population of 75 million. About 40 million Muslims remained within Indian borders. Independence resulted in bloody rioting between the religious factions, mass expulsions, and the emigration of millions of people. Perhaps a million people lost their lives before the rioting eventually died out. The territory of Kashmir remained in dispute but finally was joined to India in 1975.

Malaya, Burma, and Ceylon

Malaya, Burma, and Ceylon were other parts of the British Empire in Asia that received their independence as did India and Pakistan. All three became members of the British Commonwealth with ties to Great Britain. The Commonwealth, which also includes some former British colonies in Africa, became a significant political grouping associated on an entirely voluntary basis. Malaya suffered nine years of internal strife that delayed independence to 1957, when the Federation of Malaya was created.

The French in Indochina and Algeria

Indochina

Following World War II, the French returned to Indochina and attempted to restore their rule there. The opposition nationalist movement was led by the veteran Communist Ho Chi Minh. War broke out between the nationalists and the French forces. Despite material aid from the United States, the French were unable to maintain their position in the north of Vietnam. In 1954, their army was surrounded at Dienbienphu and forced to surrender. This military disaster prompted a change of government in France.

The 1954 Geneva Conference: French Withdrawal. This new government under Premier Pierre Mendes-France negotiated French withdrawal at a conference held at Geneva, Switzerland in 1954. Cambodia and Laos became independent and Vietnam was partitioned at the seventeenth parallel. The North, with its capital at Hanoi, became a Communist state under Ho Chi Minh. The South remained non-Communist. Under the Geneva Accords, elections were to be held in the South to determine the fate of that area. However, the United States chose to intervene and support the regime of Ngo Dinh Diem, and elections were never held. Eventually, a second Vietnamese war resulted with the United States in the role formerly played by France.

Algeria

Following World War II, nationalist agitation escalated in Algeria, Tunisia, and Morocco. The French government granted independence to Tunisia and Morocco, but it considered Algeria to be different. Algeria was legally part of metropolitan France. The government there was heavily weighted in favor of the French minority (about 10 percent of the total population), and the Arab majority had few rights. In 1954, a large-scale revolt of Arab nationalists broke out. The French government began a campaign of suppression lasting more than seven years and involving as many as five hundred thousand troops. Military casualties totaled at least one hundred thousand Arabs and ten thousand French killed with thousands more civilian casualties. The savage campaign led to torture and other atrocities on both sides.

Army Revolt and Return of General de Gaulle. Egypt and other Arab states gave aid to the Algerian Liberation Front. Algerian terrorists spread the violence as far as Paris. The government of the Fourth Republic faced a military and financial burden with no clear end in sight. French army officers in Algeria and European settlers there were adamant against any concessions, and eventually, under the leadership of General Jacques Massu (in Algeria) and General Raoul Salan (army chief of staff), the army created a committee of public safety and seized control of the government. The rebellion threatened to spread to France itself. It led to the downfall of the Fourth Republic and the return to power of General de Gaulle, who established the Fifth Republic with himself as a strong president.

Algerian Independence. De Gaulle moved step by step toward a policy first of autonomy and then independence for Algeria. In a referendum, on January 8, 1961, the French people approved of eventual Algerian self-determination. The army leaders then rebelled, forming a terrorist secret army (the Organisation armée secrete, or OAS) to oppose de Gaulle's policy with bombings and assassinations. De Gaulle prevailed in the struggle, and in July 1962, French rule ended in Algeria. General Salan (OAS leader) was arrested, tried, and sentenced to life imprisonment. There was a mass exodus of Europeans from Algeria, but most Frenchmen were grateful to de Gaulle for ending the long Algerian conflict.

The Dutch and Indonesia

During World War II, the Japanese conquered the Dutch East Indies. At the end of the war, they recognized the independence of the area as Indonesia. When the Dutch attempted to return, four years of bloody fighting ensued against the nationalist forces of Achmed Sukarno. In 1949, the Dutch recognized Indonesian independence but with some ties still with the Netherlands. In 1954, the Indonesians dissolved all ties. Sukarno's regime became one of increasing dictatorship thinly disguised by terms like "guided democracy."

The Cold War After the Death of Stalin

Following Stalin's death, Russian leaders—while maintaining an atmosphere first of tension and then of relaxation in international affairs—appeared more willing than Stalin to be conciliatory and to consider peaceful coexistence among the major competing economic and political systems.

Eisenhower and the 1955 Geneva Summit

In the United States, the atmosphere also changed with the election of President Dwight Eisenhower, and despite the belligerent rhetoric of Secretary of State John Foster Dulles, the administration did not always automatically consider conciliatory gestures as appeasement of the Communists. In 1955, a summit conference of Eisenhower, the British and French leaders, and Soviet premier Nikita Khrushchev met at Geneva in an atmosphere more cordial than any since World War II. The "spirit of Geneva" did not last long, however.

The U-2 Incident and Breakup of the Paris Conference (1960)

The U.S.'s CIA developed a high-flying reconnaissance aircraft known as the U-2. Under Eisenhower, the agency used the U-2 to make secret flights over the Soviet Union in order to take aerial photographs. At first, the Russians were unable to shoot the airplane down, but in 1960 they succeeded, shooting it down well inside the Soviet Union and capturing the plane's pilot, Francis Gary Powers. The Eisenhower administration initially denied Russian charges of spying, but when Khrushchev produced the pilot and remains of the aircraft, they admitted what had happened and accepted responsibility. A summit conference was due to convene shortly in Paris, and an indignant Khrushchev used the occasion to condemn Eisenhower and then break up the meeting.

Kennedy and Khrushchev: The Bay of Pigs Incident

John Kennedy replaced Eisenhower as president of the United States in 1960. He proved to be a hard-liner in relations with the Soviet Union and a strong opponent of communism. He inherited the American dispute with Cuban leader Fidel Castro, who had ousted the U.S.-backed, right-wing dictator Fulgencio Batista in January 1959. Castro had dealt with the problem of dependency on the United States by nationalizing many economic assets—sugar mills, oil refineries, banks—that were American owned. The United States had retaliated with economic sanctions, and Castro reacted by establishing ties with the Soviet Union, which agreed to buy Cuban sugar and provide goods denied by the United States. Before he left office, Eisenhower and the CIA had prepared a plan to overthrow Castro using Cuban exiles as an invasion force. Kennedy carried out this plan, which resulted in a fiasco at the Bay of Pigs. The Cubans landed, the population did not rise to join them, and the small force was quickly overwhelmed.

Khrushchev and Berlin

After the Berlin Blockade of 1948 to 1949, Berlin became a symbol of freedom—an oasis of Western influence in the heart of East Germany. Thinking it best to keep Germany divided, Khrushchev tried to exert pressure on the Western powers through Berlin to recognize permanent division of Germany into two states. Late in 1958, he threatened to make unilateral changes in the status of Berlin, but backed down in 1959. In June 1961, following the U-2 incident and breakup of the Paris summit, Khrushchev presented an ultimatum to President Kennedy, threatening to sign a peace treaty with East Germany and then give the new state control over access to Berlin. Shortly after, the Soviets closed the East German border and built a wall through Berlin separating the Russian and Western sectors and preventing any unauthorized travel or communication between them. Despite pressure to take a strong stand, Kennedy simply moved an additional fifteen hundred American troops to Berlin while accepting the wall rather than risk war.

The Cuban Missile Crisis

In an attempt to protect the Castro regime and to project its power to the borders of the United States, Khrushchev initiated a policy of installing Russian missiles in Cuba. Aerial reconnaissance revealed this to the American government in October 1962. A thirteen-day crisis followed. President Kennedy established a "quarantine" of Cuba using the American navy. (The administration used the term "quarantine" because a blockade is an act of war under traditional international law.) Eventually, Russian ships, carrying the missiles and nuclear warheads to complete the installation, turned back rather than risk possible war. Khrushchev did obtain an American pledge not to invade Cuba and a commitment to remove American missiles from Turkey, but he had been publicly humiliated. For this and because of the failure of his domestic agricultural development program, his colleagues forced him to retire in 1964.

The Vietnam War

Before 1954, the conflict in Vietnam involved French armies against the Communist-led nationalist movement. By the 1954 Geneva Accords, France withdrew its forces, Vietnam was divided at the seventeenth parallel, the Communists under Ho Chi Minh held the North, and the South became the Republic of Vietnam with an anti-Communist regime. Elections to unite the country were never held. Instead, the United States began to play an ever larger role in South Vietnam, believing that if South Vietnam fell, all Southeast Asia would fall like a row of dominos. First Eisenhower, then Kennedy, then Lyndon Johnson believed this and reacted accordingly, and U.S. role increased; after 1964, the United States was engaged in a full-scale second Vietnam War with the hope of establishing an anti-Communist regime that could "win the hearts and minds of the people" and provide an effective barrier to further Communist expansion. China and the Soviet Union were involved in supporting North Vietnam and the liberation movement mainly by sending supplies and equipment of various kinds. Most NATO countries gave only lukewarm, if any, support to the American war in Vietnam. Eventually, public opinion at home brought an end to the United States's most unpopular war, and western Europe could breath more easily.

The Changing Balance of Power

De Gaulle as the Leader of an Independent Europe

After his return to power in France in 1958, General de Gaulle endeavored to make France a leader in European affairs with himself as spokesman for a Europe that he hoped would be a counter to the "dual hegemony" of the United States and the Soviet Union. His policies at times were anti-British or anti-American. He vetoed British entry into the Common Market, developed an independent French nuclear force, and tried to bridge the gap between East and West Europe. Despite his prestige as the last great wartime leader, he did not have great success. Nevertheless, western Europe came into its own as a factor in international affairs.

Détente

The policy of rapprochement interrupted by the Cuban Missile Crisis resumed. Despite the continuing war in Vietnam, Soviet and American leaders exchanged visits. From 1969 on, under President Richard Nixon and National Security Adviser Henry Kissinger, the policy of better relations became known as détente. The first Strategic Arms Limitation Talks (SALT I) resulted in a treaty signed during President Nixon's 1972 visit to Moscow. In this spirit of détente, trade between western Europe and the Soviet Union increased several times. The Soviet Union, faced with agricultural problems, began to purchase large amounts of American grain. In 1975, meetings in Helsinki, Finland, yielded agreements of peaceful cooperation among thirty-five nations. All agreed to accept boundaries in Europe established following World War II, including the Oder-Neisse line between the German Democratic Republic and Poland.

Nuclear Weapons and the Arms Race

Nuclear weapons—whose enormous destructive power had been first revealed when the United States dropped atomic bombs on Hiroshima and Nagasaki in 1945—were a growing concern. Initial debates on control of nuclear weapons were held in the UN when the United States had a monopoly on the atomic bomb. The Soviet Union finally insisted by 1948 that the banning of atomic weapons was of primary importance. The Security Council of the UN could not reach agreement on inspection procedures, however.

Soon the Russians would explode their first atomic bomb. During 1949 and 1950, wars were raging in Korea, Malaya, and Indochina, and rearmament was the dominant policy, with both the United States and the Soviet Union starting programs to develop more effective nuclear weapons. These included the hydrogen bomb, whose awesome power had to be measured in terms of megatons of conventional explosive.

The war in Korea and the rearmament of West Germany within NATO prevented any serious disarmament negotiations. Europe was divided into separate armed camps: NATO and the Warsaw Pact, led by the Soviet Union. In the next several years, the world moved into the age of high-tech military material. Russia tested its first bomb in 1949. By 1952, the British had tested an atomic bomb. The United States successfully developed and tested a thermonuclear weapon (the hydrogen bomb) in 1952. In 1953, the Russians exploded a similar weapon. In 1961, the Soviet Union exploded a sixty-megaton hydrogen bomb. The French joined the nuclear powers in 1960. They tested a hydrogen bomb in 1968. China also became a nuclear power, exploding its first nuclear device in 1964. By 1998, both India and Pakistan had conducted atomic-bomb tests, and Israel reportedly possessed sufficient raw material for its own nuclear weapons. In the fall of 2006 the United Nations protested underground North Korean tests of a nuclear bomb and the intent of Iran to go ahead with nuclear power.

An international trade in weapons and military supplies flourished in the 1960s and beyond, with the United States and the Soviet Union as the chief suppliers. Between 1960 and 1975, the world's annual military expenditures nearly doubled. The United States and the Soviet Union accounted for about 60 percent of those expenditures. Before World War II, military expenditures are estimated to have been less than 1 percent of the total world gross national product. In 1983, the figure had risen to 6 percent.

Agreements on Nuclear Weapons

The radiation and fallout from the various testing programs created a fear that the atmosphere would be poisoned, damage of a genetic nature might be done to plants and animals, and unborn generations of humans might be endangered in ways that were only just beginning to be understood. These concerns prompted the United States, Britain, and the Soviet Union to sign, in April 1963, a treaty to ban nuclear testing in the atmosphere, under water, and in outer space. France and China did not join and instead went on to develop weapons of their own. The proliferation of nuclear weapons prompted the United States and the Soviet Union also to sign a nonproliferation treaty to which sixty-two nations subscribed. Among the exceptions were France, China, and West Germany. Following the Cuban Missile Crisis, a direct communications link between Washington and Moscow called the "hot line" was established in order to avoid misunderstandings that might trigger nuclear war. In 1976, in a period of relatively relaxed relations, the two superpowers agreed to limit underground testing to explosions no more than eight times the power of the Hiroshima bomb (the equivalent of twenty thousand tons of conventional explosives). Finally, for the first time, in the late 1980s the Soviet Union and the United States agreed to limited on-site inspection by outsiders of their tests as well as monitoring of the agreements.

The Space Race and Its Implications

During World War II, the Germans took the first step toward space exploration when they developed the V-2 rocket. Both the United States and the Soviet Union recruited German rocket experts, from physicists who went into exile during the war or chose to leave afterwards, to advance their own space-exploration goals, thus intensifying the competition to reach space. The Soviet Union excelled early, launching the first unmanned satellite in 1957. Later, the Soviets put the first manned spacecraft into orbit. The United States landed the first manned spacecraft on the moon in 1969, making good on a commitment President Kennedy had set in 1961 for the nation to do so "before this decade is out."

After 1960, both nations deployed many experimental space stations, unmanned probes of the planets, and satellites for communication and military purposes. The two nations achieved some level of cooperation when U.S. and Soviet astronauts orbited simultaneously and brought their ships together in outer space in 1992. Some critics complained of the enormous cost of these activities and of the neglect of problems here on Earth, but others saw future benefits for all resulting. Both Russian and U.S. astronauts worked in the Russian space station *Mir*, but the age of the project and funding difficulties led to its abandonment in 1999. Both nations agreed to cooperate with the new international space station, and construction of a laboratory for the space station began in early 2001.

Advancements in space exploration, rocketry, and related sciences led to the development of such weapons as intercontinental ballistic missiles, which could carry nuclear warheads across the continents in a matter of minutes. Neither nation was able to develop an antimissile defense system; instead, each relied on a policy of deterrence. This policy was founded in the theory known as MAD, or mutually assured destruction: if one side knew that its enemy had a missile force capable of surviving any initial attack and returning the attack against the original aggressor, then neither side would start a nuclear war because of the certainty that they, too, would be destroyed.

The Reagan Strategic Defense Initiative

To date, no sure defense against nuclear attack exists. Extensive civil defense programs designed to protect the populace in the event of nuclear attack are reported to exist in the former Soviet Union, Switzerland, and China. Unfortunately, it is doubtful that these would prove effective. Evacuation of civilians from cities that would be targets takes time—more time than would be available.

The alternative would be to use missiles to destroy incoming missiles. The United States had a program of this sort in the 1950s and 1960s but gave it up in the SALT I agreements, which also contained the Anti-Ballistic Missile Treaty limiting the use of such missiles. Thus, the United States did not devise a sufficient system to combat the possibilities of missile attacks.

The idea of a ballistic missile defense system surfaced again in the United States during the presidency of Ronald Reagan. This "Strategic Defense Initiative" (officially shortened to SDI, but quickly known among its detractors as "Star Wars," after the popular science-fiction movie) would rely on platforms in outer space from which particle beams, lasers, and other advanced devices would destroy incoming missiles. Wide disagreement in the United States over the logistics of such a system prevented its development. Reaction to SDI in the Soviet Union was predictably negative, and many in the West felt it would simply lead the Soviets to escalate the arms race once again and invest heavily in weapons to defeat the system.

Change and the Collapse of Communism

Russia after Stalin

Stalin died in March 1953. His career had been one of undoubted achievements, but at tremendous cost. Stalin established a dictatorship unparalleled in history. His ruthlessness and paranoid suspicions grew worse toward the end of his life. Postwar economic reconstruction was accompanied by ideological intolerance and a regime of terror and persecution accompanied by overtones of anti-Semitism. There were indications of a new series of purges coming when Stalin died.

A so-called troika consisting of Georgi Malenkov (chairman of the Council of Ministers), Lavrenti Beria (Stalin's chief of police), and Vyacheslav Molotov (foreign minister) took over the government. A power struggle took place in which the first event was the secret trial and execution of Beria. Eventually, a little-known party functionary, Nikita

Khrushchev, became Communist Party general secretary in 1954. Malenkov and Molotov were demoted to lesser positions and eventually disappeared from public view.

Khrushchev's Secret Speech and the Anti-Stalin Campaign

Khrushchev in 1956 delivered a "secret speech" to the Twentieth Congress of the Communist Party of the Soviet Union. It soon became public knowledge that he had accused Stalin of wholesale "violations of socialist legality" and of creating a "cult of personality." This signified the victory of Khrushchev's policy of relaxing the regime of terror and oppression of the Stalin years. The period became known as "The Thaw," after the title of a novel by Ilya Ehrenburg.

Change occurred in foreign affairs also. Khrushchev visited Belgrade and reestablished relations with Tito, admitting that there was more than one road to socialism. He also visited the United States, met with President Eisenhower, and toured the country. Later, relations became more tense after the U-2 spy plane incident. Khrushchev's policy generally was one where a period of relaxation would be followed by a period of pressure, threats, and tension.

Following the loss of face sustained by Russia as a result of the Cuban Missile Crisis and the failure of Khrushchev's domestic agricultural polices, he was forced out of the party leadership and lived in retirement in Moscow until his death in 1971.

Khrushchev's Successors: Brezhnev, Andropov, and Gorbachev

After Khrushchev's ouster, the leadership in the Central Committee divided power, making Leonid Brezhnev party secretary and Aleksei Kosygin chairman of the Council of Ministers, or premier. Brezhnev's party position ensured his dominance by the 1970s. In 1977, he presided over the adoption of a new constitution that altered the structure of the regime very little. The same year, he was elected president by the Supreme Soviet.

Stalin's successors rehabilitated many of Stalin's victims. They also permitted somewhat greater freedom in literary and artistic matters and even allowed some political criticism. They maintained, and sometimes tightened, controls, however. Anti-Semitism was still present, and Soviet Jews were long denied permission to immigrate to Israel. American pressure may have helped to relax this policy in the 1970s when about 150,000 Jews were allowed to leave Russia. Other evidences of continued tight control were the 1974 arrest for treason and forcible deportation of the writer Alexander Solzhenitsyn and the arrest and internal exile for many years of the physicist Andrei Sakharov, who was an outspoken critic of the regime and its violations of human rights.

Brezhnev occupied the top position of power until his death in 1982. He was succeeded briefly by Yuri Andropov (a former secret police chief) and then by Mikhail Gorbachev, who carried out a further relaxation of the internal regime. Gorbachev pushed disarmament and détente in foreign relations, and attempted a wide range of internal reforms known as perestroika (meaning "restructuring").

Diminishing Soviet Influence

Despite the political limits imposed by the Soviet Union on its Eastern European satellites, economic developments took place during the 1970s and 1980s that eventually led to further liberalization and change in Eastern European countries. The Soviet Union, short of capital for development, could not supply the needs of Eastern European states, and these began to turn to western banks. With increasing economic ties and more East-West trade, the political situation changed. The Czechs voiced criticism of Soviet missiles on their territory. The Bulgarian government called for making East Europe a nuclear-free zone. In Romania, too, change occurred when the government insisted with some success on greater independence in foreign affairs. The Romanians also resisted Soviet pressure for closer economic ties and greater dependence on the Soviet Union.

Reforms Lead to Change in the Soviet Union

By 1985, when Mikhail Gorbachev became leader of the Soviet Union, the country faced severe economic difficulties. Pollution of rivers, increasing incidence of health problems, a rise in infant mortality in several regions, a decline in industrial production, over-centralization of planning and control, poor worker morale, and the burden of the arms race—all led to pressure for political and economic change. Confidence in central planning and leadership was further undermined and considerable fear generated throughout Europe and around the world by the meltdown disaster at the atomic power plant at Chernobyl (near Kiev) in 1986.

Gorbachev introduced reforms that had widespread and often unanticipated consequences. The government allowed some freedom for private enterprise and began decentralizing control over industry and agriculture. It relaxed its censorship of the media and even held press conferences. Gorbachev sought favor with the cultural and scientific elite by bringing back Andrei Sakharov, the noted physicist and dissident, from internal exile. The government also allowed the hitherto proscribed works of Alexander Solzhenitsyn to be openly published. In the area of foreign affairs, the United States and the Soviet Union reached a new agreement on intermediate-range ballistic missiles in 1987.

The most radical of Gorbachev's reforms was to separate the Communist Party from the Soviet government. Between 1988 and 1991, a multiparty democracy with a parliament was introduced, and the Communist Party's monopoly of political life ended. Interest groups became free to organize as political parties, support candidates for office, and solicit votes. A new constitution was adopted in 1988. The new Parliament, consisting of a Congress of People's Deputies and a Supreme Soviet, was elected and took office in 1989. In 1990, Gorbachev was elected president.

An unexpected result of Gorbachev's policies of perestroika and glasnost (meaning "openness") was the revival of separatist movements in Eastern Europe and within the multinational Soviet Union itself. Both Lithuania and Georgia voted for independence from the Soviet Union.

The Revolution of 1991 and the Post-Soviet Republics

In 1991, conservatives and hard-liners attempted a coup d'état against Gorbachev. The revolt was overcome thanks to the determined stand taken by Boris Yeltsin, who headed popular resistance. Although Gorbachev remained in office for a few months more, the real power passed to Yeltsin, and in December—with the dissolution of the Soviet Union—Gorbachev resigned and Yeltsin took his place.

The old Soviet Union broke apart once the controls were removed. The Baltic provinces (Estonia, Latvia, and Lithuania) opted for independence, as did Ukraine and other provinces of the union dominated for so long by the huge Russian republic. A loose confederation known as the Commonwealth of Independent States emerged containing eleven of the former Soviet republics. Four—Estonia, Georgia, Latvia, and Lithuania—refused to join.

Economic difficulties associated with the transition to a free economy, the mishandled repression of the Chechnya independence movement, and the forceful dispersal of Yeltsin's parliamentary opponents in 1993 gave ammunition to Yeltsin's opponents. In the 1996 elections, Yeltsin retained office as president despite reports of poor health. Following reelection, Yeltsin underwent successful heart surgery, but his health problems and continuing political difficulties made his future as Russia's leader uncertain. After his government was forced to halt all international trading of the ruble because of economic concerns, including a stock-market plunge, Yeltsin tried different politicians as his prime minister before deciding to resign, citing declining health, in December of 1999. He designated Vladimir Putin, a former official of the KGB (the Committee on State Security), as acting president. After receiving a majority of the vote in a presidential election in March 2000, Putin secured passage of legislation limiting the power of regional governmental officials in Russia. Putin's government has continued to pursue a politically popular policy of seeking a military victory in Chechnya.

Poland and the Solidarity Movement

Khrushchev's 1956 speech denouncing Stalin was followed almost immediately by revolts in Poland and Hungary, apparently encouraged by what was happening in Russia. In Poland, Wladyslaw Gomulka, previously discredited and imprisoned for "nationalist deviationism," emerged to take over the government. Khrushchev and the Russians decided to tolerate Gomulka, who had wide support. His regime proceeded to halt collectivization of agriculture and curb the use of political terror.

In the 1980s, the trade union movement known as Solidarity and its leader, Lech Walesa, emerged as political forces, organizing mass protests in 1980 to 1981 and maintaining almost continuous pressure on the Communist government headed by General Wojciech Jaruzelski. Solidarity gained power as the government of General Jaruzelski failed to master Poland's economic problems. Power passed to the Polish parliament, and in the elections held in June 1989, the first free elections held in the Communist bloc, Solidarity won an overwhelming majority. A movement began to transform the state-run economy into one based on market forces. Lech Walesa became president of Poland. By 1993 to 1994, however, economic problems resulted in a Communist majority and a change of administration, but there was no return to the old Communist dictatorship. In 1993, Poland experienced 4 percent economic growth and appeared to be making a successful transition from a centrally planned to a market economy. In 1997, Poland approved a new constitution. In elections the same year, a Solidarity-led coalition triumphed over the government of the ex-Communist Party leader Aleksander Kwasniewski, who had held the presidency since defeating Walesa in 1995. The death penalty was abolished that same year, and two years later, Pope John Paul II visited his native country. Together with Hungary and the Czech Republic, Poland joined the NATO alliance in April of 1999. Poland is expected to be the next country to be accepted into the European Union. Kwasniewski returned to power in October 2000, handily defeating Walesa in new elections.

Hungary

In Hungary in 1956, rioting against the Communist regime broke out and brought Imre Nagy to power. Nagy's policies went too far for the Russians, and Khrushchev intervened forcibly, sending in Russian troops and tanks to replace Nagy with Janos Kadar and a regime subservient to Moscow. The outbreak of the Suez Canal crisis at this time distracted the Western powers from events in Hungary. Despite the immediate political outcome in Hungary, a more flexible economic policy evolved in Eastern Europe, with many countries slowing collectivization, and a somewhat less restrictive atmosphere resulted even in Hungary. Private farm plots were now not only allowed, but encouraged, and statistics show a rise in Soviet agricultural output based primarily on the mushrooming of such private plots.

Kadar was forced out of power in 1987. By March 1990, Hungary had formed a multiparty system and had held free elections that resulted in an overwhelming repudiation of the Communists. As in Poland, the problems of the next four years led to the return of a Communist Social Democratic majority that promised to maintain economic reforms and work for greater social justice. In 1997, the Hungarian government agreed to compensate the Catholic Church for property seized during the Communist years. Elections in 1998 produced a new government based on the winning coalition of the Civic Party, the Independent Smallholders Party, and the Democratic Forum. Viktor Orban became the new prime minister. While Hungarians have worried about the fate of their countrymen who live in nearby states, Hungary has strengthened its ties with Poland and the Czech Republic. During the ethnic crisis in the 1990s that ultimately dissolved Yugoslavia, the government issued an official apology for the deaths of more than six million Jews in the Holocaust.

Czechoslovakia: Soviet Intervention and the Brezhnev Doctrine

Early in 1968, Alexander Dubcek became leader of the Czechoslovakian Communist Party and began a process of liberalization that went further than any other Eastern European country had gone at that time. Soviet leaders in Moscow grew anxious, and in May Premier Aleksei Kosygin went to Czechoslovakia and brought back a reassuring report. However, a manifesto titled *Two Thousand Words* (issued by Czech intellectuals and calling for even faster reform) and the publication of a draft of rule changes for the Czech Communist Party (allowing an unprecedented range of freedom within the party itself) apparently convinced the Russians to use military force. On August 23, they (together with Bulgaria, East Germany, Hungary, and Poland) sent in troops and established a military occupation. The occupiers reintroduced censorship and forced changes on the country designed to crush any revolutionary tendency and prevent any democratization. In April 1969, the Soviets forced Dubcek out of power and established a new regime under Gustav Husak more compliant with Soviet wishes. Nevertheless, a few changes remained, such as the federalization of the country to give equality to the Slovaks.

In the so-called Velvet Revolution, popular demonstrations in Prague in November 1989 resulted in a new government led by the playwright-dissident Václav Havel, who was confirmed in the office of president in elections held in June 1990. Bitter national rivalry caused the nation, created at the end of the First World War, to split into the Czech and Slovak republics on January 1, 1993. Since then, the Czech Republic has experienced relative prosperity, compared with high unemployment and other problems in the Slovak Republic. Since the Czech Republic became part of the NATO alliance in March of 1999, its major foreign policy goal has been to gain eventual admission into the European Union.

The Slovak Republic has experienced more difficult economic and political times. Slovakia was not considered for admission to the European Union and NATO because of the authoritarian reputation of its first prime minister, Vladimir Meciar. Public disagreements between Meciar and the republic's first president, Michael Kovac, led to a nation-wide boycott of a referendum, held in May 1997, over whether the country should join NATO. A reform slate headed by Mikulas Dzurinda replaced Meciar's government in elections in 1998, and Meciar, charged with paying illegal bonuses to cabinet members, was arrested after a long standoff with police.

Change in Western Europe

NATO and the Common Market

The military pact called the North Atlantic Treaty Organization was originally established in 1948 and strengthened during the early 1950s as a result of the Korean War. It combined armed forces of the United States, Britain, Canada, Denmark, France, Iceland, Italy, Norway, Portugal and the Benelux countries (Belgium, Luxembourg, and the Netherlands). Greece and Turkey soon joined. West Germany became a member in 1956 and Spain joined in 1982. Currently, nineteen countries are members in NATO. It has mainly been an alliance to contain communism and to protect western Europe from any threat of Russian attack or subversion.

In addition to NATO, institutions to promote economic unity have been established in the last three decades. Six members (France, Italy, West Germany, and the Benelux countries) formed the European Steel and Coal Community in 1951. Economic collaboration progressed favorably; in March 1957, inspired chiefly by Belgian foreign minister Paul Henri Spaak, the community members signed two treaties in Rome creating the European Atomic Energy Commission (Euratom) and the European Economic Community (EEC, or the Common Market)—which eventually absorbed Euratom. The EEC was to be a customs union creating a free-market area with a common external tariff with other nations. Toward the outside world, the EEC acted as a single bargaining agent for its members in commercial transactions, and it reached a number of agreements with other European and third-world states.

In 1973, the original six were joined by three new members—Britain, Denmark, and Ireland—and the name was changed to the European Community (EC). In 1979, three more countries—Greece, Portugal, and Spain—applied. These latter states were less well off and created problems of cheap labor, agricultural products, and so forth, which delayed their induction as members. Greece was admitted in 1981, while Portugal and Spain waited until 1986. In 1995, Austria, Finland, and Sweden joined the EC. On December

10 and 11, 1991, in the two treaties of Maastricht, the EC members committed to moving toward a new common market—entailing a political and economic union of the twelve nations. (Maastricht is a provincial capital in the southeastern Netherlands.)

The EC became a section of the European Union (EU), created in order to encourage a closer integration of Europe. Today, the EU has twenty-five member states, and five others are applying, most controversially Turkey. Neither organization has been without its problems. Twenty staff members of the EC who were accused of mismanagement and of hiring friends resigned in March 1997. While eleven member states in the EU have agreed to freeze the exchange rates on their currencies and tie their value to a new European-wide monetary unit, the euro, the new monetary unit has not won universal acceptance, particularly after the value of the euro plummeted below that of the U.S. dollar. Several states have claimed the Right to opt out of using the new currency. Twelve of the EU members use the euro as their unit of currency.

Great Britain Since 1951

After the postwar Labour government under Clement Attlee had achieved reforms that transformed Britain into a welfare state, it was succeeded by Conservative governments from 1951 to 1964 under Winston Churchill, Anthony Eden, and Harold Macmillan. During this period, the Conservatives restored truck transportation and iron and steel to private control, introduced some fees into the national health insurance program, and favored private over public development of housing projects. They did not, however, fundamentally alter the social security and health insurance program initiated by Labour, but accepted the welfare state.

Labour returned to power under Harold Wilson from 1964 to 1970. His government again emphasized public housing and slum clearance, democratized the educational system, restored free medical services, and increased social security pensions. A Conservative regime under Edward Heath governed from 1970 to 1974, only to be ousted by Labour once again. Harold Wilson served as Labour prime minister from 1974 to 1976, when he retired to be succeeded by James Callahan. In 1979, the Conservatives returned under the leadership of the first woman prime minister in British history, Margaret Thatcher, whose success in a male-dominated political arena earned her the monicker "the Iron Lady."

Britain's major postwar problems were economic. The government had liquidated some $40 billion in foreign investments to pay for the British war effort. Thus, it had little investment income after the war, making necessary a considerable expansion of exports to pay for needed imports. But Britain had difficulty competing for foreign markets: labor was low in productivity and Britain was outstripped by both West Germany and Japan. Demands for austerity and sacrifice from labor unions to control inflationary pressures resulted in a nationwide coal strike and prolonged work stoppage in 1972. Inflationary pressure increased with the Arab oil embargo and the drastic increase in oil prices during the winter of 1973 to 1974.

After 1974, Labour changed its policies and sought to cut public expenditures, use public funds for private investment, and limit wage increases. It gave priority to industrial expansion in several key industries with the most promise of growth. Labour for the first time in decades favored the private sector. The pound sterling was devalued from about $4 in 1945 to $1.60 in 1976 to provide more favorable trade conditions. British industry continued to be plagued by poor management and frequent strikes. Imports and pressures for higher wages and welfare benefits continued to fuel inflation.

Relations with Northern Ireland proved a burden to successive British governments. The 1922 settlement (see chapter 8) had left Northern Ireland as a self-governing part of the United Kingdom. Of 1.5 million inhabitants, one-third were Roman Catholic and two-thirds Protestant. Catholics claimed they were discriminated against and pressed for annexation by the Republic of Ireland. Activity by the Irish Republican Army (IRA) brought retaliation by Protestant extremists. From 1969 on, the two sides engaged in considerable violence, causing the British to bring in troops to maintain order. More than fifteen hundred people were killed in the ensuing years in sporadic outbreaks of violence. Britain could find no solution satisfactory to both sides and the violence continued.

Separatist pressure of a far less violent kind was prevalent in Wales and Scotland. In 1976, Welsh and Scottish regional assemblies were established with jurisdiction over housing, health, education, and other areas of local concern. Budgets, however, remained under the control of London. The Scots were especially motivated to seek change because of the discovery of North Sea oil deposits, much of which was located in Scottish territorial waters.

Under Prime Minister Thatcher in the 1980s, the British economy improved. London regained some of its former power as a financial center. Southern England was prosperous, but the industrial midlands remained in the doldrums with continued widespread unemployment and poverty. In recent years, an influx of people from former colonies in Africa, Asia, and the West Indies has caused some racial tensions.

Prime Minister Thatcher was a partisan of free enterprise. She fought inflation with austerity and let economic problems spur British employers and unions to change for greater efficiency. She received a boost in popularity when Britain fought a brief war with Argentina over the Falkland Islands and emerged victorious. She stressed close ties with the Republican administration of Ronald Reagan in the United States. Her popularity remained undiminished, whereas the Labour opposition was plagued by internal strife. Both the old Liberal Party and the new Social Democratic party made gains at the expense of Labour, but neither gained any significant power. A Conservative victory in 1987 elections made Thatcher the longest-serving prime minister in modern British history.

Thatcher differed with her party over Britain's participation in the EEC (the Common Market) and the projected introduction of a common currency. Having lost the support of the Conservatives in Parliament, Thatcher resigned and was replaced by Chancellor of the Exchequer John Major. Under Major's leadership, Conservatives had to deal with slow economic growth, unemployment, and racial tensions caused by resentment over the influx of persons from the Commonwealth. In addition, there remained the chronic problem of Northern Ireland, with its Protestant–Roman Catholic animosities; this had been made more difficult by the IRA, which had resorted to terrorism and violence to attain unity with Ireland proper. Major's government launched negotiation with Sinn Fein.

Tony Blair became Britain's youngest prime minister in some 200 years when his Labour Party won the elections of May 1997. The so-called Good Friday Accord of April 1998 climaxed twenty-two months of talks with Sinn Fein. It provided for shared political power between Protestants and minority Catholics, and gave the Republic of Ireland a voice in Northern Irish affairs. The weapons held by the IRA proved to be the most difficult point to solve, but on May 30, 2000, Britain returned home-rule powers to the Northern Ireland Assembly after the IRA announced that it had put its arms "beyond use."

Blair announced plans to achieve partial decentralization of the government, including the creation of separate parliaments in Scotland and Wales. Blair's government also pushed successfully to trim the number of hereditary peers in the House of Lords. Blair worked closely with the U.S. president Bill Clinton in crises involving Iraq and Serbia. Britain turned its Hong Kong colony over to China in July 1997. By 1999 and into 2000, however, economic strains had emerged between Britain and other European nations. Britain was one of several states that insisted on the Right to opt out of the common European currency, the euro, and France led other European nations in banning the importation of British beef because of the fear of bovine spongiform encephalopathy, or mad cow disease. Facing defeat in the Commons, Blair now faces defeat because he has announced his decision (fall 2006) to resign in the face of his unpopular deference to U.S. president George W. Bush in the matter of wars in Afghanistan and Iraq.

France Under the Fifth Republic

The Fourth Republic established in the wake of World War II suffered from the weaknesses of the third: a strong legislature and a weak executive leading to competition between factions and instability in government together with problems in trying to maintain French rule in Indochina and Algeria. In June 1958, the assembly made General de Gaulle premier with six months' emergency powers to deal with Algeria and problems posed by a rebellious army.

Under de Gaulle, the legislature drafted and approved a new constitution establishing the Fifth Republic with a much strengthened executive in the form of a president empowered to dissolve the legislature and call for elections, to submit important questions to popular referendum, and, if necessary, to assume emergency powers. De Gaulle used all these powers in his eleven years as president.

De Gaulle eventually settled the Algerian problem by granting independence in July 1962. Elsewhere in foreign policy, de Gaulle's tenure as first president of the Fifth Republic was marked by an attempt to make France an independent force in world affairs. He saw the struggle as one between powers, not ideologies. France became the world's fourth atomic power in 1960 and developed its own nuclear striking force. De Gaulle refused to follow the lead of either Britain or the United States. At one time, he advocated that Quebec free itself from Canada and at another sided with the Arabs against Israel. Many came to view his foreign policy as quixotic.

In domestic politics, de Gaulle strengthened the power of the president by using the referendum and bypassing the assembly, as when he secured passage of a constitutional amendment providing for future direct popular election of the president. De Gaulle was reelected in 1965, but people became restless with what amounted to a republican monarch. Labor became restive over inflation and housing while students objected to expenditures on nuclear forces rather than education. In May 1968, student grievances over conditions in the universities caused hundreds of thousands to revolt. They were soon joined by some ten million workers who paralyzed the economy. De Gaulle survived by promising educational reform and wage increases. New elections held in June 1968 returned de Gaulle to power. He began the promised reforms, but in April 1969, the president suffered a defeat on a constitutional amendment that he had set up as a vote of confidence. He therefore resigned and died a year later.

De Gaulle's immediate successors were Georges Pompidou (1969–1974) and Valéry Giscard D'Estaing (1974–1981). Both provided France with firm but not particularly radical leadership, and continued to follow an independent foreign policy without de Gaulle's more flamboyant touches.

In 1981, Socialist François Mitterand succeeded Giscard D'Estaing. He inherited a troubled economy. During the 1970s, France had prospered and become the third-largest producer of aerospace technology next to the United States and the Soviet Union. Believing prosperity would continue, Giscard's government did not invest sufficiently and allowed wages and social services to increase at high rates. During his first year, Mitterand tried to revitalize economic growth, granted wage hikes, reduced the work week, expanded paid vacations, and nationalized eleven large private companies and banks. The aim was to stimulate the economy by expanding worker purchasing power and confiscating the profits of large corporations for public investment. France took out foreign loans to finance Mitterand's program. When results were poor, foreign investors were reluctant to grant more credit. Mitterand then reversed his policy and began to cut taxes and social expenditures. By 1984, this had brought down inflation but increased unemployment. The French public generally denounced big government but nevertheless wanted government benefits and services.

Mitterand's policies of nationalization and decentralization of the governmental apparatus, put in place by Napoleon almost two hundred years earlier, were slowed by conservative resistance to basic change. Slow industrial growth, inflation, and unemployment remained problematic. Mitterand lost his Socialist majority in Parliament in 1986, but regained it in 1988. At that point, his regime came to favor cooperation with the United States and a policy of moderation in domestic affairs. Mitterand retired at the end of his term in 1995 and died in January 1996.

Jacques Chirac, a Gaullist elected president in elections in May 1995, made a reduction in France's high unemployment rate one of his government's main goals. He continued Mitterand's policies favoring the integration of Europe, educational reform, and lower taxes. He resumed the testing of French nuclear weapons in the South Pacific, a decision that was reversed in 1996 amid a storm of international criticism, particularly from nations in the Pacific. A socialist coalition won a majority of seats in the National Assembly in 1997, and Lionel Jospin became prime minister, leaving France with a conservative president and socialist prime minister. Jospin's policy of seeking closer ties with the former French colony of Algeria was tempered by charges of human rights abuses in that country. France participated in the NATO operation in Kosovo (discussed later in the chapter) beginning in 1999.

Germany: From Adenauer to Reunification

Christian Democrats remained in power after West German independence for two reasons: (1) prosperity, which by the mid-1950s was reaching all classes of Germans, and (2) the unique personality of Chancellor Konrad Adenauer, who kept the country firmly allied with NATO and the West. Christian Democratic victories in 1953 and 1957 showed the public's approval of the laissez-faire policy of Adenauer's economics minister, Ludwig Erhard. Adenauer's long tenure made him the key figure, lessened the importance of Parliament, and resulted in much government bureaucracy. Adenauer claimed to want the reunification of Germany, but he insisted on free elections, which the Communists of East Germany could not accept, and thus effectively blocked any negotiated solution to the unification problem. Adenauer's last electoral victory was in September 1961. The aged chancellor spent the next years trying to remain in office despite party feeling that he should retire.

In 1963, the Christian Democrats named Erhard to succeed Adenauer. Erhard had quite a different style—treating ministers and department heads as colleagues and equals. He fostered a more collegial atmosphere but had less drive and vigor, especially in foreign affairs. By 1966, the Christian Democrats decided on a change. In November 1966, they formed a so-called great coalition with the Social Democrats. Christian Democrat Kurt Kiesinger became chancellor, and Social Democrat Willy Brandt took over as foreign minister. Brandt announced his intention to work step by step for better relations with East Germany, but found that in a coalition of two very dissimilar parties he could make no substantial progress.

In domestic affairs, pressure for change in the German universities led to outbreaks of student violence just before the similar outbreaks among students in France. Early in 1969, Gustav Heinemann (a Social Democrat) was elected president. An active campaign won the Socialists the Bundestag elections, which occurred later in 1969. Socialists were joined by the Free Democrats and obtained the majority necessary to make Willy Brandt chancellor in October 1969.

Brandt, former mayor of West Berlin, was Germany's first Socialist chancellor in almost forty years. In foreign affairs, he opened the way for British entry into the Common Market. The German mark was revalued at a higher rate, emphasizing Germany's true economic strength. Brandt was now able also to move for improved relations with the East (the policy of *Ostpolitik*). He offered improved economic relations to Poland and the Soviet Union, and in return those states labeled his approach "positive." In the summer of 1970, he negotiated a treaty with the Soviet Union in which both parties renounced the use of force in European affairs. Later that year, West Germany and Poland agreed to recognize the Oder-Neisse line as the legal border between the two countries. Relations improved also with East Germany. Walter Ulbricht, longtime First Secretary of the East German Communist Party, retired from government in 1971, and the next year Brandt signed a treaty with East Germany to normalize relations and improve communications. Both states entered the UN, bypassing the question of whether the division of Germany was permanent.

Elections in November 1972 gave Brandt's coalition a clear victory and a fifty-seat majority in the parliament. But the chancellor, who had concentrated on foreign affairs, faced domestic problems. Brandt seemed to many too tolerant of disorders among university students. Others criticized his sometimes emotional approach to foreign policy, as in relations with his pro-Israel policy, which seemed to be based on liberal German guilt. The discovery of a spy in his immediate office was an excuse for replacing him. Brandt put up little resistance, and Helmut Schmidt (a Social Democrat) became chancellor in the spring of 1974.

Problems with the economy and the environment brought an end to Schmidt's chancellorship and the rule of the Socialists in 1982. An organization called the Greens, which was a loosely organized coalition of environmentalists alienated from society, detracted from Socialist power. In 1982, the German voters turned to conservative Christian Democrats again, and Helmut Kohl became chancellor. The economy continued strong on the whole and the new leadership followed a policy of using German influence to reduce U.S.-Soviet confrontation and tension.

In East Germany, Erich Honecker's government was overthrown in October 1989, and in November the Berlin Wall was breached and removed. In elections held in March 1990, proponents of German reunification won overwhelmingly, and by October, East and West Germany were once again reunited as one country, with its capital at Berlin. By 1995, the country had made significant progress in overcoming the problems associated with reunification and a faltering East German economy. Kohl's sixteen-year tenure as German chancellor ended in September 1998, when his government lost to a coalition led by the Social Democrat Gerhard Schroeder. Schroeder, who had campaigned as a centrist, began a far-reaching program of economic reforms, lowering corporate taxes and making sizeable cuts in the national budget.

As part of the reunification of east and west, the parliament was restored to its traditional seat of power in Berlin in September 1999. Problems in integrating the eastern and western sections of the country continued, however, and in 1997, eastern Germany manufactured only about 3 percent of German exports. Neo-Nazi groups appeared to have made some gains in the economically depressed eastern sections. Germany, which had avoided participating in military conflicts since 1945, worked with other NATO nations in the Kosovo crises (discussed later in the chapter), and Germany agreed to accept more refugees from Kosovo than any other country, some forty thousand in all.

Italy

Italian politics was beset with problems caused by lack of common interests among different areas. The Christian Democrats, who were closely allied with the Roman Catholic Church, dominated the national scene. Their organization, though plagued by corruption, did provide some unity to Italian politics by supplying the prime ministers for numerous coalitions.

Italy advanced economically. In the period from 1958 to 1962, the nation moved into the top ten industrial powers. Natural gas and some oil were discovered in the North, and the Po Valley area especially benefited.

Unfortunately, business efficiency found no parallel in the government or civil service. Italy suffered from terrorism, kidnappings, and assassinations on the part of extreme radical groups such as the Red Brigades. These agitators hoped to create conditions favorable to the overthrow of the democratic constitution. The most notorious terrorist act was the assassination in 1978 of Aldo Moro, a respected Christian Democratic leader.

In 1983, the Christian Democrats received only about one-third of the popular vote and as a result of this weakness, Bettino Craxi (a Socialist) became prime minister at the head of an uneasy coalition that lasted four years—the longest single government in postwar Italian history. After Craxi's resignation, no strong leader emerged.

By the 1990s, Italian industry and the economy generally had advanced to a point where Italy was a leading center in high-technology industry, fashion design, and banking. These advances, however, were concentrated in the cities of the North. Southern Italy continued to have problems associated with economic backwardness and poverty.

Political instability has been the mark of Italian politics ever since the end of World War II. Corruption within a system dominated by the Christian Democrats resulted in criminal trials in the 1990s that sent a number of high government officials to prison. In 1993, the electoral system for the Senate of the Italian parliament was changed from proportional representation to a system that gave power to the party with the majority of votes. The 1994 elections for Parliament brought to power the charismatic, conservative Silvio Berlusconi and his *Forzia Italia* ("Let's go, Italy") movement. In 1996, Italians elected a government dominated by a center-left coalition for the first time since the Italian Republic was created. Carlo Ciampi, who as treasury secretary formulated a series of economic reforms that led to Italy's membership in the European Economic Union (EU), was elected to the presidency in May 1999. After being indicted for tax fraud, Berlusconi was reelected in 2001. Italy pursued an active role in foreign policy, leading efforts to protect international aid being sent to war-torn Albania and allowing its air bases to be used during the NATO air strikes against Serbia in the Kosovo crises (discussed later in the chapter).

Spain and Portugal

In the Iberian Peninsula, two similar events have been the most important of the postwar era. In Portugal, Europe's longest right-wing dictatorship came to an end in September 1968 when a stroke incapacitated Antonio Salazar, who died two years later. A former collaborator, Marcelo Caetano, became prime minister, and an era of change began. Under Caetano, the government relaxed censorship and granted some freedom to political parties.

In 1974, General Antonio de Spinola published his views on the long struggle of Portugal to hold on to its African colonies. This event sparked more change. Caetano dismissed the general, whose popularity grew nevertheless. In April 1974, the Caetano regime was overthrown and a "junta of national salvation" took over, headed by General Spinola. The general proved too conservative and cautious for younger officers, and he was unable to work with the strong forces of the Communist and Socialist parties that had emerged from secrecy with the collapse of the dictatorship. Spinola retired and went into exile. Portugal went through a succession of governments. Its African colonies of Mozambique and Angola were finally granted independence in 1975. Portugal joined the Common Market in 1986. After the 1996 elections, won by the Socialist Jorge Sampaio, the new government took advantage of good economic conditions and in 1999 was able to make Portugal a charter member of the European Economic and Monetary Union, established in 1990 as part of the move to full political union of member European states, which culminated in the Maastricht treaties of 1991–1993. Portugal took the lead in working to create a UN peacekeeping force when its former Indonesian territory, East Timor, was racked by violence in 1999. Portugal gave up its last colony, Macao, to China in December 1999. Sampaio was reelected in 2001, in an election marked by an unusually high number of abstentions.

In Spain, dictatorship also came to an end. Francisco Franco, who had been ruler of a Fascist regime since the end of the Civil War in 1939, held on until he designated the Bourbon prince, Juan Carlos, to be his successor. In 1975, Franco relinquished power and died three weeks later. Juan Carlos proved a popular and able leader and over the next several years took the country from dictatorship to constitutional monarchy. The new government appeased Basque and Catalan separatist movements, which had caused trouble for so long, by granting them local autonomy. Spain entered the Common Market in 1986, at the same time as Portugal. Despite the easy victories of the conservative Peoples Party in the March 1999 and March 2000 elections, regional conflicts continued to be a problem. During 1999 to 2000, Basque separatists killed nineteen people through assassinations and bombing.

Europe's Changing Role in International Relations

New Role for NATO?

NATO, which had originated as a Western alliance against the Soviet Union, lost its reason for being with the collapse of the Soviet Union and revolution in Eastern Europe. In his 1996 reelection campaign, U.S. president Bill Clinton suggested that NATO be expanded to include Eastern Europe and that it provide a collective guarantee against any aggression by one power against another. Faced with the prospect of applications for membership from the Eastern European nations that had ousted their Communist governments, NATO members, concerned about the Russian reaction, created a Partners for Peace program. More than twenty nations, including Russia, became participants in the program. On September 11, 2001, the alliance was forced to adapt to a new challenge as the United States came under terrorist attack. NATO Secretary-General George Robertson said that if the attacks—which turned commercial jetliners into guided missiles that killed thousands at New York's World Trade Center and the Pentagon—were found to be foreign (a suspicion which, in short order, came to be supported by evidence that pointed to Saudi exile Osama bin Laden's al Qaeda terrorist network), under the alliance's Article 5 it would be as if all NATO members had been attacked. This marked the first time in the alliance's history that Article 5 had been invoked.

Europe and the UN

The UN continued to play a limited but significant role in world affairs—more for Europe, which supports international organizations, than for the unilateral United States. It served as a vehicle for intervention in disputes between the Arabs and Israelis, in the Sudan, and, recently, in the Balkans. It has provided humanitarian aid and maintained international military units to police peace agreements. The UN and its constituent organizations have also played a crucial role in a number of less well-known instances such as telecommunications, international aviation, relief of distress among children, culture, and support of international work in education, the arts, and science.

The Balkan Crisis (Yugoslavia and Its Successor States)

Yugoslavia's Marshal Tito managed to hold together a nation of six republics with rival ethnic groups, despite economic difficulties and complicated relations with Stalin and the Soviet Union. Even after Tito's death in 1980, the system continued to function for a number of years. But with the turmoil in Eastern Europe and the collapse of the Soviet Union, Yugoslav unity ended in 1991 and various factions took up arms against each other that summer. Slovenes and Croats broke away from Serbian control, and Bosnia and Herzegovina declared independence by the end of the year. Armed conflict broke out between Serbs, Croats, Bosnian Muslims, and other factions and interest groups.

The UN sent Cyrus Vance (U.S. secretary of state under President Jimmy Carter) and Lord David Owen (a former British foreign secretary) to mediate the dispute, but several truces and agreements broke down. European states, including Russia, all deplored the strife in the former Yugoslavia. On several occasions, NATO intervened with air strikes and economic sanctions against the Serbs, but no agreement could be reached on military action sufficient to force an end to the conflict. In 1995, Richard Holbrook of the United States negotiated a peace agreement, and in 1996 a multinational force (which included U.S. troops for the first time) was sent in to police the agreement and maintain peace. Beginning in February 1998, the Yugoslav army and police from Serbia battled a separatist movement in the province of Kosovo, carrying out harsh reprisals against the area's largely Muslim residents. When NATO launched air strikes against Serbia in March of 1999, massacres of civilians by Serb militia increased to the point that an estimated eight hundred thousand people died in the province. Serbia agreed to a withdrawal in June, and a NATO peacekeeping contingent, including Russian soldiers, occupied Kosovo. Slobodan Milosevic, president of Serbia from 1990 to his deposition in 2001, had involved his country in almost continuous warfare since 1990, was forced out by widespread popular demonstrations after he lost the election in September 1999 to Vojislav Kostunica, a law professor. The change in leadership paved the way for the eventual rebuilding of the Serb economy. In April 2001, Milosevic was arrested for corruption. He was eventually turned over to the UN war-crimes tribunal at the Hague in the Netherlands, where he was charged with committing crimes against humanity and genocide. He is the first head of state to face an international war-crimes court.

Western Involvement with the Middle East

In August 1990, in a campaign that met little resistance and lasted only a few days, the army of Saddam Hussein, dictator of Iraq, seized control of neighboring Kuwait. The European powers and the United States—seeing a threat to their oil supplies—organized under the leadership of U.S. president George Bush. Under the mantle of the UN, they called on Iraq to withdraw. When Hussein refused, a multinational army led by the United States was mobilized in February 1991 to liberate Kuwait. Iraqi resistance soon collapsed, and within one hundred hours, the allies had freed Kuwait and driven the Iraqi army back to the Euphrates River. President Bush then called a halt to hostilities.

The greatest source of continuing instability in the Mideast since World War II has been the ongoing conflict between the state of Israel and her Arab neighbors. Through more than fifty years of intermittent violence and warfare, Western governments, motivated in large part by a desire to support a democratic state, have supplied increasing amounts of economic and military aid to Israel. In 1964, the Palestine Liberation Organization (PLO), led by Yassir Arafat, was formed among Arab refugees who had been expelled from their ancestral homes by the Israelis. The PLO adopted a long-standing policy that sought the destruction of Israel. By the 1990s, however, the PLO had abandoned this goal in favor of a policy backing separate Israeli and Palestinian states; as a result, the PLO was extended recognition by Israel. Egypt and Jordan had signed peace treaties with Israel, and now, it seemed, it might be the Palestinians' turn. But U.S.-brokered negotiations broke down during the final days of the Clinton administration.

Cultural and Social Developments Since World War II

Science and Technology

Until the Second World War, Europe enjoyed a significant lead in most scientific and technological fields, despite the rising competition of the United States and other lands. The automobile belonged as much to Daimler and Benz (Germany) as to Henry Ford (the United States); the best schools for science and technology were probably European polytechnics in France, Germany, and Switzerland; most Nobel prizes before World War II went to Europeans, especially in physics—the Curies, Becquerel, Röntgen, Lorentz, Thomson, Marconi, Bohr, Planck, de Broglie, Heisenberg, Schrödinger, among others. It was in the 1930s that a brain drain began in Europe, in large part due to fascism, and this drain only accelerated with the Second World War. After 1945, the United States became the center not only for medicine, science, and technology, but also for painting and other artistic fields—due in part to émigrés who enriched American universities and cultural life at the expense of Old Europe.

Advances in science and technology have caused considerable change in the period since World War II. In 1900, about fifteen thousand trained scientists were engaged in research and teaching—most in Europe. In the postwar years, the figure reached five hundred thousand; in addition to central and western Europe, the Soviet Union, the United States, and Japan were heavily involved in scientific research and development of technologies that applied scientific advances to everyday life. It is interesting to look at the increasing internationalization of science and technology among the Noble prizes, in which one now occasionally sees Americans sharing the prize with Europeans.

Much of the early work on such devices as rockets, the jet aircraft engine, radar, and the computer was done in England and Germany during and immediately after World War II. The English mathematician Alan Turing was influential in wartime cryptography in which machines were developed to discover, by high-speed computation, the random settings of German cipher machines. Significant research on computers was done in places such as the University of Manchester following the war; in the last three decades, however, the lead in computers has been taken by the United States and Japan. European refugees, such as John von Neumann, a mathematician of genius active in several fields, from topology to computer science, have often helped in this brain transfer.

Rapid change occurred in medicine, beginning in Europe, with the development of sulfa drugs, penicillin, cortisone, and antibiotics to cure formerly crippling infections. Prewar names show the preponderance of European doctors and scientists: Robert Koch and Alexander Fleming are examples. Their research led to the American development of vaccines for poliomyelitis (1955) and other diseases. Remarkable developments in surgery included transplantation of vital organs. Research in genetics led to genetic engineering, in which scientists actually learned to create new and different living organisms. Here, what was a continental-European bailiwick before 1930, with such names as Correns, DeVries, and Tschermak, became more and more the province of the Americans and British, with such names as Morgan, Watson, Crick, Rosalind Franklin, and others. Some of this work was done in Europe, but more than ever before the balance was shifting to other areas, including the United States, Russia, and Japan. In one notable European achievement, however, Scottish scientists in 1998 succeeded in producing a genetically identical copy of a Finn Dorset sheep they named "Dolly." This raised the scientific and ethical question of whether human beings can or should be cloned.

In other scientific developments, England became a pioneer in radio astronomy with the work of Sir Bernard Lovell, using the great radio telescope at Jodrell Bank. The disastrous accident at the nuclear reactor at Chernobyl in Ukraine in April 1986 caused many Europeans to rethink the issues of nuclear reactors and public safety. In general, European science and technology have continued to advance, just not at the level of predominance of the pre–World War II era. Europeans, more than Americans, are concerned with finding and developing alternative fuels, more eco-friendly technologies, and such.

Religion

In postwar Europe, an ecumenical movement among branches of the Christian faith was a notable achievement. The Second Vatican Council (1962–1965) supported ecumenism and called for greater toleration among Christians. Most branches of Christianity continued to espouse traditional beliefs, which has meant a continuation of conflict with the teachings of modern science and such philosophies as Marxism. The Roman Catholic Church, in particular, has been outspoken in opposition to nuclear weapons. Some Protestant sects have gone so far as to come out in support of rights for gay men and women.

Literature and Art

Writers and artists throughout Europe have produced important work since World War II. Even in Russia, despite censorship, such writers as Boris Pasternak and Alexander Solzhenitsyn wrote signal works that were published abroad, though not in Russia itself until the political changes of the 1990s. The English writer George Orwell achieved fame for his frightening portrayal of a future totalitarian society in the novel *1984* (published in 1949). Writers such as Frantz Fanon in *The Wretched of the Earth* (published in French in 1961) and Jean-Paul Sartre in his *Critique of Dialectical Reason* condemned colonialism and called attention to the enormous discrepancies between the wealth of the first world (Europe, the British Commonwealth, Japan, and the United States) and the underdeveloped nations of the so-called third world.

German writers of the older generation, such as Carl Zuckmayer and Bertolt Brecht, as well as younger writers such as Wolfgang Borchert and Günter Grass, and the Swiss Heinrich Böll, produced notable works. Zuckmayer's play *The Devil's General*, although written in the United States at the end of World War II, gave a remarkable picture of wartime Germany. Grass's novel *The Tin Drum* (1959), also set in Nazi Germany, became a best seller that was translated into English and other languages.

Censorship in the Soviet Union under Stalin and successors failed to stifle creativity and criticism. Boris Pasternak's *Doctor Zhivago* was an epic covering the period before, during, and after the 1917 Russian Revolution. Its author, however, was not allowed to leave Russia to accept the Nobel Prize for literature. Alexander Solzhenitsyn's novel *One Day in the Life of Ivan Denisovich* won critical acclaim. A later work, *The Gulag Archipelago*, was a detailed description and indictment of the whole apparatus of forced labor camps run by the secret police during the Stalin era. The author was arrested for treason and forced into exile in 1974.

In the fine arts, the art world was dominated by Pablo Picasso, who worked in many innovative styles into the late 1900s. In film, the work of the Swedish director Ingmar Bergman (*The Seventh Seal*, *Wild Strawberries*) and the Italians Roberto Rossellini (*Open City*) and Vittorio de Sica (*Bicycle Thief*) attracted attention and critical acclaim as realists who rejected the hidebound conventions of Hollywood sentimentality. Germans Werner Herzog and Rainer Werner Fassbinder pushed the boundaries of cinematic realism further, and the Russian Andrei Tarnovsky became a pioneer in a new modernist cinema of science fiction. Although Hollywood infiltrated and even dominated European markets from the 1920s on, European filmmakers have continued to distinguish themselves in an increasingly globalized world.

Music

The history of western music is conterminous with Europe until the twentieth century, when American composers finally entered the spotlight, especially in such areas as jazz, swing, movie music, and rock 'n roll, among others. But young American composers, such as Aaron Copland and Samuel Barber, continued to come to Europe to put the finishing touches on their craft with such great teachers as Nadia Boulanger (1887–1979) in Paris. Also, from the 1920s to the present, Europe has continued to give the world some of its best composers, conductors, musicians, and stage designers.

Philosophies and Cultural Politics

The First World War saw the end to many verities of old culture: no longer would old-style liberalism, realistic representations in the arts, tonal music, and such rule without challenges and subversion. The Second World War saw even the new rules of modernism, atonal music, abstract painting, and more questioned, often without the creation or substitution of any new (or old) values. A cultural vacuum seemed to ensue, into which American culture stepped for at least a decade. But European culture did revive, and some notable movements may be singled out here for mention:

Existentialism. Prewar roots had already made existentialism distinctly European. Works of the nineteenth-century Dane, Søren Kierkegaard (1813–1855), were revived, and Martin Heidegger (1889–1976) added to this. The result was an engaged philosophy inviting political involvement, rooted often in an atheistic sense of abandonment in the world and the need for "good faith" in dealing with life and the Other (other people as different, unpredictable entities). Much of this philosophy was based in a radical rereading of Immanuel Kant, but it was expanded by Jean-Paul Sartre (1905–1980) and Albert Camus (1913–1960) into areas Kant might have found frightening. Existentialism shaped the Beat movement in America and provided college students for decades with a way to confront an increasingly alienated, meaningless world with the hope of making meaning for one's self.

Feminism. Americans might boast of the honor of having hosted the Seneca Falls Convention (1848) of early feminists, but Europe could always point back to its eighteenth-century pioneers in feminist thought, Mary Wollstonecraft (1759–1797) and Olympe de Gouges (1745–1793). Furthermore, when feminism in the United States was still fighting for a platform and a champion, John Stuart Mill (1806–1873) came out as one of the first male feminists, advocating women's suffrage in Parliament; then he and his wife, Harriet Taylor, cowrote the path-breaking *The Subjection of Women* (1869), more than a pendant to Mill's radically liberal manifesto, *On Liberty* (1859). Feminists cropped up in most political persuasions, from radical socialist to right-of-center liberalism, culminating in the suffragette movement in England (circa 1890–1914). After the First World War, women began to get the vote in major European countries. After the

Second World War, Simone de Beauvoir (1908–1986) reopened the dialogue on women's rights with an important study of the nature of the relationship between sex and gender. Her *The Second Sex* (1949) pioneered in ideas of the social construction of gender roles; without Beauvoir, it is hard to conceive the works of Anglo-Australo-American feminists of the next generation: Kate Millet, Betty Friedan, Gloria Steinem, and others.

Environmentalism. At the turn of the nineteenth century, U.S. environmentalists were making waves: John Muir, Teddy Roosevelt, and others spoke up for the need for natural parks and wildlife reserves. A superficial look at European culture shows back-to-nature movements, such as the German *Wandervögel*, and later, nudism and other nature-friendly cults. After World War II, the United States continued to lead the way, with such manifestos as Rachel Carson's *The Silent Spring* (1962). But then, as America spawned Ralph Nader's consumerist environmentalism, Europe woke up to its own severe environmental problems, and the Green Party was born in Germany in 1980. This is not to say that there had not been earlier outcries about the pollution of the environment: as early as the romantics in the 1790s, prophets in the wilderness decried the despoliation of the countryside by the new belching factories and (later) locomotives. Also, efforts to clean up the Thames and Rhine rivers, for instance, came from pre–World War II initiatives. But the German Green Party showed even environmentally sensitive Americans that they could learn something about political activism from their European colleagues.

Problems Facing Europe in the Twenty-First Century

Europe faces some serious problems in this millennium that undermine its claims to a central place in the education of the world: Eurocentrism is a common charge, and the once-paramount European values of democracy, individualism, realistic representation, tonal music, and such are challenged on many fronts. A bleak view has emerged that Europe is doomed to be the second-rate boutique and tourist trap for the rest of the world, where the United States, Japan, South Korea, and the oil-exporting countries have taken an economic lead over Europe in many indicators.

Europe now suffers from a number of endemic problems:

- A workforce spoiled by tremendous benefits and high wages is no longer viable in many markets.

- European higher education no longer dominates in scientific and technological disciplines.

- The free-for-all of factions in European parliamentary politics often leads to confusion and instability.

- The former Eastern or Soviet bloc countries, undone by decades of improper state allocation of resources, along with the "poor" Balkans, south Italy, Portugal, and Spain seem to act as a drag on general European prosperity, not to mention progress.

It no longer seems germane or even defensible to study Europe as the fount of all values, if Europe is really becoming stale and rigid in its welfare-state mindsets and old modernism.

But an equally compelling case can be made that the announcement of the death of "Old Europe" (a phrase used by U.S. President George W. Bush's first secretary of defense, Donald Rumsfeld, to describe France and Germany) is rather premature. Europe has shown its resilience in the face of disaster and reversals so many times that to rule out a comeback is cynical and illogical. The ailing states of the former Soviet Union are seeking to reform their own economies and use the controlled export of oil and gas to revitalize. Turkey, though plagued by the nationalist desires of its Kurdish minority, has genuine claims to EU membership and to its share in the still-lingering prosperity of Europe. Long mired in corrupt politics, Italy has in recent decades risen in most indicators to the status of stability and prosperity. Germany continues to produce a good gross national product, despite its high labor costs and the predictable costs of reunification (predictable, it seems, for all except Chancellor Kohl and his Christian Democrats, who oversaw that process). England after the Thatcher era of austerity and mine closings has bounced back economically, as has its old rival and neighbor, Ireland, now called the "Celtic Tiger" for its vibrant, modern economy. The newly independent Baltic states, especially Estonia, are pioneering in such areas as Internet use. And, to give just one more case, Spain, long kept back by the fascism of Francisco Franco, has miraculously modernized itself under King Juan Carlos.

No, Europe is not passé, not spent, not irrelevant in a world where the media are fixated on the United States, Arab oil, fundamentalist Islam, and the economic dynamos of the Far East. The excesses and inadequacies of the rest of the world may still be amenable to solutions and models and lessons from that once backward, dirty, and religiously fanatical little subcontinent that launched its own terrorists and religious wars, sent out fleets of marauders and pirates, exploited its own poor to engorge its idle rich, and much more by way of sins and crimes. The economic revival of social-welfare states, the long-flourishing pacifism, the vital preservation of cultural heritage alongside the avid fostering of new arts and letters, the brave and adult attempt to face multicultural problems: these and many other trends in twenty-first-century Europe bear our close attention.

◄───────── TIMELINE ─────────►

Cold War, Unification, and the Decolonized World (1945–2001)

Year(s)	Event	Significance
1945	The Cold War starts in Germany.	Allied soldiers are forced to give the eastern zone of Germany to advancing Russian troops. American politicians start to grumble over the supposed betrayal of Poland to Stalin, and much else.
1945–1946	France establishes the Fourth Republic.	General Charles de Gaulle returns triumphant to France, and helps establish the Fourth Republic. The republic's strong Communist and Socialist parties worry the now very conservative United States. Like Britain, France becomes a social-welfare state.
1945	The Labour Party wins in Britain.	Clement Attlee replaces Winston Churchill as prime minister during the Yalta conferences. Pursuant to the wartime Beveridge Report, Britain starts installing a welfare state to protect the poor and sick from free-market depredations.
1945 on	Christian Democrats rise to power—and stay there—throughout the Continent.	Part of the postwar mood favored the rise of new Christian Democratic parties in France, Germany, Italy, the Benelux countries, and elsewhere. The parties wed Christian values to conservative politics, and are usually pro–United States. The Christian Democrats remain in power almost everywhere until the late 1960s.

1945–1999	European countries divest themselves of their overseas colonies.	Starting before the end of World War II, European colonies assert the desire for autonomy; postwar, they achieve it. Milestones in decolonization include Egypt (1952), Vietnam (1954), and the Congo and other African countries (1960–1961). The reversion of Hong Kong to mainland China in 1999 marks the end of the colonial era. A significant trend in European and U.S. history is the reflux of colonials to the mother country to seek jobs: Jamaicans and Nigerians in the United Kingdom, Algerians and other Francophone Africans in France, and so on. The huge rise in non-European, non-white, non-Christian workers in Europe is a lingering problem.
1947	Communist threat sparks crisis over Greece and Turkey.	Civil war breaks out in Greece between monarchists and Communists who had fought fascists. U.S. president Harry Truman articulates the Truman Doctrine promising aid to countries or minorities struggling to be free from "outside agitators" (that is, Commies).
1947	The Truman administration implements the Marshall Plan as the economic arm to its political-military doctrine.	Secretary of State George Marshall announces the United States' intent to give aid and grants to all European countries in need of money for rebuilding after World War II. Though Poland and Czechoslovakia are interested, Stalin forces them to refuse U.S. aid as a bourgeois tool. The Marshall Plan is significant as a success in economic recovery, but it was also used as a tool in the Cold War, despite the best intentions.

(Continued)

1948–1949	Currency crisis in the German zones leads to the Berlin airlift.	The three western zones cooperate too much for Soviet tastes: first the three unite, then they establish a new mark as currency. This creates instability in eastern zone. Soviet leader Josef Stalin blocks roads to Berlin to starve it. The Allied airlift of supplies to Berlin lasts a year and stymies Stalin.
1949	The two Germanies are established.	After the Berlin airlift, two Germanies are formed: the western republic firmly under Christian Democratic control (Konrad Adenauer) and the American umbrella, the eastern part as a Soviet satellite. When workers in Berlin demonstrate in 1953, their revolt is crushed, thus showing that the new government wanted to stay a docile satellite of the all-powerful Soviet Union.
1950	Six countries form the European Coal and Steel Community.	Spearheaded by French statesmen Jean Monnet and Robert Schuman, France, Italy, Germany, and the three Benelux countries agree to set up a toll-free zone among themselves and strive for economic unification. It is the first major step toward a "United States of Europe."
1949–1953	The Soviet Union acquires atomic weapons.	The Cold War heats up after the Soviet Union breaks the U.S. monopoly on nuclear weapons with an atomic, then hydrogen bomb. As China turns Communist, and as both seem bent on annexing Korea, the United States escalates its own policy of containment.
1954–1955	West Germany remilitarizes.	Over the protests of German liberals, the West German government decides to remilitarize and join NATO in order to protect German interests, but also join the U.S.-led cause of anti-communism.

1956	Unrest occurs in Poland, Hungary, and the Suez Canal zone.	After Stalin's death in 1953, countries in the Soviet bloc hope in vain for better conditions. Revolts in Poland and a revolution in Hungary ensue, but the rebels' appeals for help to the United States fall on deaf ears. The United States is more concerned to assert its control over the Suez Canal against old colonial powers of Britain and France.
1956	Nikita Khrushchev delivers his secret speech at the Twentieth Party Congress.	As new premier, Khrushchev admits to the crimes of Stalin. When his speech is leaked to the world press, hopes are raised of a thaw in Soviet attitudes. Later, there is a thaw in the arts, but the Soviet hard-line prevails in foreign affairs.
1957	Treaty of Rome establishes the European Economic Community (EEC).	The six nations of the European Coal and Steel Community (1950) expand their economic reforms beyond coal and steel to many other products. The EEC forms as a counterweight to the over mighty U.S. market.
1957	The Soviets launch the Sputnik satellite.	The launching of a Soviet satellite in outer space alarms the United States, where false reports circulate for decades of Soviet superiority in science and military.
1958	The Soviet government forbids author Boris Pasternak from attending the Nobel awards ceremony.	Awarded the Nobel Prize in Literature for his masterpiece *Doctor Zhivago* (1957), Pasternak could neither publish the work in the Soviet Union (it was smuggled to Italy) nor accept the award.
1960–1962	A series of crises tip the Cold War toward the brink of nuclear war.	The Soviets down a U.S. U-2 spy plane; U.S.-Soviet summit in Vienna fails; the Soviets erect the Berlin Wall; and, finally, the Cuban Missile crisis occurs. (U.S. bravado in the latter makes the Soviets remove missiles form Cuba.) In a few years, the United States and Soviet Union move away from old co-existence toward the opposite policy of détente.

(Continued)

1968	In Berlin, Paris, and elsewhere, radicalized university student riot.	Student riots against U.S. hegemony, ossified French education, and the Vietnam War lead to gains for parties of the Left.
1968	Prague Spring occurs.	Upset at Communist rule, Czechs revolt but are put down (cf. Hungary, 1956) by Soviet tanks. The Soviet premier announces his Brezhnev Doctrine (mirror-image to Truman's, 1947): the Soviet Union will aid any government or land striving to be free of capitalist domination.
1973	The Common Market expands by three new members.	With de Gaulle out of French politics, Britain can now be admitted to the EEC, along with Denmark and Ireland.
1975	Thirty-five nations sign the Helsinki Accords.	Though criticized in the United States as a capitulation to Soviet presence in Eastern Europe, the Helsinki Accords actually broaden the scope of reporting on human rights violations in the Soviet bloc.
1982–1985	The EEC expands to twelve nations.	Admitting Greece, Portugal, and Spain, the EEC now expands beyond the industrialized west to include agricultural powers. The prospect of poor workers flocking to rich European cities for jobs alarms many and fuels such Far Right movements as Jean Marie LePen's nationalists in France.
1992–1993	The Maastricht Treaty creates the European Union (EU).	The European Union seeks to unify the continent politically and economically. The introduction of the euro as common currency in 2001 marks a step forward, but the negative attitudes of Britain, Denmark, and others to the EU show that much remains to be done. The EU is now the trade equal of the United States and Japan.

Selected Readings

Intended for students, this short bibliography is based on criteria of readability and scope rather than scholarly rigor or narrow focus. This list is highly selective and is compiled with the hope of inspiring more interest in modern European history.

General Reference Works

Kinder, Hermann, and Werner Hilgemann. *The Anchor Atlas of World History,* Vol. 1: *From the Stone Age to the Eve of the French Revolution*. Translated by Ernst Menze. New York: Anchor/Doubleday, 1974.

Kinder, Hermann, and Werner Hilgemann. *The Anchor Atlas of World History,* Vol. 2: *From the French Revolution to the American Bicentennial*. Translated by Ernst Menze. New York: Anchor/Doubleday, 1978.

Davies, Norman. *Europe: A History*. Oxford: Oxford University Press, 1996.

Roberts, J.M. *The Penguin History of Europe*. London: Penguin, 1997.

Works by Country

MacKenzie, David and Michael Curran. *A History of Russia, The Soviet Union and Beyond*. 5th edition. Belmont, CA: Wadsworth, 1999.

Schama, Simon. *A History of Britain: At the Edge of the World? 3000 BC–1603 AD; British Wars, 1603–1776; The Fate of Empire, 1776–2001*. Vols. 1–3. New York: Harper and Collins, 2003.

Goubert, Pierre. *The Course of French History, 987 to the Present*. London: Routledge, 1991.

Holborn, Hajo. *A History of Modern Germany*. Vol. 1: *Reformation*; Vol. 2: *1648–1840*; Vol. 3: *1840–1945*. Princeton: Princeton University Press, 1959–1962.

Craig, Gordon. *Germany 1866–1945*. Oxford: Oxford University Press, 1980.

Fulbrook, Mary. *Divided Nation: A History of Germany, 1918–1990*. New York: Oxford University Press, 1992.

Taylor, A.J.P. *The Habsburg Monarchy, 1809–1918.* Chicago: University of Chicago Press, 1976.

Works by Era

Renaissance:

Plumb, J.H. *The Italian Renaissance.* New York: American Heritage, 1961/1989.

Reformation:

Chadwick, Owen. *The Reformation.* London: Penguin, 1964/1990.

Scientific Revolution:

Butterfield, Herbert. *The Origins of Modern Science, 1300–1800.* New York: Macmillan, 1957.

Age of Exploration:

Elliott, J.H. *The Old World and the New, 1492–1650.* Cambridge: Cambridge University Press, 1970.

Absolutism:

Doyle, William. *The Old European Order, 1660–1800.* Oxford: Oxford University Press, 1993.

Enlightenment:

Hampson, Norman. *The Enlightenment.* New York: Penguin, 1968.

Lieven, Dominic. *The Aristocracy of Europe, 1815–1914.* New York: Columbia University Press, 1992.

French Revolution and Napoleon:

Lefebvre, Georges. *The Coming of the French Revolution.* Translated by R.R. Palmer. Princeton: Princeton University Press, 1962–1964.

Reaction, 1815–1848, and Revolutions:

Schroeder, Paul. *The Transformation of European Politics, 1765–1848.* London: Clarendon Press, 1994.

Age of Nation-Building and Liberalism:

Taylor, A.J.P. Struggle for Mastery in Europe, 1848–1918. Oxford: Oxford University Press, 1954.

Imperialism:

Ferguson, Niall. *Empire: The Rise and Demise of the British World and Order and Lessons for Global Power.* New York: Penguin, 2003.

Modernism:

Wilson, Edmund. *Axel's Castle: A Study in the Imaginative Literature of 1870–1930.* New York: Charles Scribner's Sons, 1931.

First World War and Fascism:

Keegan, John. *The First World War.* New York: Borzoi, 1998.

Paxton, Robert O. *The Anatomy of Fascism.* New York: Vintage, 2005.

Weinberg, Gerhard. *A World at Arms: A Global History of World War Two.* Cambridge: Cambridge University Press, 1994.

Cold War, Unification and Decolonization:

Judt, Tony. *Postwar: A History of Europe Since 1945.* New York: Penguin, 2005.

PRACTICE EXAMS

AP European History

PRACTICE EXAM 1

This exam is also on CD-ROM in our
special interactive AP European History TESTware®

AP European History

Section 1

**TIME: 55 minutes
80 questions**

DIRECTIONS: Each of the questions or incomplete statements below is followed by five suggested answers or completions. Select the one that is best in each case.

1. Renaissance Humanism was a threat to the Church because it

    (A)   espoused atheism

    (B)   denounced scholasticism

    (C)   denounced neo-Platonism

    (D)   emphasized a return to the original sources of Christianity

    (E)   advanced an amoral philosophy

2. Desiderius Erasmus of Rotterdam was the author of

    (A)   *The Praise of Folly*

    (B)   *The Birth of Venus*

    (C)   *Utopia*

    (D)   *The Prince*

    (E)   *Don Quixote*

3. All of the following are characteristics of Northern Humanism EXCEPT:

    (A)   It insisted on the need for a scripture in the vernacular.

    (B)   It believed that medieval Latin was inferior to ancient Latin.

(C) It embraced Christian principles more than pagan themes.

(D) It was very supportive of the Protestant Reformation.

(E) It carried on scholarship in ancient languages to purify texts.

4. During the Reformation, Anabaptism drew its membership mostly from the ranks of the

(A) nobility

(B) middle class

(C) peasants

(D) businessmen

(E) army officers

5. The Colloquy of Marburg in 1529

(A) was an attempt by the Catholic Church to combat the Protestant heresy

(B) was a meeting where Luther was outlawed throughout the Empire

(C) was a debate between Luther and Zwingli that resulted in a formal split within Protestantism

(D) was an attempt by Charles V to reconcile Luther to the Catholic Church

(E) resulted in the fall of Thomas Wolsey as Lord Chancellor of England

6. English Puritanism developed during the reign of Elizabeth I

(A) in reaction to the failure of the Elizabethan Religious Settlement to implement the reforms of the Council of Trent

(B) because of Elizabeth I's intention to extend Protestant sentiment throughout the realm

(C) because of dissatisfaction with the scope and breadth of the Elizabethan Religious Settlement among those influenced by Calvinist views

(D) as a direct reaction to the Jesuit Mission led by Edmund Campion

(E) to reassert the hierarchical and ceremonial forms of Henry's era

7. The response of the Catholic Church to the Reformation was delayed because

(A) the Papacy feared the remnants of the Conciliar Movement

(B) Rome wanted to coordinate its policy with secular Catholic leaders

(C) church leaders thought that the opposition would self-destruct

(D) the situation did not appear to be urgent from the Roman perspective

(E) the Church did not possess the money needed to confront Protestantism

8. The Catholic Counter-Reformation included all of the following EXCEPT

    (A) the *Index of Prohibited Books*

    (B) the Council of Trent

    (C) a more assertive Papacy

    (D) the establishment of new religious orders

    (E) a willingness to negotiate nondoctrinal issues with reformers

9. The Petition of Right (1628–1629)

    (A) was an attempt by James I to secure additional tax revenues through the Parliament

    (B) resulted in Parliament voting to execute the Duke of Buckingham

    (C) addressed a range of Parliamentary grievances even as it set the stage for new sources of revenue requested by Charles I

    (D) denounced the radical religious policies of Charles I's government

    (E) was approved by the Addled Parliament

10. René Descartes has been credited with all of the following EXCEPT

    (A) being the first to publish the discovery of coordinate or analytical geometry

    (B) developing the science of optics through the laws of refraction of light

    (C) establishing as his famous philosophic starting place: "cogito ergo sum"— I think, therefore I am

    (D) holding that the concept of God was unnecessary in his concept of the universe

    (E) developing a philosophical Dualism that links the physical and spiritual worlds

11. Henry IV gave Huguenots the right to practice their religion through

    (A) the Edict of Potsdam

    (B) the Edict of Fontainebleau

    (C) the Edict of Nantes

    (D) an agreement with the Papacy

    (E) the Peace of Amiens

12. Which of these thinkers is identified most closely with the following statement? "Renounce notions, and begin to form an acquaintance with things."

    (A) Galileo   (D) Spinoza

    (B) Bacon   (E) Boyle

    (C) Descartes

13. For several decades during the late seventeenth century, Austria fought on two fronts against which two countries?

    (A) Italy and Prussia

    (B) England and Russia

    (C) France and Ottoman Turkey

    (D) Prussia and Ottoman Turkey

    (E) France and Italy

14. The *Fronde* was directed primarily against

    (A) the power of French landlords

    (B) the authority of the absolute monarchy

    (C) the influence of the nobility

    (D) the wealth of the church

    (E) the poverty of the peasants

15. The Peace of Utrecht

    (A) resulted in the political and economic collapse of France

    (B) elevated England to the status of greatest European power

    (C) terminated the Wars of Louis XIV and restored peace to Europe

    (D) transferred Canada to England

    (E) resulted in the unification of Germany

16. A moderate proposal that called on France to adopt a political system similar to Great Britain was an element espoused by Montesquieu in

    (A) *The Social Contract*

    (B) *The Spirit of the Laws*

    (C) *The Encyclopedia*

(D)   *The Declaration of the Rights of Man and the Citizen*

(E)   *Two Treatises on Civil Government*

17.   John Calvin's theology can be considered most similar to the political philosophy of which of the following?

(A)   Rousseau   (D)   Montesquieu

(B)   Condorcet   (E)   Locke

(C)   Hobbes

18.   An economic philosophy identified with "bullionism" and the need to maintain a favorable balance of trade was

(A)   Utopian Socialism

(B)   Marxism

(C)   Capitalism

(D)   Syndicalism

(E)   Mercantilism

19.   The *liberum veto*

(A)   was a critical element in the evolution of the British Parliament

(B)   was pronounced by Louis XIV as a monarchical right

(C)   restricted the national and political development of Poland

(D)   demonstrated the extent of Peter the Great's Westernization

(E)   gained the support of the Vatican after the failure of Mazzini's Roman Republic

20.   "...there is no place for industry... no arts; no letters; no society; and which is the worst of all, continual fear, and danger of violent death; and the life of man, solitary, poor, nasty, brutish, and short." This quotation from Thomas Hobbes's *Leviathan* (1651) describes the concept known as

(A)   natural rights

(B)   state of nature

(C)   social contract

(D)   reason of state (raison d'état)

(E)   nationalism

21. In *Emile*, Rousseau

   (A) advanced his views on the Social Contract

   (B) called for a "natural" education free of the artificial encumbrances imposed by institutions such as the Church

   (C) denounced Voltaire for his pedantic and unproductive lifestyle

   (D) shared Montesquieu's idealization of England's constitutional monarchy as a model for a future French government

   (E) advanced his case for atheism

22. "Men are born, and always continue free and equal in respect of their rights. Civil distinctions, therefore, can be founded only on public utility." In 1789 these statements were part of

   (A) the U.S. Bill of Rights

   (B) the Constitution of the Year III

   (C) the Declaration of the Rights of Man and the Citizen

   (D) Quesnay's statement of physiocracy

   (E) *What Is the Third Estate?* by the Abbé Sieyès

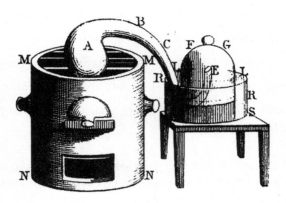

23. The drawing above represents

   (A) the "Leyden Jar"

   (B) the Gray experiment showing that electricity can be conducted by means of threads

   (C) the "Phlogiston" theory

   (D) Lavoisier's Apparatus for the Decomposition of Air

   (E) Franklin's device for the processing of alcohol

24. The following picture is of

(A) Arkwright's water frame

(B) the spinning jenny invented by Hargreaves

(C) Whitney's cotton gin

(D) Watt's silk-making machine

(E) Franklin's paper-making machine

25. English Utilitarianism was identified with the phrase

(A) all power to the people

(B) from each according to his labor, to each according to his need

(C) universal reason

(D) the greatest good for the greatest number

(E) collectivist nationalism

26. "Do you not hear them repeating unceasingly that all that is above them is incapable and unworthy of governing them; that the present distribution of good throughout the world is unjust; that property rests on a foundation which is not an equitable foundation? ... I believe that we are at this moment sleeping on a volcano." Alexis de Tocqueville made these remarks to

(A) the American Senate in 1838

(B) the French Chamber of Deputies in 1848

    (C)   the court of Napoleon III before the Franco-Prussian War

    (D)   the Chamber of Peers in the Third French Republic in 1875

    (E)   the court martial of Captain Alfred Dreyfus in 1894

27.   The achievements of the Jacobins included all of the following EXCEPT

    (A)   the abolition of slavery

    (B)   the franchise given to all adult males

    (C)   the adoption of the metric system

    (D)   decreeing the law of the maximum—fixed prices on essentials and raised wages

    (E)   the redistribution of all land among the peasants

28.   The following map indicates the thesis advanced by H. Mackinder in 1904 that

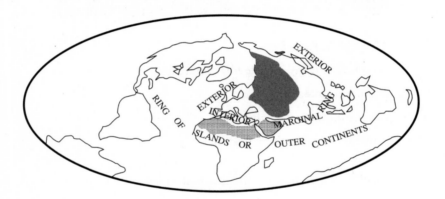

    (A)   the continental part of Eurasia forms the world's heartland and constitutes a potential threat for sea powers

    (B)   only a combined Anglo-American-Russian alliance could prevent German world domination

    (C)   the theory advanced by Alfred Mahan in *The Influence of Sea Power Upon History* was correct

    (D)   sea powers must dominate land powers through containment

    (E)   the Southern Hemisphere is as significant as the Northern Hemisphere

29.   The drawing shown below by Karl Arnold appeared in *Simplicissimus* (July, 1924) and was entitled *Neue Typen: Der Rassemensch—New Types: The Racial Man* or *The Man of Breeding*. It was a critical comment on

(A) the Prussian Junkers who condemned the Versailles Treaty

(B) the anti-Semites who supported Hitler and the emerging Nazi Party

(C) German capitalism

(D) German social decadence

(E) the ineptitude of the Social Democratic Party

30. The notion that "civilization was not the product of an artificial, international elite… but the genuine culture of the common people, the *Volk*" was advanced by

(A) René de Chateaubriand in *The Genius of Christianity*

(B) Georg Wilhelm Hegel in *Reason in History*

(C) Giuseppe Verdi in *Don Carlo*

(D) William Wordsworth in *Lyrical Ballads*

(E) Johann Gottfried Herder in *Ideas for a Philosophy of Human History*

31. The Reform Bills of 1832, 1867, and 1884–1885 in Great Britain

(A) eliminated child labor abuses in the textile industry

(B) eliminated the power of the House of Lords

(C) alleviated the most drastic problems confronting the Irish

(D) extended the franchise and redistributed seats in Parliament

(E) gave the vote to all adults over age 21

32. The Dual Alliance of 1879 may be described as all of the following EXCEPT

   (A) a defensive pact between Germany and Austria

   (B) a move, from the German perspective, directed at the diplomatic isolation of France

   (C) a move, from the Austrian perspective, directed at Italian encroachment in the Balkans

   (D) a long-term alliance renewed through the World War I

   (E) a move to address German concerns over growing anti-German sentiment in Russia

33. During the era of the French Revolution, the Thermidorian Reaction

   (A) initiated the Reign of Terror

   (B) resulted in the dissolution of the National Assembly

   (C) terminated the Reign of Terror after the execution of Robespierre

   (D) was the direct cause of the rise of Napoleon

   (E) witnessed the execution of Louis XVI and Marie Antoinette

34. The era of the Napoleonic Wars was concluded by the

   (A) Peace of Utrecht

   (B) Congress of Berlin

   (C) Peace of Westphalia

   (D) Congress of Vienna

   (E) Peace of Paris

35. Charles Fourier, Robert Owen, and Claude de Saint-Simon may be called

   (A) anarchists

   (B) Liberals

   (C) advocates of capitalism

   (D) pre-Marxist socialists

   (E) revisionists

36. The July Revolution in France resulted in the

   (A) development of democracy in France

   (B) installation of Louis Philippe as king

   (C) presidency of Louis-Napoleon Bonaparte

(D)   establishment of a republican form of government

(E)   withdrawal of Prussian troops

37.   The preceding map indicates locations of European revolutions during what year?

(A)   1820

(B)   1830

(C)   1848

(D)   1919

(E)   1825

38.   The Frankfurt Assembly was

(A)   a Pan-German assembly interested in the formulation of an integrated union of German states

(B)   Bismarck's instrument to bring about a Prussian-dominated Germany

(C)   a group of German representatives who were concerned primarily with economic issues

(D)   an Austrian effort to obstruct Bismarck's plan for German unification

(E)   a group dedicated to the *grossdeutsch* plan

39. The failure of the Revolutions of 1848 may be attributed to all the following factors EXCEPT

    (A) the continuing loyalty of the armed forces to the old leadership

    (B) the cunning of the old leadership in manipulating revolutionary forces

    (C) the lack of effective organization among nationalist revolutionaries across national boundaries

    (D) the failure of liberal revolutionaries to address social and economic needs

    (E) the rejection of liberal reforms by radical workers in the West because those reforms ignored social and economic considerations

40. The industrial economy of the nineteenth century was based upon all of the following EXCEPT

    (A) the availability of raw materials

    (B) an adequate labor supply

    (C) the availability of capital

    (D) a system to distribute finished products to market

    (E) an equitable distribution of profits among all who were involved in production

41. Which one of the following would most likely oppose laissez-faire policies in nineteenth-century Europe?

    (A) Factory owner

    (B) Liberal

    (C) Free trader

    (D) Socialist

    (E) Middle-class businessman

42. According to the graph shown below, which was the most urbanized part of Europe in the nineteenth century?

    (A) Eastern Europe

    (B) Prussia

    (C) France

    (D) Central Europe

    (E) The British Isles

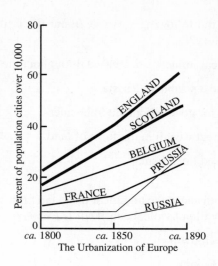

The Urbanization of Europe

43. "Anxiety, or the idea of anxiety, permeates modern thought in all its aspects. You find it almost everywhere you look: in Freudian psychology, in the philosophy of existentialism, in poetry and the novel, in the language of religion...and...of course, in contemporary political movements."
This passage is an example of writing in

(A)   intellectual history

(B)   social history

(C)   economic history

(D)   diplomatic history

(E)   political history

44. "The greatest good for the greatest number" was a belief of

(A)   Marx

(B)   Bentham

(C)   Nietzsche

(D)   Freud

(E)   de Maistre

45. Which one of the following was true about the European middle class in the nineteenth century?

    (A) Its political influence decreased throughout the century.

    (B) It was most sizable in Russia.

    (C) It called for government aid to business.

    (D) It held great wealth in the form of land.

    (E) It espoused liberalism.

46. Which author advanced the argument that anarchism would be achieved through education and without violence in *What Is Property?*

    (A) William Godwin

    (B) Mikhail Bakunin

    (C) Georges Sorel

    (D) Pierre Proudhon

    (E) Charles Fourier

47. The Revisionist Marxist movement

    (A) failed to gain a following during the late nineteenth century

    (B) supported the Marxist concept of revolution but differed with numerous other Marxist prescriptions

    (C) encompassed the Fabian Society, the Social Democratic Party in Germany, and the French Socialist movement led by Jean Jaurès

    (D) was the base upon which Lenin developed his support for the deployment of Communism in Russia

    (E) never attracted much support except in China and Vietnam

48. The New Economic Plan (NEP) was

    (A) Lenin's plan to revitalize the Russian economy after Russia's Civil War

    (B) a scheme developed by Trotsky to enhance his control over the Communist Party organization through economic concessions

    (C) Gorbachev's 1989 plan for the restructuring of the Russian economy

    (D) Nicholas II's last attempt to recover political support through economic concessions

    (E) the name given to Stalin's first economic plan, which emphasized collective farming and improvements in heavy industry

49. The 1878 Congress of Berlin resulted in all of the following EXCEPT

    (A) the recognition of Rumania, Serbia, and Montenegro as independent

    (B) the realization of Russian war aims at the expense of the Turks

    (C) the transfer of Cyprus from the Ottoman Empire to Great Britain

    (D) the establishment of the autonomous principality of Bulgaria

    (E) Austrian military occupation of Bosnia and Herzegovina

50. Czar Alexander II of Russia (1855–1881)

    (A) established *zemstvos*—assemblies that allowed nobles to retain control over rural politics, but also introduced social services there

    (B) liberated the serfs, which improved their political, social, and economic well-being

    (C) made no effort to reform the Russian judicial system

    (D) overhauled the military with sweeping reforms limiting its powers

    (E) was motivated to reform Russian society not out of fear, but because of his genuine desire to improve the condition of all of his people

51. The failure of Wilhelm II's government to continue the Reinsurance Treaty with Russia

    (A) led Russia to adopt a position of "splendid isolationism"

    (B) eventually led to the isolation of Germany

    (C) resulted in the Austrian-Russian Entente of 1894

    (D) caused Russia to undertake a massive naval building program

    (E) led Russia to support the establishment of Poland as a buffer state

52. The Russian Revolution of 1905

    (A) resulted in the abdication of the Czar

    (B) was immediately suppressed by Nicholas II

    (C) led to the removal of the Orthodox Church from politics in Russia

    (D) was the primary cause for Russia's defeat in the Russo-Japanese War

    (E) led Nicholas II to issue the October Manifesto, which called for an advisory representative assembly (the *Duma*) to be formed

53. Oscar Wilde's *Picture of Dorian Gray* and Thomas Mann's *Death in Venice*

   (A) are examples of the Romanticism that dominated literature at the turn of the twentieth century

   (B) embodied a new symbolist direction in literature that addressed previously ignored themes

   (C) emphasized a new sense of realism in literature

   (D) were representative of a literary movement known as expressionism

   (E) were not well received by the intellectuals of the era

54. All of the following statements concerning the Third French Republic are accurate EXCEPT:

   (A) The Dreyfus Affair, Panama Scandal, and Boulanger Crisis were serious threats to its continuance.

   (B) The Third Republic was established in the midst of French defeat in the Franco-Prussian War.

   (C) It was threatened upon its creation by the Paris Commune.

   (D) It established a Constitution in 1875 that provided for a republican form of government.

   (E) It supported an extension of the power of the Catholic Church in French society.

55. The Berlin Conference of 1884–1885

   (A) specified that Britain would have control over the Niger and Congo rivers

   (B) established the principle that an imperial claim had to be supported by effective control over the interior

   (C) specified that the Congo would be under Portuguese control

   (D) supported the dream of Cecil Rhodes for a Cape-to-Cairo railroad under British control

   (E) established Italian authority in Libya

56. Bismarck's *Kulturkampf*

   (A) consisted of a series of measures intended to eliminate the impact of Marxism in German politics

   (B) was a series of anti-Catholic laws directed at curtailing the influence of the Center Party

   (C) was his diplomatic strategy to maintain the diplomatic isolation of France

(D)   was intended to disrupt the progress of the Social Democratic Party

(E)   was denounced by Pope Pius X

57.   The Parliament Act of 1911 included all of the following provisions EXCEPT that the

(A)   life span of Parliament was reduced from seven to five years

(B)   revenue bills approved by the House of Commons automatically became law after being sent to the House of Lords

(C)   House of Lords had no veto power over revenue bills

(D)   House of Lords could effectively veto nonrevenue bills

(E)   House of Lords could only delay enactment of nonrevenue bills

58.   The expansion of "division of labor" and "mass production" through the development of standard parts and manufacturing was stimulated by

(A)   the institution of bank credit

(B)   the factory system

(C)   competition

(D)   economic imperialism

(E)   political rivalries

59.   Who was the dominant personality at the Congress of Vienna?

(A)   Metternich

(B)   Bismarck

(C)   Alexander I

(D)   Talleyrand

(E)   Wellington

60.   In 1829, the Ottoman Turks were forced to accept the Treaty of Adrianople, which

(A)   recognized the independence of Bulgaria

(B)   recognized the independence of Greece

(C)   granted Christians access to the Holy Places in Palestine

(D)   permitted Russia to have access to the Mediterranean

(E)   recognized the independence of Serbia

61. The Treaty of Brest-Litovsk

 (A) concluded hostilities between Great Britain and Turkey

 (B) ended the war between the Allies and Hungary

 (C) concluded hostilities between the Allies and Bulgaria

 (D) was a humiliating agreement that the Russians signed with Germany

 (E) concluded the war between the Allies and the Ottoman Empire

62. The following chart indicates that

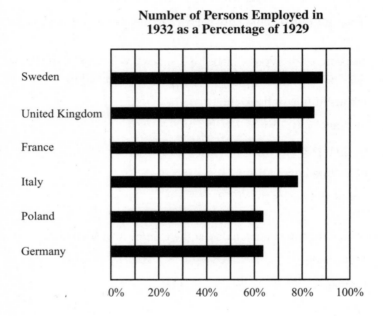

**Number of Persons Employed in
1932 as a Percentage of 1929**

 (A) Nations with large populations were better able to respond to the impact of the Depression than nations with smaller populations.

 (B) Advanced industrial societies had lower rates of unemployment during this period.

 (C) The postwar economies in Central and Eastern Europe were fragile and subject to rapid deterioration during an economic collapse.

 (D) Sweden and the United Kingdom had the strongest economic systems in the world.

 (E) Nations with small populations were better able to respond to the impact of the Depression than nations with larger populations.

63. Which of the following is NOT true of Ulrich Zwingli (1484–1531)?

    (A) He taught that it is not necessary to fast during Lent.

    (B) He banned the use of religious images in churches.

    (C) He agreed with Martin Luther on the doctrine of the Lord's Supper.

    (D) He died at a battle between Catholic and Protestant forces.

    (E) He abolished monasteries.

64. What does the following cartoon refer to?

    (A) The continuing cooperation between Hitler and Stalin during the 1930s

    (B) The contradictions inherent in the Russo-German Non-Aggression Pact

    (C) The delight shared by Stalin and Hitler

    (D) The defeat of Czechoslovakia

    (E) The defeat of Finland

65. The Glorious Revolution of 1688–1889 resulted in all of the following EXCEPT

    (A) the flight and abdication of James II

    (B) the passage of the Bill of Rights

    (C) the elevation of William III and Mary II to the throne

    (D) specification that all future monarchs must be members of the Church of England

    (E) an agreement that, in the event of no heirs, the house of Hanover would succeed the Stuarts

66. The text of Denis Diderot's *Encyclopédie* was centered primarily on

    (A) theology

    (B) technology

    (C) history

    (D) philosophy

    (E) poetry

67. In the following poem, the Hungarian-Swiss Tzara provides a sample of which twentieth-century literary movement?

    "The aeroplane weaves telegraph wires
    and the fountain sings the same song,…
    At the rendez-vous of the coachmen the aperitif is orange
    but the locomotive mechanics have blue eyes.
    The lady has lost her smile in the woods."

    (A) Symbolism

    (B) Expressionism

    (C) Deconstructionism

    (D) Dadaism

    (E) Idealism

68. The driving force behind Hegel's dialectic was

    (A) nationalism

    (B) racial superiority

    (C) universal reason

    (D) materialism

    (E) religious values

69. After 1950 the Soviet Union suppressed movements toward more liberal governments in all of the following European countries EXCEPT

    (A) East Germany

    (B) Poland

    (C) Czechoslovakia

    (D) Yugoslavia

    (E) Hungary

70. Friedrich Nietzsche advanced his philosophy in which works?

    (A) *Thus Spake Zarathustra* and *The Will to Power*

    (B) *The Golden Bough* and *The Wild Duck*

    (C) *The Return of the Native* and *Jude the Obscure*

    (D) *Civilization and Its Discontents* and *The Riddle of the Universe*

    (E) *The Descent of Man* and *The Weavers*

Art © *The Educational Alliance, Inc. / Estate of Peter Blume/*
Licensed by VAGA, Inc., New York, NY

71.   In the preceding painting entitled *The Eternal City* by the American painter
      Peter Blume (1937),

      (A)   fascist Italy is dominated by the personality of Mussolini

      (B)   fascism in Italy appears to have improved the general condition of the
            people

      (C)   Mussolini emerges as a benevolent dictator who was genuinely concerned
            with the condition of the people

      (D)   there is a sympathetic rendering of the impact of fascism on Italian life
            and institutions

      (E)   one can see his account of the March on Rome in 1922

72.   During the "June Days" in Paris (1848),

      (A)   conservative monarchists were overwhelmed by the mob

      (B)   the forces led by Louis Blanc prevailed

      (C)   the army suppressed the radical revolutionary element

      (D)   Louis Napoleon came to power

      (E)   Lamartine was recognized as the leader of the revolution

73.   In an effort to conduct a successful economic war against Britain, Napoleon
      created the

    (A)   Bank of France

    (B)   Confederation of the Rhine

    (C)   Continental System

    (D)   Napoleonic Code

    (E)   Kingdom of the Two Sicilies

74.   The 1909 budget proposed by Lloyd George advocated

    (A)   progressive income and inheritance taxes

    (B)   an end to all property taxes

    (C)   drastic reductions in funding for domestic programs

    (D)   drastic reductions in expenditures for weaponry

    (E)   a redistribution of excessive tax revenues

75.   In the painting shown below, *Guernica* (1937) by Pablo Picasso, the artist rendered his interpretation of

©2007 Estate of Pablo Picasso/
Artists Rights Society (ARS), New York, NY

    (A)   the chaos caused by the Versailles Peace Conference

    (B)   Hitler's invasion of Poland

    (C)   the impact of the aerial bombardment of a Spanish town by the German Condor Legion during the Spanish Civil War

    (D)   the effect of the Depression on French society

    (E)   the fall of France in 1940

Unemployment

(Numbers in thousands & percentage of appropriate work force)

	Germany		Great Britain	
1930	3,076	15.3	1,917	14.6
1932	5,575	30.1	2,745	22.5
1934	2,718	14.9	2,159	17.7
1936	2,151	11.6	1,755	14.3
1938	429	2.1	1,191	13.3

76. The preceding chart indicates

   (A) that Germany and Britain recovered from the Depression at about the same level and rate

   (B) that Hitler's Germany reduced unemployment at a remarkable rate during the period from 1936 and 1938

   (C) that Britain was complacent about its double-digit unemployment during the 1930s

   (D) that the German economic system was superior to that of Great Britain

   (E) that the use of the adjective "appropriate" distorts valuable data in order to make Nazi Germany look better

77. The following maps indicate changes in the western border of Russia between what years?

   (A) 1815 and 1922

   (B) 1848 and 1945

   (C) 1914 and 1921

   (D) 1914 and 1950

   (E) 1725 and 1920

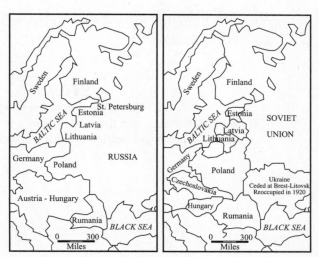

78. Article 231 of the Versailles Treaty

    (A) is known as the "War Guilt" clause and established Germany's responsibility for the war

    (B) established the new nation of Poland

    (C) denounced all secret treaties

    (D) established the League of Nations

    (E) resulted in the decentralization of Germany

79. The Russian blockade of Berlin in 1948–1949 was a reaction to

    (A) the merging of the British, French, and American zones into West Germany

    (B) the Truman Doctrine

    (C) the Marshall Plan

    (D) the formation of NATO

    (E) the Chinese revolution

80. West Germany recovered during the 1950s and early 1960s under the political leadership of

    (A) Willy Brandt

    (B) Konrad Adenauer

    (C) Heinrich Brüning

    (D) Alfred Hugenberg

    (E) Erich Honecker

STOP
This is the end of Section I.
If time still remains, you may check your work only in this section.
Do not begin Section II until instructed to do so.

Section II

PART A – DOCUMENT-BASED ESSAY

TIME: Reading Period—15 minutes
    Writing Time: 45 minutes
    1 Essay Question

> **DIRECTIONS:** Read both the document-based essay question in Part A and the choices in Parts B and C during the reading period. Use the time to organize answers. You must answer Part A (the document-based essay question) and choose ONE question from Part B and ONE question from Part C to answer.

This question is designed to test your ability to work with historical documents. As you analyze each document, *take into account its source and the point of view of the author*. Write an essay on the following topic that integrates your analysis of the documents. You may refer to historical facts and developments not mentioned in the documents.

Analyze the rivalry between Benjamin Disraeli and William Gladstone that dominated English politics from the late 1860s to 1880.

Historical Background: During the late 1860s the political rivalry between the conservative Benjamin Disraeli and the liberal Gladstone blossomed and continued until Disraeli's death in 1881. This period witnessed the extension of the franchise, a wide range of domestic legislation, and a debate on imperialism.

Document 1
"Hoity-Toity"

Document 2
Letter from Queen Victoria to William Gladstone —May 6, 1870

…The circumstances respecting the Bill to give women the same position as men with respect to Parliamentary franchise gives her an opportunity to observe that she had for some time past wished to call Mr. Gladstone's attention to the mad & utterly demoralizing movement of the present day to place women in the same position as to professions—as *men*;—& amongst others, in the *Medical Line* ….

The Queen is a woman herself—& knows what an anomaly her *own* position is:—but that can be reconciled with reason & propriety tho' it is a terribly difficult & trying one. But to tear away all the barriers w^h surround a woman, & to propose that they sh^{ld} study with *men*—things w^h c^{ld} not be named before them—certainly not *in a mixed audience*—w^{hd} be to introduce a total disregard of what must be considered as belonging to the rules & principles of morality.

The Queen feels so strongly upon his dangerous & unchristian & unnatural *cry* & movement of "women's rights,"—in w^h she knows Mr. Gladstone agrees; (as he sent her that excellent Pamphlet by a Lady) that she is most anxious that Mr. Gladstone & others sh^{ld} take some steps to check this alarming danger & to make whatever use they can of her name.

She sends the letters w^h speak for themselves.

Let woman be what God intended; a helpmate for a man—but with totally different duties & vocations.

Document 3
"The Conservative Programme"

Document 4
"The Colossus of the World"

Document 5
"On the Dizzy Brink"

Document 6
"A Bad Example"

STOP
This is the end of Section II, Part A.
If time still remains, you may check your work only in this section.
Do not begin Section II, Part B until instructed to do so.

PART B – Essay Question

TIME: 35 minutes
    1 Essay Question

> **DIRECTIONS:** Answer ONE question from the three questions below. Choose the question that you are most prepared to answer thoroughly. You should spend about 5 minutes organizing or outlining your answer.

1. Analyze and compare the motivations for the wars of Louis XIV and Napoleon.

2. Analyze and compare causes for the rise of fascism in Germany and Italy.

3. The Stuarts have been held partly accountable for the decline of monarchical power in Great Britain. Analyze the justification for such a position.

STOP
This is the end of Section II, Part B.
If time still remains, you may check your work only in this section.
Do not begin Section II, Part C until instructed to do so.

PART C – Essay Question

TIME: 35 minutes
      1 Essay Question

DIRECTIONS: Answer ONE question from the three questions below. Choose the question that you are most prepared to answer thoroughly. You should spend about 5 minutes organizing or outlining your answer.

---

4.   Discuss and analyze the ideological legacy of the French Revolution of 1789.

5.   At the Paris Peace Conference, Germany was forced to acknowledge its guilt for the World War I. Discuss and analyze the situations that led to the outbreak of the war.

6.   Assess the extent to which the overseas empires had an impact upon European economic and political life from 1870 to 1914.

END OF EXAM

PRACTICE EXAM 1

AP European History

Answer Key

1.	(D)	21.	(B)	41.	(D)	61.	(D)
2.	(A)	22.	(C)	42.	(E)	62.	(C)
3.	(D)	23.	(D)	43.	(A)	63.	(C)
4.	(C)	24.	(B)	44.	(B)	64.	(B)
5.	(C)	25.	(D)	45.	(E)	65.	(E)
6.	(C)	26.	(B)	46.	(D)	66.	(B)
7.	(A)	27.	(E)	47.	(C)	67.	(D)
8.	(E)	28.	(A)	48.	(A)	68.	(C)
9.	(C)	29.	(B)	49.	(B)	69.	(D)
10.	(D)	30.	(E)	50.	(A)	70.	(A)
11.	(C)	31.	(D)	51.	(B)	71.	(A)
12.	(B)	32.	(C)	52.	(E)	72.	(C)
13.	(C)	33.	(C)	53.	(B)	73.	(C)
14.	(B)	34.	(D)	54.	(E)	74.	(A)
15.	(C)	35.	(D)	55.	(B)	75.	(C)
16.	(B)	36.	(B)	56.	(B)	76.	(B)
17.	(C)	37.	(C)	57.	(D)	77.	(C)
18.	(E)	38.	(A)	58.	(B)	78.	(A)
19.	(C)	39.	(B)	59.	(A)	79.	(A)
20.	(B)	40.	(E)	60.	(B)	80.	(B)

PRACTICE EXAM 1

AP European History

Detailed Explanations of Answers

Section I

1. **(D)**

   Renaissance Humanism was a threat to the Church because it (D) emphasized a return to the original sources of Christianity—the Bible and the writings of the Fathers of the Church. In that light, humanists tended to ignore or denounce the proceedings of Church councils and pontiffs during the Middle Ages. While many Renaissance humanists denounced scholasticism, there was no inherent opposition to it, and many retained support of the late Medieval philosophy. Renaissance Humanism did not espouse atheism, nor did it advance an amoral philosophy; it tended to advance a neo-Platonism through the writings of such individuals as Pico della Mirandola and Marsilio Ficino.

2. **(A)**

   Erasmus of Rotterdam was the author of (A) *The Praise of Folly*, which was a criticism of the ambitions of the clergy. *The Birth of Venus* (B) was a painting by Rafael. More was the author of *Utopia* (C); Machiavelli wrote (D) *The Prince*; and Cervantes was the author of *Don Quixote*.

3. **(D)**

   Few Northern Humanists (exceptions: Melanchthon and Reuchlin) approved of the Reformation: Erasmus criticized laxness in the Catholic Church but refused to join Protestant reformers. Northern or Christian Humanism used studies of ancient languages to make Scriptures available in local languages and to produce good scholarly versions of the writings of the Church Fathers. Northern humanists acknowledged the Church's use of the Vulgate Latin Bible, mainly with the uneducated, but they themselves tried to study and use only the best Greek and Latin in their translations.

4. **(C)**

   Each of the three major Protestant groups—Lutheran, Calvinist, and Anabaptist—relied in major ways on particular social elements. Although Lutheranism drew support from a broad social spectrum, Luther himself was forced to rely on sympathetic nobles of the Holy Roman Empire in order to defend Lutheranism against the Holy Roman Emperor. Calvinism held special appeal for the new middle class, particularly business elements. Anabaptism drew most of its membership from the peasantry in western Germany and the Low Countries.

5. **(C)**

At the Colloquy of Marburg in 1529, Luther and Zwingli failed to concur on the nature of the Eucharist and the concept of predestination; this led to the fragmentation of Protestantism. (A) is incorrect because the Catholic strategy was centered on the establishment of new religious orders and the reforms of the Council of Trent. Luther was declared an outlaw by Charles V at the Diet of Worms in 1521. Charles V's attempts to reconcile Luther with the Church were confined to debates that occurred prior to 1521. Thomas Wolsey's fall from power as Henry VIII's adviser was not related to the Colloquy, but stemmed from the divorce crisis.

6. **(C)**

English Puritanism developed during the reign of Elizabeth I because of dissatisfaction with the scope and breadth of the Elizabethan Religious Settlement among exiles and others who were influenced by Calvinist views. Obviously, (A) is incorrect because the Council of Trent advanced Catholic doctrines; Elizabeth I was interested in consolidating, not extending, Protestantism in England (B); the Jesuit Mission (D) occurred in 1580 and was not related to Puritanism; Puritanism (E) opposed the earlier forms of worship, whether Roman Catholic or Henrician.

7. **(A)**

The response of the Catholic Church to the Reformation was delayed because the Papacy feared remnants of the Conciliar Movement, which had been evident at the Councils of Constance, Basel, and Florence. This movement, based in Roman Catholic tradition, asserted that authority within the Church resided in the assembly of bishops; it challenged Petrine Supremacy and the authority of the Papacy. Rome (B) had little interest in coordinating its policy with secular leaders, although the early support of Charles V and Henry VIII was well received. By the 1530s, most intelligent Church leaders did not (C) think that Protestantism would self-destruct or that (D) the situation was not serious. The monetary situation of the Church (E) was not relevant to its taking a position against Protestantism.

8. **(E)**

The Counter-Reformation did not include (E) a willingness to negotiate nondoctrinal issues with reformers; indeed, the Catholic Church considered all confrontational issues to be doctrinal. The Council of Trent (B) was convened in three sessions from 1545 to 1563 and reaffirmed traditional Catholic doctrines; new religious orders (D) such as the Jesuits appeared; the Papacy (C) became more assertive through its issuing of the *Index of Prohibited Books* in 1558–1559.

9. **(C)**

The Petition of Right addressed perceived constitutional abuses related to the proceedings of the Court of the Star Chamber, a ship tax, and the quartering of British troops in private dwellings; upon its acceptance by Charles I, additional sources of revenue were provided to alleviate the financial crisis caused by unsuccessful wars against Spain and France. (A) is incorrect because it refers to James I, who died in 1625; (B) is false because Parliament did not vote on Buckingham's execution—he was murdered in 1628; (D) Charles I's religious policies cannot be labeled radical—they were reactionary and led to the charge that Charles I was sympathetic to Catholicism; (E) the Addled Parliament convened in 1614 and was not connected with the Petition of Right.

10. **(D)**

Descartes argued that God was essential as Guarantor of the laws of the universe. Descartes discovered coordinate or analytical geometry, developed the science of optics, used "cogito ergo sum" as his starting place, and believed in a dualism between the physical and spiritual worlds, separate but linked.

11. **(C)**

The Edict of Nantes of 1598, issued by Henry IV, allowed French Huguenots to practice their religion and fortify some cities. The Edict of Fontainebleau (B), issued by Louis XIV in 1685, revoked the Edict of Nantes. The Edict of Potsdam (A), issued by Elector Frederick William of Brandenburg-Prussia in 1686, invited French Protestants fleeing France to settle in his lands. The Papacy (D) opposed the Edict of Nantes and all agreements that tolerated Protestant groups in Catholic countries. The Peace of Amiens (E) was a treaty of 1802 involving Napoleon.

12. **(B)**

Francis Bacon advanced empiricism in the early seventeenth century. (A) While Galileo accomplished much in science, his emphasis was more on math as the new language of science, not a philosophy. Descartes's *Discourse on Method* (1637) develops a mathematically oriented type of deduction; Baruch Spinoza's (D) contributions occurred later, in mathematics and ethics. In addition to formulating his law on gas and temperature, Robert Boyle (E) was a chemist who did much to discredit alchemy during the second half of the seventeenth century.

13. **(C)**

France and Ottoman Turkey. Austria was attacked twice, between 1660 and 1685, by the Ottoman Turks and confronted during the same time by wars with France. (A) and (E) are incorrect because Italy did not exist at that time. (B) is incorrect because England was allied with Austria, and Russia was undergoing political crises not resolved until Peter the Great seized power and reformed the government. (D) is incorrect because Prussia did not oppose Austria until 1740.

14. **(B)**

Beginning with terminology (*Fronde*), this question asks for an analysis of these periodic revolts by the nobility of France. A phenomenon of the sixteenth and seventeenth centuries, they were regarded as threats to royal authority by monarchical ministers Mazarin and Richelieu, who suppressed them ruthlessly. Most revolts ended when Louis XIV involved the most powerful members of the old nobility in sterile and useless ceremonial lives at his palace of Versailles.

15. **(C)**

The Peace of Utrecht terminated the wars of Louis XIV, restoring peace to Europe. (A) and (B) are incorrect because France, though defeated, was still the most powerful nation in Europe. (D) is incorrect because Canada was not transferred to England until the Treaty of Paris in 1763. (E) is incorrect because the Peace of Utrecht was unrelated to the unification of Germany, which occurred in 1871.

16. **(B)**

A moderate proposal that called on France to adopt a political system similar to that of Great Britain was an element espoused by Montesquieu in (B) *The Spirit of the Laws*. *The Social Contract* (A) was written by Jean Jacques Rousseau; *The Encyclopedia* (C) was by Denis Diderot; *The Declaration of the Rights of Man and the Citizen* (D) was produced by the National Assembly in August 1789; and John Locke wrote *Two Treatises on Civil Government*.

17. **(C)**

Hobbes's warlike state of nature accords well with Calvin's theology of sinfulness. Calvin's *Institutes* has a political agenda, namely a belief in establishing a "City of God" on earth; and the strict rules of Geneva prove this. Rousseau (A) and Locke (E) are more sanguine about human nature; Condorcet (B) was the apostle of progress, and likewise optimistic. Montesquieu (D) was firmly against absolutist government as practiced by Calvin and theorized by Hobbes; likewise, Locke's ideal of constitutional monarchy is not consonant with Hobbes's absolutism.

18. **(E)**

Mercantilism was an economic philosophy identified with "bullionism" and the need to maintain a favorable balance of trade. Utopian Socialism (A) was an early nineteenth-century philosophy that emphasized the need for a more equitable distribution of wealth; (B) Marxism and (D) Syndicalism were leftist approaches to economics and politics. (C) Capitalism was the developing condition in which Mercantilism operated.

19. **(C)**

The *liberum veto* (C) restricted the national and political development of Poland. Under this peculiar law, any member of the Polish Diet could dissolve the assembly by using his veto; this provision led to a highly decentralized Poland that was exploited by

Austria, Russia, and Prussia during the eighteenth century. The *liberum veto* had nothing to do with (A) Britain, (B) France, (D) Peter the Great's Westernization of Russia, or (E) Mazzini's Roman Republic.

20. **(B)**

Hobbes's *Leviathan* described early human society (the "state of nature") as an anarchic "war of all against all." For self-protection, citizens agreed to form the first government, an agreement termed by Hobbes the "social contract." It is important to read the quotation carefully, since two of the answers (B) and (C) are from the *Leviathan*; you may be misled into choosing (C) because you have studied it in a class, and "social contract" sounds familiar. The concept of natural rights, incorporated into the French Declaration of the Rights of Man, was summarized by John Locke as the idea that human beings are born "free, equal, and independent." "Reason of state" was the justification used by French statesmen such as Cardinal Richelieu to defend measures to create a centralized absolute monarchy in France. Answer (E), nationalism, is not only incorrect but also irrelevant to this question.

21. **(B)**

In *Emile* Rousseau (B) called for a "natural" education free of the artificial encumbrances imposed by institutions such as the Church. His view on the Social Contract (A) was advanced separately; Rousseau did not (C) denounce Voltaire for his lifestyle; nor did Rousseau in *Emile* identify with (D) Montesquieu's sympathy for the English constitutional monarchy. Since the concept of God was essential to Rousseau's thought, he did not advance a case for atheism (E).

22. **(C)**

In 1789 these statements were part of (C) the Declaration of the Rights of Man and the Citizen passed by the National Assembly in France. The English Bill of Rights (1689) was a consequence of the Glorious Revolution when William and Mary came to power. The Constitution of the Year III (1795) established the Directory in France; it was a government that was advised by experts or intellectuals. In *What Is the Third Estate?* (1788) the Abbé Sieyès maintained that the Third Estate of the Estates-General was in fact a "National Assembly" and representative of the national sovereign power.

23. **(D)**

The drawing represents (D) Lavoisier's Apparatus for the Decomposition of Air. The Leyden Jar (A) was a means of storing electricity and was used by Benjamin Franklin (E) in his kite experiment. While Stephen Gray did make contributions to the science of electricity (B) and the erroneous Phlogiston theory (C) was toppled during this period, they were not related to the illustration.

24. **(B)**

The picture is of the spinning jenny invented by James Hargreaves.

25. **(D)**

English Utilitarianism was identified with the phrase (D) "the greatest good for the greatest number." Jeremy Bentham, James Mill, and John Stuart Mill were prominent Utilitarians. "All power to the people" and "From each according to his labor, to each according to his need" (B) were elements in Lenin's rhetoric. "Universal reason" (C) is identified with Georg Wilhelm Hegel; and "collectivist nationalism" is associated with Johann Fichte.

26. **(B)**

In January 1848—only weeks prior to the outbreak of the February revolution in Paris—Alexis de Tocqueville addressed the Chamber of Deputies. In the remarks quoted, Tocqueville addressed the concerns of French liberals—the need to open the political system to the people and the urgency of the economic crisis caused by a misdistribution of wealth. Tocqueville did not (A) address the United States Senate in 1838, (C) the court of Napoleon III in 1870, (D) the Peers of the Third Republic in 1875, or (E) the court-martial of Dreyfus in 1894.

27. **(E)**

Among the achievements (some short-lived) of the Jacobins were (A) abolishing slavery, (B) giving the franchise to all adult males, (C) adopting the metric system, and (D) decreeing the law of the maximum, which fixed prices on essentials and raised wages. The Jacobins did not succeed in the (E) distribution of all land among the peasants.

28. **(A)**

The map indicates the thesis advanced by H. Mackinder in 1904 that (A) the continental part of Eurasia forms the world's heartland and constitutes a potential threat to sea powers. Mackinder and other geopoliticians influenced policy makers during this period; later, during the 1930s, Mackinder abandoned his thesis because of technological and economic trends. (D) A consequence of Mackinder's thesis may have been that sea powers must dominate land powers through containment; such a conclusion would have been supported by (C) the American strategist Alfred Mahan, who wrote *The Influence of Sea Power Upon History, 1660–1783*. Mackinder did not contend that (B) only a combined Anglo-American-Russian alliance could prevent German world domination or that (E) the Southern Hemisphere is as significant as the Northern.

29. **(B)**

The drawing *Neue Typen: Der Rassemensch* by Karl Arnold (July 1924) was a critical commentary on (B) the anti-Semites, who supported Hitler and the emerging Nazi Party. Obviously, (A), (C), (D), and (E) are incorrect responses.

30. **(E)**

The notion that "civilization was not the product of an artificial, international elite… but of some genuine culture of the common people, the *Volk*" was advanced by (E) Herder in *Ideas for a Philosophy of Human History*. Herder influenced Fichte,

Hegel (B), and other German nationalists and intellectuals. Wordsworth's (D) *Lyrical Ballads* did not advance such a directly political theme; the conservative (A) Chateaubriand emphasized the role of divine intervention and a human response to religion in *The Genius of Christianity*. Such sentiments are not reflected in Verdi's opera *Don Carlo*.

31. **(D)**

The Reform Bills of 1832, 1867, and 1884–1885 in Britain were significant milestones in the evolution of constitutional rights in Britain, mainly through extending the franchise and redistributing seats in Parliament. These measures eliminated many "rotten boroughs" and provided industrialized cities of the Midlands with parliamentary representation. Efforts to eliminate child labor abuses were embodied in a series of acts, including the Factory Act of 1833. The influence of the House of Lords was not curtailed until the passage of the Parliament Bill of 1911. The myriad political, economic, and social ills confronting the Irish were not resolved in the nineteenth century. In 1918 all men over 21 and women over 30 were given the right to vote; women over 21 were enfranchised in 1928.

32. **(C)**

From the Austrian perspective, the Dual Alliance was directed at Russian—not Italian—encroachment in the Balkans. The Dual Alliance (1879) was a defensive pact between Austria and Germany that was renewed through World War I and addressed German concerns over the diplomatic isolation of France and growing anti-German sentiment.

33. **(C)**

The Thermidorian Reaction beginning in July 1794 (C) terminated the Reign of Terror with the execution of Robespierre. The Terror was initiated in June 1793 when radical Jacobins overthrew the Girondins; the National Assembly was dissolved in 1791 when the Legislative Assembly was formed; Napoleon did not come to power until the *coup d'état* of the Eighteenth Brumaire in 1799; Louis XVI and Marie Antoinette were executed by vote of the Convention prior to the seizure of that institution by the radical Jacobins.

34. **(D)**

The Congress of Vienna concluded the wars of the Napoleonic era. The Peace of Utrecht (1713) ended the War of the Spanish Succession; the Congress of Berlin (1878) discussed the Russo-Turkish War of 1877–1878; The Peace of Westphalia closed the Thirty Years' War; and the Peace of Paris (1856) ended the Crimean War.

35. **(D)**

Charles Fourier, Robert Owen, and Claude de Saint-Simon can be described as pre-Marxist (or Utopian) socialists. Liberals believed in property, free trade, and minimal government intervention. Anarchism was introduced by Proudhon in

What Is Property?; Marx and Engels developed Scientific Socialism; the term *revisionists* is applied to Marxists who differed with some Marxian notions. Socialists and anarchists were opposed to both liberalism and capitalism.

36. **(B)**

Louis Philippe was installed as King of the French as a result of the liberal July Revolution of 1830. While he and his advisers were "liberal" at the beginning of his reign, they were not democrats (A) and became increasingly conservative. The July Revolution established a constitutional monarchy, not a republic (D). Louis Napoleon was elected President of France in 1848 (C). The withdrawal of Prussian troops (E) occurred in 1871, after the Franco-Prussian War.

37. **(C)**

The map shows the revolutions that shook Europe in 1848. The revolutions of 1820 (A) and 1830 (B) were not as significant as the revolutions of 1848. 1825 saw the Decembrist Revolt, not a revolution (E). In 1919, revolutions, often Marxist, occurred in Berlin and other cities in central and eastern Europe.

38. **(A)**

The Frankfurt Assembly was a Pan-German assembly interested in the formulation of a union of German states; its representatives were as interested in the *kleindeutsch* (Small German) solution as the (E) *grossdeutsch* (Big German). Bismarck ((B) and (D)) was not in power during the Frankfurt Assembly (1848–1849); the primary interests of the delegates (C) were political, not economic.

39. **(B)**

The failure of the Revolutions of 1848 cannot be attributed to the intelligence and cunning of the old leadership in manipulating the revolutionary forces. Indeed, the old guard proved to be inept when the revolutions broke; there was a sense of inevitability concerning the revolutions that led to despair and initial compliance with revolutionary demands. It was only after revolutionary leaders made a series of errors (A), (C), (D), and (E) that the old regime was able to restore itself to power.

40. **(E)**

The industrial economy of the nineteenth century was *not* based upon an equitable distribution of profits among those involved in production. Marxists and other critics of capitalism condemned the creed of capitalists and the abhorrent conditions of the industrial proletariat. Raw materials, a constant labor supply, capital, and an expanding marketplace were critical elements in the development of the industrial economy.

41. **(D)**

The term *laissez-faire* is the key: It is a way to signal a belief in free trade—free from government interference or guild regulations. This was a tenet of Liberalism in the nineteenth century; and by mid-century many factory owners and businessmen had been sold on free trade. Socialists, of course, tended to advocate government action to redistribute wealth—anything but ruthless laissez-faire for them!

42. **(E)**

This question requires that you not only interpret the graph correctly but also use your knowledge of history and geography. The two most urbanized areas (England and Scotland) are major parts of the British Isles.

43. **(A)**

Intellectual historians study the role of ideas and intellectuals in history. Do not let the quotation intimidate you; read the quotation and note what kind of subject matter is involved. For a careful reader, the answer is not difficult.

44. **(B)**

Jeremy Bentham, who used this slogan to describe utilitarianism, believed that one of the unfinished tasks remaining from the Enlightenment was the creation of a nonreligious system of morality that would be socially beneficial. His "moral calculus" sought to create a system that would reward the obedient with pleasure, and criminals with pain. Note that (A) is an attempt to mislead you; it seems plausible, but is not correct. De Maistre was an early nineteenth-century French conservative writer. Nietzsche hated British utilitarians. Freud invented other types of "psychic calculus" based on the libido and unconscious drives.

45. **(E)**

The impact of the middle class grew throughout the century [thus (A) is false], and its size was greatly expanded by the Industrial Revolution [thus (B) is false]. Its *laissez-faire* ideology was the opposite of (C) and, as a product of the Industrial Revolution, it did not hold its wealth in the form of large amounts of land, as the old nobility did.

46. **(D)**

Proudhon (D) justified anarchism in *What Is Property?*. He asserted that change could be realized through education and nonviolence. Godwin's (A) *Enquiry Concerning Social Justice* argued for a utopia based upon the perfectibility of individuals. Bakunin (B) was an anarchist who attacked Marx and his philosophy. Sorel (C) was a founder of anarcho-syndicalism (based on unions). Fourier (E) was a Utopian Socialist.

47. **(C)**

Revisionist Marxism encompassed the Fabian Society of Sidney and Beatrice Webb, the German Social Democratic faction of Eduard Bernstein, and French socialists led by Jean Jaurès. Revisionist Marxism gained a significant following (A) during the late 19th century; it opposed the Marxist imperative of revolution; Lenin was an orthodox Marxist who opposed (D) the revisionists; most Asian Marxists did not identify with the revisionist movement.

48. **(A)**

The New Economic Plan (NEP) was Lenin's plan (1921) to revitalize the Russian economy after their Civil War. It was not (B) a scheme by Trotsky to control the Communist Party, nor (D) Nicholas II's attempt to recover political support. Obviously, it was not (C) Gorbachev's 1989 plan for restructuring the Russian economy, although there are valid points of comparison between the 1921 and 1989 schemes. Stalin's economic plan (E) was known as the first Five-Year Plan; it resulted in a long-term commitment to collectivization and the expansion of Russian heavy industry.

49. **(B)**

The Congress of Berlin (1878) did not result in the realization of Russian war aims. Russia wanted to establish a large Bulgarian state, gain access to the Mediterranean Sea, and extend its control in the Black Sea and eastern Balkans. The small, autonomous principality of Bulgaria (D) was established; Rumania, Serbia, and Montenegro were recognized as independent states (A); Cyprus (C) was transferred to Great Britain; and Austria acquired the right to occupy Bosnia and Herzegovina militarily (E); annexation was won in 1908.

50. **(A)**

Czar Alexander II (1855–1881) (A) established the *zemstvos,* assemblies that allowed nobles to influence the votes of towns and peasants, but also introduced social services. His Emancipation Edict (1861) did not (B) improve the well-being of the serfs. Alexander II did (C) make improvements in the judiciary, but (D) no sweeping reforms of the military, only a reduction in years of service and some punishments. He was motivated (E) by fear of the masses, not by a genuine desire to improve the conditions of the Russian people.

51. **(B)**

The failure of Wilhelm II to renew the Reinsurance Treaty with Russia eventually led to the isolation of Germany. Russia was not interested in an (A) isolationist position; the German action contributed to the formation of the (C) Franco-Russian or Dual Entente of 1894—Austria was allied with Germany. Russia was opposed to (E) an independent Poland because such a development would result in a loss of territory; while the Russian navy expanded slightly during this period, the Russian economy was not able to (D) support a massive naval building program.

52. **(E)**

The Russian Revolution of 1905 led Nicholas II to issue the October Manifesto calling for an assembly (the *Duma*). It did not (A) result in his abdication (he would resign in March 1917), nor was it (B) suppressed by Nicholas II. The Orthodox Church (C) did not lose political power; the Revolution of 1905 occurred (D) as Russian forces were being defeated in the Russo-Japanese war. Defeats in the war provided a cause that sparked the Revolution.

53. **(B)**

Oscar Wilde's *Picture of Dorian Gray* and Thomas Mann's *Death in Venice* embodied a new symbolist direction in literature that addressed formerly taboo themes such as fantasies relating to perpetual "youth" and homosexuality. These works and others of this vintage could not be (A) construed as examples of Romantic literature, nor can they be categorized as examples of a (C) "new" sense of realism in literature or examples (D) of an expressionist literary movement. Both works were applauded by intellectuals at the time of their publication.

54. **(E)**

The policies of the Third Republic tended to **restrict** the influence of the Catholic Church; on occasion, those policies were downright anticlerical. The (A) Dreyfus Affair, Panama Scandal, and Boulanger Crisis were serious threats to the Third Republic, which had been established (B) in the midst of French defeat in the Franco-Prussian War (1870–1871). In the spring of 1871 the Paris Commune (C) threatened the new republic, but the Commune collapsed. In 1875 (D) a constitution was adopted that formalized the rule of law in the Third Republic.

55. **(B)**

The Berlin Conference of 1884–1885 established the principle that, for a great power to claim an area, it had to show other powers that it effectively controlled the interior, not just the coast. This Conference, directed at curtailing the growth of Britain's Empire, did not (A) say that Britain could control the Niger and Congo rivers, nor did it support (D) the dream of Cecil Rhodes for a Cape-to-Cairo railroad under British control. Further, the conference (C) turned the Congo over to Belgium, not Portugal. Italy (E) obtained Libya later (1912).

56. **(B)**

Bismarck's *Kulturkampf* was his "cultural struggle," in the name of Protestant Germany and using anti-Catholic laws, to undermine the Center (Catholic) Party. While Bismarck opposed the Marxism (A) of the Social Democratic Party (D), he used other methods to restrict that party's influence. The *Kulturkampf* had nothing to do with Bismarck's (C) diplomatic isolation of France. Popes Pius IX and Leo XIII, not Pius X, condemned the *Kulturkampf* (E).

57. **(D)**

The Parliament Act of 1911 did not permit the House of Lords to veto nonrevenue bills effectively. In addition to a brief delay, in the event of a veto by the Lords, the House of Commons could redraft the measure and transform it into a revenue bill. The Act did (A) reduce the life span of a Parliament from seven to five years; the House of Lords (C) had no veto power over revenue bills.

58. **(B)**

The expansion of the "division of labor" and of "mass production" through standard parts and manufacturing processes was stimulated by (B) the factory system. While the (A) institution of bank credit and (C) competition were elements in the development of capitalism, they did not stimulate the division of labor or mass production. (D) Economic imperialism was a byproduct of the system; (E) political rivalries were not directly related to this development.

59. **(A)**

The dominant personality at the Congress of Vienna was Metternich. Alexander (C), Talleyrand (D), and Wellington (E) attended the Congress, but none of them was considered dominant. (B) Bismarck was to dominate diplomacy a half century after the close of the Congress of Vienna.

60. **(B)**

In 1829 the Ottoman Turks were forced to accept the Treaty of Adrianople, which (B) recognized the independence of Greece. Bulgarian and Serbian independence (A) and (E) would not be recognized until the Congress of Berlin in 1878. The (C) Christian "right of access" to the Holy Places in Palestine was a factor in the origins of the Crimean War (1854), and Russian access to the Mediterranean (D) was a constant item on the agenda of East Mediterranean affairs until it was realized in 1967.

61. **(D)**

The Treaty of Brest-Litovsk (March 1918) was (D) a humiliating agreement that the Russians signed with Germany. The Treaty of Neuilly (C) concluded hostilities between the Allies and Bulgaria; the Treaty of Trianon (B) ended the war between the Allies and Hungary; the Treaty of Sèvres (E) ended the war between the Allies and the Ottoman Empire. There was no formal separate treaty concluding hostilities between Great Britain and Turkey.

62. **(C)**

The chart indicates only that postwar economies in Central and Eastern Europe were fragile—subject to rapid deterioration during economic collapse.

63. **(C)**

Zwingli was a Swiss reformer who served as the religious adviser of the city of Zürich. Although he was inspired by Luther's teaching, the two men disagreed on the subject of the Lord's Supper and were unable to reconcile their views during a meeting in 1529. Luther believed that Christ is present in the Eucharist, although he denied that the bread and wine is actually changed into the body and blood of Christ, as the Catholic doctrine of transubstantiation maintained. Luther's position is known as consubstantiation. Zwingli, however, denied that Christ is substantially present in the Eucharist, which he believed has merely a symbolic meaning. This theological disagreement prevented the German and Swiss Protestants from coordinating their efforts. As a Protestant reformer, Zwingli taught that the pope has no authority to lead the Christian people, and he rejected the Catholic tradition of fasting during the forty days before Easter known as Lent (A). He also rejected monasticism, and therefore closed down monasteries (E). For the sake of simplifying Christian worship, he banned both music and religious images (B). Zwingli converted several of the Swiss cantons besides Zürich, but a civil war broke out between the Protestant cantons and the cantons that remained Catholic. Serving as a chaplain, Zwingli was killed by the victorious Catholic forces following the Battle of Kappel in 1531 (D).

64. **(B)**

The "Rendezvous" (1939) by British cartoonist David Lou refers to contradictions inherent in the Russo-German Nonaggression Pact. It does not refer to (D) Czechoslovakia, (E) Finland, or (C) any niceties between Stalin and Hitler, both of whom suspected each other's motives and hated each other's ideologies.

65. **(E)**

The Glorious Revolution of 1688–1889 did not include an agreement that, in the event of no heirs, the Hanoverians would succeed the Stuarts. This arrangement was specified in the Act of Succession of 1701, a year before William III's death and the succession of Queen Anne, who survived all her children. Upon Queen Anne's death in 1714, George I became the first Hanoverian King of England.

66. **(B)**

The text of Diderot's *Encyclopedia* was centered primarily on (B) technology. While history (C) and philosophy (D) were elements, technological innovations and science were emphasized in this profusely illustrated work. Theology (A) and poetry (E) were not given much attention.

67. **(D)**

This poem by the Hungarian-Swiss Tzara is an example of the twentieth-century movement called Dadaism. This post–World War I literary fad was in reaction to the "order" that led to war and its horrors; though short lived, Dadaism contributed to surrealism. Symbolism (A) was an earlier movement that is illuminated by Edmund

Wilson's *Axel's Castle*. Expressionism (B) and idealism (E) are terms that relate to many facets of art—literary and other. Deconstructionism (C) is a term that applies to post-1960 literature and criticism.

68. (C)

The driving force behind Hegel's dialectic was universal reason—his "God." Marx identified materialism (D) as the key historical force. Hegel's philosophy has been used, and misused, by those who identify with (A) nationalism, (B) racial superiority, and, to a lesser extent, (E) religious values.

69. (D)

After 1950 the Soviet Union suppressed movements toward more liberalism in East Germany (A), Poland (B), Czechoslovakia (C), and Hungary (E), but not Yugoslavia (D). Marshall Tito's Yugoslavia carved out autonomy from the Soviet Union in the 1950s; its more innovative approach to Communism led to a more fluid economic system. The Soviet Union's suppression of liberalism in East Germany and Poland (1953), Hungary (1956), and Czechoslovakia (1968) was violent and followed by the installation of pro-Soviet regimes.

70. (A)

Friedrich Nietzsche wrote such works as (A) *Thus Spake Zarathustra* and *The Will to Power*. (B) *The Golden Bough* was by Sir James Frazer, an English anthropologist, and *The Wild Duck* was a play by Henrik Ibsen. (C) *The Return of the Native* and *Jude the Obscure* were novels by Thomas Hardy. (D) *Civilization and Its Discontents* was an essay by Sigmund Freud; *The Riddle of the Universe* was a tract by the biologist Ernst Haeckel. (E) *The Descent of Man* was a work by Charles Darwin, and *The Weavers* was a play by Gerhard Hauptmann.

71. (A)

In the painting *The Eternal City*, the American painter Peter Blume portrays a (A) fascist Italy that is dominated by the personality of Mussolini. The painting does not depict (B) how fascism in Italy improved the condition of the people, (C) Mussolini as a benevolent dictator, (D) a sympathetic rendering of the impact of fascism on Italian life and institutions, nor does it (E) depict the March on Rome in 1922.

72. (C)

During the "June Days" in Paris (1848) the (C) army suppressed the radical revolutionary element. Workers who had been supported by the National Workshops (Louis Blanc) opposed the conservative policies of the new Assembly; they revolted and were suppressed by military units loyal to the government. This situation indicates that (A) and (B) are incorrect. (D) Louis Napoleon did not come to power until the subsequent elections for the presidency of the Second French Republic. (E) Lamartine was a poet and republican leader who enjoyed support during the winter and spring of 1848; thereafter, his influence declined.

73. **(C)**

In an effort to conduct a successful economic war against Britain, Napoleon created the (C) Continental System. Its primary goal was the economic isolation of Britain through the closing of European markets to British goods. Earlier, Napoleon established (A) the Bank of France to consolidate the French economy; the (D) Napoleonic Code was a codification and reform of French law. The (B) Confederation of the Rhine, supported by Napoleon, was intended to subordinate German states. The (E) Kingdom of the Two Sicilies appeared earlier.

74. **(A)**

The 1909 budget proposed by Lloyd George advocated (A) progressive income and inheritance taxes. This liberal budget was designed to tax those who could afford it—the wealthy—and to raise revenues for defense and domestic social programs. (B) Property taxes did not cease, nor were there drastic reductions in funding for (C) domestic programs or (D) weapons. Obviously, the 1909 budget did not specify a (E) redistribution of excessive tax revenues.

75. **(C)**

In this painting entitled *Guernica* (1937), Pablo Picasso portrayed (C) the impact of aerial bombardment on a Basque town by the German Condor Legion during the Spanish Civil War. German and Italian military "volunteers" assisted Franco's fascist forces in the struggle against the republicans.

76. **(B)**

This chart indicates (B) that Hitler's Germany reduced unemployment at a remarkable rate from 1936 to 1938; fascist economic controls facilitated this change. (A), (C), (D) are incorrect; the German economy was not "superior" to Britain's, nor was Britain content with excessive unemployment—though one may criticize the manner in which the Labour and Conservative parties handled economic recovery, free economies are more difficult to direct than state-controlled economies. (E) alerts us to a truth about standardized tests: They never use falsifications in data or graphs without letting students know explicitly that something is wrong.

77. **(C)**

The maps indicate changes in the western border of Russia between (C) 1914 and 1921. These changes were associated with developments and decisions which were caused by World War I, the Russian Revolution, and the rise of nationalism in eastern Europe—the creation of Poland and other new nation-states.

78. **(A)**

Article 231 of the Versailles Treaty (A) is known as the "War Guilt" clause and established Germany's responsibility for the war; the case for reparations was based on the assignment and acceptance of guilt. While (B) the establishment of Poland, (C) the denunciation of secret diplomacy, and (D) the establishment of the League of Nations were provided for in other clauses of the treaty, the Versailles agreement did not (E) result in a decentralized Germany.

79. **(A)**

The Russian blockade of Berlin in 1948–1949 was a reaction to (A) the unification of the British, French, and American zones into West Germany. While the (B) Truman Doctrine was directed at preventing communist victories in Greece and Turkey, and the Marshall Plan (C) was designed to assist in accelerating the economic recovery of Europe, they were not the direct causes of the blockade. NATO (D) was formed after the blockade began and the Chinese Communist (E) victory did not occur until October 1949.

80. **(B)**

West Germany recovered during the 1950s and early 1960s under the leadership of (B) Konrad Adenauer. Willy Brandt (A) served as Social Democratic Chancellor during the 1960s. Erich Honecker (E) was the Communist leader of East Germany from 1971 to 1989. Heinrich Brüning was (C) a leader of the Center Party and chancellor of the Weimar Republic before Hitler. (D) Alfred Hugenberg, a media mogul and member of the Nationalist Party, served as Minister of Economics in the coalition cabinet headed by Adolf Hitler as Chancellor.

Section II

Sample Answer to Document-Based Question

Between the passage of the Reform Bill of 1867 and the death of Benjamin Disraeli, Disraeli and William Gladstone were the leaders of the Conservative and Liberal parties, respectively. They were classic rivals who attacked one another on every possible occasion and who appeared to prosper as a result of the antagonism. During the early 1870s Gladstone initiated a series of reforms that included the Education Act of 1870, the Ballot Act of 1872, and reforms of the military and municipal governments. Disraeli characteristically denounced the reforms as absurd or for not going far enough in resolving a particular problem. In 1872 Disraeli, in his famous "Crystal Palace Speech," introduced the concept of the New Imperialism; Disraeli advocated British imperialism and Gladstone emerged as the staunch anti-imperialist.

Punch magazine capitalized on this personal rivalry during the 1870s in scores of cartoons. In its cartoons *Punch* sought to attack those people and institutions that took themselves too seriously; no topic or issue—except the person of Queen Victoria—was immune from ridicule. In "Hoity-Toity" the lingering issue of the Alabama claims crisis with the United States was held up for scorn. In the second document, the letter from Victoria to Gladstone, the Queen advances the argument of her class in her opposition to extending the vote to women and in providing women with an equal opportunity in the professions. In "The Conservative Programme" Punch attacked Disraeli for being evasive in describing the domestic policies and programs of the Conservative Party. This criticism was targeted at Disraeli because of the absence of specific Conservative programs; this was especially noticeable when compared to the apparently endless list of Gladstone's proposals that was ridiculed in "The Colossus of the World" in 1879. Disraeli daring was the subject of "On the Dizzy Brink" when the Conservative leader appeared politically vulnerable in 1878. Within a few months, Disraeli nullified his critics when he emerged as the victor at the Congress of Berlin (June–July 1878), which settled the Russo-Turkish War of 1877–1878. The final cartoon, "A Bad Example," was critical of both Disraeli and Gladstone for their personal attacks on one another. In spite of their antagonism, Britain was well served by its two most distinguished prime ministers of the second half of the nineteenth century.

Sample Answers to Essay Questions

1.   For more than 50 years (1660–1715) the policies of Louis XIV dominated Europe. Through the War of Devolution, the Dutch War, the War of the League of Augsburg, and the War of the Spanish Succession, Louis attempted to establish personal control over Western and Central Europe. To "the sun king" war was a means to demonstrate his greatness and acquire a significant place in history. While Napoleon also catered to a vision of the greatness of France, his wars differed from those of Louis XIV because there was an ideological consideration—the Revolution—that motivated the French to support Napoleon's policies. Further, the Napoleonic wars involved a proportionately higher number of "citizens" than did the military enterprises of Louis XIV.

During the last four decades of the seventeenth century, Louis XIV's France enjoyed a position of hegemony over European affairs. The War of Devolution, which was related to property claims in small towns in the Spanish Netherlands, resulted in the establishment of an alliance, anchored with Great Britain and The Netherlands, against France. The British and Dutch feared that unless Louis XIV was contained, he would establish such an overwhelming base of power that he would eliminate the sovereignty of many nations by destroying the European diplomatic equilibrium. In the Dutch War, the War of the League of Augsburg, and the War of the Spanish Succession, European powers responded to French aggression through the formation of coalitions. The success of the coalitions maintained the balance of power and, in the end, not only thwarted Louis XIV's aspirations but also demonstrated that France was isolated. States as diverse as Britain, Austria, The Netherlands, and Prussia joined to preserve their independence. At the Peace of Utrecht in 1713–1714, France was still recognized as the greatest European power; however, France did not achieve its goals and, defeated in the War of the Spanish Succession, had to make concessions to the coalition victors.

The Napoleonic Wars (1799–1815) constituted a more serious threat to the European political structure than did the wars of Louis XIV. Napoleon carried with him the liberal ideology and some reforms of the French Revolution; indeed, the French revolutionary tradition was viewed as more dangerous than the might of French armies. Upon achieving victory, Napoleon not only would establish French control over the defeated area, but he would also introduce political and economic reforms that threatened the basis of the old order's power. Legal reforms in Spain, economic reforms in the German states, and other similar developments rendered the Napoleonic Wars much more complex than earlier struggles. The other nations of Europe responded to French power and the Revolution through resurrecting the coalition concept, which had prevailed against Louis XIV. From the outbreak of resistance in Spain in 1808 to the defeat in Russia (1812–1813) and the devastation of French defeat at Waterloo in June 1815, the coalition against Napoleon succeeded in suppressing this second French attempt to alter the European political system.

In the wars of Louis XIV many of the coalition members were motivated by dynastic considerations; Britain and The Netherlands were clearly motivated by national values. During the Napoleonic period, the coalition was generally motivated by nationalism, although dynastic priorities were not absent. In Central and Southern Europe, nationalism prevailed over the revolutionary tradition; however, in spite of efforts to suppress this tradition, it would reappear in the Revolutions of 1820, 1830, and 1848.

2.   While the development of fascism in Germany and Italy had some parallel or similar experiences, the causes for the rise of fascism in each were often unique to that nation's history and structures.

When Adolf Hitler became German Chancellor in January 1933, the fascist party achieved a victory that only a few years before was considered beyond its reach. Beginning in 1920 the National Socialists adopted the fascist approach to government, which viewed the state as an entity in its own right; the state was more important than individuals who resided in it. German fascism was Romantic, militaristic, highly nationalistic, and imbued with a racist totalitarianism that was fundamentally antidemocratic. During the 1920s, Hitler and his Nazi Party were considered a radical fringe that never would come to power; the Weimar Republic continued to rely on the support or acquiescence of Germans until the Depression began to devastate the economy in 1930. Fascist success in Germany can be attributed to (1) the continuing economic and social crisis caused by the Depression, (2) the inability of the Weimar Republic to advance a credible policy to alleviate the widespread distress, (3) the organization of the Nazi Party, (4) the continuing humiliation from defeat in the war, and (5) the charisma of Adolf Hitler. Through Hitler's direction, the Nazis gained a significant power base in the *Reichstag* from which he was able to demand a place in the new Hindenburg government in 1933. Once in power, Hitler moved quickly to consolidate his position, passing the Enabling Act and others, which gave him dictatorial powers and purged Germany of his political enemies. Within two years Hitler had purged or co-opted all power bases opposed to him, including his toughest sell, conservative army leaders. Mussolini not only took longer to achieve secure power, but often had different and more widespread problems to deal with.

The rise of fascism in Italy via Benito Mussolini can be attributed to (1) the failure to obtain the expected gains for Italy's involvement and sacrifices during World War I, (2) the postwar economic collapse, (3) "1919ism"—the fear of Bolshevism, (4) the ineptitude of the centrist Italian parties in handling the political and economic crisis that gripped Italy after the war, and (5) the opportunistic Mussolini. During the war Italians had entertained thoughts that they would acquire colonies and great power status as a result of their involvement with the Allies; at the Versailles Conference and in the subsequent treaty it was evident that these goals were not realized. At the same time Britain and the United States ceased making loans after the armistice; this action resulted in a financial crisis in Italy that was aggravated by the rapid demobilization of the Italian army, high unemployment, and inflation. "1919ism" was the Italian Red Scare, the fear that the economic crisis would provide the Bolsheviks with an opportunity to initiate a revolution; this anxiety resulted in polarizing Italian society, with the wealthy classes identifying with order and the preservation of their own interests. During the chaotic period from 1918 to 1922, the Italian political system proved unable to resolve the crisis; Italian political parties were not able to overcome their own party factionalism and sustain a durable coalition government. Into this void of leadership stepped Mussolini, a flamboyant and egocentric demagogue who promised to reestablish order and a sense of national pride to Italy. Mussolini's seizure of power—the March on Rome (1922)—was not opposed. Similarly to Hitler, Mussolini set out, as soon as possible, to undermine parliamentary forms (the rigged Acerbo Law of 1923) and to sideline socialist and communist opponents (e.g., the murder of Socialist leader Matteotti in June 1924). But in two major instances, Mussolini had, if not different problems, then those problems to a different degree.

In Mussolini's consolidation of power one sees two basic differences with the later German case: the power of religious identity in Italy, and its economic backwardness. The keystone of Mussolini's consolidation of power was his wooing of the disaffected Vatican, sealed by the compromising Lateran Accords of 1929, in which Mussolini and the Pope gave each other what they most needed. Getting the majority Catholics on his side was far more important to Mussolini than Hitler's easier co-optation of Protestants and Catholics in Germany. Second, Germany, despite the Depression, had perhaps the best economic and industrial infrastructure in Europe, second only to the United States, so Hitler's plans to get industrialists on his side and gear up the German economy for war were more solidly based; indeed, Nazi Germany emerged with breath-taking speed from the Depression, several years before the United States did. Italy was, on the contrary, still relatively backward: agrarian in the main, little infrastructure, and only moderately industrialized in the North. Mussolini's economic policies—the ambition to be self-sufficient, grabs for overseas land, and his medieval "corporatism" to reorganize industry and labor—had only limited success, compared with Nazi Germany.

3.   When James I assumed the throne upon the death of Elizabeth I in 1603, the monarchy in Britain was a strong executive position that was restricted by the English constitutional concept of the "King in Parliament." By the time that Queen Anne—the last Stuart—died in 1714, the alignment of English domestic political power had shifted. While there were many factors that led to this alteration, the Stuart monarchs contributed to this erosion of monarchical power through inept leadership and policies that did not consider the English historical tradition nor the forces that were current during the seventeenth century.

James I (1603–1625) alienated Parliament by asserting his support for royal absolutism and the "Divine Right of Kings." During his reign, James convened few Parliaments, and those that were held were confrontational—the Addled Parliament of 1614 is a good example. Further, James I did not address the continuing religious crisis that centered on Puritanism; the Hampton Court Conference reinforced the Anglican status quo and led to a loss of support for James among the Puritans. James I's personal life did not enhance his public reputation; his purported bisexuality, his awkward physical appearance, and his Scots accent rendered him "unkingly" to many. Charles I (1625–1649) succeeded his father and found himself involved with unsuccessful and costly foreign enterprises in Spain and France; in 1628, the King's favorite, the Duke of Buckingham, was assassinated and Charles I was forced to convene a Parliament for funds to pay his debts caused by the foreign wars. Parliament forced Charles to sign the Petition of Rights, which was an statement of grievances; Charles pledged not to improperly collect the ships' tax, not to abuse the use of martial law as it related to the public billeting of troops, and to respect the writ of habeas corpus. After Parliament provided the funds, Charles I decided to rule without a Parliament—from 1629 to 1640 no Parliament sat. During this period Charles I and his aid, Archbishop William Laud, attempted to suppress Puritanism throughout the country. In 1637 Charles I and Laud extended this policy in Scotland; the Scottish reaction led to war and, reluctantly, in the spring of 1640, Charles I summoned what became known as the Short Parliament—it lasted for only three weeks. The suppressed Parliamentary and Puritan forces demanded that Charles I meet their demands before they would grant funds to raise an army; Charles I dissolved the Short Parliament. With the Scottish problem becoming more acute, Charles summoned the "Long" Parliament in the fall of 1640—it sat for years. Between 1640 and 1660, English politics were in a state of flux; the English Civil War, the execution of Charles I, the establishment of the Commonwealth and the Protectorate, and the Restoration of the Stuarts in the person of Charles II transpired during those decades. The Parliament was strengthened and the monarchy weakened as a result of these developments. The monarchy that was restored in 1660 was a modified and restricted executive force.

In 1688 and 1689 another constitutional crisis gripped the nation. James II, a Catholic, had a male heir and baptized the child a Catholic. Faced with the likelihood of a series of Catholic monarchs over a Protestant nation, Tory and Whig politicians in Parliament arranged for William and Mary to replace James II, who fled the nation. This Glorious Revolution was formalized with the Bill of Rights in April 1689, which stipulated that the Parliament, through its control of finances, was the dominant force in English politics. The monarch was still very significant and exercised considerable power; however, the power enjoyed by the great Tudor monarchs, Henry VIII and Elizabeth I, would not be seen again.

4.   Any attempt to reflect upon the ideological legacy of the French Revolution of 1789 must be preceded by a brief review of the intellectual forces that impacted on the Revolution and the ideology that was manifested during the Revolution. The Revolution that broke in France in 1789 and continued for the next decade was ideologically motivated by the political and philosophic concepts that were advanced during the Enlightenment—the Age of Reason. While many varying sentiments emerged during the eighteenth century, there was a common ideological basis: Eighteenth-century intellectuals were interested in developing a rationally based human society that was free from the assumptions of the past and that would advance human progress.

During the Revolution itself, there was a great debate over how to realize these goals. This debate, which continued long after the revolutions were suppressed, was one of the major ideological legacies of the French Revolution—an open and public dialogue on issues of concern. It anticipated an environment that fostered intellectual activity; the anti-intellectualism of the past would be replaced. During the nineteenth century attempts were made to curtail the freedom of speech through varying forms of censorship; the July Ordinances and the later actions of François Guizot in the 1840s were examples of this censorship. Freedom of speech or debate was the underlying component of the radical philosophic tradition that emerged from the French Revolution. Another major factor that endured was the revision of the notion of humanity that developed during the revolutionary period. The thoughts of Rousseau, Montesquieu, and others and the historic experience of the Revolution influenced Marx, Proudhon, and John Stuart Mill in the nineteenth century as well as Sartre, Freud, and others in the twentieth century as they attempted to develop an understanding of humanity and the individual. The notion of the role and rights of "the people" were altered; the last vestiges of the medieval order were struggling to survive. Related to the changing concept of "the people" was a broadening of the idea of the "nation." Further, no longer would humans be viewed primarily in a religious context; humankind was to be examined and measured within a political, economic, or social context.

Finally, any consideration of the ideological legacy must include comments on the "cult of progress." While J. B. Bury and others have considered this issue, the impact of the concept of progress as a consequence of the French Revolution must be revised continually. Further, the interrelationship of "progress" with other developments, such as racism, democracy, and totalitarianism, makes any discussion problematic. The French Revolution of 1789 initiated a global revolutionary tradition that was not limited to France or Europe.

5.   While Germany was forced to agree with the infamous War Guilt clause (Article 231) of the Versailles Treaty, the outbreak of the World War I involved many diverse factors that render any assignment of specific national guilt a rather futile undertaking. The immediate circumstances that led to the outbreak of the war were focused on the diplomatic crisis of the summer of 1914; the Austrians, with German support, reacted to the assassination of Archduke Franz Ferdinand by directing an ultimatum at Serbia, which was supported by Russia. The alliance systems were deployed and the war was underway by early August.

The causes that led to this situation were (1) the polarization of Europe into two armed camps, (2) imperialism, and (3) militarism and the arms race. Since Bismarck's dismissal in 1890, the European diplomatic situation had become more complex; by 1907, it was clear that two separate and opposing groups of nations existed. In 1890 Germany failed to renew the Reinsurance Treaty with Russia; within four years, the Russians entered into the Dual Entente with France, which terminated the key element in Bismarck's foreign policy, the diplomatic isolation of France. During the late 1890s Germany rebuffed British overtures for an alliance; this rejection resulted in the British entering into the Anglo-Japanese alliance (1902), the Entente Cordiale (1904), and the Anglo-Russian Entente (1907). While these arrangements did not obligate Britain to any direct military action in the event of war, they did affiliate Britain with the French-oriented diplomatic system. This affiliation was evident during the Algeçiras Conference in 1906. Germany and Austria-Hungary were isolated.

Imperialistic rivalries contributed to an increasingly hostile environment among the European powers. From the Fashoda Crisis of 1898–1899 to the First and Second Moroccan Crises and the Balkan conflicts, the European powers found themselves in conflict with one another—frequently over areas that were unrelated to their national security or interests. This conflicting environment was exacerbated by the growing influence of the military within European governments. A sense of the "inevitability" of war led the great powers to develop war plans such as the German Schlieffen (1905) and the French Plan XVII (1912). These developments implied that a military resolution to a crisis was acceptable; there was dissatisfaction with the "indecisive" nature of diplomatic settlements. Further aggravating this militarism was the impact of technology on weaponry. During the two decades immediately prior to the outbreak of the war, improvements and innovations in weapons were revolutionary. The development of new classes of capital ships with enhanced ranges and armament, the revolution in artillery, and innovations in field weapons (such as the machine gun) and in the quality of repeating rifles resulted in an arms race that directed funds away from domestic needs.

In the summer of 1914 the mediation efforts that had worked on previous occasions failed, and Europe stumbled into a war for which it had longed prepared. While Germany must be faulted for William II's "Blank Check" to the Austrians, most of the major powers were responsible for contributing to a situation in which a general war was acceptable. The causes for this war and, in many incidents, most wars are to be found in the mentality of the age, which permits nations to adopt confrontational policies and procedures.

6.   From Disraeli's call for a "New Imperialism" in the early 1870s to 1914, the European powers participated in the most reckless and active era of colonial expansion. Bolstered by economic need, aspects of social Darwinism, and the zealousness of militant Christianity and European nationalism, the European powers participated in the "Scramble for Africa," for a position in China, and for Pacific islands. Considerable resources were expended in the acquisition and maintenance of these colonial empires; the consequences of imperialism resulted in national and domestic political rivalries and mixed economic results.

From the perspective of the impact of imperialism on the relations between nation-states, one can divide this era into two periods: before and after the Berlin Conference of 1884–1885. This meeting established the principle that any claim to a territory had to be supported by occupation of the whole territory in question and notification of other powers; this was intended to regulate colonial claims and to limit the expansion of the British Empire. Throughout the era, imperialism resulted in conflicts between European powers: the Afghan wars, the Fashoda crisis, the Venezuelan dispute, the Boer War, the Moroccan Crises, and the Libyan crisis illustrate the extent and frequency of these conflicts. Further, imperialism emerged as a domestic political issue in Britain, France, Germany, Italy, and Belgium. In England, Disraeli and his Conservative Party supported imperial expansion and involved the nation in a series of colonial wars, including the Ashanti and Zulu wars. Disraeli's liberal rival, William Gladstone, rejected imperialism but found that it was extremely difficult to maintain his anti-imperialist position during his four tenures as Prime Minister, due to international and national political factors. Thus, Gladstone found himself dispatching General Charles Gordon to the Sudan and then sending an expeditionary force to rescue him. Within England the Fabian Society was consistently anti-imperialist until the Boer War, when the Fabians were factionalized over British involvement in South Africa. In Germany and France, liberal and socialist political parties opposed imperialist policies advanced by the rightist and conservative governments and parties.

European economic life was stimulated by the increased trade that resulted from imperialism and the establishment of colonies. Not only did the European powers acquire new sources of raw materials, but also—and more importantly in most instances—they acquired new markets in which they could distribute their finished goods. Domestic industries that provided transport or products associated with transport and new settlements profited from the expansion. At the same time, imperial activities diverted capital away from domestic investments and programs; some contend that the Western European economies possessed excess capital during this period that could not be absorbed by the domestic economies. Another negative economic factor was the continuing costs associated with the administration and defense of colonies; this involved human as well as financial resources. It appears that the immediate economic impact was positive but that the long-term result was negative. It should also be noted that the economic gains during the early decades of this period resulted in deferring consideration of domestic economic problems that affected the working classes.

PRACTICE EXAM 2

This exam is also on CD-ROM in our special interactive AP European History TEST*ware*®

AP European History

Section 1

TIME: 55 minutes
      80 questions

DIRECTIONS: Each of the questions or incomplete statements below is followed by five suggested answers or completions. Select the one that is best in each case.

---

1.   Lorenzo Valla gained fame for

    (A)   becoming ruler of the Renaissance city of Florence

    (B)   proving the Donation of Constantine a fraud

    (C)   inventing devices for the field of navigation

    (D)   challenging the authority of the Holy Roman Emperor

    (E)   helping to unify Italy

2.   Ferdinand and Isabella's policies of Spanish nationalism led to the expulsion from Spain of large numbers of Spanish

    (A)   Protestants   (D)   Calvinists

    (B)   Catholics   (E)   monks

    (C)   Jews

3.   With papal mediation, Spain in 1494 agreed to recognize that one other nation had valid claims to parts of South and Central America. Which nation was it?

    (A)   Great Britain   (D)   Italy

    (B)   Portugal   (E)   France

    (C)   Austria

4.   The "idols" of Francis Bacon, explained in his *Novum Organum,* were

(A)   strict standards of scientific accuracy

(B)   impediments to clear scientific thinking

(C)   religious objects

(D)   famous scientists

(E)   political objectives

Part of the text in the illustration reads:

"So soon as a coin in coffer rings,
The soul into heaven springs."

5.   The individual depicted on the horse in the illustration above is

(A)   Calvin   (D)   Luther

(B)   Tetzel   (E)   Henry VIII

(C)   Boniface VIII

6.   The first Swiss leader of the movement that became Calvinism was

(A)   Jean Calvin   (D)   Menno Simons

(B)   Ulrich Zwingli   (E)   Thomas Cranmer

(C)   Balthasar Hubmeier

7.   The 1555 principle of *cuius regio, eius religio*—incorporated later into the peace settlement that ended the Thirty Years' War—signified

   (A)   a weakening of the authority of German electors

   (B)   the right of monarchs to dictate the religion of their state or principality

   (C)   an increase in papal authority in the Holy Roman Empire

   (D)   increased authority for the nobility in religious controversies

   (E)   that religion was a private matter to be decided by each individual

8.   Which of the following was most influential in the spread of Protestantism in sixteenth-century Europe?

   (A)   The universities   (D)   Lectures

   (B)   Holy Roman Emperors   (E)   Monarchical authority

   (C)   The printing press

9.   "We Italians then owe to the Church of Rome and to her priests for our having become irreligious and bad; but we owe her still a greater debt ... that the Church has kept and still keeps our country divided."
   This passage expresses the opinion of

   (A)   Luther   (D)   Machiavelli

   (B)   Calvin   (E)   Dante

   (C)   Leo X

10.   "I dissent from those who are unwilling that the sacred Scriptures should be read by the unlearned and translated into the vulgar tongue, as though Christ had taught such subtleties that they can scarcely be understood even by a few theologians. . . . "
   This passage expresses the opinion of

   (A)   Ignatius Loyola   (D)   Desiderius Erasmus

   (B)   Niccolo Machiavelli   (E)   Robert Boyle

   (C)   Galileo Galilei

11.   Although he was a Roman Catholic, which one of the following was most like Calvin in his efforts to reform the church and society?

   (A)   Girolamo Savonarola   (D)   King Louis XIII

   (B)   Ignatius Loyola   (E)   Emperor Charles V

   (C)   Thomas More

12. The Peace of Augsburg

   (A) recognized that Lutheranism was the true interpretation of Christianity

   (B) recognized the principle that the religion of the leader would determine the religion of the people

   (C) denounced the Papacy and Charles V

   (D) resulted in the recognition of Lutheranism, Calvinism, and Catholicism

   (E) authorized the seizure of all Church property in German states

13. The Price Revolution of the sixteenth century was caused by

   (A) the establishment of monopolies

   (B) the importation of silver and gold into the European economy

   (C) a shortage of labor

   (D) the wars of religion caused by the Reformation

   (E) an unfavorable balance of trade

14. All of the following statements about the Edict of Nantes are true EXCEPT:

   (A) It banned Huguenot military forces and fortresses.

   (B) It promoted religious toleration.

   (C) It guaranteed freedom of worship for French Calvinists.

   (D) It followed a major civil war in France.

   (E) It was revoked by Louis XIV.

15. Richelieu served as "Prime Minister" to

   (A) Louis XII   (D) Louis XIII

   (B) Henry IV   (E) Francis I

   (C) Louis XIV

16. The *Fronde* was directed primarily against the

   (A) power of French landlords

   (B) authority of the absolute monarchy

   (C) influence of the nobility

   (D) wealth of the church

   (E) poverty of the peasants

17. Which one of the following statements best characterizes the Russian *streltsi*?

    (A) They were a military corps with great influence in Russian politics.

    (B) As intellectuals, they were an important group at court.

    (C) They were the leaders of the Decembrist revolt of 1825.

    (D) As church leaders, they contributed to the myth of Holy Russia.

    (E) They were foreigners who chose to live in Russia.

18. "Behold, an immense people united in a single person; behold this holy power, paternal, and absolute; behold the secret cause which governs the whole body of the state, contained in a single head; you see the image of God in the king, and you have the idea of royal majesty . . . "
    This passage by the French bishop Bossuet illustrates the concept of

    (A) sovereignty

    (B) absolutism

    (C) divine right

    (D) papal authority

    (E) parliamentary government

19. Which of the following is true of the Table of Ranks of Peter the Great?

    (A) It separated the Russian population into distinct classes.

    (B) It set educational and performance levels for civil servants.

    (C) It required the nobility to serve in the Russian army.

    (D) It legalized serfdom in Russia.

    (E) It established a Russian parliament.

20. Peter the Great's principal foreign policy achievement was the

    (A) acquisition of ports on the Black Sea

    (B) acquisition of ports on the Baltic Sea

    (C) Russian gains in the three partitions of Poland

    (D) defensive alliance with England

    (E) defeat of France in the Great Northern War

21. This drawing below by Isaac Newton illustrates his experiments with

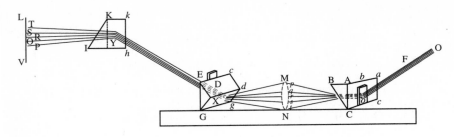

(A) fluids   (D) gravity

(B) energy   (E) gases

(C) light

22. Enclosures were required to

(A) reinforce the concept of private property

(B) eliminate continuing boundary disputes

(C) permit scientific farming

(D) assist in accurate property tax collections

(E) permit the newly rich to acquire property

23. The electors of Saxony in the seventeenth and eighteenth centuries derived power and wealth from each of the following factors EXCEPT

(A) mining operations

(B) their monopoly in Europe on the secret of porcelain production

(C) their production of the finest silks in Europe

(D) their election more than once to the throne of Poland

(E) the trade in books and furs that centered on Leipzig

24. The Royal Society of London, founded in 1662, was one of the first

(A) societies dedicated to geographic exploration

(B) groups to stage Shakespearean plays

(C) literary clubs

(D) scientific societies

(E) political clubs

25. *"Ecrasez l'infame!,"* Voltaire's slogan of "crush the infamous thing," called for the suppression of

(A) the Church

(B) immorality

(C) the French monarchy

(D) censorship

(E) French universities

26. Rousseau's concept of the ideal government was centered on

(A) the general will

(B) a strengthened monarchy

(C) a theocracy

(D) abolition of the government

(E) a strengthened army

27. The Pragmatic Sanction was an attempt to secure the throne of Austria for

(A) Frederick II

(B) Joseph II

(C) Catherine II

(D) Maria Theresa

(E) Franz Joseph

28. "By pursuing his own interest (every individual) frequently promotes that of society more effectively than when he really intends to promote it. I have never known much good done by those who affected to trade for the public good." This passage expresses the opinion of

(A) Thomas Malthus in his *Essay on Population*

(B) Adam Smith in his *Wealth of Nations*

(C) Karl Marx in his *Das Kapital*

(D) Charles Darwin in his *Origin of Species*

(E) Jane Austen in her *Pride and Prejudice*

29. All of the following statements are true about the eighteenth-century French *philosophe* Voltaire EXCEPT that

(A) he admired the British political system

(B) he was an atheist

(C) he believed that religious considerations had biased the French judicial system

(D)   he favored Enlightened Despotism

(E)   he wrote a novel in reply to the German philosopher Leibniz

30.   The Abbé Sieyès exerted a major influence on the French Revolution through his book entitled

(A)   *Essay on Human Understanding*

(B)   *What Is to Be Done?*

(C)   *The Progress of the Human Mind*

(D)   *The Third Estate*

(E)   *Letters on the English*

31.   Which of the following did the Civil Constitution of the Clergy lead to?

(A)   The clergy were given the first vote in the Estates-General.

(B)   The church was made a department of the French state.

(C)   Most of the clergy were condemned to execution during the Reign of Terror.

(D)   The office of bishop was abolished.

(E)   The church was made completely independent from the state.

32.   The battle of Valmy (September 20, 1792) was important because

(A)   the Convention, which met the first time that day, supervised the battle

(B)   the king, in losing the battle, lost important support among the army

(C)   an army pieced together from regulars and conscripts was able to beat the professional army under the Duke of Brunswick

(D)   in it the needle-nosed, breech-loading rifle was used for the first time

(E)   the royal family was caught fleeing to enemy territory during the battle

33.   Which of the following chronological sequences of the French Revolution is correct?

(A)   Directory, Consulate, Legislative Assembly

(B)   Legislative Assembly, Convention, Directory

(C)   Convention, Consulate, Directory

(D)   National Assembly, Convention, Directory

(E)   Consulate, Empire, Directory

34. For more than 250 years England had a special relationship, based on a royal marriage and a treaty guaranteeing fortified wines, with which country?

    (A) Spain   (D) France

    (B) Portugal   (E) The Netherlands

    (C) Germany

35. The "Weber thesis" attempted to explain the connections between the rise of Calvinism and the rise of

    (A) absolute monarchies   (D) Anglicanism

    (B) capitalism   (E) Lutheranism

    (C) the nation-state

36. Prussia's acquisition of the Rhineland in Germany at the Congress of Vienna proved to be a significant development because

    (A) the Rhineland became a buffer zone between Germany and France

    (B) most German industry developed in the area

    (C) it proved to be a very fertile agricultural area

    (D) in military terms, it was the easiest part of Germany to defend

    (E) it was welcomed by France

37. Which social group benefited most from British Corn Laws, 1815–1846?

    (A) Nobility

    (B) Middle class

    (C) Businessmen

    (D) Small farmers

    (E) Industrialists

38. All of the following are preconditions for the Industrial Revolution EXCEPT

    (A) an adequate road system

    (B) a failing agricultural system

    (C) adequate raw materials

    (D) a spirit of entrepreneurship

    (E) a source of financing to build factories

39. All of the following occurred during the Prussian Era of Reform, 1806–1821, EXCEPT

    (A) improvements in the number and quality of Prussian soldiers

    (B) the abolition of serfdom

    (C) the end of the Junker monopoly on landholding

    (D) universal manhood suffrage

    (E) reform of the state bureaucracy

40. All of the following are characteristics of the Romantic movement EXCEPT

    (A) a focus on emotion or intuition over reason

    (B) rejection of the study of history as useless

    (C) admiration for the Enlightenment

    (D) glorification of the Middle Ages

    (E) glorification of folk culture

41. Which of the following would a Fabian Socialist most likely approve?

    (A) Adam Smith's *Wealth of Nations*

    (B) Government-owned utilities

    (C) Laissez-faire policies

    (D) An increase in the budget for the British navy

    (E) Government subsidies to private corporations

42. According to the ideas of Karl Marx, the LAST of the major European powers to have a proletarian revolution was supposed to be

    (A) Britain   (D) Germany

    (B) Italy   (E) Russia

    (C) France

43. The Chartist movement of the nineteenth century drew much of its support from the

    (A) nobility   (D) workers

    (B) middle class   (E) factory owners

    (C) small farmers

44. *"We don't want to fight,*
But, by jingo, if we do,
We've got the ships,
We've got the men,
We've got the money too."

This saying, popular with British crowds reacting to British-Russian tensions in 1877, gave rise to the term

(A)   chauvinism

(B)   Rule, Britannia

(C)   Workshop of the World

(D)   jingoism

(E)   Fortress of Democracy

45. All of the following define the Second Industrial Revolution EXCEPT

(A)   the emergence of major steel industries

(B)   large growth in the textile industry

(C)   the emergence of the German chemical industry

(D)   the application of electricity to industrial production

(E)   the widespread use of oil

CHANGE IN NATIONAL POPULATIONS AT THE TURN OF THE CENTURY (POPULATION IN MILLIONS)

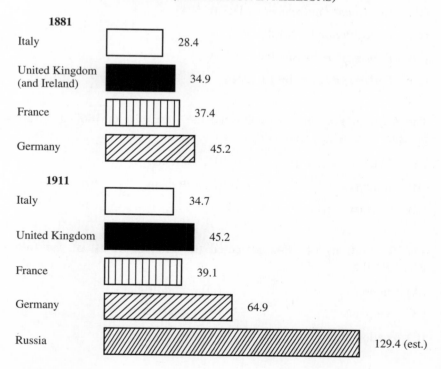

1881

Italy — 28.4

United Kingdom (and Ireland) — 34.9

France — 37.4

Germany — 45.2

1911

Italy — 34.7

United Kingdom — 45.2

France — 39.1

Germany — 64.9

Russia — 129.4 (est.)

46. All of the following statements may be deduced from the graph shown above EXCEPT:

    (A) The United Kingdom gained more people than France.

    (B) The United Kingdom gained more people than Italy.

    (C) Russia had the greatest population growth in percentage terms.

    (D) Germany gained more people than France.

    (E) Much of Europe was experiencing population growth.

47. Which of the following best characterizes the beliefs of St. Simon (1760–1825)?

    (A) admiration for industrialization

    (B) fear of modern trends

    (C) admiration for religion

    (D) rejection of the usefulness of science

    (E) concern that Europe was in decline

48. A nineteenth-century novel whose main character asserts the superiority of the new science and nihilism (taking nothing at face value) to the old idealism was

    (A) *Les Misérables* by Hugo

    (B) *Crime and Punishment* by Dostoyevsky

    (C) *Degeneration* by Nordau

    (D) *Frankenstein* by Shelley

    (E) *Fathers and Sons* by Turgenev

49. The Austrian government established the *Ausgleich* in 1867 in response to pressure from which nationality?

    (A) Poles   (D) French

    (B) Magyars   (E) Italians

    (C) Germans

50. The Revolutions of 1848 reflected the interest of all of the following EXCEPT the

    (A) liberals   (D) middle class

    (B) utopians   (E) Marxists

    (C) nationalists

51. The Schleswig-Holstein question was a contentious issue between

    (A) Prussia and Sweden

    (B) Austria and Prussia

    (C) Prussia and Russia

    (D) Prussia and the Netherlands

    (E) Prussia and Great Britain

52. Which British Prime Minister was most in favor of the Irish Home Rule bill?

    (A) Benjamin Disraeli   (D) Joseph Chamberlain

    (B) William Gladstone   (E) Robert Peel

    (C) Lord Salisbury

53. The Balfour Declaration (1917)

    (A) denounced the use of chemicals by Germans on the Western Front

    (B) was a British pledge to support a homeland for Jews in Palestine

    (C) was a mediation effort to resolve the Anglo-Irish crisis

    (D) was an attempt to persuade the United States to abandon its neutrality

    (E) repudiated the notion that the victors wanted territory or compensation

54. The map below indicates the partition of Africa in what year?

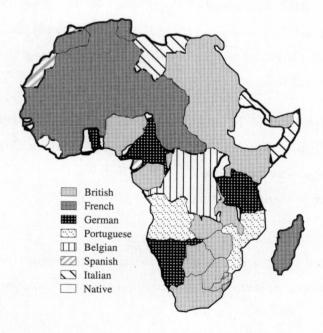

British
French
German
Portuguese
Belgian
Spanish
Italian
Native

(A) 1815

(D) 1960

(B) 1914

(E) 1848

(C) 1870

55. The Concert of Europe is an expression used to characterize which era?

(A) The decades after the Congress of Vienna in which Metternich reigned over continental diplomacy, but not over British foreign policy

(B) The decades after the Crimean War in which Great Britain exercised diplomatic domination

(C) The era of 1862–1890 in which Bismarck dominated European and colonial politics

(D) The harmony of interests during the decades of the New Imperialism

(E) The stable system of alliances in the decades before World War I

56. In 1834, German states (excluding Austria) agreed to eliminate tariffs between the states through a customs union known as the

(A) *Fürstenstaat*

(D) *Zollverein*

(B) Confederation of the Rhine

(E) Hanseatic League

(C) Frankfurt Assembly

57. Britain established direct authority over India after the suppression of the

(A) Opium Wars

(D) assassination of Gandhi

(B) Boxer Rebellion

(E) Warren Hastings affair

(C) Sepoy Mutiny

58. The British policy of "Splendid Isolationism" was terminated with the

(A) Anglo- Entente

(D) Second Moroccan Crisis

(B) Anglo-Russian Entente

(E) Boer War

(C) Anglo-Japanese Alliance

59. In the "April Theses," Lenin

(A) challenged the policies of the Provisional Government

(B) outlined a plan for a Russian class war after the Revolution of 1905

(C)   denounced the revisionist elements within socialism

(D)   called for continuing the war against Germany

(E)   designated Kerensky as his successor

60.   The Versailles Treaty resulted in the formation of several new nations, including

(A)   Yugoslavia and Hungary

(B)   Poland and Greece

(C)   Poland and Italy

(D)   Austria and Germany

(E)   Austria and Italy

61.   The Dawes Plan

(A)   was an international proposal to outlaw war

(B)   was a reparations plan designed to eliminate the friction that led to the Ruhr Crisis

(C)   was denounced by Gustav Stresemann

(D)   was a permanent reparations settlement that survived until the 1930s

(E)   resulted in the dismemberment of Czechoslovakia

62.   The rise of German fascism can be attributed to all of the following EXCEPT the

(A)   failure of the Weimar Republic to solve the crisis of the Depression

(B)   effective organization of the Nazi Party

(C)   charisma of Adolf Hitler

(D)   lingering humiliation of defeat in World War I

(E)   policies of Gustav Stresemann

63.   All of the following were significant economic trends in Germany during the 1920s EXCEPT

(A)   large amounts of money were drained out of Germany to pay reparations

(B)   periods of high inflation

(C)   a very stable currency (the mark)

(D)   periods of high unemployment

(E)   the government put large amounts of paper money in circulation

64. This Soviet poster of 1930 below was an attack on

(A) militarism   (D) capitalism

(B) war   (E) pacifism

(C) religion

65. A Dutch humanist who published an edition of the Greek New Testament was

(A) Marsilio Ficino   (D) Desiderius Erasmus

(B) John Colet   (E) Thomas More

(C) Johann Reuchlin

66. "Existence precedes essence" is a summation of the twentieth-century philosophy of

(A) nihilism   (D) logical positivism

(B) fascism   (E) existentialism

(C) communism

67. Keynesianism (the economic doctrines of the twentieth-century British economist John Maynard Keynes) teaches that during times of economic downturns governments should

(A)   practice austerity

(B)   increase taxes

(C)   create budget deficits

(D)   institute wage and price controls

(E)   nationalize major industries

68.   In 1956, which country revolted against the USSR, only to see its desire for independence crushed because the West was preoccupied by the Suez crisis?

(A)   Poland

(B)   China

(C)   Yugoslavia

(D)   The German Democratic Republic

(E)   Hungary

69.   After 1945, policies of the Soviet Union led to all of the following EXCEPT

(A)   the continuing development of Soviet military power

(B)   a slow demobilization from a war economy

(C)   consistency in the exercise of power by the Communist Party

(D)   a general improvement in the standard of living

(E)   extensive influence in the United Nations in the years immediately following World War II

70.   The map shown below indicates the

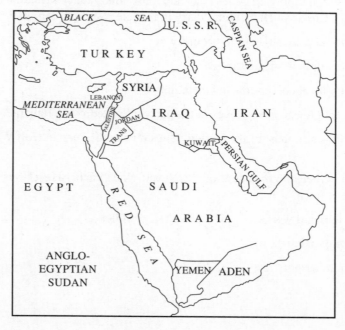

(A) political boundaries in the Near East in 1960

(B) political boundaries in the Near East during the presidency of Gamal Nasser in Egypt

(C) partition of the Ottoman Empire after World War I

(D) scope of the European colonial holdings in the Near East after 1945

(E) status of the Ottoman Empire after the Congress of Berlin

71. Which one of the following was NOT part of the early years of the Cold War?

(A) Berlin blockade

(B) Atomic monopoly by the United States

(C) Soviet occupation of Eastern Europe

(D) Rearmament of Germany

(E) A Communist government in Poland

72. In the Cold War, which of the following Soviet writers was not allowed to travel to Stockholm to receive his Nobel Prize for literature?

(A) Shostakovich

(B) Pasternak

(C) Beria

(D) Brezhnev

(E) Prokofiev

73. Which of the following issues made the most important contribution to the defeat of Italy's Christian Democratic Party in the late twentieth century?

(A) Poverty throughout the country

(B) Chronic food shortages

(C) Political corruption and instability

(D) Religious conservatives in the party alienated many Italians.

(E) Italy's support of the United States during the Persian Gulf War

74. Before he became president of Czechoslovakia, Václav Havel was known as a dissident and a

(A) shipyard worker

(B) filmmaker

(C) playwright

(D) soldier

(E) poet

75. Which of the following was the last country in western Europe to grant women the right to vote in national elections?

    (A)   the Federal Republic of Germany

    (B)   France

    (C)   Norway

    (D)   Spain

    (E)   Switzerland

76. All of the following are considered European terrorist groups EXCEPT for the

    (A)   Greens

    (B)   Red Brigades

    (C)   Baader-Meinhof gang

    (D)   Basque separatists

    (E)   Irish Republican Army

77. Of the following events or groups, which marked the FIRST major act toward European unification after World War II?

    (A)   The Maastricht Treaty

    (B)   The European Coal and Steel Community

    (C)   The formation of NATO

    (D)   The Common Market

    (E)   EURATOM

78. Which of the following was the most outspoken proponent of feminism in post–World War II Europe?

    (A)   Anna Akhmatova   (D)   Simone de Beauvoir

    (B)   A. S. Byatt   (E)   Gloria von Thurn und Taxis

    (C)   Christina Onassis

79. Which of the following is NOT considered a factor in the fall of the Berlin Wall in November 1989?

    (A)   Long-term weaknesses in the Soviet economy

    (B)   The challenge of the United States' proposed "Star Wars" defense

(C)   Pressures by Gorbachev on the East German leadership not to act

(D)   Demonstrations by East Germans in the summer and fall of 1989

(E)   The threat by president-elect George H.W. Bush to take military action

80.   The value of the euro, launched in 1999 as an electronic currency and in 2002 as a cash currency, is determined by

(A)   each member country

(B)   the new European Central Bank

(C)   free-market fluctuations

(D)   the value of the U.S. dollar

(E)   the value of gold

STOP
This is the end of Section I.
If time still remains, you may check your work only in this section.
Do not begin Section II until instructed to do so.

Section II

PART A – DOCUMENT-BASED ESSAY

TIME: Reading Period—15 minutes
      Writing Time: 45 minutes
      1 Essay Question

> **DIRECTIONS:** Read both the document-based essay question in Part A and the choices in Parts B and C during the reading period. Use the time to organize answers. You must answer Part A (the document-based essay question) and choose ONE question from Part B and ONE question from Part C to answer.

   This question is designed to test your ability to work with historical documents. As you analyze each document, take into account the source and the point of view of the author. Write an essay on the following topic that integrates your analysis of the documents. You may refer to historical facts and developments not mentioned in the documents.

   Analyze the nature and causes of the Great Fear in the French Revolution of 1789, and assess the validity of the following statement about the Great Fear.

   "The Great Fear can be explained by the economic, social, and political circumstances prevailing in France in 1789 … (it) gathered the peasants together; allowed them to achieve the full realization of their strength and reinforced the attack already launched against (feudalism) … it played its part in preparations for the (revolution) and on these grounds alone must count as one of the most important episodes in the history of the French nation."

   —Georges Lefèbvre, *The Great Fear of 1789*

   Historical Background: The Great Fear began in the spring of 1789, when peasants throughout the rural areas of France armed themselves in response to rumors of aristocratic plots and roving bands of brigands. Peasants mistakenly attacked other peasants; much of the violence was directed against local noblemen. The violence and anarchy of the Great Fear gained the attention of both royal ministers and the National Convention of the revolution. Both groups moved to release the peasants from their remaining obligations under feudalism.

Document 1

Background of the French Revolution

FRENCH POPULATION IN 1789

TOTAL: from 22,000,000 to 25,000,000

First Estate	Clergy .... 100,000 to 130,000
Second Estate	Nobility .... 400,000 or fewer
Third Estate	*Upper Bourgeoisie	
	Bourgeoisie .... 5,250,000, more or less	
	Urban Proletariat	
	Peasantry .... 16,250,000 to 21,500,000	

*Not all bourgeoisie lived in cities and towns. Often, doctors, lawyers, and *rentiers* (those living on income from investments) lived in the country or in small villages. Total *urban* population was less than 4,000,000 and perhaps as low as 2,000,000.

Document 2

"The first cause is the small yield of this year's harvest which in some districts did not even produce the quantities of a normal year. ... Second, the rains and inundations of 1787, the hail and drought of 1788. ... Third, the usury ... the closing of granaries by landed proprietors. ... Fourth, private sales from the granaries. ... Fifth, the lack of supplies at the market place. ... "

—Report to the Paris *Parlement* on increases in grain prices, December 1788

Document 3

"The backwardness of France is beyond credibility. From Strasburg hither, I have not been able see a newspaper ... well dressed people are now talking of the news of two or three weeks past, and plainly by their discourses know nothing of what has been passing. The whole town of Besançon has not been able to afford me the *Journal de Paris*, nor of any other paper that gives certain of the transactions of the states; yet it is the capital of a province, large as half a dozen English counties, and containing 25,000 souls. ... No one paper has been established in Paris for circulation in the provinces. ... "

—Arthur Young, English tourist, July 17, 1789

Document 4

" ... [I]nformation in France (is not so) diffusive as I imagined. Of the active citizens ... nearly half, particularly in the country, can neither write nor read."

—William Taylor, English tourist, June 1790

Document 5

" ... (To the south of Romilly) rumors said that brigands had appeared in the canton; they had been seen going into the woods. The tocsin was sounded and three thousand men gathered to hunt down these alleged brigands ... but the brigands were only a herd of cows."

—From a report in the *Journal de Troyes*, July 28, 1789

Document 6

(Jacques Turgot, a finance minister to King Louis XVI, made a concerted attempt to institute administrative and economic reforms during his brief tenure. Some of the reforms abolished the last feudal obligations of the peasants, including the corvée, which required the peasants to provide free labor for public works or other tasks as directed by the nobility.)

"We have noted with pain that … works have been executed, for the most part, by means of the corvée required of our subjects … while they have been paid no wages for the time they are so employed. … The weight of this obligation does not fall, nor can it ever fall, anywhere else than upon the poorest part of our subjects, upon those who have no property other than their hands and their industry, upon the peasants, the farmers. The landowners, almost all of whom are … exempt, contribute but very little."

—From a decree by Turgot abolishing the corvée, 1776

Document 7

"The high price of corn has occasioned many insurrections in some of the provincial towns, and particularly at Reims and Vendôme: at St. Quentin a barge laden with 2,000 sacks of the above-mentioned commodity belonging to the very rich individual of the place, who was accused in the neighboring villages of having made his fortune by entirely engrossing the article, was seized upon by the populace and the whole of the cargo was thrown into the river."

—Lord Dorset to Lord Carmarthen, British nobility, March 19, 1789

Document 8

"In the early Spring of 1789 … the Duc d'Orléans was very popular in Paris. The previous year he had sold many paintings from the fine collection in his palace, and it was generally believed that the eight millions raised by the sale had been devoted to relieving the suffering of the people during the hard winter which had just ended. In contrast, whether rightly or wrongly, there was no mention of any charitable gifts from the royal princes or from the king and queen. … Nor did the king ever show himself. Hidden away at Versailles or hunting in the nearby forests, he suspected nothing, foresaw nothing, and believed nothing he was told."

—*Escape from Terror: The Journal of Madame de la Tour du Pin* (ed. and trans. Felice Harcourt, Folio Society, 1979), p. 79

Document 9

"One hundred and fifty chateaux … have already burned. What should I say about the atrocities, the murders committed against the noblemen? A nobleman who was paralyzed, and left on a funeral pile. … They burned the feet of another so that he would give up his title-deeds."

—Marquis de Ferrières, French nobleman, deputy of the Estates-General, Memoirs, July 1789

Document 10

"The National Convention, after hearing the report of its committee on public safety, decreed that all persons who spread false news or cite terror in the provinces, arouse the citizens, or cause disturbances and trouble, shall be brought before the extraordinary tribunal and punished as counter-revolutionary. … It was not necessary that there should be uprisings and disturbances; only news that might lead to these."

—Durand de Maillane, historian, from his *History of the National Convention* (1820) (The Convention subsequently abolished all feudal obligations.)

STOP

This is the end of Section II, Part A.
If time still remains, you may check your work only in this section.
Do not begin Section II, Part B until instructed to do so.

PART B – Essay Question

TIME: 35 minutes
1 Essay Question

DIRECTIONS: Answer ONE question from the three questions below. Choose the question that you are most prepared to answer thoroughly. You should spend about 5 minutes organizing or outlining your answer.

---

1. Analyze the impact of the Counter-Reformation on European history.

2. Compare the origins and proposals of the Utopian Socialists, the Marxists, the anarchists, and the revisionists during the nineteenth century.

3. Compare the unification movements of Germany and Italy in the nineteenth century.

STOP
This is the end of Section II, Part B.
If time still remains, you may check your work only in this section.
Do not begin Section II, Part C until instructed to do so.

PART C – Essay Question

TIME: 35 minutes
     1 Essay Question

DIRECTIONS: Answer ONE question from the three questions below. Choose the question that you are most prepared to answer thoroughly. You should spend about 5 minutes organizing or outlining your answer.

---

4.   Assess the extent to which the English Civil War and the Glorious Revolution advanced the cause of constitutionalism in England in the seventeenth century.

5.   Assess and analyze the effects of the Second Industrial Revolution on European society in the late nineteenth and early twentieth centuries.

6.   Analyze the extent to which the aftermath of World War I led to World War II.

END OF EXAM

PRACTICE EXAM 2

AP European History

Answer Key

1.	(B)	21.	(C)	41.	(B)	61.	(B)
2.	(C)	22.	(C)	42.	(E)	62.	(E)
3.	(B)	23.	(C)	43.	(D)	63.	(C)
4.	(B)	24.	(D)	44.	(D)	64.	(C)
5.	(B)	25.	(A)	45.	(B)	65.	(D)
6.	(B)	26.	(A)	46.	(C)	66.	(E)
7.	(B)	27.	(D)	47.	(A)	67.	(C)
8.	(C)	28.	(B)	48.	(E)	68.	(E)
9.	(D)	29.	(B)	49.	(B)	69.	(E)
10.	(D)	30.	(D)	50.	(E)	70.	(C)
11.	(A)	31.	(B)	51.	(B)	71.	(D)
12.	(B)	32.	(C)	52.	(B)	72.	(B)
13.	(B)	33.	(B)	53.	(B)	73.	(C)
14.	(A)	34.	(B)	54.	(B)	74.	(C)
15.	(D)	35.	(B)	55.	(A)	75.	(E)
16.	(B)	36.	(B)	56.	(D)	76.	(A)
17.	(A)	37.	(A)	57.	(C)	77.	(B)
18.	(C)	38.	(B)	58.	(C)	78.	(D)
19.	(B)	39.	(D)	59.	(A)	79.	(E)
20.	(B)	40.	(C)	60.	(A)	80.	(B)

PRACTICE EXAM 2

AP European History

Detailed Explanations of Answers

Section I

1. **(B)**

In this case, it is not enough to be able to name a Christian Humanist or explain his ideas: This question tests your knowledge about Christian Humanism and the Renaissance. Even if you have heard of Valla, the correct answer also requires that you know the term *Donation of Constantine*. This was a document that canon (Church) lawyers used against Holy Roman emperors who challenged papal authority, so it had the opposite effect to (D). Ostensibly a signed document in which the Roman Emperor Constantine acknowledged papal superiority in both the religious and temporal realms, the Donation was proved a fraud by Valla on the basis of Latin usage not appropriate for its date, and of references to historical events that occurred at a later date.

2. **(C)**

While this question calls for fact retention, it may also require an ability to analyze the effects of policies. The first monarchs of a united Spain, Ferdinand and Isabella achieved that unity by conquering the remaining Muslim area of southern Spain. In an effort to promote cultural unity and establish a national identity, they defined *Spain* in terms of orthodox Catholicism. Those not fitting their definition of orthodoxy were condemned as disloyal or subversive. Two particular groups, Jews and Muslims who had converted to Christianity but retained old customs or dress, were forced into exile by Spanish authorities.

3. **(B)**

Portuguese navigators played a role in the explorations of the New World. If this fact is not known, there are other approaches. Consider clues that you may know: Portuguese is the language of Brazil, the largest nation in South America. Some elimination may also be done: (D) is obviously incorrect, since Italy was not finally united until 1870.

4. **(B)**

Bacon asserted that scientists should be clear-minded thinkers, untouched by religious or political biases or philosophical preconceptions. He listed a series of biases or preconceptions that might be obstacles to scientific work, terming them "idols." Answer (C) is too obvious to consider seriously.

5. **(B)**

The illustration depicts the sale of indulgences in early 1500s Germany by the Dominican monk Tetzel. The incident angered Luther and set him on the path that led to the Reformation. The wording of the question may mislead you by causing you to examine the picture for major clues. This approach is not likely to be helpful. The real clues are in the "jingle," which you may remember from a history course. If you do, the question asks for something more: the name of the monk who sold indulgences in Luther's part of Germany.

6. **(B)**

The wording of the question ("first Swiss leader") indicates that the easy answer—Calvin—must be incorrect. If the correct answer is unknown, it is possible to eliminate answer (D), the best-known Anabaptist leader. Answer (C) is a lesser-known Anabaptist, and (E) is the name of the Archbishop of Canterbury who helped Henry VIII create the Church of England. Before the French lawyer Jean Calvin assumed leadership of the movement that would bear his name, most tenets of Calvinism had been proclaimed and spread by the ex-priest Ulrich Zwingli, who founded a separate congregation in Basel (Switzerland) and beyond.

7. **(B)**

Questions may give extra information ("1555") not to mislead, but rather to help you. If you recall the Peace of Augsburg, then the answer is easy; if not, then look for answers that were not results of the Thirty Years' War. This war ended with another compromise that empowered princes and leaders in the Holy Roman Empire to dictate to their lands which religion, now to include Calvinism, they could practice [so answer (A) is wrong]. Dissenters among their subjects were expected to convert or to move to another territory.

8. **(C)**

Movable-type presses, which evolved in the sixty years before the Reformation, made the printing of cheap leaflets and even the Bible possible on a large scale. The question asks for a judgment of the "most influential." Answer (B) may be eliminated quickly. The military power of Charles V, Holy Roman Emperor during the Reformation, was an obstacle to the spread of Protestantism.

9. **(D)**

A careful reading of the passage is essential. Because it is critical of papal involvement in politics, you may eliminate answer (C). Answer (A) may sound tempting but, again, the "obvious" answer is incorrect; Luther was German, not Italian. Of the remaining answers, it may be possible to arrive at answer (D) because you have previously read Machiavelli and know of his strong criticisms of papal involvement in Italian politics.

10. **(D)**

A test of your ability to apply historical knowledge, this question cites a quotation that illustrates the Christian Humanists' interest in translating the Bible from Latin into the local languages of Europe. The only Christian Humanist listed in the answers is Erasmus. Loyola was founder of the Society of Jesus, or Jesuits; Machiavelli was a political writer during the Italian Renaissance; Galileo was a scientist during the Scientific Revolution; and Robert Boyle was one of the first prominent European physicists and chemists.

11. **(A)**

In late fifteenth-century Florence, the monk Savonarola decried worldly influences in church and society, insisting that while the church itself could not be corrupt, its leaders might be corrupted. His efforts to ban sinful influences are reminiscent of Calvin's godly government in Geneva. Charles V may have wanted to be as authoritarian as Savonarola or Calvin, but he could never do so because he was beset by French, Turkish, and German Protestant enemies. The other answers are simply wrong (e.g., Louis XIII reigned much later and was rather weak).

12. **(B)**

The Peace of Augsburg (1555) (B) recognized the principle that the religion of the leader would determine the religion of the people; it was a major victory for Lutheranism and a defeat of Habsburg aspirations to control the Holy Roman Empire. Lutheranism (A) was not recognized as the true interpretation of Christianity, and the Peace of Augsburg did not authorize the seizure of all Church property in German states (E). Calvinism (D) was not recognized until the Peace of Westphalia in 1648; (C) Charles V and the Papacy were negotiators in formulating the Peace of Augsburg.

13. **(B)**

The Price Revolution of the sixteenth century was partly caused by (B) the importation of silver and gold from Latin America; this helped eliminate the scarcity of money in Europe—and thus caused a fourfold increase in prices. The licensing of monopolies (A) and maintenance of a favorable balance of trade (E) were important elements in seventeenth-century mercantilism. While there were occasional labor shortages (C) and the wars of religion (D) did disrupt economic activities, these developments did not have a substantial impact on the Price Revolution. The other major cause of the Price Revolution—a general population rise that fed demand—is not mentioned, so you need not factor it in.

14. **(A)**

The Edict of Nantes was issued by Henry IV after the religious wars. Raised a Huguenot, Henry became king by promising to convert to Roman Catholicism. The war left France exhausted, convincing many that religion should be kept strictly separate from politics. Thus there was support for the Edict, which guaranteed the Huguenots

freedom of worship and the right to have some fortified towns. Louis XIV, most powerful of the French monarchs and a devout Catholic, later revoked the Edict, asserting
that the right of Huguenots to have their own fortresses was a violation of his royal
sovereignty, as was their competing religion.

15. **(D)**

Richelieu served as "prime minister" to (D) Louis XIII. For more than two decades
during the turbulent Thirty Years' War and the La Rochelle crisis with the Huguenots,
Cardinal Richelieu administered France for Louis XIII. Henry IV (B) was Louis XIII's
father; Louis XIV (C) was his son. Louis XII (A) and Francis I (E) were earlier French
monarchs.

16. **(B)**

Beginning with terminology ("the *Fronde*"), this question asks for an analysis of
the purpose of these periodic revolts by the nobility of France. A phenomenon of the
sixteenth and seventeenth centuries, they were regarded as threats to royal authority by
monarchical ministers Mazarin and Richelieu, who suppressed them ruthlessly. Most
ended when Louis XIV involved the most powerful members of the nobility in sterile
and useless ceremonial lives at his palace of Versailles.

17. **(A)**

The *streltsi*, or Moscow guards, created and toppled tsars; the nobility sought their
favor. Peter the Great destroyed the *streltsi* after a revolt in 1698. With some knowledge
of Russian history, one or two of the other answers may be eliminated. Answer (C) is not
likely, since the date of the Decembrist revolt places it much too late in Russian history.

18. **(C)**

This question demands knowledge of terminology and careful reading. Answers (A)
through (C) are so closely related that a second reading of the passage is recommended
in order to find differences. Although the passage deals with sovereignty and may support
absolute monarchy, the last part ("You see the image of God in the king . . .") makes clear
that the writer is using "divine right" to justify monarchies. "Divine right of kings" was
the label for an argument that monarchs held their throne by divine authority: God had
seen that they were born into the royal family, safeguarded them to adulthood, and preserved their health. Thus, revolution was contrary to God's will. Answer (D) is an attempt
to test those who see the word *God* in the passage but otherwise do not read it carefully.

19. **(B)**

The Table of Ranks set educational and training standards for Russian high civil
servants, almost all of whom were nobility; promotion was also based on the same
criteria. It was part of Peter's attempt to supplement the old boyar nobility with a new,
service-based nobility beholden to the tsar.

20. **(B)**

Peter the Great's principal foreign policy achievement was (B) the acquisition of ports on the Baltic Sea. Peter's victory over Sweden (E) in the Great Northern War—Peace of Nystadt, 1721—provided Russia with direct access to the Baltic and then to the Atlantic. His efforts to acquire ports on the Black Sea (A) were not realized; later Catherine the Great would expand in this area at the expense of the Ottoman Turks. The partitions of Poland (C) occurred after Peter's death; Russia did not enter into any alliance with England (D) during this period.

21. **(C)**

In answering this question, study the drawing. The prism-shaped objects are indeed prisms, splitting light entering from the right into a spectrum, recombining it, and splitting it again. Answer (D) may attract those who do not study the drawing, since Newton formulated laws of gravity and motion; carefully looking at the drawing should help you to avoid this mistake.

22. **(C)**

Enclosures were required (C) to permit scientific farming. Other devices were available to (A) reinforce the concept of private property, (B) eliminate continuing boundary disputes, and (D) assist in accurate property tax collections. (E) Permission for the newly rich to acquire property was not a consideration.

23. **(C)**

The Saxon capital, Dresden, was considered the loveliest city in Europe, with its great art treasures, so the wealth and power of Saxon electors must be accounted for. If you have heard of Meissen or Dresden porcelain, then eliminate that choice. You may not know of Saxon involvement in Polish affairs, their pre-eminence in mining, the Book Fair at Leipzig, or its fur trade with Russia, but you can guess that silk was then more a French affair, so (C) must be the "wrong," or correct, answer. Saxony excelled in linens and cottons, not silks.

24. **(D)**

The wars of religion in Europe had the ironic effect of stimulating interest in science, which some Europeans argued was less emotional and less likely to lead to warfare. The seventeenth century saw the establishment of scientific societies in most European nations.

25. **(A)**

An example of a question that requests knowledge of a particular kind of terminology—slogans—this question asks for your understanding of Voltaire's outlook and the major target of his writings. If enough is known about Voltaire, some answers may be eliminated; since Voltaire favored (and helped coin the name) Enlightened

Despotism, answer (C), for example, is not correct. Answer (D) sounds plausible but is not the correct answer.

26. (A)

Rousseau's political ideas remain the subject of much debate, but it is clear that he believed that political problems might be solved through the "general will," an amorphous idea that his interpreters have variously described as a democratic majority or government by a fascist oligarchy. Answer (B) summarizes Voltaire's position; (C) a theocracy, which means rule by Church elites, would have been rejected by virtually all leading French thinkers of Rousseau's day.

27. (D)

This question rewards secure knowledge: You should have studied the Pragmatic Sanction as a women's issue. Charles VI tried to secure the throne for his daughter, Maria Theresa, in spite of the Salic Law and other traditions that denied to princesses on the continent (Russia, an exception) the ability to inherit crown lands. The unwary student may be misled by the other enlightened despots: Though Frederick (A) and Catherine (C) were similar to Maria Theresa, neither was Austrian; Joseph (B) was her son: and Franz Joseph (E), though an Austrian emperor, reigned later.

28. (B)

Smith's book, which appeared in 1776, opposed mercantilism and predicted that the greatest prosperity would be reached when individuals were free to pursue their own selfish interests without government interference or regulation.

29. (B)

"Exclusion" questions, which ask you to identify one answer that does not fit the others, may be approached in different ways. One way is to identify the false choice; another is to eliminate true answers. Although he criticized Christianity as "superstition" and believed that religious bias caused Huguenots to be unjustly persecuted, Voltaire retained God in his philosophy. His type of religion, Deism, saw God as creator of the universe. The remaining answers are true: Voltaire favored the reform of French society from above by "enlightened despots"; during a stay in England, he wrote a book praising the English political system; and he wrote his skeptical *Candide* in reply to the German philosopher Leibniz, whose optimism held that this is the best of all possible worlds.

30. (D)

Sieyès's *Third Estate* sought to use a military coup d'état to create a strong, but unelected, executive. The book suggested goals that Napoleon later accomplished. *What Is to Be Done?* was the title of Vladimir Lenin's book detailing the path to revolution in Russia. In his *Essay on Human Understanding*, John Locke argued that human personality is formed entirely by the environment, rather than by innate or preconceived ideas. *The Progress of the Human Mind*, by the philosopher Condorcet, argued that human perfectibility was possible and that "nature has set no limits to our hopes." Voltaire wrote *Letters on the English*.

31. **(B)**

Passed by the National Assembly during the French Revolution, the Civil Constitution of the Clergy reflected the anticlericalism of many revolutionaries. It denied papal power to appoint bishops or other clergy, substituting popular election instead, and made them salaried officials of the state. While some clergy perished in the Reign of Terror, there was no direct connection between these events and the Civil Constitution. Note that answer (E) flatly contradicts answer (B), suggesting that one of these two must be the correct answer.

32. **(C)**

Valmy was seen as a victory of enthusiastic recruits over mercenary professionals, and this victory achieved not only the evacuation of all foreign troops from French soil, but also the victory of French revolutionary principles in the new Convention. Actually, it was the well-trained artillery that saved the day, but still the symbolic victory of revolution over reaction was clear. The king, under house arrest after the flight to Varennes, had nothing to do with Valmy; breech-loading rifles were introduced in the mid-1800s.

33. **(B)**

The correct chronological sequence is (B) Legislative Assembly (1791–1792), Convention (1792–1795), and Directory (1795–1799). The National Assembly existed from 1789 to 1791; the Consulate from 1799 to 1804; and the Empire from 1804 to 1814.

34. **(B)**

When Charles II married a Bragança of the Portuguese royal family, he got Tangier and Bombay in the dowry; this wedding also began a long friendship between the countries. In 1703 they concluded the Treaty of Methuen, which guaranteed the English a steady supply of the fortified wines, port, and Madeira; in return, the Portuguese got a powerful ally to protect them. It is no coincidence that Britain landed in Portugal in 1808 in its campaign to oust French armies from both Portugal and Spain. Napoleon had made a secret pact to dismember Portugal to punish Portugal for not joining the Continental Blockade.

35. **(B)**

Note that this question requires you to know what the Weber thesis was and what it meant. Some answers appear unlikely. Answers (A) and (C) preceded the rise of Calvinism. Anglicanism is a poor choice because it was restricted to one part of Europe and depended on the political and personal desires of Henry VIII. Weber, an early twentieth-century German sociologist, theorized that a symbiotic relationship existed between Calvinism and capitalism because both were based on common virtues such as industriousness, thrift, etc. Answer (E) is simply incorrect.

36. **(B)**

Relinquished by Austria because its distance from Vienna had made it difficult to defend against Napoleon, the Rhineland was awarded by the Congress of Vienna to Prussia, which had sought territorial rewards for its role in defeating the French emperor. After 1850, the Rhineland, with its supplies of coal and iron ore and its location along that river, became the major industrial area of Germany. This question asks for the significance of a geographical change. One way to arrive at the correct answer is to try to recall other incidents involving the Rhineland in German history. If you recall that the French invaded it in 1923 to take control of industry there, you will realize that answer (B) must be correct.

37. **(A)**

This question draws on knowledge-based analytical skills, requiring both a knowledge of the Corn Laws and an ability to analyze their social impact. Passed by the British Parliament during the Napoleonic Wars, when goods were frequently in short supply, the Corn Laws applied to grain grown within Britain. In times when the supply of grain was low, the tariff on foreign grain increased dramatically. The laws guaranteed that the owners of farms and farm lands, mainly the nobility, would make a fortune during times of food shortage. Businessmen and industrialists objected to the laws because they restricted foreign trade, since other countries could not sell their agricultural products to Britain in order to buy British factory-made goods. Thus, answers (B) through (E) are incorrect.

38. **(B)**

In the forefront of the Industrial Revolution, Britain enjoyed coal and iron ore deposits, a good road system, and a nobility willing to underwrite the risky venture of opening factories ("entrepreneurship"). If you cannot eliminate these answers, you may arrive at answer (B) by analysis. The Agricultural Revolution, which increased farm yields but put many small farmers out of work, created a surplus labor supply for the factories. Also, financing for many early factories came from nobles who owned much of the land and depended, at least initially, on farm income.

39. **(D)**

Although the first three answers plus answer (E) were achieved during the Era of Reform—including abolition of some of the power of the Junkers, the nobility who owned the large farm estates in eastern Prussia—the monarchy did not institute any type of universal manhood suffrage (all adult males allowed to vote) until 1850. Even then, the votes of the wealthy "counted" for much more than the middle class or the poor.

40. **(C)**

In general, Romantics regarded the Enlightenment as an era that elevated cold, mechanical reason and failed to appreciate the variety and spontaneity of human experience. While Enlightenment philosophers valued history for its lessons in morality and government, the Romantics emphasized history as the nurse of the emotions, therefore not "useless." The Middle Ages were admired, to the point that replicas of castles and "new" ruins were built during the Romantic era. In contrast to the cosmopolitan atmosphere of the French Enlightenment, many Romantics championed the worth of individual nations and cultures.

41. **(B)**

The Fabian Socialists were a British movement that attracted such notables as George Bernard Shaw and H. G. Wells. Led by Sidney and Beatrice Webb, the Fabian Socialists called for increased public ownership of private industry. Such changes were to come gradually, on the lines of the tactics of Fabius Maximus, the "great delayer" in Roman history, whose army wore out Hannibal's by not fighting, but rather luring them on, thus achieving his mission with less loss of blood than his more warlike rival, Scipio Africanus.

42. **(E)**

A test of your knowledge of Marx's ideas and ability to use them for analysis, this question focuses on Marx's belief that revolution is a logical outcome of the growth of capitalism. The most industrialized nations would have the first large proletarian classes, and thus the first revolutions. Nations that had not yet become industrialized would have revolutions last; Marx, in fact, ridiculed the large peasant class in Russia, which he believed would be innately opposed to change.

43. **(D)**

Convinced that liberalism spoke for the middle class, many workers joined the Chartist movement, which during the 1830s and 1840s presented several mass petitions to Parliament demanding the abolition of property qualifications for voting, secret ballots, universal suffrage, and payment for members of Parliament.

44. **(D)**

Jingoism, taken from the word *jingo* in the second line of the saying, came to mean emotional, mindless nationalism. The other answers are attempts to create plausible alternatives. For example, British citizens proudly boasted in the nineteenth century that their nation, the most highly industrialized in the world at the time, was the "Workshop of the World."

45. **(B)**

The term *Second Industrial Revolution* describes an economic shift in the second half of the nineteenth century when steel, electricity, oil, and chemicals became important parts of industrialization, supplementing the steam, iron, and textiles that had been central to the First Industrial Revolution. The one item that belongs to the First, rather than the Second, Industrial Revolution is textiles.

46. **(C)**

Answer (C) is not reasonable because the graph indicates growth in actual numbers ("population in millions") rather than percentages. The percentage of growth for Russia cannot be calculated since the graph does not give the numerical population of Russia at the start of the period (1881).

47. **(A)**

A forerunner of Comte, the founder of the philosophy of positivism, St. Simon believed that industrialization, aided by science, would bring a wondrous new age to Europe. Despite the religious sound of his name, answer (C) is incorrect.

48. **(E)**

Fathers and Sons, a Russian classic, contains the best clue in its title, which suggests generational conflict: in it Bazarov is torn between the human weaknesses of the older generation and the scientific coldness of his cohort, the "sons." Hugo dealt with social injustice. Dostoyevsky's was a psychological novel, and *Degeneration* was an alarmist diatribe by Max Nordau, not a novel, warning that modern trends were decadent. A misleading choice is *Frankenstein*, which shows that it is evil to tinker with human nature, but it is not about generations.

49. **(B)**

The clues are plentiful—a date, a German name, and the mention of Austria. The one complication is the use of the name *Magyars*, since the *Ausgleich* split Austrian government functions into Austrian and Hungarian (not Magyar) states. *Magyar* is, however, the traditional name for the Hungarian people—once again, terminology is essential. If the available clues are not sufficient, think of what Austria was called after 1867—"Austria-Hungary" should come to mind.

50. **(E)**

Marxist interests were not reflected during the Revolutions of 1848 because Marxism was hardly known. Though the *Communist Manifesto* was written at this time, it was not distributed widely and had no impact on the revolution. *Das Kapital* was not completed until the 1860s. The liberal (A) desire for constitutional government, the radical economic alternatives of the Utopian Socialists (B), the nationalist (C) call for self-determination, and the enfranchisement of the middle class (D) were all at work in the 1848 revolutions.

51. **(B)**

The Schleswig-Holstein question was a contentious issue between (B) Austria and Prussia during the 1860s; it was a contributing factor to the outbreak of the German

Civil War (1866) between these powers. Bismarck manipulated the crisis to create a favorable situation for Prussia. Neither Sweden (A), Russia (C), The Netherlands (D), nor Great Britain (E) were involved critically with the Schleswig-Holstein issue.

52. (B)

The British prime minister who was associated closely with Irish Home Rule was (B) William Gladstone. Gladstone maintained through his four ministries that one of his principal tasks was "to pacify Ireland." Robert Peel's (E) career was over before the Irish crisis broke during the second half of the nineteenth century. Benjamin Disraeli (A), Lord Salisbury (C), and Joseph Chamberlain (D) were not particularly interested in or sympathetic to the Irish.

53. (B)

The Balfour Declaration (1917) (B) was a vague pledge by Britain to support the establishment of a Jewish homeland in Palestine. It was not related to (A) the German use of chemicals, (C) the Anglo-Irish crisis stemming from the Easter Rebellion, (D) American neutrality, or (E) annexations and reparations as war aims. The Balfour Declaration conflicted with the Sykes-Picot agreement of 1916 that "promised" Arabs a homeland in Palestine if they fought against the Turks.

54. (B)

The map indicates the partition of Africa in (B) 1914 after most of the European powers had participated in establishing colonial empires.

55. (A)

The term *Concert of Europe* applies only to the decades in which Metternich, chancellor of Austria, exerted indirect influence over the foreign policies of most of Europe, but not over Britain's, which in the 1820s repudiated the Holy Alliance. (B) and (C), though correct statements, have nothing to do with the Concert; (D) and (E) are simply false.

56. (D)

In 1834, many German states (but not Austria) agreed to drop tariffs between states through a customs union, the (D) *Zollverein*. The *Fürstenstaat* (A) was a term that expressed the "state of the prices," the decentralized German political order established by the Peace of Westphalia in 1648. The Confederation of the Rhine (B) was organized by Napoleon as a means of administering some German states and manipulating German politics. The Frankfurt Assembly (C) emerged in 1848 as part of the revolution, with the aim of unifying Germany. The Hanseatic League (E) was a medieval alliance of North Sea and Baltic ports, centered on German cities.

57. (C)

Britain established direct control over India after the suppression of the (C) Sepoy Mutiny of 1857. This mutiny, caused by a perceived violation of Hindu and Muslim practices, had its roots in the way that the East India Company administered its areas. The (A) Opium Wars (1840s) involved Britain in conflicts with China over the distribution of opium. The Boxer Rebellion (1899–1900) was an antiforeign outburst against foreign influence in China; it resulted in the siege of the foreign legations in Beijing and the use of a multinational force to rescue them. The assassination of Gandhi in January 1948 occurred after Britain had withdrawn from India; India had become a free nation and held dominion status in the British Commonwealth of Nations. The Warren Hastings affair (E) was a scandal that involved British management of India during the late eighteenth century.

58. **(C)**

The British policy of "Splendid Isolationism" was terminated with the (C) Anglo-Japanese Alliance of 1902; it specified that each nation would adopt a position of benevolent neutrality in the event that the other was attacked by another state. This agreement, which was maintained through World War I, preceded the (A) Anglo-French Entente (1904), the (B) Anglo-Russian Entente (1907), and the (D) Second Moroccan Crisis (1911). The Boer War (E) preceded the Anglo-Japanese accord.

59. **(A)**

In the "April Theses" (1917) Lenin (A) challenged the policies of the Provisional Government; Lenin was opposed (D) to continuing the war against Germany. (B) is incorrect because the "April Theses" were not related to the 1905 revolution; Lenin denounced the revisionists in *What Is to Be Done?* in 1902; he did not support Kerensky (E) as his successor—Kerensky had fled to Western Europe and would later live and die in the United States.

60. **(A)**

The Versailles Treaty resulted in the formation of several new nations, including (A) Yugoslavia and Hungary; Yugoslavia was a new kingdom that was based on an expanding Serbia; Hungary came from the Austro-Hungarian Empire that was dissolved. (B) and (C) are incorrect because while Poland was a new state in 1919, both Italy and Greece had existed previously. (D) and (E) are incorrect because Germany and Italy both existed earlier; Austria was a new nation that emerged from the Austro-Hungarian Empire.

61. **(B)**

The Dawes Plan (B) of 1924 was a reparations plan designed to eliminate the friction that led to the Ruhr Crisis. The Kellogg-Briand Pact (1927) was (A) an international proposal to outlaw war. Stresemann (C) supported the Dawes Plan to gain the withdrawal of French and Belgian troops from the Ruhr Valley. The Dawes Plan was not permanent (D); in 1929, it was replaced by the Young Plan. The Munich agreement of 1938 (E) resulted in the dismemberment of Czechoslovakia.

62. **(E)**

The rise of fascism in Germany (1933) cannot be attributed to the policies of Gustav Stresemann, who died in 1929. Stresemann was one of the few able leaders to emerge during the Weimar Republic; he did much to restore German prestige and establish stability in Central Europe. The (A) failure of the Weimar Republic to address the crisis caused by the Depression, the (B) effective organization of the Nazi Party, the (C) charisma of Adolf Hitler, and (D) lingering humiliation of defeat in World War I were factors that contributed to the rise of fascism in Germany.

63. **(C)**

Answers (B) and (C) are opposites; high inflation almost always affects the value of a country's currency. If you recognize this, it will be apparent that one of these two answers is the correct answer. If necessary, guess, since your odds are 50 percent, and only 0.25 point is deducted for an incorrect guess.

64. **(C)**

Although a cannon barrel looms large in the poster, below it is a cross and a man in clerical garments. Not only are answers (A) and (B) the same—indicating that they should be eliminated—but the purpose of the cannon barrel appears to be to accuse religion of hypocrisy (of sanctioning war while preaching love and peace). Answer (D) is for those who do not study the poster carefully; it seems plausible but is not the correct answer.

65. **(D)**

Desiderius Erasmus (1466–1536), also known as Erasmus of Rotterdam, was a Dutch humanist who hoped to reform the Church by seeking inspiration from Christianity in its earliest stages. To this end he published in 1516 an edition of the original Greek text of the New Testament, including notes and a new Latin translation, which he hoped could be used to inspire spiritual renewal. He corresponded with religious reformers yet took a moderate position and never broke away from the Roman Catholic Church.

66. **(E)**

The term *existentialism* gives the key clue. Neither fascism (B) nor communism (C) is a real philosophy; nihilism (A) is a nineteenth-century phenomenon much less concerned than existentialism with ethical issues; and logical positivism (D) is a branch of philosophy preoccupied with the mathematic restatement of philosophical and linguistic propositions, hardly a concern of existentialists such as Sartre, de Beauvoir, and Camus.

67. **(C)**

For this question, you must know about Keynes and understand the logic of his economic system. Keynes asserted that governments should spend more money during economic crises—even to the point of running deficits—in order to "prime the pump" of the economy.

68. **(E)**

In 1956, Hungary revolted against Soviet rule and called on Western powers for aid; the United States, Britain, and France, however, were more concerned with Egypt's attempt to seize the Suez Canal and wage war on Israel. Neither China (B) nor Yugoslavia (C) revolted in 1956. Though Poland (A) and East Germany (D) did have unrest in 1956, their failed efforts were small in scope and much shorter in duration than events in Hungary, so the question of help from the West was moot.

69. **(E)**

After 1945 the policies of the Soviet Union resulted in (A) the continuing development of Soviet military power, (B) a slow demobilization from a war economy, (C) consistency in the exercise of power by the Communist Party, and (D) a general improvement in the standard of living. The Soviet Union did NOT (E) enjoy extensive influence in the United Nations during the years immediately following World War II; American influence there was sustained through the 1960s when the Soviets did gain considerable influence in the international assembly, especially among the new developing nations of the Third World.

70. **(C)**

The map indicates the partition of the Ottoman Empire after World War I. The further emergence of new nations from colonies and the independence of Israel in 1948 render (A), (B), and (D) incorrect. The Congress of Berlin (E) occurred in 1878 and did not result in any substantive changes in the boundaries of the Near East except for Britain obtaining the island of Cyprus.

71. **(D)**

One good approach to this sort of question is to try to identify which answer was not true of the post–World War II period. Germany, divided into two states, was not allowed to have an army until non-Communist West Germany joined the North Atlantic Treaty Organization in 1955 and Communist East Germany joined the corresponding Warsaw Pact. An alternate approach is to determine that answers (A) through (C), plus answer (E), were true of the postwar period, leaving (D) as the correct answer by elimination.

72. **(B)**

Pasternak was forbidden to travel to receive the Prize for his novel *Dr. Zhivago*, which included critical comments about the Bolshevik revolution and the subsequent civil war between Reds and Whites. Shostakovitch and Prokofiev were Soviet composers; Beria a head of the KGB, the secret police; and Brezhnev a ruler of the Soviet Union during the late 1960s and 1970s.

73. **(C)**

The correct answer is (C). Political corruption and instability were central causes in the downfall of the Christian Democrats in the 1990s. Corruption landed a number of them in jail, and the party had never been able to maintain a stable ruling coalition in the Italian Parliament for the duration of the entire postwar period. Though southern Italy's economy lagged behind the prosperous North, poverty (A) was not widespread in Italy; food shortages (B) were not a problem for Italy; the Christian Democrats, despite their name, were a centrist and largely secular political party (D), and Italy did indeed support the United States during the Persian Gulf War (E), a fact unrelated to the fortunes of the Christian Democrats.

74. **(C)**

The correct answer is (C). Havel worked as a playwright.

75. **(E)**

In 1971, Switzerland finally granted women's suffrage, last but one among major states in Western Europe (the last was Portugal in 1976). Norway was the first independent state to let women stand for national elections (New Zealand claimed that honor in 1893, but as a semiautonomous member of the British Empire; Finland gave women the right to vote as a province of Russia in 1906); Turkey allowed women to vote in 1908, Norway in 1913. Germany enacted women's suffrage in 1919, Spain in 1931, and France in 1944. The littlest European states were the last: Liechtenstein, Andorra, and San Marino.

76. **(A)**

Greens are ecological political parties in modern Europe, especially that pioneered in West Germany in the 1970s; far from being terrorists, they advocate pacifism. The Red Brigades were Italian terrorists in the 70s and early 80s; Basque separatists have engaged in terrorist tactics against Spain for decades; the Baader-Meinhof gang was a terrorist group in Germany in the late 70s; and the IRA (Irish Republican Army) engaged in violent attacks on British officers in Ireland from the 1920s to the Good Friday Accords of 1998–1999.

77. **(B)**

The ECSC, formed in 1951, was the first success in unification. An agreement among the later Six (Benelux countries, France, West Germany, and Italy), the ECSC aimed at regulating coal and steel production, pricing and marketing for the good of all. NATO (1949) signalized European dependence on the will of the United States in military matters; EURATOM (1957) deals with atomic energy, not unification. Both the EEC (1957) and Maastricht (1991) are later events in European unification.

78. **(D)**

Beauvoir produced the most important postwar work on feminism in her classic *The Second Sex* (1949). Neither Onassis (C) nor Thurn und Taxis is known as a writer (both were or are socialites). Byatt (B) is not known for feminism, nor is Akhmatova (A), though the great Russian poet is considered a strong female voice and a great model for women—a role she came to disown, since she was not, strictly speaking, a feminist and disliked bad poetry by anyone, including women.

79. **(E)**

Despite President Reagan's dramatic order to premier Gorbachev to "take down that wall!," the rhetoric of neither Reagan nor the elder Bush was a factor in its fall. Other factors, (A) through (D), are considered key causes of the decision of the East German government not to thwart West Germans' tearing down the wall or East Germans' flowing to West Berlin. Though the "Star Wars" scenario was not a realistic proposal, U.S. spending on the program alarmed the Soviets, who were unable to match our dollars with their exhausted rubles.

80. **(B)**

The new European Central Bank is empowered to set the value of the euro against other currencies. Member countries do not have a direct say (A): They work indirectly. Free trade (C) and the U.S. dollar (D) are thrown in to mislead students who have not thought about differences between European and American mind-sets. Gold (E) has not pegged world currencies since 1973.

Section II

Sample Answer to Document-Based Question

In the myriad of events that shaped the French Revolution of 1789, much attention has been given to occurrences in the capital city of Paris, where mobs in the streets weakened a royal government already under attack from an increasingly restive middle class. Less attention has been given to the reactions of the French peasants, or small farmers, whose grievances and concerns emerged during a period of anarchy and violence called the Great Fear.

The restiveness of the French peasants had been aggravated by both natural and political events. Three years of substandard harvests had contributed to economic misery in the rural areas of France. As grain prices rose, the peasants complained about the burden of their remaining feudal obligations. These included the corvée, the necessity of providing free labor for public works projects or other tasks as assigned by the local nobility.

It was not surprising that peasant grievances were initially directed against the nobility they saw as contributing to their misery. Rumors of aristocratic plots swept the countryside, including rumors of food hoarders among a greedy nobility. Some of the first violence of 1789 was in the rural areas, where peasants took control of local granaries and attacked members of the nobility.

The situation appeared to worsen because of lack of accurate information. An English observer noted the lack of rural newspapers. Word of mouth became the source of information. The most common rumor was that bands of brigands were operating in the area. Responding to such rumors, organized groups of armed peasants sometimes attacked other groups of peasants by mistake. In one case, the band of brigands turned out to be a herd of cows.

At the very least, such sporadic violence demonstrated the decline of the old regime: the decline of royal control in the rural areas of France. There were signs that peasant unhappiness was increasingly directed against the monarchy itself. It was noted that, although some noblemen contributed their personal funds to buy food for the peasants, the king made no appearance in the countryside, nor did he comment on events. The king remained a distant figure, hunting wildlife that the peasants were forbidden to hunt.

Although the leaders of the Revolution in Paris were from the middle class, the Great Fear obviously had considerable impact. When King Louis XVI called the Estates-General into session in 1789, the Third Estate—consisting of a middle-class minority and an overwhelming peasant majority—emerged as the dominant group in France. When the Third Estate was transformed into a National Convention, the Convention became so alarmed by the Great Fear that it made rumormongering a criminal offense. Later, the Convention acknowledged one of the major concerns of the peasants by abolishing the remaining feudal obligations in France.

While the peasants were less educated and sophisticated than the middle-class politicians who led France during the Revolution, they clearly had an impact on events. The Great Fear united the peasants and made them aware of their own power. In their own disorganized way, the peasants had made the end of feudalism one of the great achievements of the Revolution.

[This essay (1) uses documents in a careful way, quoting some indirectly; (2) has a clear introduction and conclusion; (3) centers each paragraph around a single theme or idea; (4) cites specific examples; (5) includes "outside" information; and (6) clearly addresses itself to the topic.]

Sample Answers to Essay Questions

1.   The Counter-Reformation or Catholic Reformation was the reaction of the Catholic Church to the spread of Protestantism. It was composed of several distinct developments that had varying impacts on European history; however, the general impact of the Counter-Reformation was negative because the Church identified with the old order and adopted a defensive ideological position that solidified doctrines and the precepts of the Church. This anti-intellectual tenor made the Church seem merely a remnant of the medieval order rather than an active power in helping its members to cope with the changing phenomena of modern European society.

    The Roman Church was slow to react to the Lutheran Reformation because of the fear that the conciliar movement within the Church would reassert itself. The conciliar movement, which maintained that the ultimate power in the Church resided in the bishops meeting in council—not the Papacy—was evident during the fifteenth century at the Councils of Constance, Florence, and Basel. During the 1520s and 1530s, other than decrees of excommunication and the like, the response of the Church was limited to the establishment of new religious orders. Among these orders were the Theatines, the Oratorians, and the Jesuits; they were intended to create a new, more positive image of the Catholic clergy and generally stressed the pastoral needs of the people. The Jesuits were founded by Ignatius Loyola, a retired Spanish military officer; this order would serve the interests of the Papacy and regain the people and territory that had been lost because of Protestantism. Reinforced by pledges of loyalty and by a deteriorating position, Rome convened the Council of Trent in 1545; this Council would meet in three sessions from 1545 to 1564 and constitute the most important component of the Counter-Reformation. Traditional Church doctrines on the sacraments and an elite ordained priesthood were reaffirmed; the Council of Trent formalized the split within Christendom—doctrinal determinations rendered any compromise with Protestant leaders impossible. During 1558–1559, the Papacy decreed that it established the *Index of Prohibited Books* (1559–1967), which listed works that were contrary to Church teaching; Catholics, under pain of sin, were directed to refrain from reading these books. During the late sixteenth century and for the next two centuries, the Roman Church relied on the Inquisition to enforce its doctrines and to defend the Church's interests.

    The anti-intellectual and reactionary characteristics of the Counter-Reformation continued to dominate Catholic thought and policy until the twentieth century. Pope Pius IX denounced most aspects of modern culture in *Syllabus of Errors* in 1864; at the First Vatican Council (1870–1871) the doctrine of papal infallibility was adopted. During the first decade of the twentieth century Pope Pius X denounced "modernism." Within the context of European history, the Counter-Reformation was equated frequently with authoritarianism and the medieval order.

2.   During the nineteenth century, several political and economic alternatives to capitalism were developed in response to the negative consequences of the Industrial Revolution, the lingering sentiments associated with the French Revolution, and the absence of participatory governments.

The Utopian Socialists emerged early in the nineteenth century under the leadership of Charles Fourier, Robert Owen, and Claude Saint-Simon. They were interested in alleviating the distress associated with the Industrial Revolution and unregulated urban life in general. They maintained that employers who provided for the economic and social well-being of their employees would be rewarded through increased productivity. Further, community-held businesses would prosper because all participants had a stake in the success of the effort. The Utopian Socialists had a rather naive understanding of history and the forces that were current during their own time—they underestimated the depth of human greed and they failed to appreciate that many Europeans did not entertain any sense of "economic" responsibility to their employees. Several attempts at establishing utopian communities were undertaken by Robert Owen; several achieved initial success and survived for several decades.

The tactics and the philosophy of Utopian Socialists were discredited by the failure of the revolutions of 1848. Marxism, or scientific socialism, emerged as a "realistic" alternative to utopian socialism. In many works, such as *The Communist Manifesto*, *Critique of Political Economy*, and *Das Kapital*, Karl Marx argued that one must understand that history was in fact a struggle—the dialectic—in which "the people" had been suppressed; material culture or economics was the driving force of Marx's dialectic. The future progress of humanity demanded that a violent revolution occur in which all aspects of *bourgeoisie* culture would be destroyed—churches, governmental institutions, capitalism, etc. After a period known as "the dictatorship of the proletariat" (led by the Communist Party), the people would overthrow the party and enter into a "classless society." The Marxist philosophy attracted the support of many intellectuals and reformers during the second half of the nineteenth century. While most accepted his conceptual arguments, many Marxists departed from Marx on the necessity of revolution. These "evolutionists," or revisionists, contended that revolution was not required when the people could elect a Marxist government to implement the revolutionary reforms. Among the revisionists were Sidney and Beatrice Webb, Keir Hardie, and George Bernard Shaw (who were all involved in the formation of the Fabian Society in Great Britain); Edward Bernstein, who led the Social Democratic Party (SDP) in Germany; and the French socialist Jean Jaurès. The revisionist approach was denounced by Lenin in *What Is to Be Done?* (1902).

Anarchism was a political philosophy that was originated by the French radical Pierre Proudhon, who wrote *What Is Property?* immediately prior to the revolutions of 1848. Proudhon and the Russian anarchists Mikhail Bakunin and Peter Kropotkin envisioned a simple society along Jacobin lines; individuals would live in harmony and equality after the artificial structures (religion, nations, etc.) had been eliminated. The people would rise in general revolution after their oppressors. Unlike the Marxists, who were literate oriented, the anarchists placed their hopes with the common uneducated people. Anarchism attracted considerable support, especially in Southern Europe.

3.   The unification movements in Germany and Italy paralleled one another during the period from 1850 to 1870. Both efforts were based on expanding an existing state; both involved domestic adjustments and international conflicts; and both movements capitalized upon national sentiments that had been expressed during the revolutions of 1848. The architect of German unification was the Prussian Otto von Bismarck; Italian unification was supported by Camillo Cavour, Napoleon III, Giuseppe Garibaldi, and King Victor Emmanuel II.

During the revolutions of 1848, many German statesmen and intellectuals had anticipated that Prussia would be the nucleus of a new Germany. While that goal was not realized at that time, Prussia emerged in the 1850s and 1860s as an aggressive state that was interested in consolidating its position in north central Europe. Under the leadership of William I and Bismarck, Prussia introduced a constitutional government in 1850, introduced domestic political and legal reforms during the 1850s, and expanded its army. During the early 1860s, Prussia was allied with Austria in a brief war (1863) with Denmark over the provinces of Schleswig and Holstein; as a result of the Danish defeat, the provinces came under the joint administration of the victors. In turn, this led to a situation that Bismarck exploited in his preparations for the showdown with Austria. With guarantees of Italian participation on a southern front and of French neutrality, Bismarck fabricated a crisis to which the Austrians responded by declaring war. The German Civil War of 1866 resulted in the humiliating defeat of Austria. Bismarck did not exact any territory from Austria; it was evident that Prussia was the pre-eminent power in Central Europe. In 1867, Bismarck established the North German Confederation as a means of transforming Prussian influence into a German state. During the summer 1870 a diplomatic crisis developed between France and Prussia over the "Ems Dispatch." Arguing that William I had been insulted by French diplomats in discussions relating to the Spanish succession, Bismarck created a crisis that led to a French declaration of war. The Franco-Prussian War of 1870–1871 resulted in the defeat of France, the surrender of Napoleon III, the end of the Second French Empire, Prussian occupation of much of France, and, in January 1871, the establishment of the German Empire.

In 1848, Italian unification was supported by King Charles Albert of Sardinia-Piedmont. After initial successes, his forces were defeated by the Austrians. In Rome, Mazzini's ill-fated Roman Republic was overthrown by French troops and an increasingly conservative Pope Pius IX was restored to power. During the 1850s, Camillo Cavour, who served as Prime Minister to Victor Emmanuel II, emerged as the leader of an expanded Sardinian state, which it was anticipated would result in a unified Italy. Cavour attracted the support of European liberals through a range of social, constitutional, and economic reforms; Sardinia was a participant with Britain and France in the Crimean War against Russia. In 1856, at the Paris Peace Conference, Cavour spoke on the need to establish an Italy that was governed by Italians—a direct attack on the continuing Austrian control of Lombardy and Venetia. His remarks were received sympathetically by Napoleon III, the French emperor who had been raised in Italy. In 1858, Cavour and Napoleon III signed the secret Plombières Agreement, which pledged French support in driving the Austrians from the two provinces if the Austrians declared war. Cavour construed a crisis and the

Austrians obliged by declaring war (1859). As a result of this brief war, Sardinia obtained Lombardy but Austria retained Venetia. Cavour died shortly thereafter. In 1860, Garibaldi and an army of 1,000 men landed in Sicily and within three months seized control of the Kingdom of the Two Sicilies. This new acquisition was incorporated into a Sardinian-dominated Italian Confederation. In 1866, the Italians acquired Venetia in return for their participation in the German Civil War. Italian unification was realized in the fall of 1870 when Italian forces, capitalizing on the withdrawal of the French garrison (Franco-Prussian War), seized Rome—the Patrimony of St. Peter.

4.   Other Europeans sometimes regarded the English as a country of madmen during the seventeenth century, when the English overthrew two monarchs, even executing one. Yet the English Civil War and the Glorious Revolution of 1688 were singular constitutional events, pushing England ahead of the rest of Europe in terms of political development.

Both events transferred some elements of royal power to the English Parliament, which had existed since the thirteenth century; in the years since, the relationships between kings and Parliament had not always been smooth. The Tudor monarchs of the sixteenth century had handled Parliament with skill, using a mixture of compromise, guile, bribes, and cleverness to maintain royal authority. Their successors, the Stuarts, proved less successful in dealing with Parliament. Parliament tried to outlaw Roman Catholic advisers to James I by passing a Test Act, which required that high civil servants be members of the Church of England. When James tried to nullify the Test Act with his own Toleration Decree, Parliament cut his funding. Like other Stuart monarchs, James relied on subsidies from foreign monarchs.

Charles I continued the Test Act–Toleration Decree cycle. He also tried to combat the growing Calvinist (Puritan) presence in the Church of England. Many Puritans became Anglicans when Elizabeth I instituted the Thirty-Nine Articles, a broad creed of faith designed to quiet religious controversy within the Church of England. When Civil War broke out in 1641, the king was confronted with two armies: the army of Parliament and the army of the Puritans.

Charles's defeat and execution at the end of the war did not directly advance constitutionalism, since the following years of Puritan rule were neither successful nor favorable to the growth of parliamentary power. Oliver Cromwell personally ruled for a time as Lord High Protector. Upon his death, parliament chose to restore the monarchy by inviting Charles II to rule.

While Charles II avoided reopening old wounds, his successor, James II, returned to the cycle of Test Acts and Toleration Decrees. The resulting Glorious Revolution saw James flee the country and Parliament once again placed in a position to select a new monarch. Parliament's choices—James's daughter Mary and her Dutch husband—conceded considerable amounts of royal power to Parliament. For example, they agreed to a Bill of Rights banning royal interference in court proceedings and guaranteeing freedom from arbitrary arrests. The events of 1688 finally established the sovereignty of Parliament.

The political violence and chaos of the seventeenth century brought changes to England that France would undergo a century later. The unwritten English constitution had been considerably revised, and Parliament had become a sovereign, significant presence in the English political system.

5.   Building on the important advances of the First Industrial Revolution in its exploitation of steam power, the use of iron as a building component, the mechanization of cotton manufacture, and more, the Second Industrial Revolution made Europe the dominant economic and military power in the world, despite rising competition from the United States. It also, however, had created major social problems as European countries became increasingly urbanized and the working classes demanded more and more rights in the workplace and in the voting booth. Because of the unwillingness of the upper middle classes and nobles to compromise with the beleaguered petite bourgeoisie, the new white-collar workers or the working classes, the ruling classes, in funding and profiting from the Second Industrial Revolution, also entrenched themselves behind a wall of protectionism in economic and militarism in diplomacy that ironically made this Second Industrial Revolution a potent cause in the slide to World War I.

The Second Industrial Revolution is generally dated from the 1870s, when steel, oil, electricity, and artificial chemicals became the leading indicators in West European economies. Urbanization and factories proceeded apace; so too the development of workers' suburbs with cheap housing, made possible by new modes of transportation (electric trams, even automobiles) and communication (telegraph, telephone, pneumatic tubes). The First Industrial Revolution had given rise to demands for unions and better working conditions, rarely granted before 1870, whence the number of workers' revolts and major revolutions in Europe after Napoleon. After Liberals gained power in many cabinets or saw their programs implemented, from 1850 to 1890, from England to Russia, urban and even agricultural workers, who were needed more than ever for the new second-wave industries, saw their chance to demand more rights and more of the affluence. Thwarted by the power and conservatism of the new plutocracy, where old nobles now made common cause with the newer financial and educational bourgeoisie, the lower-middle and working classes sought other ways to express their political and economic frustrations than in the hidebound older parties. They increasingly embraced forms of socialism or anarchism; even when these ideologies did not take hold, the now legal unions had recourse more and more often to sometimes violent, often crippling strikes, as is seen in the last years before World War I.

The ruling classes were duly alarmed. They did not want to share the wealth of the Second Industrial Revolution, nor did they wish these new working-class movements to take any power from them, so from 1870 on, European powers sought to divert workers with their best weapon: nationalism. When that could not be expressed in a war or in new colonies, nationalism took a turn toward imperialism. Many historians see the aggressive imperialist programs of Disraeli, Bismarck, Jules Ferry, and the Russian tsars as ways to distract disgruntled workers and others from problems caused at home by the very prosperity occasioned by the two industrial revolutions. With new opportunities for gain also came market fluctuations, especially in agriculture, always lagging: From 1873 to the 1890s, Europe suffered a long Depression, in spite of the new industries, and probably because of Europe's inability to cope with the agricultural competition posed by the Americas, north and south, or by the "breadbasket of Europe" in the Ukraine.

As imperialism and militarism became the preferred policies of the ruling class after 1890, the new products of the Second Industrial Revolution came to be seen in light of their uses for war. Economic competition, contrary to some classical economists, did not foster a spirit of healthy rivalry then, but rather a rise in the more rabid forms of nationalism. But now war would be far more destructive and far-flung than even the academics and scientists of the time could see. Whereas the First Industrial Revolution seemed to advance by trial and error, the Second had enthroned scientific method as its catechism. Scientists and engineers paved the way for the military to invest in armored vehicles, barbed wire, chemical gases for use against the enemy, the new airplane as a weapon, and much more. Military contracts were more reliable, and often more lucrative, for industrialists than those of normal trade. The road to world war was thus paved by advances in science and industry.

Industrialization came last to Sicily, Ireland, and Spain, perhaps, but its late arrival in Russia bore more fruit. Contrary to Marx, theoretician of the demise of capitalism made rich by the First Industrial Revolution, Russia, not an advanced industrial country, was the most fertile ground for revolutionary ideas, and the power least able to fight a sustained modern war. So when Russia had fared badly after two years of mechanized warfare, it got its revenge on the more advanced countries by adapting and adopting Marxian ideas in the Bolshevik Revolution. As Lenin and Stalin later showed, the glories of the Second Industrial Revolution were much desired; but to have any chance at them, a backward country, they discovered, might need Marxist revolution or (as in the case of Spain, Sicily, and Ireland) various forms of anarchic violence. The United States was lucky to jump on the industrial bandwagon when it was in the early stages of its second voyage.

6.   Described by wartime propaganda as the "war to end all wars," World War I was followed by peace settlements that promoted bitterness and disillusionment in Europe. In this way, the settlements may have themselves become partial causes of World War II, though we must not neglect either purely internal pressures or the changing international scene, especially world markets and naval agreements.

Three treaties ended the war—the Treaty of Versailles with Germany and the Treaties of St. Germain and Neuilly with Austria and the Ottoman Empire. The Treaty of Versailles was criticized within Germany as the "imposed treaty," so called because it was not the treaty promised when Germany asked for a cease-fire in November of 1918. Germany had been promised a negotiated treaty, but the Treaty of Versailles, written by Germany's enemies, had been forced upon Germany with the choice of signing the treaty or resuming hostilities.

Already embittered by a continuing British naval blockade of Germany in 1919, after the war ended—which, rightly or wrongly, many Germans blamed as the cause of starvation in the country—Germans were especially unhappy with some parts of the treaty. The German army was limited to 100,0000 men; training was prohibited in tanks and planes; and Germany was required to pay an unspecified amount of reparations. To many Germans it appeared that their nation was being blamed for starting the war and for all destruction resulting from the war.

The Treaty of Versailles opened the way for politicians such as Adolf Hitler, who argued that Britain and France were not to be trusted and their democracies were not to be emulated. Although Hitler's National Socialist Party was never able to garner more than 34 percent of the vote, he probably spoke for many Germans when he dismissed the Weimar Republic, the German government that was formed after the war, as an expedient and weak government formed in hopes of gaining easier peace terms from Woodrow Wilson and his allies.

In order to convince many Germans that military force was necessary to roll back the hated treaty, Hitler also could point to two other parts of the peace settlements. Germany had lost much of mineral-rich Silesia to the re-created Poland, even though the majority of Silesians had chosen, in a referendum, to remain with Germany. Hitler also exploited the issue of the "Polish Corridor," a strip of formerly German land awarded to Poland in order to give the Poles an outlet to the sea.

The treaties with Austria and the Ottoman Empire allowed the victorious Allies to create new nations in Eastern Europe. The new nations were not particularly stable, struggling with internal divisions and bickering with their neighbors over borders and territory. In his book *Mein Kampf*, Hitler, born an Austrian, looked at these areas as a natural direction for future German expansion.

Disillusionment over the peace settlement was not restricted to Germany. Britain and France had been promised a collective security agreement with the United States by Woodrow Wilson. When the United States instead withdrew from the European diplomatic system after the war, both European nations struggled to find new ways to make themselves secure. By the 1930s, many British citizens and some French citizens had come to believe that the Treaty of Versailles had been too harsh. The result, unfortunately, was a tendency to view Hitler as a mere statesman with valid grievances who needed to be "appeased."

It would be inaccurate to say the treaties at the end of World War I became the major causes of World War II. The major causes lay in the personality and ideas of Adolf Hitler. By helping Hitler's rise to power, and by failing to establish a stable diplomatic system to block him, the treaties were, however, a factor.

PRACTICE EXAM 3

This exam is also on CD-ROM in our
special interactive AP European History TEST*ware*®

AP European History

Section 1

TIME: 55 minutes
80 questions

> **DIRECTIONS:** Each question or incomplete statement below is followed by five answers or completions. Select the one that is best in each case.

1. Known as the "Prince of the Humanists," in works such as *In Praise of Folly* he criticized the clergy and abuses that he saw in the Church. He was

    (A) Francesco Petrarch

    (B) Desiderius Erasmus

    (C) Cornelius Agricola

    (D) Pico della Mirandola

    (E) Thomas More

2. A pioneer in the Age of Exploration, Prince Henry of Portugal sponsored

    (A) the exploration of the west coast of Africa

    (B) the establishment of colonies in Brazil

    (C) Hernando Cortez's conquest of the Maya

    (D) the creation of an important trading post in Goa

    (E) the earliest efforts to discover a Northwest Passage

3. All of the following are correctly matched EXCEPT

    (A) Pizarro—conquest of the empire of the Incas

    (B) Coronado—early exploration of the American Southwest

    (C) Balboa—exploration of the Mississippi Valley

    (D) Cortez—conquest of the Aztecs

    (E) Diaz—reached the southernmost tip of Africa

4.   The Protestant Reformation

(A)   rejected many aspects of primitive Christianity

(B)   weakened nationalistic feelings

(C)   tended to strengthen the power of secular rulers

(D)   launched the first Christian missionaries to convert the Far East

(E)   served to weaken the hold of spiritual beliefs on the minds of Europeans

5.   Martin Luther believed that the problem of personal sin had its solution in

(A)   good works

(B)   acceptance of the doctrine of predestination

(C)   justification by faith

(D)   an inner awakening to the spirit of God

(E)   adherence to the teachings of the Church councils

6.   In transforming the Catholic Church into the Church of England, Henry VIII

(A)   abolished Catholic sacraments

(B)   disbanded monasteries and confiscated their land

(C)   forced Calvinist doctrines on the new Church

(D)   needed the help of Scottish Presbyterians

(E)   defended the authority of Rome in English church affairs

7.   The sixteenth-century religious wars in France were largely ended with the

(A)   accession of Louis XI

(B)   Edict of Nantes

(C)   Massacre of St. Bartholomew's Day

(D)   Treaty of Cateau-Cambrésis

(E)   resolution of the Habsburg-Bourbon conflict by the Peace of Augsburg

8.   The German sociologist Max Weber advanced the thesis that a significant result of the Protestant Reformation was that

(A)   Protestantism, particularly Calvinism, fostered capitalism

(B)   Luther's support of the German peasant class weakened his appeal to German princes

(C)   a close alliance evolved between Luther and Anabaptist leaders

(D)   it greatly enhanced Europe's overseas exploration

(E)   Protestant opposition to usury hampered the growth of industry

9.   "All are not created on equal terms, but some are preordained to eternal life, others to eternal damnation; and, accordingly, as each has been created for one or the other of these ends, we say that he has been predestined to life or death ... ." This statement reflects an essential view of

(A)   Thomas Hobbes   (D)   the Council of Trent

(B)   John Calvin   (E)   Ulrich Zwingli

(C)   Martin Luther

10.   "The state of the monarchy is the supremest thing upon the earth; for kings are not only God's lieutenants upon earth, and sit upon God's throne, but even by God himself they are called gods... ." This concept of the status of monarchy would best reflect the view of

(A)   Frederick II of Prussia   (D)   William III of England

(B)   John Locke   (E)   Joseph II of Austria

(C)   James I of England and Scotland

11.   During the sixteenth and seventeenth centuries, the United Provinces (Netherlands) were noted for toleration of Jews, but which state was considered the most tolerant?

(A)   France   (D)   Poland-Lithuania

(B)   The Papal States   (E)   Russian Muscovy

(C)   Brandenburg-Prussia

12.   Which Lutheran country fought for the Protestant side in the Thirty Years' War, oversaw shipping between the North Sea and Baltic, yet in 1814 lost the kingdom of Norway as a result of supporting Napoleon against Britain?

(A)   Sweden   (D)   Finland

(B)   Denmark   (E)   The Netherlands

(C)   Prussia

13.   The Counter-Reformation was closely allied with which artistic movement?

(A)   Italian Renaissance   (D)   Neoclassical

(B)   Baroque   (E)   Flemish realism

(C)   Rococo

14. The etching above by an eyewitness shows the massacre on St. Bartholomew's Day, 1572, of

    (A) Dutch nobility   (D) Spanish Catholics

    (B) German peasants   (E) English merchants

    (C) French Calvinists

15. Which of the following forms of government would most likely win the approval of a *politique*?

    (A) Secular government in which religion plays no role

    (B) Theocracy

    (C) Parliamentary government

    (D) Huguenot government

    (E) Government based on the model of the Papacy

16. The illustration above, an early depiction of Copernicus's concept of the universe, indicates that he was in error by

    (A) retaining the medieval placement of heaven at the outermost reaches of the universe

    (B) retaining Ptolemy's geocentric theory

    (C) adhering to the view that the orbits of the planets are circular

    (D) failing to take into consideration advances made by Kepler

    (E) rejecting the heliocentric theory

17. "… I have heard him say, that after his Booke of the Circulation of the Blood came out, that he fell mightily in his Practice, and that it was believed by the Vulgar that he was crack-brained."
    This excerpt, taken from an account by John Aubrey, describes

    (A) Paracelsus   (D) Harvey

    (B) Galvani   (E) Bacon

    (C) Valla

18.   Kepler's contribution to the Scientific Revolution was his

(A)   presentation of sound mathematical proof supporting Ptolemy's geocentric theory

(B)   demonstration that the planets move at a constant speed

(C)   demonstration that the surface of the moon was not smooth

(D)   mathematical proof that the orbits of the planets are elliptical

(E)   demonstration of errors in the astronomical measurements of Brahe

19.   The phrase "Cogito ergo sum" ("I think, therefore I am"), which reflects the process of logical deduction, is associated with

(A)   Hugo Grotius   (D)   Richard Hooker

(B)   Jean Bodin   (E)   René Descartes

(C)   Galileo Galilei

20.   Locke's *Treatises on Civil Government* allowed subjects to revolt, provided that the

(A)   revolution was not violent

(B)   government had violated property rights

(C)   poor had been oppressed

(D)   government had not held elections

(E)   government was a monarchy

21.   From circa 1680 to 1725, the balance of power shifted radically in Eastern Europe. Russia, Brandenburg-Prussia, and Austria rose at the expense of which three powers in decline?

(A)   Poland—the Papacy—the Holy Roman Empire

(B)   France—Poland—Sweden

(C)   Venice—Denmark—Saxony

(D)   Poland—Sweden—the Ottoman Empire

(E)   Finland—Sweden—Poland

22.   All of the following characterized Russia when Peter I ascended the throne EXCEPT

(A)   a weak nobility

(B)   a split in the Russian Orthodox church

(C)   lack of access to the Baltic and Black Seas

(D)   limited contact with the rest of Europe

(E)   an economy based on agriculture

23.   A *philosophe* of eighteenth-century France would be likely to

(A)   advocate the nationalist aspirations of the monarchy

(B)   ridicule the idea of progress

(C)   support the political theories advocated by Hobbes

(D)   oppose religious intolerance and superstition

(E)   reject the mechanistic world-view advanced by earlier scientists

24.   The "Great Fear" that swept through the French countryside in 1789 had its origin in the rumor that

(A)   the armies of Prussia and Austria were moving toward Paris

(B)   the Reign of Terror in Paris was spreading to the rest of France

(C)   brigands were attacking villages and burning crops

(D)   the execution of Louis XVI would lead England to declare war

(E)   the overthrow of the Jacobins would result in a restored monarchy

25.   "Come forth into the light of things,
Let Nature be your teacher...
Enough of Science and of Art
Close up those barren leaves
Come forth, and bring with you a heart
That watches and receives"
Such a view would most likely be expressed by a

(A)   deist   (D)   disciple of Diderot

(B)   follower of Rousseau   (E)   *philosophe*

(C)   physiocrat

26.   The thesis that "population, when unchecked, increases in a geometrical ratio ... subsistence only arithmetically" was advanced by

(A)   Henri de Saint-Simon   (D)   Thomas Malthus

(B)   Jeremy Bentham   (E)   Henri Bergson

(C)   Herbert Spencer

27. All of the following are plausible causes of the French Revolution EXCEPT

    (A)   the desire of the middle class for a greater voice in government

    (B)   an inefficient, corrupt government infuriated most French people

    (C)   the nobility of France sought to enhance their power

    (D)   a majority of the French populace desired to abolish the monarchy

    (E)   the activities of the *philosophes* had weakened faith in traditional values and institutions

28. "Man is born free; and everywhere he is in chains … . How did this change come about? I do not know. What can make it legitimate? That question I think I can answer."
These words began the famous work treating the social contract by

    (A)   Edmund Burke   (D)   Ferdinand de Lesseps

    (B)   Jean-Jacques Rousseau   (E)   Denis Diderot

    (C)   John Locke

29. All of the following statements about Richelieu are correct EXCEPT that he

    (A)   sought to weaken the power of the nobility

    (B)   waged war on French Protestants

    (C)   deprived Huguenots of their religious rights

    (D)   supported German Protestants in their struggle with the Habsburgs

    (E)   supported Gustavus Adolfus in his military operations in Germany

30. "Whereas you … in the year 1615 were denounced to this Holy Office for holding as true the false doctrine taught by many, that the sun is the center of the world and immovable, and that the earth moves, and also with a diurnal motion… ."
This was the charge brought against

    (A)   Nicholas Copernicus   (D)   Tycho Brahe

    (B)   Johannes Kepler   (E)   Anton van Leeuwenhoek

    (C)   Galileo Galilei

31. According to mercantilist theory, colonies

    (A)   were to receive independence as soon as they were self-sufficient

    (B)   were a military burden to the mother country

(C)   should be encouraged to develop their own industry

(D)   were strongest if allowed to trade freely with other countries

(E)   should be markets and sources of raw materials for the mother country

32. "I believe in the equality of man; and I believe that religious duties consist in doing justice, loving mercy, and endeavoring to make all our fellow creatures happy. All national institutions of churches, whether Jewish, Christian, or Turkish, appear to me no other than human inventions, set up to terrify and enslave mankind, and monopolize power and profit."
This view would best reflect the attitudes of a

(A)   Quietist

(B)   Deist

(C)   member of the Moravian Brethren

(D)   Jansenist

(E)   Pietist

33. Peter the Great's purpose in building the city of St. Petersburg was to

(A)   escape the influence of Mongol forces in Moscow

(B)   establish within Russia a region free of serfdom

(C)   throw off the powerful pressure of the Greek Orthodox Church

(D)   hasten the Westernization of Russia

(E)   create a defensive barrier against the aggression of the Poles

34. "The prince is to the nation he governs what the head is to the man; it is his duty to see, think, and act for the whole community, that he may procure it every advantage of which it is capable. He must be active, possess integrity, and collect his whole powers, that he may be able to run the career he has commenced."
This concept of the obligations of the ruler would best reflect the views of

(A)   Peter the Great

(B)   James I

(C)   Frederick the Great

(D)   Louis XIV

(E)   Bishop Bossuet

35. "That the pretended power of suspending the laws, or for execution of laws, by regal authority, without the consent of Parliament is illegal.... That the raising or keeping of a standing army within the kingdom in the name of peace, unless it be with the consent of Parliament, is against the law."
The first English monarch to accept and rule in accordance with these decrees was

   (A)   George I

   (B)   William III

   (C)   Anne

   (D)   Charles II

   (E)   Henry VIII

36. In his *An Essay Concerning Human Understanding*, John Locke held that human knowledge was derived from

   (A)   heredity and faith

   (B)   conscience and emotions

   (C)   intuition and moral law

   (D)   environment and reason

   (E)   divine inspiration and innate perception

37. "The only way to erect such a common power as may be able to defend them from the invasion of foreigners and the injuries of one another, and thereby secure them in such sort as that by their own industry and by the fruits of the earth they may nourish themselves and live contentedly, is to confer all their power and strength upon one man, or upon one assembly of men, that they may reduce all their wills by plurality of voices unto one will... ."
This theory of government reflected the view of

   (A)   John Locke

   (B)   Jean Bodin

   (C)   John Napier

   (D)   Charles de Montesquieu

   (E)   Thomas Hobbes

38. Which one of the following statements best explains the political and military decline of Poland by the late eighteenth century?

   (A)   A lack of a parliamentary system

   (B)   The *liberum veto*

(C)   The impact of religious wars in Poland

(D)   The selection of any Polish monarchs from the ranks of the nobility

(E)   The strength of the Polish monarchy

39.   In the "Diplomatic Revolution" of 1756

(A)   Prussia became an ally of Britain

(B)   Austria became an ally of Britain

(C)   France fought Austria

(D)   the Holy Roman Empire was abolished

(E)   the French broke off diplomatic relations with the rest of Europe

40.   All of the following were factors in higher agricultural yields in the Agricultural Revolution EXCEPT the

(A)   introduction of nitrogen-fixating crops

(B)   use of iron-reinforced seed-drills and ploughshares

(C)   enclosure of lands once scattered about as strips

(D)   more intentional application of manure

(E)   substitution of oats for potatoes

41.   Which is the correct order of events in the career of Napoleon?

(A)   Civil Code, Concordat, invasion of Spain

(B)   Concordat, Civil Code, invasion of Spain

(C)   Invasion of Spain, Concordat, Civil Code

(D)   Invasion of Spain, Civil Code, Concordat

(E)   Concordat, invasion of Spain, Civil Code

42.   The Whigs of the late seventeenth and eighteenth centuries adhered to all the following views EXCEPT the

(A)   desire to abolish slavery

(B)   primacy of rural over mercantile interests

(C)   need to show loyalty to the Hanoverian dynasty

(D)   need for gradual political and electoral reform in Britain

(E)   value of principled dissent in public life

43. Which of the following best characterizes Burke's *Reflections on the Revolution in France*?

   (A) It condemned the French Revolution as a source of radical ideas used in the American Revolution.

   (B) It praised the French Revolution as a sincere attempt to spread liberty and promote equality.

   (C) It condemned the violence and anarchy of the French Revolution.

   (D) It praised the French Revolution but condemned the American Revolution.

   (E) It condemned all revolutions.

44. According to the graph below, which one of the following statements is true?

   (A) Industrial production had a greater impact than agricultural production in Britain in 1800.

   (B) Agricultural production had a greater impact than industrial production in Germany in 1900.

   (C) Agriculture became less significant in Britain and Germany by 1900.

   (D) Britain produced fewer industrial products than Germany.

   (E) During the period shown, industrial production was an insignificant part of the British economy.

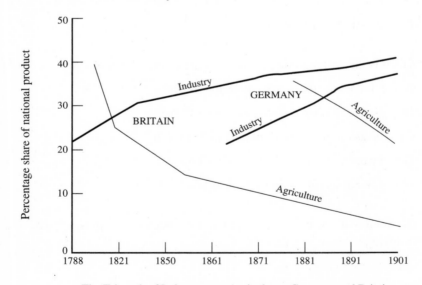

The Triumph of Industry over Agriculture: Germany and Britain

45. The 1848 Revolutions reflected the interests of all of the following EXCEPT the

   (A) Liberals   (D) middle class

   (B) Utopians   (E) Marxists

   (C) Nationalists

46.   In the nineteenth century Britain fought two major wars there—as did the USSR, from 1979 on. The country in question was and is

(A)   India   (D)   Poland

(B)   Afghanistan   (E)   Persia/Iran

(C)   China

47.   The German philosopher Friedrich Nietzsche argued that Western civilization

(A)   placed too much stress on rational thinking

(B)   required a reorientation based on Christian morality

(C)   weakened because not enough emphasis was placed on social morality

(D)   required that greater stress be placed on political democracy

(E)   placed too much emphasis on elitist elements in society

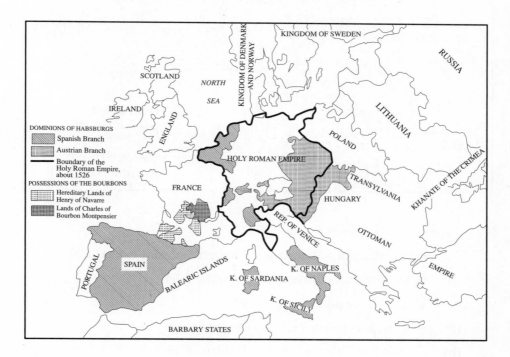

48.   The map above depicts Europe around

(A)   1800   (D)   1950

(B)   1500   (E)   1900

(C)   1700

49. After the tsar authorized general mobilization on both the Austrian and German fronts, Germany declared war on Russia. Which of the following countries did Germany invade first?

(A) Russia   (D) Britain

(B) Austria-Hungary   (E) Italy

(C) France

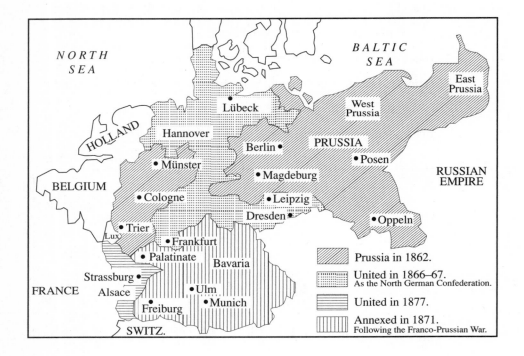

50. According to the map above, Prussia

(A) held territory in both eastern and western Germany before 1870

(B) assumed control of Alsace-Lorraine after 1866

(C) annexed Bavaria to Prussia in 1866

(D) was able to unite all of Germany in 1866

(E) occupied more territory than the Austrian Empire

51. A long-term trend that was a basic cause of World War I was

(A) the decline of the Ottoman Empire

(B) the rise of Poland

(C) Italian interest in the Balkans

(D)   Russian refusal to become involved in the Balkans

(E)   a decline in nationalist sentiment in Europe

52.   "Imperialism emerged as a development and direct continuation of the fundamental properties of capitalism. ... imperialism is the monopoly stage of capitalism." The writer quoted above would most likely accept which of the following statements as true?

(A)   Imperialism is caused by European advances in science and technology.

(B)   A desire for national prestige drove Europeans to a race to gain colonies.

(C)   Imperialism is a natural, predictable result of the growth of capitalism.

(D)   A country in an advanced capitalist phase can become the "colony" of another country.

(E)   Imperialism feeds the egos of less powerful nations of Europe.

53.   A conclusion that might be drawn from the graphs shown below is that

(A)   Russia on the eve of the World War I had still failed to develop its industrial base.

(B)   France was on the decline industrially.

(C)   Economic factors may have entered into the mounting antagonism between Great Britain and Germany.

(D)   Austrian industrial growth was lagging behind even small Belgium.

(E)   The unification of Germany had had little impact on the industrial growth of that country.

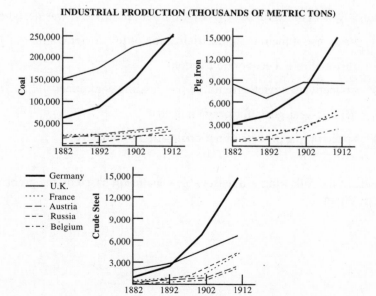

INDUSTRIAL PRODUCTION (THOUSANDS OF METRIC TONS)

54. In the wake of the failed Beer Hall Putsch, Hitler determined that

(A) it would be necessary to recruit officers from the regular army

(B) he had to eliminate paramilitary groups around him, because they fright-ened the conservative middle classes of Germany

(C) Bavaria was not a suitable region in which to build his political power

(D) the way to achieve political power was not through force, but through democratic elections and party politics

(E) it was necessary to form an alliance with the Social Democratic Party

55. A concept of Bolshevism advanced by Lenin but NOT to be found in the writings of Marx is

(A) that the industrial class of workers, exploited by the bourgeoisie, will rise in rebellion and overthrow their oppressors

(B) that there is a need for an elite cadre to control the "dictatorship of the proletariat," giving impetus and direction to the revolution

(C) that control of society throughout the ages has rested in the hands of those who control the tools of production

(D) the concept of economic determinism

(E) the view that existing governments, mere tools of the dominant economic class, would not sincerely act on behalf of the working class

56. Lenin's *New Economic Policy* (NEP), introduced in 1921, was designed to

(A) bring about the rapid industrialization of the Soviet Union

(B) restore limited economic freedom

(C) collectivize Soviet agriculture by founding communes

(D) set five-year goals for heavy industry

(E) speed up the process of nationalization of industry

57. Which of the following is a reasonable conclusion based on the graph shown on the next page?

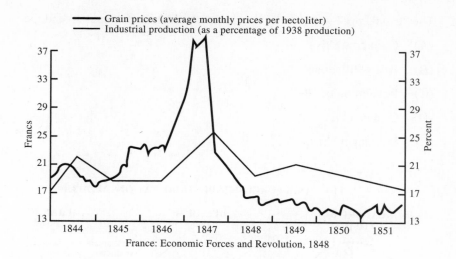

Grain prices (average monthly prices per hectoliter)
Industrial production (as a percentage of 1938 production)

France: Economic Forces and Revolution, 1848

(A)   There was no connection between grain prices and industrial production.

(B)   High grain prices were a factor in the revolution of 1848 in France.

(C)   Industrial production and grain prices sometimes declined in tandem.

(D)   High industrial production caused grain prices to rise.

(E)   Declining industrial production caused grain prices to fall.

58.   Hohenzollern authority in ruling Prussia depended on support from the

(A)   bankers   (D)   constitution

(B)   Junkers   (E)   intellectuals

(C)   courts

59.   Which of the following best characterizes the attitude of nineteenth-century Russian Slavophiles?

(A)   All Slavs should be united under a single government.

(B)   All Western influences should be rejected.

(C)   Westernization should not be allowed to destroy the distinctive aspects of Slavic culture.

(D)   Russia should have no role in the leadership of the Slavic nations.

(E)   Russia should become completely Westernized.

60. The "gap theory" was used by the German politician Bismarck to end the

    (A) Corn Law Crisis

    (B) Army Bill Crisis

    (C) Revolution of 1848

    (D) Crimean War

    (E) Boulanger Crisis

THE WORK FORCE IN INDUSTRIAL NATIONS MID-1850s

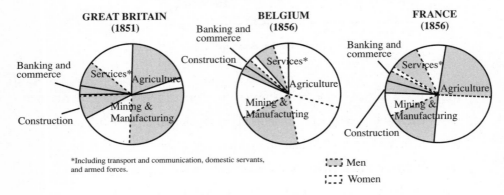

*Including transport and communication, domestic servants, and armed forces.

▪▪▪ Men

▪▪▪ Women

61. Based on the chart above, we deduce that, for these countries in the 1850s,

    (A) women were often excluded from the labor force in industrialized states

    (B) in Great Britain the role of women in agriculture was on the decline

    (C) construction remained solely a male occupation

    (D) in France and Belgium mining and manufacturing were increasing

    (E) women had yet to participate in banking and commerce in Great Britain

62. Social Darwinism gave theoretical support for all of the following EXCEPT

    (A) economic individualism

    (B) militarism

    (C) the growth of big industry

    (D) cosmopolitanism

    (E) imperialism

63. During the Third Republic, 1875–1945, which of the following phrases describes a political crisis centered on accusations of treason against a French military officer?

    (A) The Irish Question

    (B) The Panama Canal scandal

    (C) The Zabern Affair

    (D) The Dreyfus Affair

    (E) The *"Daily Telegraph* Affair"

64. The Paris Commune was suppressed by the

    (A) Prussian army

    (B) French army

    (C) workers of Paris

    (D) French rural militias

    (E) British army

65. Which British Prime Minister made Irish Home Rule his political cause?

    (A) Benjamin Disraeli

    (B) William Gladstone

    (C) Lord Salisbury

    (D) Joseph Chamberlain

    (E) Robert Peel

66. The Anglo-French Entente (also known as the Entente Cordiale)

    (A) was a defensive treaty aimed at containing German expansion in Europe

    (B) was a defensive treaty aimed at containing German expansion overseas

    (C) resolved Anglo-French colonial disputes in Egypt and Morocco

    (D) was a nineteenth-century treaty that ended the diplomatic isolation of Britain

    (E) was an agreement to finance the building of the Trans-Siberian railroad

67. The map below illustrates the

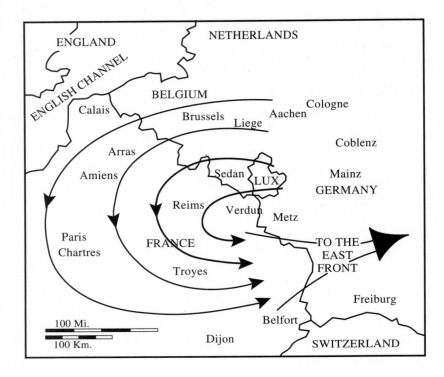

(A) Maginot Line

(B) Schlieffen Plan

(C) Invasion of France in 1940

(D) "soft underbelly of Europe"

(E) French defenses in World War I

68. Werner Heisenberg's contribution to twentieth-century science was the

(A) "Big Bang" theory regarding the origin of the universe

(B) theory of plate tectonics and continental drift

(C) hypothesis that we cannot know both position and speed for subatomic particles

(D) discovery of the oldest known *hominid* at that time in East Africa

(E) invention of the radio telescope

69. Which one of the following factors stimulated the growth of fascism in Europe during the 1920s and 1930s?

    (A) Free trade among European nations

    (B) The development of cheaper armaments

    (C) Economic prosperity

    (D) Fear of communism

    (E) The growth of parliamentary governments

70. Among the issues advocated by the *Action Française* of Charles Maurras was

    (A) opposition to monarchies

    (B) an end to Jewish influence in France

    (C) a smaller French army

    (D) loyalty to the Third French Republic

    (E) parliamentary government

71. Which slogan best describes the proclaimed policy of the Soviet Union during the late 1950s and early 1960s toward the capitalist nations of the world?

    (A) "V for Victory"

    (B) "The Third Force"

    (C) "Peaceful Coexistence"

    (D) "Peace, Land, and Bread"

    (E) "Peace in Our Time"

72. All of the following statements about Eastern Europe, 1945–1960, are true EXCEPT

    (A) all Eastern Europe nations were subservient to the Soviet government

    (B) Eastern European nations rejected the Marshall Plan

    (C) there was a revolt in Hungary

    (D) there was a revolt in East Germany

    (E) almost all of the nations of Eastern Europe were militarily allied with the Soviet Union

73. The primary problem of France when Charles de Gaulle became president of the nation during the 1950s was to

    (A) increase French participation in the North Atlantic Treaty Organization (NATO)

    (B) settle the Algerian problem

    (C) recover from the devastation of World War II

    (D) end the occupation of France by German forces

    (E) eliminate the deficit budgets of the French government

74. During the Persian Gulf War of 1991, what action did Russia take?

    (A) Russia supported Iraq by selling arms.

    (B) Russia supported Iraq with troops and weapons.

    (C) Russia supported Iraq diplomatically, but not materially.

    (D) Russia supported the international army led by the United States.

    (E) Russia remained neutral.

75. The United Nations was originally planned in a document known as the

    (A) Truman Doctrine

    (B) Atlantic Charter

    (C) Molotov Plan

    (D) Brussels Pact

    (E) Treaty of Rapallo

76. The Soviet leader Leonid Brezhnev, one may successfully argue,

    (A) continued the "Thaw" that had allowed more artistic freedom under Nikita Khrushchëv, his predecessor

    (B) reverted to Stalinist policies when he authorized military action against the "Prague Spring" in Czechoslovakia

    (C) began programs to restructure the Soviet economy that anticipated the policy of *perestroika* carried on by Gorbachev

    (D) was the author of *glasnost* (media openness), a policy for which Gorbachev wrongly took credit

    (E) led the August 1991 coup suppressed not by Gorbachev but by Boris Yeltsin, who replaced Gorbachev

77. Which of these African lands was formally put under Belgian rule in 1885?

    (A) The Congo

    (B) South Africa

    (C) Nigeria

    (D) Angola

    (E) Ethiopia

78. Martin Luther was NOT executed as a heretic because

    (A) he was able to escape to neutral Switzerland

    (B) he won the support of the Holy Roman Emperor

    (C) he won the support of many of the German princes

    (D) he sided with the German peasants in their revolt

    (E) the Roman Catholic Church no longer recommended capital punishment for religious dissidents

79. The geocentric theory of the universe was first opposed in the sixteenth century by the European astronomer

    (A) Michel de Montaigne

    (B) François Rabelais

    (C) Johannes Kepler

    (D) Galileo Galilei

    (E) Nicholas Copernicus

80. What was the original purpose of NATO?

    (A) To provide a peaceful solution to the Balkan problem

    (B) To provide an army to enforce United Nations decisions

    (C) To protect Europe from Soviet aggression

    (D) To protect human rights around the world

    (E) To safeguard the status quo in the Middle East

STOP
This is the end of Section I.
If time still remains, you may check your work only in this section.
Do not begin Section II until instructed to do so.

Section II

PART A – DOCUMENT-BASED ESSAY

TIME: Reading Period—15 minutes
Writing Time: 45 minutes
1 Essay Question

DIRECTIONS: Read both the document-based essay question in Part A and the choices in Parts B and C during the reading period. Use the time to organize answers. You must answer Part A (the document-based essay question) and choose ONE question from Part B and ONE question from Part C to answer.

This question is designed to test your ability to work with historical documents. As you analyze each document, take into account the source and the point of view of the author. Write an essay on the following topic that integrates your analysis of the documents. You may refer to historical facts and developments not mentioned in the documents.

The view expressed in Document 1 has been accepted by many historians of Imperialism, though subjected to modification or rejection by others. Utilizing the documents presented here, evaluate its validity or possible weaknesses.

Document 1

"Analysis of the actual course of modern Imperialism has laid bare the combination of economic and political forces which fashions it. The forces are traced to the sources in the selfish interests of certain industrial, financial, and professional classes seeking private advantages out of a policy of imperial expansion."
                    —J. A. Hobson, anti-imperialist economist, *Imperialism, A Study*, 1902

Document 2

"Our connection with them [the Malay States] is due to the simple fact that seventy years ago the British government was invited, pushed, and persuaded into helping the rulers of certain states to introduce order into their disorderly, penniless, and distracted households by sending trained British civil servants to advise the rulers in the art of administration and to organize a system of government which would secure justice, freedom, safety for all, with the benefits of what is known as civilization."
                    —Frank Swettenham, British Colonial Official, circa 1869

Document 3

"No one acquainted with the actual state of society in the West Indies can doubt that, if they were left, unaided by us, to settle amongst themselves in whose hands power should be placed, a fearful war of colour would probably soon break out, and civilization would be thrown back for centuries."

—Lord Grey, Head, British Colonial Office, 1853

Document 4

"Everyone will admit … the value of that commerce which penetrates to every part of the globe; and many of these colonies give harbours and security to that trade, which are most useful in times of peace, but are absolutely necessary in time of war."

—Lord John Russell, British Prime Minister, 1850

Document 5

"If persons, knowing the risks they run, owing to the disturbed state of these countries, choose to hazard their lives and properties for sake of large profits which accompany successful trading, they must not expect the British Government to be answerable if their speculation proves unsuccessful."

—Governor, Straits Settlements, circa 1860

Document 6

"Let us endeavour to strike our roots into the soil by the gradual introduction and establishment of our own principles and opinions; of our laws, institutions, and manners; above all, as the source of every other improvement, of our religion, and consequently of our morals."

—William Wilberforce, British Statesman/Humanitarian, circa 1825

Document 7

"The position of Russia in Central Asia is that of all civilized states which are brought into contact with half-savage nomad populations possessing no fixed social organization.

"In such cases, the more civilized state is forced in the interest of the security of its frontier, and commercial relations, to exercise a certain ascendancy over her turbulent and undesirable neighbors. Raids and acts of pillage must be put down. To do this, the tribes of the frontier must be reduced to a state of submission. This result once attained, these tribes take to more peaceful habits, but are in turn exposed to the attacks of the more distant tribes against whom the State is bound to protect them."

—Prince Gorchakov, Russian Foreign Minister, 1864

Document 8

"Onward Christian Soldiers, on to heathen lands,
Prayer-books in your pockets, rifles in your hands
Take the glorious tidings where trade can be done:
Spread the peaceful gospel—with a Maxim gun."

—Henri Labouchère, Anti-Imperialist Editor, *Pioneers' Hymn*, 1893

Document 9

"Throughout the Century of Peace ... man's mind had become open to the truth, had become sensible to the diversity of species, had become conscious of Nature's law of development ... . The stern logic of facts proclaimed the Negro and Chinaman below the level of the Caucasian, and incapacitated from advance towards his intellectual standard. To the development of the White Man, the Black Man and the Yellow must ever remain inferior, and as the former raised itself higher and yet higher, so did those latter seem to sink out of humanity and appear nearer and nearer to the brutes."
—W. D. Hay, Social Darwinist author, *Three Hundred Years Hence*, 1881

Document 10

"At this time, as you know, a warship cannot carry more than fourteen days worth of coal, no matter how perfectly it is organized, and a ship which is out of coal is a derelict on the surface of the sea, abandoned to the first person who comes along. Thus the necessity of having on the oceans provisions stations, shelters, ports for defense and revictualizing. And it is for this that we needed Tunisia, for this that we needed Saigon, and the Mekong Delta, for this that we need Madagascar, that we are at Diego-Suarez and Vohemar and will never leave them. Gentlemen, in Europe as it is today ... a policy of peaceful seclusion or abstention is simply the highway to decadence."
—Jules Ferry, French Imperialist, speech to French National Assembly, 1883

Document 11

Population (in millions)

	Great Britain	Russia	France	Germany	Italy
1796		29			
1800	10-9			24-5	18-1
1801			27-3		
1830	16-5			29-6	
1831			31-9		
1850	20-9			35-4	23
1851			35-8		
1858		67			
1870	26-2			40-9	26-6
1871			36-1		
1897		129			
1900	37			56-4	32-4
1901			39		
1910	40-8				
1911			39-2		34-8
1914		142		67-8	
1921	42		39-2		38-4

Document 12

"We stand on nationalism in our belief that the unfolding of economic and political power by the German nation abroad is the prerequisite for all far-reaching social reforms at home."

—Manifesto of the *Nationalsozialer Verein*, 1897

Document 13

"Nations may be roughly divided between the living and the dying.... For one reason or another—from the necessities of politics or under the pretence of philanthropy—the living nations will gradually encroach on the territory of the dying, and the seeds and the causes of conflict among civilized nations will speedily appear."

—Lord Salisbury, British Minister, 1898

Document 14

"... No doubt there will remain people like the aged savage who in his old age went back to his savage tribe and said that he had 'tried civilization for forty years, and it was not worth the trouble,' but we not take account of the mistaken ideas of unfit men and beaten races."

—Walter Bagehot, *Physics and Politics*, 1869

Document 15

"Early in November [1897] several Ministers, including myself, received a memorandum drawn up by Count Muraviëv. It pointed out that the occupation of Kiao-Chow by the Germans offered a favourable occasion for us to seize one of the Chinese ports, notably Port Arthur.... He pointed out that these ports had an enormous strategic importance."

—Count Witte, Russian Finance Minister, *Memoirs*

Document 16

"Take up the White Man's burden—
Send forth the best ye breed—
Go bind your sons to exile—
To serve your captives' need;
To wait in heavy harness,
On fluttered folk and wild—
Your new-caught, sullen peoples,
Half-devil and half-child."

—Rudyard Kipling, Imperialist poet, 1893

Document 17

"An Empire such as ours requires as its first condition an Imperial Race—a race vigorous and industrious and intrepid. Health of mind and body exalt a nation in the competition of the universe. The survival of the fittest is an absolute truth in the conditions of the modern world."

—Lord Rosebery, former British Prime Minister, *The Times*, 1900

Document 18

"In order to save the 40,000,000 inhabitants of the United Kingdom from a bloody civil war, we colonial statesmen must acquire new lands to settle the surplus population, to provide new markets for the goods produced by them in the factories and mines. The Empire, as I have always said, is a bread and butter question. If you want to avoid civil war, you must become imperialists."

—Cecil Rhodes, South African Statesman and Apostle of Imperialism, 1895

STOP
This is the end of Section II, Part A.
If time still remains, you may check your work only in this section.
Do not begin Section II, Part B until instructed to do so.

PART B – ESSAY QUESTION

TIME: 35 minutes
1 Essay Question

DIRECTIONS: Answer ONE question from the three questions below. Choose the question that you are most prepared to answer thoroughly. You should spend about 5 minutes organizing or outlining your answer.

---

1. Compare the doctrines and politics of the three main groups in the Protestant Reformation—Lutheranism, Calvinism, and Anabaptism.

2. Compare the policies and aims of the policies of mercantilism and laissez-faire capitalism.

3. Assess the extent to which the early Scientific Revolution was a triumph of mathematics over the verbally based sciences of the ancient world.

STOP
This is the end of Section II, Part B.
If time still remains, you may check your work only in this section.
Do not begin Section II, Part C until instructed to do so.

PART C – ESSAY QUESTION

TIME: 35 minutes
      1 Essay Question

> **DIRECTIONS:** Answer ONE question from the three questions below. Choose the question that you are most prepared to answer thoroughly. You should spend about 5 minutes organizing or outlining your answer.

4. In the seventeenth century "absolutist" regimes spread, with varied success, across Continental Europe. What were the conditions and forces at work to make this form of government seem desirable?

5. "The French Enlightenment was a fountainhead of humanitarian and libertarian principles; it articulated grievances and sought alternatives. The German Enlightenment was more abstract and less practical."

   Analyze and assess the validity of this statement, citing specific individuals.

6. Assess and analyze how problems in the World War II alliance of the United States, Great Britain, and the Soviet Union helped lead to the Cold War.

END OF EXAM

PRACTICE EXAM 3

AP European History

Answer Key

1.	(B)	21.	(D)	41.	(B)	61.	(E)
2.	(A)	22.	(A)	42.	(B)	62.	(D)
3.	(C)	23.	(D)	43.	(C)	63.	(D)
4.	(C)	24.	(C)	44.	(C)	64.	(B)
5.	(C)	25.	(B)	45.	(E)	65.	(B)
6.	(B)	26.	(D)	46.	(B)	66.	(C)
7.	(B)	27.	(D)	47.	(A)	67.	(B)
8.	(A)	28.	(B)	48.	(B)	68.	(C)
9.	(B)	29.	(C)	49.	(C)	69.	(D)
10.	(C)	30.	(C)	50.	(A)	70.	(B)
11.	(D)	31.	(E)	51.	(A)	71.	(C)
12.	(B)	32.	(B)	52.	(C)	72.	(A)
13.	(B)	33.	(D)	53.	(C)	73.	(B)
14.	(C)	34.	(C)	54.	(D)	74.	(D)
15.	(A)	35.	(B)	55.	(B)	75.	(B)
16.	(C)	36.	(D)	56.	(B)	76.	(B)
17.	(D)	37.	(E)	57.	(C)	77.	(A)
18.	(D)	38.	(B)	58.	(B)	78.	(C)
19.	(E)	39.	(A)	59.	(C)	79.	(E)
20.	(B)	40.	(E)	60.	(B)	80.	(C)

PRACTICE EXAM 3

AP European History

Detailed Explanations of Answers

Section I

1. **(B)**

Desiderius Erasmus, a Dutch humanist of the Northern Renaissance, was a strong critic of abuses within the Church, but did not support the Reformation launched by Luther, whom he had influenced. Petrarch was a leading literary figure in the early Renaissance in Italy (A). Agricola was a sixteenth-century scientist in the field of mining technology (C). Mirandola was a Renaissance humanist (D). Thomas More, chancellor to Henry VIII, was a humanist who wrote *Utopia* (1516) with such radical ideas as communal property and the right to divorce (E).

2. **(A)**

In the first half of the fifteenth century, Prince Henry's seamen explored the west coast of Africa as far south as the Cape Verde Islands. Brazil (B) was first discovered by the Portuguese seamen in 1500, four decades after Prince Henry's death, while Goa (D), in India, was also established by the Portuguese some time after his passing. Cortez, in the service of Spain, conquered the Aztecs (C), not the Mayas, and Portugal's explorations were directed southward, not to the northwest (E).

3. **(C)**

Balboa was the first European to gaze on the waters of the Pacific. All other matches are correct.

4. **(C)**

Religious conformity became a means by which the power of the prince was enhanced. Protestants tended strongly to look to the primitive Christian Church and community for what they saw as correct guidance (A). Nationalistic feelings were an integral aspect of the Reformation (B), while the religious enthusiasm of Europeans assumed near-fanatic proportions (E). The practice of sending missionaries to the East was, at this time, purely a Catholic matter (D).

5. **(C)**

Justification by faith constituted the central pillar of the Lutheran faith. All other concepts noted were either rejected by Luther or viewed as of secondary importance.

6. **(B)**

Henry's break with the papacy centered on his desire to get rid of his first wife because she had not produced a male heir. The sole change Henry desired was a transfer of the authority of the Church from the Pope to himself (thus answer (E) is incorrect). He retained six of the Church's sacraments and resolutely opposed all Protestant influences, keeping a close eye on his Archbishop of Canterbury, who favored a Lutheran Protestantism. In order to persuade nobles and gentry to accept his changes, Henry dissolved Catholic monasteries and distributed their wealth among influential nobles and gentry. Neither Calvinism nor the Scots were involved in Henry's decisions.

7. **(B)**

Enacted by Henry IV, the Edict of Nantes granted limited religious and political autonomy to Huguenots. Louis XI came to the throne following the Hundred Years' War (A). The St. Bartholomew's Day Massacre set off the worst phase of the Religious Wars (C). The Treaty of Cateau-Cambrésis (1559) ended the Habsburg-Valois conflict (D). The Peace of Augsburg was a settlement between German Protestants and Catholics in the Reformation (E).

8. **(A)**

The late-nineteenth-century German sociologist Weber propounded the theory of the Protestant work ethic as a cause for the rise of capitalism. Luther supported the princes, not peasants (B), who showed radical tendencies in the early days of the Reformation, or the Anabaptists (C); indeed, he called for their extermination. The Reformation, if anything, deterred Protestant involvement in overseas exploration (D), a movement Catholic Portugal and Spain had begun. Protestants publicly supported the taking of interest, whereas the medieval Church had tacitly allowed the practice, though publicly opposed it (E).

9. **(B)**

This statement spells out the doctrine of Predestination, a core tenet of Calvin's teachings. Thomas Hobbes (A) was the seventeenth-century author of the political treatise *Leviathan*. While predestination had long been a Christian doctrine, neither Luther (C), the Catholic Council of Trent (D), nor Zwingli (E) placed the extraordinary emphasis on it that was clear in Calvin's works.

10. **(C)**

This statement reflects the doctrine of the "Divine Right of Kings," a theory held by early Stuart monarchs of England. Neither Frederick the Great (A) nor Joseph II of Austria (E), both "Enlightened Despots," would have held such beliefs, while William III of England (D), king with consent of Parliament, would also have hesitated to claim such power. John Locke (B), an outspoken exponent of "constitutional monarchy," would have rejected such an idea out-of-hand.

11. **(D)**

The Union of Lublin (1569) created the largest contiguous empire west of Muscovy-Russia, though a marriage in 1385 had set the stage for the union of Lithuania and Poland. Earlier, after the Black Death, King Casimir the Great allowed Jews fleeing persecution in Western Europe to resettle in his lands (though he limited the interest they could charge to 8 percent, down from the previously acceptable 100 percent). The other choices were not as friendly to Jews. France granted Jews civil rights under Napoleon, Russia only under Alexander II (rescinded in part by Alexander III and Nicholas II), and the Papal States allowed persecution into the 1860s.

12. **(B)**

Students should learn about this major shift in Scandinavian history. From 1397 to 1523, Sweden, Norway, and Denmark were united in personal union. Swedish dissatisfaction with Danish control led to the split-up, and in 1536 Denmark managed to absorb Norway into a new union. Denmark called the shots in politics, trade, and the new Lutheran religion, but Norway retained its separate crown. An old conflict with England over Baltic trade was exacerbated by the Danes's allegiance to Napoleon. Nelson bombarded Copenhagen (1807), and the British government at the Congress of Vienna (1814) punished Denmark by awarding Norway to Sweden. Its newly elected king, the Frenchman Bernadotte, had deserted his former master and allied with Britain in 1813. Britain rewarded him for his treachery.

13. **(B)**

Counter-Reformation authorities saw that Protestants removed images and ornaments, making their churches plain; Catholic reformers counteracted that plainness with a concerted appeal to the senses, so many churches gave patronage to Baroque painters, architects, and sculptors. Though there are strongly Catholic themes in Renaissance and Rococo art, those eras did not correspond with the years of the Counter-Reformation (ca. 1540–1660).

14. **(C)**

The St. Bartholomew's Day Massacre of French Calvinists in Paris, termed "Huguenots," led to the War of the Three Henries and the first Bourbon monarch (Henry IV). When dealing with questions based on illustrations, it is important to look for explicit details or other information in the question and in the illustration itself, since it is usually not possible to arrive at a correct answer by eliminating answers. The only clue ("St. Bartholomew's Day") must suffice. Do not be misled by the use of the term *French Calvinists* instead of the name *Huguenots*, the term preferred by historians: the term *French Calvinists* is nothing more than a definition of the more arcane *Huguenots*.

15. **(A)**

The *politiques*, who emerged in the French civil wars of religion as the leading political group in France, argued that government should be based purely on political principles. Religion in politics was seen as an obstacle to good government. Answers (B) (government by religious leaders), (D), and (E) might be eliminated since they represent an opposite viewpoint. A *politique* might accept answer (D), but parliamentary government developed only later in France and was irrelevant to the central concerns of the *politiques*.

16. **(C)**

The fact that the orbits were elliptical was determined by Kepler after the death of Copernicus. Copernicus's theory rejected both the medieval (A) and Ptolemaic (B) concept of the universe while advancing the heliocentric theory (E). Kepler's work (D) was conducted after the death of Copernicus.

17. **(D)**

William Harvey, an English physician and experimenter, advanced the view in 1628 that the blood circulated and the heart acted as a pump. Paracelsus was a sixteenth-century physician who attacked long-accepted theories of "humors" as a source of disease (A). Valla, a Renaissance humanist, exposed the "Donation of Constantine" as a forgery (C). Galvani was an eighteenth-century anatomist and experimenter with electricity (B). Bacon (1561–1626) was an ardent advocate of the inductive approach to scientific research (E).

18. **(D)**

By abandoning Copernicus's concept of circular orbits, Kepler supported the validity of the heliocentric theory. He proved the error of Ptolemy's theory (A) and demonstrated that the speed of the planets in their orbits varies in relation to their distance from the sun (B). It was Galileo who, using a telescope, saw for the first time the pockmarks on the moon (C). Kepler used many measurements of Brahe, his former employer (E).

19. **(E)**

René Descartes was a seventeenth-century French geometer and mathematician and a proponent of deductive reasoning. Hugo Grotius was a Dutch legal theorist in the area of international law (A). Jean Bodin was a sixteenth-century French *politique* and advocate of religious toleration (B). Galileo was a famed Renaissance physicist and astronomer (C). Richard Hooker was a sixteenth-century English theologian (D).

20. **(B)**

Locke allowed legal revolution carried through by the educated and propertied, provided that the monarch had violated property rights. In the case of James II, ousted in the Glorious Revolution of 1688, Locke believed that his government had extracted "forced loans" from prominent citizens in order to underwrite government expenses. American forefathers copied the phrase "life, liberty, and the pursuit of happiness" from Locke, although in Locke's words it was originally "life, liberty, and the right to property."

21. **(D)**

Venice, the Holy Roman Empire, and the Papacy were no longer factors in the European balance of power in that period. Though France suffered in major wars from 1686 to 1715, it in no way ceased to be a great power. Since Finland was not independent until 1918, that leaves the only possible combination of Poland, Sweden, and the Ottoman Empire. Good students will call on their knowledge of geography to situate Sweden as northern, Poland as western, and the Ottoman Turks as the southern states adversely affected by wars with Prussia, Russia, and Austria.

22. **(A)**

By the time Peter ascended the throne, the power of the boyars, the original Russian nobility, had been weakened by previous tsars such as Ivan IV ("the Terrible"), but they still wielded considerable influence. The other statements are all true. The Russian Orthodox church had been split in the 1600s by liturgical disputes; Russia did not win access to either sea until the reign of Peter, who opened the way to the Baltic; and Russian contact with the West had been of a limited nature.

23. **(D)**

Philosophes of the Age of Reason strongly condemned religious intolerance and what they viewed as the irrational superstitions underpinning religious beliefs. Cosmopolitan in outlook and generally antimonarchial (A), they were convinced of humankind's ability to progress (B) and were strongly under the influence of earlier scientists and their concept of the universe (E).

24. **(C)**

Rumors had spread among the peasants that the monarch and aristocracy intended to crush them through the use of brigands. This sort of question shows the usefulness of timelines to history students. Prussia and Austria were not at war with France in 1789 (A), nor had the king been executed (D), nor had the Jacobin "Terror" begun or ended (B and E).

25. **(B)**

The poem reflects a romantic view, questioning the merits of science and extolling nature and the emotions. The other answers refer to men or movements that were strongly influenced by reason and science and had little regard for the "sentiments of the heart."

26. **(D)**

Thomas Malthus was an eighteenth-century forerunner in the field of human demography. Saint-Simon (A) was a prominent Utopian Socialist of the early nineteenth century. Bentham (B) was the founder of Utilitarianism. Bergson (E) was a social philosopher of the late nineteenth century, the advocate of the *élan vital*, and Spencer (C) extolled a sort of Social Darwinism, even before the *Origin of Species* (1859).

27. **(D)**

The *cahiers* or list of grievances of summer 1789 indicated that a majority of the French people wanted the monarchy reformed, not abolished. All of the other complaints or demands have been advanced as probable factors in the coming of the Revolution.

28. **(B)**

This is the opening of Rousseau's *Social Contract*. Locke (C) was an earlier English statesman and political theorist, while Burke (A) was a British politician and author of *Reflections on the Revolution in France*. Diderot (E) was a *philosophe* of the Age of Reason and editor of the monumental *Encyclopédie*. De Lesseps (D) was the architect and builder of the Suez Canal (1859–1869).

29. **(C)**

While waging war on the French Huguenots and depriving them of certain political and military privileges, he did not deny their religious rights. His major goal was the enhancement of the power of the crown, which meant weakening the influence of the aristocracy and the Habsburgs through aid to the German Protestants and King Gustavus Adolfus in the Thirty Years' War.

30. **(C)**

This is a passage from the notes of the Inquisition trial of Galileo for advancing his astronomical views. Copernicus (A), Kepler (B), and Brahe (D), all astronomers, were dead by 1615, while the Dutchman Leeuwenhoek (E) in 1676 was the first person to observe microbes through the microscope.

31. **(E)**

The utilization of colonies as "feeders" of raw materials to the mother country, and closed markets to the finished products of the mother country, was a standard concept of the mercantile system. There was no desire to see colonies gain their independence (A) in the mercantile system, develop their own industry (C), or be permitted to trade with other countries (D), all of which would serve as competition to the mother country. Colonies, as in the case of the American holdings of England, were customarily expected to defend themselves (B).

32. **(B)**

The words of Thomas Paine reflect a deistic outlook toward organized religion. The other groups were, even when heterodox, still devoutly religious. Pietism and the Moravian Brethren attempted to make Lutheranism more heartfelt and activist; Quietism was a seventeenth-century Catholic movement aimed at making the soul passive in its attitude toward Christ. Jansenism was an attempt by some French Catholics to revive an Augustinian severity to oppose Jesuit laxity.

33. (D)

He spoke of the city as his "window to the West," the avenue through which Western trade and technology would flow into Russia. When Peter came to the Russian throne, the power of the Mongols had already been broken (A) and he was to weaken that of the Orthodox Church (C) through means not related to the establishment of St. Petersburg. Poland was on a marked path of decline (E), and he tightened the controls on the serfs (B) rather than loosening them.

34. (C)

The role of the prince is seen as a "career," not a God-given right: This was the concept held by the Enlightened Despots, of whom Frederick the Great, whose words these are, was a prime example. All of the other monarchs and individuals noted were strong advocates of the concept of divine-right monarchy.

35. (B)

The words are from the English Bill of Rights, accepted by King William before he came to the throne in 1688. George I (A) and Anne (C), who came to the throne after the enactment of the Bill, accepted it, while Charles II (D) and Henry VIII (E) reigned earlier (and probably would have rejected it).

36. (D)

The human mind, a "blank tablet" at birth, gained knowledge only through sensory perception and reflection on the knowledge so acquired. Locke rejected any sources of knowledge other than the information he gained through his sensory contacts with the world about him and his integration of that knowledge through his powers of reasoning.

37. (E)

The concept, that of "absolutism," was supported by Hobbes in his *Leviathan*. John Locke (A), in his *Two Treatises on Civil Government*, clearly rejected such a concept. Bodin (B) and Montesquieu (D), French political theorists of the sixteenth and eighteenth centuries, respectively, would also have rejected such a concept of absolutism. Napier (C) was a scientist, the deviser of logarithms.

38. (B)

A major cause was the failure of the Polish parliament, the Sejm. The *liberum veto*, which allowed any member to force adjournment if he objected to proceedings, made the Sejm ineffective. The other answers are either not applicable or untrue. Poland had no religious wars *per se*. The Polish nobility, split among themselves, often raised foreigners to the throne rather than pick someone from their own ranks. (E) is also incorrect because Poland had more problems with weak monarchs than with the overly assertive sort.

39. (A)

In 1756, Britain, which had been allied with Austria, switched to Austria's great rival, Prussia. That led to a new French-Austrian alliance the same year, an even more revolutionary event, given the ages-old Habsburg-Valois rivalry.

40. (E)

In reading through (A) to (D), recall the use of clover and other plants in crop rotation, "Turnip" Townsend, iron implements, enclosure of fields for crops and sheep, and the great "gifts" left by fatter livestock. (E) is the opposite of true, since it was the introduction of potatoes into Europe by such pioneers as Sir Walter Raleigh, the French horticulturist Parmentier, and Frederick the Great that increased the caloric intake of peasants, thus making them more immune to diseases and better workers.

41. (B)

The correct chronological sequence is Concordat with the Pope (1801), Civil Code (1804), then the invasion of Spain (1808).

42. (B)

The Whigs achieved political, social, and economic prominence in British life by their support for new industries and mercantile interests, mainly the City-of-London men, at a time when Tories seemed fixated on agriculture alone. Though as aristocratic as the Tories, Whigs tended to show greater faith in the new royal house, dissent, reform, and other trends abhorrent to Tories, who, owing to their stubborn faith in the old Stuart dynasty, were often considered disloyal to the Hanoverians.

43. (C)

It is important to read answers carefully, since misreading one word (such as *not*) may cause you to pick wrongly. Like many Englishmen, Burke was sympathetic to the French Revolution's aims during its early stages, but later was appalled by its violence. Since the American Revolution preceded the French, answer (A) is not possible. Answer (D) reverses Burke's opinion.

44. (C)

Of the first three answers, the only one that is a correct interpretation of the graph is (C). Answer (D) may or may not be true, but the graph (which indicates percentage shares of national product) does not provide the kind of information required to decide.

45. (E)

Marxist agendas did not affect the Revolutions of 1848 because Marxism was still in an embryonic stage. Though the *Communist Manifesto* was written at this time, it had no impact on the Revolution. *Das Kapital* was not completed until the 1860s. The Liberal (A) desire for constitutional government, the radical economic alternatives of the Utopian Socialists (B), the nationalists' (C) call for self-determination, and the enfranchisement of the middle class (D) were all evident during the Revolutions of 1848.

46. (B)

Britain's difficulties in Afghanistan evidently did not teach either the USSR (1979–1989) or the United States (2002 onward) any lessons. Britain fought numerous conflicts in India (A), but the USSR did not invade India in the twentieth century. Both Britain and the USSR had interests in China (C) and Persia (E) at these times, but clues in the question point away from these choices. The unwary student may recall the reaction of the USSR to the Solidarity movement, but the USSR did not invade Poland (D), and *Solidarnosc* did not arise until 1980.

47. (A)

He placed great emphasis on man's utilizing his inner "will," an intuitive, irrational force. Highly contemptuous of Christian "slave mentality" (B), contemporary moral standards (C), and democracy (D), he called for an elite "superman" who depended on his "will" to lead society (E).

48. (B)

On the map, several areas of Europe are depicted with dark shading. These areas are the lands controlled by the Habsburgs in the sixteenth century. Answer (C) is incorrect, since Spain was lost by the Habsburgs in the 1600s. A further clue: The large size of the Ottoman Empire, covering the entire Balkan peninsula, precludes any answer after about 1870.

49. (C)

This question requires analytical thinking, an understanding of a complex chain of events, and knowledge of terminology (although the term *Schlieffen Plan* does not appear in the question). Answer (A) may be eliminated since it is too obvious for an advanced test. In frequent renewals of the Triple Alliance, Austria consistently pushed Germany to make specific, secret promises of aid to Austria in the event of war. According to one German promise, Russian mobilization was to lead to a German declaration of war. German military planners, however, were worried about a two-front war, in both the east (Russia) and west (France). A commission working under the German Count Alfred von Schlieffen produced his famous Plan, which required that Germany invade the weaker country of the two in overwhelming numbers, with the goal of quickly defeating the weaker country. The Schlieffen Plan considered the French army to be faster in mobilization than the Russian, but essentially weaker.

50. **(A)**

As shown by the variously marked areas of the map, Prussia was able to unite most of northern Germany in 1867 and combine it with Prussian land in both Eastern and Western Germany. Answers (B), (C), (D), and (E) will be ruled out by a careful study of the map.

51. **(A)**

Although the war began as a result of the assassination of the heir to the Habsburg throne and the ensuing dispute between Austria and Serbia, the background to these events was the steady decline of the Ottoman Empire, which had once controlled most of the Balkan peninsula. The resulting power vacuum allowed Austrian expansion into the Balkans, a development that created friction with new nations there, such as Serbia. Questions such as these test your breadth of knowledge and your analytical skills. Textbooks frequently emphasize, as causes of World War I, trends such as secret alliances or yellow journalism; background events such as the decline of the Ottoman Empire are generally implicit.

52. **(C)**

Although knowledge of terminology is a great help, in this question careful reading of statements is essential. This quotation, from Vladimir Lenin, father of the Soviet Revolution of 1917, is part of his argument that capitalism held internal contradictions that would lead to its self-destruction; a major contradiction was the uncontrolled race for colonies.

[*Source*: Lenin, *Imperialism: The Highest Stage of Capitalism* (New York: International Publishers, 1934)]

53. **(C)**

By 1902, Germany had surpassed Great Britain, in some cases markedly, in basic industrial production, a fact that created increasing tension between the two states. Russia (A), if not one of the major industrial powers of Europe, had established a base. France (B), if not as productive as Germany or England, was increasing its production, as was Austria (D). Clearly German unification in 1871 led to an explosion in Germany's industrial growth (E).

54. **(D)**

It was through the electoral process that the Nazis gained power. Hitler won the qualified support of the aristocratic officer corps only after attaining power (A). Hitler's first paramilitary backing, the SA or "Storm Troopers," were broken by him only in 1934 (B). He continued to work out of Bavaria until the early 1930s (C), while he was always in opposition to the Party (E).

55. **(B)**

The idea that an elite cadre was necessary to give leadership to the anticipated revolution was that of V. I. Lenin. For Marx, such a revolution was inevitable as the condition of the working class grew intolerable (A). Since in Marx's view the capitalists controlled the means of production and dominated society (C), including government, they would not permit the State to help the workers. Economic determinism (D) is a core concept of Marxism.

56. **(B)**

Introduced in the face of falling production and popular discontent, the NEP allowed greater economic freedom in the hope of increasing production. The First Five-Year plan (D), linked to the collectivization of agriculture (C) and the effort to expand industry greatly (A), was introduced in the late 1920s by Stalin. The NEP represented a "step back" from nationalization of industry (E).

57. **(C)**

From the information given in the graph, the only statement that is reasonable is (C) (from late 1847 to 1851). The other statements may or may not be true, but the graph does not give sufficient information to test them.

58. **(B)**

This question relies on not only knowledge but also understanding of society in Prussia—the German state that united all of Germany in 1870. The Prussian Junkers, whose income came largely from landed estates in eastern Prussia, provided most civil servants and army leadership for the Hohenzollerns (the Prussian ruling family); they were found in prominent German positions as late as World War II. Prussia had no constitution until 1850. Answer (C) might be partly correct, since Junkers often were judge and jury on their own estates and filled major judicial posts, but it is not the best answer. In the nineteenth century, middle-class German businessmen and bankers saw the Junkers as political rivals, since the Junkers pushed for tariff and tax policies that favored agriculture over industry.

59. **(C)**

This question shows the importance of knowing exact terminology. The Slavophiles did not reject all Western influences, but many wanted to retain a distinctly Russian culture. Thus (B) and (E) are incorrect. Answers (A) and (D) refer to Pan-Slavism, which was different from Slavophilism. Pan-Slavists wanted to unite all Slavs (most of the people of Eastern Europe) under a single nation, generally Russia. But not all Slavophiles espoused Pan Slavism, or vice versa.

60. **(B)**

The question asks for knowledge of terminology ("gap theory") but adds a major clue ("Bismarck"). Since the country in which the Army Bill Crisis occurred is not identified, you must know that term as well. Bismarck was brought to power in Prussia by the crisis, which was a stalemate between the Prussian king and his legislature over reforms of the Prussian army. Bismarck solved the stalemate by insisting that the Prussian constitution contained a "gap": There was no mention of what was to be done if such a logjam developed. Since the king had granted the constitution, Bismarck insisted that the monarch might ignore the liberals in the legislature and follow his own judgment. Answer (E) (the name of a political crisis in France during the 1880s) is designed to tempt those who know that the "gap theory" solved a crisis but are not certain of the name of the crisis.

61. (E)

The pie chart for Great Britain indicates that women had not yet broken into the ranks of banking and commerce. In each of the three charts, women are seen to represent a factor in all areas except banking and commerce in England.

62. (D)

Social Darwinism tended to be nationalistic rather than cosmopolitan. Using the concept "survival of the fittest," coined by Herbert Spencer, an ardent Social Darwinist, the other activities mentioned could be justified.

63. (D)

The first decades of the Third Republic were tumultuous, as monarchists bitterly tried to regain control. When doubts began to surface over the guilt of Alfred Dreyfus, a military intelligence officer convicted by a rigged court martial of passing military secrets to Germany, the rival Republicans were able to use the issue to destroy royalist credibility in France. The Irish Question involved British debates over pacifying unhappy Ireland in the nineteenth century, when all of Ireland was part of Britain. The Zabern Affair described the shooting of demonstrators in the Alsace-Lorraine section of Germany by a German army unit in 1913. The Panama Canal scandal was an attempt by royalists to turn opinion to their side; it concerned financial chicanery in a failed French project to build the canal. In the *"Daily Telegraph* Affair," German Emperor William II was embarrassed by the publication of comments that he made to a British newspaper reporter.

64. (B)

Answer (A) appears too obvious. When the French government, which had moved to Bordeaux, signed a peace agreement with Prussia in 1871, Paris, under siege by Prussia, refused to accept surrender. A separate government in Paris, the Commune, spoke of nationalizing banks in order to finance continued resistance to German invaders. French troops loyal to the government suppressed the Commune, a creation of anarchist workers (thus C is wrong). The event remained a nightmare to the middle classes, which feared that radicalism was growing in France.

65. (B)

The British Prime Minister who was associated closely with Irish Home Rule was (B) William Gladstone. He maintained through his four ministries that one of his principal tasks was "to pacify Ireland." Robert Peel's (E) career was over before the Irish crisis broke during the second half of the nineteenth century. Benjamin Disraeli (A), Lord Salisbury (C), and Joseph Chamberlain (D) were not particularly interested in or sympathetic to the Irish.

66. (C)

The Anglo-French Entente (known as the Entente Cordiale) (C) resolved Anglo-French colonial disputes in Egypt and Morocco; northeast Africa (Egypt and the Sudan) was recognized as a British sphere of influence; northwest Africa (Morocco and Algeria) was recognized as a French sphere of influence. This arrangement was not (A) directed at German expansion in Europe or (B) overseas; it was signed in 1904 and therefore was not (D) a nineteenth-century agreement; the Trans-Siberian railroad (E) had been funded by French loans during the 1880s and 1890s; it was not mentioned in this agreement.

67. (B)

The Schlieffen Plan, a German army contingency plan first formulated in the 1870s, called for a quick defeat of France in the event of a future European war. The plan was a solution to the generals' nightmare of a two-front war; after a French surrender, the German army would be prepared to fight Russia. The words *to the east front* show that this map does not describe events in World War II, since the German invasion of France in that war preceded Germany's invasion of Russia. The Maginot Line describes fortifications the French built along France's border with Germany during the 1920s. Answer (D) names Winston Churchill's belief that Germany was vulnerable to invasion through Southern Europe.

68. (C)

Heisenberg's uncertainty (or indeterminacy) principle stated that no fixed model of atoms was possible, only an approximation, since instruments of observation distorted the subatomic world. The "Big Bang" theory (A) is the work of several astronomers, while the same is true of the geological theory of plate tectonics (B)—Wegener being one of the earliest to conceive of continental drift. Claims as to who has discovered the oldest hominid (D) are contested by anthropologists. Richard Leakey is among the leading claimants. The first major radio telescope was constructed under the supervision of Bernard Lovell (E).

69. (D)

Fascist leaders often portrayed themselves as the best alternative to the spread of communism across Europe. The Depression helped bring fascist leaders such as Hitler to power, and caused European nations to enact protectionist policies, which led to a marked decline in trade. Fascism tended to gain support in nations without a tradition of successful parliamentary government.

70. **(B)**

Nurtured during the early years of the Third French Republic, when Royalists in France bitterly tried to gain control over the state, the *Action Française* advocated an authoritarian government with a strengthened military. The organization, a pre-fascist movement, also fed on anti-semitic prejudices.

71. **(C)**

Khrushchëv, ruler of the Soviet Union after the death of Stalin, proclaimed the superiority of the Soviet system and predicted a continued competition with capitalism, but he added that the struggle would be peaceful. Answer (A) was a World War II slogan of the Allies fighting Germany and Italy. Answer (B) was the slogan during the 1960s of the French president De Gaulle, who predicted increasing European independence from the "superpowers" of the United States and the Soviet Union. Answer (D) was one of Lenin's slogans in pre-revolutionary Russia. "Peace in Our Time" (E) was the prediction made by the British Prime Minister Chamberlain in 1938 following the Munich conference over the fate of Czechoslovakia.

72. **(A)**

Under the leadership of Marshall Tito, a communist and World War II hero, Yugoslavia refused to follow Soviet directives after World War II. This question may also be answered by identifying the remaining answers as true. Eastern European nations were forbidden by the Soviet government to participate in the Marshall Plan. A revolt in East Germany in 1953 was suppressed by the country's government, and a Hungarian revolt of 1956 was put down by the Soviet army. Almost all Eastern European nations were militarily allied with the Soviet Union through the Warsaw Pact.

73. **(B)**

De Gaulle, a World War II hero, later came to power due to riots in Algeria, where a native population pushed for independence while a sizable French population clamored for continued ties with France. After granting Algerian independence, De Gaulle steered France on an independent course in Europe, insisting on the withdrawal of NATO bases from the country while continuing to cooperate with NATO.

74. **(D)**

The correct choice is (D). Russia backed the international force led by the United States. Since this army was mobilized against Iraq because of Saddam Hussein's invasion of Kuwait, any choice indicating Russian neutrality or support for Iraq would, by inference, have to be dismissed.

75. **(B)**

The product of a meeting off the coast of Newfoundland in 1941 between British prime minister Churchill and U.S. President Roosevelt, the Atlantic Charter listed joint war aims in World War II, including the United Nations. The Truman Doctrine was a pledge by the American president to "contain" Communism. The Molotov Plan was a Soviet counterpart to the Marshall Plan of economic aid to postwar Europe. The Brussels Pact laid the groundwork for the NATO alliance after World War II. The Treaty of Rapallo, signed in 1922, established diplomatic ties between Weimar Germany and the new communist government of Russia.

76. (B)

Brezhnev acted like an old Stalinist in his crackdown on the "Prague Spring" of 1968. He did not (A) continue Khrushchëv's artistic Thaw, nor did he anticipate (C and D) any of Gorbachev's attempted reforms. Having died over a decade before, Brezhnev could not have led the 1991 coup (E).

77. (A)

Though students should not be expected to know the nineteenth-century map of Africa in detail, they ought to know something about European involvement in such areas as the Congo, Nigeria, Egypt, the Sudan, Abyssinia, and South Africa.

78. (C)

Luther's teachings were condemned in 1520 by Pope Leo X. He was subsequently excommunicated but refused to recant at the Diet of Worms in 1521, where the emperor, Charles V, condemned Luther (B). He was not put to death, however, because his patron, Frederick the Wise of Saxony, hid him in Wartburg Castle. Later, more princes with grievances against Rome or the emperor joined the Protestant cause, and they successfully resisted imperial attempts to crush their rebellion. In the peasant revolt of 1524–1525, Luther sided with the nobles (D).

79. (E)

The Polish astronomer Nicholas Copernicus (1473–1543) was the first European scholar to challenge the geocentric model of the Ptolemaic universe, which held that the earth is at the center and the sun travels around it. Copernicus made the case for a heliocentric, or sun-centered universe, in his book *On the Revolutions of the Celestial Orbs* (1543). He was later supported by Kepler and Galileo (C, D). Montaigne and Rabelais (A, B) were not astronomers but writers; Montaigne was renowned for his essays, and Rabelais for his satires.

80. (C)

The North Atlantic Treaty Organization was founded in 1949 to protect Europe from Soviet aggression. Following the collapse of the Soviet Union, President Clinton suggested that NATO provide a collective guarantee against any aggression by one power against another. Though NATO, among other international groups, sought a solution to the Balkan crisis (A), this was not its founding purpose. (B) is not a good answer because, while NATO has supplied troops for U.N. missions, such activity is not part of its charter. (D) is incorrect because, although NATO members have generally supported human rights, they considered preventing expansion of Soviet influence their primary objective. Finally, NATO's erratic support of Israel (E) has never been part of NATO's overall objective.

Section II

Sample Answer to Document-Based Question

J. A. Hobson, an economist and publicist with a brilliant mind, had a great impact both in his own day and in subsequent decades on the study of Imperialism and its roots. Among those he influenced were V. I. Lenin, who drew on him heavily for his work, *Imperialism, the Highest Stage of Capitalism*, the major Marxian discussion of the subject. However, in Hobson's own day and, to a greater extent, in recent years, scholars have raised questions regarding his conclusions. There are to be seen in these documents a number of the assertions, attitudes, and claims held by prominent statesmen and intellectuals of the Age of Imperialism that seem, if not to wholly discredit Hobson's views, to raise questions as to whether they alone can account for the colonial expansion of Europe in the nineteenth century.

In Document 2 there is the assertion by an English official familiar with the colonial scene that the impetus for the penetration of a region did not always come from the European governments themselves: rather, there were native elements within countries or regions that welcomed foreigners. In this case, according to the English official, princes of the Malaysian regions found it desirable to draw upon British expertise in organizing their relatively primitive governments along more efficient lines. It is possible to demonstrate that there were in many other areas of Africa and Asia native elements who found contact with Europeans advantageous. Thus in many lands, merchants, seeking to expand their own trade, found in the Europeans a ready market. Document 5 also indicates that it was not always the home government, in this case England, that pushed or even supported the economic penetration of the backward regions: If merchants wished to trade in areas of instability, they did so at their own risk and should expect no assistance from their own governments. Admittedly, both documents predate the great Age of Imperialism, an age in which, in the wake of intensified economic competition among the major states of Europe, gunboat diplomacy became more common.

Much has been written about the White Man's Burden as a factor in European Imperialism. This concept, eulogized in Kipling's poems (Document 16), held that it was a virtual obligation of Westerners, who possessed a superior civilization, to bring the benefits of that civilization—or at least those aspects of it that they could absorb—to the backward peoples of Asia and Africa. This moralistic view was seen early in the writings of William Wilberforce, a statesman and humanitarian who had demonstrated his real concern for humankind in his ardent struggle to end slavery in all English holdings and, indeed, worldwide. Certainly many of those Europeans who were involved in the colonial regions of the globe were sincere in their efforts to improve the welfare of their subjects. The activities of the British in India in seeking to eradicate suttee (i.e., widow burning) and the cult of thuggee and to improve food production and health services provides evidence of this. It could be argued, however, that this paternalistic attitude, if beneficent, still maintained the colonial peoples as subjects. Once established in a colony, it was possible to argue, not without some justification, that the continued presence of the civilizing influence of the Europeans was necessary to prevent the natives from falling back into a state of anarchy and near-barbarism (Document 3). Clearly there were those who, opposed to imperialism, questioned this humanitarianism as nothing more than a cloak to conceal more selfish motives. Thus Document 8 portrays the missionary as little more than the vanguard of a nation's political and economic interests.

It is clear that as the nineteenth century advanced, this paternalistic attitude for humankind took a less humane twist as the impact of Social Darwinism was felt. Now, rather than a humanitarian duty, the subjugation of backward peoples was seen as a natural part of the struggle for the survival of the fittest (Documents 9, 13, 14, and 17) in which the needs of the weak need not be taken into consideration. There is evident, too, a strong element of racism, for the white race is destined to triumph over the inferior black and yellow races. In Document 13, there is the suggestion that the struggle in the colonial sphere is also becoming one in which the Western states themselves are in a mounting and, in Social Darwinist terms, natural struggle in which the stronger, living nations will overcome the weaker, dying Western states.

Clearly it was not always solely or even primarily economic advantages that the colonial powers sought in imposing their rule on the peoples of Asia and Africa. Bases for strategic purposes were often a goal (Documents 4, 10, and 15). As the maritime and naval expansion of Europe took place, this became all the more true. While it might be argued that such harbors and fortified sites were utilized to enhance and expand a nation's economic interests, it is also true that they served as protection against potential threats from other European powers. British expansion into the inhospitable and costly Northwest Territories was due more to a perceived threat from Russia to India than from visions of economic gain. Clearly, a Russian foreign minister found it logical to justify his country's expansion into central Asia on the basis of the threat presented by the semicivilized peoples of that region.

Documents 11, 12, and 18 provide evidence of yet two more explanations that have been advanced to explain, if not justify, Europe's imperialistic surge. Document 11 indicates that Eastern Europe, in the course of the nineteenth century, experienced a large growth in its population. To the leaders of many of these countries this growth seemed to demand that a safety valve be found for the surplus population. To many the solution lay in the establishment of overseas colonies. This argument was seen in the claims of Cecil Rhodes, virtually the personification of Imperialism (Document 18), and in the claims of many German advocates of colonial expansion that *Lebensraum* (living space) represented a logical solution to their expanding population. Documents 12 and 18 provide yet a second motive for the acquisition of colonies: They were necessary for the economic vitality of the mother country, not solely to provide profits for Hobson's "certain industrial, financial, and professional classes," but, rather, for the working class of the nation in general. It would, in the view of the *Nationalsozialer Verein* Manifesto, contribute to social reform in Germany, while Rhodes, more dramatically, argued that it was the only alternative to civil war in England.

To argue that Hobson was wrong in arguing for the significance of economic factors in the nineteenth-century surge of European Imperialism would be in error, for it is obvious that many of the documents presented here do take note of the role of that factor, even though it might not be the central idea discussed. It would be correct, however, as many scholars have done, to insist that to explain a major movement in history such as Imperialism on the basis of monocausation is in error. Any such movement is the consequence of the interaction of numerous forces. Even where one force such as economics may be of paramount importance, it can and often is multifaceted: Profits derived from the colonial world certainly benefited certain of the capitalist elements in the state, but such prosperity could also serve the interests of the masses and make them no less eager for colonial expansion. Nor is it possible to contend that there were no Imperialists who were not motivated by truly humanitarian sentiments rather than solely visions of profit, or a statesman who was not concerned with the defense of his country rather than financial gain for privileged elements in his nation. Great historical movements are too complex to have simple, singular explanations.

Sample Answers to Essay Questions

1.   United on a major principle—the preeminence of Scriptures over theological or papal authority—the three Protestant groups of the Reformation differed in significant ways on the implications of the Scriptures and on the ideal political structures for "this world."

The two major doctrines of Martin Luther became part of most Protestant theology, although not necessarily by the names that Luther used. Like most Protestants of the Reformation, Luther found the New Testament letters of St. Paul a source of inspiration. St. Paul's statement that "the just shall live by faith" led to Luther's doctrine of "justification by faith." Arguing (somewhat erroneously) that Roman Catholic doctrines held that "good works" could compensate for sins, Luther taught that human sin was too great to be balanced out by good deeds. In his doctrine of "justification by faith," the emphasis was on God's grace and on salvation given in return for individual faith.

Luther's portrayal of individuals alone before God's judgment, penitent and seeking salvation, led to his other doctrine that became widely accepted within Protestantism: the priesthood of the believer. Rejecting priests as unnecessary intermediaries, most Protestants viewed their ministers as having no special status except as pastors to a congregation. But Lutherans, thanks to the Peasants' Revolt of 1524–1525 and other factors, came like their founder to advocate a uniform obedience to God's vicars on earth—his anointed princes.

Calvinism was distinctive for its doctrine of Predestination. The doctrine of Predestination had been considered and rejected by St. Augustine, and few other groups in Protestantism gave it much attention. John Calvin made it a central theme in his *Institutes of the Christian Religion*. Popular Calvinism added the idea that God would not allow the "elect of God" to suffer in this life; "success" became the sign of salvation. For some, success in business became a mark of salvation. Far less passive than Lutheranism, Calvinism came to advocate a very active role of the "elect" in seeking to found the "City of God" on earth—even to the point of deposing and killing "godless" princes, usually defined as Catholic.

Anabaptism, which largely drew its membership from the peasantry, tended to hold that belief should be based on the Scriptures alone. Although Anabaptist beliefs tended to vary from congregation to congregation, and from town to town, Anabaptists were generally less educated than other Protestants and regarded with suspicion any ideas or doctrines not clearly articulated in the Scriptures. The fierce persecution of Anabaptists from the beginning led them to seek a strict separation of church and state, the latter being labeled an ungodly power. Small wonder that Anabaptist sects, coming to the British colonies, helped enshrine the doctrine of separation of church and state in the U.S. Constitution.

One area of major difference between the three Protestant groups of the Reformation was in their attitudes toward the Eucharist, or Communion. Luther believed that Christ was present during Communion, but he tended to reject the Catholic belief that Christ was present in the elements of Communion, the bread and wine. Calvinists and Anabaptists were likely to regard Communion as a memorial service, without the physical presence of Christ.

In sum, while the three major groups of the Protestant Reformation drew different lessons from Scripture, they found agreement in their outlooks on the role of the churches and the relationship of sinners to God.

2.   Mercantilism, an economic policy developed during the age of absolute monarchies, and laissez-faire, preeminent during the era of industrialization and the rise of the middle class, were virtually completely opposite economic policies. Yet each was popular during its own time, largely for reasons connected with the political and economic conditions of the eras.

In many ways, mercantilism, popular during the late seventeenth and eighteenth centuries, represented an attempt to extend the powers of absolutism to trade and colonies. Assuming that resources were strictly limited and that European nations would engage in a prolonged struggle to control those resources, the ministers of European monarchs attempted to tie the economies of their colonies closely to that of the mother nation. Colonies were to function as both a market for the mother country's products and as a source of raw materials.

Mercantilist policies seldom functioned as hoped, as illustrated by the case of Britain, which had begun to gather an extensive colonial empire. North American industries frequently wanted to produce their own versions of products made in Britain, but royal ministers promoted legislation to prevent such colonial competition. Raw materials were also, at times, available more cheaply from other nations than from Britain's own colonies.

The problems involved in mercantilism were obvious by the time Adam Smith published his *Wealth of Nations* in 1776. Smith argued for an era of economic freedom, where individuals might pursue their own economic self-interest without government regulation or limitation. The result, he believed, would be economic expansions that would create new resources. His book coincided with the early stages of the Industrial Revolution, and Britain, far ahead of the rest of Europe in industrialization by the early 1800s, liked the idea of a tariff-free Europe, an era of "free trade."

The middle class, growing rapidly in size as industrialization proceeded, also liked the laissez-faire idea of keeping government separate from business. Building on the ideas of Thomas Malthus, who argued that the food supply increased much more slowly than the population, the Scottish economist Ricardo produced the iron law of wages:

Wages to the working class might not be increased in real terms. Wage hikes would only produce inflation—and no real improvement for the workers.

Ricardo's work seemed to demonstrate that natural economic law, not economic exploitation, kept the working class in dire straits. His work probably soothed the consciences of any middle-class business people who feared government regulation of factories. Yet it illustrated a basic contradiction in laissez-faire ideas: Smith argued that resources were not finite but might be expanded by free economic activity, while Ricardo argued that there was only a limited amount of wealth.

3.   Starting from the premise that the old, Earth-centered view of the solar system had become too complicated, scientists during the Scientific Revolution gradually moved to the Copernican version of a sun-centered solar system. In the process, the Copernican system challenged Church authority, helped the newer inductive reasoning triumph over the deductive reasoning of the Middle Ages, and became a testing ground for the emergence of scientific methods. In this shift it became clear, from Galileo on, that the old, word-based approach to science would have to be scrapped in favor of the new system, in which numbers were the "language" of Nature, and therefore mathematics the preferred method of science.

During the Middle Ages, the Earth-centered view had met the requirements of Scholasticism, the medieval system of deductive logic and knowledge that emphasized reliance on Church authorities. Where Church authorities had not written on a problem, an outside—even pagan—author might be approved. The Earth-centered system of the second-century Greek-Egyptian astronomer Ptolemy was given Church approval partly because it seemed to conform to Scriptures—where the sun was described as moving backward—but also because it illustrated the supreme medieval irony: Human beings were sinful and wretched, but also important enough to be at the center of not only the solar system but the entire universe. Later, Platonism would add the old Greek idea that geometry (and, by extension, all forms of math) was a necessary prerequisite to any scientific advances.

In the sixteenth century, the Polish astronomer Copernicus pointed to the increasing complexity of the Ptolemaic system as a reason to consider alternatives. As a high official in the Catholic Church, Copernicus merely suggested alternative hypotheses. His work, however, began a process in which facts gained through observation were assembled into alternative theories; "induction" replaced deduction. Brahe's laboriously collected, mathematically precise data were to prove more important than flights of fancy.

When the Italian Galileo used his observations with a telescope to support the Copernican system, he fell victim to Church discipline in a famous trial. His work on inertia, however, and on the speed of falling bodies led to research by others. The Central European astronomer Kepler added to the Copernican trend by producing three laws of planetary motion that favored the Copernican view. Devoutly religious, however, Kepler believed that he was functioning not as a critic of religion but as a prophet discovering the mysteries of God's creation.

The work of Newton illustrated the importance of mathematics for scientific work, producing another scientific "principle" to oppose Church authority. Newton's work on gravity virtually confirmed the Copernican system, which could not be proved by methods involving observations and experiments. Gravity, for Newton, was a property of all matter and was strongest in the largest bodies. His work implied that the most massive object in the solar system, the sun, would have to be at the center of the system. Newton arrived at his answers through mathematics, but others saw the virtues of inductive thinking revealed in the triumph of the Copernican view. While writers like Descartes praised deduction, Francis Bacon insisted that the new scientific method of induction would solve all of the riddles of nature in perhaps a century.

The Copernican controversy became central to the Scientific Revolution because it combined so many elements in the emergence of science—the replacement of deductive reasoning (to some degree) by induction, the emergence of the scientific method as an "authority" in itself, and calls for the freedom of scientists to pursue their work without theological restrictions. Few other developments in the Scientific Revolution were quite so broad and far-reaching.

4. The efforts of European princes to bring the affairs of their states more firmly under their control had their origins both in internal elements that constituted, or were seen as constituting, disruptive forces threatening their realm's stability and strength and, at the same time, changes in the nature of relations between states. When a realm was threatened by chaos, a return to the bullying of local old nobles, and the rise of the "wrong" religions, it seemed to the majority of people in several lands across continental Europe that a perfectly acceptable solution to this dire threat was to allow one's legitimate monarch to assume absolute power to maintain the old forms of social status, religion, and custom.

Internally, many states were, in the wake of the Reformation, confronted with the pressure of religious groups that, although in the minority, were extremely militant in their desire to gain recognition of their particular form of Christianity. France in the mid-sixteenth century had been torn apart by conflicts that, in part, had their origins in the bitter conflict between Calvinist Huguenots and the predominant Catholic population. In the sixteenth and seventeenth centuries, too, England and Germany endured, to varying degrees, bitter struggles that had their roots at least in part in the clash of Catholic and Protestant sects. The answer to many princes was uniformity, the imposition on the state's population of one faith, that of the prince. The dissenters' choices were generally limited—accept the state religion, suffer persecution, or flee. Although Cardinal Richelieu, unable to tolerate the special political and military privileges the Huguenots received as a result of the Edict of Nantes, crushed them on the battlefield, he did not deprive them of their religious rights. Such an act of toleration, however, was relatively rare for the age: King Louis XIV, in persecuting the Huguenots for their religious beliefs, was far closer to the norm. Even the recognized Church was sometimes seen as a potential threat: Such was the case in France, where the feared loyalty to Rome of Catholic ecclesiasts led to French monarchs seeking to bring their churchmen more firmly under their control in the form of the Gallican Church.

Religious groups were not the only elements in the states of Europe that were seen as threats to stability. The old nobles of Europe had emerged from the medieval period possessing many privileges and rights that acted as significant obstacles to the exercise of princely power. Jealous of their privileged position, they were determined to retain and, provided the opportunity, to expand it. They were willing to endanger the security of their country in order to do so, as was demonstrated both in the course of the French Religious Wars and, in the mid-seventeenth century, the Fronde, a revolt on the part of aristocratic elements aimed at curtailing the trend toward centralization initiated by Richelieu and Mazarin.

Nor were religious and aristocratic groups the only potentially disruptive elements in society, for in many states there were other virtually autonomous elements enjoying rights that exempted them from the complete control of the state. Such was the case with the provincial estates and law courts in several countries, including Prussia and the Habsburg lands. Russians looked back on the chaotic Time of Troubles (1598–1613) as one good reason to subordinate even the old national assembly (for them, the *zemskii sobor*) to the assumed wisdom of the tsar and his chosen advisers. Everywhere, people looked to the instability and declining prosperity of most republics (e.g., the United Provinces of the Netherlands after 1672, Venice, the Swiss cantons, the Holy Roman Empire, and especially Poland) and deduced, quite reasonably, that absolute rule was stronger and simpler.

In addition to the instability generated by various internal forces, changes in the nature of relations between states served to enhance the presumed need for concentrating power in the hands of a central administration, controlled by the prince. Competition become more intense and, for at least a few states, had assumed a "global" nature. If a nation was to survive, much less thrive, it had to be able to defend itself and, if the opportunity presented itself, to take advantage of its neighbors. Such ability was to a large extent dependent on the existence of a strong military establishment. As armies grew larger—Louis XIV maintained a standing army of 400,000—the costs entailed in maintaining them, together with the expense of extensive fortifications, arsenals, supply depots, transportation facilities, and administrative support systems necessary to sustain them, increased steadily. This, in turn, demanded more effective control of the state's revenues and, equally important, increasing those revenues as much as possible. The fiscal affairs of the state consequently entailed the expansion and centralization of the necessary organs of state. Moreover, in an age of expanding commercial activities, the economic well-being of the state was seen as requiring close state involvement in every facet of its economic activity. Mercantilism, the economic side of absolutism, was oriented toward strengthening the economic vitality of the state at the expense of one's enemies or possible enemies.

These various threats, internal and external, to the state's well-being led many to conclude that the only solution was to vest ultimate and absolute power in the hands of the prince, one whose concern would be for the welfare of the entire nation, not simply one class or element. Such was the argument advanced by Thomas Hobbes in his *Leviathan*, where he argued that the alternative to placing sovereignty in the hands of one man was, in essence, anarchy. Such was the power Louis XIV envisioned when he proclaimed "I am the state."

5.   Although the Enlightenment is taught as a single historical era, there were actually three Enlightenments—English (late 1600s), French (1700s), and German (late 1700s, early 1800s). Each was a response to the particular conditions prevailing in those nations; not surprisingly, each produced somewhat different solutions.

All tended to agree on basic tenets. All three favored Reason—the common ability of human beings to interpret nature logically and to find common, logical solutions to their problems. All tended to reject intolerance, unjustified biases, and dogmatic religion. And they shared admiration of natural science, not surprising considering that the Scientific Revolution had occurred in the previous centuries.

The French Enlightenment was a very cosmopolitan period, focused on issues that the *philosophes* believed to be of concern to all humankind. One reason was that the *philosophes*, most of whom lived in Paris, came from different lands. Baron d'Holbach, champion of materialism, was German; Beccaria, who argued that the purpose of the law was to fit the punishment to the crime, was Italian. Some scholars argue that the first appearance of the word *humanity* was in the French language during this period.

Nevertheless, purely French conditions had a significant influence. Voltaire's call for a secular French society, and his condemnation of Christianity as superstition and prejudice, reflected the traditional intolerance shown to religious minorities in France by the state. French Huguenots, who had gained freedom of worship and the right to bear arms by the Edict of Nantes, lost these when Louis XIV revoked the edict in 1685. Voltaire himself deplored the French army's destruction of the Huguenot city of Port Royal. The most famous court case in which he became involved, the Calas case, concerned a Huguenot father found guilty of murdering a son who, it was said, desired to convert to Roman Catholicism.

In order to achieve a secular society, the *philosophes* became reformers, proposing specific social arrangements or solutions. *Candide* showed Voltaire's reformist bent, since it was written in angry reaction to the German philosopher Leibniz's statement that this is the best of all possible worlds. Voltaire did not reject religion entirely; he kept God as Creator in his own Deism, in which there were to be no complicated doctrines to nurture theological arguments. God the creator sounded suspiciously like Newton's portrait of God as the "clock-winder" of the universe.

The same faith in secular reform drove Diderot to publish his famous Encyclopedia; led Voltaire and others to believe that Enlightened Despots might reform their countries in a "revolution from above"; and caused Rousseau, who in some ways was a *philosophe* and in some ways was not, to seek citizen participation in government through his idea of the "general will."

None of the *philosophes* were scientists, but it was clear that they envisioned a universe and society governed by immutable and rational laws. While it would be difficult to tie the *philosophes* directly to the French Revolution, it appears that they made criticisms of the French government and society respectable in their country.

Conditions in Germany were quite different. Germany was, according to a famous saying, a "geographic expression" of 300-odd states, many with their own petty prince. The major religious war in Germany had ended in 1648 with arrangements that allowed each prince to dictate the official religion of his area. While French absolute monarchs of the 1700s imposed censorship in an almost half-hearted way, German princes included religious authority in their sovereignty. The German middle class, smaller in numbers than the French, did not challenge monarchical power the way the French had. Observers commented about the subservience of the German burgher; that the spirit of reform was lacking.

The two major German figures of the Enlightenment, Leibniz and Kant, admired natural science, but their attitudes toward it were quite different from the French *philosophes'*. Leibniz tended to be interested in rationalism, and he, along with Newton and the French mathematician Descartes, is given credit for the discovery of calculus. Yet Leibniz rejected Newton's theory of gravity and was unimpressed with the experimental work that led to that theory or that seemed to confirm that theory.

Kant also was interested in Reason, but his emphasis was on the ability of the mind, through Reason, to shape reality. Kant had been appalled at the work of the Scottish philosopher Hume, who seemed to challenge the validity of science by demonstrating that "cause and effect" was always assumed in science but could not be proven. Kant sought to demonstrate that the mind operated in such a way that "cause and effect" was always perceived; while "cause and effect" might not be proven, the mind operated in regular and consistent ways, according to its own internal laws. Kant's *Critique of Pure Reason* was an attempt to rescue science from philosophical skepticism. It also attempted to lay the basis for a new, nonreligious morality; the "categorical imperative" was a moral rule that was logically self-evident.

Monarchical authority intervened when Kant, in his subsequent book, *Critique of Practical Reason*, speculated that while the existence of God might not be proven, belief in God was a practical necessity. After the appearance of the book, he was commanded by the Prussian monarch to halt his commentaries on religious matters. Perhaps this incident is one reason why Kant, when writing of the ideal state, wrote in terms of abstractions rather than specifics and entirely avoided reform proposals.

More likely, the German Enlightenment, and Kant, reflected the domination of German monarchs over matters of free thought and religion, as well as the deferential attitude of the German middle class toward monarchs and nobility. Kant's ideal state was a state that met certain abstract philosophic criteria, rather than a state that was judged on the basis of specific, practical results, such as prosperity or free speech.

The future direction of German thought was evident in two traits seen in Kant: (1) his "inwardness," or emphasis on the internal workings of the mind, and (2) his attempts to define the ideal government on theoretical rather than practical grounds. Beginning with German Idealism in the early nineteenth century, German thinkers were often accused of being much more abstract than French or British counterparts, of emphasizing internal freedom over external rights, and of justifying the status quo more than challenging it. That trend appeared to be clear as early as the German Enlightenment.

Despite their shared belief in similar qualities such as Reason, the German and French Enlightenments were quite different periods. The French Enlightenment sought to strengthen humanitarian impulses such as toleration and to encourage free thought and criticism. Such traits were lacking in the German Enlightenment, which spoke of the "ideal" rather than the "real."

6.   Thrust into World War II by the actions of fascist Germany and Japan, the three major or non-fascist powers—the United States, Britain, and the Soviet Union—discovered during the course of the war that the sole point of total agreement among them was their opposition to the totalitarian governments they were fighting.

Some historians have referred to the alliance as the "Accidental Alliance," the alliance created not by a common outlook of its members but by the events of the war. Britain had been brought into the war by the German attack on Poland; the Soviet Union had entered because Hitler, wanting to impress on Britain how isolated it was, had sent German troops into the Soviet Union; and the United States had entered the war because of an attack by Japan, Germany's ally, on an American naval installation in Hawaii.

While the United States and Britain shared a common language and similar forms of government, the Soviet Union had little in common with its allies. Relations between the Soviet Union and British government had been particularly cool. During the 1930s, when the aggressive diplomacy of Hitler had been met with general British-French acquiescence, Stalin appeared to believe that this "appeasement" was a deliberately anti-Soviet policy. Documentary evidence is lacking—Stalin's archives are not available to historians of either East or West—but Stalin appeared to believe that the British hoped to use Hitler, a staunch anticommunist, to rid the world of Communism. Stalin's suspicions may have deepened when a Soviet observer who attended the Munich conference of 1938 was rebuffed by Britain and France when he suggested a collective security agreement against Germany. Possibly this rebuff explains the Soviet government's decision to sign a nonaggression pact with Germany in 1939, shortly before the German invasion of Poland. But the pact contained a provision for a de facto partition of Poland between Germany and the Soviet Union. In effect, Stalin cleared the way for the start of World War II. The British government, which went to war to defend the sovereignty of Poland, did not forget Stalin's role in the events of 1939. The British Prime Minister Winston Churchill was especially suspicious of his Soviet ally, particularly when the Soviet Union announced formation of a Polish communist government in exile to replace the civilian government that had fled to London.

Representing a country that had remained distant from prewar European diplomacy, the American President Roosevelt took a more tolerant view of Stalin, whom he termed "Uncle Joe." Roosevelt worked with Churchill to solve a problem that arose when the two leaders decided to delay a landing in France until landings and victories were assured in North Africa and Italy. Stalin had been demanding a "second front" in France to relieve pressure on Soviet troops. In an attempt to assure Stalin that no separate peace would be signed with Hitler—that a German victory in the Soviet Union would not end the struggle—both men issued a proclamation that their nations would not leave the war until unconditional surrender by Germany. Despite the conciliatory offer, Stalin refused to declare war against Japan. In fact, the Soviet Union would declare war against Japan only three days before the war ended, and only after two atomic bombs had been dropped on Japanese cities.

By the time of the Normandy landings in mid-1944, German troops were retreating from the territory of the Soviet Union. Stalin appeared to believe that victory over Germany had been achieved almost entirely by his troops; the landing of his allies in France might be a mopping-up operation. Stalin's ambitions in Eastern Europe loomed large. When the Soviet army approached Warsaw, the Polish underground revolted against the German rulers of the city. The Soviet advance halted just long enough for the Germans to eliminate this politically active group of Poles.

The conferences at Yalta and Potsdam at the end of the war have been criticized for ceding Eastern Europe to Stalin, but they largely recognized what had already happened to that area, which was occupied by Soviet troops. For the British—who had gone to war to preserve Poland—the loss of that nation was particularly bitter. A Winston Churchill speech in 1946 coined the term *iron curtain* and pointed to the major issue of the Cold War: the Soviet domination of Eastern European nations that had enjoyed a brief period of self-determination between 1919 and 1939.

The reasons for Soviet occupation of Eastern Europe are probably mixed and complex. Fear of a resurgent Germany, desire for a buffer zone against a future German invasion, use of opportunities to spread communist revolutions—it is difficult to sort out which played the major role. It is clear, however, that the tensions and suspicions among the antifascist allies of World War II laid no basis for their cooperation in the postwar world. Instead, they appeared to guarantee division between the two sides once World War II had ended.

PRACTICE EXAM 4

AP European History

Section 1

TIME: 55 minutes
80 questions

> **DIRECTIONS:** Each of the questions or incomplete statements below is followed by five suggested answers or completions. Select the one that is best in each case.

1. Roughly 30 to 40 percent of Europeans died in the Black Death, 1347–1350. In about what year did Europe's population reach its pre-plague level of circa 70 million?

   (A) 1400

   (B) 1450

   (C) 1550

   (D) 1650

   (E) 1750

Saint Agatha, by Francisco de Zurbaran, 1634

2. The painting above represents

    (A) the Renaissance fusion of pagan and Christian elements

    (B) a Protestant heretic tortured by the Spanish Inquisition

    (C) an obsession with the horrors of the Thirty Years' War

    (D) the Counter-Reformation's interest in mysticism

    (E) the triumph of anatomical dissections in art academies

3. Had Pope Alexander VI's Treaty of Tordesillas been observed,

    (A) England would have remained Catholic

    (B) the Dutch would have traded the Cape Colony for Brazil

    (C) Spain and Portugal would have dominated the overseas world

    (D) England would have received the Ohio Valley in exchange for French holdings in the Caribbean

    (E) Switzerland would have remained under the control of the Habsburgs of Austria

4. Which of the following best describes how the Northern Renaissance differed from the Renaissance in Italy?

    (A) It lacked the financial foundation provided by the city-states of Italy.

    (B) While attaining triumphs in architecture, it could not compare with the glory of Italian paintings and sculpture.

    (C) It placed a greater emphasis on religious piety.

    (D) It drew more heavily on the Byzantine tradition, which had died out in the South.

    (E) It reflected more strongly its contacts with cultures of the New World.

5. "… It is, then, much safer to be feared than to be loved… for touching human nature, we may say in general that men are untruthful, unconstant, dissemblers, they avoid dangers and are covetous of gain. While you do them good, they are wholly yours… but when [danger] approaches, they revolt."

    Such was the lesson taught to rulers by

    (A) Lorenzo Valla   (D) Hugo Grotius

    (B) Niccolo Machiavelli   (E) Johan Huizinga

    (C) Michel de Montaigne

6. As a consequence of the English War of the Roses,

    (A) English territorial holdings in France were lost

    (B) Anglicanism was proclaimed the state religion

(C)   the Tudor dynasty came to the throne

(D)   Monasticism in England was abolished

(E)   the kingdoms of England and Scotland were unified

7.   The specific abuse that Luther addressed in his "Ninety-Five Theses" was

(A)   simony

(B)   the sale of indulgences

(C)   clerical marriage

(D)   lay investiture

(E)   recognition of secular authority

8.   All of the following were factors in the success of Luther's religious movement EXCEPT

(A)   the printing press

(B)   German nationalism

(C)   Luther's alliance with German princes

(D)   widespread concern in Germany over the political intentions of the Habsburg emperor

(E)   Luther's support of the new concepts of the universe resulting from the ideas of Copernicus and other scientists

9.   All of the following may be claimed for English textile production circa 1800 EXCEPT:

(A)   The mechanization of the production of woolens made English raw wool the leading indicator of gross national product.

(B)   The quality of Indian cottons sparked English interest in setting up competing mills to produce their own cottons.

(C)   The invention of the spinning jenny, water frame, and cotton gin spurred English mechanization of cotton production.

(D)   The combination of City of London merchants, the Bank of England, and the English merchant marine aided exports of all textiles.

(E)   England looked to Egypt, India, the United States, and even Saxony as sources of raw cotton.

10.   All of the following were enlightened "despots" or enlightened ministers between 1750 and 1815 EXCEPT

(A)   the Marques de Pombal of Portugal

(B)   Louis XV of France

    (C)   Joseph II of Austria

    (D)   Frederick II of Prussia

    (E)   the Baron vom und zum Stein of Prussia

11.   As a consequence of the English "Glorious" Revolution of 1688–1689,

    (A)   the Hanoverian dynasty came to the throne

    (B)   Oliver Cromwell was overthrown

    (C)   Anglicanism was proclaimed the faith of the state

    (D)   Charles I Stuart was executed

    (E)   the principle of constitutional monarchy was firmly established

12.   Napoleon Bonaparte's "Continental System," initiated in 1806, had as its goal

    (A)   the creation of a unified Germany

    (B)   placement of Napoleon's brother on the throne of Spain

    (C)   the defeat of Britain through economic warfare

    (D)   a military alliance of states under his control to wage war on Russia

    (E)   the creation of a military force drawn from many European states to undertake the conquest of the Middle East

13.   As a consequence of the Russo-Japanese War,

    (A)   Russia was forced to sell Alaska to the United States

    (B)   Russia and Japan divided Korea

    (C)   Japan annexed Manchuria

    (D)   China was forced to cede its Maritime Provinces, including Vladivostok, to Russia

    (E)   Russia abandoned its interests in Manchuria

14.   As a result of the Crimean War, Russia

    (A)   gained control of the Black Sea

    (B)   was confronted with a revolution

    (C)   saw the introduction of a number of important reforms

    (D)   tightened control over the serfs

    (E)   introduced a national Duma, or parliament

15. The basic idea of mercantilism was

    (A) to acquire colonies

    (B) the promotion of social welfare through increased economic activity

    (C) to gain access to raw materials

    (D) the maintenance of a favorable balance of trade in order to increase the country's holdings in gold and silver

    (E) pursuit of laissez-faire to maintain an equitable balance of trade

16. Which was a significant reason for the weakness of New France in comparison with British holdings in North America?

    (A) Indian tribes tended to be more favorably inclined to the British.

    (B) The population of Britain was much larger than that of France.

    (C) The French government carefully monitored who could immigrate to its colonies, whereas Britain treated America as a "dumping ground."

    (D) French explorers failed to penetrate the interior and construct forts.

    (E) The missionary activities of French missionaries alienated the Indians.

17. Under the domestic system in England, also called "putting out,"

    (A) shipbuilding was made a state monopoly

    (B) spinning and weaving were done in rural homes

    (C) factory workers were prohibited from joining unions

    (D) farmers expanded the use of crop rotation and fertilization

    (E) foreign workers were by statue forbidden to take the jobs of Englishmen

18. The *asiento* granted to the English in the Peace of Utrecht gave them

    (A) possession of Gibraltar

    (B) the exclusive right to sell slaves in Spanish colonies of the New World

    (C) permission to trade freely in the Spanish islands of the Caribbean

    (D) the French island of Guadeloupe

    (E) the territory of Florida

19. Holding that man's life in a "state of nature" was "solitary, poor, nasty, brutish, and short," a sort of absolutist government was advocated by

    (A) Thomas Hobbes   (B) John Milton

(C)   William Blackstone   (E)   Jacques Bossuet

(D)   Baron d'Holbach

20.   All of the following states sent troops to the Thirty Years' War EXCEPT

(A)   Sweden

(B)   Austria

(C)   France

(D)   Denmark

(E)   England

21.   As a consequence of the Great Northern War, Peter the Great

(A)   replaced his insane half-brother, Fyodor, as czar of Russia

(B)   drove the Turkish navy from the Black Sea

(C)   extended Russian holdings into central Siberia

(D)   gave Russia a "window to the West" on the Baltic Sea

(E)   destroyed the political influence of the *streltsi* and Old Believers

22.   Which is one of the main failures of the Peace of Augsburg (1555)?

(A)   It left Italy disunited and a prey of the great powers.

(B)   It did not provide for recognition of the Calvinists.

(C)   By recognizing the rights of the Anabaptists, it introduced a radical religious faction into Germany.

(D)   It allowed France too many special privileges in Germany.

(E)   The powers of the emperor were not clarified.

23.   The theory of the separation of powers was most clearly enunciated in the works of

(A)   Voltaire

(B)   Montesquieu

(C)   Rousseau

(D)   Locke

(E)   Hobbes

24. The picture below is a typical example of the artistic movement known as

(A) French Renaissance   (D) Neoclassicism

(B) Baroque   (E) Romanticism

(C) Rococo

25. The map below indicates which of the following?

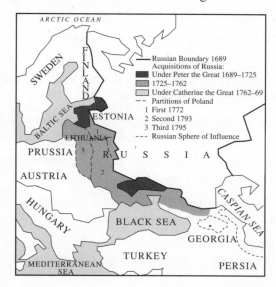

(A) Prior to the reign of Peter the Great, Russia was completely shut off from access to the open seas.

(B) Prior to 1800, the greatest acquisition of territory occurred during the reign of Catherine the Great.

(C) During the reign of Peter the Great, Russia gained access to the waters of the Mediterranean Sea.

(D) Peter the Great's expansion in the south was limited to the establishment of ports on the Black Sea.

(E) The partitions of Poland saw Russia gain the greatest share of the spoils.

26. A vocal element in the French Revolution, the *sans-culottes* were

(A) impoverished peasants

(B) urban and village priests

(C) members of the urban working class

(D) nobles who fled to the safety of the German states

(E) opponents of the Civil Constitution of the Clergy

27. Those members of the Estates-General who took the famous Tennis Court Oath swore to

(A) overthrow Louis XVI

(B) establish a republic

(C) draft a constitution for France

(D) break the ties between the French church and the papacy

(E) establish the principle of complete religious toleration in France

28. Which of the following statements is NOT true? Scientific research conducted in the seventeenth and eighteenth centuries

(A) assumed an international scope as governments supported scientific inquiry, hoping discoveries would have immediate, practical application

(B) laid firm foundations in physics, chemistry, and medicine as independent and rapidly expanding disciplines

(C) was centered primarily in the major universities, which were richly endowed by merchants and entrepreneurs

(D) was stimulated by the belief that the comprehension of and harnessing of the laws of nature would benefit humankind

(E)   received the encouragement of rulers who saw the practical value of discoveries to the mercantilist policies of their states

29.   The battle waged between Wolfe and Montcalm on the Plains of Abraham determined

(A)   that the Stuart dynasty would never again rule England

(B)   the fate of France's North American empire

(C)   that Austria had lost control of Silesia to the Prussians

(D)   the ultimate victor in the War of the Spanish Succession

(E)   whether France or Britain would have paramount influence in India

30.   All of the following statements are in accord with the theories of the Deists EXCEPT:

(A)   Absolute standards of good and evil do not exist; good simply results in pleasure, evil in pain.

(B)   God does not respond to individual petitions to intervene with the laws of nature on their behalf.

(C)   God should be perceived as the prime mover, the source of the laws of nature that are comprehensible to the human mind.

(D)   The concept of divine predestination is in opposition to the human dignity reason bestows on the individual.

(E)   The individual possesses the freedom and rational ability to determine what is good and evil and to choose between them.

31.   The English Navigation Acts were designed to

(A)   restrict the number of vessels constructed to prevent overbuilding

(B)   establish regulations for safer travel

(C)   ensure that vessels carried sufficient insurance to safeguard investors

(D)   weaken Dutch trade and encourage that of England

(E)   permit English ships to violate the monopolistic practices of the Spanish

32.   Muscovy achieved sovereign independence when

(A)   Dmitri Donskoi beat the Mongols at Kulikovo in 1380

(B)   Ivan III stopped paying tribute to the Golden Horde in 1480

(C)   Ivan the Terrible invaded and conquered western Siberia

(D)   the boyars elected Mikhail Romanov tsar in 1613

(E)   Peter the Great beat the Swedes in the Great Northern War

33.   The Royal Society of London is most logically associated with

(A)   the Scientific Revolution

(B)   James II Stuart of England

(C)   efforts to bring the Christian faith to the natives of Africa

(D)   financing the establishment of colonies in British North America

(E)   supporting commercial activities in the Far East

34.   "It appears then that wages are subject to a rise or fall from two causes: First, the supply and demand of labourers. Secondly, the price of the commodities on which the wages of labour are expanded.... With a population pressing against the means of subsistence, the only remedies are either a reduction of people or a more rapid accumulation of capital."
These words are best associated with

(A)   Jeremy Bentham   (D)   Robert Peel

(B)   David Ricardo   (E)   David Hume

(C)   Robert Owen

35.   The Levelers were

(A)   anti-industrial woolen weavers deprived of their jobs by mechanization

(B)   religious radicals of the 1600s who sought social and political reform

(C)   landowners in nineteenth-century England opposed to the imposition of duties on imported grain

(D)   followers of Gracchus Babeuf

(E)   the armed supporters of Oliver Cromwell

36.   Historical research indicates that the long-term consequence of the Industrial Revolution for members of the working class was to

(A)   reduce their standard of living by removing them from their agricultural roots

(B)   increase the length of their workday

(C)   reduce the financial contribution of women to the family income

(D)   increase their standard of living

(E)   leave their standard of living at about the same level, but deprive them of the advantages provided by rural life

37.   Catherine the Great

(A)   introduced reforms easing the burden on the serfs

(B)   inaugurated the Slavophile movement

(C)   annexed the Maritime Provinces of Manchu China

(D)   extended Russia's territorial holdings by ousting the Crimean Tatars

(E)   reduced the power of the nobility

38.   Edmund Burke

(A)   believed that revolutionary change would benefit all people

(B)   strongly advocated the use of military force to crush the American Revolution

(C)   proposed uprooting political institutions that were not as useful as they had been in the past

(D)   advocated evolution rather than revolution

(E)   in 1783 wrote his *Reflections* on the American Revolution

39.   The most serious error made by the statesmen assembled at the Congress of Vienna was

(A)   initiating a conflict with the Ottoman Turks

(B)   restoring Louis XVIII to the throne of France

(C)   ignoring nationalist and democratic movements in Europe

(D)   ceding Norway to Denmark

(E)   imposing the Carlsbad Decrees on Prussia

40.   Czar Alexander II undertook all of the following reforms EXCEPT

(A)   emancipation of the serfs

(B)   establishment of a national Duma or Parliament

(C)   relaxation of press censorship

(D)   the creation of local *zemstvos* or provincial assemblies

(E)   expansion of educational opportunities

41. The poster below is entitled "Tsar, Priest and Fat-Cat on the Shoulders of the Laboring Masses" (1918). Cultured Russians would have known that it alludes to what Russian classic?

(A) Pushkin's play, and Mussorgsky's opera, *Boris Godunov*

(B) Nikolai Leskov's satirical novel *Cathedral Folk*

(C) Leo Tolstoy's epic novel *War and Peace*

(D) Ilya Repin's painting *Barge Haulers on the Volga*

(E) a Russian play based on Harriet Beecher Stowe's *Uncle Tom's Cabin*

42. Social Darwinism gave theoretical support for all of the following EXCEPT

(A) economic individualism

(B) militarism

(C) the growth of big industry

(D) cosmopolitanism

(E) imperialism

43. Which is one significant difference between the problem created for the Austro-Hungarian empire by Czech nationalism and that of the Serbs?

(A) The Serbs were more politically advanced than the Czechs.

(B) A majority of the Serbs were willing to accept autonomy within the Dual Monarchy, while the Czechs sought complete independence.

(C) The Czechs could look to Germany for support.

(D) An independent Serbian state existed to encourage their ethnic kinsmen within the Dual Monarchy.

(E) A majority of Czechs agitated for cultural rights more than independence.

44. From 1881 to 1901, anarchists murdered heads of state, leading politicians, and members of royalty, from Alexander II of Russia to President McKinley of the United States. Other countries were rocked by such assassinations EXCEPT

(A) Spain   (D) Italy

(B) France   (E) Germany

(C) Austria-Hungary

45. In the course of World War I, Britain was faced with a serious rebellion on the part of its subjects in

(A) South Africa   (D) Palestine

(B) India   (E) Cyprus

(C) Ireland

46. In the works of Arthur de Gobineau and Houston Stuart Chamberlain were concepts that contributed significantly to the

(A) development of existentialism

(B) doctrines of the National Socialist Workers Party

(C) economic doctrines of Neo-Mercantilism

(D) policy of appeasement pursued by France and Great Britain in the 1930s

(E) Dadaist movement

47. "1. Open covenants openly arrived at ... diplomacy shall proceed always frankly and in the public view.

2. Absolute freedom of navigation ... alike in peace and war.

3. Adequate guarantees … that national armaments will be reduced to the lowest point consistent with domestic safety."

The statements above constitute a portion of those found in the

(A)   Atlantic Charter

(B)   Treaty of Versailles

(C)   Fourteen Points

(D)   Letters of McMahon

(E)   Kellogg-Briand Pact

48.   A common element among the revolutionary movements that swept through Europe in 1848 was

(A)   unity of purpose among middle-class liberals and urban workers

(B)   rejection of ethnic rivalry in the name of nationalistic aspirations

(C)   coordinated and timely action on the part of experienced leaders

(D)   initial success as a result of the hesitation of governmental leaders to use their superior forces

(E)   no fear of the intervention of external, foreign forces

49.   All of the following statements about the onset of World War I are true EXCEPT:

(A)   The idea of war was enthusiastically received by the public in all lands.

(B)   Few, including military men, anticipated the nature of the war that erupted.

(C)   Socialist politicians in every country opposed their governments' decision to enter the war.

(D)   Each side was convinced that its cause was just.

(E)   The Austrian effort was hampered by ethnic disunity.

50.   The political cartoon below, appearing in a French newspaper of 1902, suggests which of the following?

(A)   Japan's aggression in China was a threat to Western economic interests.

(B)   China was a target of Russian imperialism.

(C)   Japan was running a risk by challenging Russian power in the Far East.

(D)   Russia was planning to invade Japan.

(E)   An alliance of Japan and Russia would threaten French interests in China.

51.   World War I saw the use of all the following weapons of war EXCEPT

(A)   machine guns   (D)   incendiary bombs

(B)   flame throwers   (E)   tanks

(C)   poison gas

52.   Which of the following statements about totalitarianism is NOT true?

(A)   It frequently had a cult leader as head of state.

(B)   It demanded absolute commitment to its ideology.

(C)   It had no connections with nineteenth-century ideologies.

(D)   Extreme nationalism was a primary element of its ideology.

(E)   Its political structure was monolithic, one party alone being tolerated.

53.   War "as an instrument of national policy" was renounced by those nations that signed the

(A)   Locarno Treaties

(B)   Kellogg-Briand Pact

(C)   Versailles Treaty

(D)   Lytton Commission Report

(E)   Treaty of Rapallo

54.   All of the following have had a woman as head of state since 1947 EXCEPT

(A)   India   (D)   Pakistan

(B)   Britain   (E)   Israel

(C)   France

55.   All of the following statements regarding Great Britain's economic status following World War I are true EXCEPT:

(A)   Many of Britain's overseas investments had been liquidated.

(B)   Britain's industrial plants were growing antiquated.

(C)   As a result of immigration, Britain experienced a labor shortage.

(D)   There was a sharp rise in the cost of living.

(E)   The United States, Canada, and Germany were strong industrial rivals.

56.   "Take up the White Man's burden
Send forth the best you breed
Go bind your sons to exile
To serve your captives' need."

Thus wrote the poet laureate of imperialism,

(A)   Cecil Rhodes   (D)   W. B. Yeats

(B)   Rudyard Kipling   (E)   Matthew Arnold

(C)   Leander Jameson

57.   The mandate system established following World War I

(A)   was only applied to former German colonies

(B)   served to weaken European imperialism, since all mandates were promised
their independence in ten years

(C)   involved only France and Great Britain

(D)   quickly was the source of unrest in the Near East

(E)   was not accepted by the League of Nations

58.   In the years of its existence only one country was expelled from the League of
Nations. This country was

(A)   Japan, as a consequence of its aggression against China

(B)   Nazi Germany, in the wake of its attack on Austria

(C)   the Soviet Union, following its invasion of Finland

(D)   Italy, for its assault on Ethiopia

(E)   the regime of Francisco Franco, as a result of his brutal crushing of the
Spanish Republicans

59.   "ARTICLE III—It being obviously necessary and desirable, that British subjects should have some port where at they may care and refit their Ships, when
required, and keep stores for that purpose, His Majesty the Emperor of China
cedes to Her Majesty the Queen of Great Britain, etc., the Island of Hongkong,
to be possessed in perpetuity by her Britannic Majesty... ."

The statement above is derived from the treaty ending the

(A)   Boxer Rebellion

(D)   First Opium War

(B)   Sepoy Rebellion

(E)   Taiping Rebellion

(C)   Russo-Japanese War

60.   In the early 1930s, Stalin altered the Soviet Union's foreign policy

(A)   when he sought closer ties with Nazi Germany

(B)   by increasing the revolutionary activities of the Comintern worldwide

(C)   by drawing Russia into isolation

(D)   through seeking closer cooperation with the Western democracies

(E)   by withdrawing from the League of Nations

GERMAN ELECTIONS TO THE WEIMAR ASSEMBLY AND REICHSTAG, 1919–1933

(Number of seats obtained by the major parties, arranged with the Left at the top, the Right at the bottom)

	Jan. 1919	June 1920	May 1924	Dec. 1924	May 1928	Sept. 1930	July 1932	Nov. 1932	Mar. 1933
Communists	—a	2	62	45	54	77	89	100	81
Ind. Socialists	22	81	—b						
Social Demos	163	112	100	131	152	143	133	121	125
Democrats	74	45	28	32	25	14	4	2	5
Center	71	68	65	69	61	68	75	70	74
People's Party	22	62	44	51	45	30	7	11	2
Nationalists	42	66	96	103	78	41	40	51	52
Nazis	38	20	12	107	230	196	288		

a— The Communist Party boycotted the elections to the Weimar constituent assembly.

b— In these and succeeding elections the Independent Socialists merged with the Social Democrats.

61.   The chart above indicates which of the following?

(A)   The Nazi Party benefited most from the Great Depression.

(B)   A coalition of moderates in 1933 could have halted Hitler's rise to power.

(C)   In the 1920s the major threat to the Social Democrats came from the Center.

(D)   The French-Belgian occupation of the Ruhr resulted in loss of support for the Communists.

(E)   The economic recovery the Weimar Republic experienced in the mid-1920s substantially helped the Nazis win support.

62. "I say to the House as I said to Ministers who have joined this government, 'I have nothing to offer but blood, toil, sweat, and tears.' We have before us an ordeal of the most grievous kind. We have before us many, many months of struggle and suffering."

So spoke

(A) Otto von Bismarck

(D) Sir Edward Grey

(B) Georges Clemenceau

(E) Franklin Roosevelt

(C) Winston Churchill

63. Since the end of World War II, separatist movements have led to violence in

(A) Northern Ireland, Spain, and Yugoslavia

(B) Spain, Greece, and Holland

(C) Northern Ireland, Holland, and Portugal

(D) Greece, Yugoslavia, and Spain

(E) Portugal, Greece, and Northern Ireland

64. Most Nazi death camps (as opposed to concentration camps) were situated in which country—and why?

(A) Germany, so that Hitler and his cabinet could keep a close eye on them

(B) Austria, as "reward" for being Hitler's birthplace and the country most ardent in its support of Nazism

(C) Poland, because most of Europe's Jews lived there

(D) the Soviet Union, to show the enemy that Hitler had been sincere in his hatred of Bolshevism

(E) France, in order to make a Western democracy seem complicit in the awful crime of genocide

65. Economic aid from the United States for the reconstruction of Europe following World War II was announced in 1947 by

(A) Adlai Stevenson

(D) Dwight D. Eisenhower

(B) George Kennan

(E) John Foster Dulles

(C) George C. Marshall

66. Ecumenism, which has characterized the Catholic Church since the Second Vatican Council in 1963, is best described as

(A) calling for dogmatic adherence to church teachings

(B) increasing evangelic activity

(C)   promoting tolerance among Christians

(D)   expanding missionary work

(E)   encouraging less church involvement in politics

67.   The Soviet desire to reduce the level of international tensions during the Khrushchev era stemmed from Khrushchev's

(A)   conviction that Stalin had wholly misunderstood the intentions of the United States

(B)   desire to create in the West a false sense of security in preparation for the "final, inevitable triumph" of international communism

(C)   belief that the forces of Western capitalism were too strong to overcome

(D)   desire to move the Soviet Union away from the basic doctrines of Marxism-Leninism toward true "democratic socialism"

(E)   need to strengthen his position within the Soviet Union and avert the disintegration of the communist bloc in Eastern Europe

68.   The fact that the Nationalist Socialists were able to gain sufficient electoral support in the early 1930s to come to power was due, in part, to the anger generated by the Treaty of Versailles and the

(A)   communist efforts to seize power by force

(B)   triumph of Mussolini in Italy

(C)   achievements of Gustav Stresemann

(D)   inflation of the 1920s and depression of the early 1930s

(E)   enthusiastic support they received from revered President von Hindenburg

69.   The Green Party in West Germany is closely associated with

(A)   the interests of the country's influential agricultural bloc

(B)   the resurgence of Neo-Nazism

(C)   a strong environmentalist element in German society

(D)   social forces seeking the reunification of East and West Germany

(E)   a revived Pan-Germanic movement

70.   Factors that have contributed to the rapid rise in world population in recent decades include all of the following EXCEPT

(A)   a reversal in the traditional balance between births and deaths

(B)   medical advances eliminating or reducing earlier great plagues

(C)   the absence of any truly effective contraceptives

(D)   opposition of Third World leaders to sterilization and birth control devices, which were deemed to be a form of genocide by the West

(E)   marked declines in infant mortality

71.   On what basis did Baltic states demand independence from the USSR?

(A)   They were illegally annexed by Stalin in 1939.

(B)   Russian troops were not withdrawn in 1945, as the USSR had pledged.

(C)   They had no historical links with Russia.

(D)   They are ethnically distinct from Slavic Russians.

(E)   They wished to unite, instead, with the then unifying Germany.

72.   The march of history described by Marx appealed to workers partly because

(A)   the *Manifesto* painted a vision of workers unified throughout the world

(B)   it was based on nationalist zeal, a sentiment dear to most workers

(C)   it promised a utopia to the proletariat after the inevitable revolution

(D)   it showed how a communist cadre would rule in their best interests

(E)   it showed how workers must ally with the middle classes in order to achieve higher wages

73.   In 1958, Charles de Gaulle came to power in France in the midst of a crisis provoked by

(A)   a debate over the best policy concerning the conflict in Indochina

(B)   widespread riots on the part of French university students

(C)   the issue of French membership in NATO

(D)   controversy over the struggle against Algerian nationalists

(E)   the question of French membership in the Common Market

74.   "Aside from the demoralizing effect on the world at large, and the possibilities of disturbances as a result of the desperation of the people concerned … it is logical that the United States should do whatever it is able to do to assist in the return of normal economic health in the world, and without which there can be no political stability and no assured peace."

These sentiments, expressed in a speech given on June 5, 1947, reflected the program subsequently established by

(A) Winston Churchill   (D) Franklin Roosevelt

(B) George C. Marshall   (E) John Foster Dulles

(C) Dwight D. Eisenhower

75. The invasion of Egypt in 1956 by France, Britain, and Israel was the result of

    (A) the formation of the United Arab Republic to coordinate an attack on Israel

    (B) Egypt's announcement that it would not let the Soviet navy use its ports

    (C) Russia's announcement that it would assist Egypt in the construction of the Aswan dam in return for the right to build military bases

    (D) plans of president Nasser to nationalize the Suez Canal

    (E) Egyptian support for the communist rebels in Jordan, Israel's neighbor

76. Which is the best way to describe Willi Brandt's *Ostpolitik*?

    (A) It repudiated the lessons and practices of Bismarck's *Realpolitik*.

    (B) It sought to reconcile West German Communists with the dominant Social Democratic Party.

    (C) It was a hostile move by the FRG (West) to annex the GDR (East).

    (D) It exploited closer ties with the USSR to isolate France and Britain.

    (E) The FRG wanted to end its Cold War with the GDR and Poland.

77. What accident caused Europeans to rethink any expansion of nuclear power?

    (A) Three-Mile Island (United States)   (D) Bhopal (India)

    (B) Chernobyl (former USSR)   (E) North Korea

    (C) Nagasaki and Hiroshima (Japan)

78. Which statement is characteristic of the Brezhnev Doctrine?

    (A) The USSR had an obligation to help "socialist" revolutions anywhere.

    (B) Each country had a right to pursue its own road to communism.

    (C) The development of agriculture in the Soviet Union must take precedence over long-favored industry.

    (D) Any communist country had the right to intervene in the affairs of other communist countries in danger.

    (E) Jewish dissidents would be encouraged to leave the country.

79. All of the following were causes of Gorbachev's reforms of the USSR EXCEPT

    (A) environmental problems

    (B) increasing health problems among Soviet citizens

    (C) decline in industrial production

    (D) increasing oil prices

    (E) overcentralization of the economy

80. The scene below comes from *The Seventh Seal* (1957), a film by the Swedish director Ingmar Bergman. It is closest to which trend in postwar European cinema?

Courtesy Criterion Collection

    (A) the neo-Romanticism of Jean Cocteau

    (B) the neo-realism of the Italians Bertolucci and Pasolini et al.

    (C) the science-fiction world of the Russian Andrei Tarkovsky

    (D) the political satire of the Germans Fassbinder and Wenders

    (E) the historical docu-dramas of the Britons Merchant and Ivory

STOP
This is the end of Section I.
If time still remains, you may check your work only in this section.
Do not begin Section II until instructed to do so.

Section II

PART A – DOCUMENT-BASED ESSAY

TIME: Reading Period—15 minutes
Writing Time: 45 minutes
1 Essay Question

> **DIRECTIONS:** Read both the document-based essay question in Part A and the choices in Parts B and C during the reading period. Use the time to organize answers. You must answer Part A (the document-based essay question) and choose ONE question from Part B and ONE question from Part C to answer.

   This question is designed to test your ability to work with historical documents. As you analyze each document, take into account the source and the point of view of the author. Write an essay on the following topic that integrates historical facts and developments not mentioned in the documents.

   The last four centuries, centuries which saw the evolution of the national state in its modern form, have produced almost endless debates as to the rights and obligations of the individual citizen in relation to the state and the nature of the state itself. On the basis of the concepts advanced in the documents present here, discuss the diverse and changing views related to the citizen and the State which they reveal.

Document 1

—*The Great Leviathan or State,* Frontispiece to *Leviathan* by Hobbes, 1651

Document 2

"The state of monarchy is the supremest thing upon earth; for kings are not only God's lieutenants upon earth, and sit upon God's throne, but even by God Himself they are called gods...they may make and unmake their subjects, they have power of raising and casting down, of life and of death, judges over all their subjects and in all causes and yet accountable to none but God only."

—James I of England, Speech before Parliament, 1609

Document 3

"Princes are gods and participate somehow in divine independence....There is only God who may judge over their judgements and their persons....The prince may correct himself when he knows that he has done evil, but against his authority there is no remedy other than his own authority....The prince as prince is not regarded as an individual; he is a public personage....Let God withdraw His hand, and the world will fall into nothing; let authority cease in the realm, and all will be in confusion."

—Jacques-Bénigne Bossuet, circa 1660

Document 4

"The only way to erect such a common power, as may be able to defend them [the people] from the invasion of foreigners, and the injuries of one another, and thereby to secure them in such sort, as that by their own industry, and by the fruits of the earth, they may nourish themselves and live contentedly; is to confer all their power and strength upon one man, or upon one assembly of men ... there can happen no breach of covenant on the part of the sovereign; and consequently none of his subjects, by any pretence of forfeiture, can be freed from his subjection...."

—Excerpt from *Leviathan* by Thomas Hobbes, 1651

Document 5

"A man, as has been proved, cannot subject himself to the arbitrary power of another; and having, in the state of Nature, no arbitrary power over the life, liberty, or possession of another, but only so much as the law of Nature gave him for the preservation of himself and the rest of mankind, this is all he doth, or can give up to the commonwealth, and by it to the legislative power, so that the legislative can have no more than this. Their power in the utmost bounds of it is limited to the public good of society. It is a power that hath no other end but preservation, and therefore can never have a right to destroy, enslave, or designedly to impoverish the subjects...."

—John Locke, *Two Treatises on Civil Government,* 1690

Document 6

"Government cannot be good, if it does not have sole power....There cannot be two powers in one state....It is a great fortune for the prince and for the state when there are many philosophers to impress their teachings on the minds of men....The philosophers have no special interest, and are able to speak only in favor of reason and the public interest....The happiest thing that can happen to men, is for the prince to be a philosopher....He furthers the development of reason."

—Voltaire, *The Voice of the Sage and of the People*, 1750

Document 7

"[The prince] ought often to recollect he himself is but a man, like the least of his subjects. He is only the first servant of the state, who is obliged to act with probity and prudence; and to remain as totally disinterested as if he were each moment liable to render an account of his administrations to his fellow citizens."

—Frederick II, King of Prussia, "Duties of a Prince," 1781

Document 8

"To the end, therefore, that the social compact should not prove an empty form, it tacitly includes this engagement, which only can enforce the rest, *viz.* that whosoever refuses to pay obedience to the general will, shall be liable to it by the force of the whole body....It is agreed that what an individual alienates of his power, his possession, or his liberty, by the social compact, is only such parts of them whose use is of importance to the community; but it must be confessed also, that the sovereign is the only proper judge of this importance."

—J. J. Rousseau, *Social Contract*, 1762

Document 9

"[The liberties of Englishmen constitute an] entailed inheritance derived to us from our forefathers, and to be transmitted to our posterity as an estate specially belonging to people of this kingdom....A partnership in all art, a partnership in every virtue, and in all perfection. As the ends of such a partnership cannot be obtained in many generations, it becomes a partnership not only between those who are living, but between those who are living and those who are to be born."

—Edmund Burke, *Reflections on the Revolution in France,* 1790

Document 10

"Love your country. Your country is the land where your parents sleep, where is spoken that language in which the chosen of your heart blushing whispered the first word of love; it is the home that God has given you, that by striving to perfect yourselves therein, you may prepare to ascend to Him. It is your name, your glory, your sign among the people. Give it your thoughts, your counsels, your blood. Raise it up, great and beautiful as it was foretold by our great men."

—Giuseppe Mazzini, circa 1840

Document 11

"The citizen body is sovereign in the sense that no individual, no faction, no association can arrogate to itself a sovereignty not delegated to it by the people. But, there is a part of human life which necessarily remains individual and independent, and has the right to stand outside all social control. Where the independent life of the individual begins, the jurisdiction of the sovereignty ends. Rousseau failed to see this elementary truth, and the result of his error is that the *control social*, so often invoked in favor of liberty, is the most formidable ally of all despotisms."

—D. Constant, *Cours de Politique Constitutionnelle*, 1839

Document 12

"The sole end for which mankind is warranted, individually or collectively, in interfering with the liberty of action of any of their numbers, is self-protection ... the only purpose for which power can be rightfully exercised over any member of a civilized community, against his will, is to prevent harm to others. His own good, either physical or moral, is not sufficient warrant. He cannot rightfully be compelled to do or forebear because it will be better for him to do so, because it will make him happier, because, in the opinion of others, to do so would be wise, or even true.... No society in which these liberties are not, on the whole, respected, is free. The only freedom which deserves the name, is that of pursuing our own good in our own way, so long as we do not attempt to deprive others of theirs, or impeding their efforts to obtain it."

—John Stuart Mill, *On Liberty*

Document 13

"The State is in the first instance power, that it may maintain itself; it is not the totality of the people itself, as Hegel assumed in his deification of the State—the people is not altogether amalgamated with it; but the State protects and embraces the life of the people, regulating it externally in all directions. On principle it does not ask how the people is disposed; it demands obedience: its laws must be kept, whether willingly or unwillingly....When the State can no longer carry out what it wills, it perishes in anarchy...History wears thoroughly masculine features; it is not for sentimental natures or for women. Only brave nations have a secure existence, a future, a development; weak and cowardly nations go to the wall, and rightly so."

—Heinrich von Treitschke, *Lectures on Politics*, circa 1880

Document 14

"It is that in all places people of the same race, the same language, the same religion, and the same customs regard each other as brothers and work for independence and self-government, and organize a more perfect government to work for the public welfare and to oppose the infringement of other races."

—Liang Ch'i-ch'ao, *The Renovation of the People*, 1902

Document 15

"What is the significance of this revolution? Its significance is, in the first place, that we shall have a soviet government, without the participation of bourgeoisie of any kind. The oppressed masses will of themselves form a government. The old state machinery will be smashed into bits and in its place will be created a new machinery of government by the soviet organizations. From now on there is a new page in the history of Russia, and the present, third Russian revolution shall in its final result lead to the victory of Socialism."

—V. I. Lenin, Petrograd, November 1917

Document 16

"The State is only a means towards an end. Its highest aim is the care and maintenance of those primeval racial elements which create the beauty and dignity of a higher civilization....The dead mechanism [of the old State] must be replaced by a living organism based on the herd instinct, which appears when all are of one blood....One must never forget it: the majority can never replace the leader. It [the majority] is not only stupid but cowardly. You cannot get the wise man out of a hundred fools, and a heroic decision cannot come out of a hundred cowards."

—Adolf Hitler, *Mein Kampf,* 1924

STOP
This is the end of Section II, Part A.
If time still remains, you may check your work only in this section.
Do not begin Section II, Part B until instructed to do so.

PART B – Essay Question

TIME: 35 minutes
   1 Essay Question

> **DIRECTIONS:** Answer ONE question from the three questions below. Choose the question that you are most prepared to answer thoroughly. You should spend about 5 minutes organizing or outlining your answer.

1.   "The Crimean War, 1852–1856, was one of the silliest wars ever fought; yet its consequences were extraordinarily important for Russia and for Europe as a whole..."

   —William H. McNeill, *A History of the World Community*

   Discuss the origins of the Crimean War, whether it was "silly," and then discuss the "extraordinarily important" consequences of it on Russia and Europe.

2.   The Reformation at first was primarily a religious protest, but it soon gave rise to calls for social and political change. Discuss how Luther's ideas often inadvertently led to changes in the role of women, peasants, and princes.

3.   Historians speak of an "Old Imperialism," circa 1500–1750, and the "New Imperialism," circa 1880–1914. Compare and contrast these eras, and indicate reasons why, and to what extent, they differed.

STOP
This is the end of Section II, Part B.
If time still remains, you may check your work only in this section.
Do not begin Section II, Part C until instructed to do so.

PART C – Essay Question

TIME: 35 minutes
   1 Essay Question

> **DIRECTIONS:** Answer ONE question from the three questions below. Choose the question that you are most prepared to answer thoroughly. You should spend about 5 minutes organizing or outlining your answer.

4. "The Scientific Revolution of the sixteenth and seventeenth centuries also entailed radical changes in man's perception of and relations with the world, with society, and with his fellow man." Discuss the extent to which this statement hits the truth.

5. After World War II, key leaders sought to unify Europe in order to avoid further nationalist strife. Discuss how they began this trend and difficulties encountered along the way to the euro's introduction, 1999–2002.

6. The Industrial Revolution began in the eighteenth century and had dramatically altered most of Europe by 1914. Discuss the nature of this trend, how it spread, and its effects on society, economies, and politics of major countries in Europe.

END OF EXAM

PRACTICE EXAM 4

AP European History

Answer Key

1. (C)	21. (D)	41. (D)	61. (A)
2. (D)	22. (B)	42. (D)	62. (C)
3. (B)	23. (B)	43. (D)	63. (A)
4. (C)	24. (C)	44. (E)	64. (C)
5. (B)	25. (B)	45. (C)	65. (C)
6. (C)	26. (C)	46. (B)	66. (C)
7. (B)	27. (C)	47. (C)	67. (E)
8. (E)	28. (C)	48. (D)	68. (D)
9. (A)	29. (B)	49. (C)	69. (C)
10. (B)	30. (A)	50. (C)	70. (C)
11. (E)	31. (D)	51. (D)	71. (A)
12. (C)	32. (B)	52. (C)	72. (C)
13. (E)	33. (A)	53. (B)	73. (D)
14. (C)	34. (B)	54. (C)	74. (B)
15. (D)	35. (B)	55. (C)	75. (D)
16. (C)	36. (D)	56. (B)	76. (E)
17. (B)	37. (D)	57. (D)	77. (B)
18. (B)	38. (D)	58. (C)	78. (D)
19. (A)	39. (C)	59. (D)	79. (D)
20. (E)	40. (B)	60. (D)	80. (B)

PRACTICE EXAM 4

AP European History

Detailed Explanations of Answers

Section I

1. **(C)**

    This is a difficult question, but eliminate two unlikely choices—1400 (A) and 1750 (E). The former would mean massive procreation with little infant mortality, and the latter a suspiciously long amount of time. If you learned in your course that the plague was endemic rather than a one-time epidemic, then (C) or (D) looks likeliest, so guess. Studying **one** demographic chart of European population, 1350–2000, will prepare you for several possible questions.

2. **(D)**

    There is nothing pagan in the painting (A), a Protestant heretic would not be called a saint (B), the ecstasy on Agatha's face does not (C) point to horrors of war, and though anatomy was a part of the schooling of artists, there is nothing to indicate (E) any relation between medicine and art in this painting. The Spanish-sounding name ("Zubaran") is a clue, but you also learned the tenets of the Counter-Reformation and the hallmarks of Baroque art.

3. **(B)**

    This treaty, brokered by Pope Alexander VI in 1494, divided the world beyond Europe between Spain and Portugal. At the request of the Portuguese, the original line drawn down the Atlantic was moved westward. Since this occurred prior to the official discovery of Brazil, historians think that the Portuguese already knew of Brazil's existence. It was not on the Portuguese route to the East (A). The Spanish were not aware of its existence when the Portuguese claimed it (C) and (D). The Treaty of Utrecht (E) ended the War of the Spanish Succession several centuries later.

4. **(C)**

    The piety of the Northern Renaissance was reflected in the writings of Christian humanists such as Erasmus and Thomas à Kempis and the religious art of Dürer.

Like the Southern or Italian Renaissance, the Renaissance in the north had a strong financial basis (A), that of the wealth of the commercial enterprises of southern Germany, Flanders, and the Hansa cities. Both its architectural (B) and artistic achievements were significant. There was little Byzantine influence (D), nor was there any indication of New World influences (E).

5. **(B)**

Machiavelli wrote *The Prince*, a realistic look at the manner in which the ruler should govern his Renaissance state. Lorenzo Valla (A) was a humanist scholar of the Italian Renaissance who demonstrated that the "Donation of Constantine" was a forgery; Montaigne was a significant French humanist and philosopher of the late sixteenth century (C); while Grotius (D) was a Dutch legal theorist who wrote on international law, particularly as it related to warfare. Huizinga (E) was a modern historian of the early modern period.

6. **(C)**

The Tudor dynasty was established in the person of Henry VII. England lost its holdings in France (A) at the end of the Hundred Years' War in 1453, while Anglicanism (B) was proclaimed the religion of England during the reign of Henry VIII, and the monastic establishments were abolished (D) during the same reign. England and Scotland were unified (E) only in the first decade of the eighteenth century.

7. **(B)**

The activities of the Dominican Tetzel and his unbridled commercialism in the sale of indulgences prompted Luther to act. The other issues noted, while at various times severe problems within the church, were not of immediate concern to Luther when he posted the "Ninety-Five Theses."

8. **(E)**

Luther knew vaguely of Copernicus's view and disapproved, because it contradicted the Bible; so felt early Protestants. Careless texts single out the Galileo trial and neglect to say that Protestants were just as antiscientific as Catholics. All other factors mentioned were significant in contributing to the success of the religious revolt launched by Luther in German lands.

9. **(A)**

The fact that three choices are restricted to cottons gives a clue that something might be wrong with including woolens in this question; and the tip-off is "mechanization." (D) and (E) are plausible, even if you know little about these facts; (C) includes facts you learned; and given what you learned about the Seven Years' War, (B) is possible.

10. **(B)**

Answer (A) may trip the unwary; read on. You should know that Joseph, Frederick, and Stein (C, D, E) were reformers, so do not balk at the unfamiliar name, Pombal. He was an enlightened minister associated with the expulsion of the Jesuits from Portugal. If you recall, Louis XV of France was not associated with any reform except at the end of his reign, when he banned the *parlements*, and that was NOT done for enlightened reasons.

11. **(E)**

The new monarchs, William and Mary, were required to accept the "Bill of Rights" and the ultimate authority of Parliament. The Hanoverian dynasty (A) only assumed the throne on the death of Queen Anne (1714), while Cromwell (B) died a natural death nearly three decades prior to 1688. Anglicanism was proclaimed the religion of England in the reign of Henry VIII in the early sixteenth century (C).

12. **(C)**

It was designed to exclude England from all trade with the Continent. Joseph Bonaparte was placed on the Spanish throne in 1809 (B). France had little desire to see a unified Germany (A), although the "Redaction of 1803" did reduce the number of German states to 39. He was allied with Russia in 1806 (D), going to war with her only in 1812. After his earlier activities in Egypt, he undertook no further military operations in that region (E).

13. **(E)**

With its defeat in the war, Russian interests in the Far East were abandoned for the time being. The Japanese did not annex Manchuria (C) until 1931, while in 1910 Japan annexed all of Korea (B). Russia had sold Alaska (A) earlier and also acquired the Maritime Provinces (D) from China at an earlier date.

14. **(C)**

Alexander II began a series of reforms, including the emancipation of the serfs. Russia had acquired access to the Black Sea earlier (A), in the reign of Catherine the Great, while a Duma (E) was established in 1905. There was no revolution in the years immediately following the Crimean War (B), the first occurring in 1905.

15. **(D)**

Mercantilism might be envisioned as economic warfare in which one nation sought to gain an advantage over another through the acquisition of wealth in terms of precious metal. Items (A), (B), and (C), while facets of mercantilism, were secondary and contributory to the main goal of the acquisition of wealth. Laissez-faire economics (E) were diametrically in opposition to the fundamental principles of mercantilism.

16. **(C)**

France applied very rigid religious and political restrictions on those permitted to migrate to the New World. The Indians, in contact with the French and British, overwhelmingly supported the French (A). France's population was much larger than that of England (B). The French explorers and merchants penetrated the interior to a much greater extent than the English (D), and their missionaries were generally more successful in their relations with the Indians (E).

17. **(B)**

Raw wool was distributed to workers outside guild-regulated towns, frequently peasants who spun and wove it in their homes. The domestic system, where work was "put out," was not related to ship construction (A), which was not a state monopoly. The true factory had not yet appeared in the textile industry, though when it did, unions (C) were long prohibited. It was not related to agricultural practices (D) and had little or no relation to the admission of foreign workers (E).

18. **(B)**

The Royal African Company of Great Britain received the right to provide slaves for a period of thirty years. Gibraltar was ceded to England in the Treaty of Utrecht (A). Spain did not grant Britain a free hand to trade in Spain's Caribbean holdings (C), nor was Guadeloupe (D) or Florida (E) involved in the Treaty of Utrecht.

19. **(A)**

The phrase is from Hobbes's *Leviathan*. John Milton (B), an English poet and Cromwell's secretary, was the author of *Paradise Lost*; Blackstone was a leading English legalist (C); d'Holbach was a French *philosophe* (D); and Bossuet was a bishop who advised King Louis XIV and ardently defended the theory of divine right monarchy (E).

20. **(E)**

Sweden, France, Austria, and Denmark were all involved militarily in the conflict. England, distracted by Puritan attacks on the Stuarts, remained aloof.

21. **(D)**

Defeating Sweden in this war, Peter gained control of extensive areas of the southern shore of the Baltic Sea and built the city of St. Petersburg. Peter's half-brother (A) was Alexis. Although he temporarily gained Azov on the Black Sea, Peter lost it later (B), and it was left to Catherine the Great to secure the northern shores of the Black Sea for Russia. The push across the vastness of Siberia (C) had been carried out earlier, while the defeat of the *streltsi* (palace guards) and Old Believers (E) was unrelated to the Great Northern War.

22. **(B)**

The Peace of Augsburg related only to those of the Catholic and Lutheran faiths. The Peace of Augsburg did not touch upon either Italy (A) or France (D), while no mention was made of the Anabaptists (C), a sect persecuted by all major religions. The limited powers of the emperor *were* clearly defined (E).

23. **(B)**

In his *Spirit of the Laws*, Montesquieu divided the functions of government into the executive, judicial, and legislative bodies. The other men all wrote on the subject of government, their views ranging from favoritism of absolutistic government (Hobbes) to democracy (Rousseau), but none focused specifically on the issue of separation of power as did Montesquieu.

24. **(C)**

You should know about the main artistic movements. This is clearly Rococo from its pastels, naughty subject, and carefree air. That the young man seems to be looking up the young lady's dress disqualifies this work from inclusion in the other categories, which never allowed erotic frivolity like this.

25. **(B)**

Catherine's military victories at the expense of the Crimean Tatars, together with the extensive territories gained at the expense of the Poles in three partitions of their country, achieved a significant expansion of her country's holdings. Russian access to ports on the Mediterranean remained markedly limited by Turkish control of the Dardanelles well into the twentieth century (C). Prior to Peter the Great, direct assess to open waters in European Russia was limited to *Archangel* on the White Sea (Arctic Ocean). While Peter the Great attempted to expand toward the Black Sea, he was unsuccessful (D). On the basis of the information provided on the map, it is impossible to determine the extent of Russia's share of the partition (E).

26. **(C)**

Sans-culottes meant "without knee-breeches," which were worn by most of the upper classes. Urban workers pioneered in the wearing of long pants, more sensible (and warmer) for their needs. Opponents of the Civil Constitution of the Clergy (E), which included many peasants (A) and priests (B), were simply viewed as counterrevolutionaries, while those nobles who fled the violence of the revolution for safety in the German region (D) were designated as emigrés.

27. **(C)**

Proclaiming themselves a national assembly, they swore not to disband until they had established a constitution for the country. The other objectives noted only came as the Revolution gained momentum.

28. **(C)**

The universities, largely dominated by the Church, did not provide the proper atmosphere for scientific research. All of the other statements regarding the role of and attitude toward scientific investigation are valid.

29. **(B)**

Fought on the outskirts of Quebec, Canada, in 1759, the battle led to the annexation of virtually all French holdings in North America by the British in the Treaty of Paris in 1763. The defeat of the Stuarts in the Battle of Culloden, April 16, 1746, basically ended their efforts to reclaim the English throne (A). In the course of the Seven Years' War, Austria did, in fact, lose Silesia to Prussia, but in a struggle distinct from that between Britain and France (C). The War of the Spanish Succession (D) occurred a half-century earlier. The struggle for India (E), waged between Clive and Dupleix, was decided at the Battle of Plassey.

30. **(A)**

Deists, though critical of doctrines of the established religions, did believe in basic standards of what was right and wrong. Perceiving God as the prime creator and mover (C), they believed that, having established the natural laws by which humans should act (D), God did not intervene in humans' everyday lives (B). Humans, possessing reason, should learn to live in conformity (E) with those natural laws.

31. **(D)**

The Navigation Acts were laws designed to strengthen England's economy and foreign trade. They were initially designed to weaken Holland, in the mid-seventeenth century the most powerful mercantile state in Europe. While designed to enhance England's trade, they did not legalize infringement of Spain's monopolistic trade system—though English merchants had, in fact, and illegally, long done so.

32. **(B)**

The Mongols defeated Russian forces in the 1240s and thereafter exacted tribute from Russia well into the fourteenth century when, at the Battle of Kulikovo in 1380, Dmitri Donskoi turned the tide against them. But it was not until Ivan III stopped paying tribute in 1480 that Muscovy effectively achieved sovereign independence for all the Russias from the Golden Horde. The subsequent actions of Ivan the Terrible, Mikhail Romanov, and Peter the Great were all enabled by the bold refusal of Ivan the Great (III) in 1480.

33. **(A)**

Founded during the reign of Charles II Stuart (not James Stuart, B), the Royal Society was dedicated to scientific investigation. The Royal Society was not involved directly in religious (C), colonial (D), or economic activities (E).

34. **(B)**

The words are derived from Ricardo's writings on the so-called "Iron Law of Wages." Jeremy Bentham (A) was the founder of the Utilitarian school of social philosophy; Robert Peel was an important English politician and reformer of the early nineteenth century (D); David Hume was an English *philosophe* of the eighteenth century (E), while Robert Owen was an English utopian socialist (C).

35. **(B)**

Among other reforms they sought were the vote for virtually every male adult and parliamentary elections every year. A different group (called Luddites) opposed mechanization, which they saw as threatening their livelihood, and sought to destroy machines (A). English landowners (C) generally approved of duties to protect their agricultural interests. Babeuf (D), a proto-Communist of revolutionary France, had a handful of followers known as the Society of Equals. The Levellers were opponents of Cromwell (E).

36. **(D)**

While it was a gradual improvement, studies have shown that an improvement in the conditions of the working class in European industrial societies did take place. The standard of living in agrarian society, it has been shown, was not necessarily superior to that of the industrial worker (A). While hours were perhaps increased initially, laws gradually cut the hours of labor (B). Women's financial contribution (C) tended to increase as their numbers in the labor force mounted.

37. **(D)**

Through her military activities, Catherine added extensively to Russian territory in the Crimean and Black Sea areas. While imposing ever greater restrictions on the serfs (A), she enhanced the privileges of the nobles (E). The Slavophile movement (B), like the expansion of Russia to Vladivostok (C), was a later development in Russian history.

38. **(D)**

In his *Reflections on the Revolution in France*, Burke spoke out for evolutionary, not revolutionary, change. Opposed to the radical changes taking place in France (A), he saw the American Revolution (E) as the result of a natural, evolutionary process and held that the colonials should be allowed to go free without a struggle (B). Institutions (C) such as the French monarchy, if not attuned to the times, should be reformed, not simply destroyed.

39. **(C)**

Much of the nineteenth century was to see revolutionary violence stemming from nationalistic and liberal aspirations thwarted by the decisions made at Vienna. The decisions reached at Vienna did not touch upon the Ottomans (A). Louis (B), overall, did not prove a bad king. Norway was ceded to Sweden at Vienna (D), while the Carlsbad Decrees (E) were passed several years after the Congress of Vienna (1819).

40. (B)

The Duma was established in Russia only in 1905 by Czar Nicholas II. All of the other reforms noted were part of the program of Alexander II.

41. (D)

The Pushkin/Mussorgsky classic (A) has an evil tsar, priests abound in Leskov (B), and *Uncle Tom's Cabin* (E) exposed oppression of American slaves, but most often allusions are made to works in the same genre—words to words, images to images, etc. The title of Repin's classic gives a valuable clue. There is nothing in Tolstoy (C) to suggest this harsh indictment.

42. (D)

Social Darwinism tended to be highly nationalistic rather than cosmopolitan. With utilization of the concept of "survival of the fittest" derived from Darwin's theories, all of the other activities mentioned could be justified.

43. (D)

Serbia was extremely active in stirring up the nationalistic feelings of Serbs living within Austrian territory, an activity that contributed greatly to the coming of World War I. The Czechs were, in fact, more advanced politically than the Serbs (A). Both wanted independence (B) and (E). Germany, as a close ally of the Austrians, was not inclined to support the Slavic Czechs (C).

44. (E)

The German comic Kurt Tucholsky once lamented that no one had killed a Hohenzollern. Those assassinated were President Sadi Carnot of France (1894), conservative leader Canovas del Castillo of Spain (1897), empress Elizabeth of Austria (1898) and King Umberto I of Italy (1900). A clue is the popularity of anarchism in "Latin" countries (France, Italy, Spain). The choice is then between Austria (which would attract a more important assassin in 1914) and Germany, which did not suffer a wave of assassinations until 1922.

45. (C)

The Sinn Fein, the nationalist party in Ireland, broke out in open revolt at Easter of 1916. It was crushed. All of the other regions remained loyal during the war.

46. (B)

Both men, one a Frenchman, the other English, were ardent racists, believing firmly in the superiority of the German "race." Existentialism (A) as a philosophy developed largely after their deaths, as did the Dadaist art movement (E). They wrote little or nothing in the area of economics (C), and they died prior to 1930 (D).

47. **(C)**

These are three of the "Fourteen Points" of Woodrow Wilson that he tried to make the basis of the treaty ending World War I. The Atlantic Charter (A) was an agreement stating the vision of the postwar world signed by Churchill and Roosevelt. The Treaty of Versailles (B), ending World War I, did not incorporate any of the Fourteen Points. The McMahon Letters (D) related to Anglo-Arab relations during World War I, while the Kellogg-Briand Pact (E) was an international agreement of the 1920s.

48. **(D)**

The Austrians in Italy and their own country were slow to react to the revolutionary violence in its initial stages, as were the Prussian and French rulers. Class conflict (A), ethnic rivalries (B), and lack of strong unity among the revolutionary elements (C) tended to characterize the revolutionary movements. Fear of external intervention (E), as occurred in Hungary, where Russian troops intervened, was not uncommon.

49. **(C)**

Socialists, except for the most radical, generally strongly supported the national interests of their own countries during the conflict. All of the other statements are true.

50. **(C)**

The cartoon depicts the kimono-clad Japanese as walking a tight-wire (or in this case a wobbly bamboo pole) and clearly arousing the ire of the Russian bear. There are no indications in the cartoon of the nature of the risk Japan was running or of any outside power being involved in the affair.

51. **(D)**

Incendiary bombs were introduced in the course of World War II. All of the other weapons were utilized in World War I.

52. **(C)**

The ultra-nationalistic, elitist, and racial theories, to name a few elements of the fascist movement, all had strong roots in diverse nineteenth-century ideologies. The cult leader (A) (i.e., Der Fuehrer, Il Duce, etc.), the monolithic party (E), ultra-nationalism (D), and the demand for absolute loyalty (B) were all elements of the fascist movement.

53. **(B)**

An international accord of the Locarno Era, the Kellogg-Briand Pact was signed by a score of nations in 1928 with the overly optimistic idea of "outlawing warfare." The Locarno Treaties (A) were a series of international accords signed in 1925, including a guarantee of Germany's western borders and a mutual defense accord among France,

Poland, and Czechoslovakia. The Treaty of Versailles (C) ended World War I between Germany and the Allies. There were two Treaties of Rapallo (E), one in 1920 between Italy and Yugoslavia that made Fiume a free state and ceded Zara to Italy, the second in 1922 between Germany and the Soviet Union that cancelled the former's reparation payments. The Lytton Commission Report (D) dealt with Japanese aggression in Manchuria in 1931.

54. **(C)**

France has not had in the modern era a woman who served either as premiere or president, the two principal executive offices. All of the other nations have at one time or another had a woman as their chief executive officer: India—Nehru; England—Thatcher; Pakistan—Bhutto; Israel—Meir.

55. **(C)**

With the discharge of tens of thousands of soldiers and the general industrial slump that occurred in the years following the end of the war, Great Britain's problem was one of severe unemployment, not a labor shortage. All of the other statements regarding Great Britain's economic situation are true.

56. **(B)**

The excerpt is from the poem "The White Man's Burden" by Kipling, one of the great apostles of English imperialism. Cecil Rhodes (A) was a South African gold and diamond magnate, statesman, and a great practitioner of imperialism, while Jameson (C) was his agent in his efforts to gain control of the Transvaal from the Boers. Yeats (D) was an Irish poet, Arnold (E) a literary critic.

57. **(D)**

The Arabs, formerly under Ottoman domination, felt they had been deprived of promised independence when they were placed under mandates. Also, the struggle between Zionist and Arab claims in Palestine quickly erupted. Ottoman lands (A) as well as German were taken. The term of the mandate holdings varied (B). Japan, South Africa, and the United States also received mandates (C). The mandates were technically under the supervision of the League (E).

58. **(C)**

The Soviet Union was the only nation to be expelled from the League, this for its "Winter War" with Finland. Germany, Japan, and Italy walked out of the League, while Franco did not represent the legal Spanish government.

59. **(D)**

The excerpt is from the Treaty of Nanking (1842), which ended the First Opium War and saw the island of Hong Kong ceded to England. The Tai-ping Rebellion (E) was an internal rebellion in China in the mid-nineteenth century, while the Sepoy Rebellion (B) occurred in India at approximately the same time. The Russo-Japanese War (C) and the Boxer Rebellion (A) took place in the first decade of the twentieth century, and neither directly involves Great Britain or touched upon control of Hong Kong.

60. **(D)**

Frightened by the rise of an aggressive Japan and Germany, Stalin sought closer relations with anti-fascist (A) governments in the West. Stalin's actions represented an attempt to break with the isolation of Russia (C) that had previously existed. To win favor with the West, the Comintern was dissolved (B). Formerly not a member of the League of Nations, the Soviet Union was admitted to that organization in 1934 (E).

61. **(A)**

The elections of 1928, prior to the onset of the Depression, saw the Nazis as the smallest party of those represented on the chart; by 1933, they were the largest. A union of all the parties represented on the chart for March 1933 would still not have outvoted the Nazis (B). The major threat to the Social Democrats in the 1920s came either from the Independent Socialists, the Nationalists, or the Nazis (C). The French-Belgian occupation of the Ruhr (D), occurring in 1923, boosted the Communist representation in the Assembly notably, while the Weimar Republic's subsequent economic recovery (E) hurt the Nazis.

62. **(C)**

The excerpt is from a speech made by Winston Churchill in the days immediately following the evacuation of British military forces from Dunkirk. Otto von Bismarck (A), the "Iron Chancellor," was the chancellor of Prussia in the second half of the nine-teenth century, Clemenceau was the premiere of France during World War I (B), Sir Edward Grey was England's foreign minister during that conflict (D), while Roosevelt was the president of the United States (E) from 1934 to 1945.

63. **(A)**

Northern Ireland has been the scene of a blood struggle on the part of those Irish Catholics who wish unification with the Republic of Ireland, while the Basques in Spain and Croats of Yugoslavia have also carried on terrorists activities directed at separatism. Greece, Portugal, and Holland have experienced no such movements.

64. **(C)**

Hitler wanted to keep the mass murders in his death camps from his "constituents," the Germans and Austrians, so placing death camps anywhere in western or central Europe was never considered (so A, B, and E are wrong). The Wehrmacht secured western Poland first, and only later parts of eastern Poland and Russia, so C is most logical. The six death camps in western Poland were Auschwitz-Birkenau, Belzec, Chelmno, Majdanek, Sobibor, and Treblinka.

65. **(C)**

Marshall, Secretary of State in 1947, enunciated the so-called Marshall Plan. Stevenson (A), governor of Illinois, was a presidential candidate on the Democratic slate in 1952; he was defeated by Eisenhower. Kennan (B) was an important official with the State Department; Eisenhower (D) was supreme commander of the Western Allied forces in the invasion of Europe in World War II and twice president of the United States; and Dulles (E) was secretary of state under Eisenhower.

66. **(C)**

Ecumenism, one of several important reforms of the Catholic Church at the Second Vatican Council, is a call for toleration between different Christian denominations. While choices (B), increasing evangelic activity, and (D), missionary work, might seem plausible, there is no direct link with ecumenism. Preaching dogma (A) runs counter to this idea, and choice (E), less church involvement in politics, is again not "ecumenical" and is also belied by the church's outspoken opposition to nuclear weaponry, among other issues.

67. **(E)**

Strains were showing on the domestic scene of the Soviet Union, particularly in the area of consumer goods, as they were in the Soviet's relations with its satellite states. Khrushchev, although he initiated the de-Stalinization campaign, had no doubts, at least openly expressed, regarding the superiority of the Soviet system or the certainty of the Marxist-Leninist theory of history.

68. **(D)**

Germany was severely hit by the Depression, and many of the middle and upper class, fearing communism, turned to Hitler seemingly as the only alternative. The communists, like Hitler, sought power through the ballot box (A). Mussolini's rise to power (B), occurring a decade earlier, had little or no effect on the situation in Germany. Stresemann (C), who had pulled Germany to its feet after the disastrous depression of 1923, had actually set back Hitler's political aspirations. President von Hindenburg (E) loathed Hitler.

69. **(C)**

The Green Party has led a strong environmentalist drive in West Germany, holding that the extensive, and unchecked, industrialization of the country was destroying the atmosphere and landscape. Neither Neo-Nazi (B) nor Pan-Germanic (E), the Green Party's attitude toward German reunification (D) or agricultural (A) policies do not represent its primary goals.

70. **(C)**

Numerous contraceptive devices have been developed in the years since the end of World War II and have been available to a significant portion of the world's population.

All of the other factors mentioned have contributed significantly to the ballooning global population.

71. **(A)**

The Baltic peoples long maintained—and the Soviets under Gorbachev have conceded—that they were illegally annexed in 1939 by Stalin. The Soviets did not withdraw their troops (B), but they had given no such promise to do so at Yalta. The Baltic peoples, at least the Estonians and Latvians, were under Russian domination from the time of Peter the Great to 1919 (C), when they gained their independence in the wake of the Russian Revolution. They are ethnically different, although each of the Baltic states has a sizeable number of ethnic Russians living in them (D). They have no desire to be under German control (E).

72. **(C)**

"Come the Revolution," Marx held out the vision of the rise of a classless "workers' paradise." While the idea of the unity of the workers of the world (A) was a facet of Marx's doctrines, it was seen as merely a step in the desired end of a workers' paradise. Marx opposed nationalism (B), which he thought weakened the true goals of the ultimate revolution. He did not speak of an elite leadership (D) (this was Lenin's idea) and he did not perceive of an alliance (E) between the working and middle classes, actually seeing them as enemies.

73. **(D)**

De Gaulle came to power in the midst of the bitter conflict between the French and Algerian nationalists. By the time de Gaulle came to power, the French had withdrawn from Indochina (A); the other questions arose subsequent to his assuming power.

74. **(B)**

This speech, made by Secretary of State George C. Marshall, marked the inauguration of the idea of the Marshall Plan designed to bring about the economic rehabilitation of Europe following World War II. It was firmly supported by the other statesmen noted, save Roosevelt, who had died in 1945.

75. **(D)**

Israel invaded Egypt after Nasser attempted to nationalize the Suez Canal. The invasion was a failure, largely due to the pressure put on the invaders by the United States and the United Nations. The other diplomatic activities on the part of Egypt, while occurring, were not related to the invasion.

76 **(E)**

Linguists may see that "Ost" looks like "east"—a clue. This was the time in which the "Cold Warrior," U.S. President Nixon, inaugurated a similar program of détente toward the USSR and China, so context helps. Since (C) and (E) are mutually exclusive, unless both are wrong, one must be right. Many texts include a photograph of Brandt kneeling at a World War II shrine in Warsaw (Poland), an act (*der Kniefall*) resented by some Germans as humiliating, praised by others as an act of atonement for German atrocities in Poland.

77. **(B)**

The explosion at the Chernobyl nuclear power plant near Kiev caused Europeans to rethink expansion of nuclear power: One former Soviet scientist, Leonid Toptunov, has reported that more than 600,000 people received high doses of radiation—and their names have been entered in a medical register for the rest of their lives—because of the 1986 accident. Three-Mile Island (A), in Middletown, Pennsylvania, was the site of a nuclear power plant accident in 1979 that resulted in the release of small amounts of radioactive gases through the plant's venting system and the formation of a hydrogen gas bubble in the reactor's containment vessel. The atomic bombing of Nagasaki and Hiroshima (C), Japan, was carried out by the United States at the end of World War II. In 1984, Bhopal (D), India, was the site of a massive chemical plant explosion and poisonous gas leak.

78. **(D)**

This right of intervention was clearly seen in the invasion of Czechoslovakia by the Warsaw Pact States. The idea of assisting communist revolutions around the world (A) has been asserted from an early period, while the idea of communist states having the right to pursue their own path (B), such as Yugoslavia or China, did not sit well with most Soviet leaders. In the 1970s and 1980s dissident Jews were harassed by the Soviet government because of their appeals to foreign opinion (mainly the United States) for help in securing emigration to Israel (E).

79. **(D)**

By the 1980s, the political, economic, and environmental climate of the Soviet Union was precarious. Oil prices actually remained fairly stable during the period leading up to Gorbachev's reforms. The totalitarian regimes that preceded Gorbachev (A) had allowed environmental problems to proliferate, one consequence of which was increasing health problems for Soviet citizens (B). Declining industrial production made it difficult for the Soviet Union to compete with the West in developing arms and providing its citizens with a level of industrial output to which Western Europeans and Americans had become accustomed (C). This was due in part to an overcentralized economy (E) that provided no incentives for factory managers and industrial entities to become more efficient.

80. **(B)**

Though Bergman's film has magic realist shadings, its attention to the brutalities of plague and war align it decidedly with the related neo-realist Italian school. (A) Cocteau's *La Belle et la Bête* (1946) has none of Bergman's angst over the existence of God and meaning of life. In Bergman's film there is no science fiction (C), German-style satire (D), nor any pretense at historical veracity (E), which Merchant and Ivory only attempted for scenery and costumes, never in the gist of their novel-based romances.

Section II

Sample Answer to Document-Based Question

The major states of Western Europe had, in the course of the sixteenth century, begun to assume a more modern form. As competition among the nations both intensified and increasingly became of a global nature, the need for both internal unity and strength against potential foreign foes increased. Yet, emerging from the medieval period, there remained in the states numerous domestic forces that hampered the development of truly centralized administrations, strong administrations that were essential if the state was to survive and thrive. Feudal aristocracies jealous of the privileged position, a peasant class whose concept of political loyalty frequently did not extend beyond the local village or, at best, their own province, and deep divisions along religious lines were but a few of these divisive elements.

Lacking anything but the vaguest perception of the modern idea of nationalism, it was the princes who became—and deliberately made of themselves—the focal point of the state, the symbol about which the people of the state were expected to rally and to whom they were to give their unswerving obedience. This was the age of the absolute monarch and the divine-right monarch. Documents 1 through 4 present both visual and written portraits of, and justification for, such rulers. As is seen in the illustration from Hobbes's *Leviathan*, the monarch is conceived of as embodying in his person all of his subjects. James I Stuart of England, one of the most ardent exponents of "divine-right" rule, saw the monarchs' unchallengeable status as being derived from God: Princes were indeed, in his eyes, no less than gods on earth. Whether he actually believed this or, fearing that a state lacking a supreme, unquestioned sovereign power would fall into a state of confusion as held by Bishop Bossuet, simply sought to wrap his rule in a cloak of divinity is difficult to determine. Certainly King Louis XIV of France, tutored by Bossuet, was convinced that an aura of the divine shrouded his reign. James's vision of his status did not, in fact, go unchallenged, for in England, unlike France, there existed a strong middle-class element and a parliamentarian tradition to stand in opposition, one so strong that it eventually brought James's son Charles I to the execution block. It was as a consequence of the Puritan Revolution that Hobbes, horrified by what he perceived as anarchy, argued for the need to vest absolute power in the hands of one man or body of men: His argument was based not on any concept of the ruler possessing a mandate from God but, rather, the belief that the only alternative was the confusion Bossuet had prophesied.

Locke (Document 5), like Hobbes, admitted that humans, if completely unchecked by authority, could be a threat to the welfare of others. But while recognizing the need for authority, unlike Hobbes he did not believe that humans, in forming a covenant with a sovereign power, surrendered completely all their rights and freedoms, rights that, in the course of the "Glorious Revolution" of 1688, an event in which Locke was intimately involved, the English embodied in their Bill of Rights. That Revolution established the fact that England's monarch, far from being a divine or absolute ruler, was a constitutional monarch and that ultimate power rested in the hands of parliament and the representatives of the people—or in 1688 at least that small segment of the people who actually had a political voice.

While Louis XIV, the "Sun King," who had proclaimed "I am the State," had been extremely successful in surrounding himself with the trappings of majesty, by the time of his death in 1715 the "Age of Absolutism" had given way to the "Age of Reason." Reflecting the achievements of the men of the Scientific Revolution, emphasis was placed on reason as seen in Voltaire's (Document 6) call for a prince who "furthers the development of reason"—an "Enlightened Despot" who sought to rule according to "reason" and the "laws of nature." Such a monarch was Frederick II (Document 7), who, denying any divinity, claimed only to be the "first servant of the state." It was still absolutism, but in a new dress.

By the mid-eighteenth century, a new concept of the state was emerging in the more developed nations of Europe—that the state was not the prince, but the totality of the individuals who composed it. This is seen in Rousseau's (Document 8) *Social Contract*, where his "General Will" is conceived of as being, in essence, the consensus view as to what was in the best interests of the whole community: sovereignty is found in the people, not the prince or assembly.

The French Revolution and Napoleonic era served to reinforce this concept of the state being, in fact, the people. Indeed, it went further: The "State" or Nation came to possess an existence of its own—it was seen as a living organism that was more than the total of all its parts (i.e., its citizens). The conservative Burke (Document 9) saw the English "Nation" as a legacy of that land's long history, one the living had to nurture and pass on to future generations. This concept was greatly amplified in the course of the nineteenth century as various peoples of Europe struggled to free themselves of foreign masters or to extend their liberties against reactionary regimes. In the mind of Mazzini (Document 10), the Romantic Italian, his country became his "mother" and "father," a parent to whom he owed everything and for whom he was prepared to sacrifice everything. Increasingly the concept of the state as an entity having a life of its own came to be associated with a common language, a common heritage, a common race. Such a vision of the state was transmitted beyond Europe, as seen in the words of Liang Ch'i-ch'ao (Document 14), subsequently a founder of the Communist Party of China.

The second half of the nineteenth century saw other ideological concepts that influenced the vision of the state and citizens' relations to it. Social Darwinism, placing emphasis on the idea of "survival of the fittest," gave rise to the idea of the state in constant competition—warfare declared or undeclared—with its rivals. For Treitschke (Document 13), a Prussian historian, the state is seemingly perceived of as an army, its citizens little more than soldiers in the ranks who must obey. This vision of the ever-aggressive state, combined with an emphasis upon the unity—and superiority—of a particular race (*Volk*), and yet another ideological spin-off of Social Darwinism, elitism, combined to produce a concept of the state that plagued the first half of the twentieth century, the Fascist, or totalitarian, regime. This concept was succinctly stated in Hitler's *Mein Kampf* (Document 16), where the deification of the state as a "living organism," the exaltation of the "leader" as the personification of that state, and the ultimate contempt for the individual citizen, stupid and cowardly, is clearly set forth. Absolutism had returned in a terrifying form.

There were, of course, other views of the nature of the state and of its relations to the individual. Both Constant (Document 11) and, even more so, Mill (Document 12) argued that the authority of the state is limited and that the individual always retains certain rights that cannot be alienated: The state exists for the protection of the citizen, but it cannot infringe upon citizens' liberties as long as those do not threaten others.

Lenin (Document 15) represented a different concept of the state, one also having its roots in nineteenth-century ideology, that of Marxism. In theory what was envisioned was a classless state or, indeed, *no state*, for a state existed only as a tool of class oppression and, in a classless society, would not be necessary. What emerged from the Russian Revolution was, of course, quite different than the theory—a totalitarian State in which an elite, the Communist Party member and a cult leader, Stalin, dominated a subservient citizenry—totalitarianism in a different guise.

Sample Answers to Essay Questions

1.   The conflict, sparked by a relatively absurd conflict between Russia and France over the protection of Christian holy sites in Jerusalem, had its real roots in the "Eastern Question." Great Britain and France, having commercial, military, and political interests in the eastern Mediterranean and Near East, were opposed to any Russian encroachment upon the Turkish Straits or Turkish territory in that region. When a war broke out between Russia and Turkey, both Great Britain and France, fearing Russian intentions, quickly came to the Turks' support. The conflict itself, characterized by military ineptitude on all sides—ineptitude personified by the gallant but senseless "charge of the Light Brigade"—and the humanitarian activities of Florence Nightingale, ended in the defeat of Russia.

For Russia, defeat brought more than defeat on the battlefield. It brought clearly to the fore the backwardness of the Russian economic, social, and political structure. In the aftermath of the war the new czar, Alexander II, inaugurated a series of reforms, including the emancipation of the serfs, introduction of *zemstvos*, or provincial parliaments, and the extension and liberalization of the educational system. While these reforms did not go far enough, particularly in regard to the emancipation of the serfs, and were subsequently further hamstrung by Alexander's successors and conservative elements in Russian society, they were reflective of the severe domestic problems confronting Russia, problems that grew in subsequent decades. On the international scene, defeat in the war had served to block Russia's territorial ambitions in the Near East and Balkans temporarily: As a consequence, these were directed toward the Far East, where in the 1860s Russia annexed the Maritime Provinces, regions claimed by Manchu China, and southward toward Afghanistan. This expansion in the Asian area gave rise to increasing tensions with Great Britain and, eventually, the emerging Japan.

The Austro-Hungarian Empire, while not directly involved in the war, pursued a policy that was to have marked repercussions for it and, indeed, for all of Europe. In 1849, in accordance with the principles of the "Concert of Europe," Russia had come to the military assistance of Austria when it was confronted with a Hungarian uprising. When the Crimean War erupted, Russia looked to Austria for assistance, if only of a diplomatic nature, only to find Austria pursuing a policy of "neutrality." When, a decade later, Austria found itself faced with the threat presented by Otto von Bismarck's efforts to unify Germany under the leadership of Prussia, Russia, angered at Austria's "ingratitude," offered no help to its former ally: The "Concert of Europe" had been broken. Bismarck, on the other hand, while pursuing a policy of "friendly neutrality," secretly assisted Russia, thus reinforcing cordial relations to be utilized when the moment arrived.

The circumstances surrounding the Crimean War presented Austria with still another danger. Piedmont-Sardinia's Prime Minister Cavour, while having no real interest in the conflict, brought his country into the war on the side of Great Britain and France. Envisioning the unification of Italy, he realized that this would mean a war with Austria, a war his country could not win without the support of a powerful ally. France, whose ruler was Napoleon III, a man already sympathetic to the idea of Italian unification, was the logical choice. Permitted to plead his cause at the peace conference held in Paris, he was able to win Napoleon's promise of military support in Piedmont's inevitable war with Austria. Austria, isolated, fell victim to the unification ambitions of both Bismarck and Cavour and, with the eventual unification of Germany and Italy, the map—and history—of Europe were dramatically changed.

Britain, while a victor in the war, came away with a bitter taste, convinced of the wisdom of returning to a policy of "splendid isolation," seeking to avoid involvement in the affairs of the Continent. Time was to suggest that this policy was a serious error, coming as it did on the eve of the unification of Germany and Italy and the beginning of the formation of a series of alliances that were to contribute significantly to the outbreak of World War I.

The Crimean War, albeit a "silly war" fought on the periphery of the Continent, clearly had major consequences that extended far beyond the battlefield or the specific terms ending it, consequences that were to markedly alter the subsequent course of European history.

2.   Decades before Luther posted his "Ninety-Five Theses," religious unrest had been smoldering throughout Europe, unrest that occasionally erupted in revolt as seen in the movements of Wycliffe in England and John Hus in Bohemia. In these spiritual movements, nationalistic sentiments were also involved. This was particularly evident in England, where Wycliffe began to translate the Bible into English and called for the king of England, not the pope, to be recognized head of the English Church. Clearly Wycliffe's ideas, aside from doctrinal convictions, reflected a nationalistic spirit arising from England's involvement in the Hundred Years' War and a conviction that the Avignon papacy was a mere tool of the French. Wycliffe's movement also revealed another protest, this of a social nature. The Lollards, his followers, came largely from the lower class. Hungering for land, unhappy with the failings of the Church and jealous of its wealth, suffering from the impact of the Black Death and the war, their anger was directed as much against the feudal and manorial system, the great landowners, and a regime that imposed hated dues and taxes upon them and sought to keep them in a socially subservient position as it was against doctrinal concepts. The Peasants' Revolt of 1381, numbering among its leaders the Lollard priest John Bull, was an overt display of this social unrest.

These and other protests and calls for change emerged even more clearly following Luther's revolt. He early translated the Bible into German, a national language. In his *Address to the Christian Nobility of the German Nation*—a nation that in fact did not exist—he made a frankly patriotic appeal to his countrymen to reject the authority of the papacy and argued that, as the Church could not reform itself, the secular authorities must do so. Depending heavily upon the German princes for support, he early established the close relationship that would long exist between the Lutheran Church and the state. Nor was this alliance of state and church limited to Lutheran regions. In England, Henry VIII's "Reformation," motivated on his part more by "reasons of state" than those of a religious nature, created a national religion, Anglicanism, adherence to which was demanded as a sign of loyalty to king and state. This trend to national religions was not limited to Protestant states, for French monarchs worked to create a "Gallican Church," Catholic but controlled by the throne rather than the papacy. The unity of Christendom was giving way to national religions. Neither the Germans nor the Czechs, however, were to benefit from this trend.

Luther emphasized the Bible as the ultimate source of truth. Many took his words to heart: The problems such pursuits of truth presented quickly became evident, for the Scriptures and the picture they painted of the primitive Christian community lent themselves to diverse and at times revolutionary social, economic, and political interpretations. As early as the 1520s, peasants of southwestern Germany, suffering under the pressure of customary rents and services imposed upon them by their lords in a decaying feudal and manorial system, argued that they could find no scriptural justification for their burdens. Many revolted in 1524, seeking to throw off the hated obligations. While they found some support from religious leaders such as Zwingli, Luther was now in close alliance with the princes of Protestant Germany, and turned violently on them.

The "Anabaptists," a term of derision applied to sects holding a broad spectrum of beliefs but having in common the practice of adult baptism, were seen by more conservative Protestants and Catholics alike as a danger to the social order. Communal ownership of property, including wives, the imminent return of Christ, anarchism, and withdrawal from the affairs of the secular state were among the ideas certain sects adhered to. In 1525 in Münster, Thomas Münzer, once an associate of Luther, established a communistic theocratic society, only to be crushed before the end of the year. More radical were the Melchorites, who, under the leadership of John of Leiden, gained control over the ordinary workers and craft guilds in Münster and established their "heavenly Jerusalem." Burning all books except the Bible, abolishing private property, introducing polygamy, they lived in an atmosphere of abandon and chaos—although probably not as much as their critics maintained—awaiting the coming of the Messiah. The Protestants and Catholics allied to crush them brutally. The more moderate Anabaptists, viewing themselves as a Christian community that, while recognizing the authority of the state, sought to live as an entity apart from the state, were long cruelly persecuted by Lutherans, Calvinists, and Catholics. Interestingly, the Anabaptists were among the earliest to advocate yet another "revolutionary" idea—religious toleration.

The revolutionary calls for changes in the social, economic, and political spheres on the part of the religious groups did not end with the close of the sixteenth century, nor were they confined to the German area. Seventeenth-century England saw such movements as the Levelers, who called for the vote for all adult males and the yearly parliamentary elections; Fifth Monarchy Men; and the communist Diggers.

3.   While the term *imperialism* dates only from the 1880s, the objectives it implied are as old as history, to be seen when the first state sought to politically, economically, or culturally dominate another. The appearance of the term, however, indicated that the earlier goals, and the motives behind them, had been formulated into a more cohesive concept.

The "Old Imperialism" saw Europeans explore many corners of the globe and, where possible, colonize extensively. As with the subsequent "New Imperialism," the forces that led the Europeans to do so were varied. Much emphasis has been placed by scholars since the time of Marx upon the economic factors that drove Europeans to expand their influence in the colonial regions after circa 1871. Yet economic factors were not lacking in the earlier period. Certainly the vision of "El Dorado"—vast treasures of the Aztecs and Incas—long led men to explore uncharted lands. In addition to the dream of vast hoards of gold, silver, and precious stones that drove the earlier explorers, the spices, jewels, cottons, silk, and porcelains of India, China, and the East Indies, together with the slaves of Africa, provided an economic stimulus to the European merchants and the countries they represented. The nations of the age of the "New Imperialism" saw their colonies as sources of raw materials and as markets for their finished products: The same was no less true of the earlier period, particularly in relation to their holdings in the New World.

Yet another reason advanced for the imperialistic surge of Europe in the late nineteenth century has been the missionary zeal of many Europeans: yet the earlier "God" of the cry of "God, Gold, and Glory" symbolized the ardent, even fanatical drive on the part of explorers to spread their faith, whether by sword or teaching. Nor was the quest for "glory" on the part of men such as Cortez, Pizarro, and others wholly lacking from men such as Cecil Rhodes or Henry M. Stanley.

Any study seeking to compare the "Old Imperialism" with the "New" will disclose other factors broadly parallel. The European states of the late nineteenth century enjoyed, as a consequence of the Industrial Revolution and a strong scientific and technological orientation, marked advantages, particularly in the military area: The gunboat and machine gun came to be symbols of European imperialism. But four centuries earlier the Portuguese, Spanish, and those who followed them also enjoyed the advantage of superior ships and firepower. The acquisition of colonies for strategic purposes or to deter the expansion of rival European powers was also characteristic of imperialism in the two periods, as was the pursuit of economic policies of mercantilism or "Neo-Mercantilism."

If there are many broad parallels between the Old Imperialism and the New, are there any differences? Three stand out. In the 1500s the Spanish encountered great civilizations in the New World: These, however, were not able to resist European firepower, discipline, and disease. In North America the natives, at best, could offer only temporary resistance. The result was that the lands of the New World were largely open to European exploitation and colonization. The situation in Asia and Africa was markedly different, for such dynasties as the Moguls of India, Mings and Manchus of China, and Tokugawa of Japan were able to control the handful of Europeans who came to their ports, while the adverse health conditions of sub-Saharan Africa deterred penetration of the interior. Nor did preindustrial Europe have any items for sale really desired by those lands. As a result, European merchants went as suppliants, content to purchase the items so desired in the West. After the mid-nineteenth century, this situation altered dramatically. On one hand the Asian dynasties were undergoing internal decay, a situation the Westerners quickly exploited. Too, the rise of natives in these regions who saw advantages in cooperating with the Europeans provided another wedge the latter could exploit. In Africa, medical advances permitted the Europeans to penetrate and exploit the interior.

In the economic sphere, the Industrial Revolution and second Commercial Revolution had also altered the picture dramatically. There was now extensive surplus capital to be invested for high profits in overseas areas. As these investments mounted, it was only natural that there was a desire on the part of the investors that their governments "protect" their interests, even if this necessitated military intervention or outright annexation. As the industrial plants of Europe demanded more and more raw materials, governments sought spheres of influence where these could be guaranteed: Such spheres for the sale of the finished products of the plants were also sought. The consequence of these forces was that by 1900 virtually every nation and people of Africa and Asia was either governed directly or under the strong influence of a Western power.

In the era of the Old Imperialism the inevitable clashes of interest between the European powers in the colonial regions had often resulted in war. In the later period, while tensions remained, diplomacy often resolved before war erupted.

4.   There developed in the millennium before 1500 a concept of the universe and of humankind's place in it that provided an ordered, hierarchical structure, preordained by the creator. In this universe every object, animate or inanimate, knew its place: To upset this balance was in the eyes of the church, since it had been established by God, a sin. This "Medieval Synthesis," reaching its culmination in the eleventh and twelfth centuries, was an amalgam of the scientific ideas of Aristotle, Ptolemy, and Galen, the "authorities" of antiquity, and the doctrines of the church. At the heart of this synthesis was its conception of the cosmos. At the center of the universe was the earth, motionless, changing, and corruptible. It was surrounded by nine crystalline spheres with which the sun, moon, planets, and stars were associated. Moving in perfect circular orbits, this heavenly realm was one of perfection and incorruptibility. Beyond the ninth sphere was the empyrean, the region of the blessed spirits.

Even before the sixteenth century, questions were being raised regarding the validity of the medieval synthesis. Professors at Oxford, Padua, and Paris began to apply mathematical reasoning to problems of physics and astronomy, raising questions regarding the theories of Aristotle and Ptolemy, while the study of anatomy by Renaissance artists served to undermine the authority of Galen; humanists, in their studies of antiquity, discovered Greek philosophers who held theories in opposition to Aristotle and Ptolemy. The consequence of this doubting and questioning became clear in the sixteenth century with the publication of Vesalius's *On the Structure of the Human Body* and Copernicus's *On the Revolution of Heavenly Bodies*. Vesalius, while not rejecting wholly the authority of Galen, demonstrated the value of information gained through dissection. Copernicus's work, although advanced only as a theory, struck a sharper blow at a fundamental tenet of the Medieval Synthesis. Aware of ancient theories that the sun was the center of the universe and that the earth moved about it, he utilized mathematics to demonstrate that the universe constructed on these concepts presented a simpler, more logical explanation for the movements of the heavenly bodies than Ptolemy's complex system of epicycles. While Copernicus did not reject Ptolemy's ideas entirely, retaining the concept of the circular orbits of heavenly bodies and a finite sphere of fixed stars, he had sharply challenged authority.

In the decades that followed, Francis Bacon emphasized the need for inductive reasoning and empirical research while René Descartes reinforced the essential role of mathematical analysis and theory in scientific investigation. Others, using these new tools, steadily increased humankind's pool of knowledge, as did Gilbert in magnetism, Harvey in the circulation of blood, Torricelli with vacuums; while others were expanding humankind's mathematical tools—Descartes with analytical geometry, Newton and Leibniz with calculus. Contributing to the advance of science was the beginning of an alliance of the artisan with the skills to construct superior equipment and the scientist who used them, an alliance that proved fruitful.

The seventeenth century, the "Century of Genius," saw a seemingly unbroken chain of discoveries that totally altered humankind's conception of the universe, the forces behind it, and humans' place in it. Kepler, substituting elliptical orbits for Ptolemy's perfect circles, corrected Copernicus's error and validated the heliocentric theory. Galileo, using the newly invented telescope, revealed that the moon was not a perfect globe and that the sun was not changeless, that the earth moved, and that the earth and heavens were subject to the same forces and laws. Newton, drawing on Kepler's astronomy, Galileo's physics, his own mathematical skills, and inductive reasoning, removed the distinctions between celestial and earthly physics: The "Medieval Synthesis" had been destroyed, replaced by the "World Machine" of Newton.

Humans, in a sense, had been displaced from the center of the universe by Copernicus, Kepler, and Galileo: Humans' mind, if not their physical being, had been restored to that position by the accomplishments of Descartes, Newton, and other scientists. These scientists had demonstrated that, through the application of the proper tools—inductive reasoning, empiricism, and mathematics—the secrets of the universe could be unveiled. In doing so, they had also challenged and severely weakened the "authorities," those of antiquity and of the church. But the achievements of these scientists had provided humans with a new vision, that of an ordered universe governed by "natural" laws, and new "authorities"—science, the scientific method, and humankind's own reason. Intellectuals of Western Europe, deeply impressed with the achievements of the scientists, were convinced that through the proper application of these tools not only could the mysteries of the physical world be solved, but those of society itself. The eighteenth century, the "Age of Reason," saw men, the *philosophes*, seek to find solutions to the social, economic, and political problems they perceived to exist. Imbued with a spirit of optimism, they believed it possible to discover, through reason, the natural laws that governed society and humankind's relations with other humans. They, like the scientists, were prepared to challenge authority, whether that of the monarch, the church, or the established traditions of the day. That their conception of what was wrong in society was frequently based upon personal or class convictions did not deter their conviction that reason would lead to the reconstruction of society in accord with the laws of nature.

5.   There were other reasons that Europe suffered through two world wars: diplomatic blunders, rabid leaders, and the worldwide economy; but to those viewing the rubble and human misery in 1945, one thing was clear: National histories had led to needless economic competition, unhealthy forms of nationalism, and an unwillingness to view Europe as a single continent united by millennia of common law, culture, and interests. Postwar leaders started immediately to work to overcome artificial national boundaries any way they could. In 1946, the same year he announced the existence of an "Iron Curtain," Winston Churchill called for a United States of Europe. There would be many more steps, mostly in areas of the economy, before Europe would see anything approaching a "U.S. of E."

It is no coincidence that the first leaders of the pan-European movement were members of some form of Christian Democracy. Churchill of Britain could say that his Tory party championed Christian principles, but only loosely: The later withdrawal of Britain from unification initiatives showed that Tories were more isolationist than their old leader. But Spaak of Belgium, Adenauer of West Germany, Gasperi of Italy, and Schuman of France all represented a variation on prewar religion-based parties. Whereas Christian Socialists had gone to extremes of nationalism, even racism, the new Christian Democrats sought to inject politics with the spirit of Christian communalism, cooperation, and even compromise—all for the greater European good. Until 1949, initial meetings could simply lay the groundwork and support for a Council of Europe in Strasbourg. With the formation of a separate West Germany in 1949, the last key player was ready. The next year, the Six (the three Benelux countries, France, Germany, and Italy) signed treaties forming the European Coal and Steel Community; this marked the first manageable step to greater unification, namely the easily sellable notion that the protectionist trade barriers of earlier history had not done economies much good, so that a barrier-free trade zone would be more helpful in rebuilding war-tattered Europe. Certainly, the economic miracle of Germany helped to justify that move, so much so that in 1957 the Six extended their economic cooperation beyond coal and steel to other commodities when they signed the path-breaking Treaty of Rome (1957), establishing not only the Common Market (EEC) but also other agencies of international cooperation, such as EURATOM.

International politics, more than national, hampered further developments toward unification. The Cold War split Europe into two camps, and for every move in the West to ameliorate economic conditions, the Soviets tried (usually without success) to parrot those moves in the eastern bloc. With the formation of NATO in 1949, its West European members also had to divert energies away from unification to more pressing matters of defense and propaganda; but the refusal of a number of European countries to join NATO hurt chances of further cooperation. The old neutrality of Sweden and Switzerland was a factor; but other countries, such as Austria, threw roadblocks in the way of further unification. Also, the animus of De Gaulle's France toward Britain insured that, during the 1960s, British bids to join the EEC would be thwarted. De Gaulle's withdrawal of French forces from NATO cooperation (1966) was a parallel move, since he viewed the Anglo-American "friendship" as a dangerous encroachment on continental European power. It was only in 1973 that the Six could expand to become the Nine with the entry of Britain, Ireland, and Norway into the Common Market. Now the Nine were ready to try for more cooperation on the far thornier issues of politics by inaugurating a European parliament at Strasbourg in 1979.

In 1982 another three (Greece, Portugal, and Spain) joined, but not without necessary political changes preceding their bids and acceptance: The rest of Europe had not looked kindly on the authoritarian regime of Colonel Salazar or Franco, but by 1982 those tyrants were gone. The message of unification was clear: Internal reforms must precede entry into this exclusive club. (Turkey is still trying to amass enough internal reforms to satisfy the Euro-moralists in Brussels.) The Twelve seemed to have reached a critical mass for the next step, a common plan for integration of economies and national political structures within a truly European framework. Negotiations proceeded apace until the Maastricht Treaty of 1991. Each member nation now had to go home and discuss how and to what extent it would sacrifice the old notion of national sovereignty to a higher entity. First, as usual, the way had to be smoothed for the introduction of a common currency, which transpired over a few years in 1999–2002, as the euro was first tried for electronic transactions and then became the common cash currency. Though everyone feared that the Germans would balk, given their reverence for the almighty mark, it was the Brits who threw a monkey wrench into the works by refusing to adopt the euro. Unification has recently stalled on the political front with fierce debates over a common European constitution. Negative votes by Denmark and France show that much work has yet to be done to create a "United States of Europe"—if indeed the European Union is not already satisfied with its status.

6.   The Agricultural and Industrial Revolutions dramatically altered the economic structure of England and changed forever the physical face of the country as it shifted from a land dominated by small, peasant-operated farms to one where large industrial cities and big, capitalist-oriented agricultural establishments dotted the countryside. Many other changes, even more significant if not so visible, also took place in the ideological, social, and political structure and outlook of English society.

The Agricultural Revolution and the Enclosure Movement had seen many peasants forced from the land. Some found employment as tenant farmers or agricultural laborers. Others, moving into the blossoming industrial cities, constituted the basis of the expanding industrial working class. The new urban, industrial centers of England tended to be in Wales, the Midlands, and the north, this as a result of the location of ore and coal deposits. This population expansion was enhanced by the fact that from the early 1600s England, like many regions of the world, experienced a steady increase in its birthrate and, perhaps more significant, a lowering mortality rate and increased longevity. Previously these regions had been underpopulated and, more significant, had little or no representation in Parliament. By contrast, the south and southeast of England, in earlier days the agricultural heartland of England, dominated Parliament. Even though the population was shifting away from the south, political power long remained in the hands of the landowners and commercial class of that region, who, through their control of "rotten" and "pocket" boroughs, were in a position to manipulate large segments of the House of Commons in their own interests. The powerful House of Lords also represented the older, vested interests. In the decades before the French Revolution, tensions were mounting as the new industrial middle and upper classes demanded they receive more equitable representation. While their demands were pushed into the background by that conflict, with its end they came to the fore once again, now assuming a more threatening nature, as seen in the "Peterloo Massacre" (1819) and the abortive Cato Street Conspiracy of 1820. Following a period of repressive efforts on the part of conservative elements in the government to repress the calls for reforms, after 1822 more liberal elements began to introduce reforms, including weakening the protective mercantile system, a reform desired by manufacturers; revising antiquated criminal laws; and repealing the Combination Acts, which prohibited the formation of unions. These reforms were capped by the Third Reform Bill of 1832: This abolished more than fifty "rotten" and "pocket" boroughs, redistributing the seats in Parliament to areas previously without representation, and the extension of the vote to a larger segment of the middle class, including those in the industrial sphere. In the decades that followed, although political change came gradually, *it did come*. This was due, in part, to the competition between the two major parties for the vote, a factor that led to an increasing extension of the franchise to a larger segment of the male population (women would have to wait until the 1920s to obtain the vote). Another factor was the increasing political activism of the middle and lower classes. The working class, initially lacking political cohesion, began to become more articulate and, through the formation of political parties, gain a voice in the chambers of Parliament. By 1911, virtually every male in Great Britain had gained the right to vote, the secret ballot had been introduced, and the powers of the House of Lords, normally a reactionary body, had been dramatically curtailed. Parliament had assumed a very "modern appearance."

The changes that were taking place in the political structure of England were mirrored in and influenced by changes in the social structure of the country. Those who were in the fore of the industrialization of England came, in many cases, from a different social strata than the aristocratic, landowning, and commercial elements that had dominated Parliament since the "Glorious Revolution" of 1688. Thus many were members of the "dissenting churches," such as the Quakers and Methodists, rather than the "established" or Anglican Church. Many traced their roots back to the artisan or, in the nineteenth century, even working, class. As such, they tended to be viewed as outsiders or *nouveau riche* by the dominant element in society. However, as their economic role in society became more and more important and, eventually, dominant, they gradually gained social as well as political acceptance. Social mobility being greater in Great Britain than it was in many nations of the Continent, marriage between the industrial capitalists and the old families became increasingly common. They were becoming, politically and socially, part of the Establishment.

If the gradually enhanced status of the middle and upper classes of England's industrial society was taking place, the same was true of those who, at the outset of the Industrial Revolution, had constituted the lower strata, the working class, who endured wretched working conditions in the factories, miserable pay, and generally intolerable living conditions. Gradually, albeit very gradually, working conditions improved through the enactment of various labor regulations. Their incomes began to rise, permitting many to enter the ranks of the middle class. Increasingly their voice in the political arena became louder.

Clearly by the advent of the twentieth century the Agricultural and Industrial Revolutions had brought into being a "new" England, its face changed physically, socially, and politically.

ANSWER SHEETS

AP European History

PRACTICE EXAM 1

AP European History

Section I

Answer Sheet

1. Ⓐ Ⓑ Ⓒ Ⓓ Ⓔ
2. Ⓐ Ⓑ Ⓒ Ⓓ Ⓔ
3. Ⓐ Ⓑ Ⓒ Ⓓ Ⓔ
4. Ⓐ Ⓑ Ⓒ Ⓓ Ⓔ
5. Ⓐ Ⓑ Ⓒ Ⓓ Ⓔ
6. Ⓐ Ⓑ Ⓒ Ⓓ Ⓔ
7. Ⓐ Ⓑ Ⓒ Ⓓ Ⓔ
8. Ⓐ Ⓑ Ⓒ Ⓓ Ⓔ
9. Ⓐ Ⓑ Ⓒ Ⓓ Ⓔ
10. Ⓐ Ⓑ Ⓒ Ⓓ Ⓔ
11. Ⓐ Ⓑ Ⓒ Ⓓ Ⓔ
12. Ⓐ Ⓑ Ⓒ Ⓓ Ⓔ
13. Ⓐ Ⓑ Ⓒ Ⓓ Ⓔ
14. Ⓐ Ⓑ Ⓒ Ⓓ Ⓔ
15. Ⓐ Ⓑ Ⓒ Ⓓ Ⓔ
16. Ⓐ Ⓑ Ⓒ Ⓓ Ⓔ
17. Ⓐ Ⓑ Ⓒ Ⓓ Ⓔ
18. Ⓐ Ⓑ Ⓒ Ⓓ Ⓔ
19. Ⓐ Ⓑ Ⓒ Ⓓ Ⓔ
20. Ⓐ Ⓑ Ⓒ Ⓓ Ⓔ
21. Ⓐ Ⓑ Ⓒ Ⓓ Ⓔ
22. Ⓐ Ⓑ Ⓒ Ⓓ Ⓔ
23. Ⓐ Ⓑ Ⓒ Ⓓ Ⓔ
24. Ⓐ Ⓑ Ⓒ Ⓓ Ⓔ
25. Ⓐ Ⓑ Ⓒ Ⓓ Ⓔ
26. Ⓐ Ⓑ Ⓒ Ⓓ Ⓔ
27. Ⓐ Ⓑ Ⓒ Ⓓ Ⓔ

28. Ⓐ Ⓑ Ⓒ Ⓓ Ⓔ
29. Ⓐ Ⓑ Ⓒ Ⓓ Ⓔ
30. Ⓐ Ⓑ Ⓒ Ⓓ Ⓔ
31. Ⓐ Ⓑ Ⓒ Ⓓ Ⓔ
32. Ⓐ Ⓑ Ⓒ Ⓓ Ⓔ
33. Ⓐ Ⓑ Ⓒ Ⓓ Ⓔ
34. Ⓐ Ⓑ Ⓒ Ⓓ Ⓔ
35. Ⓐ Ⓑ Ⓒ Ⓓ Ⓔ
36. Ⓐ Ⓑ Ⓒ Ⓓ Ⓔ
37. Ⓐ Ⓑ Ⓒ Ⓓ Ⓔ
38. Ⓐ Ⓑ Ⓒ Ⓓ Ⓔ
39. Ⓐ Ⓑ Ⓒ Ⓓ Ⓔ
40. Ⓐ Ⓑ Ⓒ Ⓓ Ⓔ
41. Ⓐ Ⓑ Ⓒ Ⓓ Ⓔ
42. Ⓐ Ⓑ Ⓒ Ⓓ Ⓔ
43. Ⓐ Ⓑ Ⓒ Ⓓ Ⓔ
44. Ⓐ Ⓑ Ⓒ Ⓓ Ⓔ
45. Ⓐ Ⓑ Ⓒ Ⓓ Ⓔ
46. Ⓐ Ⓑ Ⓒ Ⓓ Ⓔ
47. Ⓐ Ⓑ Ⓒ Ⓓ Ⓔ
48. Ⓐ Ⓑ Ⓒ Ⓓ Ⓔ
49. Ⓐ Ⓑ Ⓒ Ⓓ Ⓔ
50. Ⓐ Ⓑ Ⓒ Ⓓ Ⓔ
51. Ⓐ Ⓑ Ⓒ Ⓓ Ⓔ
52. Ⓐ Ⓑ Ⓒ Ⓓ Ⓔ
53. Ⓐ Ⓑ Ⓒ Ⓓ Ⓔ
54. Ⓐ Ⓑ Ⓒ Ⓓ Ⓔ

55. Ⓐ Ⓑ Ⓒ Ⓓ Ⓔ
56. Ⓐ Ⓑ Ⓒ Ⓓ Ⓔ
57. Ⓐ Ⓑ Ⓒ Ⓓ Ⓔ
58. Ⓐ Ⓑ Ⓒ Ⓓ Ⓔ
59. Ⓐ Ⓑ Ⓒ Ⓓ Ⓔ
60. Ⓐ Ⓑ Ⓒ Ⓓ Ⓔ
61. Ⓐ Ⓑ Ⓒ Ⓓ Ⓔ
62. Ⓐ Ⓑ Ⓒ Ⓓ Ⓔ
63. Ⓐ Ⓑ Ⓒ Ⓓ Ⓔ
64. Ⓐ Ⓑ Ⓒ Ⓓ Ⓔ
65. Ⓐ Ⓑ Ⓒ Ⓓ Ⓔ
66. Ⓐ Ⓑ Ⓒ Ⓓ Ⓔ
67. Ⓐ Ⓑ Ⓒ Ⓓ Ⓔ
68. Ⓐ Ⓑ Ⓒ Ⓓ Ⓔ
69. Ⓐ Ⓑ Ⓒ Ⓓ Ⓔ
70. Ⓐ Ⓑ Ⓒ Ⓓ Ⓔ
71. Ⓐ Ⓑ Ⓒ Ⓓ Ⓔ
72. Ⓐ Ⓑ Ⓒ Ⓓ Ⓔ
73. Ⓐ Ⓑ Ⓒ Ⓓ Ⓔ
74. Ⓐ Ⓑ Ⓒ Ⓓ Ⓔ
75. Ⓐ Ⓑ Ⓒ Ⓓ Ⓔ
76. Ⓐ Ⓑ Ⓒ Ⓓ Ⓔ
77. Ⓐ Ⓑ Ⓒ Ⓓ Ⓔ
78. Ⓐ Ⓑ Ⓒ Ⓓ Ⓔ
79. Ⓐ Ⓑ Ⓒ Ⓓ Ⓔ
80. Ⓐ Ⓑ Ⓒ Ⓓ Ⓔ

Section II Essays

Use the following pages to prepare your essays.

Section II Essays *(Continued)*

PRACTICE EXAM 2

AP European History

Section I

Answer Sheet

1. Ⓐ Ⓑ Ⓒ Ⓓ Ⓔ	28. Ⓐ Ⓑ Ⓒ Ⓓ Ⓔ	55. Ⓐ Ⓑ Ⓒ Ⓓ Ⓔ
2. Ⓐ Ⓑ Ⓒ Ⓓ Ⓔ	29. Ⓐ Ⓑ Ⓒ Ⓓ Ⓔ	56. Ⓐ Ⓑ Ⓒ Ⓓ Ⓔ
3. Ⓐ Ⓑ Ⓒ Ⓓ Ⓔ	30. Ⓐ Ⓑ Ⓒ Ⓓ Ⓔ	57. Ⓐ Ⓑ Ⓒ Ⓓ Ⓔ
4. Ⓐ Ⓑ Ⓒ Ⓓ Ⓔ	31. Ⓐ Ⓑ Ⓒ Ⓓ Ⓔ	58. Ⓐ Ⓑ Ⓒ Ⓓ Ⓔ
5. Ⓐ Ⓑ Ⓒ Ⓓ Ⓔ	32. Ⓐ Ⓑ Ⓒ Ⓓ Ⓔ	59. Ⓐ Ⓑ Ⓒ Ⓓ Ⓔ
6. Ⓐ Ⓑ Ⓒ Ⓓ Ⓔ	33. Ⓐ Ⓑ Ⓒ Ⓓ Ⓔ	60. Ⓐ Ⓑ Ⓒ Ⓓ Ⓔ
7. Ⓐ Ⓑ Ⓒ Ⓓ Ⓔ	34. Ⓐ Ⓑ Ⓒ Ⓓ Ⓔ	61. Ⓐ Ⓑ Ⓒ Ⓓ Ⓔ
8. Ⓐ Ⓑ Ⓒ Ⓓ Ⓔ	35. Ⓐ Ⓑ Ⓒ Ⓓ Ⓔ	62. Ⓐ Ⓑ Ⓒ Ⓓ Ⓔ
9. Ⓐ Ⓑ Ⓒ Ⓓ Ⓔ	36. Ⓐ Ⓑ Ⓒ Ⓓ Ⓔ	63. Ⓐ Ⓑ Ⓒ Ⓓ Ⓔ
10. Ⓐ Ⓑ Ⓒ Ⓓ Ⓔ	37. Ⓐ Ⓑ Ⓒ Ⓓ Ⓔ	64. Ⓐ Ⓑ Ⓒ Ⓓ Ⓔ
11. Ⓐ Ⓑ Ⓒ Ⓓ Ⓔ	38. Ⓐ Ⓑ Ⓒ Ⓓ Ⓔ	65. Ⓐ Ⓑ Ⓒ Ⓓ Ⓔ
12. Ⓐ Ⓑ Ⓒ Ⓓ Ⓔ	39. Ⓐ Ⓑ Ⓒ Ⓓ Ⓔ	66. Ⓐ Ⓑ Ⓒ Ⓓ Ⓔ
13. Ⓐ Ⓑ Ⓒ Ⓓ Ⓔ	40. Ⓐ Ⓑ Ⓒ Ⓓ Ⓔ	67. Ⓐ Ⓑ Ⓒ Ⓓ Ⓔ
14. Ⓐ Ⓑ Ⓒ Ⓓ Ⓔ	41. Ⓐ Ⓑ Ⓒ Ⓓ Ⓔ	68. Ⓐ Ⓑ Ⓒ Ⓓ Ⓔ
15. Ⓐ Ⓑ Ⓒ Ⓓ Ⓔ	42. Ⓐ Ⓑ Ⓒ Ⓓ Ⓔ	69. Ⓐ Ⓑ Ⓒ Ⓓ Ⓔ
16. Ⓐ Ⓑ Ⓒ Ⓓ Ⓔ	43. Ⓐ Ⓑ Ⓒ Ⓓ Ⓔ	70. Ⓐ Ⓑ Ⓒ Ⓓ Ⓔ
17. Ⓐ Ⓑ Ⓒ Ⓓ Ⓔ	44. Ⓐ Ⓑ Ⓒ Ⓓ Ⓔ	71. Ⓐ Ⓑ Ⓒ Ⓓ Ⓔ
18. Ⓐ Ⓑ Ⓒ Ⓓ Ⓔ	45. Ⓐ Ⓑ Ⓒ Ⓓ Ⓔ	72. Ⓐ Ⓑ Ⓒ Ⓓ Ⓔ
19. Ⓐ Ⓑ Ⓒ Ⓓ Ⓔ	46. Ⓐ Ⓑ Ⓒ Ⓓ Ⓔ	73. Ⓐ Ⓑ Ⓒ Ⓓ Ⓔ
20. Ⓐ Ⓑ Ⓒ Ⓓ Ⓔ	47. Ⓐ Ⓑ Ⓒ Ⓓ Ⓔ	74. Ⓐ Ⓑ Ⓒ Ⓓ Ⓔ
21. Ⓐ Ⓑ Ⓒ Ⓓ Ⓔ	48. Ⓐ Ⓑ Ⓒ Ⓓ Ⓔ	75. Ⓐ Ⓑ Ⓒ Ⓓ Ⓔ
22. Ⓐ Ⓑ Ⓒ Ⓓ Ⓔ	49. Ⓐ Ⓑ Ⓒ Ⓓ Ⓔ	76. Ⓐ Ⓑ Ⓒ Ⓓ Ⓔ
23. Ⓐ Ⓑ Ⓒ Ⓓ Ⓔ	50. Ⓐ Ⓑ Ⓒ Ⓓ Ⓔ	77. Ⓐ Ⓑ Ⓒ Ⓓ Ⓔ
24. Ⓐ Ⓑ Ⓒ Ⓓ Ⓔ	51. Ⓐ Ⓑ Ⓒ Ⓓ Ⓔ	78. Ⓐ Ⓑ Ⓒ Ⓓ Ⓔ
25. Ⓐ Ⓑ Ⓒ Ⓓ Ⓔ	52. Ⓐ Ⓑ Ⓒ Ⓓ Ⓔ	79. Ⓐ Ⓑ Ⓒ Ⓓ Ⓔ
26. Ⓐ Ⓑ Ⓒ Ⓓ Ⓔ	53. Ⓐ Ⓑ Ⓒ Ⓓ Ⓔ	80. Ⓐ Ⓑ Ⓒ Ⓓ Ⓔ
27. Ⓐ Ⓑ Ⓒ Ⓓ Ⓔ	54. Ⓐ Ⓑ Ⓒ Ⓓ Ⓔ	

Section II Essays

Use the following pages to prepare your essays.

Section II Essays *(Continued)*

PRACTICE EXAM 3

AP European History

Section I

Answer Sheet

1. Ⓐ Ⓑ Ⓒ Ⓓ Ⓔ
2. Ⓐ Ⓑ Ⓒ Ⓓ Ⓔ
3. Ⓐ Ⓑ Ⓒ Ⓓ Ⓔ
4. Ⓐ Ⓑ Ⓒ Ⓓ Ⓔ
5. Ⓐ Ⓑ Ⓒ Ⓓ Ⓔ
6. Ⓐ Ⓑ Ⓒ Ⓓ Ⓔ
7. Ⓐ Ⓑ Ⓒ Ⓓ Ⓔ
8. Ⓐ Ⓑ Ⓒ Ⓓ Ⓔ
9. Ⓐ Ⓑ Ⓒ Ⓓ Ⓔ
10. Ⓐ Ⓑ Ⓒ Ⓓ Ⓔ
11. Ⓐ Ⓑ Ⓒ Ⓓ Ⓔ
12. Ⓐ Ⓑ Ⓒ Ⓓ Ⓔ
13. Ⓐ Ⓑ Ⓒ Ⓓ Ⓔ
14. Ⓐ Ⓑ Ⓒ Ⓓ Ⓔ
15. Ⓐ Ⓑ Ⓒ Ⓓ Ⓔ
16. Ⓐ Ⓑ Ⓒ Ⓓ Ⓔ
17. Ⓐ Ⓑ Ⓒ Ⓓ Ⓔ
18. Ⓐ Ⓑ Ⓒ Ⓓ Ⓔ
19. Ⓐ Ⓑ Ⓒ Ⓓ Ⓔ
20. Ⓐ Ⓑ Ⓒ Ⓓ Ⓔ
21. Ⓐ Ⓑ Ⓒ Ⓓ Ⓔ
22. Ⓐ Ⓑ Ⓒ Ⓓ Ⓔ
23. Ⓐ Ⓑ Ⓒ Ⓓ Ⓔ
24. Ⓐ Ⓑ Ⓒ Ⓓ Ⓔ
25. Ⓐ Ⓑ Ⓒ Ⓓ Ⓔ
26. Ⓐ Ⓑ Ⓒ Ⓓ Ⓔ
27. Ⓐ Ⓑ Ⓒ Ⓓ Ⓔ

28. Ⓐ Ⓑ Ⓒ Ⓓ Ⓔ
29. Ⓐ Ⓑ Ⓒ Ⓓ Ⓔ
30. Ⓐ Ⓑ Ⓒ Ⓓ Ⓔ
31. Ⓐ Ⓑ Ⓒ Ⓓ Ⓔ
32. Ⓐ Ⓑ Ⓒ Ⓓ Ⓔ
33. Ⓐ Ⓑ Ⓒ Ⓓ Ⓔ
34. Ⓐ Ⓑ Ⓒ Ⓓ Ⓔ
35. Ⓐ Ⓑ Ⓒ Ⓓ Ⓔ
36. Ⓐ Ⓑ Ⓒ Ⓓ Ⓔ
37. Ⓐ Ⓑ Ⓒ Ⓓ Ⓔ
38. Ⓐ Ⓑ Ⓒ Ⓓ Ⓔ
39. Ⓐ Ⓑ Ⓒ Ⓓ Ⓔ
40. Ⓐ Ⓑ Ⓒ Ⓓ Ⓔ
41. Ⓐ Ⓑ Ⓒ Ⓓ Ⓔ
42. Ⓐ Ⓑ Ⓒ Ⓓ Ⓔ
43. Ⓐ Ⓑ Ⓒ Ⓓ Ⓔ
44. Ⓐ Ⓑ Ⓒ Ⓓ Ⓔ
45. Ⓐ Ⓑ Ⓒ Ⓓ Ⓔ
46. Ⓐ Ⓑ Ⓒ Ⓓ Ⓔ
47. Ⓐ Ⓑ Ⓒ Ⓓ Ⓔ
48. Ⓐ Ⓑ Ⓒ Ⓓ Ⓔ
49. Ⓐ Ⓑ Ⓒ Ⓓ Ⓔ
50. Ⓐ Ⓑ Ⓒ Ⓓ Ⓔ
51. Ⓐ Ⓑ Ⓒ Ⓓ Ⓔ
52. Ⓐ Ⓑ Ⓒ Ⓓ Ⓔ
53. Ⓐ Ⓑ Ⓒ Ⓓ Ⓔ
54. Ⓐ Ⓑ Ⓒ Ⓓ Ⓔ

55. Ⓐ Ⓑ Ⓒ Ⓓ Ⓔ
56. Ⓐ Ⓑ Ⓒ Ⓓ Ⓔ
57. Ⓐ Ⓑ Ⓒ Ⓓ Ⓔ
58. Ⓐ Ⓑ Ⓒ Ⓓ Ⓔ
59. Ⓐ Ⓑ Ⓒ Ⓓ Ⓔ
60. Ⓐ Ⓑ Ⓒ Ⓓ Ⓔ
61. Ⓐ Ⓑ Ⓒ Ⓓ Ⓔ
62. Ⓐ Ⓑ Ⓒ Ⓓ Ⓔ
63. Ⓐ Ⓑ Ⓒ Ⓓ Ⓔ
64. Ⓐ Ⓑ Ⓒ Ⓓ Ⓔ
65. Ⓐ Ⓑ Ⓒ Ⓓ Ⓔ
66. Ⓐ Ⓑ Ⓒ Ⓓ Ⓔ
67. Ⓐ Ⓑ Ⓒ Ⓓ Ⓔ
68. Ⓐ Ⓑ Ⓒ Ⓓ Ⓔ
69. Ⓐ Ⓑ Ⓒ Ⓓ Ⓔ
70. Ⓐ Ⓑ Ⓒ Ⓓ Ⓔ
71. Ⓐ Ⓑ Ⓒ Ⓓ Ⓔ
72. Ⓐ Ⓑ Ⓒ Ⓓ Ⓔ
73. Ⓐ Ⓑ Ⓒ Ⓓ Ⓔ
74. Ⓐ Ⓑ Ⓒ Ⓓ Ⓔ
75. Ⓐ Ⓑ Ⓒ Ⓓ Ⓔ
76. Ⓐ Ⓑ Ⓒ Ⓓ Ⓔ
77. Ⓐ Ⓑ Ⓒ Ⓓ Ⓔ
78. Ⓐ Ⓑ Ⓒ Ⓓ Ⓔ
79. Ⓐ Ⓑ Ⓒ Ⓓ Ⓔ
80. Ⓐ Ⓑ Ⓒ Ⓓ Ⓔ

Section II Essays

Use the following pages to prepare your essays.

PRACTICE EXAM 4

AP European History

Section I

Answer Sheet

1. Ⓐ Ⓑ Ⓒ Ⓓ Ⓔ
2. Ⓐ Ⓑ Ⓒ Ⓓ Ⓔ
3. Ⓐ Ⓑ Ⓒ Ⓓ Ⓔ
4. Ⓐ Ⓑ Ⓒ Ⓓ Ⓔ
5. Ⓐ Ⓑ Ⓒ Ⓓ Ⓔ
6. Ⓐ Ⓑ Ⓒ Ⓓ Ⓔ
7. Ⓐ Ⓑ Ⓒ Ⓓ Ⓔ
8. Ⓐ Ⓑ Ⓒ Ⓓ Ⓔ
9. Ⓐ Ⓑ Ⓒ Ⓓ Ⓔ
10. Ⓐ Ⓑ Ⓒ Ⓓ Ⓔ
11. Ⓐ Ⓑ Ⓒ Ⓓ Ⓔ
12. Ⓐ Ⓑ Ⓒ Ⓓ Ⓔ
13. Ⓐ Ⓑ Ⓒ Ⓓ Ⓔ
14. Ⓐ Ⓑ Ⓒ Ⓓ Ⓔ
15. Ⓐ Ⓑ Ⓒ Ⓓ Ⓔ
16. Ⓐ Ⓑ Ⓒ Ⓓ Ⓔ
17. Ⓐ Ⓑ Ⓒ Ⓓ Ⓔ
18. Ⓐ Ⓑ Ⓒ Ⓓ Ⓔ
19. Ⓐ Ⓑ Ⓒ Ⓓ Ⓔ
20. Ⓐ Ⓑ Ⓒ Ⓓ Ⓔ
21. Ⓐ Ⓑ Ⓒ Ⓓ Ⓔ
22. Ⓐ Ⓑ Ⓒ Ⓓ Ⓔ
23. Ⓐ Ⓑ Ⓒ Ⓓ Ⓔ
24. Ⓐ Ⓑ Ⓒ Ⓓ Ⓔ
25. Ⓐ Ⓑ Ⓒ Ⓓ Ⓔ
26. Ⓐ Ⓑ Ⓒ Ⓓ Ⓔ
27. Ⓐ Ⓑ Ⓒ Ⓓ Ⓔ

28. Ⓐ Ⓑ Ⓒ Ⓓ Ⓔ
29. Ⓐ Ⓑ Ⓒ Ⓓ Ⓔ
30. Ⓐ Ⓑ Ⓒ Ⓓ Ⓔ
31. Ⓐ Ⓑ Ⓒ Ⓓ Ⓔ
32. Ⓐ Ⓑ Ⓒ Ⓓ Ⓔ
33. Ⓐ Ⓑ Ⓒ Ⓓ Ⓔ
34. Ⓐ Ⓑ Ⓒ Ⓓ Ⓔ
35. Ⓐ Ⓑ Ⓒ Ⓓ Ⓔ
36. Ⓐ Ⓑ Ⓒ Ⓓ Ⓔ
37. Ⓐ Ⓑ Ⓒ Ⓓ Ⓔ
38. Ⓐ Ⓑ Ⓒ Ⓓ Ⓔ
39. Ⓐ Ⓑ Ⓒ Ⓓ Ⓔ
40. Ⓐ Ⓑ Ⓒ Ⓓ Ⓔ
41. Ⓐ Ⓑ Ⓒ Ⓓ Ⓔ
42. Ⓐ Ⓑ Ⓒ Ⓓ Ⓔ
43. Ⓐ Ⓑ Ⓒ Ⓓ Ⓔ
44. Ⓐ Ⓑ Ⓒ Ⓓ Ⓔ
45. Ⓐ Ⓑ Ⓒ Ⓓ Ⓔ
46. Ⓐ Ⓑ Ⓒ Ⓓ Ⓔ
47. Ⓐ Ⓑ Ⓒ Ⓓ Ⓔ
48. Ⓐ Ⓑ Ⓒ Ⓓ Ⓔ
49. Ⓐ Ⓑ Ⓒ Ⓓ Ⓔ
50. Ⓐ Ⓑ Ⓒ Ⓓ Ⓔ
51. Ⓐ Ⓑ Ⓒ Ⓓ Ⓔ
52. Ⓐ Ⓑ Ⓒ Ⓓ Ⓔ
53. Ⓐ Ⓑ Ⓒ Ⓓ Ⓔ
54. Ⓐ Ⓑ Ⓒ Ⓓ Ⓔ

55. Ⓐ Ⓑ Ⓒ Ⓓ Ⓔ
56. Ⓐ Ⓑ Ⓒ Ⓓ Ⓔ
57. Ⓐ Ⓑ Ⓒ Ⓓ Ⓔ
58. Ⓐ Ⓑ Ⓒ Ⓓ Ⓔ
59. Ⓐ Ⓑ Ⓒ Ⓓ Ⓔ
60. Ⓐ Ⓑ Ⓒ Ⓓ Ⓔ
61. Ⓐ Ⓑ Ⓒ Ⓓ Ⓔ
62. Ⓐ Ⓑ Ⓒ Ⓓ Ⓔ
63. Ⓐ Ⓑ Ⓒ Ⓓ Ⓔ
64. Ⓐ Ⓑ Ⓒ Ⓓ Ⓔ
65. Ⓐ Ⓑ Ⓒ Ⓓ Ⓔ
66. Ⓐ Ⓑ Ⓒ Ⓓ Ⓔ
67. Ⓐ Ⓑ Ⓒ Ⓓ Ⓔ
68. Ⓐ Ⓑ Ⓒ Ⓓ Ⓔ
69. Ⓐ Ⓑ Ⓒ Ⓓ Ⓔ
70. Ⓐ Ⓑ Ⓒ Ⓓ Ⓔ
71. Ⓐ Ⓑ Ⓒ Ⓓ Ⓔ
72. Ⓐ Ⓑ Ⓒ Ⓓ Ⓔ
73. Ⓐ Ⓑ Ⓒ Ⓓ Ⓔ
74. Ⓐ Ⓑ Ⓒ Ⓓ Ⓔ
75. Ⓐ Ⓑ Ⓒ Ⓓ Ⓔ
76. Ⓐ Ⓑ Ⓒ Ⓓ Ⓔ
77. Ⓐ Ⓑ Ⓒ Ⓓ Ⓔ
78. Ⓐ Ⓑ Ⓒ Ⓓ Ⓔ
79. Ⓐ Ⓑ Ⓒ Ⓓ Ⓔ
80. Ⓐ Ⓑ Ⓒ Ⓓ Ⓔ

Section II Essays

Use the following pages to prepare your essays.

Section II Essays *(Continued)*

Index

A

Absinthe Drinker (Degas), 216
Absolutism, 65, 105, 106, 110, 137
Académie des Sciences, 58
Act of Annates (England), 42
Act of Restraint of Appeals (England), 42
Act of Settlement (England), 89
Act of Supremacy (England), 42
Act of Uniformity (England), 86
Act of Union (England), 90, 91
*Address to the Christian Nobility of the
   German Nation* (Luther), 39
Adenauer, Konrad, 327, 353
Adrianople, Treaty of, 171
Advancement of Learning (Bacon), 57
Afghanistan, under British rule, 228
Africa
   colonization, 205–206
   exploration of, 32–33
   North African campaigns of WWII, 302, 303
Agadir Crisis, 230–231
*Against the Murderous, Thieving Hordes of
   Peasants* (Luther), 39
Agincourt, battle of, 19
Agriculture, 61, 119–120, 280–281
Ahmed III (Ottoman Empire), 101
Airplanes, use in WWI, 243
Aisne, battle of, 250
Aix-la-Chapelle, Treaty of, 112, 115
Aix-la-Chapelle Congress, 152, 169–170
Alais, Peace of, 110
Albania, 238, 295
Albert I (Belgium), 213
Albrecht of Brandenburg, 38
Alexander I (Russia), 150, 151, 168–169,171
Alexander II (Russia), 192, 201–202
Alexander III (Russia), 202–203
Alexander VI Borgia, 33

Alexeev, M. V., 267–268
Algeçiras Conference, 230
Algeria, 326, 337–338, 351
Al Kut, 241, 251
Allenby, Edmund, 251, 254
Alliance system, 237–238
Allied Control Council, 330, 331
Allied powers, 239, 241, 242, 253–254
Alsace-Lorraine, 113, 115, 191, 208, 229,
   256, 257
Alva, Duke of, 50–51
America. *See* United States of America
Amiens, battle of, 254
Amish, 41
Amsterdam, 77
Anabaptists, 40–41, 44, 46
Anarchists, 164–165, 195
Anatomy Lesson of Dr. Tulp (Rembrandt),129
Ancient of Days (Blake), 158
Andropov, Yuri, 344
Anglicanism, 42, 46, 79–80, 86, 107
Anglo-Japanese Alliance, 228
Anglo-Russian Entente, 228–229
Anna (Russia), 97
Anne (England), 90
Anne of Austria, 109
Annunciation (da Vinci), 27
Anticlericalism, 98, 213
Anti-Semitism, 277
Antwerp, 51, 111, 114
Appeasement, 288, 293
April Theses, 247
Arafat, Yassir, 358
Aragon, 15
Architecture
   baroque style, 127–128
   medieval style, 25–26
Aristotle, 56
Arkwright, Richard, 120

Armada, 52, 76
Armies
  Russian (1864-1874), 201
  in seventeenth century, 47–48
Arminius, Jacobus, 107, 111
Arouet, Francois-Marie (Voltaire), 123, 126
Art
  baroque period of, 55, 128
  of Counter-Reformation, 45
  cubism, 236–237
  of early twentieth century, 232–237
  existentialism, 290
  impressionism, 218, 219–220
  mannerism, 54–55
  realism, 215–216
  Renaissance, 25–28, 29–30
  romantic period of, 157–158
  since WWII, 360
  surrealism, 291
Art nouveau, 234
Artois, Count of, 167
Ascendancy, 43
Ashes and Diamonds (Wajda), 320
Assembly of Notables, 138
Atheism, 125
Atlantic, battle of, 303
Atlantic Charter, 317
Atomic bomb, 308
Attlee, Clement, 297, 307, 308, 328, 349
Augsburg, Peace of, 40, 52, 53
Augsburg Confession, 39
Augustan Age, 90
Ausgleich, 204
Australia, 207
Austria (Habsburg Monarchy)
  feudalism, 71
  government structure, 70–71
  music, 71
  rulers (1658-1790), 71–72
  Seven Years' War, 115
  War of the Austrian Succession, 115
  wars with Turks, 100, 101
  war with France (1792), 141
Austria (Republic)
  alliance with Italy (1934), 279
  annexation by Nazi Germany, 294
Austria-Hungary
  assassination of Franz Ferdinand, 231

Balkan Crisis, 230, 238–239
  creation of, 204
  cultural revival, 204
  government structure, 204
  Triple Alliance, 209
  WWI, 239, 240–241
Austrian Empire
  Congress of Vienna, 150–152
  end of, 258
  formation of, 177
  Metternich era, 150, 151, 166, 168, 169,
    170, 177
  nationalism in, 177–179
  and Prussia, 190
  Schleswig-Holstein, 190
  Seven Weeks' War, 190–191
  war with Hungary (1848-1849), 178
  war with Sardinia (1859), 189
Austro-Prussian War, 190–191
Avignon Papacy, 14, 38
Azov, 101
Aztec empire, 33

B

Babylonian Captivity (Luther), 39
Babylonian Captivity at Avignon, 14, 38
Bacchus (Caravaggio), 55
Bach, Johann Sebastian, 56, 131
Bacon, Francis, 57
Bakunin, Mikhail, 195
Balance of power, 237–238
Balboa, Vasco Núñez, 33
Baldwin, Stanley, 259–260, 272, 288
Balfour, Arthur James, 210
Balfour Declaration, 256, 335
Balkan League, 238
Balkans. *See also names of specific countries*
  countries in, 238
  Crisis of 1908, 230, 238
  nationalism, 231
  Ottoman Empire, 100–101, 193, 204
  WWII, 299, 305
Ballot Act (Great Britain), 198
Baltic Sea, 112
Bank of England, 89, 329
Banks, 77, 89, 105, 111
Barbarossa, 299, 300

Barge Haulers on the Volga (Repin), 217
Baroque period, 55–56, 127–131
Basque movement, 356
Basra, 241
Bastille, storming of, 139–140
Batista, Fulgencio, 339
Battles. *See names of specific battles*
Bavaria, 70, 262
Bayle, Pierre, 125
Bay of Pigs, 339
Beauvoir, Simone de, 362
Beer Hall Putsch, 274
Beethoven, Ludwig van, 158
Belgium
    Congo, 205, 206
    democratic reform, 213
    French invasion of, 112
    independence, 173
    before independence, 51
    in Ruhr, 260–261
    within United Kingdom of Netherlands, 151
    WWI, 239, 240
    WWII, 296–297
Bellarmine, Robert Cardinal, 106
Benedetti, Count, 191
Benes, Eduard, 322
Bentham, Jeremy, 161
Bergman, Ingmar, 360
Beria, Lavrenti, 343
Berlin, Treaty of, 193
Berlin airlift, 331
Berlin Blockade, 339–340
Berlin Conference, 206
Berlin Wall, 354
Berlusconi, Silvio, 355
Bernini, Gianlorenzo, 55
Bernini, Giovanni, 127
Berri, Duke of, 167
Bessarabia, 151
Bethmann-Hollweg, Theobald, 209
Beveridge, William, 328
Bible, 14, 31–32, 39, 94, 108
Big Four, 256
Bill of Rights (England, 1689), 89
Bismarck, Otto von, 189, 190, 191, 193-194, 207–209, 238
Black Death, 13
Blair, Tony, 351

Blake, William, 158
Blanc, Louis, 164, 176
Blanqui, Auguste, 164
Blast of the Trumpet against the Terrible Regiment of Women (Knox), 106
Blenheim, battle of, 114
Blitzkrieg, 295
Bloc National, 260–261
Bloody Sunday, 203
Bluebird (Maeterlinck), 235
Blum, Leon, 289
Boccaccio, Giovanni, 24
Böcklin, Arnold, 218
Bodin, Jean, 106
Boers, 206
Boer War, 206, 228
Bohemia, 52, 178
Boleyn, Anne, 41–42
Bolsheviks, 203, 247, 248, 249, 250
Bonar-Law, 259
Bonnie Prince Charlie, 91
The Book of the Courtier (Castiglione), 24
Bosch, Hieronymus, 29
Bosnia-Herzegovina, 193, 204, 230, 231, 238, 357
Boulanger, Nadia, 361
Boulanger Crisis, 212
Bourbon dynasty, 69, 112, 151, 167
Bourgeois, Leon, 282
Bourgeoisie, 155
Boxer Rebellion, 207
Boyars, 16
Boyne, battle of, 90
Brahe, Tycho, 56
Brandenburg-Prussia, 73
Brandt, Willy, 353–354
Brazil, exploration of, 33
Breitenfeld, battle of, 53
Brest-Litovsk, Armistice at, 252–253
Brezhnev, Leonid, 344
Briand, Aristide, 260, 261
Bright, John, 197
Britain, battle of, 298–299
Brittany, 22
Brockdorff-Rantzau, Count, 257
Brueghel, Pieter, 29
Bruni, Leonardo, 29
Brüning, Heinrich, 275

Brunswick Manifesto, 141
Brusilov Offensive, 242
Bucer, Martin, 41, 44
Bucharest, Treaty of, 242
Büchner, Georg, 235
Bukharin, Nikolai, 252, 287
Bulgaria
  communization of, 321
  Neuilly Treaty, 258
  resistance to Soviet rule, 345
  Russian influence, 193, 204
  San Stefano Treaty, 193
  war with Turkey (1912), 238
  WWII, 299, 305
Bulge, Battle of the, 306
Bülow, Bernhard von, 209
Burckhardt, Jacob, 22
Burgundy, 15, 16
Burial at Ornans (Courbet), 215
The Burial of Count Orgaz (El Greco), 45
Burke, Edmund, 143
Burma, 337
Burschenschaften, 168
Byron, Lord, 171
Byzantine Empire, 100

C

Cabot, John, 33
Cabot, Sebastian, 33
Cabral, 33
Cadets, 203
Caetano, Marcelo, 355–356
Café Terrasse at Night (van Gogh), 232
Caillebotte, Gustave, 219
Callahan, James, 349
Calvin, John, 41
Calvinism
  church structure, 44
  in England, 42
  in Habsburg lands, 52
  origins of, 41
  in Prussia, 73, 74
  spread of, 49
  teachings of, 41, 46
  in United Provinces, 111
Cambrai, battle of, 251
Campo Formio, Treaty of, 142, 144

Camus, Albert, 361
Canals, 120, 154
Canning, George, 170, 172
Cano, Juan Sabastia del, 33
Canterbury Tales (Chaucer), 21
Capital (Marx), 165, 195
Capitalism, 47, 69, 118, 126, 161
Caporetto, battle of, 251
Caprivi, Count von, 209
Capuchins, 43
Caravaggio, 55, 128
Carier, Jacques, 34
Carlsbad Decrees, 168, 174
Carnot, Lazare, 141
Carson, Rachel, 362
Cartel des Gauches, 261, 272–273
Cartwright, Edward, 120
Casablanca Conference, 303, 317–318
Cassirer, Ernst, 290
Castiglione, Baldassare, 24–25
Castlereagh, Lord, 169, 170
Castro, Fidel, 339
Catalan movement, 356
Cateau-Cambrésis, Treaty of, 49
Catherine de' Medici, 49
Catherine II (Russia), 97, 101, 127
Catholic Church. *See* Roman Catholic Church
Catholic Emancipation Act (England), 172
Cato Street Conspiracy, 167
Cavaliers, 82, 86, 109
Cavour, Camillo de, 188–189
Cellini, Benvenuto, 25
Central Executive Committee (CEC), 270
Central powers, 239, 241, 242
Cervantes, 54
Ceylon, 337
Chamberlain, Neville, 288, 293, 294, 297
Champagne offensive, 250
Charles Albert (Sardinia), 179
Charles Emmanuel I (Italy), 99
Charles Emmanuel III (Italy), 99
Charles I (Austria), 242
Charles I (England), 78–84, 108–109
Charles I (Spain), 48
Charles II (England), 85–88
Charles II (Spain), 69
Charles III (Spain), 69–70
Charles IX (France), 49

Charles V (Holy Roman Empire), 38, 40, 48
Charles VI (Holy Roman Empire), 72, 115
Charles VII (France), 20
Charles X (France), 173
Charles X Gustavus (Sweden), 92
Charles XI (Sweden), 92
Charles XII (Sweden), 92, 95
Chartism, 180–181
Chatelet, Emilie de, 126
Chaucer, Geoffrey, 21
Chechnya, 346
Chemical warfare, 243–244
Chernobyl, 345, 359
Chernov, Victor, 247, 250
Chiang Kai-shek, 332–333
Chiaroscuro, 26
Child labor, 180
China
  Boxer Rebellion, 207
  British capture of Peking, 197
  Civil War, 332–333
  communism, 271
  Japanese occupation of Shantung, 258
  Korean War, 334
  Nine-Power Treaty, 284
  war with Japan (1937-1945), 300
Chirac, Jacques, 352
Chirico, Giorgio de, 290, 291
Chopin, Fryderyk, 174
Christian Democrats (Germany), 327, 353, 354
Christian Democrats (Italy), 354–355
Christian humanism, 31–32
Christianity. *See also* Calvinism; Roman
  Catholic Church
  Anabaptists, 40–41, 44, 46
  Anglicanism, 42, 46, 79–80, 86, 107
  ecumenical movement, 360
Lutheranism, 39–40, 44, 46, 52
  Methodism, 125
  Presbyterianism, 44, 87, 90
  Protestant Reformation, 37–40
  Puritans, 41, 42, 51, 86, 107
  wars of religion (1560-1648), 47–54
Christian IV (Denmark), 53
Christian IX (Denmark), 213
Christian socialism, 165
Christina (Sweden), 92, 111
Churchill, Winston

Iron Curtain speech, 330
Potsdam Conference, 307–308
prime minister, 297, 329, 349
WWI, 241
WWII, 303, 304, 305
Yalta Conference, 306–307
Ciampi, Carlo, 355
Cities, 59, 155–156
Civil Constitution of the Clergy, 140
The Civilization of the Renaissance in Italy
  (Burckhardt), 22
Civil Services Reform (Great Britain), 198
Clarendon Code, 86
Classical past, 23
Clay, Lucius, 331
Clement VII (Pope), 41–42
Clement XI (Pope), 98
Clement XIV (Pope), 98
Clergy, 44
Clinton, Bill, 356
Clones, 359
Coal, 153–154
Coercion Acts (England), 166
Colbert, Jean-Baptiste, 66, 118
Cold War, 330–335, 338–340
Coleridge, Samuel Taylor, 157
Coligny, Gaspard de, 49
Collectivization, 280–281
Colleges and universities, 57, 168
Colonna, Vittoria, 28
Columbus, Christopher, 33
Combes Laws (France), 213
Comintern, 267
Commedia (Dante), 24
Commercial Revolution, 153
Common Market, 348, 350, 356
Commonwealth (England, 1649-1653), 84
Communism. *See also* Soviet Union
  in China, 271, 332–333
  in France, 325
  in Italy, 324
  Marxism, 165, 195–196, 203, 210
Communist Information Agency
  (Cominform), 323
The Communist Manifesto (Marx and Engels),
  165, 195
Composition VII (Kandinsky), 237
Concerto, 131

Concert of Europe, 151–152, 169, 191
Concordat of 1801, 144
Concordat of Bologna, 49
Congo, 205, 206
Congress of Vienna, 150–152, 166, 169
Congress System, 152, 169–170
Conservatism, 160, 168
Conservative Party (Great Britain), 197, 198–199, 210, 272, 349, 350
Constance, council at, 14
Constantinople, fall of, 16
Constituent Assembly, 250
Constitutionalism, 105, 106
Consulate government (France), 144–145
Consul for Life, 145
Containment, 331–332
Continental Blockade, 146
Conventicle Act (England), 86
Convention Parliament (England), 86
Copenhagen, Treaty of, 92
Copernicus, Nicolas, 56
Corfu, 267
Corn Laws (England), 166, 180
The Coronation of Poppaea (Palestrina), 56
Corporation Act (England), 86
Cortes, Hernan, 33
Cotton, 120
Cotton gin, 120
Council of Constance, 14
Council of Pisa, 14
Council of Ten, 256
Council of Trent, 44
Counter-Enlightenment, 124–125
Counter-Reformation, 43–47
Courbet, Gustave, 215
Covenant, 106
Cranmer, Thomas, 42
Craxi, Bettino, 355
Crecy, battle of, 19
Crimea, 97, 101
Crimean War, 172, 188, 192–193
Critique of Dialectical Reason (Sartre), 360
Critique of Political Economy (Marx), 195
Critique of Pure Reason (Kant), 158
Crompton, Samuel, 120
Cromwell, Oliver, 82–83, 84–85, 109
Cuba, 339, 340
Cubism, 236–237

Cuno, Wilhelm, 262
Curzon line, 295
Customs Union, 168
Czechoslovakia
    communization of, 322–323
    democratic history of, 289
    formation of, 258
    Hitler's invasion of, 294–295
    Prague Spring, 347
    resistance to Soviet rule, 345
    Velvet Revolution, 347–348
    WWII, 289
Czech rebellion, 267
Czech Republic, 348
Czechs, 71

D

Daguerre, Louis, 214
Daladier, Edouard, 273, 289
Dali, Salvador, 291
Dalmatia, 258
The Dance of Life (Munch), 233
Dante, 24
Darby, Abraham, 153–154
Dark Ages, 12
Darkness at Noon (Koestler), 289
Darwin, Charles, 217
Das Kapital (Marx), 165, 195
David (Donatello), 26, 28
David (Michelangelo), 28
David, Jacques-Louis, 158
Da Vinci, Leonardo, 27
Dawes Plan, 263
Death of Sardanapalus (Delacroix), 159
December Uprising, 171–172
Declaration of Independence, 161
Declaration of Indulgence, 88
Declaration of London, 243, 251
Declaration of Pillnitz, 141
Declaration of Rights of Man (France), 161
Degas, Edgar, 215, 216
De Gaulle, Charles, 298, 325, 338, 340–341, 351–352
Deism, 125
Delacroix, Eugene, 159
Denikin, Anton, 268
Denmark

democratic reform, 213
  in fifteenth century, 16
  Great Northern War, 92
  Lutheranism, 39
  in Norway, 93
  Schleswig-Holstein, 190
  Thirty Years' War, 52–53
  war with Prussia, 204
  WWII, 296
Depression, Great, 271–272, 274
Descartes, René, 57, 122
D'Estaing, Valéry Giscard, 352
D'Este, Beatrice, 28
Détente, 341
The Devil's General (Zuckmayer), 360
De Witt, Jan, 111
Dias, Bartolomeu, 32
Diderot, Denis, 123
Diet of Worms, 38
Dimitrov, Georgi, 321
Diplomatic Revolution, 115
Directory (France), 142, 143–144
Disarmament treaties and agreements,
  284–286
Diseases, 13, 87, 117
Disquieting Muses (Chirico), 290
Disraeli, Benjamin, 193, 197, 198–199, 205
Divine Comedy (Dante), 24
Doctor Zhivago (Pasternak), 360
Doenitz, Karl, 306
Dogger Bank Incident, 228
Donatello, 26
Donation of Constantine (Valla), 29
Don John, 48
Don Quixote (Cervantes), 54
Doumergue, Gaston, 273
Dracula, 16
The Dram-Shop (Zola), 235
Dreikaiserbund, 238
Dreyfus Affair, 212–213
Dual Alliance, 208–209, 238
Dual Entente, 227
Dual Monarchy. *See* Austria-Hungary
Dubcek, Alexander, 347
Duchamp, Marcel, 235, 236
Dulles, John Foster, 339
Duma, 246
Dürer, Albrecht, 30

Dutch East Indies Company, 77
Dzurinda, Mikulas, 348

E

Eastern Accords, 284
Easter Rebellion, 259
East Germany
  Berlin Blockade, 339–340
  Cold War conflict, 330–331
  establishment of, 321–322, 327
  reunification with West Germany, 354
East India Company, 197
Ebert, Friedrich, 254, 262–263, 264
Eckart, Dietrich, 274
Eckhart, Meister, 14
Economic theory, 118, 126
Economy
  in 1500-1640s, 60–61
  capitalism, 47, 69, 118, 126, 161
  in eighteenth century, 120–121
  France (1980s), 352
  France (after WWI), 261
  France (pre-Revolution), 138
  Great Britain (after WWI), 259, 349–350
  Italy (after WWI), 355
  mercantilism, 61, 118, 138
  Netherlands (seventeenth century), 77–78
  social institutions necessary for prosperity,
    117–118
Ecstasy of Saint Teresa (Bernini), 55
Ecumenical movement, 360
Eden, Anthony, 329, 349
Edict of Nantes, 50, 67
Education, 39, 126, 162, 210
Education Act (Great Britain), 198
Edward III (England), 19
Edward VI (England), 42
Egypt, 144, 302, 336
18 *Brumarie*, 142, 144
Eighty Years' War, 50–51
Einstein, Albert, 218
Eisenhower, Dwight, 302, 304, 305–306,
  339, 344
El Alamein, 302
Elegances of the Latin Language (Valla), 29
El Greco, 31, 44, 45
Elizabeth (Russia), 97, 115, 116

Elizabeth I (England), 42, 49, 51–52
Emile (Rousseau), 123
Emilie Flöge (Klimt), 234
Empiricism, 57, 122
Ems Dispatch, 191
Encyclopedia (Diderot), 123
Engels, Friedrich, 165
England. *See also* Great Britain and American
  War for Independence, 90
  under Anne, 90
  Armada, 52
  Bill of Rights (1689), 89
  under Charles I, 78–84, 108–109
  under Charles II, 85–88
  Civil War, 78, 82–85, 109
  Clarendon Code, 86
  Commonwealth (1649-1653), 84
  in eighteenth century, 90–91
  exploration, 33–34
  farming, 61
  in fifteenth century, 16–17
  Glorious Revolution, 88–90
  Hundred Years' War, 19–21
  under James I, 107–108
  under James II, 88–90, 109
  literature, 54
  nobility in, 18–19
  population, 59
  Protectorate (1653-1659), 85
  Protestant Reformation, 41–42
  religious conflicts (1553-1603), 51–52
  Renaissance, 30
  Restoration (1660-1688), 85–88
  scientific societies, 58
  War of the League of Augsburg, 113
  War of the Roses, 20
  under William and Mary, 88–90, 109
Enlightenment, 70, 98, 121–127, 157, 169
Entente Cordiale, 228
Environmentalism, 362
Erasmus, Desiderius, 31
Erhard, Ludwig, 353
Erzberger, Matthias, 263
Essay Concerning Human Understanding
  (Locke), 126
Estaing, Valéry Giscard D', 352
Estates-General, 139
Estonia, 93, 95, 295, 346

Ethiopia, 279–280, 286, 294
Eucharist, 45
Euro, 351
Europe
  early ideas, 11
  physical geography of, 11–12
European Atomic Energy Commission
  (Euratom), 348
European Community (EC), 348–349
European Economic Community (EEC),
  348, 350, 356
European Steel and Coal Community, 348
European Union (EU), 349, 355
Evolution, 217
Existentialism, 290, 361
Exploration, 32–34, 118–119
Expressionism, 232
Expulsion of Adam and Eve (Masaccio), 26
Eyck, Jan van, 29

F

Fabian Society, 195–196, 210
Factories, 155
Factory Act (Great Britain), 180
Falkland Islands, 350
Family structure
  Industrial Revolution, 156
  seventeenth century, 59–60
Fanon, Frantz, 360
Farming, 61, 119–120, 280–281
Fascism, 265–267, 278–280, 288, 289–290.
  See also Nazi Germany
Fashoda Crisis, 230
Fassbinder, Rainer Werner, 328
Fathers and Sons (Turgenev), 202
February Revolution, 245–246
Feminism, 126, 361–362
Ferdinand (Bohemia), 52
Ferdinand I (Austria), 177–178
Ferdinand I (Holy Roman Empire), 48
Ferdinand of Aragon, 22
Ferdinand VI (Spain), 69
Ferdinand VII (Spain), 167, 170
Feudalism, 18, 21, 71, 86
Fichte, Johann Gottlieb, 159
Ficino, Marsilio, 23
Fighting Temeraire (Turner), 159

File-Mile Act (England), 86
Film, 360–361
Finland, 93, 95, 117, 151, 296
First Coalition (1792-1797), 143–144
First Coalition (Russia), 247
First Dutch War, 112
First Estate (France), 137, 139
First Five Year Plan (Soviet Union), 280–281
Fiume, 258, 265
Five-Power Treaty, 284
Flight into Egypt (Giotto), 26
Florence, 15, 24
Florentine Academy, 23
Flying shuttle, 120
Foch, Ferdinand, 253–254
Food and diet, 60
Four Holy Men (Dürer), 30
Fourier, Charles, 164
Four Points, 192
Fourteen Points, 255, 282
Foxe, John, 14
France
    Agadir Crisis, 230–231
    in Algeria, 326, 337–338, 351
    American War for Independence, 116
    Boulanger Crisis, 212
    Cartel des Gauches, 261, 272–273
    Chirac government, 352
    Civil Constitution of the Clergy, 140
    Combes Laws, 213
    Crimean War, 192–193
    Declaration of Rights of Man, 161
    De Gaulle government, 341–342,
        351–352
    Depression (1931-1935), 272
    Doumergue government, 273
    Dreyfus Affair, 212–213
    Dual Entente, 227
    Dutch Wars, 112–113
    Entente Cordiale, 228
    Estates-General, 139
    exploration, 34
    Fashoda Crisis, 230
    in fifteenth century, 15, 17
    Fifth Republic, 338, 351–353
    Five-Power Treaty, 284
    Fourth Republic, 338, 351
    Franco-Prussian War, 191, 200

    under Henry IV, 50, 110
    Huguenots, 43, 49, 50, 67, 106, 109, 110
    Hundred Years' War, 19–21
    imperialism, 205, 206, 207
    in Indochina, 326, 337
    July Revolution, 173
    Laval government, 273
    literature, 54
    Little Entente, 277, 279
    under Louis XIII, 110
    under Louis XIV, 65–67, 68, 89, 112–113
    under Louis XV, 67
    under Louis XVI, 68, 110
    Mitterand government, 352
    monarchy, 22
    music, 56
    Napoleonic era, 143–146
    under Napoleon III, 176–177, 188–189,
        191, 199–200, 211
    National Assembly, 139–140, 211–212
    nuclear weapons, 341
    Panama Scandal, 212
    Paris Commune, 211
    Popular Front, 289
    population, 59
    Renaissance, 30
    Restoration, 167
    Revolution (1789), 68, 137–143
    revolution of 1848, 176
    in Ruhr, 260–261
    scientific societies, 58
    Second Empire, 200
    Second French Republic, 199–200
    Tardieu government, 272
    Third Republic, 211–213
    Thirty Years' War, 53
    Treaty of Pyrenees, 112
    Triple Entente, 229
    War of the League of Augsburg, 74, 113
    Wars of Religion, 49–50
    war with Austria (1792), 141
    war with Prussia, 191, 200, 238
    WWI, 239, 240, 241–242, 250, 255, 256
    after WWI, 260–261
    WWII, 295, 296–298, 302–303, 304
    after WWII, 325–326
Francis I (France), 49
Francis II (France), 49

Francis Joseph (Austria), 178
Franco, Francisco, 288, 293–294, 356
Franco-Prussian War, 191, 200, 238
Frankfurt, Treaty of, 191
Frankfurt Assembly, 179–180
Franz Ferdinand, 231, 238
Franz Joseph (Austria), 189
Frederick I (Prussia), 74
Frederick III (German Empire), 209
Frederick III of Saxony, 38
Frederick the Great (Prussia), 75–76, 115, 126–127
Frederick V (Bohemia), 52
Frederick William (Prussia), 73–74
Frederick William I (Prussia), 74–75
Frederick William IV (Prussia), 179, 180
Freedom of the Christian Man (Luther), 39
Free enterprise, 121
French and Indian War, 115–116
French Revolution, 68, 137–143
Freud, Sigmund, 217–218
Friedrich, Caspar David, 158
Fromm, Erich, 290
Frondes, 65–66, 110
Frontier, battle of, 239
Fulton, Robert, 154
Fundamental Laws (Russia), 244

G

Gabrieli, Giovanni, 131
Galileo, 57
Gama, Vasco da, 32–33
Gambetta, Leon, 212
Gargantua and Pantagruel (Rabelais), 30
Garibaldi, Giuseppe, 188, 189
Gasperi, Alcide de, 324
Gauguin, Paul, 233
Gaulle, Charles de, 298, 325, 338, 340–341, 351–352
Gaza, 251
Gender roles, 156
Geneva Conference (1954), 337
Geneva Summit (1955), 339
Genoa, 15, 99
Gentilleschi, Artemisia, 28
Geography, 11–12
George, David Lloyd, 259
George I (England), 90
George II (England), 90
George III (England), 90
George IV (England), 90, 174
George VI (Great Britain), 272
Gericault, Theodore, 159
German Confederation, 151, 162, 168, 174, 190, 207
German Democratic Republic (GDR). *See* East Germany
German Empire
    formation of, 207, 237
    imperialism, 205–206, 207
    militarism, 229
    Morocco, 230–231
    music, 217
    political structure, 207–208
    Reinsurance Treaty, 194, 209, 227
    WWI, 239, 240–243, 252–254, 255
German National People's Party (DVP), 263
German Workers Party (DAP), 274
Germany. *See also* German Empire; Nazi Germany
    Depression, 274
    environmentalism, 362
    in fifteenth century, 16
    German Confederation, 151, 162, 168, 174, 190, 207
    Industrial Revolution, 155
    nationalism in, 163
    Oder-Neisse line, 307, 318, 341, 353
    reunification of, 354
    Social Democratic Party, 196
    space exploration, 342
    Thirty Years' War, 52–53
    Treaty of Versailles, 257
    unification of, 152, 174, 179–180, 189–191
    Weimar Republic, 261–264, 275–276
    WWI reparations, 256–257, 260–261, 262, 263, 273–274
    after WWII, 307, 319, 326–328, 330–331, 353–354
Germinal (Zola), 235
Gestapo, 276, 277
Gilbert, William, 58
Gilles (Watteau), 132
Giolitti, Giovanni, 264
Giotto, 26

Giraud, Henri, 302
Girl with the Pearl Earring (Vermeer), 130
Gladstone, William, 197–198, 199, 206, 211
Glasnost, 345
Gleichschaltung, 276, 277
Glencoe Massacre, 91
Glorious Revolution, 88–90
Goebbels, Joseph, 275
Goethe, 141
Gold, 206
Gomulka, Wladyslaw, 346
Gonzaga, Isabella, 28
Good Friday Accord, 351
Gorbachev, Mikhail, 344, 345
Göring, Hermann, 274, 276
Gottwald, Klement, 322
Gouges, Olympe de, 361
Goya, Francisco G., 159
Grand Alliance, 114
Grass, Günter, 360
Great Britain. *See also* England
  Anglo-Japanese Alliance, 228
  Anglo-Russian Entente, 228–229
  appeasement policy, 288, 293
  Blair government, 351
  Boer War, 206
  Cato Street Conspiracy, 167
  Congress of Vienna, 150–152
  Crimean War, 192–193
  Depression (1929-1931), 271–272
  Disraeli era, 193, 197, 198–199
  Dogger Bank Incident, 228
  Egypt, 336
  Entente Cordiale, 228
  Fashoda Crisis, 230
  Five-Power Treaty, 284
  Gladstone era, 197–198, 199
  India, 197, 336–337
  Industrial Revolution, 152–156
  New Imperialism, 205–207
  newspapers, 214
  Northern Ireland, 350–351
  Palestine, 335
  Palmerston era, 196–197
  recognition of Soviet Union, 271
  reform (1820s-1830s), 172, 174
  reform (1870-1914), 209–210
  repressive legislation (1815-1820), 166-167

  Salisbury era, 227–228
  Seven Years' War, 115–116
  Thatcher government, 349, 350
  Triple Entente, 229
  Victorian Compromise, 180–181
  WWI, 239, 240, 241, 242–243, 251, 252, 255, 256
  after WWI, 259–260
  WWII, 295, 296, 297, 298–299, 302, 303, 304, 305
  after WWII, 328–329, 349–351
Great Depression, 271–272, 274
Great Northern War, 92–93, 95
Great Purge Trials, 287
Great Reform Bill (Great Britain), 174
Great Schism, 14, 16
Grebel, Conrad, 40
Greece, ancient, 11, 23
Greece, modern
  Balkan crisis, 238
  independence, 171
  Revolution, 170, 171
  Truman Doctrine, 332
  WWII, 299, 305
Green Party (Germany), 362
Grey, Earl, 174
Groote, Gerard, 14
Grosz, Georg, 291, 292
Grotewohl, Otto, 321–322
Guise family, 50
Guizot, François, 176
The Gulag Archipelago (Solzhenitsyn), 360
Gunpowder, 47
Gustavus Adolfus (Sweden), 53, 91–92, 111–112
Gustavus III (Sweden), 93
Gustavus V (Sweden), 213
Gutenberg, Johann, 30

H

Habeas corpus, 166
Habsburg Monarchy, 48, 54, 70. *See also* Austria (Habsburg Monarchy)
Haig, Douglas, 241, 251
Haldane Mission, 229
Händel, Georg Friedrich, 131
Hanover dynasty, 90

Hansa League, 16
Hardenberg, Karl von, 150
Hargreaves, James, 120
Harvey, William, 58
Hasidism, 125
Havel, Václav, 347–348
Haydn, Franz Josef, 132
Heath, Edward, 349
Hegel, Georg Wilhelm, 159, 165
Heidegger, Martin, 361
Heinemann, Gustav, 353
Henry II (France), 49
Henry III (France), 49, 50
Henry IV (France), 50, 110
Henry of Navarre, 50
Henry the Navigator, 32
Henry VIII, 41–42
Herder, Johann Gottfried, 163
Herriot, Edouard, 261
Hess, Rudolf, 274
Heuss, Theodor, 327, 328
Heydrich, Reinhard, 276
High Middle Ages, 12–13
Himmler, Heinrich, 275
Hindenburg, Paul von, 240, 264, 275, 276, 277
Hitler, Adolf. *See also* Nazi Germany
    appointment to Chancellor, 276
    assassination attempt, 305
    background, 274
    Beer Hall Putsch, 263, 274
    consolidation of power, 277, 287
    death of, 306
    entry into politics, 274
    presidential election of 1932, 275
Ho Chi Minh, 337, 340
Hohenlohe, Prince, 209
Hohenzollerns, 73–76, 168
Holbach, Baron d', 125
Holbrook, Richard, 357
Holland. *See* Netherlands
Holocaust, 298, 347
Holy Alliance, 151
Holy Roman Empire
    Congress of Vienna, 151
    and Habsburg Monarchy, 70
    and papacy, 16
    population, 59
    and Reformation, 39

    sack of Rome, 43
    structure of, 16, 70–71
Honecker, Erich, 354
Hong Kong, 351
Horn of Africa, 32
Huguenots, 43, 49, 50, 67, 106, 109, 110
Huizinga, Johann, 13, 289
Humanism, 23, 24, 29, 31–32
Hume, David, 122, 125
Hundred Days, 146
Hundred Years' War, 19–21
Hungary. *See also* Austria-Hungary
    alliance with Italy (1934), 279
    anti-Soviet revolution (1956), 347
    communization of, 320–321
    end of Soviet influence, 347
    in fifteenth century, 15
    nationalism, 172, 177, 178–179
    seizure of Slovakian lands before
        WWII, 295
    Treaty of Szatmar, 72
    Turk lands ceded to Austria (1718), 101
    war with Austria (1848-1849), 178
    after WWI, 258
    WWII, 299, 305
Huss, John, 14
Hussein, Sadam, 358
Hussites, 14

I

Ignatius of Loyola (Saint), 43
Illiberalism, 231
Imperialism, 204–207, 229–231
Impression: Sunrise (Monet), 219
Impressionism, 218, 219–220
Inca empire, 33
India
    British control, 197, 336–337
    exploration of, 32
    independence, 337
Individualism, 23, 47
Indochina, 326, 337
Indonesia, 338
Induction, 57
Indulgences, 38
Industrialization, in Soviet Union, 281
Industrial Revolution, 152–156, 194

Inflation, 60
Innocent III (Pope), 13
Innocent X (Pope), 98
Innocent XI (Pope), 98
In Praise of Folly (Erasmus), 31
Inquisition, 22
Institutes of the Christian Religion
    (Calvin), 41
Intendants, 110
Inter-Balkan Wars, 231
Interest rates, 118
Iran, 331
Iraq, 241, 358
Iraq War, 351
Ireland
    Act of Union, 91
    Catholic rebellions, 81, 108
    Cromwell's invasion of, 84–85
    in eighteenth century, 90–91
    independence, 259
    Irish Home Rule, 211
    Reformation, 43
    Ulster, 259, 350–351
Irish Republican Army (IRA), 259, 350, 351
Isabella of Castile, 22, 33
Island of the Dead (Böcklin), 218
Israel, 256, 335–336, 358
Italy
    alliance with Austria (1934), 279
    under Austrian rule, 151
    Ethiopia invasion, 279–280, 286, 294
    Five-Power Treaty, 284
    music, 56
    under Mussolini, 264–267, 278–280,
        286, 288
    nationalism, 163–164
    population, 59
    Renaissance, 22–24
    revolutions and uprisings, 170–171, 177
    scientific societies, 58
    in seventeenth-eighteenth century, 98–99
    Triple Alliance, 209
    unification of, 99, 188–189
    uprisings (1831-1832), 174
    war with Turkey (1911), 231
    WWI, 240, 251, 254, 255, 256
    after WWI, 258, 264–267
    WWII, 298, 302, 303
    after WWII, 324–325, 354–355

Ivan III (Russia), 93
Ivan IV (Russia), 93
Ivanov, Nikolai, 240

J

Jacobins, 141
Jacobites, 91
James I (England), 107–108
James II (England), 88–90, 109
Jansenism, 67, 98, 125
Japan
    Anglo-Japanese Alliance, 228
    Five-Power Treaty, 284
    invasion of Manchuria, 282, 286, 300
    war with China (1937-1945), 300
    war with Russia (1904-1905), 202, 203,
        207, 244
    after WWI, 258
    WWII, 300–301, 307–308
Jaruzelski, Wojciech, 346
Jaurès, Jean, 196, 213
Jesuits, 43, 67, 98
Jews
    Hasidism, 125
    Holocaust, 298, 347
    Israel, 256, 335–336, 358
    in Nazi Germany, 277, 287
    in Soviet Union, 344
    in United Provinces, 111
Joan of Arc, 19–20
Jodl, Alfred, 306
Joffre, Joseph, 241
John III (Poland), 100
Joseph II (Holy Roman Empire), 72, 127
Jospin, Lionel, 352–353
Joyce, James, 220
Juan Carlos (Spain), 356
Jugendstil, 234
Julius II, 24
July offensive, 248
July Revolution (France), 173
June Days, 176
Jutland/Skagerrak, battle of, 243

K

Kadar, Janos, 347
Kamenev, Lev, 250, 269–270, 287

Kandinsky, Wassily, 237
Kant, Immanuel, 125, 158, 361
Karlowitz, Treaty of, 100
Kashmir, 337
Katharine of Aragon, 41–42
Kay, John, 120
Kellogg-Briand Pact, 285
Kempis, Thomas à, 14
Kennan, George, 332
Kennedy, John F., 339–340
Kepler, Johannes, 56–57
Kerensky, Alexander, 247, 248–249
Khrushchev, Nikita, 339, 340, 343–344
Kierkegaard, Søren, 361
Killiecrankie, battle of, 91
King George's War, 115
Kingsley, Charles, 165
King William's War, 113
Kirchner, Ernst Ludwig, 291
Kirov, Sergei, 282
Kissinger, Henry, 341
Klimt, Gustav, 234
Knox, John, 41, 43, 106
Koestler, Arthur, 289
Kohl, Helmut, 354
Kolchak, Alexander, 268
Koniggratz, battle of, 190
Korean War, 328, 333–334
Kornilov affair, 248–249
Kossuth, Louis, 177, 178
Kostunica, Vojislav, 358
Kosygin, Aleksei, 344, 347
Kotzebue, August von, 168
Kovac, Michael, 348
Kovacs, Bela, 320
Kronstadt rebellion, 268
Kruger, Paul, 206
Kuchuk-Kainardji, Treaty of, 101
Kulturkampf, 208
Kuwait, 358
Kwasniewski, Aleksander, 346–347

L

Labour Party (Great Britain), 210, 272,
    328–329, 349, 351
Laibach Congress, 152, 170, 171
Laissez-faire capitalism, 118, 126, 161
Lake Victoria, 205

Lamartine, Alphonse, 176
Lamentation of the Dead Christ
    (Mantegna), 25
Land Act (Great Britain), 198
Las Meninas (Velazquez), 128
Lateran Accords, 278–279
Latin America, 170
Latvia, 95, 295, 346
Laud, William, 79, 81, 107, 108
Laval, Pierre, 273, 298
Lawrence, T. E., 251
Lay piety, 14
League of Augsburg, 113
League of Nations, 255, 257, 258–259,
    277, 282–283, 286
Lebrun, Albert, 273
LeBrun, Vigée, 158
Lefevre d'Etaples, Jacques, 31
Legislative Assembly (France), 140–141
Leibniz, Gottfried Wilhelm, 74, 122
Leighton, Alexander, 80
Leipzig, battle of, 146
Lend-Lease Program, 299, 301
Lenin, Vladimir, 203, 247, 249–250, 252,
    267–269, 269
Leonardo da Vinci, 27
Leopold I (Holy Roman Empire), 71, 114
Leopold II (Belgium), 213
Leopold of Saxe-Coburg (Belgium), 173
Leo X (Pope), 38
Les Demoiselles d'Avignon (Picasso), 236
Letter of Majesty, 52
LeVau, Louis, 128
Ley, Robert, 276
Liberalism, 161–162
Liberal Party (Great Britain), 197, 198,
    210–211, 271
Liberty, 162
Literature
    Augustan Age, 90
    in early twentieth century, 220
    during Hundred Years' War, 21
    naturalism, 235
    Renaissance, 24–25
    romantic period, 157
    since WWII, 360
    in sixteenth-seventeenth centuries, 54
    symbolism, 235
Lithuania, 295, 346

Little Entente, 277, 279
Livingston, David, 205
Locarno Pact, 263, 284, 286
Locke, John, 122, 125, 126
Lollards, 14
Lombardy, 151
London, 59, 87
London, Treaty of, 240, 258
London Naval Disarmament Treaty, 285
Louis Napoleon (Napoleon III), 176–177, 188–189, 191, 199–200
Louis-Philippe (France), 173, 176
Louis XI (France), 22
Louis XIII (France), 110
Louis XIV (France), 65–67, 68, 89, 112–113, 127–128
Louis XV (France), 67
Louis XVI (France), 68, 110, 138–140, 141
Louis XVIII (France), 167, 173
Lovell, Bernard, 359
Lovesick (Grosz), 292
Lublin Committee, 320
Ludendorff, Erich, 240, 253, 254
Luftwaffe, 278, 298
Lusitania, 243, 252
Luther, Martin, 31, 37–39
Lutheranism, 39–40, 44, 46, 52
Lützen, battle of, 53, 92
Lvov, George, 246, 247, 248
Lytton Report, 286

M

Maastricht treaties, 356
Macadam, John, 120
MacArthur, Douglas, 308, 334
MacDonald, Ramsey, 260, 271–272, 288
Machiavelli, 29
Mackensen, August von, 241
Macmillan, Harold, 349
Madagascar, 206
Maeterlinck, Maurice, 235
Magellan, Ferdinand, 33
Magenta, battle of, 189
Magnetism, 58
Magritte, René, 291, 292
Magyars, 177
Major, John, 350
Majuba Hill, battle of, 205

Malaya, 337
Malenkov, Georgi, 343
Manchuria, Japanese invasion of, 282, 286, 300
Manet, Edouard, 215, 216
Mannerism, 54–55
Man on Balcony (Caillebotte), 219
Mantegna, Andrea, 25
Manutius, Aldus, 30
Mao Zedong, 332
Maria de' Medici, 109, 110
Maria Theresa, 72, 76, 115
Marie Antoinette, 68, 140, 141
Marlborough, Duke of, 114
Marne, battle of, 240
Marriage, 59–60, 156
The Marriage of Maria Braun (Fassbinder), 328
Marshall, George C., 332
Marshall Plan, 324, 329
Marsiglio of Padua, 14
Martin V (pope), 14, 16
Marx, Karl, 47, 159, 165, 195
Marxism, 165, 195–196, 203, 210
Mary, Queen of Scots, 51–52, 106
Mary I (England), 42, 49, 51
Mary II (England), 88, 109
Mary of Burgundy, 22
Masaccio, 26–27
Materialism, 125
Matthias (Holy Roman Empire), 52
Matthys, Jan, 40
Mazarin, Cardinal Jules, 110
Mazzini, Giuseppe, 163–164, 174, 177
Meciar, Vladimir, 348
Medicine, 359
Medieval art, 25–26
Mein Kampf (Hitler), 274
Melanchthon, Philip, 39
Menaced Assassin (Magritte), 292
Mendel, Gregor, 218
Mennonites, 41
Mensheviks, 247
Mercantilism, 61, 118, 138
Mesopotamian campaign, of WWI, 251
Mesta, 22
Methodism, 125
Metternich, Klemens Wenzel von, 150, 151, 166, 168, 169, 170, 177
Michael II (Romania), 305, 321

Michelangelo, 24, 27–28, 127
Michelet, Jules, 164
Middle Ages, 12–14, 18, 100
Middle class, 155, 182
Mikolajczyk, Stanislas, 320
Milan, 15
Militarism, 229
Military, 47–48
Miliukov, Paul, 247
Miliutin, D. A., 202
Mill, John Stuart, 361
Millerand, Alexandre, 260, 261
Milosevic, Slobodan, 357–358
Milton, John, 54
Mindszenty, Josef Cardinal, 321
Mitterand, François, 352
Molotov, Vyacheslav, 343
Monarchy. *See also names of specific*
    monarchs
        Bellarmine's writings on, 106
        Enlightenment, 126–127
        in France, 65–68
        rise of, 21–22
        women, 49
Monet, Claude, 219
Mongolia, 271
Monnet, Jean, 326
Monroe Doctrine, 170
Montagu, Mary, 126
Montaigne, Michel de, 54
Montenegro, 193, 204, 238
Montesquieu, Baron de, 123
Monteverdi, Claudio, 56
Montgomery, Bernard, 302, 305–306
More, Thomas, 31, 42
Morgenthau Plan, 318
Moro, Aldo, 355
Morocco, 230–231, 337
Mozart, Wolfgang Amadeus, 132
Muhammad IV (Ottoman Empire), 100
Müller, Hermann, 264
Müller, Ludwig, 277
Munch, Edvard, 233
Municipal Reform Law (Great Britain), 180
Music
    baroque period, 56, 130–131
    rococo influences, 132
    romantic period, 158

since WWII, 361
in Vienna, 71
Wagner, 217
Mussolini, Benito, 264–267, 278–280, 286,
    288
Mussorgsky, Modest, 94
Mustapha II (Ottoman Empire), 100–101
Mutual Guarantees, Treaty of, 284
Mutually assured destruction (MAD), 343

N

Nader, Ralph, 362
Nagy, Imre, 347
Nana (Zola), 235
Napoleon Bonaparte, 142, 143–146
Napoleonic Code, 144
Napoleonic Wars, 145–146
Napoleon III, 176–177, 188–189, 191,
    199–200, 211
Narva, battle of, 95
Nasser, Gamal Abdel, 336
National Assembly (France), 139–140,
    211–212
National Convention (France), 141–142
National Covenant of Scotland, 80
Nationalism, 20, 162–164, 177–179
National Land League, 211
National Socialist German Workers Party.
    See Nazi Germany
Native Americans, 34
NATO. *See* North Atlantic Treaty Organization
    (NATO)
Naturalism, 26, 232, 235
Natural law, 58
Natural religion, 125
Natural selection, 217
Naval strategy, during WWI, 242–243
Navarino Bay, 171
Navarre, 22
Navigation Acts (England), 118, 180
Nazi Germany. *See also* World War II
    (WWII)
    annexation of Austria, 294
    anti-Semitism, 277
    elections of 1924, 263–264
    elections of 1930, 275
    foreign policy, 277–278
    formation of, 263

Holocaust, 298
occupation of Czechoslovakia, 294–295
organization of, 287–288
rearmament, 286
religion, 277
reoccupation of Rhineland, 293
resistance to, 289–290
rise of, 274–276
Netherlandish Proverbs (Brueghel), 29
Netherlands
art, 129–130
Calvinism, 41
Congress of Vienna, 151
democratic reforms, 213
economy (seventeenth century), 77–78
Eighty Years' War, 50–51
First Dutch War, 112
independence, 77, 78
Indonesia, 338
Napoleonic occupation, 142
productivity, 118
Second Dutch War, 112–113
Spanish Habsburgs, 50, 76
WWII, 296–297
Neuilly, Treaty of, 258
Neumann, John von, 359
Newcomen, Thomas, 120
New Imperialism, 204–207, 229–231
New Poor Law (Great Britain), 180
Newspapers, 214
Newton, Isaac, 58
Nicholas I (Russia), 171, 192, 200–201
Nicholas II (Russia), 203, 244, 246
Nightingale, Florence, 192
Nijmegen, Peace of, 113
9/11/01, 357
Nine-Power Treaty, 284
1984 (Orwell), 360
Nixon, Richard, 341
Nobility
in fifteenth century, 21–22
in France, 22, 65, 66–67, 110, 137
in Middle Ages, 18–19
in Spain, 22
Normandy invasion, 304
North Atlantic Treaty Organization (NATO)
formation of, 348
Germany, 328

Italy, 324
Korean War impact, 334–335
new role for, 356–357
and NSC-68, 333
original members, 348
Partners for Peace program, 356–357
Poland, 347
Serbia, 357
Vietnam War, 340
Northern Ireland, 259, 350–351
North German Confederation, 191
North Korea, 331–332, 333–334
Norway, 16, 93, 151, 213, 296, 298
NSC-68, 333–334
Nuclear power, 359
Nuclear weapons, 308, 333, 341–342
Nude Descending a Staircase (Duchamp), 236
Nuremburg trials, 326–327
Nystad, Treaty of, 95

O

Oath of the Horatii (David), 158
O'Connell, Daniel, 172
October Manifesto, 203, 244
October Revolution, 249–250
Octobrists, 203
Oder-Neisse line, 307, 318, 341, 353
Oldenbarneveldt, Jan van, 111
Olivia, Treaty of, 92
Olympia (Manet), 216
One Day in the Life of Ivan Denisovich
    (Solzhenitsyn), 360
On Liberty (Mill), 361
Opera, 56
Operation Sea Lion, 298–299
Orange, House of, 111
Orban, Viktor, 347
Orfeo (Palestrina), 56
The Origin of Species (Darwin), 217
Orwell, George, 360
Osman Pasha, 193
Otradovic, Michna z, 71
Ottoman Empire, 15, 100–101, 192–193,
    204, 231
Owen, David, 357
Owen, Robert, 164
Oxenstierna, Axel, 111
Oxford, University of, 88

P

Pacification of Berwick, 80
Pact of Paris, 285
Painlevé, Paul, 261
Paintings. See art
Pakistan, 337
Palatinate, 52
Palestine, 192, 251, 256, 335, 358
Palestine Liberation Organization (PLO),
  336, 358
Palestrina, Giovanni, 56
Palmerston, Lord, 196–197
Panama Scandal, 212
Pan-Slav Congress (1848), 178, 187
Papacy
  Counter-Reformation, 43
  decline in seventeenth century, 97–98
  and Holy Roman Empire, 16
  in Middle Ages, 13
  and Mussolini, 278–279
  in Renaissance, 24
  Vatican, 189
Papen, Franz von, 275–276
Paradise Lost (Milton), 54
Paris, Treaty of
  (1763), 116
  (1783), 116
Paris Commune, 211
Paris Peace Conference, 254–255
Parliament (England)
  before Civil War, 78, 79, 80, 81, 108
  during Civil War, 82
  after Civil War, 83, 84, 85
  Bill of Rights (1689), 89
  Convention Parliament (1660), 86
  power of, 107
  reforms (1820s), 172
Parliament Act (1911), 210
Parri, Ferruccio, 324
Partners for Peace program, 356–357
Pascal, Blaise, 58, 67
Passarowitz, Treaty of, 101
Pasternak, Boris, 360
Paul III (pope), 43
Paulus, Friedrich, 302
Pearl Harbor, 300–301
Peasant Land Bank, 202
Peasant revolts

in England, 14
in France, 140
in Germany, 39
in Russia, 97
Peasantry
  in early modern era, 18
  in fifteenth century, 21
  in Habsburg lands, 71
  in Russia, 201, 202, 280–281
Peel, Robert, 172
Pelléas et Mélisande (Maeterlinck), 235
Peninsular War, 145
Perestroika, 345
Perrault, Claude, 127
Perseus (Benvenuto), 25
Pershing, John J., 253
Persia, 228
Persistence of Memory (Dali), 291
Petain, Henri, 242, 250
Pétain, Philippe, 297
Peter III (Russia), 97, 116
Peterloo Massacre, 167
Peter the Great (Russia), 58, 93, 94–97, 101
Petition of Right (England), 79, 108
Petrarch, Francesco, 24
Petrograd Soviet, 246–247, 248
Philibert, Emmanuel, 99
Philip II (Spain), 48, 49, 50, 52, 76
Philip IV (Spain), 68
Philip V (Spain), 69, 115
Philippines, 207
Philosophes, 123–124, 126–127
Photography, 214
Picasso, Pablo, 235, 236, 290, 360
Pico della Mirandola, 23
Pieck, Wilhelm, 321–322
Piedmont, 188
Piedmont uprising, 171
Pietism, 74, 125
Pilsudski, Joszef, 268, 288
Pisa, council at, 14
Pitt, William (the Elder), 116
Pius IX (Pope), 177
Pius VI (Pope), 98
Pizan, Christine de, 28
Pizarro, Francisco, 33
Plague, 13, 87
Planck, Max, 218
Platonic Academy, 23

Plombières Agreement, 188
Poincaré, Raymond, 260, 272
Poitiers, battle of, 19
Poland
  communization of, 320
  Congress of Vienna, 151
  creation of Second Polish Republic, 258
  end of Soviet influence, 346
  First Partition of, 76
  Great Northern War, 95
  nonaggression pact with Nazi Germany, 277
  Oder-Neisse line, 307, 318, 341, 353
  under Pilsudski, 288
  rebellion (1830-1831), 173–174
  revolutions (1830-1831), 172
  Solidarity movement, 346–347
  Teschen, 295
  War of Polish Succession, 97, 99
  war with Ottoman Empire, 100
  war with Soviet Union, 268
  WWI, 240, 241
  WWII, 295–296, 304
  after WWII, 307, 318
Poland-Lithuania, 15, 111
Pole, Reginald, 51
Political thought or theory, 106, 125–126
Politique, 50
Pompidou, Georges, 352
Popular Front (France), 289
Popular Republican Movement (MRP), 325
Population, 59, 121
Portugal
  annexation by Spain (1580), 48
  exploration, 32–33
  in fifteenth century, 16, 17
  under Salazar, 288
  Treaty of Tordesillas, 33
  after WWII, 355–356
Potsdam Conference, 307–308, 318–319
Power loom, 120
Powers, Gary, 339
Prague, Peace of, 190
Prague, Treaty of, 92
Prague Spring, 347
Presbyterianism, 44, 87, 90
The Prince (Machiavelli), 29
Princip, Gavrilo, 231, 238
Principia Mathematica (Newton), 58
Printing, 30

Protectorate (England, 1653-1659), 85
Protestantism, 44–46, 47, 67
Protestant Reformation, 37–40
Proudhon, Pierre Joseph, 165, 195
Proust, Marcel, 220, 235
Prussia
  in 1815, 189–190
  Congress of Vienna, 150–152
  Franco-Prussian War, 191, 200, 238
  German Confederation, 168
  and German unification, 179–180
  and Hohenzollerns, 73–76
  population, 70
  Schleswig-Holstein, 190
  Seven Weeks' War, 190–191
  War of Austrian Succession, 115
  war with Denmark, 204
Psychology, 126, 217–218
Ptolemy, 56
Pugachëv Revolt, 97
Puritans, 41, 42, 51, 86, 107
Pushkin, Alexander, 94
Putin, Vladimir, 346
Pym, John, 108
Pyrenees, Treaty of, 68, 112

Q

Quadruple Alliance, 151, 167, 169
Queen Anne's War, 114–115
Quisling, Vidkun, 298

R

Rabelais, Francois, 30
Radetzky, Joseph von, 177
Raft of the Medusa (Gericault), 159
Railway locomotive, 154
Rakosi, Matyas, 320
Ramillies, battle of, 114
Rapallo, Treaty of, 258, 271
Raphael, 27
Rasputin, Grigorii, 245
Rassemblement du Peuple Français (RPF), 325
Rathenau, Walter, 263
Rationalists, 122
Reagan, Ronald, 343, 350
Realism, 202, 214–217
Red Shirts, 189
Reformation, 37–43

Reichskristallnacht, 287
Reichstag, 196, 207–208, 275, 276
Reign of Terror, 141
Reinsurance Treaty, 194, 209, 227
Religion. *See* Christianity
Religion, Wars of (1560-1648), 47–54
Rembrandt van Rijn, 129
Renaissance, 22–32, 57
Repin, Ilya, 217
Restoration (England), 85–88
Restoration (France), 167
Return of the Prodigal Son (Rembrandt),
  129
Revisionism, 195–196
Revolutions
  of 1820-1829, 169–172
  of 1830-1833, 172–175
  of 1848, 175–181, 187–188
  American, 90, 116, 127
  French, 68, 137–143
  Russian, 244, 245–250
Reynaud, Paul, 297
Rhenish lands, 151
Rhineland, 151, 256, 293
Rhineland Pact, 284
Richard II, 20
Richelieu, Cardinal Armand Jean de, 53, 110
Riga, Treaty of, 268
Rijksdag, 111
Rite of Spring (Stravinsky), 235
Roads, 120, 154
Robertson, George, 357
Robespierre, Maximilien, 141
Rococo movement, 131–132
Rodzianko, M. V., 246
Röhm, Ernst, 274, 277
Roland, Marie, 126
Roman Catholic Church
  Counter-Reformation, 43–47
  Crusades, 48
  in Czechoslovakia, 322–323
  doctrine, 44–46
  in early modern era, 18
  in England, 51, 88, 172
  in Germany, 208
  in Hungary, 321
  indulgences, 38
  in Ireland, 81, 90–91, 108
  in Middle Ages, 13–14

  in Nazi Germany, 277
  in Northern Ireland, 350
  Second Vatican Council, 360
  in Spain, 69
  transubstantiation, 45–46
Romania
  communization of, 321
  Crimean War, 192
  in fifteenth century, 16
  independence of, 193, 204
  resistance to Soviet rule, 345
  WWI, 242, 256
  WWII, 299, 305
Romanov dynasty, 94
Roman Republic, 177
Romanticism, 157–160
Rome, ancient, 11, 12, 23
Rome, modern, 189
Rome, Sack of, 43
Rome, Treaty of, 258
Rome-Berlin Axis, 294
Rome Protocols, 279
Rommel, Erwin, 302, 303
Roosevelt, Franklin Delano, 301, 303, 304,
  306–307, 308
Rosenberg, Alfred, 274
Rossellini, Roberto, 360
Rothschild brothers, 169–170
Roundheads, 82, 86, 109
Rousseau, Jean-Jacques, 123, 125
Royal Observatory, 58
Royal Society, 58
Rubens, Peter Paul, 55, 129
Ruhr, 260–261, 262, 263, 327
Russia. *See also* Soviet Union
  under Alexander I, 150, 151, 168–169
  under Alexander II, 192, 201–202
  under Alexander III, 202–203
  Anglo-Russian Entente, 228–229
  art, 215, 217
  Balkans, 230, 238
  under Catherine II, 97, 101
  Congress of Vienna, 150–152
  Crimea, 97, 101
  Crimean War, 172, 192–193
  December Uprising, 171–172
  Dogger Bank Incident, 228
  Dual Entente, 227
  under Elizabeth, 97, 115, 116

February Revolution, 245–246
in fifteenth century, 15
Great Northern War, 92–93, 95
and Greek Revolution, 171
under Ivan III, 93
under Ivan IV, 93–94
literature, 360
military reform, 201
Napoleonic invasion, 145
under Nicholas I, 171, 192, 200–201
under Nicholas II, 203
under Peter the Great, 58, 93, 94–97, 101
Poland, 173–174
Reinsurance Treaty, 194, 209, 227
Revolution of 1905, 203, 244
Revolutions of 1917, 244, 245–250
Romanov dynasty, 94
scientific societies, 58
serfdom, 201
Seven Years' War, 97, 115–116
"Time of Troubles," 94
Triple Entente, 229
War of Polish Succession, 97
wars with Turks, 97, 193–194
war with Japan (1904-1905), 202, 203, 207, 244
war with Sweden, 93
WWI, 239, 240, 241, 242, 245, 248,
    252–253, 255, 256
Yeltsin era, 345–346
Russian Campaign, 146
Russian Orthodox Church, 94, 96–97
Russian Social Democratic Party, 203, 247
Ruthenia, 295
Rykov, Alexei, 287
Ryswick, Treaty of, 99, 113

S

Sadat, Anwar, 336
Saint Francis Xavier, 43
Saint Ignatius of Loyola, 43
Saint Matthew Passion (Bach), 131
Saint Petersburg, 95–96
Saint Quentin, battle of, 254
Saint-Simon, Henri de, 164
Saint Teresa of Avila, 43
Sakharov, Andrei, 344, 345
Salan, Raoul, 338
Salazar, Antonio, 288, 355

Salisbury, Lord, 227–228
Salomé (Wilde), 235
Salvation, 46
Sampaio, Jorge, 356
Sand, Karl, 168
San Stefano Accord, 193
Sardinia, 179, 188–189
Sartre, Jean-Paul, 360, 361
Savoy, 99
Saxony, 70, 151
Scheidermann, Phillip, 262
Schelling, Friedrich, 159
Schleicher, Kurt von, 276
Schleswig-Holstein, 190
Schlieffen, Alfred von, 229, 239
Schlieffen Plan, 229, 239
Schmalkaldic League, 39
Schmidt, Helmut, 354
Scholars
    of Renaissance, 28–29
    women during Enlightenment, 126
The School of Athens (Raphael), 27
Schools, in Germany, 39
Schroeder, Gerhard, 354
Schuman Plan, 329–330
Schuschnigg, Kurt von, 288
Schwarzenberg, Felix von, 178
Schwenckfeld, Caspar, 46
Science, 217, 218, 358–359
Scientific Revolution, 56–59, 153
Scotland
    Act of Union with England, 90
    Calvinism in, 41
    conflicts with England, 108
    and English Civil War, 83, 85, 109
    independence, 87
    Jacobite rising, 91
    National Covenant (1638), 80
    Reformation in, 43
    separatism (1970s), 350
Scots, 19
Sculpture
    medieval, 25
    Renaissance, 26
Second Congress of Soviets, 250
Second Dutch War, 112–113
Second Empire (France), 200
Second Estate (France), 137, 139
Second Five-Year Plan (Soviet Union), 281

Second French Republic, 176, 199–200
The Second Sex (de Beauvoir), 362
Seneca Falls Convention, 361
Sepoy Mutiny, 196
September 11, 2001, 357
Serbia, 193, 204, 231, 238–239, 241, 357–358
Serfdom, 18, 21, 201
Servetus, Michael, 46
Seurat, Georges, 220
Seven Weeks' War, 190–191
Seven Years' War, 72, 97, 115–116
Sevres, Treaty of, 258
Shakespeare, William, 54
Siberia, 94
Sicily, 99, 189, 303
Sieyès, Abbé, 139, 142, 144
The Silent Spring (Carson), 362
Silesia, 76, 115
Silver, 34
Simons, Menno, 41
Simony, 13
Sinn Fein, 259, 350, 351
Sitzkrieg, 296
Six Acts of Parliament (England), 167, 172
Sixtus IV (Pope), 24
Slovakia, 295, 348
Smith, Adam, 118, 161
Snowden, Philip, 272
Social Contract (Rousseau), 123
Social Darwinism, 217
Social Democratic Federation (Great
    Britain), 210
Social Democratic Party (SDP) (Germany),
    196, 208, 209, 327, 353–354
Socialism, 164–166, 195
Sokolovsky, Marshal, 331
Solferino, battle of, 189
Solzhenitsyn, Alexander, 344, 345, 360
Somme, battle of, 243
Sorel, Georges, 195
South Africa, 205, 206, 228
South Korea, 331–332, 333–334
Soviet Union. *See also* Russia
    Brezhnev era, 344
    Civil War (1919-1920), 267–268
    Cold War, 330–335, 338–340
    collectivization of agriculture, 280–281
    constitutional development, 270, 286–287
    end of, 345–346
    foreign policy, 271, 282
    Gorbachev era, 344, 345
    industrialization, 281
    Khrushchev era, 339, 340, 343–344
    literature, 360
    New Economic Policy, 268–269
    nuclear weapons, 341–342
    occupation of Germany, 327
    power struggle after Lenin's death, 269–270
    purges under Stalin, 281–282, 287, 319
    recognition of, 261, 271
    space exploration, 342
    under Stalin, 250, 269–270, 280–282,
        286–287
    treaties and agreements with Nazi
        Germany before WWII, 295
    war with Poland, 268
    WWII, 296, 299, 300, 301–302, 304, 305
    after WWII, 319
Sozzini, Lelio, 46
Space race, 342
Spain
    annexation of Portugal (1580), 48
    Armada, 52
    under Charles II, 69
    under Charles III, 69–70
    Civil War (1936-1939), 288, 293–294
    exploration, 33
    under Ferdinand VI, 69
    in fifteenth century, 16, 17
    Inquisition, 22
    Latin America, 170
    literature, 54
    military, 69
    monarchy, 22
    Napoleonic invasion, 145
    Netherlands, 50, 76, 112
    under Philip V, 69
    population, 59, 68
    rejection of Protestantism, 43
    Renaissance, 30
    Revolution, 167, 170
    in seventeenth century, 68–69
    Thirty Years' War, 52, 53
    Treaty of Pyrenees, 112
    Treaty of Tordesillas, 33
    War of the Spanish Succession, 69, 70,
        71, 74, 78, 90, 98
    after WWII, 356

Spartacist Rebellion, 262
Spencer, Herbert, 217
Speransky, Mihkail, 169
Spinning frame, 120
Spinning jenny, 120
Spinola, Antonio de, 356
Spinoza, Baruch, 122
Spirit of the Laws (Montesquieu), 123
SS *(Schutzstaffel)*, 275, 277
St. Bartholomew's Day Massacre, 49–50
St. Germain, Treaty of, 258
Stakhanov, Alexei, 281
Stalin, Josef
  authoritarianism, 286–287
  collectivization of agriculture, 280–281
  as commissar of nationalities under
    Lenin, 250
  death of, 343
  foreign policy, 282
  industrialization, 281
  Potsdam Conference, 307–308
  power struggle after Lenin's death, 269–270
  purges, 281–282, 287, 319
  Yalta Conference, 306–307
Stalingrad, battle of, 301–302
State, growth of, 105–106
Stavisky, Serge, 273
Steamboats, 154
Steam engine, 120
Stephenson, George, 154
Stewart, Robert, 150
Stolypin, Pyotr, 244
Strafford, Earl of, 81, 108
Strategic Arms Limitation Talks (SALT I), 341
Strategic defense initiative (SDI), 343
Stravinsky, Igor, 235
Stresa Front, 286
Stresemann, Gustav, 263, 273, 284
Stuart, Charles Edward, 91
Stuart, James Francis Edward, 91
Stuarts, 88
The Subjection of Women (Mill and Taylor),
  361
Submarines, 242–243, 252, 303
Sudan, 206
Sudetenland, 294–295
Sue, Eugene, 215
Suez Canal, 205, 336
Sukarno, Achmed, 338

Suleiman the Magnificent, 100
Sully, Duke of, 110
*Sunday Afternoon on the Isle of Grande-
  Jette* (Seurat), 220
Sun Yat-sen, 271
Surrealism, 291
Sweden
  in Baltic, 92
  democratic reform, 213
  in eighteenth century, 93
  in fifteenth century, 16
  Great Northern War, 92–93
  under Gustavus Adolfus, 53, 91–92,
    111–112
  Lutheranism, 39
  neutrality before WWII, 289
  in Norway, 151
  population, 59
  in seventeenth century, 92
  in Thirty Years' War, 53, 91–92
Switzerland, 40, 41, 151, 289
Sykes-Picot Treaty, 256
Symbolism, 232, 235
Syndicalist-corporate system, in Italy,
  266–267
Syphilis, 34
Szatmar, Treaty of, 72

T

Tabula rasa, 122, 126
Taiwan, 333
Talleyrand-Périgord, Charles-Maurice de, 150
Tanks, 243, 251
Tannenberg, battle of, 240
Tardieu, André, 272
Tariffs, 329–330
Tarnovsky, Andrei, 360
Tennis Court Oath, 139
Teresa of Avila (Saint), 43
Terrorism, 164, 357
Teschen, 295
Textiles, 61, 120
Thälmann, Ernst, 275
Thatcher, Margaret, 349, 350
Theatines, 43
Theocracy, 46
Thermidorian Reaction, 142
Thiers, Adolphe, 173, 211

Third Estate (France), 137, 139
Third French Republic, 200, 211–213
The Third of May (Goya), 159
Third Reich. *See* Nazi Germany
Thirty Years' War, 52–54, 73, 91–92
Tibet, 228
Tildy, Zoltan, 320
"Time of Troubles" (Russia), 94
The Tin Drum (Grass), 360
Tito, Marshal, 323–324, 357
Tocqueville, Alexis de, 162
Toleration Act (England), 89
Tolstoy, Dmitri, 202
Tordesillas, Treaty of, 33
Tories, 87–88, 89, 174, 197
Toynbee, Arnold, 153
Trade, 34, 77–78, 118–119, 329–330
Trade Unions Act (Great Britain), 260
Transubstantiation, 45–46
Transvaal, 205, 206
Treaties. *See specific treaty names*
Trench warfare, 243
Trent Affair, 197
Trials for Treason Act (England), 89
Trianon, Treaty of, 258
Tribute Money (Masaccio), 27
Triple Alliance, 112, 209, 238
Triple Entente, 229
Troppau Congress, 152, 170
Trotsky, Leon, 249, 250, 252, 268, 269–270
Truman, Harry, 308, 332, 334
Truman Doctrine, 332
Tudors, 20
Tukhachevski, Michael, 287
Tunisia, 302–303, 337
Turgenev, Ivan, 202
Turing, Alan, 359
Turkey, 193, 231, 238, 241, 254, 258
Turks, 15, 100–101, 192–193, 193, 204, 231
Turner, J.M.W., 159
Tuscany, 99
Two Men Looking at the Moon (Friedrich), 158
Two Thousand Words, 347

U

U-2 incident, 339
U-boats, 242–243
Ukraine, 94, 268, 300, 346

Ulbricht, Walter, 353
Ulster, 259, 350–351
Utrecht, Treaty of, 70, 115
Umberto II (Italy), 324
Union Nationale, 261
Unitarianism, 46
United Kingdom. *See* Great Britain
United Nations (UN), 319, 357–358
United Provinces, 51, 77, 111. *See also*
    Netherlands
United States of America
    Civil War, 197
    Cold War, 330–335, 338–340
    Declaration of Independence, 161
    exploration of, 33, 34
    Five-Power Treaty, 284
    League of Nations rejection, 258–259
    Monroe Doctrine, 170
    NSC-68, 333–334
    space exploration, 342
    War for Independence, 90, 116, 127
    WWI, 251–252, 253, 255
    WWII, 299, 300–301, 302, 303, 304
University Act (Great Britain), 198
Uomo universale, 28
Urbanization, 119
Ursulines, 43
U.S.S.R. *See* Soviet Union
Utilitarians, 161
Utopia (More), 31
Utopians, 164, 194–195

V

Valla, Lorenzo, 29
Valois family, 49
Vance, Cyrus, 357
Van Gogh, Vincent, 232
Vasa dynasty, 92
Vatican, 189, 278–279
Velazquez, Diego, 128
Velvet Revolution, 347–348
Venetia, 99, 189, 190
Venice, 15
Verdun, battle of, 241–242, 243
Vermeer, Jan, 130
Verona Congress, 152, 170
Versailles, 66–67, 128
Versailles, Treaty of, 257, 278, 279

Vespucci, Amerigo, 33
Vichy France, 298
Victor Amadeus II (Italy), 99
Victor Emmanuel II (Sardinia), 99, 179, 188, 189
Victor Emmanuel III (Italy), 265, 324
Victoria (England), 90, 180
Victorian Compromise, 180–181
Vienna
    nationalism in, 177–178
    Turks' siege of, 100
Vienna, Congress of, 150–152, 166, 169
Vienna, Treaty of, 190
Vienna Act (German Confederation), 168
Vietnam, 337
Vietnam War, 340
Villon, Francois, 21
Virtù, 23
Volksgeist, 163
Voltaire, 123, 126

W

Wagner, Richard, 217
Wajda, Andrzej, 320
Wales, 350
Walesa, Lech, 346
Wandervögel, 362
War against the Turks, 97
War of Devolution, 112
War of Liberation, 146
War of Polish Succession, 97, 99
War of the Austrian Succession, 72, 99, 115
War of the Fourth Coalition, 146
War of the League of Augsburg, 74, 113
War of the Roses, 20
War of the Second Coalition, 145
War of the Spanish Succession, 69, 70, 71, 74, 78, 90, 98, 113–115
War of the Third Coalition, 145
Warsaw Pact, 341
Wars of Religion (1560-1648), 47–54
Wartburg Festival, 168
Washington Conference, 286
Watt, James, 120
Watteau, Antoine, 131–132
Wealth of Nations (Smith), 118, 161
Weapons and warfare
    arms race before WWI, 229

Enfield rifle, 197
Hundred Years' War, 19
Wars of Religion (1560-1648), 47–48
WWI, 243–244
Weber, Max, 47
Wedemeyer, Albert, 333
Weimar Republic, 261–264, 275–276
Wesley, John, 125
Westphalia, Treaty of, 53, 68, 73, 77, 78, 92, 98, 189
What is Property? (Proudhon), 195
Whigs, 87–88, 89, 174, 197
White Mountain, battle of, 52
White Terror, 167
Whitney, Eli, 120
Widows', Orphans', and Old Age Pensions Act (England), 260
Wilde, Oscar, 235
Wilhelm I (Prussia/German Empire), 207, 209
Wilhelm II (Prussia/German Empire), 194, 209, 230, 254, 257
William I (Prussia/German Empire), 190, 191
William III (England), 88–90, 109, 114
William IV (England), 90, 174
William of Orange (William the Silent), 50, 76
Wilson, Harold, 349
Wilson, Woodrow, 251, 255, 256, 258, 282
Windischgrätz, Alfred, 178, 187
Winter Palace, 203, 249
"Winter War," 296
Witchcraft, 60
Witte, Sergei, 202
Wollstonecraft, Mary, 126, 361
Wolsey, Thomas, 42
Women
    feminism, 126, 361–362
    during Industrial Revolution, 156
    monarchs, 49
    Renaissance artists, 28
    voting rights in Great Britain, 259, 260
Wordsworth, William, 143, 157
World Disarmament Conference, 285
World War I (WWI)
    Allied counteroffensive, 254
    casualties, 255
    causes of, 237–238
    early stages, 239–242
    eastern front, 240–241, 242

end of, 254
events leading to, 227–231
final phase (1917-1918), 250–254
German offensive, 253–254
military technology, 243–244
naval strategy, 242–243
Paris Peace Conference, 254–255
Russia's exit, 252–253
Russia's July offensive, 248
U.S. entry, 251–252, 253
western front, 239–240, 241–242
World War II (WWII)
Balkan Campaign, 299
Battle of Britain, 298–299
Battle of Stalingrad, 301–302
Battle of the Bulge, 306
European theatre, 296–306
events leading to, 293–295
German invasion of France, 297–298
German invasion of Poland, 295–296
German invasion of Soviet Union, 299, 300
German surrender, 306
Japanese surrender, 308
Normandy invasion, 304
North African campaigns, 302–303
Pacific theatre, 300–301, 307–308
Yalta Conference, 306–307, 318
Woyzeck (Büchner), 235
Wrangel, Peter, 268
The Wretched of the Earth (Fanon), 360
Wycliffe, John, 14

X

Xavier, Francis (Saint), 43
Ximenes de Cisneros, Francesco, 32

Y

Yalta Conference, 306–307, 318, 319
Yellow Christ (Gauguin), 233
Yeltsin, Boris, 345–346
Young Plan, 273–274
Yugoslavia
breakup of, 357–358
communization of, 323–324
establishment of, 258
WWI causes, 238–239
WWII, 299, 305

Z

Zarco, Joao Gonçalvez, 32
Zemskii sobor, 93
Zemstvos, 201
Zeppelins, 243
Zimmerman telegram, 252
Zinoviev, Grigory, 269–270, 287
Zinoviev Letter, 271
Zinzendorf, Count von, 125
Zola, Emile, 235
Zuckmayer, Carl, 360
Zürich, Treaty of, 189
Zwingli, Ulrich, 40, 41